THE BIOLOGY
AND EVOLUTION OF
LUNGFISHES

Cover: Reconstructions of *Chirodipterus australis* (top) and *Griphognathus whitei* (bottom), Upper Devonian lungfishes from Gogo, West Australia. Well preserved skulls of the Gogo dipnoans have contributed greatly to our understanding of the structure and relationships of lungfishes. Illustration by R.E. Barwick.

THE BIOLOGY
AND EVOLUTION OF
LUNGFISHES

Based on proceedings of a symposium held
during the American Society of Zoologists meeting in Denver, Colorado,
December 27, 1984

Editors

WILLIAM E. BEMIS
WARREN W. BURGGREN
Department of Zoology
University of Massachusetts
Amherst, Massachusetts

NORMAN E. KEMP
Division of Biological Sciences
The University of Michigan
Ann Arbor, Michigan

Published dually as The Biology and Evolution of Lungfishes and as a Centennial Supplement (Supplement 1, 1986) to the
Journal of Morphology, Carl Gans, Editor.

Alan R. Liss, Inc., New York

Address all Inquiries to the Publisher
Alan R. Liss, Inc., 41 East 11th Street, New York, NY 10003

Library of Congress Cataloging in Publication Data
Main entry under title:

The biology and evolution of lungfishes.

Papers based on a symposium of the 1984 meeting of the American Society of Zoologists.
"Bibliography of lungfishes, 1811–1985,"
Elizabeth B. Conant: p. 305.
Includes index.
1. Lung fishes—Congresses. 2. Lung-fishes—Evolution—Congresses. 3. Lung-fishes, Fossil—Congresses. 4. Lung-fishes, Fossil—Evolution—Congresses. I. Gans, Carl, 1923–   II. American Society of Zoologists.
QL638.3.B56   1987   597'.48   87-4183
ISBN 0-8451-4225-9

Contents

Contributors

R.E. Barwick, p. 93
Department of Zoology, Australian National University, Canberra, A.C.T. 2601, Australia

William E. Bemis, pp. 3, 249
Department of Zoology, University of Massachusetts, Amherst, Massachusetts 01003

Warren W. Burggren, pp. 3, 217
Department of Zoology, University of Massachusetts, Amherst, Massachusetts 01003

K.S.W. Campbell, pp. 25, 93
Department of Geology, Australian National University, Canberra, A.C.T. 2601, Australia

Elizabeth Babbot Conant, pp. 5, 305
Department of Biology, Canisius College, Buffalo, New York 14208

Richard G. DeLaney, p. 237
Department of Medicine, University of Pennsylvania School of Medicine, Philadelphia, Pennsylvania 19104

Alfred P. Fishman, p. 237
Cardiovascular Pulmonary Division, Department of Medicine, University of Pennsylvania School of Medicine, Philadelphia, Pennsylvania 19104

Peter L. Forey, p. 75
British Museum of Natural History, London SW7 5BD, England

Raymond J. Galante, p. 237
Cardiovascular Pulmonary Division, Department of Medicine, University of Pennsylvania School of Medicine, Philadelphia, Pennsylvania 19104

Carl Gans, p. 1
Division of Biological Sciences, The University of Michigan, Ann Arbor, Michigan 48109

P.Humphry Greenwood, p. 163
Department of Zoology, British Museum of Natural History, London SW7 5BD, England

Kjell Johansen, p. 217
Department of Zoophysiology, of University of Aarhus, Aarhus DK-8000C, Denmark

A. Kemp, p. 181
Queensland Museum, Fortitude Valley, Brisbane, Queensland 4006, Australia

Karel F. Liem, p. 299
Museum of Comparative Zoology, Harvard University, Cambridge, Massachusetts 02138

Charles R. Marshall, p. 15
Department of Geophysical Sciences, University of Chicago, Chicago, Illinois 60637

Deborah K. Meinke, p. 133
Department of Zoology, Oklahoma State University, Stillwater, Oklahoma 74078

R. Glenn Northcutt, p. 277
Department of Neuroscience, University of California at San Diego, La Jolla, California 92093

Allan I. Pack, p. 237
Cardiovascular Pulmonary Division, Department of Medicine, University of Pennsylvania School of Medicine, Philadelphia, Pennsylvania 19104

Hans-Peter Schultze, p. 25, 39
Museum of Natural History, University of Kansas, Lawrence, Kansas 66045

Marvalee H. Wake, p. 199
Department of Zoology and Museum of Vertebrate Zoology, University of California, Berkeley, California 94720

Preface

This is the first supplement published by the Journal of Morphology since its founding in 1887; indeed it represents a Centennary Supplement to the Journal. Based on a symposium organized by Dr. William Bemis for the 1984 meetings of the American Society of Zoologists, this supplement brings together in one volume what is currently known about a fascinating group of animals central to any understanding of the transition of vertebrates from aquatic to land-dwelling forms. As this record of the symposium will show, studies on this group, the lungfishes, continue to lead both to insights and to controversy about the lungfishes' placement and the implication of their affinities. Not only does the volume reflect the current interest in the group, but it also contains an indexed bibliography concentrating on the literature of Recent dipnoans.

It is a pleasure to acknowledge a grant from the National Science Foundation, which made it possible to assemble the speakers who participated in the symposium and which provided some support for the cost of publishing this volume.

In introducing this volume, I wish to express my personal appreciation to Professor Norman E. Kemp who carried out most of the editorial responsibility, as well as to Professor Byron Doneen who assisted him. Beyond this, I am grateful to Drs. William Bemis and Warren Burggren who assembled the papers and did the preliminary editing. I express my appreciation to Ms. Katherine Vernon for her committed assistance with handling of the manuscripts and correspondence involved in preparation of this volume. All of us thank the contributors of these papers and also the many reviewers and editorial staff members who donated their time and talent to insure the maintenance of quality. Finally, we deeply appreciate the cooperation of Alan R. Liss, Inc. in undertaking this pioneer publishing venture for the Journal of Morphology.

Carl Gans
Editor

Introduction

Lepidosiren paradoxa and *Protopterus annectens* were discovered nearly simultaneously in the late 1830's. From the first, *Lepidosiren* and *Protopterus* stood out because they defied easy classification as fishes or tetrapods. They aroused immediate and widespread interest, and the further excitement surrounding the discovery of *Neoceratodus forsteri* in 1870 has only been equaled in this century by the discovery of the coelacanth, *Latimeria chalumnae* (Jarvik, '80). As "intermediate" forms, the lungfishes easily fit into the developing evolutionary paradigm of the second half of the 19th century. Huxley (1876:57) accorded them a "central position" among lower vertebrates, a position which continues to inspire us today.

The Dipnoi are a monophyletic group of osteichthyan fishes with a geologic range from the lower Devonian to the Recent. They are usually considered to be more or less closely related to the "Rhipidistia" and Actinistia (coelacanths). A great many zoologists and paleontologists including such prominent scientists as Louis Agassiz, Richard Owen, Marcel de Serres, Thomas H. Huxley, Carl Gegenbaur, Robert Wiedersheim, Louis Dollo, Edwin S. Goodrich, Gavin R. de Beer, Homer W. Smith, Ivan I. Schmalhausen, Bashford Dean, and Alfred S. Romer have contributed to dipnoan morphology, physiology, and evolutionary biology. As a result there is both a long history of studies on Dipnoi and a great deal of information about the living and fossil forms.

The pivotal systematic position of the Dipnoi as well as their fascinating natural history and excellent fossil record keep the group at the forefront of vertebrate biology. The jumping off point for this book is Thomson's ('69) synthesis, "The Biology of the Lobe-finned Fishes," an excellent introduction to the biology of sarcopterygians. Since 1969, however, there have been many advances, particularly in dipnoan paleontology. New Devonian dipnoans have been prepared with state-of-the-art techniques, and many previously discovered fossils have been reinterpreted, as in Miles' ('77) major study of dipnoan skulls. The application of cladistic methodology to old systematic problems has yielded new ideas on relationships and pre-cipitated excitement (if not anxiety) among evolutionary biologists focusing on the origin of the tetrapods. There have also been major advances in the biology of the living species.

Together, the new information and the fervor of a new systematic methodology have rekindled the 19th century controversy concerning the relationship of dipnoans, actinistians, "rhipidistians," and tetrapods. Rosen, Forey, Gardiner, and Patterson ('81), in their paper "Lungfishes, Tetrapods, Paleontology and Plesiomorphy," challenged conventional wisdom, and focused interest on the scientific historical understanding of the dipnoan–tetrapod problem as well as on the systematics and morphology of all sarcopterygians.

It was against this background that a symposium entitled "The Biology and Evolution of Lungfishes," sponsored by the National Science Foundation's Program in Systematic Biology, was held at the Denver meeting of the American Society of Zoologists in December, 1984. This book includes papers developed from the presentations at that meeting as well as some additional contributions. Its primary objective is to summarize current knowledge of both fossil and living lungfishes in order to provide an integrated framework for the entire radiation. A secondary goal is to place this information in the context of vertebrate evolution as a whole through a treatment of the major systematic and evolutionary problems which involve lungfishes, actinistians, "rhipidistians," and the origin of tetrapods. Finally, we wish to provide a synthesis of the vast literature on the Dipnoi while it is still possible to fit such a review between two covers.

The book has three sections followed by a summarizing review and indexed bibliography. The first section provides a reference list of the recognized fossil and living species of Dipnoi (C. Marshall) and a historical overview of the discovery and classification of lungfishes (E.B. Conant).

The second section discusses paleontology, systematics, and phylogeny. Two contributions focus on the origin, structure, and relationships of Paleozoic Dipnoi (K.S.W. Campbell and R.E. Barwick, C.R. Marshall). The structure and development of the dermal skeleton is analyzed (D.K. Meinke). In addressing questions raised by Rosen et al. ('81), several authors present divergent views on the relationships of lungfishes to other groups of vertebrates (H.-P. Schultze, H.-P. Schultze and K.S.W. Campbell, P.L. Forey).

The third section deals with the biology of the living species. Natural histories are provided for *Protopterus* (P.H. Greenwood) and *Neoceratodus* (A. Kemp). Studies of feeding (W.E. Bemis), the urogenital system (M.H. Wake), cardiovascular and respiratory functions (W.W. Burggren and K. Johansen), neuroanatomy (R.G. Northcutt), and estivation (A. Fishman, A.I. Pack, R.G. DeLaney, and R.J. Galante) are presented in detail.

The closing summary (K.F. Liem) presents an excellent critique of the entire symposium record. Documentation of the extensive work on lungfishes is provided by an indexed bibliography consisting of more than 2200 publications focusing on living species (E.B. Conant).

These divisions are for convenience and are not intended to isolate disciplines. Throughout the development of this volume, there has been an attempt to maintain continuity between divisions and the chapters within them; also, authors were encouraged to review each others' manuscripts to add to overall coherence.

For many kinds of assistance we extend thanks to T. Bemis, R. Boord, M. Coombs, M.

Feder, E. Findeis, B. Fink, L. Grande, J.T. Gregory, J. Hanken, S. Herring, J. Hopson, D. Klingener, G. Lauder, K. Liem, E. Lombard, B. Mader, G. Nelson, C. Patterson, J. Roberts, B. Schaeffer, K.S. Thomson, P. Ulinski, T.S. Westoll, E. Wiley, and many others including the regular reviewers of the Journal of Morphology. We also would like to thank the staff of ASZ for their help before, during, and after the meeting. In addition, our special personal thanks go to C. Gans,

Finally, it is appropriate to acknowledge the impact our late colleague Donn Eric Rosen had on the study of lungfishes and the friendship he shared with one of us particularly.

LITERATURE CITED

Huxley, T.H. (1876) Contributions to morphology. Ichthyopsida. No. 1. On *Ceratodus forsteri*, with observations on the classification of fishes. Proc. Zool. Soc. London *1876*:24–59.

Jarvik, E. (1980) Basic Structure and Evolution of Vertebrates. London: Academic Press.

Miles, R. (1977) Dipnoan (lungfish) skulls and the relationships of the group: a study based on new species from the Devonian of Australia. Zool. J. Linn. Soc. *61*:1–328.

Rosen, D.E., P.L. Forey, B.G. Gardiner, and C. Patterson (1981) Lungfishes, tetrapods, paleontology, and plesiomorphy. Bull. Am. Mus. Nat. Hist. *167*:159–276.

Thomson, K.S. (1969) The biology of the lobe-finned fishes. Biol. Rev. *44*:91–154.

William E. Bemis
Warren W. Burggren
Associate Editors

JOURNAL OF MORPHOLOGY SUPPLEMENT 1:5–13 (1986)

An Historical Overview of the Literature of Dipnoi: Introduction to the Bibliography of Lungfishes

ELIZABETH BABBOTT CONANT
Department of Biology, Canisius College, Buffalo, New York 14208

ABSTRACT   The 2,200 citations of a bibliography of literature on the dipnoan fishes provide an overview of 150 years of work on lungfishes. Starting with Agassiz's volumes on fossil fishes in the 1830s and extending to papers from 1985, one can document the debate on the systematic position of dipnoans, the successive areas of research interest, and the continuing use of lungfish for comparative and evolutionary studies. The papers from 1837–1860 trace the misidentification and confusion surrounding the early discovery and description of *Ceratodus, Lepidosiren,* and *Protopterus,* centering on the uncertainty about whether to place the living genera among the fishes or the amphibians. The papers of the latter half of the 19th century show the influence of evolutionary theory, of the discovery of *Neoceratodus,* and of interest in embryology. The trends in the 20th century reflect those of the larger scientific community. The listing will thus be useful both to the historian and to the active research scientist.

At the end of this volume is an annotated bibliography of papers published on the dipnoan fishes. Numbering over 2,200 titles and concerned with both living and fossil forms, it spans all the relevant years, namely, 1811–1985. The listing was gathered with two constituencies in mind: the research scientist and the historian. For the researcher, computerized library services find many of the titles of the last decade or more, but some of the earlier classics are not so generally accessible. For the historian, the crucial work from the 19th century is included here. My goal has been to find all the relevant papers in which lungfish are the primary focus or are handled comparatively in an interesting way.

The listing will be less useful for the paleontologist. For fossil material, my guidelines have been to include all papers dealing with fossil forms of the extant genera, a cross section of papers on some of the species of *Ceratodus,* and some classic references on other fossil dipnoans. More complete paleontological references can be found in the catalogues of Woodward (1891) and Deecke ('26), in the manuscript by Hans-Peter Schultze to be included in the new edition of "Fossilum Catalogus," and in the "Bibliography of Fossil Vertebrates" (Camp, '28).

In this introductory paper, I will first make a few observations about the listing itself, then describe some of the confused early accounts of the dipnoan fishes, and, finally, make suggestions on how to use the bibliography and its indexes.

OBSERVATIONS

The bibliography reveals some quantitative characteristics. The papers appear in 17 languages in 785 different journals, books, and newspapers (Table 1). Some authors have dealt with lungfish only once or twice; other authors have many papers cited (Table 2). About 7% of the papers have been written with a woman as the primary author. Lungfish have appeared on national stamps (Ghana), candy wrappers, the comic pages, Ripley's "Believe It or Not," and nature TV shows. The popular interest in these animals has undoubtedly been stimulated by the publicity attending the speculations of scientists relative to their evolutionary status. Figure 1 shows the pattern of research interest over time. Surges in publications sometimes are related to successive waves of topical interest, a phenomenon discussed below, and sometimes to external events, as exemplified by the reduced output during two world wars.

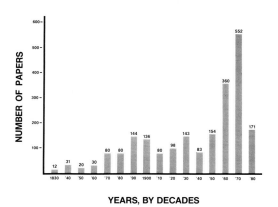

Fig. 1. Bar graph of the number of papers cited per decade.

TABLE 1. *Incidence of languages and reference sources[1] for citations in the bibliography*

Languages	No. of papers (%)
English	1,453 (66.4)
German	328 (14.9)
French	299 (13.7)
Russian	32 (1.5)
Portugese	32 (1.5)
Spanish	16 (0.8)
Dutch	5
Japanese	3
Flemish	3
Swedish	3
Afrikaans	2
Chinese	2
Latin	2
Polish	2
Czech	1
Hungarian	1
Total[2]	2,188

[1]No. of different journals, 636; books, 146; newspapers, 3.
[2]Since some books are listed as book titles independently of the papers cited in them, the total in this table is different from the total number of titles in the listing.

TABLE 2. *Ranking of numbers of papers published by authors cited in the bibliography.*

No. of papers authored	No. of authors[1]
1	681
2	179
3	79
4–5	49
6–7	30
8–9	17
10–11	6
12–13	5
14–15	4
16–17	2
>20	6

[1]No. includes multi-authored papers.

A listing such as this allows an overview of both science and scientists. It is a story of mistaken identities, of rival camps, of forgotten heroes, and even of hoaxes (Whitely, '33). The papers published prior to 1855 are especially interesting, for they focus on the discovery and the naming of the lungfish taxa and the debate over their systematic position. Indeed, if you follow the history of *Ceratodus* and the three living genera, you will find that errors in identification, systematics, and/or anatomical observation mark each one.

EARLY ACCOUNTS

The first published account of lungfish material is a case in point. It is found in the 1811 Volume 3 of "Organic Remains," by James Parkinson. The full title of the volume is more florid: "Organic Remains of a Former World: An Examination of the Mineralized Remains of the Vegetables and Animals of the Antediluvian World; Generally Termed Extraneous Fossils." In it, Parkinson published a figure of a lungfish toothplate but attributed it to "the digitated termination of the sternal plate" of a tortoise. He placed it in or near the genus *Trionyx*. His account of those black, polished fossils continued: "I would not conceal from you that the ingenious gentleman who possesses these fossils is disposed to entertain a different opinion, and to believe that they are the parts of the jaw or palate of some fish. This must remain to be determined by some more illustrative and analagous specimen: until then, I shall hold my opinion with diffidence; for, as I have had already occasion to notice, errors in these inquiries are very easily fallen into." Woodward (1891) is the first to correct the mistaken identity; his catalogue references Parkinson (1811) under *Ceratodus latissimus*.

In the 1830s, *Ceratodus, Lepidosiren,* and *Protopterus* were all described for the first time. The legacy of Linneaus was a binomial classification scheme based on a hierarchy of dichotomies, namely, the Aristotelian Doctrine of the Excluded Mean. Lungfish anatomy posed a special problem to the classical dichotomies. The early 1800s were also a time of extensive collecting on all continents. In 1758, Linneaus described 4,236 animals; a century later, a new listing by Agassiz and Bonn enumerated 129,370 animals (Storrer, '51). One of the collectors of the 1830s was the Viennese naturalist Johann Natterer, the discoverer of *Lepidosiren*. He returned from

18 years of travel in Brazil with a collection that increased the content of the Imperial Museum in Vienna six-fold. He discovered and named more than a third of the then known Brazilian mammals and over 200 Brazilian birds (Goeldi, 1896).

Paleontological material was catalogued as well. In 1833, Louis Agassiz (then 26 years old) began publication of his monumental work on fossil fishes, including the identification of a new genus, *Ceratodus* (Agassiz, 1838). He described 14 species from Triassic and Jurassic sites and mused in some detail about how to classify them. In the end, he assigned *Ceratodus* to the Selachians near the Port Jackson Shark. Thirty-two years later, when a living *Ceratodus* was discovered in Queensland, Agassiz reiterated his belief in "synthetic types" in a letter to Nature (1870). He wrote in part:

The recent discovery by Krefft has added fuel to the fire, and I. . . desire to revise the facts bearing upon the relations of the Ganoids and Selachians in general, and more particularly those of the Coelacanthi, to which, from examination of the skeleton sent me by Krefft, I find his *Ceratodus* belongs. I have little doubt already that this genus will turn out to be one of the most curious "synthetic types" in the animal kingdom, exhibiting characters of the placoids in the teeth, Ganoids in the scales, their embryonic characters in the preservation of a dorsal chord, and finally, hollow bones as in birds.

I take it some of your naturalists will crow over what they will be pleased to call my stupendous mistake in referring the teeth of *Ceratodus* to the Selachians, and yet. . . it settles beyond dispute the existence of what I have called "synthetic types" but of which naturalists have taken little or no notice.

The first report of a living lungfish came in 1836; it concerned the animal collected by Natterer near the mouth of the Amazon and sent to Leopold Fitzinger, Curator of Reptiles at the Imperial Museum in Vienna. Details came in the form of a letter (of September 17, 1836) from Fitzinger to Count von Sternberg, which was read before the Society of Natural History in Jena by "the private medical advisor Lichenstein" (Fitzinger, 1837). Fitzin-ger described the anomalous creature as similar to both the eel and to *Amphiuma*. Classification was hampered by the fact that both specimens were gutted (as he wrote, "victims of Natterer's too passionately executed chase"), but because of a remnant of lung still attached to the glottis and the placement of nostrils near the lip, it was described as "undoubtedly a reptile."

Natterer returned to Vienna and published a fuller anatomical monograph with the title: "*Lepidosiren paradoxa*, eine neue Gattung aus der Familie der fischähnlichen Reptilen"(Natterer, 1837). The opening paragraph (translated) reads in part as follows:

Among the most interesting discoveries of my stay in Brazil undoubtedly belongs the uncovering of a new species of animals of the family of fish-like reptiles (Ichthyodea). It deviates in all its characteristic details so significantly from other representatives of that group, and resembles a fish so closely in its overall formation that even the most experienced natural investigator can be misled. Through this deceptive similarity in external form with the murine-like fishes, I considered this animal to be really a fish until dissection convinced me of my error, and the investigation of my friend Fitzinger left me with no doubt concerning the proper place of this animal in the system of classification.

Shortly thereafter, Ludwig Bischoff, Professor of Anatomy at Heidelberg, obtained permission from the Vienna Museum to do a more complete dissection of *Lepidosiren*, with particular reference to the structure of the nostrils. Bischoff's publication was delayed when the Annals of the Vienna Museum went bankrupt and a new printer had to be sought; the paper was not published until 1840 (Bischoff, 1840).

In the meantime, Thomas B. Weir collected a specimen from the Gambia River in West Africa and in June 1837 presented it to the Royal College of Surgeons where Richard Owen was Curator of the Hunterian Museum. Weir's gift was accompanied by a second "dried specimen inclosed in indurated clay" (Owen, 1841). In 1839, Owen published a note in Volume 1 of the Procedings of the Linnaean Society of London (Owen, 1839), with a fuller description in the Society's

Transactions (Owen, 1841). In the 1841 paper, he expressed regret that his reluctance to publish an incomplete description prevented him from being the "original proposer" of the generic name, for he had registered the African specimen in the MS Catalogue of the Museum of the College of Surgeons in June 1837 with the designation *Protopterus anguilliforms*. On receiving Natterer's paper in 1838 and finding *Lepidosiren* both similar to his animal and more eel-like, he changed the name to *Lepidosiren annectens* (Owen, 1839). Owen (1841) compared fishes, batrachians, and reptiles for traits to be used in classification and concluded that the traditional dichotomy of lungs versus gills is not sufficient. He ended with what is now a famous quote:

> In the organ of smell we have, at last, a character which is absolute in reference to the distinction of Fishes from Reptiles. In every Fish it is a shut sac communicating only with the external surface; in every Reptile it is a canal with both an internal and an external opening. According to this test, *Lepidosiren* is a Fish. . . not by its gills, not by its air bladders, not by its spiral intestine, not by its unossified skeleton, nor its extremities nor its skin nor its eyes nor its ears, but simply by its nose;. . .

It is ironic that despite Owen's emphasis on the nostrils, he was incorrect in describing them as blind nasal sacs. In the end, he put *Lepidosiren* in its own family forming a "link connecting the higher Cartilaginous Fishes with the Sauroid genera *Polypterus* and *Lepidosteus*; and at the same time makes the nearest approach in the class of Fishes to the Perrennibranchiate Reptiles" (Owen, 1841).

Bischoff, who was still waiting for his plates to be engraved, read Owen's papers. He wrote a Supplement to his monograph (Bischoff, 1840), noting that Owen had never spoken about the African fish when the two men met the previous autumn. He then compared the two species, restated his observations about the nostrils, two auricles, and lung function, and affirmed his belief that *Lepidosiren* was an amphibian. Five years later, Joseph Hyrtl published his own monograph (Hyrtl, 1845) on *Lepidosiren paradoxa*, 60 pages long and well illustrated. He, too, pondered relevant characteristics of fish and amphibians, but,

in contrast to Bischoff, declared the Brazilian specimen to be a fish, proposing the new Family name, Pneumoichthyes.

And so, two schools of thought emerged. One, associated with Natterer and Bischoff, placed *Lepidosiren* among the amphibians. In 1840, Milne-Edwards persuaded the museum of the Jardin du Roi to allow dissection of their *Lepidosiren* by M. Bibron. The posterior nostrils, double auricle, and dorsal position of the glottis convinced Bibron and Milne-Edwards that Bischoff was correct (Milne-Edwards, 1840). Melville (1847) agreed, based on skeletal as well as soft characteristics. Duvernoy (1846) stated that lungfish have "singularly embarrassed taxonomists" and then, after a classic litany of on-the-other-hands, sided with the opinion of their amphibian placement. Gray (1856) observed living specimens at the Crystal Palace, and came to the same conclusion.

The other school of thought, led by Owen (1839), placed lungfishes among the fishes. Others agreed. Agassiz (1843) included a sentence in the second volume of his work on fossil fishes in support of Owen's views. Both Hyrtl (1845) and Peters (1845) published similar views. Under the declarative title "Lepidosiren ist kein Reptil," Wiegmann (1839) admitted that he was too timid to contradict such luminaries as Natterer and Bischoff, but once Owen claimed *Protopterus* to be a fish, he was finally free to express his similar opinion. Editorial comment matched editors against authors. Vogt, who translated Müller's paper (see Müller, 1844), added his opinion that the *Lepidosiren* was a reptile, not a fish. Oken (1841) interrupted his summaries of other's work with his own opinion that *Lepidosiren* was a chimaerid. The editor of the Annals and Magazine of Natural History used a footnote to disclaim Hogg's renaming of *Lepidosiren* (Hogg, 1841).

By the early 1860s, the controversy had abated, although in 1859 Edward Newman titled a paper, "Is the Mud-fish a Fish or an Amphibian?" (Newmann, 1859). Retractions by the Natterer and Bischoff school are hard to find. Fitzinger's changed opinion is embedded in a footnote (in Latin) in his "Systema Reptilium" (1843). That of Milne-Edwards is in a single sentence in the 1857 edition of "Lectures on Comparative Anatomy and Physiology" (Milne-Edwards, 1857). Bibron acknowledged the placement of the animals among fishes in the second volume of "Erpetologie Generale" (Dumeril et Bibron, 1854).

The era was characterized by an extravagant coinage of names to symbolize the double nature of the group. It was Müller (1844) who proposed the name Dipnoi to describe the "double breathing" of both lungs and gills in the lungfishes. He suggested Subclass Dipnoi, Order Sirenoidei to show the closeness of lungfishes to the perennibranchiate urodeles. In the same vein, Castelnau (1855) proposed the Order Ichthyosirenes, and Hyrtl (1845) suggested Family Pneumoichthyes. M'Donnel (1860) tried two new terms: Ichthyosirens and Pneumoichthyes. Duvernoy (1846) also offered two: Ichthyopteres or Ichthyo-Batrachians. And Hogg (1841) put them under Tribe Fimbribranchia, Family Amphibichthydae, Genus *Amphibichthyes*. It is interesting that most of this nomenclature was rejected, and also that pockets of inconsistency remained. For example, in Owen's catalogue of osteological specimens in the Royal College of Surgeons (1853), *Protopterus* was listed under Class Pisces, Order Protopteri, Family Sirenoidei. In Owen's catalogue of specimens in alcohol in the Royal College, published 6 years later (1859), *Protopterus* appeared under Class Amphibia, Order Pseudoichthyas, Family Lepidosirenidae.

Nevertheless, by 1860, the theory of evolution by natural selection was the new paradigm. The effects of evolutionary thought rippled through the papers of the 1870s and 80s. The authors were the champions of comparative anatomy: Humphrey, Hertwig, Furbringer, Wiedersheim, Balfour, Huxley, Sanders. The titles changed strikingly: "On the homology of the conario-hypophysial tract, or the so-called pineal and pituitary glands" (Owen, 1882); "Study of the comparative anatomy of the hind limbs of fishes" (Davidoff, 1883); "On the homologies of the shoulder-girdle of dipnoans and other fishes" (Gill, 1873).

Rosen et al. ('81) contended that the search for fossil evolutionary links detracted from the prior emphasis on living forms and thereby derailed the study of vertebrate relations and tetrapod origins into genealogies of the osteolepiform fishes. This bibliography lends some support to their thesis. It is clear that the papers of the latter half of the 19th century emphasize fossils and their evolutionary significance. There are more paleontological reports, for example, papers on *Ceratodus* teeth by Cope (1876, 1877), his archrival Marsh (1878), Woodward (1889), Miall (1878), Traquair (1878), and others. Dollo's paper on the phylogeny of the Dipneustes (1895) is a clear example of the search for prior relationships and origins.

Advocates used lungfish to reinforce their views of evolution. Huxley (1880) wrote of *Neoceratodus*: "This wonderful creature seems contrived for the illustration of the doctrine of Evolution. Equally good arguments might be adduced for the assertion that it is an amphibian or a fish, or both, or neither." Speaking of *Protopterus*, Melville (1860) wrote: "I know no animal more calculated to throw light on the philosophy of Natural History, and better fitted as an antidote to the doctrines coming into fashion regarding transitional forms, or leading to the adoption of the theory of Darwin, than the *Lepidosiren*" (*Protopterus annectens*). The British lungfish embryologist J. Graham Kerr sent a letter to Nature in 1925 (Kerr, '25) in oblique reference to the Scopes Trial, writing on evolution from the perspective of the embryologist.

In 1870, William Forster presented a new fish to Gerald Krefft, Curator and Secretary of the Australian Museum, the announcement coming in a letter to the Sydney Morning Herald on January 18, 1870 (for text of letter, see Stanbury, '78). In April of 1870, Krefft read a paper before the Zoological Society of London titled "Description of a gigantic amphibian allied to the genus *Lepidosiren* from the Wide-Bay District of Queensland" (Krefft, 1870). Gunther was in the audience and at the time finishing his "Catalogue of the Fishes of the British Museum." He published an authoritative anatomical description of the new animal and declared it to be a fish (Günther, 1871). Subsequent decades are marked by comparative studies of this newest and most archetypal lungfish.

Papers in the decades on either side of 1900 show a focus on embryology; indeed, nearly a third of papers cited between 1893–1913 deal with developmental themes. Three names are prominent: Richard Semon on *Ceratodus*, J. Graham Kerr on *Lepidosiren*, and John Samuel Budgett on *Protopterus*. Each organized expeditions to collecting areas and each published extensively, frequently noting the similarity of development with that of the urodele amphibians.

LATER ACCOUNTS

Work on lungfish in the 20th century is a microcosm of larger currents of science. The first physiological experiments appeared in the literature of the late 1920s and 30s. These were the studies of Cunningham and Reid ('32) on the pelvic filaments of *Lepidosiren* and Homer Smith's seminal work on the metabolism and excretory function of *Protopterus* ('30, '35). Ultrastructural studies are first found in the 1960s (e.g., Scharrer and Wurzelmann, '69); comparative endocrinology and cardiorespiratory physiology emerged in the late 1960s and 1970s. New phylogenetic trees trace the evolution of molecular structure in relation to function (e.g., Sawyer, '67) or compare amino acid sequencing in immunoglobulins (Marchelonis, '69, Litman et al., '71) or pancreatic trypsinogens and other enzymes (de Ha:en et al., '77).

Anatomical and developmental studies continued as an undercurrent, with special emphasis on head structures. Owen's (1841) query persisted: Is the excurrent nostril homologous to the tetrapod choanae? Does the embryology of the head skeleton permit meaningful correlations among taxa? Bertmar's study ('66) of dipnoan embryos led him to conclude that the posterior nostrils assumed their position secondarily, due to a reduction in cranial bones, and that they are thus homologous with the excurrent nostrils of other fishes rather than with the choanae of tetrapods. Harold Fox ('65), also describing embryonic material, reported a mix of specialized and common characteristics and concluded that dipnoans and amphibians have common derivation but that dipnoans are not ancestral to amphibians.

There is also the question of whether tetrapods are monophyletic or not. Holmgren ('33, '49) derived urodeles from dipnoans on the basis of similarities between the groups, whereas Jarvik ('42) emphasized the rhipidistian-tetrapod link. Kestevan ('50) believed dipnoans to be primitive amphibians. Rosen et al. ('81) postulated that lungfishes are a sister group of the amphibia.

Paleontological studies have underlain all these controversies. Westoll ('49), Schaeffer ('52), Jarvik ('68), and Thomson ('71) have postulated evolutionary relationships on the basis of fossil material. Using new finds, Campbell and Barwick (e.g., '84) have clarified cranial structure in primitive dipnoans. And Rosen et al. ('81) also used paleontological evidence for their thesis of amphibian/dipnoan relationships.

Thus this symposium could attest to the truth of Duvernoy's (1846) rueful comment, 140 years ago, that lungfish have "singularly embarassed taxonomists." They have at least given us controversy, which is the basis for a rich historical literature. For the research scientist, lungfish hold some of the answers to interesting evolutionary and systematic questions. For the historian, the study of the literature of this group is a study of the currents and cross currents, of many controversies, and of the slow growth of understanding over 150 years. So perhaps Huxley's characterization of the lungfish as "this wonderful creature" (Huxley, 1880) is still closer to the truth.

USE OF THE BIBLIOGRAPHY

For users of the listing who are unfamiliar with the literature, it seems appropriate to suggest a few leads. These are offered only as places to begin or names to look for first. The indexes should be used for a fuller reference guide.

For excellent historical reviews, see Duméril (1870), Patterson ('80), and Rosen et al. ('81). For an overview of the biology of the various living species, start with Homer Smith ('31), Johnels and Svenson ('54), Semon (1893b), Miall (1878), Brien ('59, '64), Kerr ('50), Greenwood ('58), Poll ('38), and Sawaya and Shinomiya ('72). Westoll ('49), Martin ('82), and Miles ('77) are good places to begin for the paleontological perspective.

The early monographs on the living genera are as follows: for *Lepidosiren*, Natterer (1837), Bischoff (1840), and Hyrtl (1845); for *Protopterus*, Owen (1841) and Parker (1892); and for *Neoceratodus*, Günther (1871).

The following section will consist of names of authors associated with various areas of dipnoan research; since most have authored more than one paper, I will not try to include dates. For work on embryology, turn to J.G. Kerr for *Lepidosiren*, Budgett and Brien for *Protopterus*, and for *Neoceratodus* Fox, Kemp, and the authors in Semon's Denkschrift titled, "Zoologische Forschungsreisen in Australien und dem malayischen Archipel" (Semon, 1893a). Bertmar has also published on embryology. Respiratory, cardiovascular, and estivation research has been done by McMahon, Kjell Johansen and his colleagues, and by DeLaney and his co-workers.

Godet, Dupe, and Mohsen have also done numerous studies on estivation in *Protopterus*. The names of Chavin, Hansen, Pang, and Sawyer are associated with endocrinology. Ultrastructural studies of the various species have been made on skin (Imaki), eggs (Scharrer), sperm (Jespersen), scales (Meunier), intestine (Purkerson), liver (Byczkowska-Smyk), olfactory organ (Derivot), lungs (Gannon, de Groodt, Hughes, Laurent), heart (Scheuermann), and teeth (M. Smith). Recent papers on neuroanatomy have been written by Clairambault, Nieuwenhuys, Northcutt, and Schnitzlein. Biochemical studies have been made by Haslewood, Hochachka, Isaaks, Janssens, Litman, Reeck, and others.

The papers have been sequenced alphabetically by primary author and date of publication. Each has been annotated by code, the representations of which are listed at the beginning of the bibliography. The living genera and *Ceratodus* are identified by the letters PLN and C; D by itself suggests unspecified dipnoans, and D with F (FD) means fossil dipnoans other than *Ceratodus*. The letter F for fossil is thus used adjectively, i.e., FD for fossil dipnoi, FL for fossil *Lepidosiren*, etc. When a paper is devoted entirely to one species, the annotation is clear. When other species are included in the report, the letter O (for other) is also used: after the genus (e.g., LO) if the lungfish material is primary, before the genus (e.g., OL) if the dipnoan coverage is lesser or is part of a larger series of animals.

The subject of the paper is annotated by number, the sequence roughly following that used in Dean's "Bibliography of Fishes". The numbers 1 and 2 refer to anatomy and physiology, respectively. If associated with systems, 1 or 2 gives a clue as to the focus of the paper, e.g., 1 11 implies circulatory anatomy whereas 2 11 suggests studies on cardiovascular function. Category 18 concerns natural history and zoogeography. Used after paleontological papers, 18 notes that the paper gives site locations for fossil finds. Again, in papers on fossils, a 4 usually refers to teeth or fossil skeletal material whereas 3 refers to fossil scales. If a 1 is included in fossil notation, e.g., 1 4 18, then the details of the fossil tooth anatomy are also described. Behavior (19) is a general category, often referring to locomotion or territoriality. Used with, say reproduction (14), it denotes reproductive behavior.

Special behaviors of estivation (20) or feeding (21) are given categories of their own.

An index is provided at the end of the listing. Each of the living genera and *Ceratodus* has been indexed by category. Other paleontological papers have not been indexed, nor are those which are too general or are about unspecified dipnoans. Once the index has led you to a specific paper, the full code will suggest the range of material covered.

Finally, a word of acknowledgment. This undertaking has required a good deal of help. Reference librarians at the University of Virginia, the State University of New York at Buffalo, The American Museum of Natural History, and the Museum of Comparative Zoology have been extremely helpful. Angelika Powell and Anneliesa Garver worked with me on the German papers and Kenneth Rasmussen did the Portugese translation. Numerous other translators were needed for other languages. Assistance in handling the material on a computer was given by several people, but most especially by George Conant and Joseph Sabin. It is my hope that this corporate effort prove itself useful to others. If it stimulates more interest and provides a background for work with these interesting animals, then it will have served its purpose.

LITERATURE CITED

Agassiz, L. (1838) Recherches sur les Poissons Fossiles. Vol. III. Neuchâtel: Imprimerie de Petitpierre, pp. 129–136.

Agassiz, L. (1843) Recherches sur les Poissons Fossiles. Vol. II. Neuchâtel: Imprimerie de Petitpierre, p. 46.

Agassiz, L. (1870) Letter on synthetic types. Nature *3:*166–167.

Bertmar, G. (1966) The development of skeleton, blood vessels and nerves in the dipnoan snout, with a discussion on the homology of the dipnoan posterior nostrils. Acta Zool. (Stockholm) *47:*81–150.

Bischoff, T.L.W. (1840) *Lepidosiren paradoxa.* Anatomische Untersuch und Beschreiben. Leipzeig: Leopold Voss.

Brien, P. (1959) Ethologie de la reproduction de *Protopterus dolloi* Blgr. Ann. Mus. R. Congo Belge Ser. 8 Sci. Zool. *71:*3–21.

Brien, P. (1964) The African Protoptera: Living fossils. Afr. Wildlife *21:*213–233.

Camp, C.L. et al (1928–58) Bibliography of Fossil Vertebrates. Geol. Soc. Amer. Sp. Pap. #27, #42; Mem. #37, #57, #84, #92.

Campbell, K.S.W., and R.E. Barwick (1984) The choanae, maxillae, premaxillae and anterior palatal bones of early dipnoans. Proc. Linn. Soc. N.S.W. *107:*147–170.

Castelnau, F. de (1855) Poissons. Animaux Nouveaux or Rares dans l'Amerique de Sud. Paris: P. Bertrand, pp. 104–106.

Cope, E.D. (1876) Descriptions of some vertebrate remains from the Fort Union beds of Montana. Proc. Acad. Sci. Phil. *1876:*248–261.

Cope, E.D. (1877) On the vertebrata of the bone bed in eastern Illinois. Proc. Am. Philos. Soc. *17*:52–63.

Cunningham, J.T., and D.M. Reid (1932) Experimental researches on the emission of oxygen by the pelvic filaments of the male *Lepidosiren* with some experiments on *Symbranchus marmoratus*. Proc. R. Soc. Lond. *1932*:234–248.

Davidoff, M. (1883) Beiträge zur vergleichenden Anatomie der hintern Gliedmasse der Fische. Dritter Theil: *Ceratodus*. Morphol. Jahrb. *9*:117–162.

Deecke, W. (1926) Pices triadici. Fossilium Catalogus. I. Animalia. Berlin: Junk, pp. 74–86.

de Ha:en, K.A. Walsh, and H. Neurath (1977) Isolation and amino-terminal sequence analysis of a new pancreatic trypsinogen of the African lungfish *Protopterus aethiopicus*. Biochemistry *16*:4421–4425.

Dollo, L. (1895) La phylogénie des Dipneustes. Bull. Soc. Belge Geol. Paleontol. Hydrol. *9*:79–128.

Duméril, A. (1870) Histoire Naturelle des Poissons. Vol. II. Paris: Librairie Encyclopedique de Roret, pp. 427–472.

Duméril, A.-M.-C., and G. Bibron (1854) Erpétologie Générale ou Histoire Naturelle des Reptiles. Vol. II. Paris: Bonet, p. 211.

Duvernoy, G.L. (1846) Cours d'histoire naturelle des corps organisés. Rev. Zool. *1846*:390–405.

Fitzinger, L. (1837) Vorläufiger Berichte über eine höchst interessante Entdeckung Dr. Natterers in Brasil. Isis *1837*:379–380.

Fitzinger, L. (1843) Systema Reptilium. Vol. I. Vienna: Braumüller et Seidel, p. 34.

Fox, H. (1965) Early development of the head and pharynx of *Neoceratodus* with a consideration of its phylogeny. J. Zool. (London) *146*:470–554.

Gill, T. (1873) On the homologies of the shoulder-girdle of the dipnoans and other fishes. Ann. Mag. Nat. Hist. *11*:173–178.

Goeldi, E.A. (1896) Johannes von Natterer. Bol. Mus. Paraense *1*:189–217.

Gray, J.E. (1856) Observations on a living African *Lepidosiren* in the Crystal Palace. Proc. Zool. Soc. Lond. *24*:342–348.

Greenwood, P.H. (1958) Reproduction in the East African lung-fish *Protopterus aethiopicus* Heckel. Proc. Zool. Soc. Lond. *130*:547–567.

Günther, A. (1871) Description of *Ceratodus*, a genus of ganoid fishes, recently discovered in rivers of Queensland, Australia. Trans. R. Soc. Lond. *161*:511–571.

Hogg, J. (1841) On the existence of branchiae in young Caeciliae, and on a modification and extension of the branchial classification of the amphibia. Ann. Mag. Nat. Hist. *7*:355–363.

Holmgren, N. (1933) On the origin of the tetrapod limb. Acta Zool. *14*:185–295.

Holmgren, N. (1949) Contributions to the question of the origin of tetrapods. Acta Zool. *30*:459–484.

Hyrtl, J. (1845) *Lepidosiren paradoxa*. Abh. K. Bohm. Ges. Wiss. *3*:605–668.

Huxley, T.H. (1880) On the application of the laws of evolution to the arrangement of the Vertebrata and more particularly of the Mammalia. Proc. Zool. Soc. Lond. *1880*:649–662.

Jarvik, E. (1942) On the structure of the snout of Crossopterygians and lower Gnathostomes in general. Zool. Bidr. Uppsala *21*:235–675.

Jarvik, E. (1968) The systematic position of the dipnoi. In T. Ørvig (ed): Nobel Symposium 4: Current Problems of Lower Vertebrate Phylogeny. Stockholm: Almqvist and Wiksell, pp. 223–246.

Johnels, A.G., and G.S.O. Svensson (1954) On the biology of *Protopterus annectens*. Ark. Zool. *7*:131–164.

Kerr, J.G. (1925) On evolution. Nature Suppl. *116*:80.

Kerr, J.G. (1950) A Naturalist in the Gran Chaco. Cambridge: Cambridge University Press, pp. 169–229.

Kesteven, H.L. (1950) The origin of the tetrapods. Proc. Roy. Soc. Victoria *59*:93–138.

Krefft, G. (1870) Description of a gigantic amphibian allied to the genus *Lepidosiren*, from the Wide-Bay District, Queensland. Proc. Zool. Soc. Lond. *1870*:221–224.

Litman, G.W., A.C. Wang, H.G. Fudenberg, and R.A. Good (1971) N-terminal amino-acid sequence of the African lungfish immunoglobulin light chains. Proc. Natl. Acad. Sci. U.S.A. *68*:2321–2324.

Marchelonis, J.J. (1969) Isolation and characterization of immunoglobulin-like proteins of the Australian lungfish (*Neoceratodus forsteri*). Aust. J. Exp. Biol. Med. Sci. *47*:405–419.

Marsh, O.C. (1878) New species of *Ceratodus*, from the Jurassic. Amer. J. Sci. *15*:76.

Martin, M. (1982) Nouvelles données sur la phylogénie et la systematique des Dipneustes postpaleozoiques, consequences stratigraphiques et paleogéographiques. Geobios, Mem. Sp. *6*:53–64.

M'Donnel, R. (1860) Observations on the habits and anatomy of the *Lepidosiren annectens*. Nat. Hist. Rev. *7*:93–112.

Melville, A.G. (1847) On the *Lepidosiren*. Rep. Br. Assoc. *17*:78.

Melville, A.G. (1860) Appendix to M'Donnel's paper, Nat. Hist. Rev. *7*:110–112.

Miall, L.C. (1878) Monograph of the Sirenoid and Crossopterygian ganoids. Paleontol. Soc. *32*:1–34.

Miles, R.S. (1977) Dipnoan (lungfish) skulls and the relationships of the group: A study based on new species from the Devonian of Australia. Zool. J. Linn. Soc. *61*:1–328.

Milne-Edwards, H. (1840) Remarques sur les affinities naturelles du *Lepidosiren*. Ann. Sci. Nat. *14*:159–162.

Milne-Edwards, H. (1857) Leçons sur la Physiologie et l'Anatomie Comparée de l'Human et des Animaux. Vol. II. Paris: V. Masson, pp. 365–367.

Müller, J. (1844) Über den Bau und die Grenzen der Ganoiden, and über das natürliche System der Fische. Ber. Akad. Wiss. Berlin *1844*:67–85. Translation by Vogt (1845) in Ann. Sci. Nat. *4*:5–53.

Natterer, J. (1837) *Lepidosiren paradoxa*, eine neue Gattung aus der Familie der fischähnlichen Reptilien. Ann. Wien Mus. *II*:165–170.

Newman E. (1859) Is the mud-fish a fish or an amphibian? Zoologist *17*:6450–6461.

Oken, L. (1841) Über *Lepidorisen paradoxa*. Isis *1841*:462–469.

Owen, R. (1839) A new species of the genus *Lepidosiren*. Proc. Linn. Soc. Lond. *1*:27–32.

Owen, R. (1841) Description of *Lepidosiren annectens*. Trans. Linn. Soc. Lond. *18*:327–361.

Owen, R. (1853) Descriptive Catalogue of the Osteological Series Contained in the Museum of the Royal College of Surgeons of England. Vol. I. London: Taylor and Francis, pp. 85–89.

Owen, R. (1859) Descriptive Catalogue of the Specimens of Natural History in Spirit Contained in the Museum of the Royal College of Surgeons of England. Vertebrata. London: Taylor and Francis, pp. 57–58.

Owen, R. (1882) On the homology of the conario-hypophysial tract, or the so-called pineal and pituitary glands. J. Linn. Soc. Lond. *16*:131–149.

Parker, W.N. (1892) On the anatomy and physiology of *Protopterus annectens*. Trans. R. Irish Acad. *30*:109–216.

Parkinson, J. (1811) Organic Remains. Vol. III. London:

Sherwood, Neely, and Jones, p. 269, pl.18.

Patterson, C. (1980) Origin of tetrapods: Historical introduction to the problem. In A.L. Panchen (ed): The Terrestrial Environment and the Origin of Land Vertebrates. New York: Academic Press, pp. 159–175.

Peters, W. (1845) Über einen den *Lepidosiren annectens* verwandten Fische von Quellimane. Arch. Anat. Physiol. *1845:*1–14.

Poll, M. (1938) Les protoptères. Bull. Cercle Zool. Congolais *15:*16–28.

Rosen, D.E., P.L. Forey, B.G. Gardiner, and C. Patterson (1981) Lungfishes, tetrapods, paleontology, and plesiomorphy. Bull. Am. Mus. Nat. Hist. *167:*159–276.

Sawaya, P., and N. Shinomiya (1972) Biologia da Tambaki-M'Boya, *Lepidosiren paradoxa* (Fitz. 1836). Bol. Zool. Biol. Marinha Nova Ser. (Sao Paulo) *29:*1–44.

Sawyer, W.H. (1967) Evolution of antidiuretic hormones and their functions. Am. J. Med. *42:*678–686.

Schaeffer, B. (1952) Rates of evolution in the coelacanth and dipnoan fishes. Evolution *6:*101–111.

Scharrer, B., and S. Wurzelmann (1969) Ultrastructural study on nuclear-cytoplasmic relationships in oocytes of the African lungfish, *Protopterus aethiopicus.* Z. Zellforsch. Mikrosk. Anat. *101:*1–12.

Semon, R. (ed) (1893a) Zoologische Forschungsreisen in Australien und dem malayischen Archipel. Denkschr. Med.-Naturwiss. Ges. Vol. *4.* Jena: Gustav Fischer 1893–1913.

Semon, R. (1893b) Verbreitung, Lebensverhaltnisse und Fortpflanzung des *Ceratodus forsteri.* Denkschr. Med-Naturwiss. Ges. Jena *4:*11–28.

Smith, H. (1930) Metabolism of the lung-fish, *Protopterus aethiopicus.* J. Biol. Chem. *88:*97–13.

Smith, H. (1931) Observations on the African lung-fish, *Protopterus aethiopicus,* and on evolution from water to land environment. Ecology *12:*164–181.

Smith, H. (1935) The metabolism of the lung-fish. J. Cell. Comp. Physiol. *6:*335–349.

Stanbury, P. (1978) Australia's Animals: Who Discovered Them? Sydney: The Macleay Museum, p. 48.

Storrer, T.I. (1951) General Zoology. 2nd Ed. New York: McGraw-Hill, p. 255.

Thomson, K.S. (1971) The structure and relationships of the primitive Devonian lungfish—*Dipnorhynchus sussmilchi* (Etheridge). Bull. Peabody Mus. Nat. Hist. *38:*1–109.

Traquair, R.H. (1878) On the genera *Dipterus, Palaedaphus, Holodus* and *Cheirodus.* Ann. Mag. Nat. Hist. *2:*1–17.

Westoll, T.S. (1949) Evolutionary trends in the dipnoi. In G.L. Jepson, G.G. Simpson and E. Mayr (eds): Genetics, Paleontology and Evolution. Princeton: Princeton Univ. Press, pp. 121–184.

Whitley, G.P. (1933) *Ompax spatuloides castelnau,* a mythical Australian fish. Am. Natur. *67:*563–567.

Wiegmann, A.F.A. (1839) *Lepidosiren* ist kein Reptil. Arch. Naturgeschichte 1839:398–403.

Woodward, A.S. (1889) Note on a tooth of *Ceratodus* from the Stormberg Beds of the Orange Free State, South Africa. Ann. Mag. Nat. Hist. *4:*243.

Woodward, A.S. (1891) Catalogue of the Fossil Fishes in the British Museum (Natural History). Part II. London.

A List of Fossil and Extant Dipnoans

CHARLES R. MARSHALL
Department of Zoology, Australian National University,
Canberra, A.C.T. 2601, Australia

ABSTRACT   The six known extant species of lungfish, their familial designation, and continental distribution are listed. A second list includes 55 genera and 112 species described from the fossil record, their age, geographical distribution, a brief description of the material preserved, and literature sources. The second list includes two monotypic genera thought to have dipnoan affinities. Although the list of fossil material does not include all genera and species described, it does include all the better preserved taxa. Some of the important features of the fossil record of the Dipnoi are summarized.

The lists of taxa presented in this paper include both extant and fossil dipnoans. The primary aim of this paper is to give a reasonably comprehensive introduction to the quality and extent of the fossil record of the Dipnoi.

EXTANT DIPNOANS

Table 1 lists the six known species of extant dipnoans. All three genera have a fossil record that begins in the Cretaceous (see Table 2). For information on the identification and distribution of *Protopterus* species, see Greenwood (this volume), Gosse (1984), and Trewavas (1954). Those species with a fossil record are identified in Tables 1 and 2.

EXTINCT DIPNOANS

Table 2 lists the majority of described fossil dipnoans, their geological age, geographical range, a brief description of the fossil material and one or more literature sources. The author of each genus name is given in the adjacent "Data Source" column but is not listed in the references for Literature Cited. The author of each species name is the first entry given in the adjacent "Data Source" column, and likewise is not included in Literature Cited unless the entry is the only one for the species or unless it is particularly informative. Brackets were applied according to the normal rules of synonymy. The last (or only) entry under "Data Source" is the best available account with reference to previous work on the taxon. Genera and species with living representatives are indicated in the Table. Fifty-five genera and 112 species are included in the table. Two monotypic

genera thought to have dipnoan affinities are listed at the end of the table. No generally accepted phylogeny or higher taxonomic scheme exists for the Dipnoi (cf. Miles, '77; Campbell and Barwick, '83; Marshall, this volume); hence I have listed the taxa in stratigraphic order with the youngest forms appearing first. Taxa of the same age are listed alphabetically.

While Table 2 is not a comprehensive list of all fossil remains, it does include most of the described genera and all the better preserved forms. A number of species only known from fragmentary remains (usually tooth plates) were omitted. The majority of omitted species belong to *Ceratodus*, *Ctenodus*, *Sagenodus*, and *Dipterus*. Hence the geographical ranges, and to a lesser extent, the temporal ranges for some of the genera

TABLE 1. *Extant species of dipnoans*

Species	Family	Continent found
Neoceratodus forsteri[1]	Ceratodontidae	*Australia*
Lepidosiren paradoxa[1]	Lepidosirenidae	*South America*
Protopterus aethiopicus	Lepidosirenidae	*Africa*
Protopterus amphibius	Lepidosirenidae	*Africa*
Protopterus annectens	Lepidosirenidae	*Africa*
Protopterus dolloi	Lepidosirenidae	*Africa*

[1]Species represented in the fossil record.

Address reprint requests to Mr. Marshall's current address: Department of Geophysical Sciences, University of Chicago, 5734 South Ellis Avenue, Chicago, Illinois 60637

TABLE 2. Species of fossil dipnoans

Species	Data source	Age[1]	Occurrence[2]	Material
Lepidosiren[3]	Fitzinger, 1837			
paradoxa[3]	Fitzinger, 1837; Fernandez et al., '73	Eog-R	SAm	Extant, fossil tooth plates
sp.	Sige, '68	UCr	SAm	Tooth plates
Protopterus[3]	Owen, 1839			
protopteroides[3]	(Tabaste, '63); Martin, '82a	Ter	Af	Tooth plate
sp.	de Broin et al. '74	UCr	Af	Tooth plates, pterygoids, mandibles
Neoceratodus[3]	de Castelnau, 1876			
djelleh	Kemp, '82a	Mi	Au	Tooth plates
eyrensis	(White, '25); Kemp, '82b	Mi	Au	Tooth plates
gregoryi[3]	(White, '25); Kemp, '82b	Eo-Ple	Au	Skull material and tooth plates
forsteri[3]	(Krefft, 1870); Kemp and Molnar, '81	LCr-R	Au	Extant, fossil tooth plates
Arganodus	Martin, '79			
atlantis	Martin, '79	UT	Mo	Incomplete skull, tooth plates, lower jaw, many isolated bones
Tellerodus	Lehman '75			
sturii	(Teller, 1891); Lehman, '75; Martin, '82b	UT	E	Isolated skull plates, tooth plates
Ptychoceratodus	Jaekel, '26			
rectangulus	(Linck, '36); Schultze, '81	UT	E	Tooth plates, skull roof
serratus	(Agassiz, 1838); Schultze, '81	MT-UT	E	Tooth plates, skull roof, pterygoids
Asiatoceratodus	Vorobjeva, '67			
sharovi	Vorobjeva, '67	LT	USSR	Complete skeletons, poorly preserved skulls, tooth plates
Ceratodus	Agassiz, 1838			
humei	Priem, '24; martin, '81	UCr-LTer	Af	Tooth plates
madagascariensis	Priem, '24; Martin, '81	UCr	Mad	Tooth plates
wollastoni	Chapman, '14; Kemp and Molnar, '81; Long and Turner, '84	LCr-Mi	Au	Tooth plates
africanus	Haug, '05; Martin, '81	LCr	Af	Tooth plates
pectinatus	Tabaste, '63; Kemp, '82a	LCr	Af	Tooth plates
tiguidiensis	Tabaste, '63; Martin, '81	LCr	Af	Tooth plates, palatines
nargun	Kemp, '83	LCr	Au	One tooth plate
szechuanensis	Young, '42; Martin and Ingavat, '82	UT or LJ	Ch,Th	Tooth plates
minor	Liu and Yeh, '57	UT-LJ	Ch	Tooth plates
arganensis	Martin, '79	UT	Mo	Tooth plates, isolated dermal plates
concinnus	Plieninger, 1844; Martin, '80	UT	E	Tooth plates, splenial, palatopterygoid ceratohyal
dorotheae	Case, '21; Kemp, '82a	UT	US	Tooth plates
hislopianus	Oldham, 1859; Jain, '68	UT	I	Tooth plates

formosus	Wade, '35; Kemp, '82b	MT	Au	Laterally flattened specimen
avus	Woodward, '06; Kemp, '82b	T-Cr	Au	One specimen; central trunk, poor head preservation, tooth plates
donensis	Vorobjeva and Minikh, '68	LT-UT	USSR	Tooth plates
kaupi	Agassiz, 1838; Martin et al., '81	LT-UT	E	Tooth plates
multicristatus	Vorobjeva and Minikh, '68; Kemp, '82a	LT	USSR	Tooth plates
?sp.	Dziewa, '80	LT	Ant	One tooth plate
Gosfordia	Woodward, 1890			
truncata	Woodward, 1890; Ritchie, '81	LT	Au	One complete specimen—head preservation poor; fragments
Microceratodus	Teixeira, '54			
angolensis	Teixeira, '54	LT	Af	Skull roof
Paraceratodus	Lehman et al., '59			
germaini	Lehman et al., '59	LT	Mad	Skull roof
Beltanodus	Schultze, '81			
ambilobensis	Schultze, '81	T	Mad	Skull roof
Conchopoma	Kner, 1868			
gadiforme	Kner, 1868; Schultze, '75	P	E	Skull roof, palate, axial skeleton, fins branchial basket; good preservation
sp. G	Schultze, '75	P	E	Crushed speciman showing part of skull roof, palate and axial skeleton
arctatum	(Cope, 1877); Schultze, '75	UCa	US	Basihyal tooth plate
edesi	Denison, '69; Schultze, '75	UCa	US	Crushed skull, palate, part of axial skeleton, shoulder girdle, parasphenoid
exanthematicum	(Cope, 1873); Schultze, '75	UCa	US	Fragments of skull roof, lower jaw, palate
Gnathorhiza	Cope 1883			
bothrotreta	Berman, '76, '79	LP	US	Two nearly complete skulls, fragments of postcranial skeleton, tooth plates
dikeloda	Olson, '51; Carlson, '68; Berman, '79	LP	US	Tooth plates, isolated fragments
noblensis	Olson and Daly, '72	LP	US	Skull and tooth plates
serrata	Cope, 1883; Carlson, '68; Berman, '79	LP	US	Isolated skull bones and tooth plates
pusillus	(Cope, 1877); Carlson, '68; Berman, '79	UCa	US	One tooth plate
Megapleuron	Gaudry, 1881			
rochei	Gaudry, 1881; Schultze, '77	LP	E	Skull roof, part of shoulder girdle and axial skeleton
zangerli	Schultze, '77	UCa	US	Nearly complete specimen; skull in dorsal palatal views, part of axial skeleton
Monongahela	Lund, '70			
dunkardensis	Lund, '73	UCa-P	US	Tooth plates, isolated jaws
stenodonta	Lund, '70	UCa-P?	US	Tooth plates, isolated jaws

TABLE 2. (con't)

Species	Reference	Age	Locality	Remarks
Proceratodus carlinvillensis	Romer and Smith, '34; Romer and Smith, '34; Vorobjeva and Obruchev, '64; Thomson, '69	UCa-P	NAm	Tooth plates, pterygoids
Ctenodus cristatus	Agassiz, 1838	Ca	E	Palate, lower jaw, tooth plates, skull roof
interruptus	Agassiz, 1838; Lehman, '66; Barkas, 1869; Thomson, '65	LCa	E	Skull roof, tooth plates
romeri	Thomson, '65	LCa	E	Tooth plates
Parasagenodus sibiricus	Vorobjeva, '72	LCa	USSR	Isolated skull bones, tooth plates
Tranodis castrensis	Thomson, '65; (Romer and Smith, '34); Thomson, '65	LCa	US	Isolated skull plates, tooth plates, lower jaw, operculum, fragments
Sagenodus inaequalis	Owen, 1867; Owen, 1867; Watson and Gill, '23	LCa-LP	E,US	Skull roof, lower jaw, palate, shoulder girdle, opercula series
Straitonia watersoni	Thomson, '65	LCa	E	One complete, flattened, specimen
Uronemus lobatus	Thomson, '65; Agassiz, 1844	LCa	E	Body remains
splendens	Agassiz, 1844; Westoll, '49; (Traquair, 1881); Watson and Gill, '23	LCa	E	Partial skull roof, palate, lower jaw, poor body remains
Archaeonectes pertusus	von Meyer, 1859; Bernacsek, '77	UD	E	Palate with tooth plates, fragments
Conchodus elkneri	McCoy, 1848; Gorizdro-Kulczycka, '50	UD	E	Tooth plates
jerofejewi	Pander, 1858; Vorobjeva and Obruchev, '64	UD	E,USSR	Tooth plates
ostreaeformis	McCoy, 1848; Vorobjeva and Obruchev, '64	UD	E	Tooth plates
parvulus	Bryant and Johnson, '36	UD	US	Tooth plates
Devonosteus proteus	Jaekel, '27	UD	E	Skull, palatal view
Fleurantia denticulata	Jaekel, '27; Miles, '77; Graham-Smith and Westoll, '37; Graham-Smith and Westoll, '37	UD	Ca	Skull roof, cheek, palate, most of lower jaw, axial skeleton and fins
Griphognathus minutidens	Gross, '56	UD	E	Lower jaw, palate
sculpta	Gross, '56; Shultze, '69	UD	E	Whole specimens, excellent detail
whitei	Schultze, '69; Miles, '77	UD	Au	Complete, exquisitely preserved, 3D skulls, axial skeleton elements
Grossipterus crassus	Obruchev, '64; (Gross, '33); Vorobjeva and Obruchev, '64	UD	E	Tooth plates, operculum
Heliodus lesleyi	Newberry, 1875	UD	US	Tooth plates
Holodipterus gogoensis	Newberry, 1875; Vorobjeva and Obruchev, '64; White and Moy-Thomas, '40; Miles, '77	UD	Au	Fairly complete skull in palatal aspect, skull roof, lower jaw

Species	Reference	Age	Location	Remarks
kiprijanoue	(Pander, 1858); Miles, '77	UD	E	Only incomplete lower jaw described
santacrucensis	(Gorizdro-Kulczycka, '50); Miles, '77	UD	E	Lower jaw
Jarvikia arctica	Lehman, '59	UD	Gr	Skull roof, palate, ceratohyal, hypohyal
Nielsenia nordica	Lehman, '59	UD	Gr	Partial skull roof
Oervigia nordica	Lehman, '59	UD	Gr	Skull roof, palate, tooth plates
Palaedaphus insignis	van Beneden and Koninck, 1864; van Beneden and Koninck, 1864; Vorobjeva and Obruchev, '64	UD	E	Tooth plates
livnensis	Obruchev, '60; Vorobjeva and Obruchev, '64	UD	USSR	Tooth plates
Phaneropleuron andersoni	Huxley, 1861; Huxley, 1861; Watson and Day, '16; Westoll, '49	UD	E	Good skull material, post cranial fragments
Rhynchodipterus elginensis	Säve-Söderbergh, '37; Säve-Söderbergh, '37; Schultze, '69	UD	E,Gr	Not properly described; skull material; roof, palate, lower jaw, body remains
Scaumenacia curta	Traquair, 1893 (Whiteaves, 1881); Lehman, '66	UD	Ca	Skull roof, palate, tooth plates, body fins
Soederberghia groenlandica	Lehman, '59; Lehman, '59	UD	Gr	Good skull roof material; parasphenoid, part of lower jaw rami; operculum
sp.	Campbell and Bell, '82	UD	Au	Skull roof
Sunwapta grandiceps	Thomson, '67; Thomson, '67	UD	Ca	Single specimen, tooth plates and symphysis of lower jaw
Synthetodus trisulcatus	Eastman, 1896; Eastman, 1896; Vorobjeva and Obruchev, '64	UD	US	Fused upper and lower tooth plates
Chirodipterus australis	Gross, '33; Miles, '77	UD	Au	Exquisite 3D preservation; almost complete skull, lower jaw, part of shoulder girdle-branchial basket
paddyensis	Miles, '77	UD	Au	Exquisite 3D preservation; posterior of cranium, most of lower jaw, branchial basket, shoulder girdle, anterior of flank
wildungensis	Gross, '33; Säve-Söderbergh, '52; Schultze, '82	UD	E	Exquisite 3D skull preserved
onawayensis	Sedgwick and Murchison, 1828	MD	US	Cheek and ventro-lateral view of skull, small medial section of body
Dipterus microsoma	(Hills, '29); Long and Turner, '84	UD	Au	Tooth plates
nelsoni	(Newberry, 1889); Hay, '29	UD	US	Tooth plates
oervigi	Gross, '64	MD	E	Ethmoidal region of skull, symphasis of lower jaw

TABLE 2. (con't)

Taxon	Reference	Period	Location	Material
valenciennesi	Sedgwick and Murchison, 1828; Forster-Cooper, '37; Westoll, '49; White, '65	MD	E	Skull roofs, palate, axial skeleton and fins, tooth plates, lower jaw
sp.	Bernacsek, '77	MD	US	Tooth plates, fragments
Ganorhynchus				
caucasius	Traquair, 1873	UD	USSR	Tooth plate, anterior margin of snout
splendens	Krupina, '79	MD	E,US	Snout, anterior margin of palate
Pentlandia	Gross, '37, '65; Watson and Day, '16			
macropterus	(Traquair, 1888); Watson and Day, '16	MD	E	Skull roof, fins
Rhinodipterus				
secans	Gross, '56; (Gross, '33); Ørvig, '61	UD	E	Skull roof, lower jaw, snout
ulrichi	Ørvig, '61	MD	E	Skull roof, tooth plates, lower jaw
Stomiahykus	Bernacsek, '77			
thlaodus	Bernacsek, '77	MD	Ca	Incomplete skull roof and palate, good neurocranium, tooth plates
Dipnorhynchus				
kiandrensis	Jaekel, '27; Campbell and Barwick, '82a	LD	Au	Skull roof
lehmanni	Lehmann and Westoll, '52; Campbell and Barwick, '84	LD	E	Skull roof and palate
sussmilchi	(Etheridge, '06); Thomson and Campbell, '71; Campbell and Barwick, '82b	LD	Au	Excellent 3D preservation; complete skull, one nearly complete skull, palate, with part of neurocranium
Melanognathus	Jarvik, '67			
canadensis	Jarvik, '67	LD?	Ca	Lower jaw
Speonesydrion	Campbell and Barwick, '83			
iani	Campbell and Barwick, '83, '84	LD	Au	Excellent 3D cranial material; lower jaw, palate, skull roof, opercular series
Uranolophus	Denison, '68			
wyomingensis	Denison, '68	LD	US	One nearly complete specimen; relatively abundant good skull material
Dongshanodus	Wang Junqing, '81			
qujingensis	Wang Junqing, '81	D	Ch	Tooth plate
Archaeotylus	von Meyer, 1864			
ignotus	Miles, '77	?	E	Fragmentary lower jaw
Species thought to have dipnoan affinities				
Iranorhynchus	Janvier and Martin, '78			
seyedemamii	Janvier and Martin, '78	UD	As	Incomplete lower jaw
Diabolichthys	Chang and Yu, '84			
speratus	Chang and Yu, '84	LD	Ch	Skull roof, palate

[1] U, Upper; M, Middle; L, Lower; R, Recent; Ple, Pleistocene; Pli, Pliocene; Mi, Miocene; Eo, Eocene; Eog, Eogene; Ter, Tertiary; Cr, Cretaceous; J, Jurassic; T, Triassic; P, Permian; Ca, Carboniferous; D, Devonian.
[2] Af, Africa; Ant, Antarctica; As, Asia; Au, Australia; Ca, Canada; Ch, China; E, Europe (including the U.K.); Gr, Greenland; I, India; Mad, Madagascar; Mo, Morocco; NAm, North America; SAm, South America; Th, Thailand; US, the United States; USSR, the Soviet Union.
[3] Extant taxon.

and species may not be complete. Some species and genera may not be valid, especially many of the extinct post-Palaeozoic taxa and those based solely on tooth plates or other fragmentary remains. In particular, many of the species assigned to *Ceratodus* may not be valid. The brief description of the material preserved for each species provides a simple index to the quality of the fossils; it is not intended to be complete or comprehensive. Taking into account these limitations, several generalizations can be made concerning the fossil record of the Dipnoi.

Approximately half the known genera are Devonian in age, and about four-fifths of these occur in the Upper Devonian. One quarter of the known genera are found in Carboniferous and Permian rocks and only one quarter are known from post-Paleozoic strata. Most of the morphological change within the Dipnoi occurred within in a relatively short period of time (compared with the entire history of the group) very early in the history of the order (Westoll, '49).

Fossil dipnoans are found on all continents. One quarter of the described genera are known from more than one continent. Of the total number of genera known, half occur in Europe, a fifth are found in Australia, a fifth in the United States, and a tenth in each of Canada, Greenland, Madagascar, and the USSR. These abundances probably reflect the relative intensities of collecting in each of the locations rather than any special feature of dipnoan evolution.

Six of the 55 genera listed are known from relatively complete three-dimensionally-preserved cranial material. About 12 genera have all or most of the post-cranial body preserved. Approximately 15 genera and 20 species are known from at least the skull roof, palate, and lower jaw, and on the order of 30 genera and 40 species are known from at least the skull roof. Nineteen genera and over 60 of the species listed have been described only from tooth plates or other fragmentary remains.

Overall the fossil record provides an excellent source of information for the study of dipnoan evolution. The earliest representatives of the group are among the best preserved. The most abundant and highest quality material occurs in the Devonian, the period in which the dipnoan fossil record begins. Fossil dipnoans are known from all the major stratigraphic intervals since their record began. In addition, the existence of modern representatives and the conservative evolution shown by the Dipnoi in the later part of their history suggests that reasonable inferences concerning the biology of the more recent fossil forms can be made.

ACKNOWLEDGMENTS

This paper stems from my Honors work done at the Australian National University. I thank my supervisor R.E. Barwick for his support throughout my Honors year and K.S.W. Campbell for introducing me to much of the literature. An anonymous reviewer made valuable suggestions on an early draft of the manuscript. W. Bemis provided much encouragement as the paper reached completion.

LITERATURE CITED

Berman, D.S. (1979) *Gnathorhiza bothrotreta* (Osteichthyes: Dipnoi) from the Lower Permian Abo Formation of New Mexico. Ann. Carnegie Mus. *48:*211–30.

Bernacsek, G.M. (1977) A lungfish cranium from the Middle Devonian of the Yukon Territory, Canada. Palaeontographica *157:*175–200.

de Broin, F., E. Buffetaut, J.C. Koeniguer, J.C. Rage, D. Russell, P. Taquet, C. Vergnaud-Grazzini, and S. Wenz (1974) La faune de Vertébrés continentaux du gisement d'In Beceten (Senonien du Niger). C.R. Acad. Sci. Paris D *279:*469–472.

Bryant, W.L., and J.H. Johnson (1936) Upper Devonian fish from Colorado. J. Paleontol. *10:*656–659.

Campbell, K.S.W., and R.E. Barwick (1982a) A new species of lungfish *Dipnorhynchus* from New South Wales. Palaeontology *25:*509–527.

Campbell, K.S.W., and R.E. Barwick (1982b) The neurocranium of the primitive dipnoan *Dipnorhynchus sussmilchi* (Etheridge). J. Vert. Paleontol. *2:*286–327.

Campbell, K.S.W., and R.E. Barwick (1983) Early evolution of dipnoan dentitions and a new genus *Speonesydrion*. Mem. Assoc. Australas. Palaeontol. *1:*17–49.

Campbell, K.S.W., and R.E. Barwick (1984) *Speonesydrion*, an Early Devonian dipnoan with primitive toothplates. Palaeontol. Ichthyol. *2:*1–48.

Campbell, K.S.W., and M.W. Bell (1982) *Soederberghia* (Dipnoi) from the Late Devonian of New South Wales. Alcheringa *6:*143–149.

Carlson, K.J. (1968) The skull morphology and estivation burrows of the Permian lungfish, *Gnathorhiza serrata*. J. Geol. *76:*641–663.

Chang, M.M., and X.B. Yu (1984) Structure and phylogenetic significance of *Diabolichthys speratus* gen. et sp. nov., a new dipnoan-like form from the Lower Devonian of eastern Yunan, China. Proc. Linn. Soc. N.S.W. *107:*171–184.

Denison, R.H. (1968) Early Devonian lungfishes from Wyoming, Utah and Idaho. Fieldiana Geol. *17:*353–413.

Dziewa, T.J. (1980) Note on a dipnoan fish from the Triassic of Antarctica. J. Paleontol. *54:*488–490.

Fernandez, J., P. Bondesio, R. Pascual (1973) Restos de *Lepidosiren paradoxa* (Osteichthyes, Dipnoi) de la Formacion Lumbrera (Eogeno, ?Eoceno?) de Jujuy. Consideraciones estratigraficas, paleoecologicas y paleozoogeograifcas. Ameghiniana *10:*152–172.

Forster-Cooper, C. (1937) The Middle Devonian fish fauna of Achanarras. Trans. R. Soc. Edinburgh 59:223–239.

Gorizdro-Kulczycka, Z. (1950) Les Dipneustes Devoniens du Massif de Ste. Croix. Acta Geol. Polonica 1:53–105.

Gosse, J.-P. (1984) Protopteridae. In J. Daget, J.-P. Gosse, and D.F.E. Thys van den Audenaerde (eds): Checklist of the Freshwater Fishes of Africa. Paris: ORSTOM, pp. 8–17.

Graham-Smith, W., and T.S. Westoll (1937) On a new long-headed dipnoan fish from the Upper Devonian of Scaumenac Bay, P.Q., Canada. Trans. R. Soc. Edinburgh 59:241–266.

Gross, W. (1964) Uber Die Randzahne des Mundes, die ethmoidal-region des Schadels und die unter kiefer-symphyse von Dipterus oervigi n. sp. Palaont. Z. 38:7–25.

Gross, W. (1965) Uber den Vorderschadel von Ganorhynchus splendens Gross (Dipnoi, Mitteldevon). Palaont. Z. 39:113–133.

Hay, O.P. (1929) Second bibliography and catalogue of fossil vertebrates of North America. Publ. Carnegie Institute, Washington 1:1–916.

Jain, S.L. (1968) Vomerine teeth of Ceratodus from the Maleri Formation (Upper Triassic, Deccan, India) J. Paleontol. 42:96–99.

Janvier, P., and M. Martin (1978) Les Vertébrés Devonions de l'Iran Central. I: Dipneustes. Geobios 11:819–833.

Jarvik, E. (1967) On the structure of the lower jaw in dipnoans: With a description of an early Devonian dipnoan from Canada, Melanognathus canadensis gen. et sp. nov. J. Linn. Soc. (Zool.) 47:155–183.

Kemp, A. (1982a) Neoceratodus djelleh, a new ceratodont lungfish from Duaringa, Queensland. Alcheringa 6:151–155.

Kemp, A. (1982b) Australian Mesozoic and Cenozoic lungfish. In P.V. Rich and E.M. Thomson (ed): The Fossil Vertebrate Record of Australasia. Monash University Offset Printing Unit, pp. 133–143.

Kemp, A. (1983) Ceratodus nargun, a new early Cretaceous ceratodont lungfish from Cape Lewis, Victoria. Proc. R. Soc. Vict. 95:23–24.

Kemp, A., and R.E. Molnar (1981) Neoceratodus forsteri from the Lower Cretaceous of New South Wales, Aust. J. Paleontol. 55:211–217.

Krupina, N.I. (1979) A new dipnoan species from the Famennian of Transcaucasia. Paleontol. J. 13:261–263.

Lehman, J.-P. (1959) Les Dipneustes du Devonian supérieur du Groenland. Medd. Gronland 160:1–58.

Lehman, J.-P. (1966) Dipnoi et Crossopterygii. In J. Piveteau (ed): Traité de Paleontologie Vol. 4. Paris: Masson et Cie, Paris, pp. 243–412.

Lehman, J.-P. (1975) A propos de Ceratodus sturii Teller, 1891. Bull. Mus. Natl Hist. Nat. Paris (Sci. Terre), Ser. 3 375:241–246.

Lehman, J.-P., C. Chateau, M. Laurain, and M. Nauche (1959) Paleontologie de Madagascar XXVIII—Les poissons de la Sakamena Moyenne. Ann. Paleontol. Paris 45:177–219.

Lehmann, W.M., and T.S. Westoll (1952) A primitive dipnoan fish from the Lower Devonian of Germany. Proc. R. Soc. Lond. (B) 140:403–421.

Liu, H.T., and H.K. Yeh (1957) Two new species of Ceratodus from Szechuan, China. Vert. Palasiat. 1:305–311.

Long, J., and S. Turner (1984) A checklist and bibliography of Australian fossil fish. In M. Archer and G. Clayton (eds): Vertebrate Zoogeography and Evolution in Australasia. Hesperian Press, pp. 235–254.

Lund, R. (1970) Fossil fishes from Southwestern Pennsylvania. Part I: Fishes from the Duquesne Limestones

(Conemaugh, Pennsylvanian). Ann. Carnegie Mus. 41:231–261.

Lund, R. (1973) Fossil fishes from Southwestern Pennsylvania, Part II: Monongahela dunkardensis, new species (Dipnoi, Lepidosirenidae) from the Dunkard Group. Ann. Carnegie Mus. 44:71–101.

Martin, M. (1979) Arganodus atlantis et Ceratodus arganensis, deux nouveaux Dipneustes du Trias supérieur continental marocain. C. R. Acad. Sci. Paris (D) 289:89–92.

Martin, M. (1980) Revision of Ceratodus concinnus Plieninger. Stuttgarter Beitr. Naturk., Ser. B 56:1–15.

Martin, M. (1981) Les Ceratodontiformes (Dipnoi) de Gadoufaoua (Aptien superier, Niger). Bull. Mus. Natl. Hist. Nat. Paris (Sci. Terre Paleont. Geol. Miner.) Vol. 4 Ser. 3, Section C 3:267–283.

Martin, M. (1982a) Paleontologie—Nouvelles données sur la phylogénie et la systematique des Dipneustes postpaleozoiques. C. R. Acad. Sci. Paris (II) 294:611–614.

Martin, M. (1982b) Revision von Tellerodus sturii (Teller) 1891. Verhand. Geol. Bund., Wien 1982:21–31.

Martin, M., and R. Ingavat (1982) First record of an Upper Triassic ceratodontid (Dipnoi, Ceratodontiformes) in Thailand and its paleogeographical significance. Geobios 15:111–114.

Martin, M., D. Sigogneau-Russel, P. Coupatez, and G. Wouters (1981) Les ceratodontides (Dipnoi) du Rhetien de Saint-Nicolas-de-Port (Meurthe-et-Moselle). Geobios 14(6):773–791.

Miles, R.S. (1977) Dipnoan (lungfish) skulls and the relationships of the group: A study based on new species from the Devonian of Australia. Zool. J. Linn. Soc. 61:1–328.

Olson, E.C., and E. Daly (1972) Notes on Gnathorhiza (Osteichthyes, Dipnoi). J. Paleontol. 46:371–376.

Ørvig, T. (1961) New finds of acanthodians, arthrodires, crossopterygians, ganoids and dipnoans in the upper Middle Devonian calcareous flags (Oberer Plattenkalk) of the Bergisch Gladbach-Paffrath Trough (Part 2). Palaont. Z. 35:10–27.

Ritchie, A. (1981) First complete specimen of the dipnoan Gosfordia truncata Woodward from the Triassic of New South Wales. Rec. Aust. Mus. 33:606–616.

Säve-Söderbergh, G. (1937) On Rhynchodipterus elginensis n. g., n. sp., representing a new group of dipnoanlike Choanata from the Upper Devonian of East Greenland and Scotland. Ark. Zool. B 29:1–8.

Säve-Söderbergh, G. (1952) On the skull of Chirodipterus wildungensis Gross, an Upper Devonian dipnoan from Wildungen. Kgl. Sven. Vertenskapsakad. Handl. 3:5–29.

Schultze, H.-P. (1969) Griphognathus Gross, ein langschnauziger Dipnoer aus dem Oberdevon von Bergisch-Gladbach (Rheinisches Schiefergebirge) und von Lettland. Geol. Palaeontol. 3:21–61.

Schultze, H.-P. (1975) Die Lungenfisch-Gattung Conchopoma (Pisces, Dipnoi). Senckenbergiana Lethaea 56:191–231.

Schultze, H.-P. (1977) Megapleuron zangerli. A new dipnoan from the Pennsylvanian, Illinois. Fieldiana Geol. 33:375–396.

Schultze, H.-P. (1981) Das Schadeldach eines ceratodontiden Lungenfisches aus der Trias Suddeutschlands (Dipnoi, Pisces). Stuttgarter Beitr. Naturk., Ser. B 70:1–31.

Schultze, H.-P. (1982) A dipterid dipnoan from the Middle Devonian of Michigan, U.S.A. J. Vert. Paleontol. 2:155–162.

Sige, B. (1968) Dents de Micromammifères et fragments de coquilles d'oeufs de Dinosauriens dans la faune de

Vertébrés du Cretace supérieur de Laguna Umayo (Andes peruviennes). C.R. Acad. Sci. Paris D *267:*1495–1498.

Teixeira, C. (1954) Sur un Ceratodontide du Karroo de l'Angola. Mem. Acad. Cient. Lisboa Cl. Ci. *7:*1–7.

Teller, F. (1891) Uber den Schädel eines fossilen Dipnoers *Ceratodus sturii* nov. spec. aus den Schichten der oberen Trias der Nordalpen. Abhandl. Der Kaisen Kongi. Geolog. Reichsanstalt Wien *15:*1–38.

Thomson, K.S. (1965) On the relationships of certain Carboniferous Dipnoi, with descriptions of four new forms. Proc. R. Soc. Edinburgh B *69:*221–245.

Thomson, K.S. (1967) A new genus and species of marine dipnoan fish from the Upper Devonian of Canada. Postilla *106:*1–6.

Thomson, K.S. (1969) The biology of the lobe-finned fishes. Biol. Rev. *44:*91–154.

Thomson, K.S., and K.S.W. Campbell (1971) The structure and relationships of the primitive Devonian lungfish *Dipnorhynchus sussmilchi* (Etheridge). Bull. Peabody Mus. Nat. Hist. *38:*1–109.

Trewavas, E. (1954) The presence in Africa east of the Rift Valley of two species of *Protopterus, P. annectens* and *P. amphibius.* Ann. Mus. R. Congo Belg. (N.S.) 4to Zool. *1:*83–100.

Vorobjeva, E.I. (1967) Triassic ceratodonts from South Fergana and remarks on the systematics and phylogeny of certaodontids. Paleontol. J. Transl. *1:*80–87.

Vorobjeva, E.I. (1972) A new dipnoan genus from the Paleozoic Emyaksin suite of Yakutia. Paleontol. J. Transl. *6:*229–234.

Vorobjeva, E.I., and M.G. Minikh (1968) Experimental application of biometry to the study of ceratodontid dental plates. Paleontol. J. Transl. *2:*217–227.

Vorobjeva, E.I., and D.V. Obruchev (1964) Subclass Sarcopterygii. In D.V. Obruchev (ed): Osnovy Paleontologii. Izd. Nauka Moskva *12:*268–323.

Wang Junqing (1981) A tooth plate of dipnoan from Qujing Yunan. Vert. Palasiat. *19:*197–199.

Watson, D.M.S., and H. Day (1916) Notes on some Palaeozoic fishes. Mem. Proc. Manchester Lit. Philos. Soc. *6:*1–52.

Watson, D.M.S., and E.L. Gill (1923) The structure of certain Palaeozoic Dipnoi. J. Linn. Soc. Lond. (Zool.) *35:*163–216.

Westoll, T.S. (1949) On the evolution of the Dipnoi. In G.L. Jepson, G.G. Simpson and E. Mayr (eds): Genetics, Paleontology and Evolution. Princeton: Princeton University Press. Reissued by Atheneum Press, New York (1963), pp. 121–184.

White, E.I. (1965) The head of *Dipterus valenciennesi* Sedgwick and Murchison. Bull. Br. Mus. Nat. Hist. Geol. *11:*1–45.

JOURNAL OF MORPHOLOGY SUPPLEMENT 1:25–37 (1986)

Characterization of the Dipnoi, a Monophyletic Group

HANS-PETER SCHULTZE AND K. S. W. CAMPBELL
Museum of Natural History, The University of Kansas, Lawrence, Kansas
66045 (H.-P.S.) and Department of Geology, Australian National University,
Canberra, A.C.T., 2601, Australia (K.S.W.C.)

ABSTRACT   Fossil and extant dipnoans form a well-defined group of osteichthyans. Tooth plates, a feature in common for extant and the majority of fossil dipnoans, are not found in all dipnoans. Nevertheless primitive dipnoans can be defined by 21 characters of the head skeleton: bone arrangement in the posterior part of the skull roof, relation between supraorbital sensory line and bones, five extrascapulars, ossified (soft in post-Devonian dipnoans) upper lip, lack of premaxilla and maxilla, number and arrangement of bones in cheek region, lack of coronoids, the presence of an adsymphysial plate, ossified (soft in post-Devonian dipnoans) lower lip, relationship of oral and mandibular sensory canal to "infradentaries," course of neurovascular system in lower jaw, symphysial tubuli in lower jaw, gular-shaped submandibulars, anterior naris at the edge and posterior naris within the mouth, median contact of pterygoids back to jaw articulation, posterior position of parasphenoid (buccohypophysial foramen very anterior in parasphenoid), unpaired "vomer," autostyly, neurocranial support of posterior dermal skull roof, no isolated hypobranchials, and pharyngobranchials reduced or lacking. These 21 features distinguish the dipnoans from all other sarcopterygians. The Lower Devonian genus *Diabolepis*, which is said by some authors to have a closer relationship to dipnoans than to any other sarcopterygian, is considered to be inadequately known at present for definite statements about its relationship.

This paper was not presented at the symposium, "The Biology and Evolution of Lungfishes," American Society of Zoologists annual meeting, Denver, Colorado, December 27–30, 1984. It arose from symposium discussions at which questions about the diagnostic characters of the Dipnoi and the monophyly of the group were raised. We were concerned that some speakers were prepared to use characters that we considered had been evolved within the Dipnoi as a basis for comparison with other groups. Naturally, therefore, the discussion returned several times to the question of characters used to define the Dipnoi. From our perspective a far easier task, that also leads to more useful results, is the characterization of the group at the time of its first appearance in the record. Though such an approach will not allow us to use many features of soft anatomy or physiology, it does permit us to distinguish the unique skeletal features that differentiated the group at the time it arose. Obviously it also permits the identification of subsequently evolved characters that have no part in a discussion of group interrelationships.

This is the main purpose of the paper. Consequently we have not attempted to survey the anatomy of the group as a whole; nor have we become involved in a discussion of its relationships. These issues are dealt with in other contributions to the symposium. However, in view of the special position assigned by some authors to *Diabolepis*, we have felt it necessary to comment on that genus.

We assert that the Dipnoi are a monophyletic group because, although the matter was raised in discussion, we know of no published attempt to establish diphyly or polyphyly. The view that two lineages were present at the time the group appeared in the fossil record has never been used to promote such a view (see Campbell and Barwick, this volume). Nor has any acceptable published attempt been made to show that the group is paraphyletic (Campbell and Barwick; Schultze, this volume).

Only three genera of dipnoans survive today, though approximately fifty are known from the fossil record (see Marshall, this volume). They have changed in many features since the first appearance of the group in the Early Devonian (Westoll, '49). Tooth plates, commonly considered a characteristic feature of dipnoans, are found in all extant and most fossil dipnoans, but genera without tooth plates occur in the Paleozoic. Some workers have considered the lack of tooth plates to be primitive for the group (Denison, '74; Miles, '77), but Campbell and Barwick ('83; this volume) distinguished two evolutionary lines within dipnoans, one with denticulate dentition and another with tooth plates. One problem has been conflict over the definition of the term "tooth plate." For this reason, Campbell and Barwick ('83) have preferred to distinguish the lineages by the way in which the dentition grows. The denticulate dipnoans shed and renewed their denticles throughout the growth of the animal. In contrast, dipnoans with tooth plates add dentine to the margins of the tooth plates, which then grow from the base. The Devonian genera are the most primitive members of the group (Miles, '77; Campbell and Barwick, '83; Schultze, this volume), and they are more strongly ossified than any post-Devonian dipnoan. We will use the Devonian dipnoans, and especially the Early Devonian members (*Dipnorhynchus, Speonesydrion, Uranolophus*), to identify derived features of the primitive members of the group. For the here accepted relationship of osteichthyans see Schultze (this volume, Fig. 12).

DIPNOAN SKELETAL CHARACTERISTICS
Skull roof (Fig. 1)

The bone arrangement of the skull roof is so different from that of other osteichthyans that the special nomenclature of Forster-Cooper ('37) is used.

1. On the posterior skull roof, one median bone (B-bone) is surrounded laterally by paired I- and J-bones and bordered anteriorly by C-bones. The cephalic division of the main lateral line pass through a series of smaller bones (Y_2-, Y_1-bones), which lie lateral to I and J. The posterior skull roof of dipnoans is thus characterized by a cluster of nine bones (B-, two I-, two J-, Y_2- and Y_1-bones; contrary to Rosen et al., '81, and Gardiner, '84), while there are six or fewer in actinopterygians (Fig. 1a), crossopterygians (Fig. 1b,c), and tetrapods (for definition of crossopterygians and rhipidistians see Schultze, this volume).

In early dipnoans the B-bone is surrounded posteriorly by the I-bones (Fig. 1e), whereas it reaches the posterior margin of the skull roof in almost all Middle Devonian and younger genera (Fig. 1f). The B-bone becomes the major median bone in modern forms. The only other form with a B-like bone is *Diabolepis* (Fig. 1d; Chang and Yu, '84), an Early Devonian genus of uncertain systematic position. The B-like bone in *Diabolepis* is not bordered anteriorly by two C-bones (the bone mosaic reaches far back); it is very small and may be homologous to the posterior end of the B-bone in *Uranolophus, Dipnorhynchus,* or *Speonesydrion*. All other osteichthyans lack a median bone comparable with the B-bone.

Dipnoan roofing bones cannot be homologized with those of primitive tetrapods. In earlier analyses (Watson and Day, '16; Holmgren and Stensiö, '36) the B-bone was considered to be homologous with the parietal or central parietal, and the I- and J-bones with the intertemporal and tabular or the lateral parietals. Gardiner ('84) has suggested two slightly different homologies in his Table I and Figure 89, neither of which matches the previous proposals. In addition, he has suggested new names—posterior and anterior lateral parietals—for bones I and J. All this points up the difficulty of attempting to assess pattern without a knowledge of pattern development.

2. In the primitive genera the supraorbital line passes through a series of bones (J-, K-, L-, M-, and N-) lateral to the paired C-bones (Fig. 1e), and several more anteriorly placed bones (paired E-bones and others). In all Paleozoic forms, supraorbital bones separate the lateral line series from the orbit (Figs. 1e,f, 3d). Bones-3 and -2 are lost in post-Paleozoic dipnoans.

In actinopterygians and crossopterygians, the supraorbital canal passes through the medial paired bones, the parietals (the so-called frontals in actinopterygians), and through the more anteriorly placed paired frontals in panderichthyid rhipidistians (Schultze and Arsenault, '85) and tetrapods.

In the most primitive dipnoans, the supraorbital sensory lines does not connect anteriorly with the infraorbital sensory line, and the latter does not develop an anterior commissure. Both conditions are distinct

Abbreviations

A, B,	skull roofing bones of dipnoans
C, E,	
H, I, J,	
K, L,	
M, N,	
X, Y,	
Z,	
ad. hyo,	Attachment of adductor hyomandibulae
a.m.b,	Anterior median bone
ana,	Anterior naris
Ang,	Angular
"Ang",	So-called angular of dipnoans
a.Pt,	Anterior pterygoid of actinopterygians
at.op,	Opercular attachment
Bb,	basibranchial
Bh,	Basihyal
cao,	Aortic canal
c.dl,	Dorsolateral crista
c.l,	Lateral crista
Ch,	Ceratohyal
c.m,	Median crista
cmc,	Commissure of mandibular canals
cmor,	Commissure between mandibular and oral canal
com,	Occipital commissure
cv,	Cranial cavity
De,	Dentary
"de",	Dentary of actinopterygians
Dhy,	Dermohyal
Dmpt,	Dermopterygoid
Dpl,	Dermopalatine
"Dpl," Dpl₂,	So-called dermopalatines of dipnoans
Dpl₃,	
d.sk,	Dermal skull roofing bones
Eb,	Epibranchial
Ecpt,	Ectopterygoid
"Ecpt",	So-called ectopterygoid of dipnoan *Griphognathus*
Esc,	Extrascapular
Et,	Extratemporal
fa.hyo,	Hyomandibular facet
f.bh,	Buccohypophysial foramen
f.m,	Fossa for masseter muscle
f.mm,	Divisions of foramen for masseter muscle
Fr,	Frontal
"Fr",	So-called frontal of actinopterygians
f.t,	Fossa for temporalis muscle
f.v,	Ventral otic fissure
f.VIII,	Foramen of hyomandibular ramus of facial nerve, jugular vein, and orbital artery
f.IX,	Foramen of glossopharyngeal nerve
f.X,	Foramen of vagus nerve
Gl,	Lateral gular
Gm,	Median gular
Gp,	Principal gular
Hh,	Hypohyal
Ib,	Infrapharyngobranchial
i.j,	Intracranial joint
ioc,	Infraorbital sensory line

It,	Intertemporal
J,	Jugal
j.a,	Jaw articulation
La,	Lacrimal
lc,	Cephalic division of main lateral line
ll,	Ossified lower lip (so-called dentary) of dipnoans
l.o,	Lateral otic
mc,	Mandibular sensory canal
Mx,	Maxilla
nc,	Notochordal canal
O.acc,	Accessory opercular
orc,	Oral sensory canal
Pa,	Parietal
'Pa',	So-called parietal of actinopterygians
pa.os,	Parachordal ossification
PF,	Field Museum of Natural History, Chicago, Illinois, U.S.A
Pm,	Postmandibular
Pmx,	Premaxillar
pna,	Posterior naris
Po,	Postorbital
p.o,	Posterior otic
Pop,	Preopercular
Pp,	Postparietal
pro.em,	Preoral eminence
Prsp,	Prespiracular
Psb,	Presubopercular
Psph,	Parasphenoid
Pspl,	Postsplenial
"Pspl",	So-called postsplenial of dipnoans
Pt,	Pterygoid
Ptm,	Posttemporal
q,	Quadrate
Qj,	Quadratojugal
Rbr,	Branchiostegal rays
r.sbn,	Subnasal ridge
r.sp,	Spiracular recess
Ro,	Rostral
Sang,	Surangular
"Sang",	So-called surangular of dipnoans
Sb,	Suprapharyngobranchial
Sbm,	Submandibular
Sbml,	Lateral submandibular
Sbmm,	Median submandibular
Sbmp,	Principal submandibular
Sl,	Sublingual rod (= basihyal)
So,	Supraorbital
soc,	Supraorbital sensory canal
Sop,	Subopercular
Sp,	Spiracular bone
Spl,	Splenial
'Spl',	So-called splenial of dipnoans
Sq,	Squamosal
Sql,	Lower squamosal
Squ,	Upper squamosal
St,	Supratemporal
'St',	Supratemporal of actinopterygians
Ta,	Tabular
Vo,	Vomer
v.o,	Ventral otic
2, 3, 4, 5, 6, 7, 8, 9a–g, 10, 13, 14,	Cheek bones of dipnoans

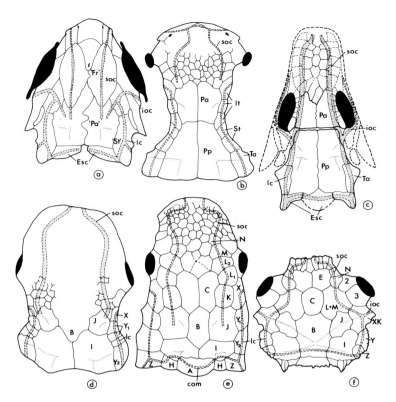

Fig. 1. Comparison of skull roof of representative osteichthyans. a) Primitive actinopterygian (*Cheirolepis trailli* from Pearson and Westoll, '79, Fig. 20c). b) Primitive rhipidistian (*Powichthys thorsteinssoni* from Jessen, '80, Fig. 3A). c) Primitive actinistian (*Diplocercides kayseri* from Stensiö, '37, Fig. 1). d) *Diabolichthys speratus* (from Chang and Yu, '84, Fig. 1D). e) Primitive dipnoan (*Dipnorhynchus sussmilchi* from Thomson and Campbell, '71; Fig. 6A; and Campbell and Barwick, '82a; Fig. 9c,e). f) Advanced dipnoan (*Sagenodus inaequalis* from Watson and Gill, '23, Fig. 1; and Westoll, '49; Fig. 8A).

from that in actinopterygians and crossopterygians.

3. Behind the I- and B-bones, a series of five bones (Z-H-A-H-Z) lies posterior to the neurocranium (Fig. 1e). These bones have the same position as the extrascapulars in other osteichthyans. The course of the commissure and the number of bones are unique to dipnoans. The commissure may have passed through all five bones as is suggested by one specimen of *Dipnorhynchus sussmilchi* (Campbell and Barwick, '82a, Fig. 9c). Most Devonian and all post-Devonian dipnoans (Fig. 1f) lack the extrascapular bone H; A and Z are lost in some Late Paleozoic and in all post-Paleozoic dipnoans.

Primitive actinopterygians (Fig. 1a) have two, and crossopterygians (Fig. 1c) three extrascapulars (Gardiner, '84). The higher number of extrascapulars in some actinistians is a feature of advanced members of that group (Schultze, this volume; Forey, '81).

4. Primitive dipnoans have an ossified snout (the soft upper lip of extant forms) formed of many small bones as in *Uranolophus* (Fig. 2a; Denison, '68). They do not have identifiable premaxillae. The ossified snout is characterized by a subnasal ridge, nasal notch, and preoral eminence (Miles, '77). The snout is so strongly ossified that it separates easily from the skull roof during the fossilization process, and one such snout has been described as the distinct genus *Ganorhynchus* (see Jarvik, '80, "the lost snout problem").

An ossified or soft upper lip with ventral nasal notch is not known in any other osteichthyan.

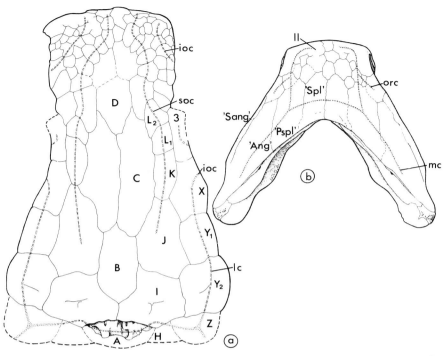

Fig. 2. Primitive dipnoan *Uranolophus wyomingensis* showing bone mosaics of snout and lower jaw. a) Snout (reconstruction of skull roof after specimens PF 1427, 3795, 3805, 3816, and 3874; X 2). b) Anterior end ("dentary" = ossified lower lip) of lower jaw of specimen PF 3797 × 1.5.

5. All dipnoans lack a premaxilla and maxilla (Fig. 3d), contrary to the statement of Rosen et al. ('81) and Gardiner ('84); see Campbell and Barwick ('84a) for discussion.

Cheek region (Fig. 3)

In the cheek region, as in the skull roof, the nomenclature of Forster-Cooper ('37), specific for dipnoans, is in use to avoid ambiguous homologization with cheek bones in other osteichthyans.

6. The cheek region is covered by many small bones (Fig. 3d). The infraorbital sensory line passes through four bones (bones 4 to 7) around the posterior to posteroventral margin of the orbit, compared to two (jugal and postorbital) in all other osteichthyans. We follow Pearson ('82) and Gardiner ('84) in homologizing the so-called "dermosphenotic" in actinopterygians with the postorbital in tetrapods. The dermosphenotic proper (= intertemporal of osteolepiforms and tetrapods;

Gardiner, '84) contains the point where infraorbital and supraorbital sensory lines branch off from the cephalic division of the main lateral line. It lies lateral to the parietal in actinopterygians (the so-called "frontal"), youngolepiforms, osteolepiforms, and tetrapods. The intertemporal is followed by the lateral line bones, supratemporal and tabular, which accompany the postparietals in osteolepiforms and primitive tetrapods. In primitive actinopterygians, only one long lateral line bone, the supratemporal, follows the intertemporal (Gardiner, '84). It may include the tabular. The relation to the medial bones indicates (as do the pitlines on the posterior paired bones of the skull roof) that the posterior paired bones of actinopterygians are homologous to the postparietals of crossopterygians and tetrapods (Jollie, '62).

Synapomorphies are also evident posterior to bones 4 to 7. The T-bone corresponds to (though of course it is not necessarily homol-

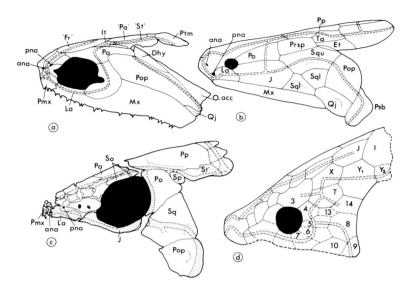

Fig. 3.   Lateral side of the head of representative osteichthyans. a) Primitive actinopterygian (*Cheirolepis trailli* from Pearson and Westoll, '79, Fig. 20a). b) Rhipidistian (*Porolepis brevis* from Jarvik, '72, Fig. 63A). c) Actinistian (*Rhabdoderma elegans* from Forey, '81, Fig. 6). d) Primitive dipnoan (*Dipnorhynchus sussmilchi* from Campbell and Barwick, '82a, Fig. 4b).

ogous with) the postorbital of other osteich-thyans insofar as it has a position ventral to bone X (dermosphenotic = intertemporal). In addition, a short sensory line canal runs from the T-bone into bone 3 above the orbit, though it is not as close to the orbit as in other osteichthyans. The high number of bones ventral to bone T is unmatched in any other plesiomorphous osteichthyans (Fig. 3a–c), though in higher actinopterygians a large number of infraorbitals and suborbitals are known. In dipnoans (contrary to Gardiner, '84), there is no bone that could be homolo-gized with the jugal (bones 5, 6, 7 in Table 1, Gardiner, '84), squamosal (missing even after Gardiner, '84), preopercular (bone 8 and 9a–f, Gardiner, '84), or quadratojugal (bone 10 after Rosen et al., '81 and Gardiner, '84, but position not posterior to jugal and postero-ventral to squamosal) in tetrapods or other osteichthyans.

Lower jaw (Fig. 4)

The lower jaw of dipnoans is so distinctive that Jarvik ('67) suggested a new nomencla-ture similar to that used by Forster-Cooper ('37) for the skull roof and cheek bones. How-ever, Jarvik's ('67) nomenclature has not

been accepted. The prearticular is the only bone that can be homologized with some cer-tainty with that in other osteichthyans.

7. The dipnoans do not possess coronoids. Actinopterygians and actinistians have many coronoids, and rhipidistians and tetrapods have three (not counting the parasymphysial plate), in their primitive states (Schultze, this volume, Fig. 16).

8. Dipnoans possess a median adsymphy-sial plate, above the symphysis of the lower jaw. This plate is fused to the prearticulars in primitive adult dipnoans (*Speonesydrion* and *Dipnorhynchus*, Campbell and Barwick, '84b) but is separate in more advanced gen-era (Jarvik, '67; Schultze, '69; Miles, '77; Campbell and Barwick, '84b).

9. Dipnoans do not have an elongate den-tary. The so-called "dentary" of dipnoans is an ossification of the anterior end of the lower jaw, the ossified "lower lip" (Fig. 4d,e), which is composed of many bones in *Uranolophus* (Fig. 2b).

10. Four "infradentaries" form the outer dermal bones of the lower jaw. They have positions comparable to the "infradentaries" of rhipidistians (Fig. 4c); without implying homology, we continue to use the rhipidis-

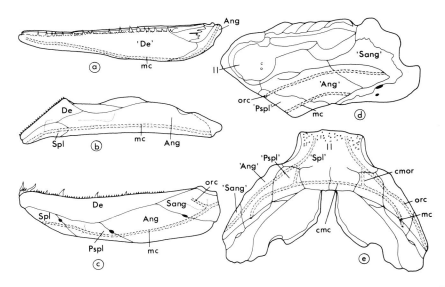

Fig. 4. Lower jaw in lateral view of representative osteichthyans. a) Primitive actinopterygian (*Mimia toombsi* from Gardiner, '84, Fig. 90). b) Primitive actinistian (*Diplocercides kayseri* from Stensiö, '37, Fig. 7A.

c) Rhipidistian (*Holoptychius* sp. from Jarvik, '72, Fig. 47C). d) Dipnoan (*Chirodipterus australis* from Miles, '77, Fig. 103). e) Dipnoan lower jaw in ventral view (*Chirodipterus australis* from Miles, '77, Fig. 102b).

tian terminology. All of the primitive dipnoans have long "surangulars" that may extend forwards almost to the "dentary." Later genera such as *Dipterus* and *Chirodipterus* have much shorter "surangulars" and enlarged "angulars." Unlike the rhipidistians, in which the mandibular sensory canal enters the lower jaw through the surangular and sends off a short oral canal in that bone, the mandibular sensory canal system enters the dipnoan mandible through the "angular." In primitive forms the oral canal is connected with the mandibular canal by a short commissure that lies near the anterior end of the "postsplenial." Anteriorly only a single canal is present, and it becomes intimately related to the symphysial tubule system. Details are presented by Campbell and Barwick (this volume). Suffice it to say that such a canal system is unlike that found in any other osteichthyan (Fig. 4a–c), and that the differences are so great that the homologies of the canal-bearing bones are questionable.

11. The neural and vascular systems of the lower jaws of *Dipnorhynchus* and *Speonesydrion* were discussed by Thomson and Campbell ('71) and Campbell and Barwick ('84b).

Unpublished work on *Uranolophus* has shown that it had an almost identical system. Of course the same nerves and vessels pass into the jaw as in other osteichthyans, but the massive median region, the symphysial tubule system, and the large anterior furrow all require a special neural and vascular organization. Details are set out by Campbell and Barwick (this volume). There is no evidence of these systems in post-Devonian dipnoans.

12. A richly branched system of small canals, the symphysial tubuli (Thomson and Campbell, '71; Miles, '77; Campbell and Barwick, '84b), is developed in anterior part of the lower jaw in primitive dipnoans (*Dipnorhynchus, Speonesydrion, Dipterus, Griphognathus, Chirodipterus*). These are analogues of the rostral tubuli in the snout. Rostral tubuli also occur in primitive rhipidistians (Chang, '82), but symphysial tubuli are unknown in primitive members of other osteichthyan groups. The development of symphysial tubuli may be correlated with the formation of the ossified dipnoan lower lip (character 9).

13. A series of large gular-shaped submandibular bones (Fig. 5c,d) lies between the

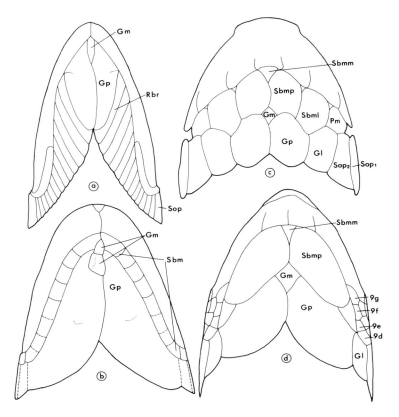

Fig. 5.   Gular region of representative osteichthyans. a) Primitive actinopterygian (*Cheirolepis trailli* from Pearson and Westoll, '79, Fig. 20d). b) Rhipidistian (*Porolepis brevis* from Jarvik, '72, Fig. 43B). c) Primitive dipnoan (*Speonesydrion iani* from Campbell and Barwick, '84b, Fig. 26). d) Advanced dipnoan (*Scaumenacia curta* from Jarvik, '67, Fig. 5B).

lower jaw and gular series. There are two pairs of large submandibular plates and one small median submandibular plate in *Dipterus* (Forster-Cooper, '37), *Griphognathus* (Miles, '77), and *Scaumenacia* (Fig. 5d; Jarvik, '67), but Campbell and Barwick ('84b) reconstructed three pairs of large submandibulars and one small median submandibular in *Speonesydrion* (Fig. 5c). Rhipidistians have a series of many narrow submandibular plates (Fig. 5b). Actinopterygians lack submandibulars (Fig. 5a).

Palate (Fig. 6)

14. In all dipnoans the anterior nares are situated at the posterior edge of the upper lip, at the anterior edge of the mouth; the posterior nares are within the oral cavity (Fig. 6c–e). This condition is unknown in any other osteichthyans. Both openings lie on the ventral side of the nasal capsule, which has no endoskeletal floor.

15. The pterygoids (entopterygoids or endopterygoids) meet along the midline from their anterior ends almost back to the level of the jaw articulation (Fig. 6c–e). They are fused together in most primitive dipnoans (*Dipnorhynchus*, Fig. 6c, and *Speonesydrion*). In all dipnoans, except perhaps *Uranolophus* in which its shape is a matter of contention, the parasphenoid is therefore excluded from the anterior region of the skull, whereas it reaches far forwards between the pterygoids in all other osteichthyans. In tetrapods the pterygoids meet only in the most anterior region (Panchen, '70).

16. The bucco-hypophysial foramen opens in the broad anterior portion of the para-

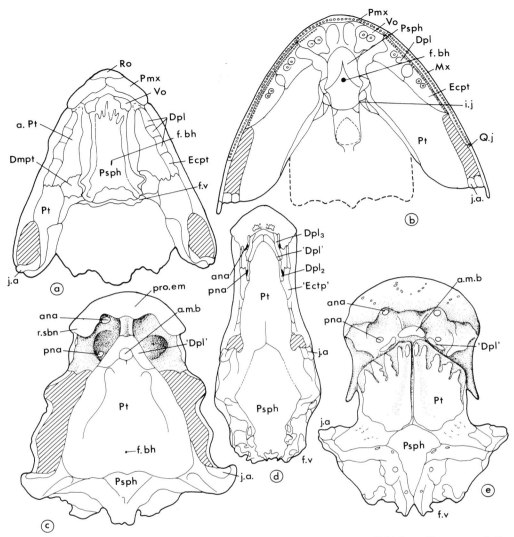

Fig. 6. Palate region of representative osteichthyans. a) Primitive actinopterygian (*Mimia toombsi* from Gardiner, '84, Fig. 75A). b) Rhipidistian (*Glyptolepis groenlandica* from Jarvik, '72, Fig. 31). c) Primitive dipnoan (*Dipnorhynchus sussmilchi* from Thomson and Campbell, '71, Fig. 75). d, e) Advanced dipnoans (d, *Griphognathus whitei* from Miles, '77, Fig. 6; e, *Chirodipterus australis* from Miles, '77, Figs. 18, 67).

sphenoid in primitive dipnoans (Fig. 6c), but in the posterior part of the parasphenoid of all other osteichthyans (Fig. 6a,b) and tetrapods. Posteriorly the parasphenoid lies below the ventral fissure (Miles, '77), and does not end at that structure as in actinopterygians and crossopterygians (Gardiner and Bartram, '77; Gardiner, '84). In primitive dipnoans (*Uranolophus, Dipnorhynchus, Speonesydrion*), the parasphenoid is fused with the pterygoids, but it is distinguishable as a short, plow-shaped bone with broad anterior part and narrow posterior stem in such later

forms as *Chirodipterus* in which it is sutured to the pterygoids (Fig. 6e; Campbell and Barwick, '82b). However, it makes weak contact with the pterygoids in primitive members of actinopterygians, crossopterygians. In these groups and in primitive tetrapods it also extends as far as, or almost as far as, the anterior ends of the pterygoids.

17. The arrangement and numbers of the plates anterior and anterolateral to the pterygoids is different from those of other osteichthyans. The occurrence and arrangement of these plates is variable in dipnoans

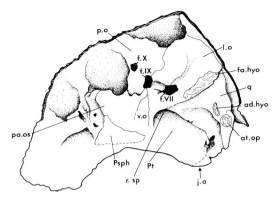

Fig. 7. Composition of the otic region. Posterior neurocranium of *Dipnorhynchus sussmilchi* (from Campbell
and Barwick, '82b, Figs. 2c–9) in ventrolateral view.

as a whole, and even within one species (*Griphognathus whitei*; Fig. 6d; Miles, '77; Campbell and Barwick, '83, '84a). Details of these
bones and their homologies are discussed by
Campbell and Barwick (this volume).

18. Autostyly occurs within osteichthyans
only in dipnoans. The autostyly of dipnoans
is distinct from that of holocephalans and
tetrapods (see Schultze, this volume). Three
processes of the palatoquadrate fuse with the
neurocranium as in tetrapods. This is unlike
the arrangement in holocephalans. A fourth
process, the pterygoid process of the tetrapods, which corresponds to the pars autopa-
latina in a parasphenoid not fused to the
neurocranium, is missing in dipnoans. This
feature, together with the occurrence of an
intracranial joint in the primitive tetrapod
Ichthyostega (Jarvik, '80), and the formation
of the neurocranium in two parts in extant
amphibians, indicate that the autostyly of
tetrapods arose in parallel.

Dipnorhynchus has a distinctive otic series
dorsal and medial to the quadrate (Fig. 7;
Campbell and Barwick, '82b) not known in
other osteichthyans. The otic capsule shows
no suture lines in all other Devonian dipnoans in which it is known. Therefore it cannot at present be decided if these four
ossifications are a feature of all primitive
dipnoans and lost in advanced dipnoans, or
an autapomorphy of *Dipnorhynchus*.

19. The posterior part of the dermal skull
roof is supported in dipnoans by narrow cristae (median, dorsolateral, lateral) of the neurocranium (Fig. 8c,d); it does not lie flat on

the neurocranium as in primitive actinopterygians (Fig. 8a; Gardiner, '84) or crossopterygians (Fig. 8b; Chang, '82). A fossa bridgei
is not developed in primitive actinopterygians (Gardiner, '84:242), or actinistians (Gardiner, '84:243). A well-developed post-temporal fossa (fossa bridgei of Jarvik, '80) is
present in advanced rhipidistians. Axial
musculature enters the post-temporal fossa
of advanced rhipidistians and the fossa
bridgei of advanced actinopterygians posteriorly. In dipnoans the jaw musculature occupies the space between neurocranium and
dermal skull roof, which is divided into the
masseter and temporalis fossae by the dorsolateral cristae (Fig. 8d). These spaces have
only a narrow opening posteriorly (Miles, '77;
Campbell and Barwick, '82b). We agree with
Jarvik ('80) and Gardiner ('84) that the masseter and temporalis fossae are not homologous with the post-temporal fossa of rhipidistians, but are a unique derived feature of
all dipnoans.

Gill arches (Fig. 9)

The gill skeleton is only known from extant and very few Devonian dipnoans (Miles,
'77). Thus supporting evidence for the following points is necessary from the study of other
Devonian genera.

In the only Devonian dipnoans in which
the gill arches are well preserved, viz., *Griphognathus* (Fig. 9d) and *Chirodipterus*, there
are two basal elements. The anterior one is
formed by the fusion of the basihyal (= sublingual rod) and an anterior basibranchial as
interpreted by Miles ('77) and Campbell and
Barwick (this volume) but contrary to Rosen
et al. ('81) and Gardiner ('84). The similarities between the ventral gill skeleton of
Eusthenopteron (Fig. 9b; Jarvik, '54) and that
of *Griphognathus* (Miles, '77) are convergent.
On the other hand, there is no proof that the
single basibranchial in *Latimeria*, and *Glyptolepis* is the primitive condition for sarcopterygians (Rosen et al., '81). These genera
are not primitive members of their groups. Like
the extant dipnoan *Neoceratodus*, which has
one basibranchial and one basihyal, they
may exhibit a derived reduced state.

20. Isolated hypobranchials are not present
in the known gill skeleton of dipnoans, although a separate hypohyal is still developed as in other osteichthyans (Fig. 9d). The
presence of hypobranchials is primitive for
gnathostomes (Fig. 9b,c). The loss of hypobranchials in urodeles occurs within that

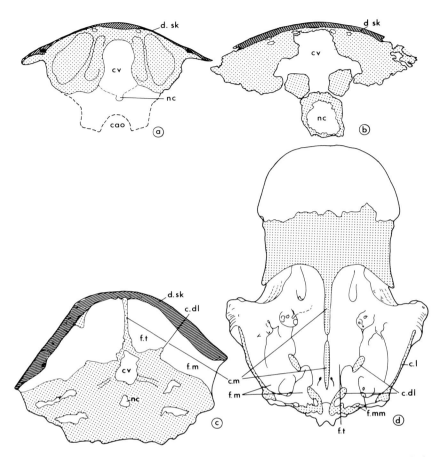

Fig. 8. a–c, Cross sections through posterior neuro-cranium with overlying dermal skull roof. a) Primitive actinopterygians (*Moythomasia durgaringa* from Gardiner, '84, Fig. 27). b) Primitive rhipidistian (*Youngolepis praecursor* from Chang, '82, Fig. 4, section 460). c) Prim-itive dipnoan (*Dipnorhynchus sussmilchi* from Campbell and Barwick, '82b, Fig. 17a). d) Neurocranium of dip-noan *Chirodipterus australis* (from Miles, '77, Fig. 34) in dorsal view; dermal skull roof removed.

group (Jarvik, '62), and cannot be used as a synapomorphy of dipnoans and tetrapods (contrary to Gardiner, '84:360).

21. Primitive dipnoans do not possess pha-ryngobranchials (Miles, '77). Nelson ('68, Fig. 5D) figured cartilaginous nodules off the me-dial ends of the epibranchials in *Neocerato-dus*, but these must be secondary structures. The loss of pharyngobranchials is paralled in tetrapods.

CONCLUSIONS

During their long evolutionary history, dipnoans either lost or grossly modified many skeletal characters known to have been pres-ent in primitive members of the group. We have no direct knowledge of features of the soft anatomy that left no traces on the skele-ton; nor do we at present have an adequate knowledge of the post-cranial skeleton of any primitive dipnoan. Soft anatomical charac-ters of the post-cranial skeleton of the ad-vanced genera should not be taken as representative of the whole of the Dipnoi in the absence of corroborative evidence. The use of outgroups to provide such evidence is dubious if the results are in conflict with those derived from the comparative study of known primitive skeletal characteristics.

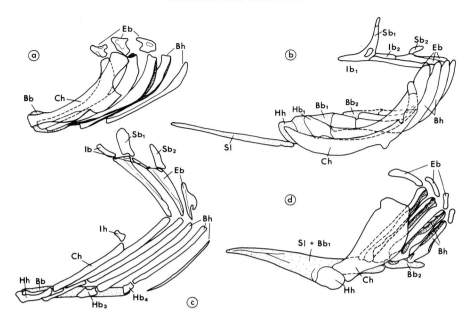

Fig. 9. Gill arch skeleton in lateral view of representative osteichthyans. a)Actinistian (*Rhabdoderma elegans* from Forey, '81, Fig. 3A,B,C). b) Rhipidistian (*Eusthenopteron foordi* from Jarvik, '54, Figs. 8A, 17). c) Primitive actinopterygian (*Mimia toombsi* from Gardiner, '84, Figs. 108, 119). d) Dipnoan (*Griphognathus whitei* from Miles, '77, Fig. 138b).

Consequently, any attempt at discussion of relationships between Dipnoi and other groups at present must rest on a comparison of the known derived cranial characters of primitive group members, and these we have outlined above.

The lower Devonian osteichthyan, *Diabolepis*, (Chang and Yu, '84) is discussed elsewhere in this volume from different points of view (Schultze, Campbell and Barwick). However, in response to editorial and reviewer's comments we summarize our main conclusions herein. Four of the cranial characters listed above for the Dipnoi (numbers 1, 2, 7, 9) may be regarded as occurring also in *Diabolepis*. Nine characters (numbers 4, 5, 8, 14–19) are not present; seven (3, 6, 11, 12, 13, 20, 21) are not known in *Diabolepis*; and one (number 10), the bone arrangement on the lower jaw, cannot be determined.

All the characters listed above as common to dipnoans and *Diabolepis* are questionable. The homologies of the median B-bone and the long series of small canal-bearing supraorbital bones (numbers 1 and 2), have not been established by the normal methods of bone interrelationship and relation to other

features such as the brain case and the orbits. Characters 7 and 9 are in dispute because it has not been shown that the lower jaws and the skull described as belonging to the species *D. speratus*, are in fact representative of a single species.

Mention should be made of the presence of rostral tubules in *Diabolepis*. Such tubules are also known in *Youngolepis* and *Powichthys*. Their significance in both these groups, however, remains unknown and further work on their innervation and relation to the lateral line system is necessary before they can be shown to be the homologues of the tubules in the Dipnoi. In any case the presence of similar tubules in *Youngolepis* and *Powichthys*, acknowledged rhipidistians, indicates that care is needed in the interpretation of these structures.

Diabolepis shows the primitive osteichthyan condition in all nine features in which it differs from dipnoans.

In summary, we consider the evidence for considering *Diabolepis* as the sister group of the Dipnoi as weak at present. Further work on the lower jaw and the rostral tubuli may strengthen the case, but meanwhile we regard the position of the genus relative to the Dipnoi as indeterminate.

ACKNOWLEDGMENTS

The authors thank very much Mrs. C. Kaubisch, Geol.-Paläontologisches Institut, Universität Göttingen, West Germany, who prepared the figures, and the typing service, Biological Division, University of Kansas, Lawrence, Kansas, for typing the final copy. H.-P. Schultze was very pleased to have the support of Prof. O. H. Walliser and the Geol.-Paläontologisches Institut, Universität Göttingen, West Germany during his sabbatical year.

LITERATURE CITED

Campbell, K.S.W., and R.E. Barwick (1982a) A new species of the lungfish *Dipnorhynchus* from New South Wales. Palaeontology 25:509–527.

Campbell, K.S.W., and R.E. Barwick (1982b) The neurocranium of the primitive dipnoan *Dipnorhynchus sussmilchi* (Etheridge). J. Vert. Paleont. 2:286–327.

Campbell, K.S.W., and R.E. Barwick (1983) Early evolution of dipnoan dentitions and a new genus *Speonesydrion*. Mem. Assoc. Australas. Palaeontol. 1:17–49.

Campbell, K.S.W., and R.E. Barwick (1984a) The choana, maxillae, premaxillae and anterior palatal bones of early dipnoans. Proc. Linn. Soc. N.S.W. 107:147–170.

Campbell, K.S.W., and R.E. Barwick (1984b) *Speonesydrion*, an Early Devonian dipnoan with primitive toothplates. Palaeo Ichthyologica 2:1–48.

Chang, M.-M. (1982) The Braincase of *Youngolepis*, a Lower Devonian Crossopterygian from Yunnan, Southwestern china. Stockholm: GOTAB, 113 p.

Chang, M.-M., and Yu (1984) Structure and phylogenetic significance of *Diabolichthys speratus* gen. et sp. nov., a new dipnoan-like form from the Lower Devonian of eastern Yunnan, China. Proc. Linn. Soc. N.S.W. 107:171–184.

Denison, R.H. (1968) Early Devonian lungfishes from Wyoming, Utah and Idaho. Fieldiana Geol. 17:353–413.

Denison, R.H. (1974) The structure and evolution of teeth in lungfishes. Fieldiana Geol. 33:31–58.

Forey, P.L. (1981) The coelacanth *Rhabdoderma* in the Carboniferous of the British Isles. Palaeontology 24:203–229.

Forster-Cooper, C. (1937) The Middle Devonian fish fauna of Achanarras. Trans. R. Soc. Edinburgh 59:223–239.

Gardiner, B.G. (1984) The relationships of the palaeoniscid fishes, a review based on new specimens of *Mimia* and *Moythomasia* from the Upper Devonian of Western Australia. Bull. Br. Mus. (Nat. Hist.), Geol. 37:173–428.

Gardiner, B.G. and A.W.H. Bartram (1977) The homologies of ventral cranial fissures in osteichthyans. In S.M., Andrews, R.S. Miles and A.D. Walker (eds): Problems in Vertebrate Evolution. Linn. Soc. Symp. Ser. Vol. 4, pp. 227–245.

Holmgren, N., and E. Stensiö (1936) Kranium und Visceralskelett der Akranier, Cycostomen und Fische. In L. Bolk, E. Göppert, E. Kallius and W. Lubosch (eds): Handbuch der vergleichenden Anatomie der Wirbeltiere, Vol. 4. Berlin: Urban & Schwarzenberg, pp. 233–500.

Jarvik, E. (1954) On the visceral skeleton in *Eusthenopteron* with a discussion of the parasphenoid and palatoquadrate in fishes. Kgl. Svenska VetenskAkad. Handl. Stockholm (4) 5:1–104.

Jarvik, E. (1962) Les porolépiformes et l'origine des urodèles. Coll. Internat. Centre National Rech. Sci. [Problèmes actuels de Paléontologie (Évolution des vertébrés), Paris 1961] 104:87–101.

Jarvik, E. (1967) On the structure of the lower jaw in dipnoans: With a description of an early Devonian dipnoan from Canada, *Melanognathus canauensis* gen. et sp. nov. In C. Patterson and P.H. Greenwood (eds): Fossil vertebrates. J. Linn. Soc. (Zool.) 47:155–183.

Jarvik, E. (1972) Middle and Upper Devonian Porolepiformes from East Greenland with special reference to *Glyptolepis groenlandica* n. sp. and a discussion on the structure of the head in the Porolepiformes. Medd. Grønland 187:1–307.

Jarvik, E. (1980) Basic Structure and Evolution of Vertebrates. Vol. I. London, New York: Academic Press, p. 575.

Jessen, H.L. (1980) Lower Devonian Porolepiformes from the Canadian Arctic with special reference to *Powichthys thorsteinssoni* JESSEN. Palaeontographica Abt. A 167:180–214.

Jollie, M. (1962) Chordate Morphology. New York: Reinhold Books, p. 478.

Miles, R.S. (1977) Dipnoan (lungfish) skulls and the relationships of the group: A study based on new species from the Devonian of Australia. J. Linn. Soc. Lond. (Zool.) 61:1–328.

Nelson, G. (1968) Gill-arch structure in *Acanthodes*. In T. Ørvig (ed): Current Problems of Lower Vertebrate Phylogeny. Proc. Nobel Symp. 4. Stockholm: Almqvist & Wiksell, pp. 129–43.

Panchen, A.L. (1970) Anthracosauria. In O. Kuhn (ed): Handbuch der Paläoherpetologie. Pt. 5A. Stuttgart: Fischer, p. 84.

Pearson, D.M. (1982) Primitive bony fishes, with special reference to *Cheirolepis* and palaeonisciform actinopterygians. Zool. J. Linn. Soc. Lond. 74:35–67.

Pearson, D.M., and T.S. Westoll (1979) The Devonian actinopterygian *Cheirolepis* Agassiz. Trans. R. Soc. Edinburgh 70:337–399.

Rosen, D.E., P.L. Forey, B.G. Gardiner, and C. Patterson (1981) Lungfishes, tetrapods, paleontology, and plesiomorphy. Bull. Am. Mus. Nat. Hist. 167:159–276.

Schultze, H.-P. (1969) *Griphognathus* GROSS, ein langschnauziger Dipnoer aus dem Oberdevon von Bergisch-Gladbach (Rheinisches Schiefergebirge) und von Lettland. Geologica Palaeontologica 3:21–79.

Schultze, H.-P. and M. Arsenault (1985) The panderichthyid fish *Elpistostege*: A close relative of tetrapods? Palaeontology 28:293–309.

Stensiö, E.A. (1937) On the Devonian coelacanthids of Germany with special reference to the dermal skeleton. Kgl. Svenska VetenskAkad. Handl. Stockholm (3) 16:1–56.

Thomson, K.S., and K.S.W. Campbell (1971) The structure and relationships of the primitive Devonian lungfish—*Dipnorhynchus sussmilchi* (Etheridge). Bull. Peabody Mus. Nat. Hist. 38:1–109.

Watson, D.M.S., and H. Day (1916) Notes on some Palaeozoic fishes. Manchester Mem. 60:1–48.

Watson, D.M.S., and H. Day (1916) Notes on some Palaeozoic fishes. Mem. Proc. Manchester Lit. Phil. Soc. 60:1–48.

Westoll, T.S. (1949) On the evolution of the dipnoi. In G.L. Jepsen, E. Mayr, and G.G. Simpson (eds): Genetics, Paleontology, and Evolution. Princeton, N.J.: Princeton Univ. Press, pp. 121–184.

JOURNAL OF MORPHOLOGY SUPPLEMENT 1:39–74 (1986)

Dipnoans as Sarcopterygians

HANS-PETER SCHULTZE
*Museum of Natural History, Department of Systematics and Ecology,
The University of Kansas, Lawrence, Kansas 66045*

ABSTRACT   Dipnoans are osteichthyans, and are the sister group of crossopterygians (actinistians, onychodontiforms, porolepiforms, osteolepiforms, and including tetrapods). They share with crossopterygians the following derived features: anocleithrum, connection between the preopercular and infraorbital sensory lines, true enamel on teeth, cosmine, sclerotic ring with more than four plates, submandibular series, archipterygium, and process of endochondral bone formation. These features characterize the sarcopterygians (crossopterygians and dipnoans), whereas the intracranial joint, double-headed hyomandibula, and three extrascapulae are synapomorphies of crossopterygians. Rhipidistians (onychodontiforms, porolepiforms, osteolepiforms, and including tetrapods) are characterized by two synapomorphies, the presence of an extratemporal and narrow submandibular bone(s). Plicidentine, four infradentaries, three coronoids, and a fenestra ventro-lateralis are synapomorphies of porolepiforms, osteolepiforms, and tetrapods. The tetrapods are most closely related to panderichthyid osteolepiforms (with which they share labyrinthodont plicidentine, three pairs of median skull roof bones, flat skull with high dorsally situated orbits, and marginal position of external naris). The common ancestor of dipnoans and tetrapods is also the common ancestor of crossopterygians (including tetrapods) and dipnoans; in other words, the hypothetical common ancestor of all sarcopterygians. The dipnoans are not the closest sister group of tetrapods, independently if living forms only are considered, or fossil forms included.

In 1967, while I was in Sweden studying the Late Devonian lungfish *Griphognathus sculpta*, the ichthyologist Dr. William A. Gosline visited Stockholm and asked how I knew I was working on a lungfish if the specimen did not have tooth plates, the main feature of dipnoans. After initial astonishment on my part, it was very easy to convince him that *Griphognathus* (Fig. 2B), like other Devonian lungfishes, can be characterized by many advanced features of the skull roof, the cheek region, and the composition of the lower jaw (see Schultze and Campbell, this volume). These features distinguish all dipnoans very clearly from other osteichthyans and tetrapods, so that it was a surprise recently to see *Griphognathus* used as the basis for returning to the old idea that lungfish are closely related to tetrapods (Rosen et al., '81). A close relationship between lungfishes and tetrapods was first discussed after the discovery of living lungfishes in the middle of the last century (Owen, 1839; Bischoff,

1840). Increasing knowledge of fossil fishes changed that viewpoint during the last century, a change largely accomplished by zoologists (Conant, this volume).

The specializations of lungfishes are so obvious that there has never been a problem in assigning a specimen to the dipnoans since Dollo (1896) clearly defined and assigned the proper genera to the group and clarified their phylogeny. *Powichthys* (Fig. 10B) is clearly not a dipnoan, contrary to the opinion of Rosen et al. ('81:165), because it lacks all dipnoan synapomorphies (see Schultze and Campbell, this volume). Jessen ('75, '80) has shown that *Powichthys* possesses a rhipidistianlike arrangement of bones in the posterior skull roof, an intracranial joint, pointed teeth with enamel and plicidentine, external nasal openings, and additional features typical of rhipidistians.

There are, however, fossil forms difficult to assign to either rhipidistians or tetrapods. *Elpistostege* has been considered a labyrinthodont amphibian (Westoll, '38, '43) or a panderichthyid rhipidistian (Worobjewa, '73). Worobjewa's suggestion is supported by new material of *Elpistostege* (Schultze and Arsenault, '85). Comparing *Panderichthys* and *Elpistostege* with *Ichthyostega* (Worobjewa, '73, Fig. 1) or with a labyrinthodont that has paired postparietals (Schultze and Arsenault, '85, Fig. 8) demonstrates a close similarity in the arrangement of skull roof bones in panderichthyid rhipidistians and labyrinthodont amphibians. *Panderichthys* (Fig. 2A) and *Elpistostege* do possess paired frontals, unknown in other rhipidistians.

Campbell and Bell ('77) described an isolated lower jaw, *Metaxygnathus*, from the Late Devonian of Australia as a labyrinthodont. It is difficult to assign isolated bones of either rhipidistians or early tetrapods, because the morphology of many elements in the two groups is very similar. The only advanced feature that justifies the determination of a lower jaw as tetrapod is the passage of the mandibular sensory line through an open groove rather than a closed tube. The latter condition is the case in the lower jaw of *Metaxygnathus* (Fig. 15H), and in addition the jaw possesses an adsymphysial tooth plate like that in osteolepiforms (Jessen, '66). Thus like *Elpistostege, Metaxygnathus* has to be considered a rhipidistian, not a labyrinthodont (see Schultze and Arsenault, '85, for further discussion).

How can one support a close relationship between dipnoans and tetrapods when the many strong similarities between rhipidistians and tetrapods have often made it difficult to assign specimens to one or the other of the latter groups? There is no case known where a fossil specimen first assigned to tetrapods later had to be reassigned to dipnoans. However, the assignment of primitive rhipidistians and dipnoans can be problematical. The assignment of *Powichthys*, clearly a rhipidistian in the author's opinion, is questioned by Rosen et al. ('81:165). On the other hand, the position of *Diabolepis* (Chang and Yu, '84) within dipnoans is doubtful, because it has a premaxilla and the anterior naris is not within the mouth cavity. These are both plesiomorphic crossopterygian features, whereas the skull roof pattern approaches that of primitive dipnoans.

Are the similarities betwen dipnoans and tetrapods convergent, synapomorphies of all sarcopterygians (tetrapods, rhipidistians, actinistians and dipnoans), or true synapomorphies of dipnoans and tetrapods (Rosen et al.,

'81)? This discussion cannot be approached by studying soft anatomy (Rosen et al., '81, character 61); therefore I will limit the argument (as Rosen et al., '81, have done) to structures that can be observed in fossil and Recent fishes and tetrapods. Many of these features have been used in previous attempts to align dipnoans with nearly every major fish group: skull roof with placoderms (Woodward, 1891; Eastmann, '06); tooth plates with holocephalans (Jarvik, '67; Ørvig, '67); autostyly with holocephalans and amphibians (Kesteven, '31, '50); embryology with actinopterygians (Bertmar, '66); cosmine with crossopterygians (Miles, '75); and choana and paired fins with tetrapods (Rosen et al., '81, and earlier authors).

To determine synapomorphies of a clade, e.g., a large group, and to minimize the number of homoplasies (convergent characters found outside the clade and derived secondarily within the clade), one must use derived features that define the clade at the level of their most primitive members—the basal taxa. I will use an abbreviated terminology, e.g., "plesiomorphic dipnoans, actinistians, etc." to refer to the basal taxa or taxon of dipnoans, actinistians, etc. In using the notion of a basal taxon (plesiomorphic member), I assume that each taxon is a monophyletic clade. It is not assumed that plesiomorphic members of a group are plesiomorphic in *all* their features. Derived features found in advanced ingroup members but not in plesiomorphic members of that group are evolved within the group. Such features have to be interpreted as convergent if they occur in other groups and if it cannot be shown that they are features common to an even larger clade. By that reasoning, soft anatomical features are difficult to assess; they are known (with very few exceptions) only in the living members of each group (terminal taxa of a clade) and rarely in the plesiomorphic members.

Figure 12 gives the terminology of the groups dealt with in this paper. The Sarcopterygii include dipnoans and crossopterygians (including tetrapods). The Crossopterygii comprise actinistians, onychodontiforms, porolepiforms (including youngolepiforms), osteolepiforms, and tetrapods. Tetrapods are members of the rhipidistian clade because rhipidistian synapomorphies are shared by tetrapods (see Ax, '84, for an extensive discussion of methodology). The clades Rhipidistia, Crossopterygii, and Sarcopterygii are monophyletic only by including tetrapods.

Nevertheless, the terms rhipidistian, crossopterygian, and sarcopterygian are regularly used to refer to the piscine members only.

I will discuss here the major features that have been used to argue for different affinities of dipnoans. I hope to demonstrate the importance of these features as either autapomorphies, convergences within dipnoans, or synapomorphies relating dipnoans with crossopterygians.

A critical evaluation of suggested relationships of dipnoans will be followed by an assessment of plesiomorphic members in different groups of osteichthyans so that a sister group relationship between dipnoans and crossopterygians can be justified. Finally, I will discuss and refute all characters supporting the sister group relationship between dipnoans and tetrapods that was proposed by Rosen et al. ('81).

ARTHRODIRAN PLACODERMS AND THE SKULL ROOF

Median, unpaired bones are found in dipnoans and arthrodires. Woodward (1891:234) believed that this indicates a close relationship:

> The dermal or membrane bones of the cranial roof in this subclass [Dipnoi including the arthrodires] exhibit little conformity with the arrangement almost invariably observed in Teleostomi; and it seems impossible to apply to them the nomenclature adopted in the case of the latter subclass.

The arrangement of skull roofing bones, especially the occurrence of median, unpaired elements, was used by Woodward (1891), Dean (1895) and Eastmann ('06) to align ceratodontid dipnoans with arthrodiran placoderms (Fig 1A). Eastman ('06) opposed Dollo's (1896) sequence from heavily ossified Devonian lungfishes with a heterocercal caudal fin to Recent ceratodontid dipnoans with skulls of many cartilaginous parts and a diphycercal caudal fin. Ontogenetic data suggest that the cartilaginous skull and diphycercal caudal fin are primitive features and ceratodontids primitive dipnoans. Cartilage appears earlier in ontogeny than bone, and a protocercal caudal tail (an early ontogenetic feature) looks similar to a diphycercal tail. Eastman interpreted this early ontogenetic appearance as an indication of primitiveness. Therefore, he considered living dipnoans to be more primitive than the Devonian forms and arrived at a trichotomy

between Paleozoic (for him advanced) dipnoans, ceratodontid dipnoans, and arthrodires. It will, however, be shown below that Dollo was justified in considering the skull roof bone arrangement and heterocercal caudal fin of Devonian dipnoans to be primitive.

The skull roof pattern in dipnoans is unique within fishes, and as distinct from other osteichthyans (including the tetrapods; Fig. 2) as it is from arthrodires (Fig. 1B,C). Many attempts have been made to compare the pattern with that of other osteichthyans (Watson and Day, '16; Watson and Gill, '23; Goodrich, '25; Holmgren and Stensiö, '36). Today, the noncommittal A-, B-, C- nomenclature of Forster-Cooper ('37) is commonly used because indisputable homologies cannot be demonstrated between bones in the skull roof of dipnoans and those of osteichthyans and tetrapods. The A-, B-, and D- bones are unpaired elements along the midline; the paired C- and E- bones meet in the midline posterior and anterior to the D-bone (Fig. 2B). Neither the cephalic division of the main lateral line nor the supraorbital sensory line passes through these bones. In addition, neither of these sensory lines passes through the I- and J-bones (lateral to the B-bone), except in early dipnoans in which the supraorbital sensory line does not join the cephalic division of the main lateral line as it does in primitive actinopterygians. Instead, the supraorbital sensory line reaches backward onto the J-bone. The occipital commissure passes through the I-bones. There is a "cluster of five bones (B- and the pairs of J- and I-bones) in the occipital region of dipnoans" (Rosen et al., '81:226); nevertheless, this cluster is not comparable with the five bones (unpaired fused postparietal and paired supratemporals and tabulars) in the posterior skull roof of *Ichthyostega* as proposed by Gardiner ('80) and Rosen et al. ('81). The bones of the cephalic division of the main lateral line (tabular and supratemporal) are included in the cluster of five bones in *Ichthyostega* (Fig. 2C) but not in dipnoans (Fig. 2B). The comparable cluster would have to include the Y_1- and Y_2-bones, which results in a cluster of nine bones not known outside of dipnoans. The basic, most common pattern in the posterior region of the skull roof of tetrapods (*Ichthyostega* excepted) and osteichthyans is a cluster of an even number of (paired) bones: four in palaeoniscoid actinopterygians (Figs. 10A, 13A) and actinistians and porolepiforms (Figs. 13C, 14A; type Y of Andrews, '73); six in tetrapods, osteolepiforms (Figs. 2A,C, 14B-D) and onychodonts

Abbreviations

A, B, C, D, E, H, I, J, X, Y, Z, bones in the dipnoan skull roof
a.n., anterior naris
An, angular
?An, questionable angular of dipnoans (Md Oc2 of Jarvik, '67)
b, bone
ch, ceratohyal
cho, choana
Co, coronoid
c.t. cornu trabecula
c.V$_1$, V$_{2,3}$, 4, VII, canals for nervus profundus, trigeminus, facialis
d, dentine
De, dentary
?De, questionable dentary of dipnoans (Md X of Jarvik, '67)
Dpl, dermopalatine
> >Dpl< < palatine of Rosen et al. ('81) = dermopalatine 2 of Miles ('77)
Dspl, dentalosplenial of actinopterygians
e, enamel
> >e.d.b.< < , extra dermal bone of Rosen et al. ('81) = dermopalatine 3 of Miles ('77)
eh, epihyal
Ept, ectopterygoid
Esc, extrascapular
Et, extratemporal
f, flask-shaped part of pore-canal system
Fr, frontal
h.p., horizontal partition of flask-shaped part of pore-canal system
It, intertemporal
lj, lower jaw
mc, mandibular canal
mtp, metapterygoid
Mx, maxilla
> >Mx< < , maxilla of Rosen et al. ('81) = ectopterygoid + tooth-plates forming lateal nasal field + subnasal ridge of Miles ('77)
N, nasal
na, external naris of tetrapods
nc, notochord
orc, oral sensory canal

Pa, parietal
p.a., processus ascendens
p.b., processus basalis
ph, pharyngohyal
ple, pleromin
Pmx, premaxilla
> >Pmx< < , premaxilla of Rosen et al. ('81) = preoral area of Miles ('77)
p.n., posterior naris
po, external pore of pore-canal system
p.o., processus oticus
Pp, postparietal
pq, palatoquadrate
Prart, prearticular
pr.bp, processus basipterygoideus
pr.c, processus connectens
pr.d, processus descendens of sphenoid
Pro, postrostral
Psp, parasphenoid
Pspl, postsplenial
?Pspl, questionable postsplenial in dipnoans (Md Mc2 of Jarvik, '67)
Pt, entopterygoid
pt, processus pterygoideus
ptp, propterygium
pu, pulp canal
ra, radius
Ro, rostral
San, surangular
?San, questionable surangular in dipnoans (Md Oc3 of Jarvik '67)
sc, scapulocoracoid
sh, stylohyal (= interhyal)
Spl, splenial
?Spl, questionable splenial of dipnoans (Md Mcl of Jarvik '67)
St, supratemporal
Ta, tabular
ul, ulna
Vo, vomer
> >Vo< < , vomer of Rosen et al. ('81) = dermopalatine 1 of Miles ('77) Y, pre- (holocephalan) or adsymphysial (dipnoan) plate

(type X of Andrews, '73). The number of paired bones increases in some early rhipidistians (e.g., eight in *Powichthys*, Fig. 10B).

The unpaired D-bone is lost in advanced dipnoans. Rosen et al. ('81, Fig. 42) choose such dipnoans for comparison with tetrapods and osteichthyans in "the position of the eye in relation to the junction between two pairs of large bones (p. 225)." *Griphognathus* and most other dipnoans do not show that feature; the osteolepiform *Panderichthys* is actually closer to tetrapods in this character. In the latter case, the bones of the skull roof can be homologized directly (topographically,

by the course of the sensory lines, and by the position of the pineal opening; Schultze and Arsenault, '85), independent of the names commonly used for these bones. In conclusion, the comparison between skull roof bones of dipnoans and tetrapods utilized by Rosen et al. does not demonstrate a close relationship of the two groups.

HOLOCEPHALANS AND TOOTH PLATES

The presence of a crushing dentition formed by tooth plates has been used to postulate a relationship between dipnoans and arthrodiran placoderms (Eastman, '06; Fig. 1A), and

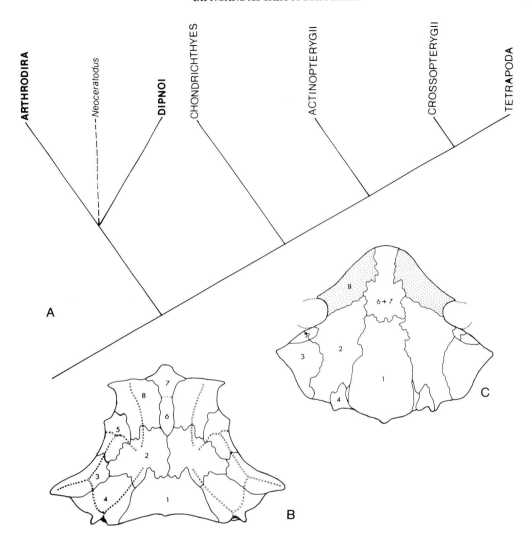

Fig. 1. A. Relationship of dipnoans to arthrodires after Eastman ('06). B, C. Proposed homologies (identical numbers identify proposed homologies) of skull roof bones between the arthrodire *Dunkleosteus* (B) and the dipnoan *Neoceratodus* (C), following Eastman ('06, Figs. 3,4).

between dipnoans and holocephalans (Jarvik, '67; Fig. 3A). An additional argument for a dipnoan-holocephalan (and ptyctodontid) relationship is that the same kind of hard tissue (pleromin) forms the tooth plates (Ørvig, '67). Pleromin occurs in psammosteid agnathans, ptyctodontids, holocephalans and lungfishes. Ørvig ('76a,b) considers these tissues indistinguishable from one another, ex-

cept in regard to their relationship with surrounding hard tissues. Pleromin, which is a hypermineralized, continously growing dentinous hard tissue, forms between aspidin in psammosteid agnathans, between "bony hard tissue" in ptyctodonts, between osteodentine in holocephalans (Fig. 3E), and between dentine or bone (Fig. 3D) in dipnoans (= petrodentine of Lison, '41, or Smith, '77).

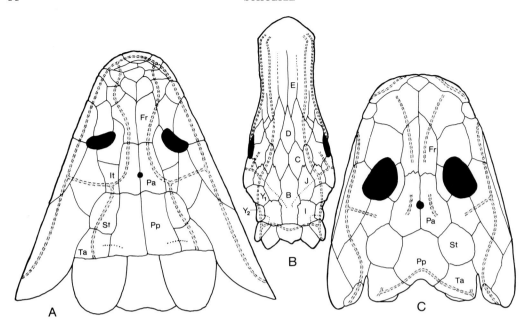

Fig. 2. Comparison of the skull roof. A. *Panderichthys* (from Vorobyeva, '77, Fig. 2B). B. *Griphognathus* (from Miles, '77, Fig. 111). C. *Ichthyostega* (from Jarvik, '80, Fig. 171A).

It also occurs in plectognath teleosts (Ørvig, '80:20). The first occurrence of pleromin in dipnoans is more important for this discussion than the differences to surrounding hard tissues. Pleromin is not a synapomorphy for all dipnoans, as it does not occur in *Griphognathus* (Ørvig, '76b; Smith, '77, '84) or the plesiomorphic forms *Uranolophus, Dipnorhynchus* and *Speonesydrion* (Campbell and Barwick, '83). Pleromin appears "gradually" in tooth plates of *Dipterus* (Denison, '74), forming first only on the elevated parts of tooth ridges and later occupying the whole crushing area of the plate in more advanced forms. The pattern of appearance of pleromin in different groups of fishes and its relation to surrounding hard tissues clearly indicates parallel development.

Ørvig ('76b) argues that the tissue forming the core of the tuberclelike teeth of *Griphognathus* is a combination of denteons and a hypermineralized interstitial substance. That tissue, according to Ørvig ('76b:94), is indistinguishable from similar tissue in the teeth of "most bradyodonts and certain selachians" (e.g., *Ptychodus*). Elasmobranchs, un-like *Griphognathus*, have no enamel covering the tubercles. The teeth of elasmobranchs are not fused to a bony base. The coexistence with different tissues implies parallel development in these two cases, or even in all three, because bradyodonts and *Ptychodus* are not closely related elasmobranchs. In conclusion, histological arguments concerning the tooth plates do not support a direct relationship between dipnoans and elasmobranchiomorphs.

Jarvik ('52) and Mookerjee et al. ('54) postulate a relationship of dipnoans to elasmobranchiomorphs based on the histology and formation of the vertebral centra in the two groups. The arrangement of hard tissue into rings (Jarvik, '52) is a very superficial similarity. Elasmobranch centra are formed by calcified cartilage, the centra of the lungfishes *Soederberghia, Jarvikia,* and *Griphognathus* by bone. Similarity in the formation of the centra does exist between dipnoans, crossopterygians, and tetrapods (Schultze, '70:316, 330). Unfortunately, the specimen studied by Mookerjee et al. ('54) is lost, and no other specimen of *Protopterus* with centra

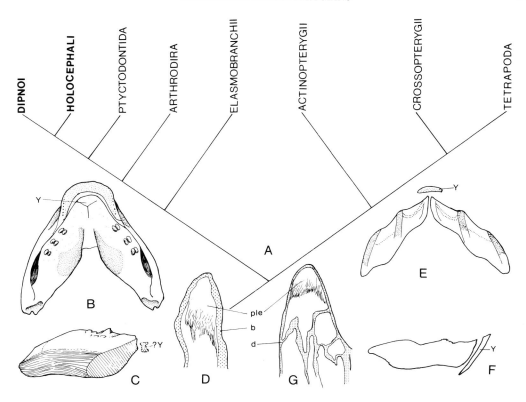

Fig. 3. A. Relationship of dipnoans to holocephalans after Jarvik ('80; for details see Schultze and Trueb, '80). B-D, Dipnoan jaws. B. *Holodipterus santacrucensis*, lower jaw in dorsal view. C. *Chirodipterus wildungensis*, lower jaw in medial view. D. *Protopterus aethiopicus*, vertical section of upper jaw plate of embryo. E-G. Holocephalan jaws. E, F, *Myriacanthus paradoxus*, lower dental plates in dorsal view (E) and medial view (F). G. *Chimaera monstrosa*, vertical section of upper jaw plate of juvenile. B, C, E, F, after Jarvik ('67, Fig. 9); D, after Lison ('41, Fig. 9); G, after Brettnacher ('39, Fig. 6).

has been described. Presence of a cell-bearing chordal sheath seems to be either a convergent or primitive feature, as it is not restricted to dipnoans and elasmobranchiomorphs (Schultze, '70).

The arrangement of tooth plates (Eastman, '06; Jarvik, '67) is also difficult to accept as an indication of relationship. Jarvik ('80) noted differences in relation to other structures: Tooth plates are fused to bony plates in dipnoans, but not in holocephalans; Meckel's cartilage is surrounded by bony plates in dipnoans, but not in holocephalans. The radial arrangement of ridges on dipnoan tooth plates is not found in holocephalans. Most importantly, the formation of dipnoan tooth plates by fusion of isolated denticles during ontogeny (Semon, 1899; Kemp, '77) and phylogeny (Denison, '74) contradicts assertions

of homology, and thus argues against a common ancestry with holocephalans. In contrast, tooth plates of holocephalans develop from a single entity (Schauinsland, '03; Kemp, '84); they evolve phylogenetically by reduction of number of teeth per tooth family and per jaw quadrant (Zangerl, '81). Thus, ontogenetic and phylogenetic development indicate an independent origin of tooth plates in the two groups.

Holocephalans have a deep presymphysial dental plate (Fig. 3F). A flat median bone above the Meckel's cartilage lies in a comparable region in dipnoans (Fig. 3B); it is not as deep as the one figured by Jarvik ('67, Fig. 9C) for *Chirodipterus*. The figured piece "MdY" in *Chirodipterus* is a piece of the prearticular or the Meckel's cartilage (Schultze, '69b). This flat bone lies in the medial continuation of the suture between the prearticular and the lower jaw, bordering bones labially, in the position of the missing coronoids. Therefore, this element (possibly paired, Schultze, '69b) is homologous with the adsymphysial plate in crossopterygians (Schultze, '69b; Miles, '77). Tooth plates in the arthrodire *Mylostoma* differ in both arrangement (Denison, '78) and histology (Ørvig, '57) from that in dipnoans.

Tooth plates and pleromin are independently evolved features of dipnoans, evolved in a parallel manner to similar structures in other fishes. The appearance in early ontogeny of pointed teeth, and also their occurrence in plesiomorphic dipnoans, supports such an interpretation. Small, tuberclelike teeth in *Uranolophus* are formed by dentine (which surrounds a pulp cavity) and enamel. These plesiomorphic dipnoan teeth do posses one feature, namely, enamel, that is a synapomorphy with other sarcopterygians (Smith, '79). Primitive dipnoans do not show differentiation of dentine into plicidentine, which is a plesiomorphic feature of tetrapods (Schultze, '69a, '70).

HOLOCEPHALANS, AMHIBIANS AND AUTOSTYLY

Autostyly, the fusion of the palatoquadrate with the endocranium, has been used to relate dipnoans with holocephalans (Jarvik, '67, '80) or with amphibians (Kesteven,'31; Fox, '65; Rosen et al., '81). Kesteven ('50) combines the two views and derives both dipnoans and amphibians (the latter by two lineages) from holocephalans (Fig. 4A).

In holocephalans (Fig. 4B), the palatoquadrate is fused totally to the endocranium (holostyly), but the hyoid arch is still completely developed with a hypohyal, ceratohyal, epihyal (= hyomandibula) and a posteriorly directed suprapharyngohyal. The holostyly of holocephalans is usually considered to be quite different from that of dipnoans (de Beer, '37; Stahl, '67; but see Kesteven, '50, and Jarvik, '80).

In dipnoans (Fig. 4C), the palatoquadrate fuses to the endocranium with three processes (basal, ascending, and otic). In embryonic stages, the hyoid arch is formed by hypohyal, ceratohyal, stylohyal (an osteichthyan character, equivalent to character 15 of Rosen et al., '81), epihyal (= hyomandibula), and laterohyal (after Fox, '65). These elements can be recognized in fossil dipnoans (Miles, '77), except for the stylohyal

(which may be fused to the quadrate portion of the palatoquadrate) and the laterohyal (which may be included in the broad dorsal epihyal of *Griphognathus*).

The autostylic condition develops differently in amphibians (Fig. 4D). The palatoquadrate embryologically has an anterior pterygoid portion (Edgeworth, '23, '25; Fox, '54) as in actinopterygians, actinistians, and rhipidistians. It is fused to the endocranium by two processes posteriorly (otic and ascending) and anteriorly by the ethmoidal process. The existence of a pterygoid process with an ethmoidal process indicates a more primitive palatoquadrate in the hypothetical amphibian ancestor than in dipnoans. The hyoid arch of amphibians is reduced to a hypohyal and a ceratohyal, and the epihyal is transformed into the columella auris (= stapes). The amphibian endocranium, in contrast to dipnoans, is formed by the fusion of two divisions (an anterior orbito-ethmoidal and a posterior otico-occipital portion; Fox, '54). These more primitive palatoquadrate and two divisions of the endocranium, in combination with the probable occurrence of a remnant of an intracranial joint in *Ichthyostega* (Jarvik, '80), indicate that autostyly has been independently acquired in dipnoans and tetrapods. The occurrence of autostyly in some actinopterygians (e.g., Gymnarchidae), and in holocephalans, dipnoans, and tetrapods, points to functional convergence (Hofer, '45). Although Miles ('75) interpreted most of the features used by Kesteven ('50) and Jarvik ('64, '67, '68) for relating holocephalans and dipnoans as convergences (or "chance"), and others as primitive, the differences in structure and ontogenetic development of the endocranium let me agree with Hofer ('45) and Miles ('75) that autostyly evolved independently within dipnoans.

ACTINOPTERYGIANS AND EMBRYOLOGY

Dipnoans have been related to actinopterygians in recent literature only by Bertmar ('66). Bertmar opposed Fox's ('65) use of embryological data to relate dipnoans with tetrapods. It is true that Fox's ('65) argument is weakened because he made comparisons only with tetrapods, whereas Bertmar ('66) also considered embryological features of actinopterygians. However, Bertmar ('66) found only symplesiomorphies of actinopterygians and dipnoans (Jarvik, '68; Miles, '75): basic similarities in the development and composition of the ethmoidal and orbito-temporal

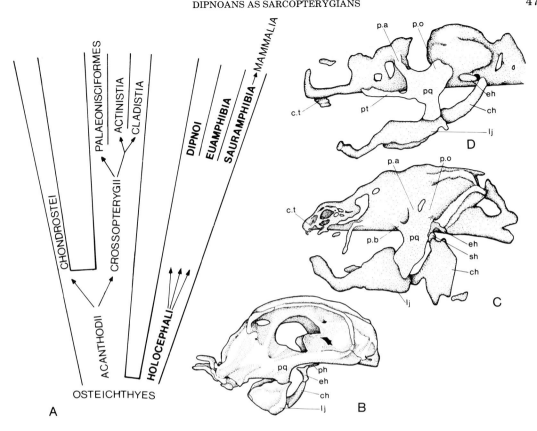

Fig. 4. A. Relationship of dipnoans to holocephalans and amphibians after Kesteven ('50). B-D, Embryonic endocrania. B. Holocephalan *Callorhynchus antarcticus*, after Schauinsland ('03). C. Dipnoan *Neoceratodus forsteri*, after Fox ('65, Figs. 24, 31). D. Urodele amphibian *Andrias japonicus*, after Fox ('54, Figs. 14, 15).

region, and in the endoskeleton of the snout. These symplesiomorphyes do not tell us anything about the closest relatives of dipnoans; they demonstrate only that dipnoans are osteichthyans.

CROSSOPTERYGIANS AND COSMINE

Even though a close relationship between dipnoans and crossopterygians (specifically osteolepiforms) was postulated early in this century (Gregory, '15; Watson, '26; Westoll, '49), Miles ('75) recently tested the arguments for a close affinity of the two groups (Fig. 5A). The feature that unites crossopterygians and dipnoans is cosmine (Miles, '75, '77). Miles ('75) includes actinistians within crossopterygians based on their possession of an intracranial joint and the absence of any indication that an intracranial joint has ever

existed in dipnoans. Later, Miles ('77) excluded actinistians from crossopterygians based on four "negative" characters (lack of an extensive supraotic cavity, lack of cosmine, lack of submandibular, lack of maxilla). He related dipnoans to crossopterygians (excluding actinistians) based on cosmine. The actinistians, following Miles ('77), thus become the sister-group of dipnoans and rhipidistians.

Like early dipnoans, osteolepiforms and porolepiforms possess rhombic scales and dermal bones with cosmine (Fig. 5). Cosmine is described in onychodontiforms (Jessen, '66, '67), but not with certainty in actinistians, causing Rosen et al. ('81) to doubt the usefulness of the character as a whole. Gross ('56), Schultze ('69b) and Ørvig ('69) demonstrated that the cosmine in dipnoans, porolepiforms,

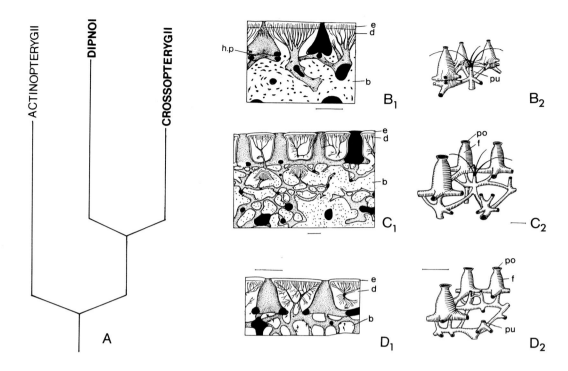

Fig. 5.   A. Relationship of dipnoans to crossopterygians after Miles ('75). B-D. Cosmine and pore-canal system in crossopterygians and dipnoans; B_1-D_1, vertical section through scales; B_2-D_2, restoration of canal system. B. Osteolepidid. C. *Porolepis posaniensis.* D. *Dipterus* sp. Scale bars, 0.1 mm. (B-D, from Schultze, '69b, Fig. 42b-d.)

and osteolepiforms, and especially that in dipnoans and porolepiforms, is very similar (Fig. 5C,D). The osteolepiforms (Fig. 5B), unlike porolepiforms and dipnoans, have a horizontal partition in the flask-shaped portions of the pore canal system. I now agree with Rosen et al. that the latter condition is a derived state within crossopterygians (contrary to Schultze, '69b; Thomson, '75, '77). Still, both Miles ('75, '77) and I maintain that cosmine is a synapomorphy uniting dipnoans and crossopterygians. It has been lost many times within dipnoans and osteolepiforms and at least once in porolepiforms, onychodontiforms, and possibly actinistians (Schultze, '77). Rosen et al. ('81:253) believe (following Smith, '77) that the dipnoan genera *Griphognathus* and *Holodipterus* have secondarily lost cosmine. That is correct at least for *Griphognathus* where scales on the venter still have patches of cosmine (Schultze, '69b, Fig.32b). I also agree with them that it is difficult, if not impossible, to distinguish precosmoid and postcosmoid status. In the case of *Griphognathus*, the loss of cosmine on skull roof bones is one indication that the genus is not as primitive within dipnoans as Rosen et al. postulate.

TETRAPODS AND CHOANA

In connection with the formation of the nasolacrimal duct, Rosen et al. ('81:197) hypothesize that the choana forms by failure of the nasal placode "to migrate outward and upward to the side of the snout as in other fishes." This simple explanation for the differences in position of the nasal openings in fishes is not necessarily the correct one. Rosen et al. suggest that the migration upward of the divided placode accounts for the two external nares in actinopterygians, actinistians, and onychodontiforms, but in osteolepiforms and tetrapods the posterior part of the placode fails to migrate upwards, thus

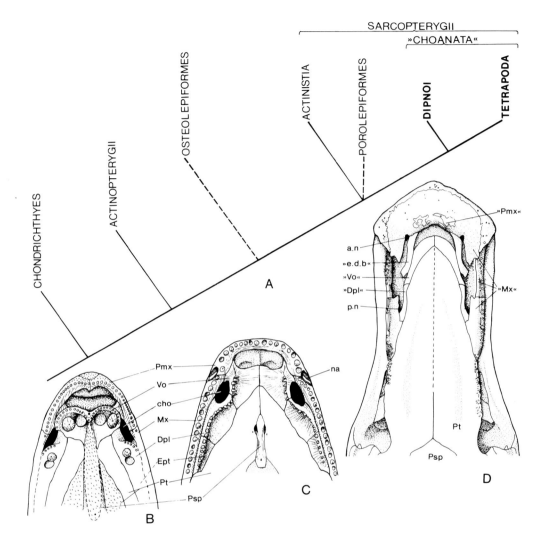

Fig. 6. A. Relationship of dipnoans to tetrapods after Rosen et al. ('81). B-D. Anterior part of palate region. B. Osteolepiform *Panderichthys rhombolepis* (from Worob-jewa '75; Fig. 2). C. Tetrapod *Ichthyostega* sp. (from Jarvik, '52, Fig. 36). D. Dipnoan *Griphognathus whitei* (from Miles, '77, Fig. 57; with terminology by Rosen et al., '81).

forming the choana. However, this does not explain the anatomy of porolepiforms, where two external nares and a fenestra endochoanalis exist with the latter covered by the vomer (Chang, '82). In dipnoans, both the anterior and posterior parts of the nasal placode fail to migrate upward (Bertmar, '68), so that both nares lie inside the mouth (Rosen et al., '81, Fig. 6). We can then call both nares choana (anterior and posterior choana), or anterior and posterior naris depending on our definition of choana.

I prefer to use here the term "choana" as it is used in tetrapods (Fig. 7H). It can be defined in two complementary ways:

1) an opening in the palate surrounded primitively by four dermal bones of the premaxilla, maxilla, vomer and palatine
2) a palatal opening for a pathway beginning with one opening outside the mouth, the external naris (in tetrapods, the pathway for air with the mouth closed)

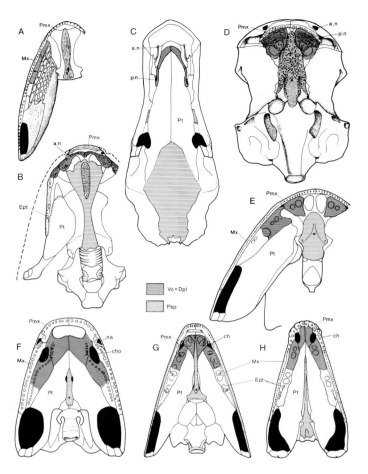

Fig. 7.　Palate region of osteichthyans. A. Actinopterygian *Cheirolepis trailli* (from Pearson and Westoll, '79, Fig. 86). B. Actinistian *Latimeria chalumnae*. C. Dipnoan *Griphognathus whitei* (from Miles, '77, Fig. 6). D. Porolepiform *Youngolepis praecursor* (from Chang, '82, Figs. 10 and 7B). E. Porolepiform *Glyptolepis groenlandica* (from Jarvik, '72, Fig. 31). F. Tetrapod *Ichthyostega* sp. (from Jarvik, '80, Fig. 171B). G. Osteolepiform *Eusthenopteron foordi* (from Jarvik, '54, Fig. 25). H. tetrapod *Eogyrinus attheyi* (from Panchen, '72, Fig. 7).

By these criteria, the posterior palatal openings in dipnoans cannot be called true choanae and are not homologous to the openings in tetrapods (for further differences see Bertmar, '65, '66, '69; Jarvik, '42, '80).

Jarvik ('80) explains the palatal position of the dipnoan nares by the same ontogenetic process as Rosen et al., but arrives at the conclusion that the position of both nares on the palate supports a relationship between dipnoans and holocephalans. In elasmobranchs, the fenestra nasalis communis, the opening for both anterior and posterior naris, is situated ventral to the snout, whereas in holocephalans it is inside the mouth (Jarvik, '80 Fig. 305); Jarvik calls this latter condition "pseudochoana." The "pseudochoana" is a common opening for both nares in holocephalans, and is not comparable to the paired separate openings in dipnoans.

A compelling example of nasal placode migration is seen in the Early Devonian *Diabolepis* (Chang and Yu, '84). *Diabolepis* possesses a premaxilla similar in shape and position to that in plesiomorphic crossopterygians (*Powichthys, Youngolepis*), with the added feature that the posterior part of the premaxilla extends onto the palate. A still further shifting of the premaxilla onto the palate would result in the position of the premaxilla and anterior nostril on the palate as postulated by Allis ('32a,b), for *Neoceratodus*. Based on their interpretation of additional tooth plates in the palate of *Griphognathus* as "marginal teeth", Rosen et al. dismiss Allis' (32a,b) comparative anatomical argument. Instead they argue that the failure of dipnoans to form a continuous infraorbital lateral line canal is an indication that the posterior part of the nasal placode has not migrated dorsally. Accepting such a hypothesis, both nares in dipnoans have moved from a rostral position onto the palate (as seen in *Diabolepis*) and not from a lateral position as have the choana in tetrapods. The anterior naris of *Diabolepis*, already ventral to the upper lip, is still outside the premaxilla, and the posterior naris lies at the posterolateral margin of the premaxilla on the palate. The endoskeletal posterior opening of the nasal capsule (fenestra ventralis of Chang, '82) is situated close to the margin and is supposedly covered by the vomer in *Powichthys, Youngolepis* (Fig. 7D), and porolepiforms (Chang, '82); it is open in osteolepiforms (Jarvik, '80; Rosen et al., '81; Fig. 7G).

Rosen et al. follow earlier interpretations of the posterior naris of dipnoans as choana (for earlier authors see Jarvik, '42:273). They use three lines of evidence:

1) palatal bones around the two nasal openings in *Griphognathus whitei*
2) palatal fenestra in *Polypterus*
3) restoration of fenestra exochoanalis in *Eusthenopteron foordi* (different from that in Jarvik, '42)

Each of these arguments will be discussed.

Miles ('77) describes more bones in the palate of *Griphognathus whitei* than had previously been known in dipnoans (Fig. 7C), other fishes, or tetrapods. There is much variation in the shape, size, and number of the bones (Miles, '77:163; Campbell and Barwick, '84b) lateral to the pterygoids. Miles ('77) interprets all of these as palatal bones (ectopterygoid and dermopalatines), but Rosen et al. ('81) rename the bones to fit their hypothesis of relationship (Table 1).

The nomenclature of Miles ('77) again indicates the difficulties involved in homologizing the bones of dipnoans with those of other fishes or tetrapods. Rosen et al. homologize parts of the ossified upper lip (which is soft in living dipnoans) with the premaxilla, based on a reinterpretation of posteriorly following bones as maxillaries. The toothlike tubercles on the upper lip ("preoral area" of Miles, '77), subnasal ridge, and lateral lamina of *Griphognathus* are interpreted by Rosen et al. as an outer dental arcade, which they divide into premaxilla and maxilla. It seems curious that a combination of bones and parts of bones are homologized with a single element — the maxilla of other fishes and tetrapods.

Except for comparing *Eusthenopteron* with tetrapods, Rosen et al. do not explain why they homologize the dermopalatine 1 of Miles ('77) with the vomer. They may be correct here, but there exists an additional unpaired median bone in most dipnoans that has been named a vomer for which they do not give an explanation (both the "vomer" and dermopalatine 1, are shown in Miles, '77: Fig. 67).

They do propose not a reasonable homologue of the "extra" dermal bone (see Rosen et al., '81:181 in contrast to p. 230). If we accept the homologies of these bones indicated by Rosen et al., we are faced with the anterior naris being positioned medial to the anterior part of the maxilla and lateral to an "extra" dermal bone, and the posterior naris (their choana) medial to the posterior part of

TABLE 1. *Identification of palatal bones of* Griphognathus whitei[1]

Regions identified by Miles	Regions identified by Rosen et al.
Preoral area	Premaxilla
Dermopalatine 1	Vomer
Dermopalatine 2	Palatine
Dermopalatine 3	"Extra" dermal bone
Ectopterygoid	
Tooth plates form lateral nasal field	Maxilla
Subnasal ridge	
Entopterygoid	Pterygoid

[1]Identifications according to Miles (77; Fig 7C), or Rosen et al. ('81, Fig 6D).

the maxilla and lateral to the palatine. None of these topographic relationships occur in any tetrapod. In addition, an ectopterygoid present in rhipidistians and tetrapods is missing in Rosen et al.'s reinterpretation of *Griphognathus*.

The comparison of the palate of a juvenile (4 cm standard length) *Polypterus ornatipinnis* (Rosen et al., '81, Fig. 12) with the palate of adult fishes, especially *Eusthenopteron*, is curious. Only a few of the palatal bones of *Polypterus* (see Allis, '22; Jarvik, '54; Rosen et al., '81, Fig. 45B) are developed in the figured specimen (Rosen et al., '81, Fig. 12). The "opening" that is covered by soft tissue lies in the anteroventral part of the nasal capsule, close to the anterior part of the premaxilla. This "opening" is covered in adults by a medial process of the premaxilla and the mesial dermopalatine (Allis, '22, Fig. 23; Jarvik, '54, Fig. 27B). Even in the juvenile *Polypterus* the "opening" is not surrounded by the same bones as the choana in *Eusthenopteron*. The choana of *Eusthenopteron* and of tetrapods opens at the posteroventral, not anteroventral, part of the nasal capsule. *Polypterus* is not similar to either tetrapods or to *Eusthenopteron*. Perhaps Rosen et al. interpreted the fenestra endonasalis in ventral view as a palatal fenestra (see Allis, '22, Figs. 8, 13).

The only difference in the restorations of the anterior palate of *Eusthenopteron* by Jarvik ('42, Fig. 56) and Rosen et al. ('81, Fig. 14) is in the different shape of the anterior head of the dermopalatine, not in the size of the opening. The anterior head of the dermopalatine has the ability to articulate with the vomer. The tooth row on the dermopalatine does not reach the vomer; the same is the case in *Panderichthys rhombolepis* (Worobjewa, '75, Fig. 2; Fig. 6B). These are minor differences in comparison with the surprising similarity of the two figures. Rosen et al. ('81, Fig. 14) reconstruct the choana as being smaller than the size seen in their photograph of *Eusthenopteron* (Rosen et al., '81, Fig. 13).

Another similarity between osteolepiforms and tetrapods is the relationship in each between the enlarged teeth of the lower jaw and the choana. In all labyrinthodonts with a marginal position of the choana, the teeth of the lower jaw reach into the fenestra exochoanalis. They are also enlarged in some labyrinthodonts (for example, *Limnoscelis*) in that area of the lower jaw. This does not seem to have affected the choana's function. On the other hand, the lower jaw dentition in *Griphognathus* is opposed to the nares, "closing" them (Miles, '77:290–291; Campbell and Barwick, '84b) without affecting the function of the openings.

Campbell and Barwick ('84b) provide a more detailed discussion on the impossibility of homologizing the posterior naris of lungfishes and tetrapods. Northcutt (this volume) also shows that the nerve supply is quite different in tetrapods and dipnoans.

TETRAPODS AND PAIRED FINS

Holmgren ('33, '39, '49a,b) derived urodele limbs from the dipnoan archipterygium, but considered anuran and amniote limbs to represent an independent origin of tetrapod limbs. Rosen et al. ('81) extended Holmgren's viewpoint to derive the paired appendages of all tetrapods from a dipnoan archipterygium, despite the differences between the appendages of urodeles and anurans/amniotes. They specify "seven general conditions of the tetrapod limb" in which the dipnoan archipterygium and tetrapod limb should agree (character "44" and subsequent descriptions inside quotation marks refer to those used by Rosen et al., '81:207–208).

1) "An unpaired basal element (humerus or femur)" is known in all sarcopterygians, not just dipnoans and tetrapods (Fig. 8A–D,F,G). Furthermore, there are many features of the basal element in crossopterygians in common with tetrapods that do not occur on the basal element of dipnoans. For example, the basal element has a dorsomedial process in actinistians and osteolepiforms that is comparable to the entepicondylar process in tetrapods. Rackoff ('80) and Jarvik ('80) identified additional structures of tetrapods that are seen in the humeri of osteolepiforms.

2) "Paired, subequal, sub-basal elements (ulna-radius and fibula-tibia)" [character "44"] are known only in osteolepiforms (Fig. 8C,G) and tetrapods (Fig. 8F). Rosen et al. ('81, Fig. 31) figured a juvenile specimen (15 mm) of *Neoceratodus* showing a colateral element aligned with the second axial element. However, the variation in endoskeletal elements of the pectoral fin of *Neoceratodus* is so great (Howes, 1887) that any of a number of arrangements of the radius could be made. The broad sec-

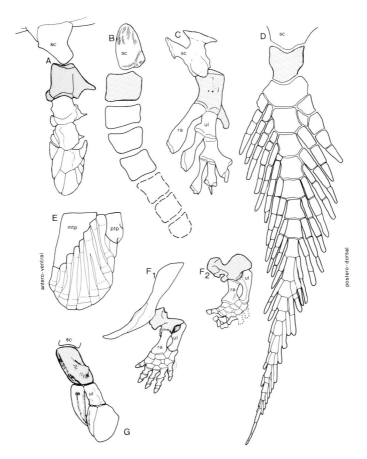

Fig. 8. Endoskeleton of pectoral appendages of os-teichthyans. A. Actinistian *Latimeria chalumnae* (from Millot and Anthony, '58, Fig. 1 and Pl. 64.2). B. Poro-lepiform *Glyptolepis groenlandica* (from Jarvik, '80, Fig. 200C). C. Osteolepiform *Eusthenopteron foordi* (from An-drew and Westoll, '70, Fig. 6a). D. Dipnoan *Neoceratodus forsteri* (from Semon, 1898, Fig. 34). E. Actinopterygian *Amia calva* (from Jessen, '72, Pl. 3, Fig. 3). F. Tetrapod *Eryops attheyi* (from Gregory and Raven, '41, Fig. 24C): F_1, restored with cleithrum; F_2, unrestored. G. Advanced osteolepiform *Panderichthys rhombolepis* (from Worob-jewa, '75, Fig. 3A). Unpaired basal element (humerus) stippled.

ond element of adult dipnoans could indicate fusion (see Semon, 1898; Braus, '01), but that is not clear when using other sarcopterygians as an out-group for comparison, because actinis-tians (Fig. 8A) and porolepiforms (Fig. 8B) have an unpaired second element as do dipnoans. Osteolepiforms alone fulfill the condition of having paired sub-basal elements. These elements are not subequal as claimed by Rosen et al., not even in *Ichthyostega* (Jarvik, '80, Figs. 163, 164); the radius (tibia) is bigger than the ulna (fibula).

3) "Two primary joints (shoulder or hip and elbow or knee)" [character "45"] are present in dipnoans (after Rosen et al., '81), actinistians, osteolepiforms (Rackoff, '80), and tetrapods. The "ball" of the first joint is formed by the sca-pulocoracoid or pelvic girdle in dip-noans and actinistians, and on the proximal limb element (humerus, fe-mur) in osteolepiforms and tetrapods. Andrews and Westoll ('70) compared the "screw-shaped" glenoid fossa on the scapulocoracoid of *Eusthenopteron* with that of tetrapods. Rosen et al. consid-

ered that feature invalid because of the similar shape of the glenoid in *Chirodipterus australis*; however, the latter glenoid is convex (Janvier, '80, Fig. 12A) and not truly a fossa. The second joint is a proximal ball and distal socket arrangement in living dipnoans (Rosen et al., '81, Figs. 30A, 31); in actinistians and porolepiforms it is a flat articulation. Only in osteolepiforms do the two elements articulate with the humerus in the same manner found in tetrapods (Rackoff, '80).

4) "Distal bony elements (carpals or tarsals and digits) arising on postaxial side of appendage" is an assumption for tetrapods made by Rosen et al. They interpret the radius as being homologous to the metapterygium of actinopterygians (Fig. 8E) or elasmobranchs and put the metapterygial axis through the ulnar elements in *Eusthenopteron*. A long axis forms the center of the paired fins in dipnoans, actinistians and porolepiforms. Preaxial and postaxial radials are known in dipnoans and actinistians, and may be present in porolepiforms. Only in osteolepiforms are the radials reduced on one side of the axis as in tetrapods. It is possible that these represent opposite sides of the axis in osteolepiforms and tetrapods, but the position of the axis in osteolepiforms and tetrapods proposed by Rosen et al. is as arbitrary as that proposed by Holmgren ('33). The similarity of the elements in osteolepiforms and tetrapods suggests the same position; this explanation is more parsimonious as it requires only one change.

5) "Pectoral and pelvic appendages alike in structure (i.e., structurally similar and with at least four or five primary segments)" is plesiomorphic for all sarcopterygians if one accepts that the number of elements is lower in the pelvic appendages of all sarcopterygians except tetrapods. Four or five primary segments occur in actinistians, osteolepiforms, and tetrapods, but dipnoans have a long extended axis with many elements (at least in living representatives and in the few known fossil examples).

6) An "extensive muscular lobe" is always connected with an extensive endoskeleton; thus, porolepiforms and dipnoans have the most extensive muscular lobe. This feature is only another way of stating that porolepiforms and dipnoans have a long endoskeleton (see no. 5). A long axial endoskeleton of the paired appendages is plesiomorphic for sarcopterygians. This assumption is more parsimonious than to postulate the parallel developments of archipterygia three times: in actinistians, porolepiforms, and dipnoans (Schultze, '77). "Reduction or loss of dermal rays" [character "46"] is a feature of Mesozoic and Recent dipnoans, not Devonian representatives, which have dermal rays as do all other Devonian sarcopterygians.

In conclusion, Rosen et al.'s seven conditions of the paired appendages are not synapomorphies uniting dipnoans and tetrapods. A comparison of these structures made without preassumptions clearly aligns osteolepiforms with tetrapods (Rackoff, '80).

The shoulder girdle in Devonian dipnoans is very poorly known. Rosen et al. ('81, Fig. 39G) illustrate the shoulder girdle of *Chirodipterus* with posttemporal, supracleithrum, anocleithrum, cleithrum, clavicle, and an unpaired interclavicle. These are the same elements known in other sarcopterygians (Jarvik, '44). The incorporation of an anocleithrum between the supracleithrum and cleithrum is e.g., a common primitive feature of sarcopterygians (Rosen et al., '81, "character 24"). Although *Chirodipterus*, with many bones in the shoulder girdle, is more primitive than Recent dipnoans, it is not a plesiomorphic member of the group as indicated by Rosen et al. The position of the anocleithrum is unknown in plesiomorphic dipnoans; therefore, its relation to the skin, one important feature after Rosen et al., is debatable. On the other side, the anocleithrum could be lost even in advanced osteolepiforms as in tetrapods.

The position of the pectoral fin on the cleithrum is variable in sarcopterygians. Rosen et al. show a high position in dipnoans, actinistians, and porolepiforms, and a low position in osteolepiforms. Contrary to the statement of Rosen et al. ('81:219), dipnoans are not similar to tetrapods in the position of their pectoral appendage and the relationship of cleithrum/clavicle. In *Ichthyostega*, the front limb inserts as low down on the shoulder girdle as it does in osteolepiforms (cf. Jarvik, '80, Figs. 170, 75, 100, or 137). The cleithrum/

clavicle ratio is even higher in *Ichthyostega* than it is in *Eusthenopteron*.

The pelvic girdle of Recent dipnoans is formed by one entirely cartilaginous unpaired element. Rosen et al. compare it with the pelvic girdle of *Necturus maculosus*, which is formed mainly by cartilage, with an ossified ilium and ischium. Recent dipnoans show no similarity to plesiomorphic tetrapods or other osteichthyans in the morphology, composition, or position and shape of the acetabulum. I can see no possibility of deriving the plesiomorphic tetrapod pelvic girdle from the condition found in recent dipnoans.

PRIMITIVE FORMS

A major problem in most comparisons among large groups is that a "typical" form is chosen for each group. Preconceptions about similarities in selected features influences an author's choice of forms. For example, *Griphognathus* was chosen as a "key" dipnoan by Rosen et al. ('81), based on the presence of "true choanae." Ideally, the whole group should be evaluated to find the basal and thus the most plesiomorphic member (see above), or a form close to it, to use in comparisons with other groups. In any case, one should avoid using "the only well-known members of each group" (Rosen et al., '81:255). Here, I will use a simpler method to identify the plesiomorphic members of each osteichthyan group by utilizing those plesiomorphic osteichthyan features that have tendencies to change from group to group. Let us consider plesiomorphic members as those that have combined occurrences of seven consistently primitive features (Fig. 9).

1) Heterocercal caudal fin without epaxial lobe; by outgroup comparison (with elasmobranchs and acanthodians) this is a plesiomorphic feature of osteichthyans (Gardiner, '73).

2) The occurrence of two dorsal fins is, by the same reasoning, plesiomorphic for osteichthyans.

3) The supraorbital sensory canal is not connected with the cephalic division of the main lateral line in early dipnoans and actinopterygians. This is plesiomorphic for osteichthyans by outgroup comparison with acanthodians and placoderms.

4) An open pineal foramen is known in many osteichthyans. The occurrence of this feature in placoderms and even agnathans demonstrates that it is plesiomorphic for osteichthyans.

5) The buccohypophysial foramen can be found in the parasphenoid of most primitive osteichthyans, and is described from placoderms (Stensiö, '63). Therefore, it is considered a plesiomorphic feature.

6) Rhombic scales with a peg-and-socket articulation occur in all the major osteichthyan groups and have to be considered plesiomorphic for osteichthyans (Schultze, '77).

7) A mesomeric skull roof pattern with a mosaic of bones in the snout region (Pearson, '82) has to be considered plesiomorphic for osteichthyans based on its occurrence in all osteichthyan groups.

Because primitive features can be retained in phylogenetically advanced forms, I will indicate that the supposed plesiomorphic forms occupy a position close to the initial branching point of the group. The basal forms may possess all seven primitive features, nevertheless, they are not primitive in all their features; they are neither ancestors nor archetypes.

Plesiomorphic actinopterygians

The development from rhombic to round scales occurs many times within actinopterygians, and the combination of rhombic scales with a heterocercal caudal fin is present in palaeoniscoids and even some more advanced actinopterygians. Palaeoniscoid actinopterygians possess the more primitive, three-layered, rhombic ganoid-scale (Gross, '66). Combined with rhombic scales and a heterocercal caudal fin are such apomorphic actinopterygian features as tooth tips formed by acrodin, ganoin on scales and bones, four sclerotic dermal plates, one dorsal fin, and others (see Rosen et al., '81, features 20–23; Pearson, '82) that are not shared by dipnoans or other sarcopterygians. As in early dipnoans, the supraorbital sensory line in palaeoniscoids does not join the infraorbital sensory line, but reaches back onto the postparietals. The pineal foramen lies in a separate bone in *Cheirolepis*, as it does in early dipnoans and other sarcopterygians. A buccohypophysial foramen is described in the parasphenoid of *Cheirolepis* (Pearson and Westoll, '79) and other Devonian palaeoniscoids (Gardiner, '73). The parasphenoid is confined to the prechordal part of the endocranium as in crossopterygians. The skull roof is covered by relatively few large bones: paired postparietals (Romer, '45; Jollie, '62; usually so-called parietals), paired parietals

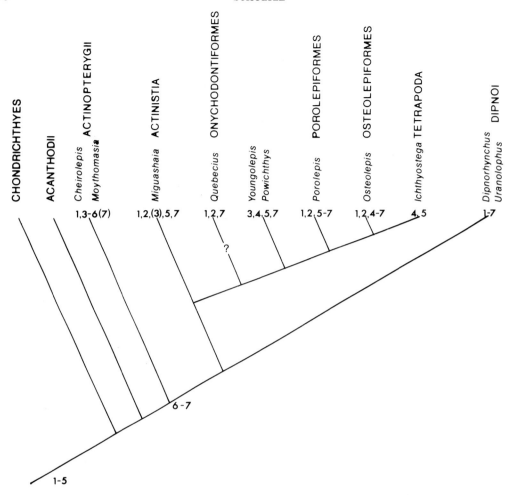

Fig. 9. Primitive (plesiomorphic) genera of osteichthyans with plesiomorphic features: 1, heterocercal caudal fin; 2, two dorsal fins; 3, supraorbital sensory line canal not connected with cephalic division of main lateral line; 4, open pineal foramen; 5, buccohypophysial foramen in parasphenoid; 6, rhombic scales; 7, mesomeric skull roof pattern with bone mosaic in snout region. Scheme based on Figure 12.

(usually so-called frontals), large unpaired postrostral (? frontal), and paired nasals. The snout is constructed of a few bones except in *Cheirolepis* (Pearson, '82, Fig. 4); a bone mosaic like that in the snout of sarcopterygians is not yet known in primitive actinopterygians. The bone mosaic in the skull of *Acipenser* and other actinopterygians is secondarily derived. It is not important to the present discussion if *Cheirolepis* (Pearson, '82; Lauder and Liem, '83) or a stegotrachelid palaeoniscoid (Gardiner, '73) is used as the most plesiomorphic actinopterygian.

Plesiomorphic characters of crossopterygians

The group of fishes usually called crossopterygians (see Andrews, '73) includes actinistians, onychodontiforms, porolepiforms, and osteolepiforms (including rhizodontiforms). These groups are united mainly by one feature, the intracranial joint (Andrews, '73). They share other features with dipnoans (cosmoid scales, dermal sclerotic ring consisting of numerous small plates, endoskeletal structure of paired fins, etc.) and with all osteichthyans (heterocercal caudal fin, two

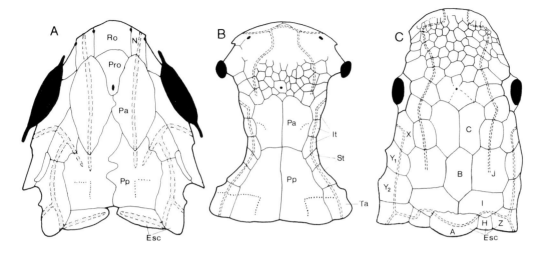

Fig. 10. Comparison of the skull roof. A. Actinopterygian *Cheirolepis trailli* (from Pearson and Westoll, '79, Fig. 20c). B. Rhipidistian *Powichthys thorsteinssoni* (from Jessen, '80, Fig. 3A). C. Dipnoan *Dipnorhynchus sussmilchi* (from Thomson and Campbell, '71, Fig. 6A, and Campbell and Barwick, '82a, Fig. 9c,e).

dorsal fins, two external nares, pointed teeth, supraorbital sensory canal not connected with cephalic division of main lateral line, open pineal foramen, buccohypophysial foramen in parasphenoid, and a mesomeric skull roof pattern with a mosaic of bones in the snout region).

Rosen et al. and Lauder and Liem ('83) split crossopterygians into subgroups that appear sequentially between actinopterygians and dipnoans on their cladogram. They deny both the intracranial joint and cosmine as synapomorphies for groups comprising the crossopterygians. There is controversy about the importance of the intracranial joint. It is considered as a synapomorphy either for sarcopterygians (Forey, '80) or — more commonly — for crossopterygians (Schultze, '81). Bjerring ('73) used embryological data concerning the position of cranial nerves to refute a close relationship between actinistians and rhipidistians. However, Bjerring's reasoning is inconsistent if one takes into account rhipidistians other than *Eusthenopteron*. Accepting *Eusthenopteron* as the "standard" for osteolepiforms, the nervus profundus emerges in the intracranial joint. The nervus trigeminus in the anterior part of the oticooccipital portion of the endocranium (Fig. 11A). In contrast these nerves in actinistians emerge respectively in the posterior part of the ethmoidal region and the intracranial

joint (Fig. 11B). The actinistian situation is also seen in *Youngolepis* and *Powichthys* (Fig. 11C,D; Chang, '82). Jessen ('80) places both openings in the posterior part of the ethmoidal region in *Powichthys* (Fig. 11D). It follows that the different exit position of these nerves is not sufficient to negate the homology of the intracranial joint as Bjerring ('73) asserts. An intracranial joint is known in all four crossopterygian groups, although it may not be a synapomorphy of crossopterygians because it is absent in *Youngolepis* (Chang, '82), and the close relative *Powichthys* has a weakly developed intracranial joint (Jessen, '80). It cannot be determined if the undivided endocranium of *Youngolepis* is primitive for rhipidistians and sarcopterygians, or an autapomorphy for *Youngolepis*. Either possibility contradicts Forey ('80) and Rosen et al.: The lack of an intracranial joint is not a synapomorphy for tetrapods and dipnoans but rather a primitive feature for sarcopterygians or a convergence occurring at least three times. The undivided endocranium in *Youngolepis* (in contrast to *Powichthys*) and "neotetrapods" (in contrast to *Ichthyostega*) *sensu* Gaffney ('79) indicates the evolution of fusion of the bipartite endocranium at least two times. The undivided endocranium of dipnoans does not show any indication of fusion from two parts, and is considered here as primitive in comparison with actinopte-

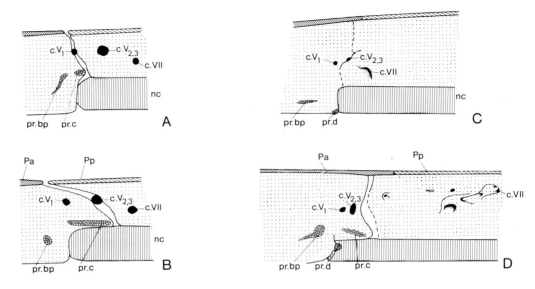

Fig. 11. Comparison of position of intracranial joint. A. Osteolepiforms. B. Actinistians (from Jarvik, '80, Fig. 214A,B). C. *Youngolepis praecursor* (Chang, '82, Fig. 15B). D. *Powichthys thorsteinssoni* (from Jessen, '80, Figs. 5, 6).

rygians. It is most parsimonious to interpret the intracranial joint, with all its specialized features, as a synapomorphy of crossopterygians. The parasphenoid in all crossopterygians is limited to the anterior moiety. This is primitive in comparison with actinopterygians, in which it terminates at the ventral occipital fissure (Gardiner '73). Three large extrascapularia may be another synapomorphy of crossopterygians, compared with four in actinopterygians and five (A-, H- and Z-bones) in dipnoans.

Plesiomorphic actinistians

Actinistians have changed little since the Devonian (Huxley, 1861; Jarvik, '80). They are easily recognized by their rounded triphycercal tail with widely spaced fin rays, unpaired fins having an endoskeleton similar to that of the paired fins, sutural position of the sensory line canals, lack of maxilla, short dentary, and additional features (Forey, '81). Forms with rhombic scales are not known. The Devonian *Miguashaia* is the only form with a heterocercal caudal fin (Schultze, '73) and may possess cosmine; the anocleithrum is ornamented. Two dorsal fins persist in all known members of the group. The supraorbital canal ends close to but does not connect with the cephalic division of the main

lateral line canal (Chang, '82). An open pineal foramen has not been described in any actinistian.

Devonian forms are more primitive than later forms in some features (Stensiö, '38). They have a greater degree of ossification in the endocranium, a larger extent of bone mosaic in the snout region, presence of a buccohypophysial foramen (groove in *Latimeria* only) in the parasphenoid, three extrascapulars, and a basipterygoid process. Taking into account the few changes seen in actinistians since the Devonian (Jarvik, '80), with care one could use features of *Latimeria* for comparison with other groups.

Plesiomorphic rhipidistians

Porolepiforms, osteolepiforms, and sometimes onychodontiforms (not discussed here because of incomplete knowledge) are grouped together as rhipidistians. Plesimorphic porolepiforms and osteolepiforms have most of the seven previously mentioned primitive osteichthyan features (Fig. 9). In both groups, the supraorbital sensory canal enters the cephalic division of the main lateral line, but it does not in the Early Devonian forms *Powichthys* and *Youngolepis*. These two forms combine features (Chang, '82) that have been defined as characters of either porolepiforms or osteolepiforms. They have two external nares, but the fenestra endonarina posterior is not separate from the fenestra ventro-lateralis (Jarvik, '42; fenestra ventralis of Chang, '82) as it is in porolepiforms. After Chang ('82), the fenestra ventralis is covered by the vomer on the palate in porolepiforms, *Powichthys*, and *Youngolepis*. *Powichthys* (Fig. 10B) has an open pineal foramen as do osteolepiforms, but it is in front of the parietals. No pineal foramen is developed in *Youngolepis*. Separate premaxilla, tabular, supratemporal, and intertemporal bones as well as simple plicidentine are other osteolepiform features expected to be present in primitive porolepiforms. These features are also found in onychodontiforms with the exception of plicidentine. An extratemporal bone occurs in osteolepiforms, porolepiforms, *Youngolepis*, and onychodontiforms. In summary, *Youngolepis* and *Powichthys* combine characters of porolepiforms and osteolepiforms (Chang, '82). At the same time, they are more primitive in some features than those two groups: the number of bones through which the cephalic division of the main lateral line passes is higher than in dipnoans; the intracranial joint has the actinistian position; and the infraorbital sensory canal and ethmoidal commissure run between bones in the suture as in actinistians.

The wide separation of osteolepiforms and porolepiforms (advocated by Jarvik in many publications; for example, see Jarvik, '72, '80) is not justified. *Youngolepis* and *Powichthys* support a close similarity between porolepiforms and osteolepiforms, and justify even more strongly the Rhipidistia as a monophyletic taxon.

Plesiomorphic onychodontiforms

Onychodontiforms are Devonian and Carboniferous sarcopterygian fishes that possess characteristic teeth (Jessen '67). They have the primitive gnathostome feature of two dorsal fins and, at least in one form, a heterocercal caudal fin (*Quebecius*, Schultze, '73). All known forms have round scales; cosmine may be present in *Onychodus* (Jessen, '67). Small forms such as *Strunius* or *Quebecius* have an actinopterygianlike appearance, also seen in other juvenile crossopterygians (e.g., *Eusthenopteron*, see Schultze, '84); nevertheless, the snout region is covered by a mosaic of bones. They lack, at least in juvenile forms, fleshy lobate fins. The main character that onychodontiforms share with other crossop-

terygians is the presence of an intracranial joint in the endocranium, even though there is no external joint between the dermal bones. The arrangement of bones in the skull roof (Jessen, '67; Andrews, '73) agrees with osteolepiforms in one respect (tabular and supratemporal lateral to postparietal) and with actinistians in another (very long postparietals). Presently, onychodontiforms are too poorly known to be placed with certainty on a cladogram.

Plesiomorphic porolepiforms

Porolepiforms are accepted here as a monophyletic group based on their possession of dendrodont plicidentine (Schultze, '69a; Rosen et al., '81). They have two external nares (as do actinistians and actinopterygians) and a heterocercal caudal fin and two dorsal fins (as in all plesiomorphic sarcopterygians). Porolepiforms possess a fenestra endochoanalis (Jarvik, '42, '72) covered by the vomer; this means that only a sharply angled choanal tube course would maintain porolepiforms as choanate fishes (see Chang, '82, for discussion). The occurrence of the three openings (anterior and posterior external nares, and fenestra endochoanalis) casts doubt on the hypothesis that the choana is the posterior external naris. Bertmar ('68, '69) postulates a derivation of the posterior external naris and fenestra endochoanalis from the posterior half of the nasal placode. In osteolepiforms, the upper portion of the posterior part of the nasal placode (the posterior external naris of porolepiforms) forms the nasolacrimal duct (Jarvik, '42; Bertmar, '69). Although it is not functional, the fenestra endochoanalis of porolepiforms has a similar position to that in osteolepiforms. The plesiomorphic form within porolepiforms is *Porolepis*, with rhombic scales and cosmine; a heterocercal caudal fin and two dorsal fins can be present in porolepiforms with round scales. The snout region is covered by a bone mosaic in all members of the group including *Porolepis* (Jarvik, '72, Fig. 34A, Pl. 8, Fig. 1) in which cosmine normally covers the snout region. All members of the group possess a buccohypophysial foramen in the parasphenoid. An open pineal foramen in the dermal skull roof has not been found in any porolepiform. The supraorbital sensory canal connects with the cephalic division of the main lateral line in the dermosphenotic.

Jessen ('75, '80) changed the diagnosis of porolepiforms to include the Lower Devonian *Powichthys*. *Powichthys* has osteolepiform plicidentine, and many other osteolepiform features (Chang, '82), and therefore was discussed above together with rhipidistians.

Plesiomorphic osteolepiforms

Osteolepiforms are characterized by having only one external nasal opening, and a palatal opening of the nasal cavity surrounded by the premaxilla, maxilla, palatine, and vomer. Among fishes, these features are known only within osteolepiforms. Rosen et al. postulate two narial tubes emerging from the single opening in osteolepiforms. They justify that interpretation by comparison with *Polypterus* and the situation shown in Worobjewa's ('73) restoration of *Panderichthys*. Two narial tubes emerging from one nasal opening should be primitive for all osteichthyans; that cannot be reconciled with the cladograms proposed here or in Rosen et al. The situation in *Polypterus* and (if correct) in *Panderichthys* must be interpreted as autapomorphies for those forms because they do not occur in close relatives. Actinopterygians, the closest relatives of *Polypterus*, have two nares as do plesiomorphic sarcopterygians. In addition, I could not find a narial opening in *Elpistostege* (Schultze and Arsenault, '85), the closest relative of *Panderichthys*. Worobjewa ('73) compares the second small opening (possibly only the opening of the infraorbital canal?) with a similar one in theriodonts. This small opening in *Panderichthys* is unique within osteolepiforms.

Osteolepiforms (with the exception of small forms) have plicidentine that is more primitive than that of porolepiforms. In addition, the scales and bones of primitive forms (those with heterocercal caudal fin, two dorsal fins, and rhombic scales) are covered by cosmine. A bone mosaic in the snout region is definitely known only in forms without a cosmine cover but can be postulated for cosmine-covered forms such as *Osteolepis*, *Gyroptychius*, or *Thursius*. The pineal foramen already lies between the parietals in these primitive osteolepiforms, not in front of the parietals as in other plesiomorphic sarcopterygians. A buccohypophysial foramen is found in all members of the group in which the parasphenoid is known. As in porolepiforms, the supraorbital sensory canal enters the cephalic division of the main lateral line in the dermosphenotic (= intertemporal).

Plesiomorphic tetrapods

Since Säve-Söderberg ('32), all authors have agreed that the Late Devonian amphibian *Ichthyostega* is the most primitive tetrapod. *Elpistostege*, from the earliest Late Devonian (Westoll, '38, '40, '43), is not a primitive tetrapod but rather a panderichthyid osteolepiform (Schultze and Arsenault, '85). Jarvik ('52) described typical piscine features in *Ichthyostega*: a posteriorly situated dorsal fin continuous with the caudal fin and with endoskeletal radials and dermal fin-rays (lepidotrichia); scales; subopercle; and preopercle. The division of the endocranium into two moieties with a notochordal canal in the otico-occipital region (Jarvik, '52, '80) is disputed. Rosen et al. reject that feature for reasons of parsimony: In their view, the intracranial joint is primitive for sarcopterygians, and the fusion of both moieties occurred only once in the common ancestor of dipnoans and tetrapods. Therefore, they accept only five of the six synapomorphies for "neotetrapods" (i.e., tetrapods excluding *Ichthyostega*), given by Gaffney ('79). I agree with all sixteen characters cited by Gaffney ('79) as synapomorphies for tetrapods including *Ichthyostega*. In addition to Gaffney's ('79) list the following characters are also primitive features of plesiomorphic tetrapods: three median pairs of bones (postparietal, parietal, frontal) on the skull roof between the lateral line bones (tabular, supratemporal, and intertemporal = dermosphenotic), and between the supraorbital and lacrimal; pineal foramen between parietals; one large squamosal; lacrimal, jugal, postorbital, supraorbital, and prefrontal surrounding the orbit; narrow, elongate parasphenoid with a buccohypophysial foramen and ending anterior to the otico-occipital region; paired premaxilla, maxilla, vomer, dermopalatine, ecto- and entopterygoid; lower jaw with long dentary four infradentaries (surangular, angular, postsplenial, splenial), three coronoids and a prearticular; pointed teeth with enamel and (labyrinthodont) plicidentine; one external nasal opening surrounded by maxilla, premaxilla, lacrimal and lateral and anterior tectal; and one palatal opening (choana) surrounded by premaxilla, maxilla, vomer, and dermopalatine.

Ichthyostega is derived with respect to two skull roof features (Fig. 2C): The postparietals are fused to form one median bone, and an intertemporal is missing. The postparietals are paired in the only other tetrapod known from the Late Devonian (*Acanthostega*) and in all other labyrinthodonts. Therefore, a paired postparietal is proposed as a primitive tetrapod feature. Occurrence or absence of an intertemporal is not as clear. All three lateral line bones—tabular, supratemporal, and intertemporal—occur in anthracosaurs (Fig. 14D; Panchen, '72), but the intertemporal is found only sporadically within temnospondylous labrinthodonts. Variations in dermal bone pattern occur within species and between closely related forms. For example, the osteolepiform *Panderichthys* has an intertemporal (Fig. 14C), whereas the closely related *Elpistostege* lacks such a separate bone. The intertemporal is a separate bone in other osteolepiforms, actinistians, dipnoans (equivalent to the X-bone), and actinopterygians, and its occurrence in early tetrapods has to be considered a primitive feature.

All of these plesiomorphic features must be present in the common ancestor of tetrapods, and one should expect at least a large portion of them in the closest sister group.

Plesiomorphic dipnoans

Many derived features characterize dipnoans (see Schultze and Campbell, this volume): pattern of the posterior skull roof, composition of lower jaw, lack of maxilla and premaxilla, thickened "upper lip," tooth plates or tubercles with syndentine, and two nasal openings in palate, to name just a few. The archipterygium and a united endocranium with fused palatoquadrate are disputed as dipnoan apomorphies. Most Devonian dipnoans possess a heterocercal caudal fin and two dorsal fins. The Early Devonian dipnoans with these two features possess rhombic scales with cosmine, a tissue composed of a combination of dentine, a pore-canal system, and a thin enamel layer. The Early Devonian genera *Uranolophus* and *Dipnorhynchus* (Fig. 10C) possess all of these plesiomorphic features; therefore, it seems most parsimonious to regard these as the most primitive known dipnoans. They also have additional features found in other plesiomorphic osteichthyans:

1) The supraorbital sensory line does not join the cephalic division of the main lateral line as it does in primitive actinopterygians (Fig. 10A), *Latimeria*, and *Youngolepis* (Chang, '82).

2) Bone mosaic in the snout region, as in porolepiforms and osteolepiforms in which the snout region is not covered by a complete cosmine layer (for actinopterygians see Pearson, '82). An osteichthyan macromeric pattern cannot be justified (contrary to Miles, '75) by comparison with acanthodians as an outgroup or even by the distribution of bone mosaic in the snout of different osteichthyan groups. The possibility of homologizing a few dipnoan bones with those of other osteichthyans (Miles, '75) does not justify the postulation of a common ancestor with a stable skull roof pattern. Here, I agree with Pearson ('82), who postulated an ancestral mesomeric pattern for osteichthyans.

3) An open pineal foramen is known in *Dipnorhynchus* and *Speonesydrion* (Campbell and Barwick, '84a) but seems to be closed in all other dipnoans.

4) A buccohypophysial foramen in the parasphenoid has been described from a few dipnoans (Jarvik, '80; Campbell and Barwick, '82b). Contrary to other osteichthyans, the foramen lies in the most anterior part of the parasphenoid. The parasphenoid is shaped differently in dipnoans than in other osteichthyans, mainly covering the posterior region of the endocranium. In plesiomorphic forms it is already excluded from the ventral side of the anterior moiety by the entopterygoids, which meet in the midline.

5) Only the neural and haemal arches are ossified (no vertebral centra).

6) All the additional features that characterize crossopterygians, dipnoans and tetrapods (Rosen et al., '81, characters "1–19" and "24–27"; Lauder and Liem, '83, characters "1–23") have to be added here.

A median, unpaired B-bone (see, e.g., Fig. 2B) is one key character of dipnoans. It is well developed in all Middle Devonian and younger dipnoans, and sometimes even incorporates other bones. In Early Devonian forms, the B-bone is relatively smaller and surrounded posteriorly by paired I-bones that meet in the midline. The pineal opening lies in a bone mosaic anterior to the C-bones. This position (combined with the failure to develop unpaired D- and paired E-bones) is plesiomorphic for dipnoans and reminiscent of the situation in *Powichthys* (Fig. 10B) and *Diabolepis* (Chang and Yu, '84).

This brief discussion shows clearly that Early Devonian dipnoans are the most primitive (i.e., cladistically most plesiomorphic) lungfishes. Such a position was taken by Dollo (1896), and more recently by Miles ('77) and Campbell and Barwick ('82a,b; this volume), who give additional arguments for the plesiomorphic position of Early Devonian dipnoans.

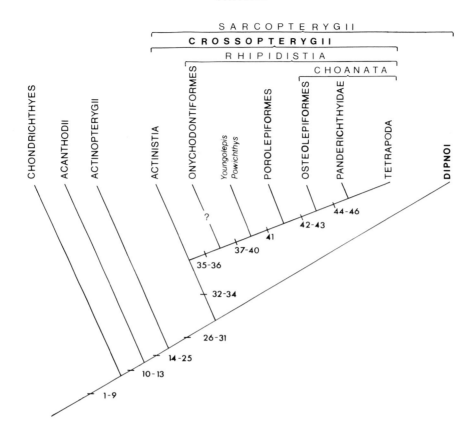

Fig. 12.   Interrelationships of osteichthyans; for explanation of synapomorphies (numbers) see text.

DIPNOANS AS SARCOPTERYGIANS

Plesiomorphic dipnoans possess the following features that are also primitive for gnathostomes (Fig. 9): heterocercal caudal fin, two dorsal fins, open pineal foramen. After Janvier ('81), these are features that gnathostomes also have in common with osteostracan agnathans, although it has yet to be proven that the notochord of agnathans extends into the upper lobe of the epicercal caudal fin, or that the dorsal fins of agnathans are formed by fin rays as in gnathostomes.

Other primitive dipnoan features are synapomorphies (Fig. 12) for all gnathostomes (including placoderms) as shown by Rosen et al. ('81) and Lauder and Liem ('83):

1) Parasphenoid with buccohypophysial foramen. The homologization of the parasphenoid in placoderms with that of osteichthyans assumes that it is lost in chondrichthyans and acanthodians. A buccohypophysial foramen is present on the ventral side of the endocranium of chondrichthyans (fenestra basalis) and acanthodians.

2) A cephalic lateral-line system that includes a supraorbital line, infraorbital line, central sensory line, cephalic division of main lateral line, occipital cross commissure, supramaxillary (jugal) line (homologous to the supraoral line of placoderms following Stensiö, '47), preopercular line (homologous to the postmarginal line of placoderms after Stensiö, '47), and an oral and mandibular line on the lower jaw (not known in placoderms). The supraorbital line does not join the cephalic divi-

sion of the main lateral line in plesiomorphic placoderms, acanthodians, actinopterygians, dipnoans, actinistians, *Youngolepis*, or *Powichthys*. A central sensory line is known in placoderms, acanthodians, actinopterygians (*Cheirolepis trailli*, Pearson, '82), and possibly actinistians (according to Stensiö, '47). A central line is not present in primitive tetrapods, dipnoans, or rhipidistians—in the latter group, a similarly positioned line can be homologized with the posterior end of the supraorbital line. The appearance in Triassic tetrapods of a groove in the same position as the central line (Stensiö, '47) has to be interpreted as a neomorphic structure. Fully developed oral and mandibular canals are known among osteichthyans only in dipnoans (Rosen et al., '81: no. "4" changed).

3) Lower jaw supported by palatoquadrate and hyomandibula (Rosen et al., '81, no. "1").

4) A hyoid bar connecting the branchial apparatus with the hyomandibula (not known in placoderms) (Rosen et al., '81, no. "2").

5) Anterior branchial arches consisting of basibranchial, hypobranchial, ceratobranchial, epibranchial, and pharyngobranchial elements (not known in placoderms) (Rosen et al., '81, no. "3").

6) Paired pectoral and pelvic appendages with endoskeletal supporting girdles (Rosen et al., '81, no. "5").

7) Three semicircular canals in the otic capsule (Rosen et al., '81, no. "6").

8) Ventral otic fissure between embryonic trabecular and parachordal segments of endocranium (not in placoderms) (Lauder and Liem, '83, Fig. 1, no. "2").

9) Lateral occipital fissure (not present in placoderms) (Lauder and Liem, '83, Fig. 1, no. "3").

The following primitive dipnoan features are synapomorphies for osteichthyans plus acanthodians:

10) Ossified dermal opercular plate(s) (Lauder and Liem, '83, Fig. 1, no. "5").

11) Stylohyal (=interhyal) in the hyoid arch (Lauder and Liem, '83, Fig. 1, no. "6").

12) Dermal branchiostegal rays (Lauder and Liem, '83, Fig. 1, no. "7").

13) Sclerotic ring (Lauder and Liem, '83, Fig. 1, no. "9").

There are many primitive features that previous authors (Rosen et al., '81; Lauder and Liem, '83) have used as symplesiomorphies for dipnoans and primitive members of all the other osteichthyan groups:

14) Dermal skull bones with descending laminae attaching to the endocranium (Rosen et al., '81, no. "8").

15) Endochondral bone (Rosen et al., '81, no. "9").

16) Lepidotrichia (Rosen et al., '81, no. "10").

17) Dermal sclerotic ring (Rosen et al., '81, no. "13").

18) Marginal upper and lower jaw teeth (dental arcades) on dermal bones lateral to the palatoquadrate and dorsal to Meckel's cartilage (Rosen et al., '81, no. "14"). However, dipnoans do not have true marginal teeth; the necessary corresponding bones are missing. Toothlike structures are formed on the thickened anterior region of the lower and upper jaws. Therefore, this feature cannot be correctly considered as shared by dipnoans and other osteichthyans.

19) Long dentary and coronoids above Meckel's cartilage (Figs. 15,16). Coronoids, which occur in all other osteichthyans and tetrapods, are lacking in dipnoans. The thickened anterior part of the dipnoan lower jaw is usually considered homologous to a dentary; if that interpretation is correct, the dentary is short in dipnoans (as in actinistians). Thus, these two characters cannot be demonstrated in dipnoans, which have reduced the dentary and lost the coronoids.

20) Hypohyal in hyoid arch (Lauder and Liem, '83, Fig. 1, no. "12").

21) Dermal shoulder girdle formed by posttemporal, supracleithrum, cleithrum, clavicle, and unpaired median interclavicle (Lauder and Liem, '83; Fig. 1, no. "16").

22) Rhombic scales with a peg-and-socket articulation (Schultze, '77).

23) Mesomeric skull roof pattern with bone mosaic in snout region (Fig. 10; Pearson, '82).

24) A forward (rather than backward) orientation of infrapharyngobranchials (Rosen et al., '81, no. "16").

25) Suprapharyngobranchials present on first two gill arches (Rosen et al., '81, no. "17").

Primitive dipnoans share features with crossopterygians that have to be considered sarcopterygian synapomorphies:

26) Anocleithrum as an intermediate bone between supracleithrum and cleithrum (Rosen et al., '81, no. "24").

27) True enamel on teeth (Rosen et al., '81, no. "26").

28) Sclerotic ring formed by more than four plates (Rosen et al., '81, no. "27").

29) Archipterygium, pectoral, and pelvic appendages with a central axis and pre- and postaxial radials (Fig. 8A, B,D). To consider the archipterygium as a synapomorphy of sarcopterygians assumes that a long endoskeletal girdle on which the metapterygium and radials articulate is primitive for gnathostomes. This character would become another primitive sarcopterygian character (Fig. 9) if it could be shown that the archipterygium is also primitive for chondrichthyans and that the lobed paired fins of some early actinopterygians have a similar arrangement.

30) Cosmine present (Fig. 5).

31) Submandibular series present.

Synapomorphies of dipnoans have been cited throughout the paper and are presented in Schultze and Campbell (this volume). Here, only a few synapomorphies of crossopterygians will be discussed. This is not intended to be a complete list—that is outside the scope of the present paper. Crossopterygians have the following advanced features in common:

32) Double-headed hyomandibula. After Campbell and Barwick ('82b:324), the hyomandibula of *Dipnorhynchus* is single-headed with a long facet. The double-headed hyomandibula of *Griphognathus* (Miles, '77) is therefore a convergent development in dipnoans and crossopterygians.

33) Intracranial joint (Fig. 11). Unlike tetrapods, there is no indication for loss of the intracranial joint in dipnoans.

34) Three extrascapulars (Figs. 13C, 14 A–C). Extrascapulars carry the occipital commissure in osteichthyans. There are four or more in actinopterygians (Fig. 13A) and five in dipnoans (the A-, H- and Z-bones, Fig. 13B). In actinistians, the number of extrascapulars is secondarily increased.

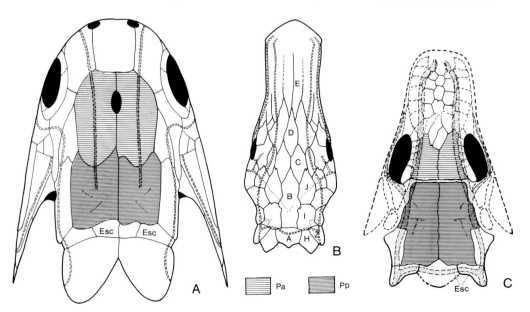

Fig. 13. Comparison of median bones on the skull roof. A. Actinopterygian *Moythomasia nitida* (from Jessen, '68, Fig. 1B). B. Dipnoan *Griphognathus whitei* (from Miles, '77, Fig. 111). C. Actinistian *Diplocercides kayseri* (from Stensiö, '38, Fig. 1).

Rhipidistians do not all possess an external dermal joint above the intracranial joint. Such a joint is found only in porolepiforms and osteolepiforms (in parallel with actinistians), whereas onychodontiforms, *Youngolepis,* and *Powichthys* do not have such a transversing suture between the parietal and the postparietal shield. Panderichthyids have secondarily lost the external dermal joint. Rhipidistians can be characterized by the following derived features:

35) Extratemporal present. The extratemporal in onychodontiforms is large

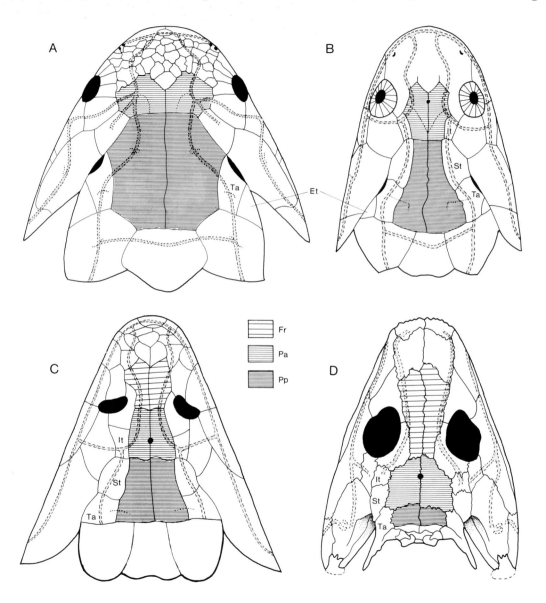

Fig. 14.   Frontals, parietals, and postparietals on the skull roof. A. Porolepiform *Holoptychius* sp. (from Jarvik, '72, Fig. 45A). B. Osteolepiform *Osteolepis macrolepidotus* (from Jarvik, '72, Fig. 61C). C. Advanced osteolepiform *Panderichthys rhombolepis* (after Vorobyeva, '77, Fig. 2B). D. Tetrapod *Paleoherpeton decorum* (after Panchen, '70, Fig. 1a).

and lateral to the tabular at the middle of the postparietal (Andrews, '73, Fig. 2F). In porolepiforms (Fig. 14A) and osteolepiforms (Fig. 14B) it is lateral to the tabular at the level of the posterior part of the postparietal. An extratemporal is not yet known in *Youngolepis* or *Powichthys*. It is lost in panderichthyids (Fig. 14C) and some osteolepiforms.

36) Narrow submandibular bone(s). The long and narrow submandibular bone is undivided in onychodontiforms, whereas in porolepiforms (Jarvik, '80, Fig. 187C,D; Schultze and Campbell, this volume, Fig. 6b) and osteolepiforms (Jarvik, '80, Fig. 144B) it is divided into many small bones. The situation is quite different in dipnoans, which have large gularlike submandibulars (Miles, '77, Fig. 126; Jarvik, '80, Fig. 333C; Schultze and Campbell, this volume, Fig. 6c,d).

Excluding onychodontiforms from rhipidistians, there are many advanced features shared by porolepiforms and osteolepiforms:

37) Fenestra ventro-lateralis. In both porolepiforms and osteolepiforms, and in *Powichthys* and *Youngolepis,* the fenestra ventro-lateralis is present dorsal to the junction of the premaxilla, maxilla, vomer, and dermopalatine. Jarvik ('42, '72, '80) and Jessen ('80) noted a ventral opening (choana) in all rhipidistians; after Chang ('82) the fenestra ventro-lateralis in *Youngo-lepis* (Fig. 7D), *Powichthys,* and porolepiforms is covered by the vomer. Only in porolepiforms is the posterior external nasal opening the exoskeletal exit of the fenestra ventro-lateralis; in osteolepiforms and tetrapods it is the choana (see character 42).

38) Four infradentaries in an anterior to posterior sequence and below a long dentary (Fig. 15D,G,H) with a submandibular series of many bones (see character 36). Actinopterygians (Fig. 15A) have only developed two posterior infradentaries (angular and surangular); the deepened dentary is usually considered to be a dentalosplenial, a bone that takes the position of the dentary, splenial, and postsplenial. In actinistians (Fig. 15B)

two infradentaries are known, a small anterior one (splenial) and a large posterior one (angular and ?surangular). Only rhipidistians (Fig. 15D,G,H) and tetrapods (Fig. 15E,I) have four infradentaries (splenial, postsplenial, angular, and surangular). The mandibular sensory line passes through the infradentaries; a short oral line branches off the mandibular line in the surangular of rhipidistians and tetrapods. The external side of the dipnoan lower jaw is difficult to compare with that of other sarcopterygians (Jarvik, '67; Schultze, '69b; Miles, '77) The oral and mandibular sensory lines pass through the four dipnoan "infradentaries" (Miles, '77; Campbell and Barwick, '84a). The oral sensory line enters the lower jaw in the "surangular" (Fig. 15J); the mandibular sensory line enters in the "postsplenial" (only in *Melanognathus*, Fig. 15J) or in the "angular" (Miles, '77), Fig. 102b, 108b; Campbell and Barwick, '84a, Figs. 18A, 20B). Both lines pass through the "angular" and "postsplenial" and meet in the "postsplenial" (the "splenial" of *Melanognathus*). The mandibular lines of each lower jaw are connected by a commissure ventral to the symphysis. The arrangement of lower jaw elements of dipnoans, the course of the two sensory lines, and the lack of a true dentary (see above) are all very different from other osteichthyans, and specifically from rhipidistians and tetrapods (see Jarvik, '67). The composition of the lower jaw of dipnoans can therefore only be interpreted as an synapomorphy of dipnoans.

39) Three coronoids (Fig. 16C–E,G,H). This feature unites all rhipidistians and early tetrapods. The number of coronoids is higher in actinopterygians (Fig. 16A) and actinistians (Fig. 16B), but dipnoans lack coronoids (Fig. 16F,I). In dipnoans, the labial side of Meckel's cartilage is covered by a large tooth-bearing bone, the prearticular, which has a length similar to that in other sarcopterygians; in actinopterygians (Fig. 16A) the comparable element is relatively short.

40) Plicidentine. Simply folded plicidentine is primitive for rhipidistians, including *Youngolepis* and *Powichthys*

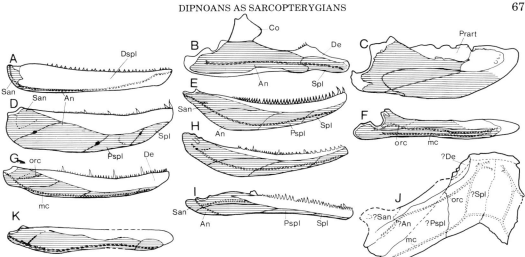

Fig. 15. Lower jaws in external view showing dentary and infradentaries in osteichthyans. A. Actinopterygian *Glaucolepis magna* (after Nielsen, '42, Fig. 39). B. Actinistian *Latimeria chalumnae* (after Nelson, '73, Fig. 1A,B). C. Dipnoan *Holodipterus gogoensis* (after Miles, '77, Fig. 109a). D. Porolepiform *Holoptychius* sp. (after Jarvik, '72, Fig. 47C). E. Primitive tetrapod *Ichthyostega* sp. (after Jarvik, '80, Fig. 174A). F. Dipnoan *Griphognathus minutidens* (after Schultze, '69b, Figs. 1,3). G. Osteolepiform *Eusthenopteron foordi* (after Jarvik, '80, Fig. 125A). H. Osteolepiform *Metaxygnathus denticulus* (after Campbell and Bell, '77, Fig. 6A). I. Tetrapod *Dvinosaurus primus* (after Bystrow, '38, Fig. 19A). J. Primitive dipnoan *Melanognathus canadensis* (after Schultze, '69b, Fig. 40b). K. Advanced osteolepiform *Panderichthys rhombolepis* (after Gross, '41, Figs. 15, 16, 19). Infradentary series hatched.

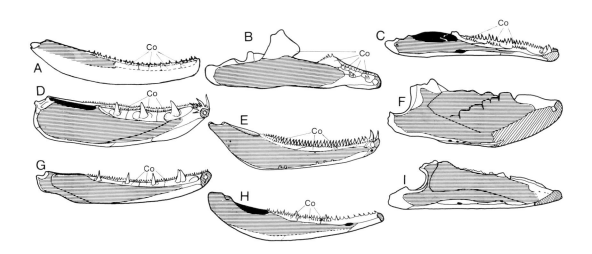

Fig. 16. Lower jaws in internal view showing prearticular and coronoids in osteichthyans. A. Actinopterygian *Cheirolepis trailli* (after Pearson and Westoll, '79, Fig. 10a). B. Actinistian *Latimeria chalumnae* (after Nelson, '73, Fig. 1B). C. Tetrapod *Dvinosaurus primus* (after Bystrow, '38, Fig. 19B). D. Porolepiform *Holoptychius* sp. (after Jarvik, '72, Fig. 47A,B). E. Primitive tetrapod *Ichthyostega* sp. (after Jarvik, '80, Fig. 174B). F. Dipnoan *Holodipterus gogoensis* (after Miles, '77, Fig. 109b). G. Osteolepiform *Eusthenopteron foordi* (after Jarvik, '80, Fig. 125B). H. Osteolepiform *Metaxygnathus denticulus* (after Campbell and Bell, '77, Fig. 6C). I. Dipnoan *Griphognathus whitei* (after Miles, '77, Fig. 100b). Prearticular hatched horizontally.

(Jessen, '80). Porolepiforms have complexly folded dentine (= dendrodont plicidentine), and i.e. the polyplocodont dentine in panderichthyids and early tetrapods (Schultze, '69a) is even more extensively folded (= labyrinthodont). The similarity between these two groups is so great that distinguishing tooth sections is not possible. The occurrence of plicidentine in lepisosteids (gars) can be interpreted only as a convergence, for the following two reasons: a) The plicidentine occurs in typical actinopterygian teeth that have an acrodin tip and lack enamel; b) Lepisosteids are actinopterygians according to many other features, and are not even very primitive actinopterygians. Plesiomorphic actinopterygians do not possess plicidentine.

Porolepiforms and osteolepiforms are advanced over *Youngolepis* and *Powichthys* in the following features:

41) The supraorbital sensory line joins the cephalic division of the main lateral line (Fig. 14A–C). This feature is independently acquired in actinopterygians and some dipnoans; in plesiomorphic forms of those groups the supraorbital sensory line ends in the postparietal (Text-Fig. 10A) or in the I-bone (Fig. 10C).

The number of bones in the palate region is reduced to four: vomer, dermopalatine, ectopterygoid, and a large entopterygoid (Fig. 7E–H); this could also be the case in *Youngolepis* and *Powichthys*, but the palate of these forms is incompletely known (Fig. 7D). The maxilla and quadratojugal have a common suture. The identification by Rosen et al. ('81) of bone 10 in *Griphognathus* as a quadratojugal seems very doubtful. Bone 10 is surrounded by a number of bones that cannot be compared with those of rhipidistians and tetrapods. Three bones (the lacrimal, jugal, and postorbital) surround the ventral and posterior margin of the orbit in rhipidistians, whereas primitive dipnoans have six bones in the same position (Campbell and Barwick, '82a, Figs. 4, 5; Schultze and Campbell, this volume, Fig. 4d). Porolepiforms and actinistians have many supraorbitals, but only two bones form the dorsal

and anterior border of the orbit in dipnoans (Campbell and Barwick, '82a, Figs. 4, 5; Schultze and Campbell, this volume, Fig. 4d), osteolepiforms, and tetrapods.

There are many synapomorphies of osteolepiforms and early tetrapods; the following are several of the most important:

42) Choana. Despite Rosen et al.'s attempt to homologize the posterior naris of dipnoans with the choana of tetrapods, the position of the two openings is quite different (see above). The choana in osteolepiforms and tetrapods has an identical position relative to surrounding bones, combined with the presence of only one external naris in the two groups.

43) Cheek region formed by jugal, postorbital, one squamosal, quadratojugal, and a fully anchored preopercle. Porolepiforms have a higher number of squamosals, and primitive dipnoans a greater number of bones in the cheek region (Campbell and Barwick, '82a, Fig. 4a,b; Schultze and Campbell, this volume: Fig. 4d).

The open pineal foramen lies between the parietals. This is a position convergently acquired to that in actinopterygians because primitive sarcopterygians and even rhipidistians (Fig. 10B,C) have an open pineal foramen in front of the parietals. The reduction of endoskeletal radials in the paired appendages to one side of the axis is accepted here as another synapomorphy.

Within osteolepiforms, tetrapods most closely resemble panderichthyids (Schultze and Arsenault, '85) based on the following derived features:

44) Three pairs of bones along the midline of the skull roof (Fig. 14C,D). Paired postparietals and parietals without an external division between them cover the posterior region of the skull roof. Anteriorly, they reach between the orbits in osteolepiforms. Paired frontals extending between the orbits (*Acanthostega, Ichthyostega, Panderichthys;* Fig. 2A,C) or just in front of the orbits (*Elpistostege*) are known only in plesiomorphic tetrapods and panderichthyids.

45) External naris very close to the margin of the upper jaw. There is only one

external naris in panderichthyids (see above). The infraorbital line passes between the external naris and the margin of the upper jaw in panderichthyids (Worobjewa, '73, Fig. 2A) and through a tube-shaped bone in *Ichthyostega* (Jarvik, '80). Rosen et al. do not accept a bone in the position of the tube-shaped bone. They instead postulate an interruption of the infraorbital line in *Ichthyostega* as in dipnoans. The infraorbital line continues rostrad into the premaxilla of *Ichthyostega* (Jarvik, '80); the postulated interruption lies just above the choana. In dipnoans, the infraorbital sensory line extends rostrad to the posterior and anterior naris (see Campbell and Barwick, '82a, Fig. 4b for *Dipnorhynchus;* Miles, '77, Fig. 112 for *Griphognathus);* anteriorly, the ethmoidal commissure is missing (Fig. 10C). The postulated interruption of the infraorbital line in *Ichthyostega* and the missing ethmoidal commissure of dipnoans are not comparable features.

46) Flat skull with high dorsally situated orbits. The skull of panderichthyids so closely resembles that of tetrapods that misidentification can occur (e.g., *Elpistostege* was treated as a tetrapod by Westoll '38, '43). Only the ventral side, with a large median gular and narrow submandibular plates, identifies panderichthyids as osteolepiform fishes.

LUNGFISH/TETRAPOD SISTER-GROUP RELATIONSHIP: A CRITIQUE

The relationship I have proposed of dipnoans to crossopterygians contradicts the recently advanced closest relationship of dipnoans to tetrapods proposed by Rosen et al. ('81). Their proposal has already been criticized in brief by Schultze ('81) and Jarvik ('81), and methodologically by Holmes ('85). It seems important to deal here with all the synapomorphies presented by Rosen et al. to complete the preceding partial critique.

In the synapomorphy scheme presented here (Fig. 12) I accept the characters used by Rosen et al. to define sarcopterygians (characters "1–19" and "24–27"; Lauder and Liem, '83, Fig. 1, characters "1–23"). Soft

tissue features will not be considered here because they are unavailable in the fossils. The major difference between the present scheme and that of Rosen et al. lies in their hypothesis of a sister-group relationship between dipnoans and other sarcopterygians (including tetrapods). Like Holmes ('85), I interpret differently the characters "28–61", which Rosen et al. used to support that hypothesis. Some have already been dealt with, but for the sake of convenience I will list all of them here in sequence, with direct reference to the character numbers used by Rosen et al.

Character "28" (anocleithrum without surface ornamentation) cannot be evaluated because the condition of the anocleithrum is not known in plesiomorphic dipnoans, or rhipidistians. Plesiomorphic actinistians have an ornamented anocleithrum; tetrapods have no anocleithrum.

Character "29" (clavicle large relative to cleithrum) is not acceptable because the cleithrum is much larger than the clavicle in all sarcopterygians and early tetrapods. "The relative size of bones is known to be a highly variable character" (Holmes, '85:393). The pectoral appendage inserts as ventrally on the cleithrum in *Eusthenopteron* (Jarvik, '80, Fig. 100) as it does in *Ichthyostega* (Jarvik, '80, Fig. 170) or *Griphognathus* (Schultze, '69b, Fig. 31).

Character "30" ("archipterygium") is a primitive character for all sarcopterygians, whereas the reduction of endoskeletal radials to one side of the axis is considered to be advanced (see above).

Character "31" (rotation of preaxial side to postaxial) is based on a debatable position of the metapterygial axis (see above). Holmes ('85) demonstrates that the ulnar side in the tetrapod forelimb is postaxial, and that the interpretation by Rosen et al. would require a rotation of almost 180°.

Character "32" (supraorbital canal-bearing bones lateral to paired bones) is a dipnoan feature not known in other sarcopterygians or tetrapods.

Character "33" (absence of hyostyly) is convergent (see above).

Character "34" (slope of posterior margin of palatoquadrate) is a convergence between dipnoans and advanced tetrapods. The jaw articulation in primitive tetrapods is placed behind the occipital region (Jarvik, '80, Fig. 171B) so that the posterior margin of the palatoquadrate slopes forward from the jaw articulation (Panchen, '70) as it does in actinistians and actinopterygians.

Characters "35" and "43" (possible synapomorphy of the rostral organ of actinistians with the dipnoan labial cavity and the nasolacrimal duct of tetrapods) are "ambiguous" (Rosen et al., '81:257). Northcutt (this volume) shows that the innervation around the nasal capsule is quite different in dipnoans and tetrapods.

Character "36" (single, broad, triangular basibranchial) as indicated by Rosen et al. is a convergent feature that also occurs in primitive actinopterygians, and develops parallel within dipnoans. *Griphognathus* has two basibranchials (Miles, '77, Figs. 137, 138).

Characters "37–39" (reduction and loss of parts of the gill arch) are "lost" characters without any indication that they developed only once (Holmes, '85:389). Characters ("40, 41, 48, and 61") are not dealt with here because they are soft tissue features and the plesiomorphic state cannot be determined. It is not possible to decide if these characters are sarcopterygian symplesiomorphies or convergent.

Character "42" (choana) cannot be accepted as a synapomorphy uniting dipnoans and tetrapods, but rather as a character shared by osteolepiforms and tetrapods (see above).

Character "43" is ambiguous—see number "35" above.

Characters "44" (paired and subequal subbasal elements) and "45" (two primary joints in each appendage) are characters joining osteolepiforms and tetrapods (see above).

Character "46" (reduction in dermal fin rays) is not correct for Devonian dipnoans. They have a ratio of dermal fin rays to endoskeletal elements similar to that found in rhipidistians.

Characters "47" (tetrapodous locomotion) and "48" (segmented muscles in the paired fins) cannot be checked in plesiomorphic sarcopterygians.

Character "48"—see number "40" above.

Character "49" (fusion of the two halves of the pelvic girdle) is not known in plesiomorphic sarcopterygians. Jarvik ('80) hypothesizes a cartilaginous connection between the halves of the pelvis in *Eusthenopteron*, which Rosen et al. doubt. Comparing the pelves of a Recent dipnoan with those of a Recent urodele does not eliminate the possibility of convergence, and in addition the shape of the compared pelves is quite different (Rosen et al., '81, Fig. 61A,B).

Characters "50" (hyomandibula not involved in jaw suspension) and "52" (hyomandibula reduced) must be reconsidered as convergencies. Campbell and Barwick ('82b:324) state that dipnoans have a "hyomandibula/ceratohyal relationship of normal teleostome type." The hyomandibula in *Dipnorhynchus* is not ventrally connected to the quadrate, in contrast to the situation seen in *Griphognathus* and Recent dipnoans. The hyomandibula is not reduced in plesiomorphic tetrapods; the large hyomandibula supports the cheek region (Carroll, '80).

Characters "51" (loss of interhyal), "53" (loss of dorsal gill arch elements), "54" (opercular bones reduced in extant forms, but not in plesiomorphic dipnoans), and "56" (loss of autopalatine) can likewise be best explained as convergent losses.

Character "55" (pterygoids joined in midline and excluding parasphenoid from palate anteriorly) is not a correct synapomorphy. The entopterygoids in plesiomorphic dipnoans are fused along the entire midline (Campbell and Barwick, '82b), a situation quite different from that in tetrapods where the entopterygoids meet only in the anterior part of the palate and have an elongate parasphenoid lying between them for most of their length (Fig. 7F,H). The presence of a narrow, elongate parasphenoid with a posterior position of the buccohypophysial foramen indicates a close relationship between osteolepiforms (Fig. 7G) and early tetrapods (Fig. 7F,H). On the other hand, the parasphenoid of dipnoans is broad and restricted to the posterior part of the ventral surface of the endocranium (Fig. 7C), with the buccohypophysial foramen lying in the bone's anterior part (Campbell and Barwick, '82b). The position of the parasphenoid in all crossopterygians is anterior to the jaw articulation, distinct from its position posterior to the articulation in dipnoans. The latter condition appears advanced, and not a synapomorphy with tetrapods (compare Holmes, '85:388).

Character "57" (elongation of snout) is ambiguous (Holmes, '85:388). The snout is long relative to the posterior skull roof in panderichthyid osteolepiforms (Fig. 14C), which have a snout length approaching that of primitive tetrapods (Fig. 14D). Other osteolepiforms (Fig. 14B) have a relatively short snout. *Griphognathus* (Figs. 2B, 13B) has a much longer snout than early tetrapods; this is another convergent development because plesiomorphic dipnoans have relatively short snouts (Fig. 10C).

Character "58" (posterior position of eye at level of juncture between two principal bones) is also a convergence (Holmes, '85:384), found in some dipnoans but not in the most primitive forms (Fig. 10C).

Character "59" (five bone pattern in posterior skull roof) is postulated on an incorrect homologization (see above). The number of bones alone is not as important as their relationship to the lateral line system and to endocranial structures (not dealt with by Holmes, '85). Osteolepiforms and tetrapods have four bones between the bones of the main lateral line's cephalic division, whereas dipnoans have seven in the same region (Fig. 2).

Character "60" (resorption of calcified cartilage and deposition of bone tissue) is a primitive feature for all sarcopterygians; it occurs in the same manner in dipnoans, rhipidistians, and tetrapods.

In summary, the synapomorphies proposed by Rosen et al. to relate dipnoans and tetrapods as sister groups are either convergent features (nos. "33, 34, 36, 38, 57, 58"); primitive for sarcopterygians (nos. "30, 50, 52, 60"); ambiguous (nos. "28, 31, 35, 37–39, 43, 47, 51, 53, 54, 56"); deal with soft tissues (nos. "40, 41, 48, 61"); advanced for dipnoans (nos. "32, 55"); or unacceptable, i.e., nonhomologous (nos. "29, 42, 44–46, 49, 59"). Holmes ('85) rejects all the synapomorphies of Rosen et al. in a far harsher and more unequivocal manner.

CONCLUSIONS

Dipnoans are sarcopterygian osteichthyans, closely related to crossopterygians. A relationship to arthrodires or holocephalans is refuted. Plesiomorphic dipnoans do not exhibit synapomorphies with tetrapods. Therefore, it is cladistically inappropriate to postulate a sister-group relationship between the two groups. Pointed teeth with enamel and plicidentine, the composition of the lower jaw, the arrangement of bones between the orbits and in the posterior part of the skull roof, the position of the nasal opening, presence of choana, composition of the palate, etc. (see Fig. 12, characters "32–46") are synapomorphies of crossopterygians and tetrapods, specifically with the advanced panderichthyid osteolepiform rhipidistians. The hypothetical common ancestor of tetrapods and dipnoans is the common ancestor of all sarcopterygians. The choice of well-known or derived forms rather than the plesiomorphic members (or characters) of groups being compared can result in falsely postulated sister-group relationships.

ACKNOWLEDGMENTS

This paper was written while on sabbatical leave at the Institut und Museum für Geologie und Paläontologie der Georg-August-Universität, Göttingen, West-Germany, and delivered at the 1984 American Society of Zoologists meeting as part of the symposium "Biology and Evolution of Lungfishes." I thank Prof. Dr. O. H. Walliser, Institut und Museum für Geologie und Paläontologie der Georg-August-Universität, Göttingen, for his hospitality and financial help; Frau M. Noltkämper for typing part of the manuscript; and my wife, Gloria Arratia, for help in preparing the figures. Mr. M. Gottfried and Mr. R. Cloutier, Museum of Natural History, University of Kansas, Lawrence, Kansas, read the manuscript and improved the English. Jan Elder, Fran Williams, and Coletta Spencer, Word Processing Service, Division of Biology, University of Kansas, typed the final manuscript.

LITERATURE CITED

Allis, E. P., Jr. (1922) The cranial anatomy of *Polypterus*, with special reference to *Polypterus bichir*. J. Anat. *56:* 190–294.

Allis, E. P., Jr. (1932a) Concerning the nasal apertures, the lachrymal canal and the buccopharyngeal upper lip. J. Anat. *66:*650–658.

Allis, E. P., Jr. (1932b) The pre-oral buccal cavity and the buccopharyngeal opening in *Ceratodus*. J. Anat. *66:*659–668.

Andrews, S. M. (1973) Interrelationships of crossopterygians. In P. H. Greenwood, R. S. Miles, and C. Patterson (eds): Interrelationships of Fishes. Zool. Linn. Soc. London (Suppl.1) *53:*137–177.

Andrews, S. M., and T. S. Westoll (1970) The postcranial skeleton of *Eusthenopteron foordi* Whiteaves. Trans. R. Soc. Edinburgh *68:*207–329.

Ax, P. (1984) Das Phylogenetische System. Stuttgart, New York: Fischer. 349 p.

Beer, G. R. de (1937) The Development of the Vertebrate Skull. Oxford: Oxford University Press. 552 p.

Bertmar, G. (1965) The olfactory organ and upper lips in Dipnoi, an embryological study. Acta Zool. Stockholm *46:*1–10.

Bertmar, G. (1966) On the ontogeny and homology of the choanal tubes and choanae in Urodela. Acta Zool. Stockholm *47:*43–59.

Bertmar, G. (1968) Lungfish phylogeny. In T. Ørvig (ed): Current Problems of Lower Vertebrate Phylogeny. Proc. Nobel Symp. 4. Stockholm: Almquist and Wiksell. pp. 259–283.

Bertmar, G. (1969) The vertebrate nose, remarks on its structural and functional adaptation and evolution. Evolution *23:* 131–152.

Bischoff, T. L. W., von (1840) *Lepidosiren paradoxa.* Anatomisch untersucht und beschrieben. Leipzig. 34p.

Bjerring, H.C. (1973) Relationships of coelacanthiforms. In P. H. Greenwood, R. S. Miles, and C. Patterson (eds): Interrelationships of Fishes. Zool. J. Linn. Soc. London (Suppl. 1) *53:* 179–205.

Braus, H. (1901) Die Muskeln und Nerven der Ceratodusflosse. In R. Semon, Zoologische Forschungsreisen in Australien und dem Malayischen Archipelago. I. *Ceratodus.* Denkschr. Med.-Naturwiss. Ges. Jena *4:* 137–300.

Brettnacher, H. (1939) Aufbau und Struktur der Holocephalenzähne. Jb. Morph. Mikrosk. Anat., 2. Abt. *46:* 584–616.

Bystrow, A.P. (1938) *Dvinosaurus* als neotenische Form der Stegocephalen. Acta Zool. Stockholm *19:* 209–295.

Campbell, K. S. W., and R. E. Barwick (1982a) A new species of the lungfish *Dipnorhynchus* from New South Wales. Palaeontology *25:* 509–527.

Campbell, K. S. W., and R. E. Barwick (1982b) The neurocranium of the primitive dipnoan *Dipnorhynchus sussmilchi* (Etheridge). J. Vert. Paleont. *2:* 286–327.

Campbell, K. S. W., and R. E. Barwick (1983) Early evolution of dipnoan dentitions and a new genus *Speonesydrion.* Mem. Assoc. Australas. Palaeont. *1:* 17–49.

Campbell, K. S. W., and R. E. Barwick (1984a) *Speonesydrion,* an Early Devonian dipnoan with primitive toothplates. Palaeo Ichthyologica *2:* 1–48.

Campbell, K. S. W., and R. E. Barwick (1984b) The choana, maxillae, premaxillae and anterior palatal bones of early dipnoans. Proc. Linn. Soc. New South Wales *107:* 147–170.

Campbell, K. S. W., and M. W. Bell (1977) A primitive amphibian from the Late Devonian of New South Wales. Alcheringa *1:* 369–381.

Carroll, R. L. (1980) The hyomandibular as a supporting element in the skull of primitive tetrapods. In A. L. Panchen (ed): The Terrestrial Environment and the Origin of Land Vertebrates. Newcastle-upon-Tyne: Syst. Assoc. Spec. Vol. 15, pp. 293–317.

Chang M.-M. (1982) The Braincase of *Youngolepis,* a Lower Devonian Crossopterygian from Yunnan, South-Western China. Stockholm: Dept. of Geology, University of Stockholm. 113 p.

Chang M.-M., and X. Yu (1984) Structure and phylogenetic significance of *Diabolichthys speratus* gen. et sp. nov., a new dipnoan-like form from the Lower Devonian of eastern Yunnan, China. Proc. Linn. Soc. New South Wales *107:* 171–184.

Dean, B. (1895) Fishes, Living and Fossil; an Outline of Their Forms and Probable Relationships. New York, London: MacMillan and Co. 300 p.

Denison, R. H. (1974) The structure and evolution of teeth in lungfishes. Fieldiana, Geol. *33:*31–58.

Denison, R. H. (1978) Placodermi. In H.-P. Schultze (ed): Handbook of Paleoichthyology, Vol. 2. Stuttgart, New York: Fischer. 128p.

Dollo, L. (1896) Sur la phylogénie des dipneustes. Bull. Soc. Belge Géol. Paléont. Hydrologie *9:* 79–128.

Eastman, C. R. (1906) Dipnoan affinities of arthrodires. Am. J. Sci. *21:* 131–143.

Edgeworth, F. H. (1923) On the quadrate in *Cryptobranchus, Menopoma,* and *Hynobius.* J. Anat. London *57:* 238–244.

Edgeworth, F. H. (1925) On the autostyly of dipnoi and amphibia. J. Anat. London *59:* 225–264.

Forey, P. (1980) *Latimeria:* A paradoxical fish. Proc. R. Soc. London B *208:*369–384.

Forey, P. (1981) The coelacanth *Rhabdoderma* from the Carboniferous of the British Isles. Palaeontology *24:* 203–229.

Forster-Cooper, C. (1937) The Middle Devonian fish fauna of Achanarras. Trans. R. Soc. Edinburgh *59:* 223–239.

Fox, H. (1954) Development of the skull and associated structures in amphibia with special reference to the urodeles. Trans. Zool. Soc. London *28:* 241–304.

Fox, H. (1965) Early development of the head and pharynx of *Neoceratodus* with a consideration of its phylogeny. J. Zool. London *146:* 470–554.

Gaffney, E. A. (1979) Tetrapod monophyly: a phylogenetic analysis. Bull. Carnegie Mus. Natur. Hist. *13:* 92–105.

Gardiner, B. G. (1973) Interrelationships of teleostomes. In P. H. Greenwood, R. S. Miles, and C. Patterson (eds): Interrelationships of Fishes. Zool. J. Linn. Soc. London (Suppl. 1) *53:* 105–135.

Gardiner, B. G. (1980) Tetrapod ancestry: a reappraisal. In A. L. Panchen (ed): The Terrestrial Environment and the Origin of Land Vertebrates. Newcastle-upon-Tyne: Syst. Assoc. Spec. Vol. 15, pp. 177–185.

Goodrich, E. S. (1925) Cranial roofing-bones in Dipnoi. J. Linn. Soc. (Zool.) *36:* 79–86.

Gregory, W. K. (1915) Present status of the problem of the origin of the Tetrapoda, with special reference to the skull and paired limbs. Ann. New York Acad. Sci. *26:* 317–383.

Gregory, W. K., and H. C. Raven. (1941) Studies on the origin and early evolution of paired fins and limbs. Ann. New York Acad. Sci. *42:* 273–360.

Gross, W. (1941) Über den Unterkiefer einiger devonischer Crossopterygier. Abh. Preuss. Akad. Wiss. Phys.-Math. Kl. *7:* 3–51.

Gross, W. (1956) Über Crossopterygier und Dipnoer aus dem baltischen Oberdevon im Zusammenhang einer vergleichenden Untersuchung des Porenkanalsystems paläozoischer Agnathen und Fische. Kgl. Svenska VetenskAkad. Handl. (4) *5:* 1–140.

Gross, W. (1966) Kleine Schuppenkunde. N. Jb. Geol. Paläont. Abh. *125:* 29–48.

Hofer, H. (1945) Zur Kenntnis der Suspensionsformen des Kieferbogens und deren Zusammenhänge mit dem Bau des knöchernen Gaumens und mit der Kinetik des Schädels bei den Knochenfischen. Zool. Jb. Abt. Anat. Ontog. Tiere *69:* 321–404.

Holmgren, N. (1933) On the origin of the tetrapod limb. Acta Zool. Stockholm *14:* 195–292.

Holmgren, N. (1939) Contribution to the question of the origin of the tetrapod limb. Acta Zool. Stockholm *20:* 89–124.

Holmgren, N. (1949a) Contributions to the question of the origin of tetrapods. Acta Zool. Stockholm *30:* 459–484.

Holmgren, N. (1949b) On the tetrapod limb problem—again. Acta Zool. Stockholm *30:* 485–508.

Holmgren, N., and E. Stensiö (1936) Kranium und Visceralskelett der Akranier, Cyclostomen und Fische. In L. Bolk, E. Göppert, E. Kallius, and W. Lubosch (eds): Handbuch der vergleichenden Anatomie der Wirbeltiere, Vol. 4. Berlin: Urban & Schwarzenberg, pp. 233–500.

Holmes, E. B. (1985) Are lungfishes the sister group of tetrapods? Biol. J. Linn. Soc. *25:* 379–397.

Howes, G. B. (1887) On the skeleton and affinities of the paired fins of *Ceratodus,* with observations upon those of the elasmobranchii. Proc. Zool. Soc. London *1887:* 3–26.

Huxley, T. H. (1861) Preliminary essay upon the systematic arrangement of the fishes of the Devonian epoch. Mem. Geol. Surv. United Kingdom, decade *10:* 1–40.

Janvier, P. (1980) Osteolepid remains from the Devonian of the Middle East, with particular reference to the endoskeletal shoulder girdle. In A. L. Panchen (ed):

The Terrestrial Environment and the Origin of Land Vertebrates. Newcastle-upon-Tyne: Syst. Assoc. Spec. Vol. 15, pp. 223–254.

Janvier, P. (1981) The phylogeny of the Craniata, with particular reference to the significance of fossil "agnathans." J. Vert. Paleont. *1*:121–159.

Jarvik, E. (1942) On the structure of the snout of crossopterygians and lower gnathostomes in general. Zool. Bidrag Uppsala *21:* 235–675.

Jarvik, E. (1944) On the exoskeletal shoulder-girdle of teleostomian fishes, with special reference to *Eusthenopteron foordi* Whiteaves. Kgl. Svenska VetenskAkad. Handl. (3) *21:* 1–32.

Jarvik, E. (1952) On the fish-like tail in the ichthyostegid stegocephalians with descriptions of a new stegocephalian and a new crossopterygian from the Upper Devonian of East Greenland. Medd. Grønland *114:* 1–90.

Jarvik, E. (1954) On the visceral skeleton in *Eusthenopteron* with a discussion of the parasphenoid and palatoquadrate in fishes. Kgl. Svenska VetenskAkad. Handl. (4) *5:* 1–104.

Jarvik, E. (1964) Specializations in early vertebrates. Ann. Soc. Roy. Zool. Belg. *94:* 1–95.

Jarvik, E. (1967) On the structure of the lower jaw in dipnoans: with a description of an early Devonian dipnoan from Canada, *Melanognathus canadensis* gen. et sp. nov. J. Linn. Soc. London (Zool.) *47:* 155–183.

Jarvik, E. (1968) The systematic position of the Dipnoi. In T. Ørvig (ed): Current Problems of Lower Vertebrate Phylogeny. Proc. Nobel Symp. 4. Stockholm: Almquist and Wiksell. pp. 223–245.

Jarvik, E. (1972) Middle and upper Devonian Porolepiformes from East Greenland with special reference to *Glyptolepis groenlandica* n. sp. and a discussion on the structure of the head in the Porolepiformes. Medd. Grønland *187:* 307 p.

Jarvik, E. (1980) Basic Structure and Evolution of Vertebrates. Vol. 1. London, New York: Academic Press. 575 p.

Jarvik, E. (1981) Lungfishes, Tetrapods, Paleontology, and Plesiomorphy. - Donn E. Rosen, Peter L. Forey, Brian G. Gardiner, and Colin Patterson. 1981. Bull. Amer. Mus. Nat. Hist. $6.80. Syst. Zool. *30:* 378–384 [review].

Jessen, H. (1966) Die Crossopterygier des Oberen Plattenkalkes (Devon) der Bergisch-Gladbach - Paffrather Mulde (Rheinisches Schiefergebirge) unter Berücksichtigung von amerikanischem und europäischem *Onychodus*-Material. Arkiv Zool. *18:* 305–389.

Jessen, H. (1967) The position of the Struniiformes *Strunius* and *Onychodus* among the crossopterygians. Coll. Int. Centre National Rech. Sci. [Problèmes actuels de paléontologie (Évolution des Vertébrés), Paris 1966] *163:* 173–180.

Jessen, H. (1968) *Moythomasia nitida* GROSS und *M.* cf. *striata* GROSS, devonische Palaeonisciden aus dem Oberen Plattenkalk der Bergisch-Gladbach - Paffrather Mulde (Rheinisches Schiefergebirge). Palaeontographica A *128:* 87–114.

Jessen, H. (1972) Schultergürtel und Pectoralflosse bei Actinopterygiern. Fossils and Strata *1:* 1–101.

Jessen, H. (1975) A new choanate fish, *Powichthys thorsteinssoni* n.g., n. sp., from the early Lower Devonian of the Canadian Arctic Archipelago. Coll. Int. Centre National Rech. Sci. [Problèmes actuels de paléontologie (Évolution des Vertébres), Paris 1973] *218:* 213–225.

Jessen, H. (1980) Lower Devonian Porolepiformes from the Canadian Arctic with special reference to *Powichthys thorsteinssoni* Jessen. Palaeontographica A *167:*

180–214.

Jollie, M. (1962) Chordate Morphology. New York: Reinhold Books. 478p.

Kemp, A. (1977) The pattern of tooth plate formation in the Australian lungfish *Neoceratodus forsteri.* Zool. J. Linn. Soc. London *60:* 223–258.

Kemp, A. (1984) A comparison of the developing dentition of *Neoceratodus forsteri* and *Callorhynchus milii.* Proc. Linn. Soc. N.S.W. *107:* 245–262.

Kesteven, H. L. (1931) The evolution of Anamniota. Rec. Austr. Mus. *18:* 167–200.

Kesteven, H. L. (1950) The origin of the tetrapods. Proc. R. Soc. Victoria, n. ser. *59:* 93–138.

Lauder, G. V., and K. F. Liem. (1983) The evolution and interrelationships of the actinopterygian fishes. Bull. Mus. Comp. Zool. *150:* 95–197.

Lison, L. (1941) Sur la structure des dents des Poissons Dipneustes. La Petrodentine. C. R. Soc. Biol. Paris *135:* 431–433.

Miles, R. S. (1975) The relationships of the Dipnoi. Coll. Int. Centre National Rech. Sci. [Problèms actuels de paléontologie (Évolution des Vertébrés), Paris 1973] *218:*133–148.

Miles, R. S. (1977) Dipnoan (lungfish) skulls and the relationships of the group: a study based on new species from the Devonian of Australia. Zool. J. Linn. Soc. London *61:* 1–328.

Millot, J. and J. Anthony (1958) Anatomie de *Latimeria chalumnae.* Vol. 1, Squelette, muscles et formations de soutien. Centre National Rech. Sci. Paris. 122 p.

Mookerjee, H. K., D. N. Ganguly, and S. K. Brahma (1954) On the development of the centrum and its arches in the Dipnoi *Protopterus annectens.* Anat. Anz. *100:* 217–230.

Nelson, G. (1973) Relationships of clupeomorphs, with remarks on the structure of the lower jaw in fishes. In P.H. Greenwood, R. S. Miles, and C. Patterson (eds): Interrelationships of Fishes. Zool. J. Linn. Soc. London (Suppl. 1) *43:* 333–349.

Nielsen, E. (1942) Studies on Triassic fishes from East Greenland. I. *Glaucolepis* and *Boreosomus.* Palaeozoologica Groenlandica *1:* 1–394.

Ørvig, T. (1957) Notes on some Paleozoic lower vertebrates from Spitsbergen and North America. Norsk Geol. Tidskr. *37:* 285–353.

Ørvig, T. (1967) Phylogeny of tooth tissues: evolution of some calcified tissues in early vetebrates. In E. A. W. Miles (ed): Structural and Chemical Organization of Teeth. Vol. I. New York and London: Academic Press. pp. 45–110.

Ørvig, T. (1969) Cosmine and cosmine growth. Lethaia *2:* 241–260.

Ørvig, T. (1976a) Palaeohistological Notes. 3. The interpretation of pleromin (pleromic hard tissue) in the dermal skeleton of psammosteid heterostracans. Zool. Scripta *5:* 35–47.

Ørvig, T. (1976b) Palaeohistological Notes. 4. The interpretation of osteodentine, with remarks on the dentition in the Devonian dipnoan *Griphognathus.* Zool. Scripta *5:* 79–96.

Ørvig, T. (1980) Histologic Studies of Ostracoderms, Placoderms and Fossil Elasmobranches. 4. Ptyctodontid tooth plates and their bearing on holocephalan ancestry: the condition of *Ctenurella* and *Ptyctodus.* Zool. Scripta *9:* 219–239.

Owen, R. (1839) On a new species of the genus *Lepidosiren* of Fitzinger and Natterer. Proc. Linn. Soc. London *1:* 27–32.

Panchen, A. L. (1970) *Anthracosauria.* In O. Kuhn (ed): Handbuch der Paläoherpetologie, Pt. 5a. Stuttgart: Fischer. 84 p.

Panchen, A. L. (1972) The skull and skeleton of *Eogyrinus attheyi* Watson (Amphibia: Labyrinthodontia). Phil. Trans. R. Soc. London B *263:* 279–326.

Pearson, D. M. (1982) Primitive bony fishes, with special reference to *Cheirolepis* and palaeonisciform actinopterygians. Zool. J. Linn. Soc. London *74:* 35–67.

Pearson, D. M., and T. S. Westoll (1979) The Devonian actinopterygian *Cheirolepis* Agassiz. Trans. R. Soc. Edinburgh *70:* 337–399.

Rackoff, J. S. (1980) The origin of the tetrapod limb and the ancestry of tetrapods. In A. L. Panchen (ed): The Terrestrial Environment and the Origin of Land Vertebrates. Newcastle-upon-Tyre: Syst. Assoc. Spec. Vol. 15, pp. 255–292.

Romer, A. S. (1945) Vertebrate Paleontology. 2nd Ed. Chicago: University of Chicago Press. 687 p.

Rosen, D. E., P. L. Forey, B. G. Gardiner, and C. Patterson (1981) Lungfishes, tetrapods, paleontology and plesiomorphy. Bull. Am. Mus. Natur. Hist. *167:* 159–276.

Säve-Söderbergh, G. (1932) Preliminary note on Devonian stegocephalians from East Greenland. Medd. Grönland *94:* 1–107.

Schauinsland, H. (1903) Beiträge zur Entwicklungsgeschichte und Anatomie der Wirbeltiere. I-III. Zoologica, Stuttgart *16:* 1–168.

Schultze, H.-P. (1969a) Die Faltenzähne der rhipidistiiden Crossopterygier, der Tetrapoden und der Actinopterygier-Gattung *Lepisosteus.* Palaeontographica Ital. *65:* 60–137.

Schultze, H.-P. (1969b) *Griphognathus* GROSS, ein langschnauziger Dipnoer aus dem Oberdevon von Bergisch-Gladbach (Rheinisches Schiefergebirge) und von Lettland. Geologica et Paleontologica *3:* 21–79.

Schultze, H.-P. (1970) Die Histologie der Wirbelkörper der Dipnoer. N. Jb. Geol. Paläont. Abh. *135:* 311–336.

Schultze, H.-P. (1973) Crossopterygier mit heterozerker Schwanzflosse aus dem Oberdevon Kanadas, nebst einer Beschreibung von Onychodontida-Resten aus dem Mitteldevon Spaniens und aus dem Karbon der U.S.A. Palaeontographica A *143:* 188–208.

Schultze, H.-P. (1977) Ausgangsform und Entwicklung der rhombischen Schuppen der Osteichthyes (Pisces). Paläont. Zeitschr. *51:* 152–168.

Schultze, H.-P. (1981) Hennig und der Ursprung der Tetrapoda. Paläont. Zeitschr. *55:* 71–86.

Schultze, H.-P. (1984) Juvenile specimens of *Eusthenopteron foordi* Whiteaves, 1881 (osteolepiform rhipidistian, Pisces) from the Upper Devonian of Miguasha, Quebec, Canada. J. Vert. Paleont. *4:* 1–16.

Schultze, H.-P., and M. Arsenault (1985) The panderichthyid fish *Elpistostege:* A close relative of tetrapods? Palaeontology *28:* 293–309.

Schultze, H.-P., and L. Trueb (1980) Basic Structure and Evolution of Vertebrates by Erik Jarvik. Vol. 1, 1980, 576 p.; Vol. 2, 1981, xii + 338 pp. London, New York: Academic Press. J. Vert. Paleont. *1:* 389–397 [review].

Semon, R. (1898) Die Entwickelung der paarigen Flossen des *Ceratodus forsteri.* Jen. Denkschr. 4, Semon Zool. Forschungsreisen *1:* 61–111.

Semon, R. (1899) Über die Entwickelung der Zahngebilde der Dipnoer. Sitzber. Ges. Morph. Physiol. München *15:* 75–85.

Smith, M. M. (1977) The microstructure of the dentition and dermal ornament of three dipnoans from the Devonian of western Australia: a contribution towards dipnoan interrelations and morphogenesis, growth and adaptation of the skeletal tissues. Phil. Trans. R. Soc. London (B) *281:* 29–72.

Smith, M. M. (1979) SEM of the enamel layer in oral teeth of fossil and extant crossopterygian and dipnoan fishes. Scanning Electron Microscopy *1979/II:* 483–490.

Smith, M. M. (1984) Petrodentine in extant and fossil dipnoan dentitions: Microstructure, histogenesis and growth. Proc. Linn. Soc. New South Wales *107:* 367–407.

Stahl, B. (1967) Morphology and relationships of the Holocephali with special reference to the venous systems. Bull. Mus. Comp. Zool. *135:*141–213.

Stensiö, E. (1938) On the Devonian coelacanthids of Germany with special reference to the dermal skeleton. Kgl. Svenska VetenskAkad. Handl. (3) *16:* 56 pp.

Stensiö, E. (1947) The sensory lines and dermal bones of the cheek in fishes and amphibians. Kgl. Svenska VetenskAkad. Handl. (3) *24:* 1–195.

Stensiö, E. (1963) Anatomical studies on the arthrodiran head. 1. Preface, geological and geographical distribution, the organization of the arthrodires, the anatomy of the head in the Dolichothoraci, Coccosteomorphi and Pachyosteomorphi. Taxonomic appendix. Kgl. Svenska VetenskAkad. Handl (4) *9:* 1–419.

Thomson, K. S. (1975) On the biology of cosmine. Bull. Peabody Mus. Nat. Hist. Bull. *40:* 1–59.

Thomson, K. S. (1977) On the individual history of cosmine and a possible electroreceptive function of the pore-canal system in fossil fishes. In S. M. Andrews, R. S. Miles, and A. D. Walker (eds): Problems in Vertebrate Evolution. Linn. Soc. London Symp. Ser., Vol. 4, pp. 247–270.

Thomson, K.S., and K. S. W. Campbell (1971) The Structure and Relationships of the Primitive Lungfish *Dipnorhynchus sussmilchi* (Etheridge). Peabody Mus. Nat. Hist. Bull. *38:* 109 p.

Vorobyeva, E. (1977) Morphology and nature of evolution of crossopterygian fishes. Trudy paleont. Inst. *163:* 1–239. (In Russian.)

Watson, D. M. S. (1926) The evolution and origin of the Amphibia. Phil. Trans. R. Soc. London (B) *214:* 189–257.

Watson, D. M. S., and H. Day (1916) Notes on some Palaeozoic fishes. Mem. Proc. Manchester Lit. Phil. Soc. *60:* 1–52.

Watson, D. M. S., and E. L. Gill (1923) The structure of certain Palaeozoic Dipnoi. J. Linn. Soc. (Zool.) *35:*163–216.

Westoll, T. S. (1938) Ancestry of the tetrapods. Nature *141:* 127–128.

Westoll, T. S. (1940) New Scottish material of *Eusthenopteron.* Geol. Mag. *77:* 65–73.

Westoll, T. S. (1943) The origin of the tetrapods. Biol. Rev. *18:* 78–98.

Westoll, T. S. (1949) On the evolution of the Dipnoi. In G. L. Jepsen, G. G. Simpson, and E. Mayr (eds): Genetics, Paleontology and Evolution. Princeton, NJ: Princeton University Press, pp. 121–184.

Woodward, A. S. (1891) Catalogue of the Fossil Fishes in the British Museum (Natural History). Vol. 2. London: British Museum (Natural History). 567 p.

Worobjewa, E. (1973) Einige Besonderheiten im Schädelbau von *Panderichthys rhombolepis* (GROSS) (Pisces, Crossopterygii). Palaeontographica A *142:* 221–229.

Worobjewa, E. (1975) Bemerkungen zu *Panderichthys rhombolepis* (GROSS) aus Lode im Lettland (Gauja-Schichten, Oberdevon). N. Jb. Geol. Paläont. Mh. *1975:* 315–320.

Zangerl, R. (1981) Chondrichthyes I. Paleozoic Elasmobranchii. In H.-P. Schultze (ed): Handbook of Paleoichthyology, Vol. 3A. Stuttgart, New York: Fischer, 115p.

JOURNAL OF MORPHOLOGY SUPPLEMENT 1:75–91 (1986)

Relationships of Lungfishes

PETER L. FOREY
British Museum of Natural History, Cromwell Road, London,
SW7 5BD, England

ABSTRACT   Problems surrounding the relationships of lungfishes are intricately connected with the search for the origin of tetrapods. Early in the history of lungfish research, the emphasis was on attempts to determine whether lungfishes were more closely related to fishes or to tetrapods. Later there was a shift toward a search for particular ancestors and ancestral groups, an approach that not only introduced problems relative to the concept of ancestry but also stultified attempts to classify the sarcopterygians. Cladistic analysis, on the other hand, has placed the inquiry into lungfish relationships on a surer footing, in which alternative theories are more open to criticism. It is concluded that, among Recent taxa, lungfishes and tetrapods are sister-groups, with coelacanths as the plesiomorphic sister-group to that combined group. Rhipidistians are a paraphyletic group distributed amongst the Recent taxa.

There are a mere six species of lungfishes living today, the legacy of some 380 million years of dipnoan evolution. This phenomenon would probably confine them to obscurity were it not for the fact that, from time to time, they have been introduced into discussions about tetrapod origins. In recent years their role in such discussions has usually been one of physiological exemplars (e.g., Schmalhausen, '68), exemplifying by analogy how the tetrapod ancestor may have coped with problems of gas exchange and desiccation. Many workers have noted similarities between lungfishes and tetrapods, particularly amphibians, in aspects of gas exchange and excretory physiology, pulmonary circulation, and heart structure. Moreover, some have speculated that these and other similarities demonstrate that lungfishes and tetrapods, or lungfishes and amphibians, should be classified together (Bischoff, 1840; Goodrich, '24; Kerr, '32; Kesteven, '50; Fox, '65; Rosen et al., '81). At present, however, the prevailing opinion is that lungfishes and tetrapods should not be classified together; rather, their similarities should be rated as convergences, that is, as accidental acquisitions of like morphology or function.

The theory that lungfishes are the nearest living relatives of tetrapods is now generally rejected in favor of theories based on palaeontological data. Those theories favor rhipidistians as the nearest relatives of tetrapods with *Latimeria* as the living derivative (Romer, '66, Fig. 67). If correct, this means that *Latimeria* should show special similarities with tetrapods not found in lungfishes or other fishes. In fact, however, *Latimeria* lacks many of the soft anatomical characters shared by lungfishes and tetrapods. *Latimeria*, for instance, has a largely fishlike circulatory system, a typically fishlike heart, and lacks choanae and lungs.

The apparent discrepancy between systematic conclusions derived from neontological data, viz., that lungfishes are the nearest relatives of tetrapods, and those derived from paleontological data, viz., that *Latimeria* is the nearest living relative of tetrapods, entitles us to question the validity of the different methodologies that have been used in an attempt to solve the problems of lungfish relationships. Inevitably, any essay dealing with relationships of lungfishes also impinges on theories of tetrapod origins as well as wider issues of systematic methods. Within these few pages it is not possible to discuss all the diverse theories of lungfish relationships, nor is it possible to dwell on all facets of different systematic methods. Much of this ground has already been adequately covered in a few recent papers dealing with relationships of lungfishes (Jarvik,

'68a; Patterson, '80; Rosen et al., '81; Conant, this volume). The intent here is to concentrate on *specific* methods and *particular* theories in the hope that these will exemplify more general problems of lungfish relationship and tetrapod origins. It is my belief that disagreement over methods has been the primary factor preventing a solution to the problem of relationships; paucity of data is only a secondary factor. This paper deals with issues that have nearly all been addressed by Rosen et al. ('81) in greater depth. Some of the conclusions in that paper are re-evaluated here in the light of recent discoveries or reinterpretations.

HISTORICAL SOURCE OF A METHODOLOGICAL PROBLEM

When lungfishes were discovered in the 1830s there was initial disagreement over whether they should be classified with fishes or with amphibians. Bischoff (1840) and followers (Milne Edwards, 1840; Hogg, 1841; Heckel, 1845; Melville, 1848, 1860; Vogt, 1845, 1851; Asmuss, 1856; Gray, 1856) suggested, or implied through their writings, that lungfishes and amphibians should be classified together. As Patterson ('80) records, Bischoff identified several amphibian-like characters in *Lepidosiren* such as internal nostrils (choanae), lungs connected to the oesophagus by a glottis guarded by an epiglottis, reduced gills with corresponding reduction in vascularization compared to fishes, a heart with two auricles with the left auricle receiving blood directly from the lungs, and a conus with valves that separate pulmonary from branchial blood.

Not all of the early contemporary workers agreed. Müller (1840), Oken (1841), and Agassiz (1843), for instance, preferred to regard lungfishes as fishes because lungfishes have scales, sensory canals, opercular bones, and a weakly developed vertebral column. These are features commonly — but, it should be noted, not exclusively — found in fishes. Yet a third group of workers (Heckel, 1851; M'Donnell, 1860) suggested that it was impossible to say if lungfishes were fishes or amphibians because they are so clearly intermediate in structure.

We can translate these nineteenth century ideas into cladistic terms. The theory advocated by Bischoff and followers ranks lungfishes and tetrapods as sister-groups among Recent animals based on characters unique to them, and still known to be so. "Fishes" form the primary twin (terminology of Løvtrup, '77). Ideas expressed by Müller, Oken, and Agassiz suggest that lungfishes and "fishes" are secondary twins with tetrapods as the primary twin. This idea was supported by characters now known in all three taxa, which must therefore be judged to be primitive characters. The third suggestion simply says that there are three taxa whose interrelationships remain to be established.

The dispute over how to classify lungfishes was never settled, because a new way of looking at the order of life developed following Darwin's theory of evolution. That theory prompted a new question — which group of fish-like vertebrates were ancestral to tetrapods? At first lungfishes, sometimes regarded as structurally borderline, were placed as ancestors (Haeckel, 1889), but by the turn of the century they were quickly pushed aside to be replaced by crossopterygians (coelacanths and the extinct rhipidistians). The precise way in which this was done was historically complicated (see Patterson, '80; Rosen et al., '81; Conant, this volume) but stemmed from an expectation that ancestors would be found and could be identified.

Criteria necessary in an ancestor are that it be more primitive than its descendant, that it occur earlier, and that structural and physiological transition between putative ancestor and descendant be deemed to be evolutionarily plausible. Lungfishes were considered to fail the first and third criteria chiefly because they showed a specialized autostylic jaw suspension (Cope, 1892) and dentition (Boas, 1882) with no outer jaw bones (Cope, 1892). It was difficult to visualize how the crushing mode of lungfish feeding could be transformed into an essential biting and holding method of feeding. This viewpoint, prevalent around the turn of the century, is still with us today, as the following quote demonstrates:

> The known dipnoans, living or fossil, possess many specialised characters (autapomorphies) not present in many osteolepiforms, and were much farther from the morphotype expected for tetrapod ancestors. Although many of the characters used to define osteolepiforms may be primitive for choanate fish and do not necessarily indicate affinity with tetrapods, these fish nevertheless provide a more plausible basis for the origin of tetrapod structures" (Holmes, '84:436).

Parenthetically, it should be noted that we now know of lungfishes that appear not to have been wholly crushing feeders (Campbell and Barwick, '84a) and some lungfishes such as *Griphognathus* are known to have outer jaw bones, albeit the terminology of these bones is disputed (cf. Rosen et al., '81; Campbell and Barwick, '84b).

Once removed from their position as tetrapod ancestors (Cope, 1892; Haeckel, 1889), lungfishes were allied with a wide variety of vertebrate groups. They have been regarded as collateral descendants of holocephalans (Jarvik, '68a), of actinopterygians (Bertmar, '68), as the most primitive osteichthyans (Wahlert, '68), as the most primitive sarcopterygians (Westoll, '61; Schultze, this volume), or as unrelated to any other fish group (Bjerring, '84). Some workers (Miles, '77; Wiley, '79) regard them as the nearest living relatives of tetrapods — the popular nineteeth century view — but with the proviso that the extinct rhipidistians are more closely related to tetrapods.

Crossopterygians, in particular the rhipidistians (osteolepiforms and porolepiforms), do not show the specialized features that were deemed to preclude lungfishes from tetrapod ancestry and appear to most workers to be primitive enough — that is, to lack enough characters — to be considered as ancestors. Accordingly, investigators have set out to demonstrate how rhipidistians could have been transformed into Paleozoic "amphibians" on one or more occasions (for review see Rosen et al., '81).

The particular rhipidistian or rhipidistian subgroup chosen often depends upon the whim of the investigator and the regional anatomy chosen for comparison. Some workers have suggested that *Sauripterus* (Gregory, '15) or *Sterropterygion* (Rackoff, '80) are the best candidates because details of limb structure foreshadow those in tetrapods most closely. Others suggest that *Elpistostege, Panderichthys* or *Eusthenodon* are better candidates because of similarity with early "amphibians" in the configuration of skull roofing bones (Schultze and Arsenault, '85). On the other hand Panchen ('77) favors *Osteolepis* because of its high degree of ossification, deemed necessary in the transition from an aquatic medium to the less buoyant life on land. In other words, there is no agreement that one species is suitable, or known completely enough, in all organ systems. One interesting observation is that the one species that is known in greatest detail (*Eusthenopteron*) is rarely selected as *the* ancestor except in the most popularly written texts.

This approach — to search for ancestors using assumed transformations, best candidates, and relative primitivity — is fraught with problems that, in my view, have stultified attempts to answer the question of relationships. There are three important problem areas: difficulties inherent in theories of transformation, difficulties surrounding the concept of ancestry, and the special difficulties posed by fossils. The problems are interrelated and to deal with them separately is largely a convenience.

With regard to the first problem, the notion that particular structures in one organism are better precursors than those in another is sometimes employed to favor one candidate over another. Examples have been given above but one may choose especially the pattern of skull roofing bones, so often cited in theories of tetrapod origin. The pattern exhibited by lungfishes (Säve-Söderberg, '32) or various rhipidistians (Westoll, '43; Schultze and Arsenault, '85; or Säve-Söderberg, '32) has at one time or another been treated as the forerunner of the tetrapod condition. Always, however, there is a morphological gap between descendant (tetrapods) and ancesteral candidate, and this is filled with a theory of process to explain the transformation (e.g., movements of dermal bones relative to endocranium, relative movement of sensory canals, bone fusion, or fragmentation). No doubt such processes existed at the time of tetrapod origin, just as they do today; but precisely *which* theory of process we choose, and therefore *which* particular transformation we accept, is not open to question in an event that must have taken place some 350 million years ago. Having agreed on the start and end points of a transformation series, we are then entitled to speculate on the process. To use a particular theory of process to decide on the starting point (the ancestor), however, introduces an unacceptable level of assumption.

The second problem concerns the fact that, by definition, ancestors are wholly primitive relative to their presumed descendants. But no one accepts that any particular species satisfies this criterion, and very rarely are individual species named. Instead, it is usual to designate an ancestral family or order. This category is presumed to contain members that between them have enough primitive characters and, at the same time, some indications that they could have transformed into tetrapods. As has been noted above, the most popular group chosen is the osteolepiforms (variously including rhizodontids and panderichthyids), despite the fact that their exemplified primitive characters "do not necessarily indicate affinity with tetrapods" (Holmes, '84:436).

Another author, who has for many years advocated the diphyletic origin of tetrapods from the two rhipidistian subgroups, proffers these cautionary remarks about the use of primitive characters:

> If we want to prove relationship between two distinct fossil groups, we have to disregard all structural features that characterise each of the two groups and distinguish them from each other. ... Nor can we use with any confidence characters that are suspected to be primitive or known to be shared by other groups. (Jarvik, '68b:499–500).

The reason for this is implied in the term "primitive characters" because these characters are more widely distributed than in the groups under discussion. For instance, it has been suggested that the common presence in osteolepiforms and primitive tetrapods of an opercular series, double-headed hyomandibular, and a fishlike tail as occurs in *Ichthyostega*, indicates close relationship between these groups. These are all primitive characters at the tetrapod level; they specify larger groups (Osteichthyes, Sarcopterygii and Gnathostomata respectively). Using these primitive characters, we have no reason to favor osteolepiforms over porolepiforms, lungfishes, or coelacanths etc. Thus if primitive characters are of little use to indicate relationship, and further, if ancestors by definition display primitive characters, then the search for ancestors must be fraught with difficulty from the beginning. Many people have questioned the search for ancestors, whether those ancestors be species or supraspecific groupings (e.g., Eldredge, '79; Forey, '82; Wiley, '79). This is not a denial of the former existence of ancestors but rather an acceptance that they cannot be recognized.

The third major problem area concerns the fact that although ancestors of living taxa are expected to be found as fossils, it is necessary that such fossils be interpreted in the light of Recent models. Choice of the Recent model may influence our ideas of what filled grooves or passed through foramina in fossil organisms, and this in turn may influence our ideas of relationship between fossil and Recent taxa [e.g., Stensiö's ('68) hypothesis that extinct heterostracans are ancestral to Recent hagfishes]. With respect to the taxa under consideration in this paper, Rosen et al. ('81) raised the possibility that the opening between the vomer, palatine, and outer jaw bones of *Eusthenopteron* was not a choana, which would have implied relationship with tetrapods, but may have been for the reception of fangs of the lower jaw or was perhaps a simple palatal fenestra. Choosing the Recent actinopterygian *Polypterus* as the model for *Eusthenopteron* would suggest that the foramen in question is a palatal fenestra (Rosen et al., '81), but choosing tetrapods (e.g., a frog; see Jarvik, '42) would suggest it to be a choana. The point is that structures in fossils are not self evident but have to be interpreted in the light of theories of relationship with Recent organisms (Patterson, '77). But just as it is difficult to interpret structures in fossils, it is also easy to ascribe attributes that might not be directly observable. For instance, it is often claimed that *Eusthenopteron* has dorsal ribs and this is used as evidence of tetrapod affinity (Andrews and Westoll, '70; Rackoff, '80). The identification of ribs as dorsal or ventral, however, is not entirely dependent on topographic position but involves some knowledge of how the ribs grew (Rosen et al., '81:244).

It is apparent therefore that fossils may introduce an extra tier of problems that need to be recognized and allowed for in any debate of conflicting classifications. When these difficulties are considered alongside the difficulties surrounding the concept of ancestry, it is apparent that a different methodological approach is needed. Many workers have recognized this and have abandoned the search for ancestors; instead they have posed the question, "which group shows special similarities with tetrapods not found in other groups?" To answer this, a cladistic approach has been adopted whereby theories are expressed as cladograms specifying nested sister-group relationships. Several theories have been suggested, varying in the scope of the taxa considered, the initial assumptions, and the weighting of conflicting character distributions.

CLADISTIC THEORIES OF LUNGFISH RELATIONSHIPS

In the previous section it was pointed out that there are special problems introduced with the inclusion of fossils and fossil groups. The initial inquiry is therefore best conducted using Recent taxa to which the fossils can be added later. The osteichthyan taxa under consideration are Actinoptergyii, Actinistia (coelacanths), Dipnoi, and Tetrapoda. In this essay I am assuming that each of these taxa is a monophyletic group each characterized by synapomorphies. This would be in agreement with most workers, although Säve-Söderberg ('33) and Jarvik ('42) would not accept that Tetrapoda is a monophyletic group. I am also disregarding theories suggesting that coelacanths or lungfishes are most closely related to chondrichthyans or included subgroups (Lövtrup, '77, and Lagios, '81, *contra* Compagno, '81, and Forey, '80; Jarvik, '68a, *contra* Miles, '75, '77). I regard both coelacanths and lungfishes as osteichthyans based on synapomorphies shown at the basal node in Figure 2.

The most commonly discussed theories are illustrated in Figure 1. Theories 3, 4, and 5 accept a group Sarcopterygii, with numbers 4 and 5 being two possible resolutions of theory number 3. The advantage of expressing theories in this way is that they are clearly stated and can be easily criticized. The theories (numbered 1 and 5) that suggest that lungfishes and tetrapods are sister-groups constituting the group Choanata are by far the best supported (see legend to Fig. 2). Theory number 5 is the one favored in this paper. This theory might be criticized by showing that theory number 4, for instance, is a more parsimonious solution, but to my knowledge this has not been done.

One other way in which one theory is often favored over another is by weighting, that is by claiming that some synapomorphies that suggest one grouping are more important than others that suggest a different grouping. Holmes ('85:381–382), in a paper designed to criticize theory 5 (Fig. 1), advocated by Rosen et al. ('81), suggested that it was reasonable to weight each character. Holmes argues that it should be possible to decide if one character rather than another is more likely to yield the "correct" phylogenetic result. He follows Hecht and Edwards ('76) in suggesting that structurally (and presumably genetically) complex characters are more significant than structurally simple characters. The converse belief is also implied, namely, that simple characters are more prone to convergence and parallelism and hence are false guides to relationship. This is hardly a testable idea with our present ignorance of the relationship between genotye and phenotype. It is theoretically possible that a genetically simple change, if affecting early stages of ontogeny, may have profound consequences in the adult (Riedl, '78; Arthur, '83). Holmes agrees that the overriding factor in choosing between hypotheses should be parsimony when "...a large number of character distributions support a given nested pattern and few conflict with it" (Holmes, '85:381). Support for theory 5 would appear to fall into this category. According to Holmes, weighting of characters becomes important when there are nearly equal numbers of synapomorphies supporting conflicting solutions. As many of the synapomorphies of lungfishes and tetrapods involve details of soft anatomy, it is only with the introduction of fossils — where soft anatomy cannot be compared — that weighting apparently becomes important when the balance of osteological characters supporting conflicting hypotheses is ostensibly more equal.

Theories presented in Figure 1 are predictive in the sense that some additional, newly examined characters should be congruent with the chosen hypothesis. One entire field of new data is molecular information. Unfortunately surprisingly little comparative information exists so far. Biochemistry of the coelacanth is virtually unknown, only a few actinopterygians (teleosts) have been examined, and amongst lungfishes only *Lepidosiren* has been analyzed for amino acid sequences of α- and β-hemoglobins (Rodewald et al., '84). The results and implications of analyzing these sequences are rather ambiguous. Cladistic analysis conducted on the α-hemoglobin ranks sharks as the sister-group of *Lepidosiren*, while the amino acid sequence of β-hemoglobin suggests that *Lepidosiren* be grouped with osteichthyans. In both hemoglobins *Lepidosiren* is unique in many amino acid positions, probably reflecting the long independent history of this lungfish. Clearly, a great deal more comparative information (e.g., hemoglobin and myoglobin sequences from *Latimeria*, the other living lungfishes, and *Polypterus*) is needed. All we are entitled to say at present is that information from hemoglobin sequences is either totally inconsistent with all theories shown in Figure 1 (α), or is uninformative (β).

We now attempt to insert consideration of the fossils, bearing in mind problems mentioned above. Some fossils can of course be assigned unequivocally to existing taxa because they show one or more synapomor-

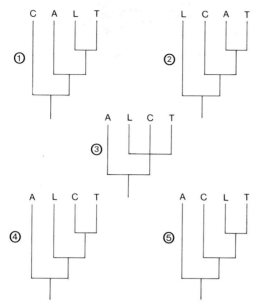

Fig. 1. Five classifications of Recent osteichthyans. Classifications 1,3, and 4 include the prior assumption that extinct rhipidistians are immediate relatives of tetrapods. Classification 5 is supported in this paper with reasons enumerated in the legend to Figure 2. 1. Classification of Wiley ('79). 2. Classification of Wahlert ('68). 3. Classification of Schultze ('81), Romer ('66). 4. Classification of Westoll ('61). 5. Classificataion of Rosen et al. ('81). Abbreviations: A, Actinopterygii; C, Actinistia (coelacanths); L, Dipnoi (lungfishes); T, Tetrapoda.

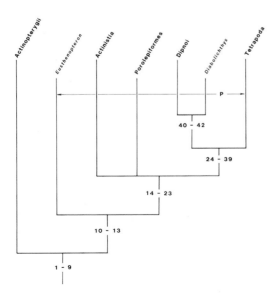

phies of the terminal taxa. If they can be classified within the Recent group, they may give us considerable information about the history of that group. Fossils may extend the morphological variation known to occur in the group and thereby change our ideas about the primitive conditions for that group (examples below). Other fossils may occupy positions between two nodes. This is because they show some but not all of the characters

Fig. 2. Preferred solution of osteichthyan classification. *Eusthenopteron* is interchangeable with most "osteolepiforms" except possibly Panderichthyidae (P) Vorobjeva. Many of the synapomorphies listed here are discussed more fully in Rosen et al. ('81) where those authors also cite further similarities between lungfishes and tetrapods in soft anatomy. Porolepiformes are placed in a trichotomy here that might be resolved with further knowledge of their structure. Rosen et al. ('81:257) record that porolepiforms are like dipnoans in having long, leaf-like pectoral fins and in details of the cosmine pore canal system. They appear more plesiomorphic than coelacanths in retaining hypobranchials. Characters 1–42 are as follows: 1, swimbladder/lung; 2, gular plates; 3, interarcual muscles; 4, separate branchial levators; 5, lepidotrichia; 6, toothed marginal upper and lower jaw bones; 7, toothed dermal bones on palate; 8, infrapharyngobranchials directed anteriorly; 9, suprapharyngobranchials present on the first two branchial arches; 10, exclusively metapterygial fin axis supported by a single basal element; 11, enamel on teeth; 12, sclerotic ring composed of more than four plates; 13, anocleithrum in shoulder girdle; 14, inferior vena cava; 15, pulmonary vein; 16, branchial levators inserting to ceratobranchials; 17, pectoral and pelvic appendages each with long muscular lobes extending well below body wall and with similar endoskeletons; 18, anocleithrum beneath skin; 19, preaxial side of pectoral fin rotated to postaxial position (see Rosen et al., '81 for discussion) resulting in pectoral and pelvic fins being the structural reverse of each other; 20, hyomandibular short, not in series with hyoid bar; 21, last gill arch articulating with penultimate arch; 22, single broad basibranchial; 23, reduction or loss of hypobranchials; 24, hyomandibular that buttresses palate and decoupled from ceratohyal; 25, ceratohyal expanded posteriorly and reaching far dorsally; 26, abbreviated palatine region; 27, loss of pharyngobranchials; 28, rib gradient with longest ribs immediately behind the head, thereafter descreasing posteriorly; 29, levator hyoideus muscle inserting directly to ceratohyal instead of hyomandibular; 30, pectoral and pelvic limb skeletons of equal size, each having two ball-and-socked joints, 31, second axial segment of fin skeleton formed by two subequal bones, in pectoral appendage the postaxial member articulating on postaxial margin of basal element; 32, muscles of paired fins segmented; 33, ontogenetic subdivision of levator hyoideus, part of which forms the depressor mandibulae muscle; 34, efferent branchial arteries joining each other before they join those of the other side to form the dorsal aorta; 35 noncompartmentalized adenohypophysis; 36, divided auricle; 37, mesotocin; 38, glottis and epiglottis; 39, lens proteins D_1, D_2 and D_5 (Løvtrup, '77); 40, rostral tubuli, 41, inturned premaxilla; 42, otic region of braincase covered by a B bone flanked by parietals.

specifying those nodes. As Patterson ('77) has pointed out, these fossils are particularly problematic because fossils are always incomplete in some respect or another, and we have no way of checking if the absence is real or an artifact or preservation.

Fossils that have been invoked in theories of lungfish relationships and in theories of tetrapod origins are the osteolepiforms and porolepiforms. The Porolepiformes is demonstrably a monophyletic group in which members possess an unusual dendrodont infolding of dentine of the larger teeth (Schultze, '69). Osteolepiformes appears to be a paraphyletic group, with different authorities including or excluding various subgroups such as Rhizodontidae, Panderichthyidae, or Rhizodopsidae (see Andrews, '73, '85; Vorobjeva, '77; Long, '85a,b; Thomson, '69). Many of these "osteolepiforms" are incompletely known or incompletely documented and their classification is influenced accordingly. Thus panderichthyids have been documented primarily on the basis of skull material, and inevitably classifications incorporating these fishes will stress these characters and exclude consideration of other portions of anatomy that in other fishes suggest different classifications. It may not be possible to consider *all* fossils without restricting the scope of comparison to one character complex (e.g., skull roofs or fin structure). As far as the "osteolepiforms" are concerned, Rosen et al. ('81) chose the best-known representative (*Eusthenopteron*). In prior discussion of tetrapod origins this has usually stood in place of "osteolepiforms" or "osteolepids." In this paper "osteolepiforms" is regarded as a paraphyletic group.

Confusion over inclusion or exclusion of various taxa referred to the Osteolepiformes and the characterization of that group is exemplified in two recent papers. Long ('85a) suggests that the Osteolepiformes is a monophyletic group. By Osteolepiformes he meant Osteolepididae and Eusthenopteridae. He excluded Panderichthyidae, Rhizodopsidae, Lamprotolepididae, and especially the Rhizodontidae. In a later paper ('85b:373) he clarified his ideas of the membership of the family Osteolepididae as the subfamilies included by Vorobjeva ('77). He could not find a synapormorphy of Osteolepididae, claiming them as a paraphyletic sister-group to higher osteolepiforms, which now include eusthenopterids, and, as a change of mind, rhizodontids and panderichthyids. In his earlier paper

Long ('85a) suggests four synapomorphies that are supposed to hold for his enlarged "osteolepiforms" ('85b). These are: a unqiue cheek in which the lachrymal is large, equal in size to the jugal, and postorbital; a barlike vertical preoperculum; exposed (ornamented) anocleithrum and enlarged basal scutes on all fins except the caudal. Few of these withstand critical examination. The relative sizes of the cheek bones and the shape of the preoperculum vary considerably (*Osteolepis, Thursius, Gryoptychius*, Jarvik, '48, Fig. 22) and are certainly not of equal size in *Panderichythys or Elpistostege* (Schultze and Arsenault, '85). The basal scutes are widespread and may possibly be a synapomorphy; but we must assume secondary loss in some (e.g., *Glyptopomus*, Jarvik, '50). The ornamented anocleithrum was considered by Rosen et al. ('81:218) as the plesiomorph end of a morphocline leading to eventual sinking beneath of skin (porolepiforms, coelacanths, lungfishes) and final loss (tetrapods). Such differing assessments in polarity of character transformation may be resolved by congruence with other characters. It is clear from this discussion that the status of Osteolepiformes remains debatable.

One solution incorporating *Eusthenopteron* and Porolepiformes was provided by Rosen et al. ('81) and is shown in Figure 2. This solution has been criticized by Holmes ('85:395), who notes that there are "...unique similarities between primitive tetrapods and *Eusthenopteron* (described by Jarvik, '80) in the pattern of bones of the mandible, the cheek, the palate and paired appendages...." Unfortunately Holmes does not put forward a counter-theory supported by these unique similarities, but these points of comparison are worth attention because they figure prominently in theories that consider osteolepiforms (*Eusthenopteron*) as the sister-group of tetrapods (see Rosen et al., '81:177). It becomes necessary to consider what these similarities amount to.

One of the strongest pieces of evidence cited in support of a sister-group pairing is the similarity in the structure of the lower jaw of early tetrapods and osteolepids, described as "almost identical" by Westoll ('43:85). Holmes ('85:395) states that the basis for this description is that "*Ichthyostega* and *Eusthenopteron* share a dermal mandibular pattern of one dentary, four infradentaries, three coronoids, and a prearticular on each side..." It is true that the lower jaws of these animals look very similar, and we also have to admit that the jaws of lungfishes look very different. In lungfishes the dentition on the lower jaw is confined to the prearticular as either a shagreen of denticles or toothplates; there is a deep labial pit laterally and in Recent lungfishes, the outside of the jaw is covered, at most, by two dermal bones. When comparing these jaws, however, we must remember Jarvik's methodological caution cited above and disregard structural features that are characteristic of each group. Thus, if we strip away the autapomorphies (labial pit, complex internal ramification of tubuli, for instance), we find that a Devonian lungfish such as *Chirodipterus* or *Uranolophus* has almost the same number of elements as osteolepiforms or tetrapods. It has, for instance, a dentary and four infradentaries, notwithstanding Jarvik's attempt to deny homology by applying unique names to the lungfish bones (Jarvik, '67). The only feature apparently lacking from the osteolepid-*Ichthyostega* comparison is the coronoid series. There may, in fact, be a transitory coronoid in young *Neoceratodus* (Jarvik, '67, Fig. 2), but this is debatable. The presence of a coronoid series, however, can hardly be used as evidence of osteolepiform-tetrapod relationship, because similar series are also found in porolepiforms (Jarvik, '72) and actinopterygians (Gardiner, '84). This must be a character of a larger, more inclusive group of which lungfishes may be a derived subgroup.

This discussion of the lower jaw is not an attempt to suggest that there are contained synapomorphies exclusively shared by lungfishes and tetrapods — although it may be noted that the equal development of mandibular and oral canals in lungfishes and Triassic stegocephalians (Nilsson, '44: 10) is remarkably similar. Rather, it is a caution that the alleged similarity of osteolepid and tetrapod jaws have to be more carefully specified beyond "almost identical." In this instance, therefore, the inclusion of fossil lungfishes has extended our knowledge of morphological variation.

The second area in which fossil lungfishes have helped us is increased knowledge of the hyoid arch. In Recent lungfishes the hyomandibular is a tiny structure seemingly unconnected with anything (Fox, '65). It does not appear to be comparable with either the fish hyomandibular or the tetrapod stapes.

On the other hand, one of the the cited similarities between osteolepiforms and tetrapods is the double-headed hyomandibular/stapes (Jarvik, '54). The hyomandibular is known in very few fossil lungfishes, but in *Griphognathus* it is a large structure with a double head and with similar relationships to surrounding foramina (Miles, '77). Outgroup comparison suggests that a large hyomandibular is a primitive feature. Carroll ('80) pointed out that the stapes (hyomandibular) of some early tetrapods was large and acted as a support for the cheek, perhaps to be reduced on several occasions to a sound-conducting stapes. Holmes ('85:387) regards Carroll's observations as "extremely damaging to the hypothesis that lungfishes are the sister group of tetrapods." But, in fact, the hyomandibular of *Griphognathus* is similarly developed, serving as a brace between palate and braincase. In both, the upper end of the hyomandibular lies free from the palate, and from here it sweeps down and forward to contact the palate where there is often a small process developed to receive it. In lungfishes, like tetrapods, the hyomandibular is free from the more ventral elements of the hyoid arch. The ceratohyal is posteriorly expanded so that it reaches up almost enough to contact the braincase, meaning that the hyomandibular has become decoupled from the ceratohyal.

This morphology contrasts with the fish condition, including that in *Eusthenopteron* (Jarvik, '54), in which the hyomandibular is tightly bound to the rear edge of the palate throughout its length and is in series with the ceratohyal by way of an interhyal or stylohyal. Conditions in porolepiforms are as yet poorly known, but the hyomandibular is of elongate shape as in *Eusthenopteron* and actinopterygians. *Latimeria* (and fossil coelacanths where known) show a highly specialized hyoid arch in which the hyomandibular lies completely free from the palate and ventrally is connected to both the ceratohyal and lower jaw via an interhyal and symplectic respectively. Such a configuration is surely related to the unusual jaw mechanisms of this fish (Lauder, '80; Alexander, '73). To summarize this information from the hyoid arch, one can say that in all aspects in which *Eusthenopteron* (osteolepids) is (are) similar to tetrapods lungfishes are also similar. Lungfishes additionally share with tetrapods the decoupling of the ceratohyal from the hyomandibular. Within living taxa this feature is also known to be associated with realignment of levator hyoideus musculature (Edgeworth, '35).

It is pertinent at this point to emphasize one further aspect of gill arch morphology. Rosen et al. ('81:238–239) pointed out that in coelacanths, lungfishes, and urodeles (tetrapods retaining reasonably well developed gill arches) the copular region is reduced to a short cartilage/bone receiving the ventral ends of the ceratobranchials or hypobranchials. The posterior arch, however, articulates with the penultimate arch, not with the copular. This pattern, which seems also to be present in porolepiforms (Jarvik, '72, Fig. 29A; Vorobjeva, '80), contrasts with that seen in chondrichthyans and actinopterygians (Rosen et al., '81; Gardiner, '84), and also that in restorations of *Eusthenopteron* (Jarvik, '54) in which all gill arches articulate with an elongate copular. Additionally, lungfishes, coelacanths, and tetrapods lack hypobranchials, and lungfishes and tetrapods lack pharyngobranchials as well. Holmes ('85:389) would rank such loss characters as insignificant and of no support for the lungfish/tetrapod hypothesis because of an (assumed) high probability of independent origin. Presumably the loss of mobility of the intracranial joint, cited as a character supporting osteolepiform tetrapod (Westoll, '43) or panderichthyid/tetrapod (Schultze and Arsenault, '85) pairings, would also fall into this category.

The anatomy of the paired appendages is another area in which Rosen et al. ('81) identified a transformation series supporting the theory that lungfishes and tetrapods are sister-groups. Those authors discussed polarity of several fin characters across a variety of lower gnathostome groups and specified several synapomorphies of lungfishes and tetrapods. The most significant of these are: 1) the basal segment articulates with the shoulder girdle proximally and the axial member of the second segment by way of ball and socket joints, meaning that there are two functional joints in the fin axis; 2) the second segment of the fin endoskeleton is composed of paired, subequal elements (corresponding to the radius/ulna or tibia/fibia); 3) the fin muscles are segmented; and 4) there are relatively few fin rays in relation to the endoskeletal support and these are confined to a narrow fringe.

As in coelacanths it appears also that the pectoral fin is the structural reverse of the pelvic fin (Rosen et al., '81, Figs. 30, 34), a pattern similar to that of tetrapod limbs. In *Neoceratodus* this arises by a 90° rotation of the fin axis during early ontogeny (Semon, 1898).

The counterclaim is that the fin of *Eusthenopteron*, or *Sauripterus* or *Sterropterygion* shares more similarity with the limb of an early tetrapod such as *Ichthyostega* or *Eryops* (Andrews and Westoll, '70; Rackoff, '80) than does the lungfish fin. Particular points of similarity emphasized are: 1) the complex shape of the basal segment equipped with various processes for muscle attachment; 2) screw-shaped glenoid process (*Eusthenopteron*) implying torsional movement; and 3) general similarity in the pattern between the axial and radial series of these "osteolepiform" fins and the humerus/femur, radius, ulna/tibia, fibula, and carpal/tarsal, and phalangeal bones. The significance of these similarities, however, is tempered by the fact that patterns 1 and 2 above are known in lungfishes (Rosen et al., '81, Figs. 30, 40). These characters may therefore be primitive or accidental similarities. With respect to the similarity in axial and radial series then, the match between any one "osteolepiform" and a tetrapod is not perfect (just as the match between lungfishes and tetrapods is not perfect). Indeed, one could find a match between the series in *Eusthenopteron* and the metapterygial axis of the actinopterygian *Acipenser* (Rosen et al., '81, Fig. 28). The most obvious difference between these two endoskeletons is that *Eusthenopteron*, like all sarcopterygians, including lungfishes, has a fin restricted to the metapterygium. Thus, arguments relying on "The greater similarity in skeletal pattern of the paired appendages between tetrapods and *Eusthenopteron*..." (Holmes, '85:395) may be diluted with the introduction of additional taxa. The fins of the "osteolepiform" taxa used for tetrapod comparison differ from the tetrapod and the lungfish limb in that the second segment, which is double, is composed of very unequal components. In specimens of *Eusthenopteron* one of these elements, usually called the radius, is nearly twice as long. Moreover, in *Sterropterygion*, which is considered closer to tetrapods than *Eusthenopteron* because of a possible elbow joint (Rackoff, '80), the "radius" is well over twice a long as the "ulna." Such disproportionate elements would not be expected in a tetrapod forerunner.

If there are characters of tetrapod/"osteolepiform" level in the fin structure, they need to be more carefully specified and the particular "osteolepiform" taxa need to be specified. It must also be acknowledged that lungfish fins also share some alleged "key" similarities of tetrapods/"osteolepiforms"; and the same may also hold true for porolepiforms, the fin structures of which are very poorly known at present. So far as I am aware, the two skeletal characters (19,30) specified at the lungfish/tetrapod, lungfish/tetrapod/coelacanth levels in Figure 2 have not been described in any "osteolepiform" so far.

To this point in the essay I have discussed the introduction of lungfish fossils that have extended our knowledge of morphological variation to the extent that they have embraced characters formerly thought to be restricted to "rhipidistians" and tetrapods. These fossils have therefore reduced the effectiveness of the traditional argument that places "rhipidistians" as the sister-group of tetrapods.

On the other hand, some fossils have provided evidence that questions some of the characters used to support the theory of lungfish/tetrapod pairing. Recently, Chang and Xiaobo ('84) have described a new Lower Devonian fish from China as *Diabolichthys*. This fish is known only from isolated braincases plus associated palatal bones and lower jaws referred to the braincase material because of similarity of the teeth (Chang and Xiaobo, '84:179). Chang and Xiaobo suggest that *Diabolichthys* is the sister-group of lungfishes and I agree with their opinion. In both, the otic region of the braincase is covered with parietals (I-bones) and a median bone (B)[*], and it is flanked by a series of small bones (X-Y series) that in lungfishes carry the otic canal; also in both the snout is inwardly turned with premaxillae facing into the mouth cavity; and the snout is penetrated by a highly complex system of rostral tubuli.

In accepting this theory of relationship, two lungfish/tetrapod synapomorphies listed by Rosen et al. ('81:230) must be ranked as parallelisms: medially united pterygoids and a long parasphenoid. The information currently available for *Diabolichthys* suggests that the pterygoids were separated by a well toothed parasphenoid that terminated at the level of the ventral fissure (Chang and Xiaobo, '84, Fig. 2D). This said, it is still possible that the anterior region of the palate was reduced and that the palate was immovable on the braincase (see Rosen et al., '81:234).

In *Diabolichthys*, therefore, we see an instance where recognition of a fossil sister-group of a Recent taxon may change ideas about the nature of a character transformation, but its ability to do so depends on the confidence with which it is classified. Parenthetically, we may note that *Diabolichthys* has a conspicuous and well-toothed dentary and premaxilla, emphasizing the fact that the early members of the dipnoan clade were typically osteichthyan in this respect. It also shows an external nasal opening very close to the jaw and no external intracranial joint; these two features are said by Schultze and Arsenault ('85:305) to link panderichthyids and primitive amphibians.

The pattern of cheek bones is one final area mentioned by Holmes ('85) as showing unique similarity between *Eusthenopteron* and primitive tetrapods. Accepting that *Eusthenopteron* stands for "osteolepiforms" of other authors (Westoll, '43), this similarity amounts to there being just seven cheek bones, thus fewer than in porolepiforms or primitive lungfishes (rhizodontiforms are very incompletely known, Andrews, '85), and disposed in a pattern totally unlike that in coelacanths in which a maxilla and quadratojugal are missing. Despite there being considerable variation among "osteolepiforms" in the relative sizes of constituent bones and consistent differences between the "osteolepiform" cheek and that of the primitive tetrapod (in which the lachrymal fails to enter the orbital margin but the jugal forms a considerable length, *contra* the "osteolepiform" condition), we could accept the seven-bone pattern as a shared derived character. Whether it can be regarded as a synapomorphy of "osteolepiforms" and tetrapods depends on congruence with other characters. If "osteolepiform" taxa straddle porolepiforms, coelacanths, or lungfishes, then it must be rated as a plesiomorph condition at the sarcopterygian level. The position of onychodonts, which have also been tentatively restored with a seven-bone pattern (Jessen, '66, Fig. 6), may also be relevant to discussions of patterns of cheekbones.

---

[*]Recognition that configuration of bones involving a "B" bone as part of that pattern is a synapomorphy of *Diabolichthys* and lungfishes means that I no longer have confidence in the lungfish/tetrapod synapomorphy as stated by Rosen et al. ('81:259 — character No. 59).

The pattern of cheek bones may be a potential falsifier of the lungfish/tetrapod hypothesis, but why the acquisition of a similar pattern of cheek bones should be rated as more significant than the loss of pharyngobranchials (a lungfish/tetrapod character) (Holmes, '85:389) or decoupling of the hyoid arch is not clear to me. One might argue that for the function of feeding the loss of pharyngobranchials with attendant muscle modification is more significant than similarity in the pattern of elements within an essentially immobile cheek plate (or roofing bones). My purpose is not to argue for one or the other solution, but rather to suggest that weighting in this manner can be so easily accomplished yet so difficult to justify.

So far in this essay I have suggested that the insertion of fossils into a Recent classification may change ideas of the hierarchical rank at which a character fits (e.g., jaw structure, hyomandibular articulation) or may overturn a previous hypothesis of synapomorphy (pterygoids, long parasphenoid). Nevertheless, I see no evidence that inclusion of fossils might refute the hypothesis that, among living taxa, lungfishes and tetrapods are sister-groups and that *Latimeria* is the primary twin. To do so would require the demonstration that one or more "rhipidistian" groups shared synapomorphies with coelacanths, and further that the combined group shared synapomorphies with tetrapods. The one "rhipidistian"/coelacanth synapomorphy claimed is the presence of an intracranial joint, a complete division of the braincase into ethmosphenoid and otic portions. This is the bastion of the paleontological argument resolving coelacanths as the nearest living relatives of tetrapods.

Much has been written about the intracranial joint. Bjerring ('73) asserts that the joint is topographically non-homologous in coelacanths and rhipidistians, based on his vertebral theory of the head. In so doing he denies relationship between coelacanths and tetrapods or coelacanths and rhipidistians (Bjerring, '84, Fig. 1). Others have taken the view that part (Wiley, '79) or all (Miles, '77) of this joint is homologous in coelacanths and rhipidistians but that, based on parsimony arguments, it should be considered a character of sarcopterygians, including dipnoans — even though the latter have lost it (Gardiner and Bartram, '77). This is the view adopted here, primarily because any grouping based on the intracranial joint is inconsistent with any classification so far proposed. There is no dermal joint, for instance, in the rhipidis-

tians, *Panderichthys*, *Elpistostege*, *Powichthys*, *Youngolepis*. The evidence for an intracranial joint is still unclear for *Ichthyostega*, but I note that Schultze and Arsenault ('85:305) rank *absence* of an external intracranial joint as a character of panderichthyids and labyrinthodonts.

My conclusions from consideration of fossils and fossil groups, are shown in Figure 2. This figure acknowledges that the extinct Panderichthyidae (*Elpistostege*, *Panderichthys*) may be more closely related to tetrapods than to dipnoans. I agree with Schultze and Arsenault ('85:305) that panderichthyids and labyrinthodonts share a flattened skull with similarly positioned orbits, although I hesitate to put these forward as synapomorphies. These authors stress similarity in pattern of skull roofing bones, a line of argumentation that I would reject, recognizing the great variability amongst rhipidistians generally and also recognizing that the actinopterygian *Polypterus* satisfies their criterion of three principal pairs of roofing bones. The theory given in Figure 2 includes some predictions about presently undescribed parts of *Panderichthys* and *Elpistostege*. Both would be expected to show characters 17–28, 30, 31.

THE CHOANA

I have left the choana for separate discussion, since historically it has been so central to ideas of sarcopterygian interrelationship, especially to the notion that rhipidistians are immediately related to tetrapods (Jarvik, '42, '80; Schultze, '81; Andrews, '73). Rosen et al. ('81) have discussed in detail the previous ideas relating to the choana. Since my prejudices have not changed substantially, I will only stress a few points without stating a definite conclusion.

Initial studies of lungfishes in the nineteenth century concluded that they had true choanae, similar in position to those in a tetrapod. Opinion changed when Allis ('19) developed his theory that the posterior nostril of a lungfish (the nostril in question) was just like an ordinary fish nostril that had moved inside the mouth, as in chimaeriforms. A consequence of Allis's argument is that the tetrapod choana is a neomorph. Allis's arguments are complicated because they rely on the assumption that there are three upper lips, a condition that remains unknown in any vertebrate.

Jarvik ('42) accepted Allis's general conclusion but gave new, far more detailed arguments based on comparative morphology.

Jarvik's arguments are difficult to summarize in a few words, but there were two key points put forward (Jarvik, '68a). He suggested that the lungfish posterior nostril is homologous to the fish excurrent nostril and not to a tetrapod choana, which he considered to be a neomorph because: 1) the infraorbital sensory canal passes above (aborally to) the anterior (incurrent), nostril and this position is presumed to imply an inward phylogenetic shift of both anterior and posterior (excurrent) nostrils; and 2) the ramus maxillaris V passes posteromedially to the posterior nostril in typically fishlike fashion. The first condition is matched in holocephalans, and there is indeed a close similarity supporting Jarvik's claim for topographic homology if not on the presumed process by which the posterior nostril "moved" into the mouth. This would appear to be a shared derived character, but whether it is regarded as a synapomorphy depends on congruence with other characters. The second point implies that there is a clear distinction between a fish posterior nostril and a choana with respect to the path of the associated nerves. Thomson ('65) has dissected several specimens of *Protopterus* and found that some specimens showed the "fish condition" while others showed the "tetrapod condition." Such observations must question the assumed distinction between nostril and choana with respect to nerve paths.

Another line of argumentation is to consider the posterior nostril/choana of a lungfish in relation to surrounding skeletal structures. The tetrapod choana is bordered by bones of the palate and the outer toothed jaw bones. It is the fenestra exochoanalis of Jarvik ('42). Modern lungfishes lack such bones and the tooth plates lining the roof of the mouth are very specialized, but a few fossil lungfishes, best exemplified by *Griphognathus*, are more complete. Rosen et al. ('81) have suggested that the posterior nostril bears the same morphological relationship to toothed palatine, ectopterygoid, and maxillary bones as does the choana in a primitive tetrapod. Identification of the marginal bones as maxillae and premaxillae in a fossil lungfish such as *Griphognathus* is based, in turn, on the fact that these bones bite outside the lower jaw teeth. Identification of palatine bones is based on comparison with bones lining the mouth of other osteichthyans. On these criteria the foramen in the roof of the mouth is like the choana of a tetrapod; therefore, that in a Recent lungfish must also be a choana.

One recent criticism of this point of view (Campbell and Barwick, '84a) suggests that all of these dermal bones lying lateral and anterior to the pterygoids in *Griphognathus* are neomorphic, developed in response to an assumed specialized feeding mode for long-snouted dipnoans. The consequent reasoning suggests that it is invalid to use bone comparison to imply homology of an enclosed nostril/choana. In my view such an argument avoids questions of homology and implies an alternative theory of relationship whereby lungfishes are thought more closely related to a group of fishes known to be primitively without these bones (? chondrichthyans). As a final thought, if *Diabolichthys* be accepted as the sister-group of lungfishes then the identification of at least paired premaxillae and vomers in primitive lungfishes becomes highly likely.

The conservative conclusion that may be drawn from this discussion is that, even with the benefit of the comparative anatomy of Recent forms, there remains debate over whether lungfishes have or do not have choanae. Most workers (Panchen, '67; Rosen et al., '81; Campbell and Barwick, '84a) agree that the excurrent nostril in a lungfish is homologous with the fish posterior nostril. Deciding whether this is homologous with the tetrapod choana depends, in part, on whether we accept the consequence of Allis's theory and Jarvik's arguments that the tetrapod choana is a neomorph. This, in turn, is partly dependent upon interpretation of a choana in fossils.

Rosen et al. ('81:187) reviewed the evidence for a choana in rhipidistians ("osteolepiforms" and porolepiforms) and found it lacking in conviction. The best recorded evidence still rests with *Eusthenopteron*. However, these authors record several important differences in size and shape of the presumed choana between the separate restorations provided by Jarvik ('42, '54) based on serial grinding series or an acid prepared specimen (Rosen et al., '81). Which of these restorations (Jarvik, '54, Fig. 25, or Rosen et al., '81, Fig. 14) is the more faithful may eventually be decided when more specimens with intact and articulated palates are prepared. Additionally Rosen et al. ('81:191–192) have recorded several problems with restoring the expected soft anatomy related to a nostril within the confined space allowed by the restored skeletal structures. Even if we do acknowledge the choana in *Eusthenopteron* on grounds of position and relationship to surrounding structures, the same argument must also apply to a fossil lungfish such as *Griphognathus*.

Conditions in porolepiforms are relevant both to the identification of a choana in *Eusthenopteron* and to the idea that the choana is a new, third opening from the nasal capsule. Porolepiforms have two external narial openings piercing dermal bones, and a third perforation called the choana, located between the vomer, dermopalatine, premaxilla, and maxilla, has been restored in *Glyptolepis* (Jarvik, '72:Fig. 31). Porolepiforms would therefore be unique among vertebrates in having three openings exiting the nasal capsule and piercing dermal bones. In Jarvik's scenario this represents an intermediate stage (morphological, not phylogenetic) between the fish condition (two external narial openings) and the *Eusthenopteron*/tetrapod condition where a new opening — the choana — has arisen in the roof of the mouth and the old posterior fish nostril has transformed into the nasolachrymal duct. In porolepiforms it is suggested that the choana has arisen but that the posterior nostril persists in fishlike form.

The so-called choana in porolepiforms is only known in *Glyptolepis* (although a ventral opening within the endoskeleton has been described in a variety of forms), where it is a tiny triangular opening (Jarvik, '72, Pl. 22, Fig. 1; Rosen et al., '81:193). Its size and shape is totally unlike the large ovoid choana of a tetrapod, or the opening in a lungfish, or the opening in *Eusthenopteron* (although in this form it is triangular rather than oval). It is very doubtful whether such a small opening could have functioned as a choana/excurrent nostril. If it is not a choana (see also Chang and Xiaobo, '84:183), but is instead a palatal fenestra as in *Polypterus* (Rosen et al., '81, Fig. 12), then it reaffirms the belief that the choana is a modified fish posterior nostril that has migrated ventrally, or failed to migrate dorsally from a primitive ventral position (Rosen et al., '81:186).

More importantly, it means that there may be two groups of sarcopterygians without a choana, i.e., coelacanths and porolepiforms. If *Eusthenopteron* is cladistically more plesiomorphic than either (Fig. 2), then the identity of the "choana" in *Eusthenopteron* must be called into question. An alternative strategy is to argue that all sarcopterygians have true choanae (except coelacanths, now definitely known to lack choanae) and therefore that this character is of no use for choosing between hypotheses (Holmes, '85:388).

In the final analysis it may not be possible to agree, on purely morphological grounds, if *Eusthenopteron* has a choana. And it may be of little consequence if we agree with Jarvik's view ('68b:500) that "... the fenestra endochoanalis is different in the two groups [osteolepiforms and porolepiforms] (Jarvik, 1942) and because the origin of the choana is still obscure (see Panchen, 1967) it may very well have arisen independently [in porolepiforms and osteolepiforms]." If we accept Jarvik's classification, then a nasolachrymal duct and a pentadactyl limb must also have arisen at least twice.

At present therefore I accept that choana as an homology specifying a group lungfishes and tetrapods. This homology might be shown to be a parallelism if the sister-group of lungfishes (*Diabolichthys*) were shown to be achoanate (see Chang and Xiaobo, '84:182, for discussion).

CONCLUSIONS

In this essay I have tried to show that the characters used by Bischoff (1840) and followers to group lungfishes with tetrapods are as valid today as they were when first enumerated. However, the conclusion that lungfishes were the nearest living relatives of tetrapods was challenged and eventually overturned at the end of the nineteenth century. This was a result of the acceptance of Darwin's theory of evolution with the consequent widespread desire to discover ancestors and the belief that they would be found as fossils. Expectation of success was prevalent among vertebrate workers (Huxley, 1868), because it was known that the major classes of vertebrates appeared at successively younger stages within the known stratigraphic record. This contrasted with the invertebrate record, in which major groups had appeared by the beginning of the known fossil record. There was, therefore, a chance that ancestors would be found to link together classes of vertebrates.

Among fossil fishes the Devonian rhipidistians were chosen as the link between fishes and tetrapods because they were thought to satisfy the necessary attributes of an ancestor: They were stratigraphically suitable; they were primitive in all respects; and they gave some indication that, given a theory of process, they might have transformed into tetrapods.

There are, however, various problems surrounding the recognition of ancestors (the nature of primitive characters, introduction of hypotheses of process, paraphyletic status, etc.) that conspire to render any hypothesis of ancestry an authoritative statement rather than a theory capable of being criticized. The additional complication provided by fossil material (incompleteness, inherent difficulties in interpretation) has meant that there is still little agreement about the tetrapod ancestor. Many of these problems have now been acknowledged and new attempts are being made using cladistic analysis, in which the emphasis has shifted away from searching for ancestors toward a preference for searching for sister-groups.

The objective of such analysis is to identify an hierarchy of monophyletic groups based on shared derived characters. Amongst living taxa lungfishes share many derived characters with tetrapods (numbered 24–39 in Fig. 2), suggesting strongly that these two are sister-groups; coelacanths share more universal attributes (numbered 14–23, Fig. 2) with lungfishes and tetrapods.

Rhipidistians are acknowledged here, as by many workers (e.g., Jarvik, '80; Schultze, '81), to be a paraphyletic group; this has always been implied in theories suggesting rhipidistians to be tetrapod ancestors. Porolepiform rhipidistians are a monophyletic group that Rosen et al. ('81) placed in a trichotomy with coelacanths and choanates (lungfishes and tetrapods) because of conflicting character distributions (see legend to Fig. 2). The osteolepiforms are more problematical. They probably constitute a paraphyletic group (Vorobjeva, '77, Fig. 22). The various families as listed by Vorobjeva ('77:12) may be distributed throughout the sarcopterygian classification shown in Figure 2. Many of them have as yet been poorly described. For these reasons Rosen et al. ('81) chose to examine *Eusthenopteron*, which is by far the best known example. Based on parsimony analysis this turns out to be more plesiomorphic than either the lungfish or the coelacanth.

The systematic conclusions arrived at by Rosen et al. have been criticized on at least two counts. Campbell and Barwick ('84a) have maintained that Rosen et al. misinterpreted the primitive condition of lungfishes,

taken by those authors to be exhibited by *Griphognathus*. Campbell and Barwick believe that there are two separate evolutionary lines of dipnoans, with *Griphognathus* as one specialized feeding type. They argue that many of the bones of *Griphognathus* (maxillae, palatines, vomers etc) are neomorphic and thus any arguments that depend on their homology with topographically similar bones in other fishes are invalid. Campbell and Barwick ('84a:169) list as one of their conclusions: "The attempt to homologize bones by matching their patterns in other groups, and then using the inferred homologies as evidence of taxonomic relationship between the groups, is obviously flawed." But it has been precisely this technique that has led to the many variants of the theory that rhipidistians are most closely related to tetrapods (e.g., Schultze and Arsenault, '85; Westoll, '43). The conclusion that bone matching is a flawed technique further suggests that detailed bone by bone comparisons of one lungfish with another (e.g., Campbell and Barwick, '82) are pointless; or that the assignment of *Dipnorhynchus lehmanii* to *Speonesydrion* on roofing bone pattern (Campbell and Barwick, '84b:5) is suspect. These criticisms introduced by Campbell and Barwick are rejected mainly because they lead to no systematic conclusions.

Throughout this essay I have chosen to cite Holmes ('85) because his criticism of Rosen et al. ('81) covers much of that voiced, but as yet unpublished, by many supporters of the traditional theory of rhipidistian relationships. Jarvik ('81) has also written a long, critical review of the concepts of Rosen et al. ('81). Over half that review deals with the choana. The remainder contains certain valid points but also contains references to assumed (non-observable) components of the neurocranium and visceral arches and also to statements of process that are, in themselves, difficult to justify. Perhaps most importantly, the systematic conclusions to which Jarvik's arguments lead (that dipnoans arose separately from all other fish groups, Jarvik, '60, Fig. 28) do not lend themselves to further analysis.

Another line of criticism has come from Holmes ('85) who disagrees with the failure of Rosen and his collaborators to weight characters, that is, to discriminate between "good" and "bad" characters. Holmes speaks of "improper weighting," but how this differs from disagreement with alternative classifications is not made clear. Application of *ad hoc* weighting procedures always leads to irresolvable arguments. Parsimony must be overall criterion of choice between hypotheses in order to reduce assumptions of parallelism and convergence to a minimum. If the hypothesis that lungfishes and tetrapods are sister-groups is found to be incorrect, it will be judged so on grounds of parsimony.

The consequences of the traditional classification whereby coelacanths are the Recent sister-group of tetrapods assumes many convergencies between lungfishes and tetrapods (those numbered 24–39 in Fig. 2), which I am unwilling to accept at present. Some authors (Burggren and Johansen, this volume) have argued that in certain of these features (heart structure, respiratory physiology) *Protopterus* and *Lepidosiren* are more like amphibians than *Neoceratodus*. The systematic consequences would presumably deny a group Dipnoi, although no author has suggested this. I do, however, following consideration of *Diabolichthys* as the sister-group of lungfishes, accept the possibility that *some* of the characters used by Rosen et al. ('81) to group lungfishes and tetrapods may have arisen independently. I further accept that some taxa (e.g., panderichthyids) may be the sister-group of tetrapods but that decision may be made only after parsimony analysis. The Rhizodontidae *sensu* Andrews ('85) have long been recognized as very distinctive crossopterygians but have always been very incompletely known. Andrews ('85) is the only detailed work on this group and suggests that the dermal shoulder girdle lacks dorsal elements (supratemporal and anocleithrum) and has a high fin insertion; additionally, from recent descriptions it appears as though the scaled lobe of the fin is very long in comparison to the fringe of fin rays. These features would suggest rhizodonts to be more cladistically derived than *Eusthenopteron*.

ACKNOWLEDGMENTS

I wish to thank P.H. Greenwood, British Museum (Natural History), for reading a manuscript of this paper and Dr. W. E. Bemis, University of Massachusetts, for the invitation to participate in the A.S.Z. lungfish symposium, Denver, 1984, at which this paper was read.

LITERATURE CITED

Agassiz, J.R.L. (1843) Recherches sur les Poissons Fossiles. Vol. II. Neuchâtel: Imprimerie de Petitpierre, pp. 2–46.

Alexander, R. McN. (1973) Jaw mechanisms of the coelacanth *Latimeria* Copeia *1973:*156–158.

Allis, E.P. (1919) The lips and the nasal apertures in the gnathostome fishes. J Morphol. *32:*145–205.

Andrews, S.M. (1973) Interrelationships of crossopterygins. In P.H. Greenwood, R.S. Miles, and C. Patterson (eds): Interrelationships of Fishes. London: Academic Press, pp. 137–177.

Andrews, S.M. (1985) Rhizodont crossopterygian fish from the Dinantian of Foulden, Berwickshire, Scotland, with a re-evaluation of the group. Trans. R. Soc. Edinburgh, Earth Sci. *76:*67–95.

Andrews, S.M., and T.S. Westoll (1970) The postcranial skeleton of *Eusthenopteron foordi* Whiteaves. Trans. R. Soc. Edinburgh *68:*207–329.

Arthur, W. (1983) Mechanisms of Morphological Evolution. Chichester: John Wiley and Sons.

Asmuss, H. (1856) Das vollkommenste Hautskelet der bisher bekannten Thierreihe. Abhandl. Erlangung der Magisterwürde, Dorpat.

Bertmar, G. (1968) Lungfish phylogeny. In T. Ørvig (ed): Current Problems of Lower Vertebrate Phylogeny. Stockholm: Almqvist and Wiksell, pp. 259–283.

Bischoff, T.L.W., von (1840) Description anatomique du *Lepidosiren paradoxa.* Ann. Sci. Nat. *14:*116–159.

Bjerring, H.C. (1973) Relationships of coelacanthiforms. In P.H. Greenwood, R.S. Miles, and C. Patterson (eds): Interrelationships of Fishes. London: Academic Press, pp. 179–205.

Bjerring, H.C. (1984) Major anatomical steps toward craniotedness: A heterodox view based largely on embryological data. J. Vert. Paleontol. *4:*17–29.

Boas, J.E.V. (1882) Uber den Conus arteriosus und die Arterienbogen der Amphibien. Morphol. Jahrb. *7:*488–572.

Campbell, K.S.W., and R.E. Barwick (1982) A new species of the lungfish *Dipnorhynchus* from New South Wales. Palaeontology *25:*509–527.

Campbell, K.S.W., and R.E. Barwick (1982) Early evolution of dipnoan dentitions and a new genus *Speonesydrion.* Mem. Assoc. Australas. Palaeontol. *1:*17–49.

Campbell, K.S.W., and R.E. Barwick (1984a) The choana, maxillae, premaxillae and anterior palatal bones of early dipnoans. Proc. Linn. Soc. N.S.W. *107:*147–170.

Campbell, K.S.W., and R.E. Barwick (1984b) *Speonesydrion,* an early dipnoan with primitive toothplates. Palaeo Ichthyologica *2:*1–48.

Carroll, R.L. (1980) The hyomandibular as a supporting element in the skull of primitive tetrapods. In A.L. Panchen (ed): The Terrestrial Environment and the Origin of Land Vertebrates. London: Academic Press, pp, 293–317.

Chang, M.-M., and Y. Xiaobo (1984) Structure and phylogenetic significance of *Diabolichthys speratus* gen. et sp. nov., a new dipnoan-like form from the Lower Devonian of Eastern Yunnan, China. Proc. Linn. Soc. N.S.W. *107:*171–184.

Compagno, L.J.V. (1981) Coelacanths: Shark relatives or bony fishes? Occ. Pap. Calif. Acad. Sci. *134:*45–52.

Cope, E.D. (1892) On the phylogeny of the Vertebrata. Proc. Am. Phil. Soc. *30:*278–281.

Edgeworth, F.H. (1935) The Cranial Muscles of Vertebrates. Cambridge: Cambridge University Press.

Eldredge, N. (1979) Cladism and common sense. In J. Cracraft and N. Eldredge (eds): Phylogenetic Analysis and Paleontology. New York: Columbia University Press, pp. 165–198.

Forey, P.L. (1980) *Latimeria:* A paradoxical fish. Proc. R. Soc. Lond. (Biol) *208:*369–384.

Forey, P.L. (1982) Neontological analysis versus palaeontological stories. In K.A. Joysey and A.E. Friday (eds): Problems of Phylogenetic Reconstruction. London: Academic Press, pp. 119–157.

Fox, H. (1965) Early development of the head and pharynx of *Neoceratodus* with a consideration of its phylogeny. J. Zool. Lond. *146:*470–554.

Gardiner, B.G. (1984) The relationships of the palaeoniscid fishes, a review based on new specimens of *Mimia* and *Moythomasia* from the Upper Devonian of Western Australia. Bull. Br. Mus. (Nat. Hist.), Geol. *37:*173–428.

Gardiner, B.G., and A.W.H. Bartram (1977) The homologies of ventral cranial fissures in osteichthyans. In S.M. Andrews, R.S. Miles, and A.D. Walker (eds): Problems in Vertebrate Evolution. London: Academic Press, pp. 227–245.

Goodrich, E.S. (1924) The origin of land vertebrates. Nature *114:*935–936.

Gray, J.E. (1856) Observations on a living African Lepidosiren in the Crystal Palace. Proc. Zool. Soc. Lond. *24:*342–346.

Gregory, W.K. (1915) Present status of the problem of the origin of the Tetrapoda, with special reference to the skull and paired limbs. Ann. N. Y. Acad. Sci. *26:*317–383.

Haeckel, E. (1889) Natürliche Schöpfungsgeschichte. 8th Ed. Berlin: G. Reimer.

Hecht, M.K., and J.L. Edwards (1976) The determination of parallel or monophyletic relationships: The proteid salamanders — a test case. Am. Nat. *110:*653–677.

Heckel, J. (1845) Bemerkung über *Lepidosiren paradoxa*. Arch. Anat. Physiol. *1845:*534–535.

Heckel, J. (1851) Uber einer neue Fisch-Species aus dem Weissen Nil, *Protopterus aethiopicus*. Sitzber. Akad. Wiss. Wein *6:*685–689.

Hogg, J. (1841) On the existence of branchiae in the young Caeciliae; and on a modification and extension of the branchial classification of the Amphibia. Ann. Mag. Nat. Hist. *7:*353–363.

Holmes, E.B. (1985) Are lungfishes the sister group of tetrapods? Biol. J. Linn. Soc. *25:*379–397.

Holmes, R. (1984) The Carboniferous amphibian *Proterogyrinus scheeli* Romer, and the early evolution of tetrapods. Philos. Trans. R. Soc. Lond. (Biol.) *306:*431–524.

Huxley, T.H. (1868) On the animals which are most nearly intermediate between birds and reptiles. Geol. Mag. *5:*357–365.

Jarvik, E. (1942) On the structure of the snout and lower gnathostomes in general. Zool. Bidrag Uppsala *21:*235–675.

Jarvik, E. (1948) On the morphology and taxonomy of the Middle Devonian osteolepid fishes of Scotland. K. Svenska Vetensk. Akad. Handl. *25:*1–301.

Jarvik, E. (1950) On some osteolepiform crossopterygians from the Upper Old Red Sandstone of Scotland. K. Svenska Vetensk. Akad. Handl *2:*1–36.

Jarvik, E. (1954) On the visceral skeleton in *Eusthenopteron* with discussion of the parasphenoid and palatoquadrate in fishes. K. Svenska Vetensk. Akad. Handl. *5:*1–104.

Jarvik, E. (1960) Théories de l' Evolution des Vertébrés Reconsidérées à la Lumière des 'Recentes Découvertes sur les Vertébrés Inférieurs. Paris: Masson.

Jarvik, E. (1967) The homologies of frontal and parietal bones in fishes and tetrapods. Colloques Internatal. Centre Natl. Rech. Sci. *163:*181–213.

Jarvik, E. (1968a) The systematic position of the Dipnoi. In T. Ørvig (ed): Current Problems of Lower Vertebrate Phylogeny. Stockholm: Almqvist and Wiksell, pp. 223–245.

Jarvik, E. (1968b) Aspects of vertebrate phylogeny. In T. Ørvig (ed): Current Problems of Lower Vertebrates Phylogeny. Stockholm: Almqvist and Wiksell, pp. 497–527.

Jarvik, E. (1972) Middle and Upper Devonian Porolepiformes from East Greenland with special reference to *Glyptolepis groenlandica* n. sp. and a discussion on the structure of the head in the Porolepiformes. Meddel. Grønland *187:*1–307.

Jarvik, E. (1980) Basic Structure and Evolution of Vertebrates. Vol. I. London: Academic Press.

Jarvik, E. (1981) Lungfishes, tetrapods, paleontology and plesiomorphy. Rev. Syst. Zool. *30:*378–384.

Jessen, H. (1966) Die Crossopterygier des Oberen Plattenkalkes (Devon) der Bergish-Gradbach-Paffrather Mulde (Rheinisches Schiefergebirge) unter Berücksichtigung von amerikanischem und europäischem *Onychodus*-material. Arkir Zool. *18:*305–389.

Kerr, J.G. (1932) Archaic fishes — *Lepidosiren, Protopterus, Polypterus* — and their bearing upon problems of vertebrate morphology. Jena Zeitschr. Naturwiss. *67:*419–433.

Kesteven, H.L. (1950) The origin of the tetrapods. Proc. R. Soc. Victoria *59:*93–138.

Lagios, M.D. (1981) The coelacanth and the Chondrichthyes as sister groups: A review of shared apomorph characters and a cladistic analysis and reinterpretation. Occ. Pap. Calif. Acad. Sci. *134:*25–44.

Lauder, G.V. (1980) The role of the hyoid apparatus in the feeding mechanism of the coelacanth *Latimeria chalumnae*. Copeia *1980:*1–9.

Long, J.L. (1985a) The structure and relationships of a new osteolepiform fish from the Late Devonian of Victoria, Australia. Alcheringa *9:*1–22.

Long, J.L. (1985b) A new osteolepid fish from the Upper Devonian Gogo Formation, Western Australia. Rec. West. Aust. Mus. *12:*361–377.

Løvtrup, S. (1977) The Phylogeny of the Vertebrata. London: John Wiley.

M'Donnell, R. (1860) Observations on the habits and anatomy of the *Lepidosiren annectens*. J. R. Dublin Soc. *2:*3–20.

Melville, G. (1848) On the *Lepidosiren*. Rept. Br. Assoc. Adv. Sci.*17:*78.

Melville, G. (1860) Appendix to M'Donnell's paper. J. R. Dublin Soc. *2:*405–406.

Miles, R.S. (1975) The relationships of the Dipnoi. Colloques Internatl. Centre Natl. Rech. Sci. *218:*133–148.

Miles, R.S. (1977) Dipnoan (lungfish) skulls and the relationships of the group: A study based on new species from the Devonian of Australia. Zool. J. Linn. Soc. *61:*1–328.

Milne Edwards, H. (1840) Remarque sur les affinités naturelles du *Lepidosiren*. Ann. Sci. Nat. *14:*159–162.

Müller, J. (1840) Bericht über die Fortschritte der vergleichenden Anatomie im Jahre 1839. Arch. Anat. Physiol. *1839:*159–198.

Nilsson, T. (1944) On the lower jaw of *Stegocephalia* with special reference to Eotriassic Stegocephalians from Spitzbergen. II, General part. K. Svenska Vetensk. Akad. Handl. *21:*1–70.

Oken, L. (1841) *Lepidosiren paradoxa*. Isis *34:*462–469.

Panchen, A.L. (1967) The nostrils of choanate fishes and early tetrapods. Biol. Rev. *42:*374–420.

Panchen, A.L. (1977) The origin and early evolution of tetrapod vertebrae. In S.M. Andrews, R.S. Miles, and A.D. Walker (eds) Problems in Vertebrate Evolution. London: Academic Press, pp. 289–318.

Patterson, C. (1977) The contribution of palaeontology to teleostean phylogeny. In M.K. Hecht and P.C. Goody (eds): Major Patterns in Vertebrate Evolution. New York: Plenum Press, pp. 579–643.

Patterson, C. (1980) Origin of tetrapods: Historical introduction to the problem. In A.L. Panchen (ed): The Terrestrial Environment and the Origin of Land Vertebrates. London: Academic Press, pp. 159–176.

Rackoff, J.S. (1980) The origin of the tetrapod limb and the origin of tetrapods. In A.L. Panchen (ed.): The Terrestrial Environment and the Origin of Land Vertebrates. London: Academic Press, pp. 255–292.

Riedl, R. (1978) Order in Living Organisms. Chichester: John Wiley and Sons.

Rodewald, K., A. Stangl, and G. Braunitzer (1984) Primary structure, biochemical and physiological aspects of hemoglobin from South American lungfish (Lepidosiren paradoxus, Dipnoi). Hoppe Seyler's Z. Physiol. Chem. 365:639–649.

Romer, A.S. (1966) Vertebrate Paleontology. 3rd Ed. Chicago: University of Chicago Press.

Rosen, D.E., P.L. Forey, B.G. Gardiner, and C. Patterson (1981) Lungfishes, tetrapods, paleontology and plesiomorphy. Bull. Am. Mus. Nat. Hist. 167:159–276.

Säve-Söderbergh, G. (1932) Preliminary note on Devonian stegocephalians from East Greenland. Meddel. Grønland 94:1–107.

Säve-Söderbergh, G. (1933) The dermal bones of the head and the lateral line system in Osteolepis macrolepidotus. Ag. with remarks on the terminology on the lateral line system and on the dermal bones of certain other crossopterygians. Nova Acta R. Soc. Sci. Uppsala 9:1–130.

Schmalhausen, I.I. (1968) The Origin of Terrestrial Vertebrates. New York: Academic Press.

Schultze, H.-P. (1969) Die Faltenzähne der rhipidistiiden Crossopterygier, der Tetrapoden und der Actinopterygien-Gattung Lepisosteus. Palaeontographia Ital. 65:60–137.

Schultze, H.-P. (1981) Hennig und der Ursprung der Tetrapoda. Paläont. Z. 55:71–86.

Schultze, H.-P., and M. Arsenault (1985) The panderichthyid fish Elpistostege: A close relative of tetrapods?

Palaeontology 28:293–309.

Semon, R. (1898) Die Entwickelung der paarigen Flossen des Ceratodus forsteri. In R. Semon (ed): Zoologische Forschungsreisen in Australien und dem Malayischen Archipelago. I. Ceratodus, pt. 2. Jena: G. Fischer Verlag, pp. 55–111.

Stensiö, E. (1968) The cyclostomes with special reference to the diphyletic origin of the Petromyzontida and Myxinoidea. In T. Ørvig (ed): Current Problems of Lower Vertebrate Phylogeny. Stockholm: Almqvist and Wiksell, pp. 13–71.

Thomson, K.S.W. (1965) The nasal apparatus in Dipnoi, with special reference to Protopterus. Proc. Zool. Soc. Lond. 145:207–238.

Thomson, K.S.W. (1969) The biology of the lobed-finned fishes. Biol. Rev. 44:91–154.

Vogt, C. (1845) Translator's comments on Müller's paper. Ann. Sci. Nat. (Zool.) 4:31.

Vogt, C. (1851) Zoologische Briefe. Vol II. Frankfurt-am-Main: J. Rütter.

Vorobjeva, E.I. (1977) Morfologiya i osobennosti evolyustii kisteperykh ryb. Trudy Paleont. Inst. SSSR 163:1–240.

Vorobjeva, E.I. (1980) Observations on two rhipidistian fishes from the Upper Devonian of Lode, Latvia (Lode). Zool. J. Linn. Soc. 70:191–201.

Wahlert, G. von (1968) Latimeria und die Geschichte der Wirbelthiere. Eine evolutionsbiologische Untersuchung. Stuttgart: G. Fischer Verlag.

Westoll, T.S. (1943) The origin of tetrapods. Biol. Rev. 18:78–98.

Westoll, T.S. (1961) A crucial stage in vertebrate evolution: Fish to land animal. Proc R. Inst. Gr. Britain 38:600–618.

Wiley, E.O. (1979) Ventral gill arch muscles and the interrelationships of gnathostomes, with a new classification of the Vertebrata. Zool. J. Linn. Soc. 67:149–179.

JOURNAL OF MORPHOLOGY SUPPLEMENT 1:93–131 (1986)

Paleozoic Lungfishes—A Review

K.S.W. CAMPBELL AND R.E. BARWICK
*Departments of Geology and Zoology, Australian National University,
Canberra, A.C.T., 2601 Australia*

ABSTRACT   Stratigraphical and paleoecological evidence indicates that lungfishes evolved in shallow marine conditions. Devonian genera had large gill chambers, and the details of bony supports of the gill arches of the Late Devonian *Griphognathus whitei* demonstrate that the arches were all functional. These data, together with an analysis of the body forms of the Devonian genera, indicate that they were dependent on gill (and possibly skin) respiration. The oldest known dipnoans, *Uranolophus* and *Speonesydrion*, are held to be representative of two lineages that can be recognized by their buccal and branchial features. One had a "rasping" dentition formed of denticles and marginal ridges that were continually shed and remodelled; the other had a "crushing" dentition characterized by the presence of variously modelled dentine masses that continued growth throughout the life of the animal. A list of buccal and branchial characters associated with these modes of feeding is presented. Because the relations of the Dipnoi have to be examined in terms of the features possessed by the group when it first appeared as a separate entity, the final part of the paper makes an attempt to define the primitive dipnoan morphotype. It is shown that many features taken to be diagnostic of the Dipnoi by some workers were not present in its early members; failure to recognize this fact has led to erroneous hypotheses about dipnoan-amphibian relations.

Since 1968, when several authors reviewed the structure and relationships of the group in the Nobel Symposium on "Current Problems of Lower Vertebrate Phylogeny," our knowledge of the early evolution of the Dipnoi has increased dramatically. More has been learned about this topic in the period since 1968 than had been learned by all previous study. By far the most significant advances have resulted from the availability of new specimens from Australian Devonian limestones. These have been preserved uncrushed, and they can be extracted from the matrix by the use of acetic acid, revealing structural details that cannot be observed using other methods. Specimens of *Dipnorhynchus* Jaekel and *Speonesydrion* Campbell and Barwick from the Emsian (Lower Devonian) rocks of the Murrumbidgee region, New South Wales, and of *Holodipterus* White and Moy-Thomas, *Chirodipterus* Gross, and *Griphognathus* Gross from the Frasnian (Upper Devonian) rocks of the Gogo region of Western Australia have been prepared using these

methods (Thomson and Campbell, '71; Miles, '77; Smith, '77; Campbell and Barwick, '82a,b, '83, 84a,b, '85). Similarly prepared material of *Stomiahykus* Bernacsek ('77) has been described from the Eifelian of Western Canada.

A second factor has been the recovery of relatively complete, though crushed, material of *Uranolophus* from the Siegenian (Early Devonian) of Wyoming, Utah, and Idaho (Denison, '68a,b, '74). Previously a single specimen of a dipnoan referred to *Dipnorhynchus lehmanni* Westoll, had been recorded from the Siegenian Hunsrückschiefer of Germany (Lehmann and Westoll, '52) but the flattened skull was difficult to prepare and hence lacked all except the crudest information on bone arrangement. The skulls, mandibles, and a single moderately well preserved body of *Uranolophus* added a great deal of information, particularly as it may be the oldest dipnoan material yet discovered. Also the description by Schultze ('69) of complete though crushed specimens of *Griphognathus* from the Upper Devonian of Germany and the Baltic States added another dimension to our understanding.

The impact of these new discoveries has been enhanced by the resurgence of interest in the fine structure of dipnoan hard tissues with the advent of scanning electron microscopy and with the refinement of older methods for application to the histology of fossils. This work has brought into better perspective the significance of such tissues as cosmine (Ørvig, '69a, Denison, '74; Thomson, '77; Meinke, '84), isopedin (Denison, '68b), dentine (Denison, '74; Ørvig, '76; Smith, '77, '79a, '84; Kemp, '77, '79, '84; Campbell and Barwick, '83), and enamel or enameloid (Kemp, '79; Smith, '79b). Studies of these tissues have taken on special significance for the discussion of relationships within the early Dipnoi and between the Dipnoi and other groups.

Even methodological disputes have contributed, because paleoichthyologists have been amongst the strongest advocates of cladistic methods for attempting to unravel the relationships of major taxa, and the Dipnoi have figured extensively in the ensuing polemics (Miles, '75, '77; Rosen et al., '81). Some of these attempts have sought to use the new methods to define primitive dipnoan characters in the light of the new Devonian discoveries (Miles, '77; Schultze, '82); others have laid stress on the characters of the living dipnoan genera (Fox, '65; Wiley '79); and yet others have deprecated the use of palaeontological data, especially where these have been used in an attempt to establish the nature of ancestral groups (Rosen et al., '81).

Finally, the detailed description of the living coelacanth *Latimeria* provided much information that was at variance with what had been "expected in a tetrapod relative" (Forey, '80:369). Most of this information related to soft tissue structure (rectal and pituitary glands and pancreas) or to the physiology of osmoregulation. To some workers (Lagios, '79, for references) these new data implied that the interpretation of the relationships of some major groups within the so-called Sarcopterygii, based on fossil skeletal material, had been grossly in error. Such an interpretation has placed an onus on paleontologists to refine their data on the morphology of other primitive lobe-finned fishes so that more reliable estimates of relationships can be attempted.

THE ENVIRONMENT OF EARLY DIPNOANS

Thomson ('69) listed the then known Devonian dipnoans with their stratigraphic, geographic, and environmental distributions, and these data were later updated (Thomson, '80:206–207). Since then the genus *Speonesydrion* has been described from the marine rocks of the Goodradigbee River, Wee Jasper, New South Wales. We note also that Gregory et al. ('77) listed *Rhynchodipterus* rather than *Griphognathus* from the marine basal Frasnian rocks of Nevada.

Allowing that *Holodipterus* and *Devonosteus* may be synonyms (Miles, '77:12), that *Conchodus* is a valid genus (though it is known only from tooth plates), and that *Uranolophus* and *Ganorhynchus* are marine, the environmental distribution of Devonian genera known at present is as shown in Table 1.

In addition to those listed above, a new undescribed genus is known from marine Lower Devonian rocks in Novaya Zemlya, and two undescribed genera are known from freshwater Upper Devonian rocks in Victoria, Australia.

Taken at face value, these data mean that 71% of the Devonian genera overall, and 90% of Early and Middle Devonian genera contained species that were entirely marine, or species that were marine for part of their life histories. These figures take on added significance when it is appreciated that almost all post-Devonian dipnoan occurrences are in freshwater rocks. Three questions have been raised about this presumptive evidence that the earliest members of the group were marine: 1) could the marine occurrences result from the transport of cadavers from rivers into the sea; 2) is there a possibility that the absence of Early and Middle Devonian freshwater sediments skews the figures; and 3) could the genera known only from marine rocks be anadromous or catadromous? These questions will now be examined *seriatim*.

1) The problem of transport after death has been examined in three ways. Thomson and Campbell ('71) considered that the preservation of detail and the lack of disintegration of two skulls of *Dipnorhynchus sussmilchi* indicated rapid burial of the specimens. The general absence of coarse sediment indicative of the presence of nearby streams draining onto the shallow carbonate bank environment argued in favor of burial in the area where the animals lived. Similar argu-

TABLE 1. Environmental distribution of Devonian dipnoan genera

Type	Devonian genera	Lower and Middle
Total number	24	9
Marine rocks only	10	5
Doubtful marine rocks	1	0
Marine and freshwater rocks	6	3
Freshwater rocks only	7	1

ments may be used for the genera *Chirodipterus, Holodipterus*, and *Griphognathus* from the Gogo Formation. These animals are not uncommonly preserved as whole fish in a slightly muddy carbonate rock that is thought to have been deposited in an inter-reef environment (Playford and Lowry, '66; Gardiner and Miles, '75).

A second approach involves the use of strontium isotopes (Dasch and Campbell, '70:1159). This element has a long residence time in the sea, and the variations of its isotopic ratios through time are reasonably well known. The isotopic ratios of fresh water will vary widely at any time depending on the composition of the rocks in the catchment area. Organisms that build carbonate or phosphate skeletons are known to incorporate the ambient strontium ratios into their skeletons. Samples of *Dipnorhynchus* and the placoderm *Buchanosteus* from Wee Jasper, New South Wales, gave isotopic ratios consistent with a marine or euryhyaline environment. Further work on other localities should be undertaken.

Finally, the fact that almost all post-Devonian occurrences of dipnoans are in coal-measure, swamp, lake, or river deposits argues in favor of the genuine marine occurrence of the Devonian forms, for the capacity of streams to transport cadavers to the sea would presumably be the same in Devonian and post-Devonian times.

2) Fish-bearing freshwater deposits of Early or Middle Devonian age are known, but their volume is small in comparison with known marine sediments of that age. Young ('81, '84) has reviewed the distribution of Early Devonian fishes and has concluded that five biogeographic provinces can be recognized. All provinces have stratigraphic sequences in which there are freshwater deposits containing fishes. In some, the faunas are not well known, and at least in the Galeaspid-Yunnanolepid Province of South China the number of endemic genera is high. Unless dipnoans evolved in that province, their ab-

sence from its freshwater rocks would have no significance for the present argument. On the other hand, the Cephalaspid Province of Euramerica and the Wuttagoonaspid-Phyllolepid Province of East Gondwana both have relatively well known faunas (by no means all described), and neither contains Early Devonian dipnoans. The Old Red Sandstone facies in the Cephalaspid Province is one of the best known fish sequences in the world, and it has failed to produce dipnoans at this level. This applies not only to Western Europe, but also to Spitzbergen, where, from many thousands of feet of sequence, much of which contains fishes (Friend, '61; Ørvig, '69a,b) no dipnoans have been described. The Australian occurrences of the East Gondwana Province are particularly instructive, since in the southeastern part of the continent the early marine record of dipnoans is better than anywhere else. In the Taemas-Wee Jasper area, non-marine sediments occur in the Sugarloaf Volcanics below the productive marine rocks and in the Hatchery Creek Conglomerate above them (Young and Gorter, '81). Despite this close association, no dipnoans have been recovered from the non-marine rocks though they do contain thelodonts, placoderms, "crossopterygians," and acanthodians. The Middle Devonian Bunga Beds and their equivalents (Fergusson et al., '79) have also yielded a moderately diverse fish fauna without dipnoans. Finally, the Lower-Middle Devonian Mulga Downs Beds, from which Ritchie ('73) has recovered many hundreds of placoderms and occasional "crossopterygians," have failed to yield a single recognizable dipnoan.

3) In his summary of the environmental distribution of early dipnoans, Thomson ('80:206) contended that "it is not possible to establish the anadromous model with certainty on the basis of environmental and distributional data alone. Some further evidence relating more directly to physiology would be needed...." Our review, however, suggests that anadromy is a highly improbable expla-

nation. If that hypothesis were true, one might expect more occurrences in freshwater rocks than have actually been recorded. This scarcity has been indicated above. In addition, what is known of the body and fin form of early dipnoans suggests that they are sluggish bottom-feeding animals, quite unlike any modern anadromous fishes.

The objections to the thesis that Early and Middle Devonian dipnoans were predominantly marine are therefore considered to carry little weight. The available evidence favors a marine origin for the group and an initial radiation under marine conditions during the Early Devonian. So far as is known at present, the group did not become widely represented in freshwater environments until the Middle and Late Devonian. There is no palaeontological evidence available to support the hypothesis of a short initial freshwater stage followed by a marine stage and a subsequent return to freshwater (see Thomson, '69:144 for summary).

The discovery that *Latimeria* varies the osmolarity of its blood and other body fluids by the retention of urea and trimethylamine oxide suggests a means of osmoregulation by which early dipnoans could have survived in a marine environment (Lagios, '79; Griffith, '80), a point already made by Thomson ('80). Aestivating lepidosirenids retain urea in their body tissues (see Fishman et al., this volume), though *Neoceratodus*, which spends all its life in water, apparently does not exhibit this capacity. Retention of urea may have been first developed to regulate osmosis in a marine environment. Urea is used for osmoregulation by chondrichthyans and some frogs that have adapted to estuarine conditions (*Rana cancrivora*), as well as by *Latimeria*, and hence such a mechanism in dipnoans would be in no way unusual. It is unlikely to be a primitive mechanism inherited by all these groups. More probably it has been evolved independently many times (Griffith and Pang, '79).

One of the main implications of this analysis is that because the earliest known members of the group were marine bottom dwellers, they were unlikely to have been air breathers. The popular notion that air breathing was a decisive innovation at the appearance of the Dipnoi, and that the group evolved in response to hypoxic conditions in freshwater lakes and streams, must be abandoned. It is probably true that the capacity to breath air developed in freshwater forms but, if so, that phase must have been at some later time. As the earliest marine genera have the marginal anterior and the internal posterior nasal openings characteristic of the group as a whole, it is impossible to argue that the internal opening evolved in association with the adoption of air breathing. That it is not a choana has already been demonstrated on morphological grounds (Campbell and Barwick, '84a).

The conclusion that early dipnoans were not air breathers has important implications for any analysis of dipnoan relationships. For example, structures of the heart and circulatory systems of modern lungfish, which show special features related to air breathing and suggest an affinity with amphibians, must have been derived after the dipnoans became a separate group. Such similiarities with amphibians would be the result of convergence.

AN EARLY DICHOTOMY

So far as we are aware, all workers now regard the Dipnoi as a monophyletic group (Schultze and Campbell, this volume). However, from their appearance in the middle Early Devonian two lineages can be recognized (see Marshall, this volume, for consideration of these lineages). They may be characterized most simply by their dentitions, but many additional characters, which are outlined below, also serve to distinguish them. However, because the dentition is their most obvious differentiating feature, we refer to them as the tooth-plated and the denticulated types. This designation has the advantage of drawing attention to the point that the division is based essentially on an integrated set of characters related to the buccal-branchial systems.

Formation of the dental surfaces

The tooth-plated types produced grinding or crushing plates on the pterygoids and the prearticulars. The earliest forms are represented by *Speonesydrion*, an Early Devonian genus represented in Europe by *S. lehmanni* (Westoll), formerly *Dipnorhynchus lehmanni*, and in Australia by *S. iani* Campbell and Barwick. By growth from their bases at the dentine/bone boundary, the denticles increased in height and in area until they joined to each other and to the adjacent continous sheets of dentine (Fig. 1). In other words, all the denticles were retained throughout growth, apart from a few that were occasionally resorbed as they become involved with remodelling of the plate mar-

TABLE 2. *Paleozoic dipnoan genera of tooth-plated and denticulate lineages with genera arranged in stratigraphic order*[1]

Tooth plated		Denticulate	
Speonesydrion	L. Dev.	*Uranolophus*	L. Dev.
Dipnorhynchus	L. Dev.	*Holodipterus*	U. Dev.
? *Melanognathus*	L. Dev.	*Griphognathus*	U. Dev.
Ganorhynchus	M.-U. Dev.	*Fleurantia*	U. Dev.
Dipterus	M.-U. Dev.	*Soederberghia*	U. Dev.
Conchodus	M.-U. Dev.	*Rhynchodipterus*	U. Dev.
Stomiahykus	M. Dev.	*Jarvikia*	U. Dev.
Pentlandia	M. Dev.	*Uronemus*[2]	L. Carb.
Rhinodipterus	M.-U. Dev.	*Conchopoma*	U. Carb.-Perm.
Palaedaphus	U. Dev.		
Chirodipterus	U. Dev.		
Scaumenacia	U. Dev.		
Archaeonectes	U. Dev.		
Phaneropleuron	U. Dev.		
Devonosteus	U. Dev.		
Grossipterus	U. Dev.		
Sunwapta	U. Dev.		
Oervigia	U. Dev.		
Tranodis	L. Carb.		
Sagenodus	L. Carb.-Perm.		
Ctenodus	L. Carb.		
Delatitia	L. Carb.		
Straitonia	L. Carb.		
Monongahela	U. Carb.		
Megapleuron	U. Carb.-Perm.		
Gnathorhiza	U. Carb.-Perm.		

[1]Lower, Middle and Upper Devonian; Lower and Upper Carboniferous; Permian.
[2]Placed by Miles ('77) with denticulate genera but now shown by Smith, Smithson, and Campbell ('86) to be a highly modified tooth-plated form.

gin (Campbell and Barwick, '83). Within this tooth-plated lineage advances were made rapidly along two lines. In the first, the number of denticles was reduced after the initial growth stages, and the plate became more consolidated by accretion of larger elements as is shown by *Dipterus valenciennesi*. In the Carboniferous *Sagenodus* and *Ctenodus* the tooth plates were produced by upward growth of dentine from the base and by the addition of spaced enlarged denticles or teeth at intervals along the labial margin (Smith, '79a, 84). The disposition and size of these marginal teeth controlled the spacing and height of the tooth ridges (Fig. 2). Each tooth plate was entirely surrounded by a layer of enamel formed from essentially parallel incremental bands. This pattern of growth is very similar to that occurring in the extant *Neoceratodus forsteri* (Kemp, '77, '79). The major changes between the Carboniferous and the Recent involved the production of a basal pulp cavity between the dentine and the bone, and the development of the so-called tubular dentine. In the second tooth-plated group, the plates increased marginally by the addition of denticles of fairly uniform size, and the surface

of the tooth plates was differentiated into crude, somewhat irregular tuberosities, as in the species of *Dipnorhynchus*. These grew by remodelling the underlying bone and thickening the dentine by differential growth from the base (Campbell and Barwick, '83).

The primitive tooth plates of both groups completely covered the palate so that it is impossible to differentiate bone boundaries on the buccal surface. The sutures are even indistinguishable in thin section (Fig. 3) (Campbell and Barwick, '85). The dentine of the tooth plates formed a continuous sheet extending down into the deep furrow occupying the symphysial region of the mandible. More advanced forms, beginning with *Dipterus*, have distinctly paired upper and lower tooth plates which do not meet in the midline.

The distinctive feature of the denticulated group is not that their buccal cavities are covered with denticles, but that growth takes place by the shedding of all the dentine-covered elements in the buccal cavity, and by their replacement with other denticles or large masses of dentine in the form of ridges or tusks (Figs. 4a, b). This process has been

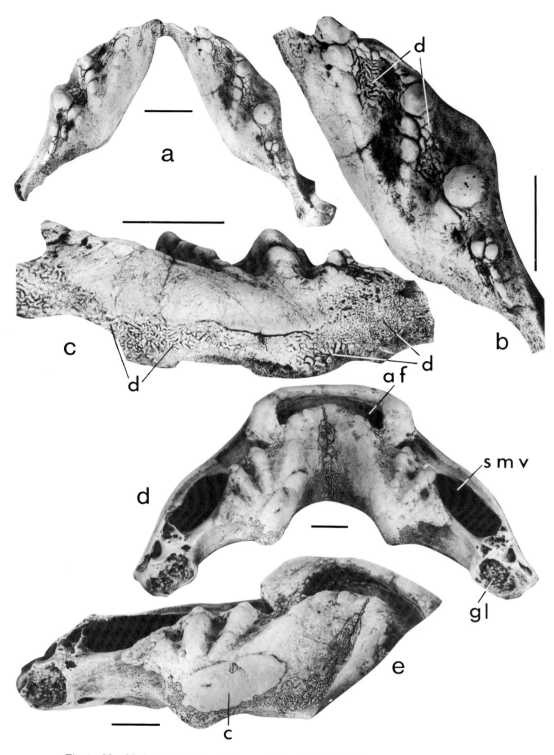

Fig. 1. Mandibular tooth plates of *Speonesydrion iani*. a) Eroded specimen ANU 35648. b, c) Right ramus of same specimen in dorsal and medial view. d) Posterodorsal view of holotype, ANU 35647. e) Oblique dorsomedial view of same specimen. af, anterior furrow; c, dentine cushion on heel of tooth plate; d, denticles; gl, glenoid fossa; smv, suprameckelian vacuity. Scales = 10 mm.

Fig. 2. Unidentified isolated tooth plate from Upper Devonian rocks at Mt. Green, Lashly Mountains, Antarctica, AMF 54320. Numbers 1–7 indicate successive teeth added to the medial tooh row. The enamel layers associated with each tooth are clearly shown. The enamel layer of tooth 7 (arrowed) obscures the layers of teeth 5 and 6, and that of tooth 4 obscures 3. Scale = 10 mm.

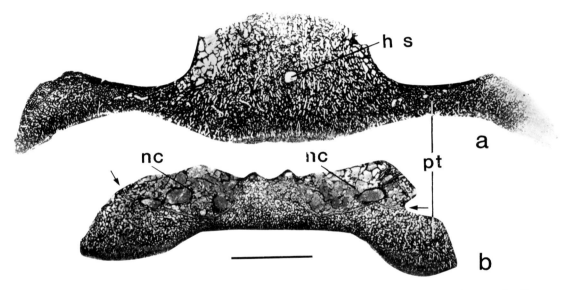

Fig. 3. Transverse sections of a palate of *Dipnorhynchus kurikae*, ANU 36508. a) Posterior section through the hypophysial stalk. b) Anterior section showing the well defined boundary between the pterygoids and neurocranium; note the absence of a suture between the pterygoids and the parasphenoid. Note the resorption areas within and on the margins of the tooth ridges, some of them occupied by new denticles. Arrows indicate suture between pterygoids and neurocranial bone. h s, hypophysial stalk; nc, neurocranial bone with numerous neurovascular canals; pt, pterygoids. scale = 10mm.

most completely recorded in *Griphognathus whitei* (Smith, '77; Campbell and Barwick, '83), but it is also well known in *Uranolophus wyomingensis* (Denison, '68a), which is the earliest known representative of the group. The palate and the prearticulars usually have a ridge or number of cusps along their margins, but occasional genera such as *Fleurantia* and *Holodipterus* have rows of enamel-covered teeth that form simulated tooth plates. All of these marginal structures and simulated tooth plates were resorbed during growth and replaced by uniformly small denticles, as is well shown in Figure 4a. This phenomenon was appreciated by Graham-Smith and Westoll ('37), Denison ('68a) and Smith ('77).

Palatal shape

In ancient species with tooth plates as in modern species (Bemis, this volume), the food was crushed between tooth rows or tuberosities that occluded in a complementary fashion. As a consequence, their palates could not

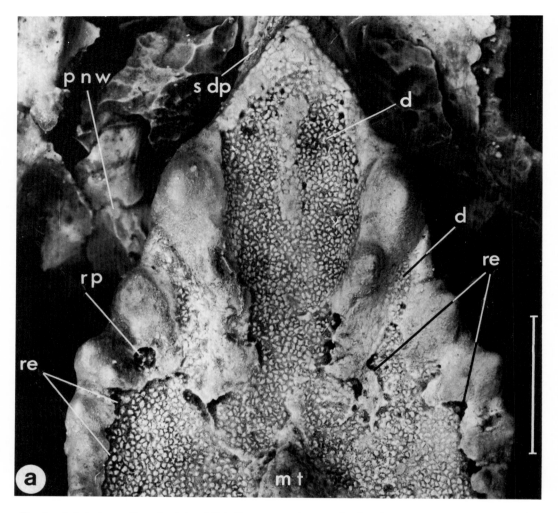

Fig. 4. a) Anterior portion of palate of *Holodipterus gogoensis*, CPC 25342, to show resorption of the marginal tooth ridges and their replacement by denticles. b) Anterior portion of palate of *Griphognathus whitei*. d, denticles; l n t p, lateral nasal tooth plates; m t, median tooth; p a, palatal arch; pn w, postnasal wall; re, resorption areas; r p, resorption pit, with newly formed denticle; s dp, surface for attachment of dermopalatine; t, marginal tooth. Scales = 10 mm.

have been highly arched. Occlusion in these Paleozoic forms normally took place only around an outer zone, the mandibular plates sloping downwards into the lingual furrow. This allowed large objects to be crushed on the medial surfaces of the plates and further comminution to take place on the outer surfaces. This is well shown in the articulated specimens of *Chirodipterus australis* (Fig. 5a).

In contrast, the denticles on the palates and mandibles of members of the denticulated group could not come into contact during occlusion because both form concave surfaces (Fig. 5b). The nature of the occlusion varies from genus to genus. In *Uranolophus* the upper and lower marginal ridges probably came into direct contact and, judging from the lack of wear on the crenulated sides of the ridges, they never slid past each other to produce a shearing action. In *Griphognathus whitei*, on the other hand, the mandible passed outside the palate around its entire lateral and anterior margins, presumably producing a shear (Fig. 8). In *Holodipterus*

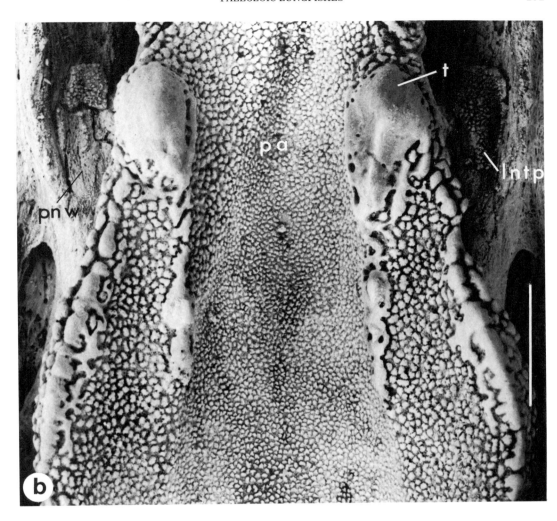

b

gogoensis the simulated tooth plates occluded at their margins. All three genera have palates that are more transversely concave than members of both tooth-plated groups, but, as might be expected, H. gogoensis is the least concave of the three.

Basibranchial/basihyal tooth plates

As most of the denticulated types had no possibility of triturating food, and the denticulated surfaces of lower and upper jaws did not even approach contact, an alternative method of food reduction must have operated. This involved the transport of food within the mouth by means of tooth plates mounted on enlarged basihyal and basibran-

chial elements, a mode we term "rasping" (Fig. 6a). These elements are best known in Griphognathus (Schultze, '69; Miles, '77), but they are also known from Conchopoma gadiforme and C. edesi (Schultze, '75; Marshall, personel communication), and they are inferred to have been present in Holodipterus gogoensis (personal observation). In Griphognathus the large basihyal and basibranchial elements are fused to form two units that are ossified perichondrially and have extensive surfaces for the articulation of the hypohyals and ceratobranchials. The concavity of the palates provided the two pairs of denticulated basihyal/basibranchial tooth plates, which were aligned to form a tongue-like

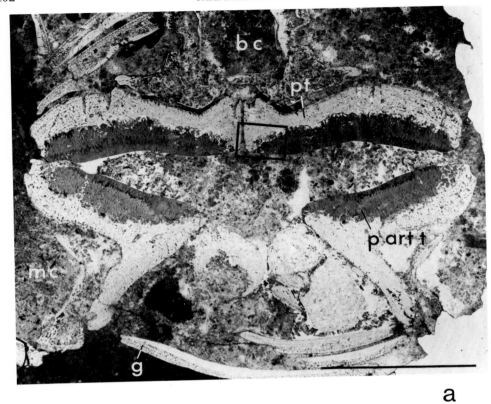

a

b

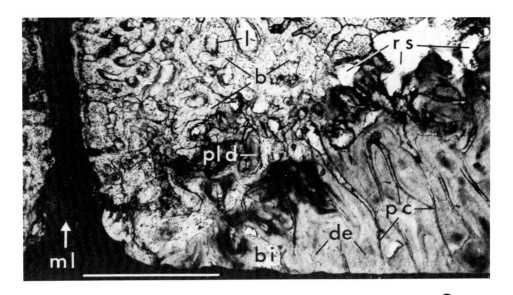

c

Fig. 5. a) Transverse section of head of *Chirodipterus australis*, CPC 22592, to show tooth plates in approximately occlusal position. b) Transverse section of partial skull of *Griphognathus whitei*, CPC 22593, showing height of palatal arch and the large marginal teeth. c) Part of the palatal tooth plate outlined in Figure 5a, to show the mode of growth of the dentine in the region along the mid-line of the palate. b, bone; b c, brain cavity; b i, bone included in dentine; d, denticles; de, dentine; g, gular plate; l, bone lacunae; l n t p, lateral nasal tooth plate; m c, meckelian cavity; m l, mid line; p a, palatal arch; p c, pulp canal; p art t, prearticular tooth plate; pl d, pleromic dentine; p n c, posterior region of nasal cavity; pt, pterygoid; t, marginal tooth. Scales for a, b = 10 mm, c = 1.0 mm.

rasp, with a suitably arched surface to work against. No such dental apparatus has been described from any tooth-plated form.

Ceratohyals/ceratobranchials

For the effective operation of a food reduction system such as that described above, considerable movement of the whole branchial/hyoid system must have been produced. The only muscle systems that could have provided such movement were those attached to the ceratohyal (Miles, '77), which one would therefore expect to be a large bone. Once again the ceratohyal is best known in *Griphognathus whitei*, but fortunately it is also relatively well known in *Uranolophus wyomingensis* in which it occupies more than two-thirds the length of the buccal cavity. In *G. whitei* the preservation of single specimens is sufficiently good to permit reconstruction of the amount of movement possible. This is because the points of attachment of the ceratohyal to the back of the skull by the hyosuspensory ligament are clearly identifiable, as also are the attachment points of the epibranchial 1 and possibly epibranchial 2 to the occiput lateral to the parasphenoidal stalk. These articulations controlled the amount of dorsoventral, lateral, and rotational movement possible by the whole system. It transpires that in all senses the amount of such movement was considerable, as is shown in Figure 7.

The full reconstruction of the musculature required to operate the system is beyond the scope of this review, but the main argument may be established by the reconstruction of the ceratohyal musculature. This is fortunate because the ceratohyal is the most distinctive and the most commonly preserved of all the branchial elements. The interpretation given by Miles ('77:264–267, Fig. 136) is in need of revision. The presence or absence of a cranial rib, which plays an important role in the movement of the hyoid system in recent lungfishes, is obviously also an important point to establish. So far as we are aware, this element has not been found in specimens of *G. whitei*.

Though the ceratohyal of *Uranolophus* is not well enough known to permit such a pre-

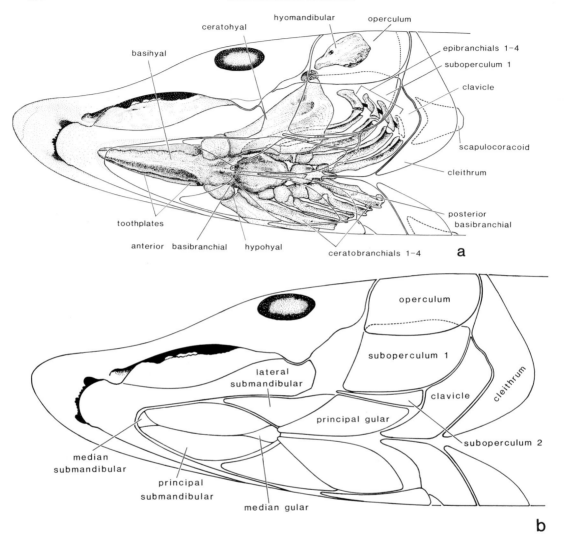

Fig. 6. a) Ventrolateral view of restored hyobranchial skeletal elements of *Griphognathus whitei*. Positions of pectoral girdle and opercular bones superimposed as reference points. b) Ventrolateral view of restored gill cover plates of *Griphognathus whitei* showing relationship to the pectoral girdle and the mandible.

cise interpretation, many of its features are closely comparable to those of *G. whitei*.

Jaw articulation

The mandible in *Neoceratodus* has a "double" jaw articulation, in which a large medial fossa is flanked by a smaller one set obliquely to it. This allows rotation of the mandible, enabling the tooth ridges to cut food by sliding the ridges down the flanks of their counterparts on the opposing palatal plate. The mechanics of the system are quite complex and need further study (Perkins, '73). Similar glenoid fossae are known in all the Devonian tooth-plated forms. An analysis of the movement in *Speonesydrion* has been given by Campbell and Barwick ('84b). It is impossible to confirm that this type of structure was present in late Paleozoic genera because the articular is not ossified, but the structure of the tooth plates implies that such jaw articulations were present in most

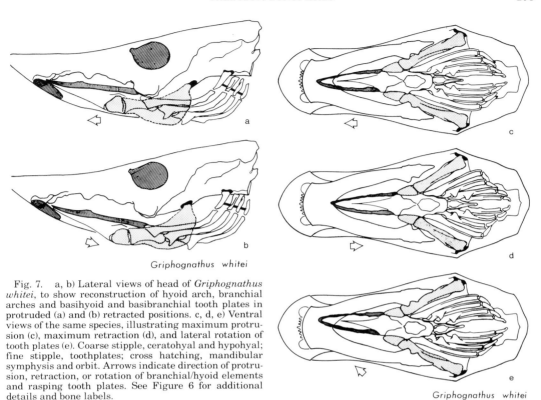

Fig. 7. a, b) Lateral views of head of *Griphognathus whitei*, to show reconstruction of hyoid arch, branchial arches and basihyoid and basibranchial tooth plates in protruded (a) and (b) retracted positions. c, d, e) Ventral views of the same species, illustrating maximum protrusion (c), maximum retraction (d), and lateral rotation of tooth plates (e). Coarse stipple, ceratohyal and hypohyal; fine stipple, toothplates; cross hatching, mandibular symphysis and orbit. Arrows indicate direction of protrusion, retraction, or rotation of branchial/hyoid elements and rasping tooth plates. See Figure 6 for additional details and bone labels.

Griphognathus whitei

genera with the possible exception of *Gnathorhiza*. In that genus the tooth plates have a precise interlocking occlusion that would restrict the degree of lateral movement (Carlson, '68; Berman, '76). Bemis ('84) has shown that *Lepidosiren* lacks the double structure because of the nature of its occlusion, and the situation in *Gnathorhiza* was probably analogous. Such a condition is highly evolved.

In *Griphognathus whitei*, on the other hand, no lateral movement of the mandible was possible because its anterior end locked in between subnasal ridges, and the mandibular rami passed neatly beside the margins of the palate. Consequently the jaw articulation was narrow and almost ginglymoid in form (Fig. 8). Also, whereas in tooth-plated Devonian forms the glenoid was open posteriorly so that some forward movement of the jaw was possible and a strong pterygoid/mandibular ligament was present to restrain excessive movement, in *G. whitei* a posterior lip on the glenoid prevented anterior movement. The articulations of *Soederberghia* and

Fleurantia were also of this type. Even *Holodipterus*, which might be expected to have at least some possible lateral and anterior movement, still shows the basic *Griphognathus* feature of a single crescentic articulation facet, which would not permit lateral rotation of the mandible (Fig. 9). It is of particular interest, therefore, to note that in *Uranolophus* the glenoid fossa more closely resembles that of *Speonesydrion* than *Griphognathus*. The reason presumably is that *Uranolophus* retained a powerful bite and was not so strongly dependent on the rasping system of food reduction as were the later Devonian members of this lineage. This is an important point, to which we return later. In our interpretation, Early Devonian members of both the denticulate and tooth-plated lineages had comparable "double" jaw articulations, but this was rapidly lost in the denticulate types as they became less dependent on a crushing mode of feeding. Members of the tooth-plated lineage retained the primitive condition except those genera that de-

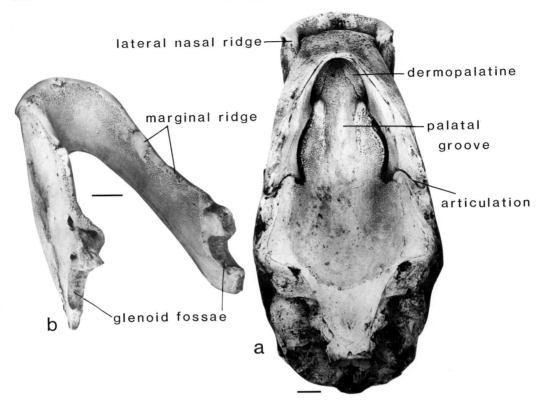

lateral nasal ridge

dermopalatine

marginal ridge

palatal groove

articulation

glenoid fossae

b

a

Fig. 8. a) Posteroventral view of skull with articulated mandible of *Griphognathus whitei*, CPC 21186, to show lack of occlusion of the pterygoid and prearticular tooth ridges. b) Oblique posterodorsal view of the mandible of the above specimen to illustrate the narrow and deeply excavated glenoid fossa. Both illustrations emphasize the lack of lateral movement of the mandible. Scales = 10 mm.

veloped a deep, precise interlocking occlusion that prevented lateral movement of the mandible.

Shape and proportions of the head

In general, forms with tooth plates are short headed. There may be some exceptions to this generalization. For example, *Ctenodus* has large, long tooth plates and it may have had a relatively long snout that was not ossified. In *Rhinodipterus* the tooth plates were set well back in the mouth for some unknown reason, and its head was unusually long. However, all the other Paleozoic tooth-plated genera have shorter heads. Where their cheeks are known, as for example in *Dipterus, Scaumenacia*, and *Chirodipterus*, the bones in front of the orbit have only a slightly arcuate ventral edge (see Fig. 13b).

All the so-called long-headed dipnoans such as *Griphognathus, Fleurantia*, and *Soeder-*

berghia, are denticulated. These have elongated depressed snouts that in lateral profile show two very significant features. First, the mandible fits up into the snout very snugly to produce a shovel-like appearance, and second, the ventral edge of the cheek bones below and in front of the orbit form a strong arch that is matched by the remarkably long and deep labial surface on the mandible. These features suggest a bottom-feeding suctorial habit with a small angle of gape. The existence of long, deep excavations in the edges of the external dermal bones of both lower and upper jaws indicates the presence of soft tissues that were more extensive than the lips of the recent genera. We consider that muscular cheek pouches were present. This would be consistent with the "rasping mode" interpretation of the food reduction system given above. The following sequence of movements could be reasonably hypothesized: 1) the jaw would open by movement of

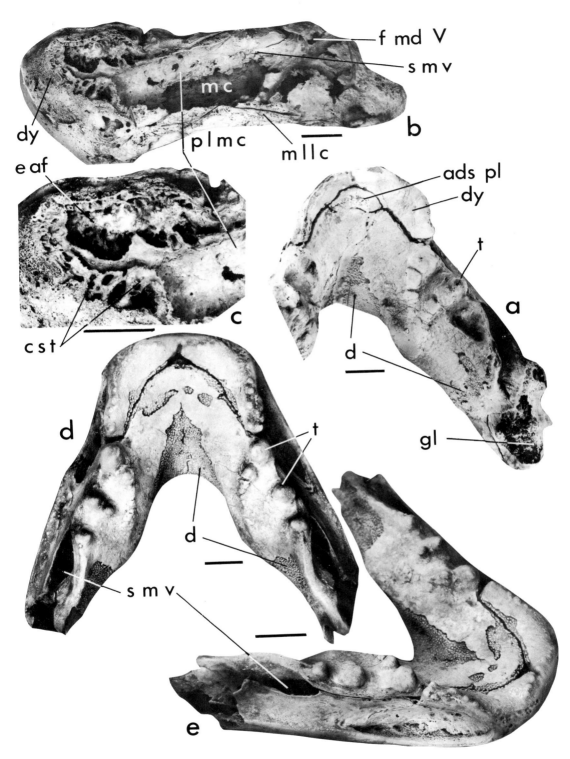

Fig. 9. a, b) Partial mandible of *Holodipterus gogoensis*, CPC 25341 in dorsal view (a) and left lateral view (b). c) Enlargement of anterior portion of b. d, e) Small, almost complete mandible, CPC 25738, in dorsal view (d) and dorsolateral view (e). ads pl, adsymphysial plate; c s t, canals for the symphysial tubuli; d, denticles; dy, dentary; e af, enclosed anterior furrow; f md V, foramen for mandibularis V; gl, glenoid fossa; mc, opening into space occupied by Meckel's cartilage; m l l c, mandibular lateral line canal; p l m c, perichondral lining of Meckel's cartilage; s m v, suprameckelian vacuity; t, tooth. Scales = 10 mm.

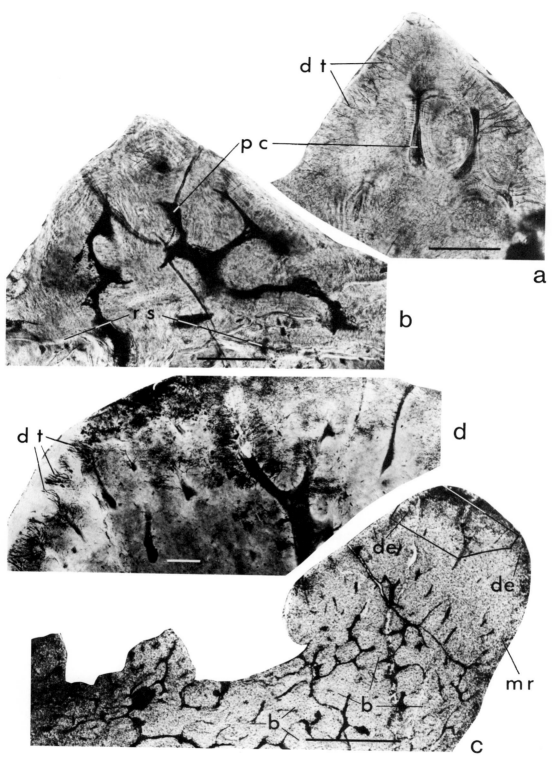

Fig. 10. Detail of denticles and marginal tooth ridges of *Uranolophus wyomingensis*. a, b) Isolated denticles in vertical section. c) Vertical section of marginal tooth ridge and adjacent denticles. d) Detail of area outlined in c. b, bone; de, dentine; d t, dentine tubules; m r, marginal ridge; p c, pulp canals, r s, resorption surfaces. Scales a, b, c = 0.1 mm; d = 1.0 mm.

both mandible and skull (Bemis and Lauder, '85; 2) at the same time the whole branchial/hyoid system would retract, dropping the floor of the buccal cavity, thus adding to its volume; 3) as the hyoid arch dropped, the posteroventral edge of the ceratohyal would force the submandibular/gular series open; and 4) the hyomandibula, a large saddle-shaped structure, would at the same time push the operculars open. The first three movements would have increased the volume of the buccal cavity significantly, producing considerable suction to draw food into the mouth. With the fourth movement they would have provided a buccal/opercular pump for gill ventilation. Closing the mouth and subsequent protrusion of the basihyal/basibranchial system would have allowed food to be manipulated and reduced by rasping it against the palate. Some food may have been transferred to the cheek pouches to be returned later to the main buccal cavity by the action of the muscular cheek.

We are not suggesting that this is anything like a complete analysis of the system, details of which are being presented elsewhere, but it does provide an integrated analysis of a number of apparently unconnected morphological features, and it establishes the denticulated long-headed forms as distinctive and highly derived. Nor do we mean to imply that all denticulated forms functioned in precisely this way. On the contrary, we consider that short headed genera like *Conchopoma* were not bottom-dwelling suction feeders like *Griphognathus*. However, we suggest that the skulls of denticulated genera were, in general, more elongated than their tooth-plated counterparts, and this can be substantiated by measurements of the palates of the short-headed denticulates *Uranolophus* and *Holodipterus*. Unfortunately, the cheeks of these genera are not well enough known to decide whether they had cheek pouches, but the structure of the mandible indicates that if they did, the pouches were relatively shorter and shallower than those of *Griphognathus*.

Dentine types

Complex dentines develop only in those genera with large basal pulp cavities. As might be expected, denticles and ridges that are frequently shed never develop a basal pulp cavity, and hence the dentine of members of the denticulate group remains very simple (Fig. 10a–c). In *Uranolophus* the denticles have a cap of enamel over dentine with highly irregular pulp canals, surrounded by circumpulpal dentine with many tubules, and interstitial dentine without tubules (Campbell and Barwick, '83). The structure of the relatively thin dentine on the marginal tooth ridges is essentially the same (Fig. 10c,d). *Griphognathus* shows few differences apart from the development of somewhat more regular pulp canals. Details of *Conchopoma* are unknown, and data are sparse for *Holodipterus*. Two points are clear—denticulated types never develop basal pulp cavities, and normal petrodentine is not present except possibly in *Holodipterus* (Smith, '84). This latter genus is under investigation at present.

Primitive tooth-plated forms also have relatively simple trabecular dentine with no sign of a cavity between the dentine and the bone. Unfortunately, the only available representatives of the most primitive genera, *Speonesydrion* and *Dipnorhynchus*, are too poorly preserved to permit an interpretation of the fine structure of the dentine, but some distinguishing details are available. Where the dentine is thickest, for example on the posteromedial "heel" of the prearticular tooth plate, it has long, sub-parallel, occasionally dividing pulp canals surrounded by circumpulpal dentine, with interstitial dentine forming the intervening matrix (Campbell and Barwick, '83). The presence of petrodentine has not been confirmed (Smith, '84). The oldest recognized petrodentine is in *Dipterus valenciennesi*, in which it is confined to the teeth on the tooth ridges. Petrodentine is also known in the Late Devonian *Scaumenacia* and *Chirodipterus* as well as in the Carboniferous *Sagenodus* (Smith, '84). Petrodentine is a widespread tissue in most, if not all, later tooth-plated forms. Its development is related to the existence of a pulp chamber between the bone and the dentine, whether this be small and irregular as in the primitive forms, or continuous as in the later ones. Petrodentine is therefore common in the later tooth-plated forms though it may not be present in their most primitive representatives. In essence then, the most primitive tooth-plated forms are characterized by simple trabecular dentine without basal pulp cavities, but there is a rapid change towards thicker dentine with longer straighter pulp canals, larger basal pulp cavities, and the development of petrodentine.

Buccohypophysial opening

The buccohypophysial opening is found in Early and Middle Devonian tooth-plated genera (see Fig. 20), and even in some Late Devonian forms such as *Scaumenacia* (Clouthier, personal communication), but it is never found in denticulated genera. While this cannot be used as a defining characteristic, it nevertheless is clear that the opening, which is a primitive feature, was lost in the denticulated line prior to its appearance in the fossil record. It is not known how this loss may be related to feeding, but it may well be a necessary concomitant of the rasping mechanism.

Pineal foramen

The pineal foramen is known from primitive tooth-plated forms such as *Dipnorhynchus* and *Speonesydrion* in which it opened between a group of "D" bones, or rarely through a single "D" in the dermal roof. It was rapidly lost in the tooth-plated lineage, but it was not present in *Uranolophus* or any other denticulate genus.

Pectoral girdles

Pectoral girdles are now known for a number of Devonian and Carboniferous genera from each lineage, and they form a clear pattern. *Scaumenacia* (see Jarvik, '80, Fig. 335) and *Chirodipterus* (Fig. 11) are representative of the Devonian tooth-plated forms. Both of these have the cleithrum and the clavicle partly buried in soft tissue, their outer surfaces being strongly concave. Only along their anterior edges and the ventral surface of the clavicle do these bones lie in the dermis. The most remarkable features of the pectoral girdle, however, are the high branchial laminae that extend steeply from the external surfaces of both cleithrum and clavicle and reach a sharp peak opposite the upper third of the scapulocoracoid. From the peak a narrow septum runs anteriorly to the edge of the cleithrum. The scapulocoracoid has a three-legged form with large foramina at its base to transmit the various neural and vascular elements (Janvier '80). The anocleithrum is a deeply buried paddle-shaped structure, its posterior blade lying flat against the dorsal interior face of the cleithrum, and its anterior process articulating with the process on the back of dermal skull bone "I." Little is known in detail of the girdle in *Dipterus,* but the external surfaces

of its cleithrum and clavicle are at least partly buried and carry little or no cosmine, the branchial laminae stand at high angles to the external surfaces of the cleithrum and the clavicle, and the anocleithrum is paddle-shaped (personal observation).

The same types of structures are known in the Carboniferous *Sagenodus*, but in the Permian *Gnathorhiza* they are greatly modified.

Pectoral girdles of *Uranolophus* and *Griphognathus*, the two best known Devonian denticulates, show many characters that set them apart from *Chirodipterus* and *Scaumenacia*. Their cleithra and clavicles are ornamented in the same way as the adjacent opercilars and head bones, and their external surfaces are not concave. Clearly they were not deeply buried but were surface structures whose outer faces conformed to the body contours. Their branchial laminae are small and lie at a low angle to the planes of the external surfaces of the cleithrum and clavicle, and the lamina of the cleithrum continues as a strong septum to join the anterior edge of that bone forming a pair of slot-like spaces (Fig. 11). The scapulocoracoid of *Uranolophus* is poorly preserved, but from its attachment areas it is inferred to be essentially similar to that of *Griphognathus*. It is very deeply concave on its anterior face, has a very widespread attachment surface, small slit-like foramina anteriorly for the passage of neurovascular elements, and a very posteriorly oriented glenoid fossa. It is impossible to generalize too far from this single example to Devonian and Carboniferous denticulates as a whole. Further work should be done on *Jarvika* and *Conchopoma*. However, we suspect that the shape of the scapulocoracoid is functionally correlated with the shape of the flat branchial laminae, and we predict that it is a feature of the group as a whole.

This analysis suggests that the pectoral girdle of Paleozoic tooth-plated forms had prominent branchial laminae that formed an abrupt posterior wall to the branchial chamber and a large surface for the attachment of limb and body muscles. In contrast, the denticulated type had a smoothly curved low posterior wall to the branchial chamber and only limited surfaces for the attachment of muscles. Further work is required to understand the functional significance of these features.

In summary, then, we have concentrated in the above discussion on cranial features to stress the point that the two lineages are

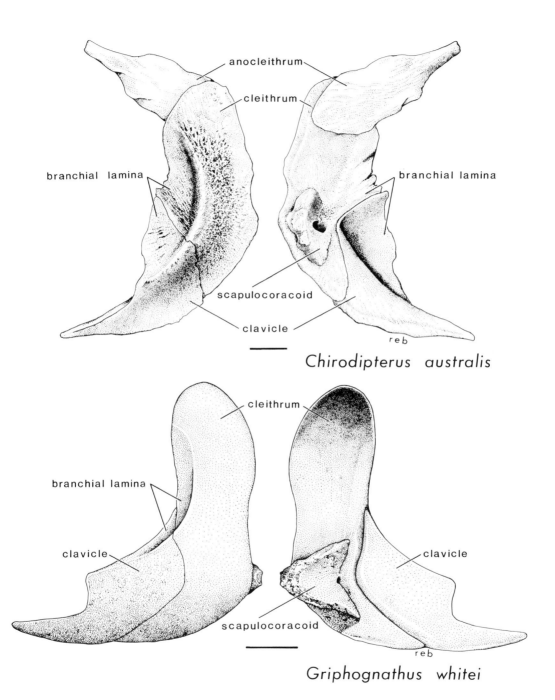

Fig. 11. Pectoral girdles of *Chirodipterus australis* and *Griphognathus whitei* in external (left) and internal (right) views. Anocleithrum in *G. whitei* is not known. Scale = 10 mm.

defined by a set of interrelated characters that form part of the feeding and respiratory systems. They are correlated character complexes. Among the listed characters, the pineal foramen is the only exception to this statement. We conclude that the sets of characters have been modified in concert to elaborate each of the functional mechanisms, thus providing a functional assurance that the lineages are monophyletic. The denticulate lineage became extinct in the Permian with *Conchopoma*. The tooth-plated lineage is still extant.

This analysis has many implications for the study of dipnoan phylogeny. Perhaps the most significant point is the extent to which parallelisms occur in the two lines. For example, the bones of the skull roof reduce in number; the suspensorium becomes more inclined; bone "A" is lost and the occipital commissure of the lateral line passes through bone "B" instead; bone "Z" becomes incorporated in the skull roof; ossification of the "dentary" is reduced; cosmine is lost. This is by no means a complete list, but it points up the necessity of recognizing the pervasive nature of parallelisms. The skill of the comparative anatomist and phylogeneticist lies not in declaring minimum parallelism and convergence on the basis of the philosophical principle of parsimony, but in the careful evaluation of the morphological, functional, and stratigraphic evidence for each proposed instance of these phenomena. Residents of the land of marsupials tend to be inherently suspicious of philosophies that *a priori* exclude or minimize parallelisms and convergences.

THE PRIMITIVE DIPNOAN MORPHOTYPE
Some remarks

Any understanding of the relationships within the Dipnoi, or among the Dipnoi and other groups, must be made using the characters of the primitive dipnoan morphotype. If this is not done we will almost certainly be misled by hapless appeals to comparisons between reduced, parallel, or convergent characters in highly derived fossil or extant taxa. This is obviously one of the main errors of the work of Rosen et al. ('81) who failed to appreciate the extent to which the paleontological data can provide evidence to falsify hypotheses based on the apparently more complete information provided by extant taxa. They complained (Rosen et al., '81:264) of "futile paleontological searches for ances-tors," "dispensible scenarios about the fish-amphibian transition, and hapless appeals to plesiomorphy," all of which could have been avoided by the postulation of relationships "developed directly from comparison among living gnathostomes." In our view such polemics do not help to clarify matters in the least. On the contrary, they conceal the fact that it is impossible to determine the characters of primitive dipnoans either from extant species or from the highly derived *Griphnognathus whitei*, to which Rosen et al. turn for a substantial part of their argument in apparent contradiction of their stated principles.

We accept the view that morphological/stratigraphical evidence may be used to define a number of trends (or polarized morphoclines), many of which have been recognized for several decades. From these it is possible to reconstruct the morphotype of the primitive dipnoan. Westoll ('49) made an analysis of dipnoan trends for a different purpose, and much of his work remains valid. Any modifications are the result of the influx of new data. We are not attempting a complete analysis but concentrate on cranial structures, and then only on those structures that figure most prominently in discussions of dipnoan relationships. The prospects for the success of such an attempt are increased if our previous statement about an early dichotomy is correct. Trends in the two lineages provide a double perspective on the primitive morphotype.

In this section we are not attempting to distinguish between so-called plesiomorphic and apomorphic characters of the morphotype. That is not our task. In our opinion too much has been written with that objective in mind, and too little care has been given to the establishement of the nature of the entities to be compared. We take the latter issue as our focus and draw the attention of readers to the point that our data are taken by Schultze (this volume) and developed from the point of view of dipnoan relationships. However, a major problem immediately presents itself. Until recently paleontologists have found no difficulty in assigning new taxa to the Dipnoi. For example, *Dipnorhynchus, Speonesydrion*, and *Uranolophus* have all been placed in the group without question. The genus *Diabolichthys* (Chang and Yu, '84), from the Gedinian (Early Devonian) of China (Fig. 12), is in a different category. It does not fall within the morphological

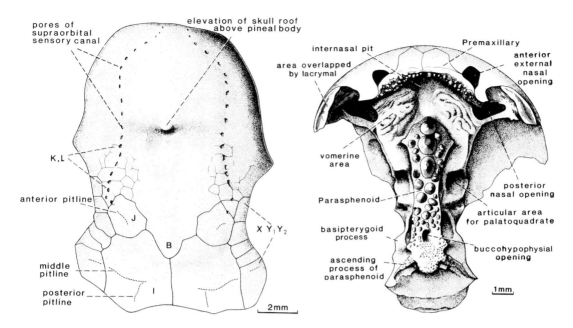

Fig. 12. Skull roof and palate of *Diabolichthys speratus* from Chang Mee-mann and Yu Xiaobo, '84.

range of the Dipnoi as previously conceived. However, on the basis of the work of Chang and Yu it would be possible to define the Dipnoi to include *Diabolichthys* and all previously described dipnoans, together with the common ancestor of both groups. This judgement would be of considerable importance, because discussion of the structure of the morphotype that gave rise to all described dipnoans would then have to take account of the morphology of *Diabolichthys* also. Consequently, we attempt to define the features of the primitive morphotype for all described lungfishes first and then make a judgement about its possible relationship to *Diabolichthys*.

A list of primitive dipnoan characters
1. Heavy ossification

This applies to all the bones including the neurocranium, dermal head bones, and scales. It is true that much of the neurocranium of *Uranolophus* remains unknown, but that is a preservation problem, the material being preserved in shale and badly crushed. Fragments of the neurocranium of the holotype of *U. wyomingensis* show that it was heavily ossified.

2. Complex roofing and cheek bone patterns (Fig. 13)

i. There were numerous small bones anterior to the orbits and they continued to the margin of the lip. The extension of the small bones to the lip is not known in *Dipnorhynchus* and *Speonesydrion* (i.e., "dipnorhynchids", but it was present in *Uranolophus*. In "dipnorhynchids" there is a single ossification forming the buccal margin, but this is of variable width. This element is assumed to have formed (but see Miles, '77) from fused small bones similar to those immediately behind it.

ii. No paired premaxillae were present. In fact no dipnoan shows paired bones in a position where they could be interpreted as premaxillae.

iii. Multiple "D" bones formed around the pineal foramen. These are not known in *Uranolophus* but are present in "dipnorhynchids." Because of the general tendency to bone reduction during evolution in both lineages, it is assumed that multiple "D" bones were primitive. Incidentally, *Dipterus* and *Chirodipterus* sometimes retain several bones in that position, although the pineal foramen is lost. *Dipnorhynchus kurikae*

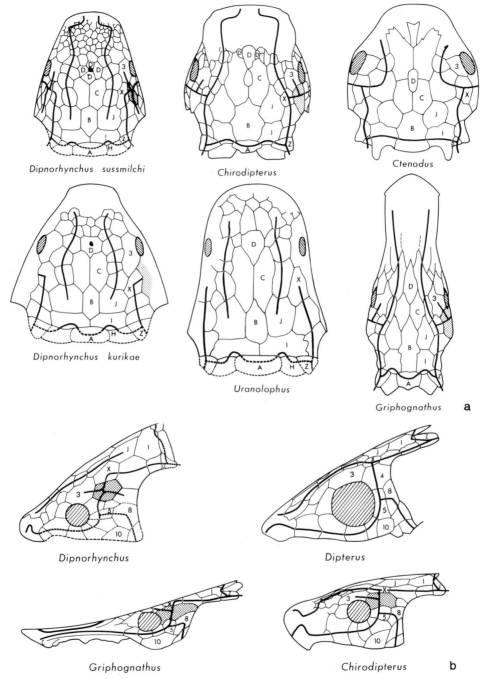

Fig. 13.   a, b) Roofing and cheek bones of a number of Devonian lungfish genera (*Dipnorhynchus, Chirodipterus, Uranolophus, Griphognathus, Dipterus*) and a single Carboniferous genus (*Ctenodus*), to show differences in the arrangement of dermal roofing and cheek bones, and the changes in pattern of the lateral line canals in the bones above and behind the orbits. Note that the occipital commissure in the species of *Dipnorhynchus* and *Uranolophus* is shown as passing through I, though this is only one of the possibilities mentioned in the text. Redrawn from various sources. Fine stipple, bone T.

Campbell and Barwick ('85) has a reduced number and one specimen has the pineal foramen in a single "D." Clearly this group of bones has been reduced more than once in the tooth-plated lineage and it was independently reduced in the denticulated lineage before its fossil record began.

iv. There were three or four "L" bones.

v. A bone "T" was present between "X" and "4." This is known only from *Dipnorhynchus*, in which it has the completely distinctive character of four lateral line canals. No such bone is known in *Uranolophus*, but no specimens with cheeks are known. On the other hand, the roof of *Uranolophus* is very wide posteriorly and the vault of the skull must have been high, leaving space for a "T." It is argued, therefore, that "T" is primitive for all dipnoans (Campbell and Barwick, '82a).

vi. There was at least one extra bone in the upper cheek behind "T," as can be inferred from the backwardly directed lateral line canal in that bone in *Dipnorhynchus*. The cheek in *Uranolophus* was not only high but also long, as is shown by the position of the orbit, and hence it was probably similar to *Dipnorhynchus* in this respect.

vii. Bones "A", "Z", and "H" were present across the posterior margin of the skull. These were roofing bones and not scales, but they were articulated with, rather than fused to, the back of the skull. It is probable that the occipital commissure passed through "H" rather than "I," or at least through "H" as well as "I." These bones are not preserved in *Uranolophus*, but "A" and "Z" are known in *Griphognathus* though they are not in contact. This suggests that a bone has been lost from the intermediate position and replaced by a scale (Miles, '77, Fig. 111). Species of *Dipnorhynchus* have no "A", "Z," or "H" preserved, but their presence may be inferred from the outlines on the back of bones "Y$_2$" and "I". The argument for their presence was developed by Campbell and Barwick ('82a).

viii. The supraorbital bone "3" carried a branch of the lateral line canal from "T," as is shown in *Dipnorhynchus sussmilchi*. The canal is retained in a number of later Devonian genera such as *Chirodipterus* and *Griphognathus*.

ix. The supraorbital and infraorbital lateral line canals did not anastomose—that is, the canals in "X" and "K" were not connected. This condition is known in *Uranolophus*, *Dipnorhynchus*, and *Speonesydrion*.

3. External dermal bones of the skull and the mandible, and the scales covered with cosmine

The cosmine varies in character from specimen to specimen of *Uranolophus*, and even on different parts of the one specimen. In "dipnorhynchids" it is much more uniform. However, the tissue is invariably present in one form or another on all Early Devonian specimens known to us.

4. All lateral line canals deeply buried

In some specimens the courses of the canals can be traced by rows of enlarged pores, particularly towards the anterior part of the head, but elsewhere the canals open to the surface through pores that are indistinguishable from the normal cosmine pores.

5. Four so-called "infradentaries" present in the mandible

Only three were reported for *Uranolophus* by Denison ('68a), but our observations show that there are four. Four "infradentaries" are known in the more advanced denticulates *Holodipterus* and *Griphognathus sculpta* (Miles, '77; Schultze, '69), as well as in all Devonian tooth-plated genera.

6. No "dentary" present

There is no evidence for the presence of paired dentaries in any dipnoan. In *Uranolophus* the "infradentaries" are preceded by a large number of small bones that continue to the buccal margin, but in "dipnorhynchids" a single ossification occupies the same space (Fig. 14a). The condition in *Uranolophus* (Fig. 14b) is considered to be primitive because some specimens of *Chirodipterus australis* also have three or four small bones as well as the large anterior one occupying the "dentary space. Presumably, therefore, this condition was primitive for the tooth-plated lineage also.

7. The mandibular lateral line entered the "infradentaries" through the posterolateral corner of the "angular"

The canal turned abruptly forwards in the "postsplenial" to join the oral canal. The position of this junction in relation to the external dermal bone is obscure because the anterior end of the oral canal lies in a tube attached to the inner surface of the "dentary." In both *Speonesydrion* and *Dipnorhynchus* the junction is forward of the anterior end of the "surangular," and this is taken as

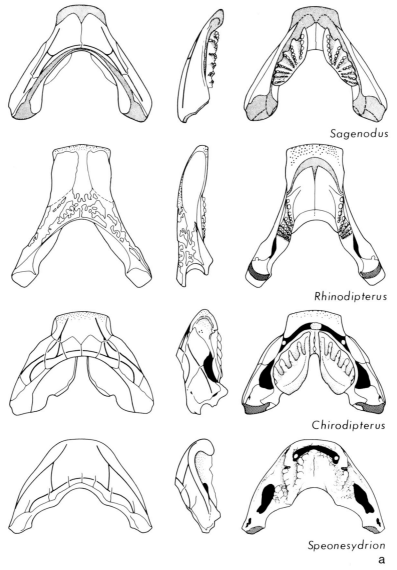

Sagenodus

Rhinodipterus

Chirodipterus

Speonesydrion

a

Fig. 14. a) Mandibles of four tooth-plated genera (*Sagenodus, Rhinodipterus, Chirodipterus, Speonesydrion*) in ventral, lateral, and dorsal views. b) Mandibles of three denticulate genera (*Holodipterus, Griphognathus, Uranolophus*) in ventral, lateral, and dorsal views. Light stipple, cartilage; dark stipple, glenoid fossa.

the primitive condition. A posterior commissure joins the two sides of the mandibular canal towards the posterior margin of the "splenials" and "postsplenials."

8.   The oral canal terminated posteriorly at or near the posterior end of the "surangular"

The oral canal may have extended out of that bone a short distance into one of the

submandibulars in one specimen of *Speonesydrion iani*, but in other "dipnorhynchids," *Uranolophus*, and all Middle and Upper Devonian genera it terminated within the "surangular." This is taken to be the primitive condition. There is no evidence that the oral canal had a connection primitively with the infraorbital canal as in *Neoceratodus* (Fig. 15). Instead, in primitive forms numerous

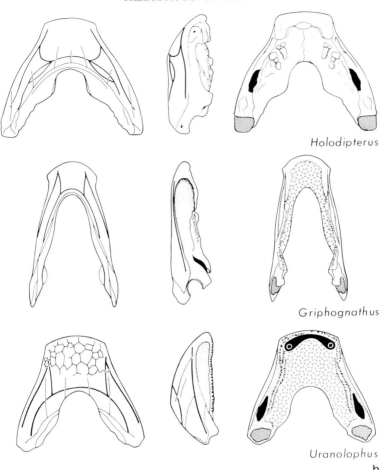

Holodipterus

Griphognathus

Uranolophus

b

small pores pass into the canal on its inner face from a parallel groove that contained the *N. mentalis externus VII*. These can be seen on "dipnorhynchids" and *Chirodipterus*. Specimens of *Chirodipterus australis* are sufficiently complete to show the canals of both the cheek and mandible, and so we have chosen to illustrate it rather than a "dipnorhynchid." No denticulate genus available to us is well enough preserved to show such detail, but we consider the "dipnorhynchid" pattern to be primitive for all dipnoans.

9. Complex bone-sheathed canals formed part of a sensory system beneath the external dermal bones of both the skull and the mandible

They are most diverse and abundant in the rostral and symphysial regions, where they consist of long tubes that ramify to form a roughly bilateral interconnected pattern beneath the dermal bones. We refer to these as rostral-symphysial tubules (Fig. 16). The larger canals open in places through large pores to the external surface. Connections with the lateral line canals are numerous. On their ventral surfaces the lateral line canals are surrounded by porous bony tissue similar to that surrounding the rostral-symphysial tubules. Proximal to the dermal bones the tubules continue to ramify and ultimately penetrate the bones making connections with the basal canals of the pore canal system to the cosmine. In "dipnorhynchids" this fine canal and tubule system extends back beneath the skull roofing bones in all areas where the median and dorsolateral cristae spread out to meet the dermal bones (Campbell and Barwick, '82a). Tubules are missing above the adductor chamber

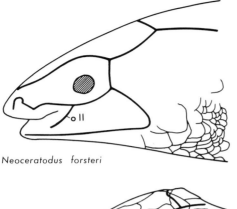

Neoceratodus forsteri

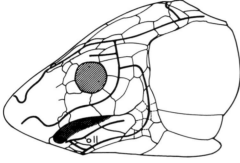

Chirodipterus australis

Fig. 15. Diagrams to show different relationships of the oral lateral line canal (o 11) in the Recent *Neoceratodus* and the Devonian *Chirodipterus*. The canal is not homologous to the two genera. Stippling indicates the position in the lateral recess of the mandible of *Chirodipterus*.

where the muscles are attached directly to the dermal bone. In the mandible of dipnorhynchids similar canals extend back along each ramus from the symphysial region, being embedded in a thin sheet of Meckel's cartilage (Fig. 17).

Such detail is not available for *Uranolophus*, but canals were clearly present in the snout and mandibular symphysial regions, and traces of their presence can be found beneath some skull roofs. Canals are also present in the rostral regions of *Griphognathus* and *Holodipterus*, and the latter genus also shows canals extending back beneath the external dermal bones.

Comparisons have been made between the canal system and the ampullae of Lorenzini found in chondrichthyans, but the distribution and pattern of branching of the two are quite different. Ampullary organs are known from modern dipnoans, but they also are distributed differently and have no associated

bony tubules. Actinistians have a rostral sensory organ (Bemis and Hetherington, '82), but its form and position are not comparable with the dipnoan system described above. Hence there are no precise analogies for the complex snout canal system in modern dipnoans or any other group of fishes, but its function may be inferred from three of its most obvious features. The first is the clear association with the lateral line system; the second is the innervation from the *N. opthalmicus profundus V* and the *N. ophthalmicus facialis VII;* and the third is the connection with the pore canal system of the cosmine. Recent work by several authors has suggested that electroreception is a primitive sensory system of vertebrates (Northcutt and Gans, '83). Other workers have interpreted the pore canal system of cosmine as being electroreceptive (Thomson, '77; Meinke, '84; Meinke, this volume). Innervation of the electroreceptors in extant fishes is normally via the *lateralis* system, and hence the relationships noted above would be consistent with an electroreceptive function. As Northcutt and Gans ('83) pointed out, the array of electroreceptors around the buccal cavity keeps the field in a fixed frame relative to the head, and to avoid interference from various extraneous sources they are deeply buried. Hence the connections, the distribution, and the form of the canal systems in the rostral region suggest that they are electroreceptors of a distinctive kind. The only other fishes with a similar system of canals are *Youngolepis* and *Powichthys* (Chang and Yu, '84).

10. Mandible with a large open anterior furrow

In both groups it is completely contained by the "dentary" in front and the "prearticulars" behind, and it is floored by a thin layer of Meckelian bone. The neurovascular supply to this furrow appears to be identical in the two groups. One or two large foramina open down into the Meckelian cavity; another large foramen opens through the posterior wall and connects with a canal that exits the mandible at a foramen on the posterior edge between the Meckelian bone and the post-splenial; and several small foramina open down into the symphysial canals (Fig. 17). These structures have been interpreted for *Speonesydrion* and *Dipnorhynchus* by Campbell and Barwick ('84). Details of the anterior furrow in *Uranolophus* are not so completely preserved, but where seen they

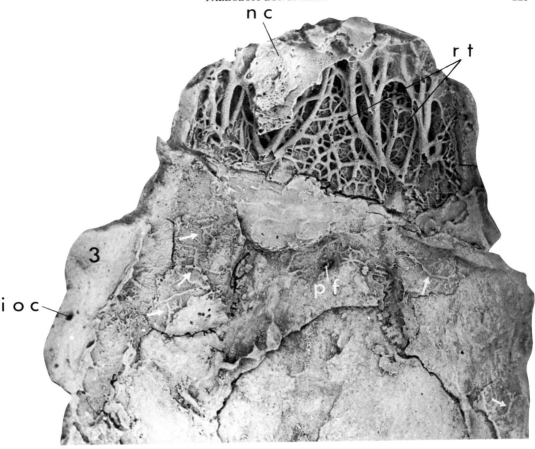

Fig. 16. Ventral surface of skull roof of *Dipnorhynchus kiandrensis* showing rostral tubule complex with symmetrically arrayed bone-sheathed canals for the *ophthalmicus profundus* and *ophthalmicus VII* nerves. White arrows indicate related tubule system connecting with the cosmine of the skull roof. i o c, infraorbital canal; n c, bone forming roof of nasal cavity, p f, pineal foramen; r t, rostral tubules. Scale = 10 mm.

are entirely comparable and may be interpreted in the same way.

The function of the anterior furrow is very difficult to assess. It could have contained sensory or glandular tissue. The postulated innervation and the position at the entrance to the mouth suggest that it was sensory, but this view is difficult to reconcile with its position in *Holodipterus gogoensis*. In that species it is present as a sausage-shaped tube with neurovascular canals as in the "dipnorhynchids," but it is completely or almost completely roofed by the "prearticulars," the adsymphysial plate, and the "dentary" (Fig. 9). Only a small hole is left in this roof (Miles, '77, Fig. 108), so that it is unlikely to have housed tactile, chemosensory, mechanosensory, or electrosensory tissue. It may have housed a gland, but this is only conjectural. In some Late Devonian genera, and all later ones, the "prearticulars" become more closely appressed to the external dermal bones ventrally, and they are separated only by a thin layer of Meckelian cartilage. The symphysial canals and the anterior furrow are lost, so there is no direct derivative of these structures to allow a satisfactory interpretation to be made.

11. A median adsymphysial plate at the anterior end of the prearticulars but behind the anterior furrow

The adsymphysial plate is difficult to distinguish in the Early Devonian genera, but

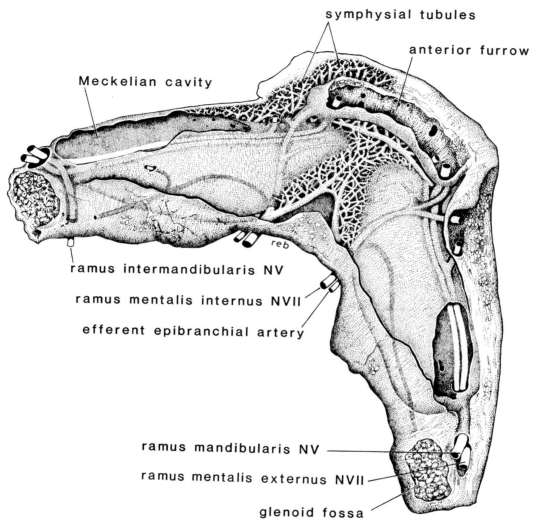

Fig. 17. Reconstruction of mandible of *Speonesydrion iani* in posterodorsolateral view, with the prearticular bones removed to show symphysial tubule complex and principal associated nerves and arteries. Particularly note the extent of the tubule system along the medial and lateral regions of each mandibular ramus. The mandible is shown rotated horizontally to the right.

its outline can be discerned indistinctly in species of *Dipnorhynchus* and *Speonesydrion*. In some species of *Dipnorhynchus* the plate joined the "dentary" to divide the anterior furrow into two (Thomson and Campbell, '71, Fig. 50). It is clearly present in *Chirodipterus* and *Holodipterus*, Late Devonian examples of the tooth-plated and denticulated lineages respectively.

12. Parasphenoid short and not extending much further forward than a line joining the jaw articulations

This bone is almost impossible to distinguish in all Early Devonian species. In the "dipnorhynchids" the thick dentine cover obscures the sutures, and even in thin section it is impossible to define boundaries (see Fig.

3). In *Uranolophus* the situation is little better, but several specimens indicate that the parasphenoid was short. *Uranolophus wyomingensis* and *Speonesydrion lehmanni* have been interpreted as having parasphenoids that extend forward between the pterygoids (Lehmann and Westoll, '52; Denison, '68a), but examination of the material has convinced us that cracks have been misinterpreted as sutures. We are encouraged in this view by the fact that in all known Middle Devonian-Carboniferous genera the parasphenoid is short, and the hypophysial pouch (with its stalk, if present) lies at its anterior end. The positions of the hypophysial structures are known in "dipnorhynchids" and *Uranolophus* and they are consistent with a short parasphenoid of the type found in later genera.

13.   Anterior naris situated in a notch in the anterior margin of the mouth, and the posterior naris within the mouth.

The nasal capsule was large, bounded behind by a post-nasal wall that was deeply buried in soft tissues, and was not protected on its ventral surface by denticulated dermal bone. It was situated high above the level of the margins of the tooth plates (Campbell and Barwick, '84a, Fig. 6A). The nasal capsule of *Uranolophus* was similar to that of *Dipnorhynchus* in these respects and is quite unlike that of *Griphognathus,* which represents a derived state.

14.   Bones around the anterior end of the palate consisting of a pair of "dermopalatines" that met in the mid-line and an unpaired median bone immediately behind them

This is the situation in *Dipnorhynchus* and *Speonesydrion.* Though the "dermopalatines" have precisely the same arrangement in *Uranolphus,* no unpaired median bone has been found. This is probably because sutures in the palate of that genus are very difficult to see. We do not accept that the bone had been lost already in the denticulate lineage, because there is good evidence of its presence in *Holodipterus gogoensis.*

With further evolution the "dermopalatines" retreated from the mid-line and became free of the pterygoids, so that they are rarely preserved. The anterior median bone became exposed anteriorly and was also free of the pterygoids. This more advanced condition is well shown in *Chirodipterus australis,* where the median bone has been referred to

as a fused pair of vomers (Miles, '77). In still later genera this median bone and the "dermopalatines" are lost. The so-called vomerine tooth plates of later genera such as *Gnathorhiza* and *Neoceratodus* are probably relics of the median part of the upper lip left after the remainder of the snout has failed to ossify.

We do not accept the idea that the anterior palatal pattern of *Griphognathus whitei* is primitive. The bones referred to by Rosen et al., ('81) as the "extra dermal bone," the "ectopterygoid", and the posterior part of the "maxilla" are all new structures developed in relation to the special nature of the bite in that genus (Fig. 18). The snout is long and highly depressed. At full occlusion, the mandible passed lateral to the palate and met the ventral surface of the small and flat nasal capsule, as well as the surface of the post-nasal wall. All these surfaces had to be protected, and denticles grew in the skin covering them, producing thin bones. In addition the inner surface of the external dermal bones met the outer edge of the mandible and a protective denticulated layer of bone (called the lateral nasal tooth plates by Miles, '77) was produced to cover them. All these denticulated bones were neomorphic in long headed denticulate genera (Campbell and Barwick, '84a).

15.   Nasal capsules at the end of a long olfactory stalk even in the short headed forms

There is no evidence in any Devonian form that the nasal capsules were crowded above the telencephalon (Northcutt, this volume).

16.   Braincase suspended from the roof by a high median crista, a pair of dorsolateral cristae, and the lateral cristae

These form a clear pattern in most Devonian lungfishes. The skull vault was highest in the most primitive genera, and a large adductor cavity was present, divided into two chambers by the dorsolateral crista (Fig. 19).

17.   Lateral walls of braincase well ossified

Separate canals were present for the jugular vein and the orbital artery in *Dipnorhynchus sussmilchi* and *Chirodipterus australis,* producing a divided cavum epiptericum (Miles, '77; Campbell and Barwick, '82b). Miles ('77) regarded the undivided condition of the cavum epiptericum in *Griphognathus whitei* as primitive, partly because of its ontogeny in *Neoceratodus* and partly because

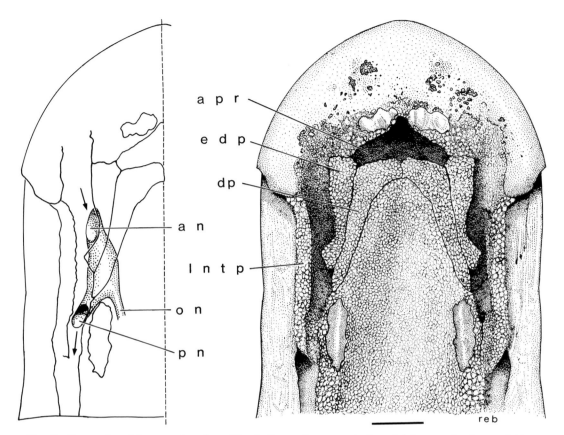

Fig. 18.   Restoration of the ventral surface of the skull of *Griphognathus whitei*, based on CPC 21186 and ANU 35641. At left, outline drawing of the nasal capsule to show relationship to the bones of the palate. a n, anterior naris; a p r, anterior palatal recess; dp, dermopalatine; e d p, extra dental plate; l n t p, lateral nasal tooth plate; o n, olfactory nerve; p n, posterior naris. Scale = 10 mm.

of its inferred primitive structure as judged from its form in adult lower tetrapods. We consider the undivided condition in *Griphognathus* to be the result of a decrease in ossification related to the loss of the full palatal bite (see below).

18.   An otic series of bones present

In Late Devonian genera no individual ossifications can be recognized, and it is assumed that the arrangement in *D. sussmilchi,* the only species in which separate bones have been recognized, represents the primitive condition (Fig. 20). The pattern consisted of a posterior otic, which included the dorsolateral crista and contained the vertical semicircular canals; the lateral otic (also referred to as the parotic crista or lateral commissure by some authors) contained the horizontal semicircular canal; and a small ventral otic lay ventral to the posterior otic. These bones are not obviously homologous with the otic series of any other teleostomes, and they probably appeared as an independent series within the Dipnoi.

19.   A large, deep cavity near the junction of the quadrate and the ventral otic for the internal carotid artery and the *N. mentalis internus VII*

This structure is known for certain only in two *Dipnorhynchus* species, though it is probably present in *Speonesydrion* and *Stomiahykus* also. The relevant part of the skull of *Uranolophus* is unknown. Later genera of both lineages show no such arrangement, but we accept it as truly primitive rather than a new feature in "dipnorhynchids." *Uranolo-*

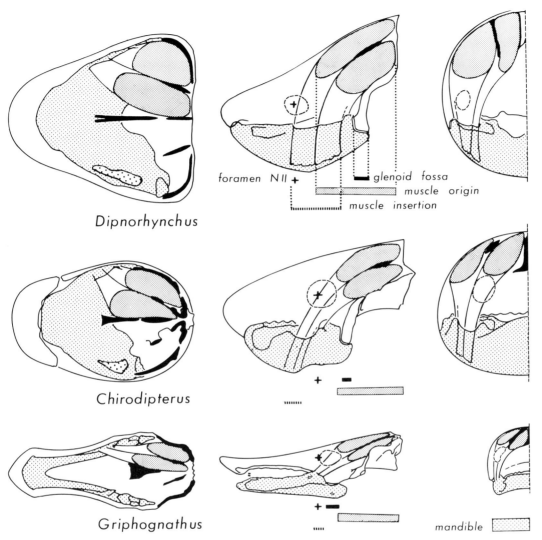

foramen N II +

▬ glenoid fossa
▭ muscle origin
▭ muscle insertion

Dipnorhynchus

Chirodipterus

Griphognathus

mandible ▭

Fig. 19. The adductor musculature of the tooth plated genera *Dipnorhynchus* and *Chirodipterus*, and the denticulate genus *Griphognathus*. Specimens drawn in dorsal, lateral, and transverse perspectives to show the relative sizes and positions of muscle masses (hatched areas). Positions of the medial, dorsolateral, and lateral cristae shown in black; Position of suprameckelian vacuity in mandible is shown by larger stippling. Muscle origins and insertions and relative positions of the optic nerve and glenoid fossa are shown as projections for each genus. Each skull is drawn at approximately the same length. The positions, masses, and orientations of the muscles' relation to the main skull elements in the crushing genera *Dipnorhynchus* and *Chirodipterus* are compared with those of the rasping genus, *Griphognathus*.

phus had a high posterior skull vault, and one of the palates of *U. wyomingensis* has the base of the internal carotid canal leading to the hypophysial pouch in much the same way as in specimens of *Dipnorhynchus*. Thomson and Campbell ('71) considered that this deep pit also housed the remnants of a spiracular organ, a view we consider to be valid. Note that specimens of *Dipnorhynchus kurikae* (Campbell and Barwick, '85), indicate that only the *N. mentalis internus VII* issued from this structure. The nerve la-

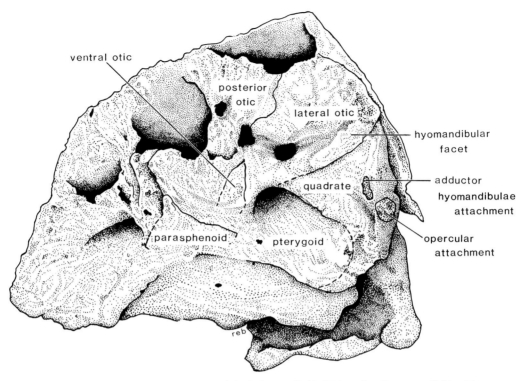

Fig. 20. Posteroventrolateral view of the holotype skull of *Dipnorhynchus sussmilchi*, with the position of the otic bones and associated structures indicated. This is the only dipnoan species in which distinct otic bones can be seen. The hyomandibular facet is undivided.

belled *ramus hyomandibularis VII* by Campbell and Barwick ('82, Fig. 11), is the *externus branch of VII*.

20. Bite massive and involving a large part of the palatal surface

This is inferred from the fact that the adductor chambers in the skull and the mandible of all Early Devonian genera are large, and that in both lineages they were greatly reduced by the Late Devonian. It is not unusual for the Meckelian chamber in Late Devonian and Carboniferous forms to be closed and for the adductor mandibulae to be attached to a short preglenoid process. This is the condition, for example, in *Griphognathus*.

21. Quadrate steeply inclined with respect to the median line of the palate

The angle of the quadrate, the shape of the adductor chambers in the skull, and the angle of insertion of the adductor mandibulae are all intimately related (Fig. 19). Reduction of the force of the bite, which is correlated with the evolution of more intricate surfaces

on the tooth plates or with the assumption of a rasping mode of feeding, permitted a reorientation of the bones forming the posterior part of the skull. This also produced a significant change in the form of the branchial chamber, and consequently changes in the shapes of the various elements of the hyoid and branchial arches.

22. Tooth plates with crudely differentiated surfaces forming the primitive adult dentition

Though tooth plates and shedding denticles appear in the record at approximately the same time, we conclude that the former condition is the more primitive for the following reasons. The evidence from *Speonesydrion* and *Dipnorhynchus* is that primitive tooth plates had poorly differentiated surfaces compared with *Dipterus* or any of the Late Devonian or subsequent genera. The ancestral form presumably would have had relatively smooth tooth plates. The most primitive forms of both lineages had powerful bites and consequently continuous den-

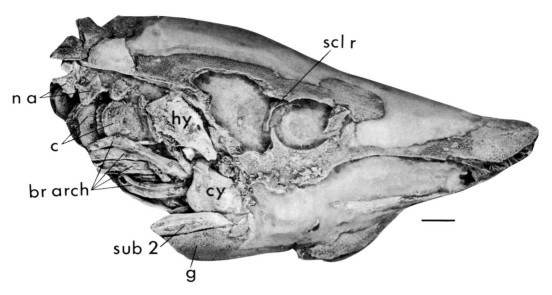

Fig. 21. Lateral view of a partly prepared skull of *Griphognathus whitei*, ANU 21634, showing the hyoid and branchial arches, elements of the vertebral column, and ventral gill cover plates. Sediment remains on the skull roof and filling the deep labial excavation on the mandible. br arch, branchial arches; c, centra; cy, ceratohyal; g, gular; hy, hyomandibula; n a, neural arch; scl r, sclerotic ring; sub 2, subopercular 2. Scale = 10 mm.

tine sheets rather than shedding denticulated surfaces would be expected. Note that this argument does *not* imply that there were no denticles in the mouths of the primitive forms, but rather that the denticles were continuously growing and became incorporated in tooth plates, as is well illustrated by *Speonesydrion.* The development of a rasping feeding system dependent on the presence of basibranchial/basihhyal tooth plates necessitated the retention of a shagreen of denticles at least on the median part of the palate. Such a shagreen can be produced only by shedding and replacement, because wear of a retained and continuously growing cover of conical denticles would soon produce a continuous smooth sheet of dentine. Therefore the shedding mode must be derived.

We are well aware that at first sight this conclusion is counter-intuitive and contradicts conclusions others have drawn from outgroup comparisons, but we contend that functional morphological study of the dipnoans themselves provides the only reliable basis for judgement.

23. Hyomandibula large, situated high upon the posterior face of the skull, and attached by a single continuous surface to the lateral otic; no hyosuspensory attachment to the quadrate present (Figs. 20,21)

This interpretation is based on the condition in *Dipnorhynchus* in which the preservation is excellent (Campbell and Barwick, '82b). No specimen of *Uranolophus* showing these structures is available. The double-headed hyomandibular attachment and the hyosuspensory ligament attachment described from the Late Devonian *Griphognathus* and *Chirodipterus*, considered by Miles ('77) to be significant in determining relationships, are conditions independently derived within the Dipnoi. As might be expected, the primitive hyomandibula articulated directly with the ceratohyal; only the hyomandibula was attached to the back of the skull, and then at a single point. The modifications found in the Late Devonian genera result from the loss of the primitive hyomandibular function.

24. Strong hypohyal present and weak hypobranchials may have been present

The former point is not at issue, but the latter point has been commented on by Miles ('77:285) and by Rosen et al., ('81:237). There is no clear evidence either way. The expanded proximal ends of the ceratobranchials do not suggest fusion between primitive ceratobranchials and hypobranchials. These expanded ends, so prominent in *Griphognathus,* permitted appropriately large articula-

Fig. 22. Ventral view of right hyoid and gill arches in restored position of specimen shown in Figure 21. Note particularly the shallow longitudinal grooves with their lateral branches represented on each of the ceratobranchials labelled 1–4. These carried the branchial arteries and their branches. cy, ceratohyal; p d, palatal denticles; tp, displaced basibranchial/basihyal tooth plate; 1–4, ceratobranchials. Scale = 10 mm.

These structures are known in detail only from *Griphognathus* and *Chirodipterus*, which are advanced representatives of the two lineages. As pointed out above, the roles of these elements in feeding are different in the two groups. Thus the fact that essentially the same paired structure occurs in each group indicates that it is a primitive feature within the Dipnoi.

26. Ceratobranchials and epibranchials deeply furrowed on their posterior faces

This information is available in detail only for *Griphognathus* and *Chirodipterus*, but fragments of the ceratobranchials in the holotype of *Uranolophus wyomingensis* suggest that they had a similar structure. The posterior groove presumably housed the branchial nerves and arteries. Branches of these structures lay in notches along one side of the posterior groove (Fig. 22) in specimens of *Griphognathus whitei*. These supplied the gill filaments. They are most closely spaced in the dorsal parts of the ceratobranchials. On the first, third, and fourth arches they are approximately equally spaced, but on the second arch they are more closely spaced. Moreover, the lengths of the rows of notches on the ceratobranchials and the epibranchials decrease considerably from the first to the fourth arch. Even if there is not a one-to-one relationship between the number of notches and the number of filaments, it may be inferred that the number of filaments on the second arch was slightly greater than the number on the first arch, and that the third and fourth arches had progressively fewer filaments. The number on the fourth arch is about half the number on the second.

In the aestivating modern genera, *Lepidosiren* and *Protopterus,* the filaments are greatly reduced on the first and second arches because the oxygenated blood from the lungs is shunted over these arches, whereas the unoxygenated blood is preferentially directed over the third and fourth arches (Burggren and Johansen, this volume). *Neoceratodus*, which does not aestivate, has well developed filaments on all gill arches, but for the lung to operate in hypoxic environments it has developed a system that allows blood pumped by the heart to bypass the respiratory capillaries of the gills selectively (Johansen et al., '67). This alternative strategy suggests that primitive dipnoans had a full array of filaments on the arches and that the circulatory systems in particular species have adapted in different ways to cope with life styles in hypoxic conditions.

tions with the basibranchials and allowed the attachment of powerful musculature to operate the feeding mechanism. We have found small bones, serving a spacing function, between the proximal ends of adjacent ceratobranchials in *Griphognathus whitei* (Fig. 6a), and these could be interpreted as modified hypobranchials. However, we are reluctant to accept such an interpretation for so highly derived a species.

25. Basibranchial/basihyal system consisting of a large anterior and a small posterior element

Fig. 23. Internal face of the operculum of *Uranolophus wyomingensis*, PF 3835, with a clearly shown (arrowed) internal muscle scar. Scale = 10 mm.

The significance of the pattern of *Griphognathus* is that although the lengths of the arches were unusual in that they were modified to meet special mechanical needs, with the consequent reduction of filament numbers on the posterior arches, filaments were present throughout. There is no evidence of reduction on the first and second arches as in *Lepidosiren* and *Protopterus.*. This, together with the good geological evidence that the most primitive dipnoas lived in well oxygenated marine conditions, supports the inference from the living genera that the primitive forms had equally developed gills with uniformly distributed filaments. In any case *Griphognathus* demonstrates that the condition in *Lepidosiren* and *Protopterus* is derived and that similarities between the circulatory systems of these extant genera and those of living tetrapods should not be used to infer phylogenetic relationships.

27. Operculum and two subopperculars present

This is inferred from *Uranolophus* and *Speonesydrion* as well as the large majority of later Devonian genera (see Fig. 6b).

28. Large adductor operculae muscle making a large sausage-shaped scar high up on the inner anterior face of the operculum

An adductor scar is now known in both *Uranolophus* and *Speonesydrion* (Fig. 23).

Specimens of *Chirodipterus australis* have ill-defined muscle scars in the same region, but our material of *Griphognathus whitei* is not well enough preserved to indicate their presence.

29. Submandibular series consisting of a median and three large plates lateral to it, together with large principal and lateral gulars

Although this arrangement is not known in position in any Early Devonian form, large isolated plates are known for both *Uranolophus* and *Speonesydrion*, and the posterior margins of their mandibles have embayments showing how the plates were arranged (Campbell and Barwick, '84b). Although with subsequent evolution the median length of the jaw decreased, thus transforming the shape of the base of the branchial chamber, the pattern of plates in *Dipterus, Scaumenacia*, and *Chirodipterus* confirms the above interpretation.

30. Scales rhombic and articulated by peg-and-socket

These are best known in *Uranolophus*, but also occur in *Dipnorhynchus*. They are clearly primitive.

31. Bases of the median and caudal fins covered with modified body scales and their more distal parts with elongated cosmine-covered scales

There is no evidence that the distal cosmine-covered scales became submerged to form the lepidotrichs of later genera. It is more probable that the lepidotrichs were primitively present, but were unossified or incompletely ossified. They extended as a fringe beyond the limits of the elongate scales.

32. Paired median dorsal fins present

The arrangement in *Uranolophus* has been misinterpreted by Denison ('68a). It is essentially similar to that of *Dipterus,* the oldest member of the tooth-plated group in which the fin arrangement is known.

THE POSITION OF *DIABOLICHTHYS*

As indicated at the beginning of the previous section, any discussion of the relationship of *Diabolichthys* to the group of previously described dipnoans must depend on an assessment of the primitive morphotype of such dipnoans. Our estimate of this morphotype has now been outlined.

Chang and Yu ('81) listed four features that they considered to be uniquely shared by *Diabolichthys* (Fig. 12) and dipnoans: 1) There is a median roofing bone separating, or partly separating, the most posterior paired bones of the skull roof ("B" separating the "I"s); 2) the buccal margin of the snout is reflexed so that a considerable part of the premaxilla lies in the mouth cavity and the anterior naris is at the margin of the mouth cavity; 3) the animal had a palatal bite—that is, the prearticular tooth plates occluded with the pterygoid tooth plates; and 4) the anterior part of the skull is short relative to the posterior part.

We are of the opinion that none of the above features has the status they suggested, for the following reasons:

1. The bone Chang and Yu designated as bone "B" is not a complete, large entity of dipnoan type—rather, it is an isolated small median bone not unlike that found in some osteolepids (Jarvik, '80, Fig. 145).

2. The buccal margin is certainly reflexed, but dipnoans have no identifiable premaxillary and the anterior nasal openings are not confined within the external dermal bones. The similarity between *Diabolichthys* and *Youngolepis* in this feature is more striking than the similarity between *Diabolichthys* and any known dipnoan.

3. The reduction of the marginal tooth-bearing bones and the production of a prearticular/pterygoid bite in *Diabolichthys* is certainly dipnoan-like, though nothing is known of maxillae or premaxillae in dipnoans. We note, however, that the Actinistia also reduced their maxillae and dentaries, producing toothed pterygoids and prearticulars. Although actinistians seem never to have produced occluding tooth plates on these bones, they demonstrate that the tendency to palatal rather than marginal biting existed in primitive teleostomes other than the dipnoans.

4. Finally, the relative shortness of the anterior part of the skull is not distinctively dipnoan. It is noteworthy that *Diabolichthys* and *Youngolepis* have long- and short-headed members. Comparison between the short-headed and the long-headed representatives of these two genera (Chang and Yu, '84, Figs. 1B and 1D, with Chang, '82, Figs. 5C and 5E) seem to us to be closer than comparisons between either type of *Diabolichthys* and any known dipnoan. The eye in *Diabolichthys*, like that in *Youngolepis* seems to be in a very anterior position similar to that of Devonian "crossopterygians," and unlike that of any primitive dipnoan.

We conclude, therefore, that Chang and Yu have not made a case for the existence of any synapomorphies between *Diabolichthys* and the Dipnoi. This conclusion is strengthened by a consideration of the unique shared characters of *Diabolichthys* and *Youngolepis*. Both have a supra-pineal eminence but no sign of pineal foramen; the pores of the supra-orbital lateral line canal terminate anterolateral to the anterior pit line; the bones lateral to the parietal (or "I") do not contain lateral line canals; and the anterior section of the infraorbital canal and the ethmoid commissure lie in the suture along the posterior edge of the premaxillae. These features are not primitive, inherited from an osteichthyan ancestor. Nor do they remotely resemble the primitive dipnoan morphotype, or indeed any primitive dipnoan. In addition, the distribution of the canals coupled with the very anterior position of the orbits in *Diabolichthys* suggests that the identification of X, Y_1, Y_2, and K, L series in that genus by Chang and Yu, is incorrect.

All these points, together with the remarkable similarity between the premaxillae, vomers, vomerine areas of the neurocranium, internasal pits, small postnasal bars, articulating areas for the palatoquadrates, and long denticulated parasphenoids with a posteriorly situated hypophysial opening in *Youngolepis* and *Diabolichthys*, allied with the fact that they occur in the same beds, indicate that these two genera are close relatives. *Diabolichthys* should be regarded as a modified "crossopterygian" that shares no unique derived characters with primitive dipnoans.

CONCLUSIONS

1. The Dipnoi evolved in the sea. The geological evidence indicates that at least some of them lived in shallow quiet water on carbonate platforms and between reefs. They give evidence of being bottom dwellers in 50–100 m of water. This information, together with their body form, the disposition of gills on the gill arches, and the size of their gill chambers, indicates that they were not air breathers.

2. From the beginning of the fossil record of the Dipnoi, two lineages can be recognized—those with denticulated buccal cavities in which growth of the denticles took

place by shedding and replacement, and those with tooth plates, which grew by the addition of dentine marginally.

3. Evolution in these lineages provides a double perspective on the primitive dipnoan morphotype. An attempt is made to define its main features.

4. A large number of parallelisms and convergences occur within and between the two lineages. Evolution was anything but parsimonious.

5. Functional study of the jaw mechanisms of a variety of Devonian forms indicates that the primitive dipnoan had a massive bite, with relatively undifferentiated dentine-covered palatal and mandibular tooth plates. The denticulated types with shedding denticles are considered to be derived. This correlates with the heavy ossification of the skulls and mandibles of the primitive members of both lineages.

6. *Griphognathus*, considered by several authors to be primitive in a number of its characters, is shown to be highly derived in almost every feature. The attempt to demonstrate the presence of a choana in this genus by relating the position of the posterior nasal opening to a series of surrounding bones, said to be the homologues of similarly placed bones in tetrapods, cannot be sustained. The surrounding bones are neomorphic in *G. whitei* and possibly in other long-headed dipnoans.

7. The remarkable tubule system in the rostral and mandibular symphysial regions of all Devonian dipnoans is most extensive in the Early Devonian forms. The innervation and distribution of this system indicates that it was electrosensory in function. Further, it had an intimate connection with the pore-canals of the cosmine, which are also thought to have had an electrosensory function.

8. Several features of the primitive dipnoan morphotype, including the absence of paired maxillae, premaxillae and dentaries, the unique pattern of bones in the extrascapular series and the posterior part of the skull roof, the distinctive otic ossifications, the arrangement of the external dermal bones on the mandible with a distinctive disposition of lateral line canals, the absence of coronoids, the short parasphenoid with the buccohypophysial opening near its anterior end, nasal openings in the mouth, and absence of a bony floor to the nasal capsules all indicate that the group became isolated before the alternative conditions that characterize the "crossopterygians"/actinopterygians became established. The view that all the above features are apomorphies of dipnoans developed from pre-existing primitive conditions that are exhibited by "crossopterygians" and actinopterygians has no basis in observation. The above requires a radical reassessment of the relation between the Dipnoi and other lobe-finned groups.

9. The appearance of the Dipnoi in the fossil record as fully developed, heavily ossified palatal biters, without any evidence of intermediate more lightly ossified forms, suggests that the complex of characters defining the group evolved quickly in a short series of coordinated steps. This is consistent with what is known of the establishment of other primitive fish groups such as the various groups of placoderms. Subsequent evolution during the Palaeozoic involved modification or loss of structures already present when the group appeared.

ACKNOWLEDGMENTS

Dr. D.G. Holloway and Mr. A.R. Coleman prepared much of the Gogo material; Dr. G.C. Young of the Bureau of Mineral Resources, Canberra, Dr. A. Ritchie of the Australian Museum, Sydney, Mr. J.C. Bruner of the Field Museum, Chicago, and Dr. H. Rémy of the University, Bonn, have made specimens available to us; Drs. D. Gouget, E. Mark-Kurik, and P. Forey made specimens collected during the Symposium on the Evolution and Biogeography of Early Vertebrates, Canberra 1983, available to us; we have benefited greatly from discussion with Drs. Chang Mee-mann, P. Forey, J. Long, H.-P Schultze, M.M. Smith, and G.C. Young; Mr. C. Marshall has provided much discussion and information on possible dipnoan relationships; M. Coleman, L. Wittig, C. Foudoulis, and T. Bowden have assisted with various aspects of the illustrations. Our thanks are extended to all these co-workers.

Repositories

A.M.F. = Palaeontological collections of the Australian Museum, Sydney

A.N.U. = Collections of the Geology Department, Australian National University, Canberra

C.P.C. = Commonwealth Palaeontological Collections, Bureau of Mineral Resources, Canberra

P.F. = Paleontological Collections, Field Museum, Chicago

LITERATURE CITED

Bemis, W.E. (1984) Morphology and growth of lepidosirenid lungfish tooth plates (Pisces: Dipnoi). J. Morphol. *179*:73–93.

Bemis, W.E., and T.E. Hetherington (1982) The rostral organ of *Latimeria chalumnae:* Morphological evidence of an electoreceptive function. Copeia *1982*:467–471.

Bemis, W.E., and G.V. Lauder (1985) Morphology and function of the feeding apparatus of the lungfish *Lepidosiren paradoxa* (Dipnoi). J. Morphol. *187*:81–108.

Berman, D.S. (1976) Cranial morphology of the Lower Permian lungfish *Gnathorhiza* (Osteichthyes: Dipnoi). J. Paleontol. *50*:1020–1033.

Bernacsek, G.M. (1977) A lungfish cranium from the Middle Devonian of the Yukon Territory, Canada. Palaeontographica B. *157*:175–200.

Campbell, K.S.W., and R.E. Barwick (1982a). A new species of the lungfish *Dipnorhynchus* from New South Wales. Palaeontology *25*:509–527.

Campbell, K.S.W., and R.E. Barwick (1982b) The neurocranium of the primitive dipnoan *Dipnorhynchus sussmilchi* (Etheridge). J. Vert. Paleontol. *2*:286–327.

Campbell, K.S.W., and R.E. Barwick (1983) Early evolution of dipnoan dentitions and a new species *Speonesydrion*. Mem. Assoc. Australas. Palaeontol. *1*:17–49.

Campbell, K.S.W., and R.E. Barwick (1984a) The choana, maxillae, premaxillae and anterior bones of early dipnoans. Proc. Linn. Soc. N.S.W. *107*:147–170.

Campbell, K.S.W., and R.E. Barwick (1984b) *Speonesydrion*, an Early Devonian dipnoan with primitive toothplates. Palaeo Ichthyologica *2*:1–48.

Campbell, K.S.W., and R.E. Barwick (1985) An advanced massive dipnorhynchid lungfish from the Early Devonian of New South Wales. Rec. Aust. Mus. *37*:301–316.

Carlson, K.J. (1968) The skull morphology and estivation burrows of the Permian lungfish, *Gnathorhiza serrata*. J. Geol. *76*:641–663.

Chang, M.-M (1982) The Braincase of *Youngolepis,* a Lower Devonian Crossopterygian from Yunnan, Southwestern China. Stockholm: GOTAB.

Chang, M.-M, and X. Yu (1981) A new crossopterygian, *Youngolepis precursor,* gen. et sp. nov., from Lower Devonian of E. Yunnan, China. Scientia Sinica *24*:89–97.

Chang, M.-M, and X. Yu (1984) Structure and phylogenetic significance of *Diabolichthys speratus* gen. et sp. nov., a new dipnoan-like form from the Lower Devonian of eastern Yunnan, China. Proc. Linn. Soc. N.S.W. *107*:171–184.

Dasch, E.J., and K.S.W. Campbell (1970) Strontium-isotope evidence for marine or freshwater origin of fossil Dipnoans and Arthrodires. Nature *227*:1159.

Denison, R.H. (1968a) Early Devonian lungfishes from Wyoming, Utah and Idaho. Fieldiana Geol. *17*:353–413.

Denison, R.H. (1968b) The evolutionary significance of the earliest known lungfish, *Uranolophus*. In T. Ørvig (ed): Current Problems of Lower Vertebrate Phylogeny, Nobel Symposium 4. Stockholm: Almqvist and Wiksell, pp. 247–257.

Denison, R.H. (1974) The structure and evolution of teeth in lungfishes. Fieldiana Geol. *33*:31–58.

Fergusson, C.L., R.A.F. Cas, W.J. Collins, G.Y. Craig, K.A.W. Crook, C.McA. Powell, P.A. Scott, and G.C. Young (1979) The Upper Devonian Boyd Volcanic Complex, Eden, New South Wales. J. Geol. Soc. Aust. *26*:87–105.

Forey, P.L. (1980) *Latimeria:* A paradoxical fish. Proc. R. Soc. Lond. B. *208*:369–384.

Fox, H. (1965) Early development of the head and pharynx of *Neoceratodus* with a consideration of its phylogeny J. Zool. *146*:470–554.

Friend, P.F. (1961) The Devonian stratigraphy of North and Central Vestspitsbergen. Proc. Yorks. Geol. Soc. *33*:77–118.

Gardiner, B.G., and R.S. Miles (1975) Devonian fishes of the Gogo Formation, Western Australia. Colloques Int. Centre Natl. Rech. Sci. *218*:73–79.

Goldstein, L., and R.P. Forster (1970) Nitrogen metabolism in fishes. In J.W. Campbell (ed): Comparative Biochemistry of Nitrogen Metabolism. New York and London: Academic Press, pp. 496–518.

Graham-Smith, W., and T.S. Westoll (1937) On a new long-headed dipnoan fish from the Upper Devonian of Scaumenac Bay, P.Q., Canada. Trans. R. Soc. Edinb. *59*:241–266.

Gregory, J.T., T.G. Murphy, and J.W. Reed (1977) Devonian fishes in Central Nevada. In M.S. Murphy et al. (eds): Western North American: Devonian. Univ. Calif. Riverside Mus. Contribs. *4*:112–120.

Griffith, R.W. (1980) Chemistry of the body fluids of the coelacanth, *Latimeria chalumnae*. Proc. R. Soc. Lond. B. *208*:329–347.

Griffith, R.W., and P.K.T. Pang (1979) Mechanisms of osmoregulation in the Coelacanth: Evolutionary implications. Occas. Papers Calif. Acad. Sci. *134*:79–93.

Janvier, P. (1980) Osteolepid remains from the Devonian of the Middle East, with particular reference to the endoskeletal shoulder girdle. In A.L. Panchen (ed): The Terrestrial Environment and the Origin of Land Vertebrates. London and New York: Academic Press, pp. 223–254.

Jarvik, E. (1980) Basic Structure and Evolution of Vertebrates. London: Academic Press.

Jessen, H.L. (1980) Lower Devonian porolepiformes from the Canadian Arctic with special reference to *Powichthys thorsteinssoni* Jessen. Palaeontographica B *167*:180–214.

Johansen, K., C. Lenfant, and G.C. Grigg (1967) Respiratory control in the lungfish *Neoceratodus forsteri* Krefft. Comp. Biochem. Physiol. *20*:835–854.

Kemp, A. (1977) The pattern of tooth plate formation in the Australian lungfish, *Neoceratodus forsteri* Krefft. Zool. J. Linn. Soc. *60*:223–258.

Kemp, A. (1979) The histology of tooth formation in the Australian lungfish *Neoceratodus forsteri* Krefft. Zool. J. Linn. Soc. *60*:223–258.

Kemp, A. (1984) A comparison of the developing dentition of *Neoceratodus forsteri* and *Callorhynchus milii*. Proc. Linn. Soc. N.S.W. *107*:245–262.

Lagios, M.D. (1979) The coelacanth and the chondrichthyes as sister groups: A review of shared apomorph characters and a cladistic analysis and reinterpretation. Occas. Papers Calif. Acad. Sci. *134*:25–44.

Lehmann, J.P., and T.S. Westoll (1952) A primitive dipnoan fish from the Lower Devonian of Germany. Proc. R. Soc. Lond. B *140*:403–421.

Meinke, D.K. (1984) A review of cosmine: Its structure, development and relationship to other forms of the dermal skeleton in osteichthyans. J. Vert. Paleontol. *4*:457–470.

Miles, R.S. (1975) The relationships of the Dipnoi. Colloques Int. Centre Natl. Rech. Sci. *218*:133–148.

Miles, R.S. (1977) Dipnoan (lungfish) skulls and the relationships of the group: A study based on new species from the Devonian of Australia. Zool. J. Linn. Soc. *61*:1–328.

Northcutt, R.G., and C. Gans (1983) The genesis of neural crest and epidermal placodes: A reinterpretation of vertebral origins. Q. Rev. Biol. *58*:1–28.

Ørvig, T. (1969a) Cosmine and cosmine growth. Lethaia 2:241–260.

Ørvig, T. (1969b) Vertebrates from the Wood Bay Group and the position of the Emsian-Eifelian boundary in the Devonian of Vestspitsbergen. Lethaia 2:273–328.

Ørvig, T. (1976) Paleohistological notes 4. The interpretaion of osteodentine, with remarks on the dentition in the Devonian dipnoan *Griphognathus*. Zool. Scripta 5:79–96.

Perkins, P.L. (1973) Mandibular Mechanics and Feeding Groups in the Dipnoi. Ph.D. Thesis, Yale University.

Playford, P.E., and D.C. Lowry (1966) Devonian reef complexes of the Canning Basin, Western Australia. Western Aust. Geol. Surv. Bull. *118.*

Ritchie, A. (1973) *Wuttagoonaspis* gen. nov., an unusual arthrodire from the Devonian of western New South Wales, Australia. Palaeontographica B *143A:*58–72.

Rosen, D.E., P.L. Forey, B.G. Gardiner, and C. Patterson (1981) Lungfishes, tetrapods, paleontology and plesiomorphy. Bull. Am. Mus. Nat. Hist. *167:*159–276.

Schultze, H.-P. (1969) *Griphognathus* Gross, ein langschnauziger Dipnoer aus dem Oberdevon von Bergisch-Gladbach (Rheinisches Schiefergebirge) und von Lettland. Geol. Palaeontol. Marburg *3:*21–79.

Schultze, H.-P. (1975) Die Lungenfisch-Gattung *Conchopoma* (Pisces, Dipnoi). Senckenbergiana Lethaia *56:*191–231.

Schultze, H.-P. (1982) A dipterid dipnoan from the Middle Devonian of Michigan, U.S.A. J. Vert. Paleontol. 2:155–162.

Smith, M.M. (1977) The microstructure of the dentition and dermal ornament of three dipnoans from the Devonian of Western Australia: A contribution towards dipnoan interrelations, and morphogenesis, growth and adaptation of the skeletal tissues. Phil. Trans. R. Soc. Lond. B. *281:*29–72.

Smith, M.M. (1979a) Structure and histogenesis of toothplates in *Sagenodus inaequalis* Owen considered in relation to the phylogeny of post-Devonian dipnoans. Proc. R. Soc. Lond. B *204:*15–39.

Smith, M.M. (1979b) SEM of the enamel layer in oral teeth of fossil and extant crossopterygian and dipnoan fishes. Scan. Electron Microsc. *1979 II:*483–490.

Smith, M.M. (1984) Petrodentine in extant and fossil dipnoan dentitions: Microstructure, histogenesis and growth. Proc. Linn. Soc. N.S.W. *107:*367–407.

Smith, M.M., T.R. Smithson, and K.S.W. Campbell (1986) The relationships of *Uronemus*—a Carboniferous Dipnoan with highly modified tooth plates. Phil. Trans. R. Soc. Lond. B. (In press).

Thomson, K.S. (1969) The biology of the lobe-finned fishes. Biol. Rev. *44:*91–154.

Thomson, K.S. (1977) On the individual history of cosmine and a possible electroreceptive function of the pore-canal system in fossil fishes. In S.M. Andrews, R.S. Miles, and A.D. Walker (eds): Problems in Vertebrate Evolution. London: Academic Press, pp. 247–270.

Thomson, K.S. (1980) The ecology of Devonian lobe-finned fishes. In A.L. Panchen (ed): The Terrestrial Environment and the Origin of Land Vertebrates. London and New York: Academic Press, pp. 187–222.

Thomson, K.S., and K.S.W. Campbell (1971) The structure and relationships of the primitive Devonian lungfish—*Dipnorhynchus sussmilchi* (Etheridge). Bull. Peabody Mus. Nat. Hist. *38:*1–109.

Westoll, T.S. (1949) On the evolution of the Dipnoi. In G.L. Jepson, G.G. Simpson, and E. Mayr (eds): Genetics, Paleontology and Evolution. Princeton, N.J.: Princeton University Press, pp. 121–184.

Wiley, E.O. (1979) Ventral gill arch muscles and the interrelationships of gnathostomes, with a new classification of the Vertebrata. Zool. J. Linn. Soc. *67:*149–179.

Young, G.C. (1981) Biogeography of Devonian vertebrates. Alcheringa *5:*225–243.

Young, G.C. (1984) Comments on the phylogeny and biogeography of antiarchs (Devonian placoderm fishes) and the use of fossils in biogeography. Proc. Linn. Soc. N.S.W. *107:*443–473.

Young, G.C., and J.D. Gorter (1981) A new fish fauna of Middle Devonian age from the Taemas/Wee Jasper region of New South Wales. Bureau Mineral Resources Geol. Geophys. Bull. *209:*83–147.

JOURNAL OF MORPHOLOGY SUPPLEMENT 1:133–149 (1986)

Morphology and Evolution of the Dermal Skeleton in Lungfishes

DEBORAH K. MEINKE

Department of Zoology, Oklahoma State University, Stillwater, Oklahoma 74078

ABSTRACT   The dermal skeleton of lungfishes is primitively composed of thick cosmine-covered bones and scales. Many Devonian lungfishes exhibit cosmine, while others have denticles of dentine and enameloid that may be arranged in several superposed layers; still others show denticles early in ontogeny superseded by cosmine later. Cosmine is a set of hard and soft tissues that includes bone, dentine, and enameloid, and a vascular and sensory pore-canal network. It is the latter that uniquely distinguishes cosmine from other forms of the dermal skeleton and its presence determines the arrangement of the skeletal tissues. I have proposed that the appearance of denticles or cosmine is dependent on the stage of development of the pore-canal system, which may be fully developed as a network or arrested at the free neuromast stage. Other evolutionary trends in the dipnoan dermal skeleton have resulted from repression of the tissue interactions that produce the skeletal tissues.

The dermal skeleton has figured prominently in studies of the evolution of fishes because it is the part of the organism most often preserved in the fossil record. Morphological differences in dermal bone and scale patterns and variations in skeletal microstructure have been used to differentiate groups of fishes at high taxonomic levels. One of these groups, the lungfishes, has been notoriously difficult to place in relation to other major taxa (e.g., Miles, '77). I will describe the dermal skeleton of lungfishes, discuss its relationships to that of other bony fishes, and comment on the systematic significance of some characters. Many of the observations made in this paper resulted from my examination of *Uranolophus wyomingensis* at the Field Museum of Natural History and *Dipterus* sp. at Washington University in St. Louis. Other data were gathered from the literature on fossil and extant lungfishes.

TISSUES IN THE DERMAL SKELETON

The variety of forms taken by the dermal skeletal tissues has often obscured fundamental developmental similarities among them. I will define as a tissue those cells and their products that have followed a similar developmental program. Given this definition, there are three major tissue types that occur in the dermal skeleton of lungfishes,

fossil and Recent. First, cellular bone appears as the deepest component of the dermal skeleton. Cellular bone, as the name implies, contains osteoblasts that secrete the bone matrix. This type of bone is normally found as two distinct arrangements, lamellar and vascular bone. Lamellar bone is usually present at the base of scales and dermal bones. It consists of sequentially deposited sheets in which the collagen fibers and mineral elements are oriented parallel to one another within sheets, and osteocytes lie flattened parallel to the lamellae. Dorsal to the lamellar bone lies an area of vascular bone, in which the bone matrix and osteoblasts are arranged concentrically around vascular canals.

The second type, dentine, is an acellular tissue that was first defined with reference to teeth that form from an involuted dental lamina. However, many varieties of dentine have been described in dermal structures of fishes (see Ørvig,'67) and these differ structurally from the orthodentine found in teeth of tetrapods and many fish. Dentine normally exhibits tubules that contain cell processes of the odontoblasts that produce the collagenous dentine matrix. Dentine is specifically formed in association with the epithelio-mesenchymal interface and often occurs with the third tissue to be described, enamel/enameloid. The toothplates of lung-

TABLE 1. *Dermal skeleton characters in dipnoans*

Taxon	Dermal bones	scales	Superpositional growth	Westoll-lines	Resorption
Uranolophus	Denticles Cosmine	Denticles Cosmine	In scales (denticles beneath cosmine)	Follow sutures	Denticles and cosmine
Dipnorhynchus	Cosmine	Denticles Cosmine	In scales (denticles beneath cosmine)	Follow sutures	Cosmine
Dipterus	Cosmine	Bony ridges Cosmine	None	Follow sutures	Cosmine and bone
Rhinodipterus	Cosmine	Cosmine	None	Some form by over-lap of cosmine	Cosmine
Chirodipterus	Cosmine	Cosmine	None	Some form by over-lap of cosmine	Cosmine
Holodipterus Griphognathus	Denticles	Denticles	In scales and dermal bones	None	Denticles
Fleurantia	Bone only	Bone only	None	None	None
Sagenodus	Bone only	Bone only, thin	None	None	None
Ceratodus	Bone only, thin and deep	Bone only, thin	None	None	None

fishes are remarkable in showing great diversity in their dentine structure (e.g., Smith, '77, '79, '84; Ørvig, '76).

Enameloid and enamel are two closely related tissues that form in association with the epithelio-mesenchymal interface and are the most superficial of the dermal tissues. Enamel, characteristic of tetrapod teeth, is deposited by ameloblasts, cells of the dental epithelium, and begins to form only after dentine deposition commences. The organic matrix of enamel is non-collagenous, and is removed as mineralization proceeds so that the mature tissue is very highly mineralized and lacking in organic material. Enameloid is distinct from enamel in that enameloid develops prior to dentine and consists primarily of collagenous matrix that is deposited by odontoblasts. This organic matrix is then removed during mineralization (Shellis and Miles, '74; Meinke, '82b). Shellis and Miles ('74) proposed that the evolution of enamel resulted primarily from regulatory changes in protein secretion rather than from structural changes in the proteins themselves.

The dermal skeletal tissues, with the possible exception of enamel, are present in the earliest vertebrate fossils from the Ordovician Period (Hall, '75). Evolutionary changes in the dermal skeletal system of vertebrates are largely the result of developmental changes in timing of appearance and rate of growth of the various tissues (e.g., Hall, '75; Maderson, '75). The developmental relationships among the tissues in living vertebrates

are widely considered to hold true for fossil vertebrates as well, an important assumption for establishing the systematic importance of dermal skeletal characters in the lungfishes where the most complex dermal skeletons exist only in fossil forms.

THE DERMAL SKELETON IN FOSSIL
LUNGFISHES (EXCLUDING TOOTHPLATES)

The dermal skeleton in lungfishes is comprised of a variety of structures (e.g., dermal bones, scales, and toothplates) that contain combinations of the tissues described above—bone, dentine, and enamel/enameloid. This condition is widespread among early fishes. A discussion of the dermal skeleton in lungfishes must focus on one such combination of tissues, cosmine, because the presence of cosmine has often been used as a diagnostic character for this group and has thus figured in discussions of lungfish relationships to other taxa (e.g., Miles, '77; Rosen at al., '81). It is well known, however, that not all fossil lungfishes had cosmine and it is notably lacking in extant forms. There have been few attempts to relate cosmine to the toothlike denticles (containing dentine and enameloid) found on scales and dermal bones in some genera (see however, Ørvig, '69, and Thomson, '75, for discussion of cosmine morphology and growth). The ensuing paragraphs describe cosmine morphology and other dermal skeletal structures such as denticles in various lungfish genera. A relationship between these apparently unrelated morphologies is then proposed. Toothplate structure in lungfishes is not discussed in this contribution because it would easily require an entire paper in its own right (see Smith, '79, '83, for excellent discussions of this topic). Also, phylogenetic changes in toothplate structure (i.e., the variety of dentinous tissues) largely bear on reconstruction of phylogeny within the Dipnoi and not on the relationship of lungfishes to other bony fishes.

Cosmine is an association of hard and soft tissues located superficially in the dermal skeleton (Fig. 1). The hard tissues include vascular bone, dentine, and enameloid, generally arranged as a single sheet and sometimes covering sutures between dermal bones (e.g., Thomson, '75). This group of tissues normally rests on a thicker base of vascular and lamellar bone. The soft tissues are inferred from generally accepted interpretations of thin sections and comparisons with similar structures in living fishes. Such soft tissues consisted of a layer of epithelium covering the entire dermal skeleton, a vascular system, and a pore-canal system that was probably a sensory network. Cosmine's structural features, however, represent only part of the unusual biological role of these tissues. Westoll ('36) was the first to propose that cosmine was resorbed at intervals to accommodate growth of the dermal skeleton. Further research into cosmine growth (Jarvik, '48; Thomson, '75, '77; Gross, '56; Ørvig, '69) has led to the generally accepted hypothesis that one cosmine sheet represents a single depositional event. This notion is in contrast to the growth of the bony portion of the bone or scale (also ganoid scales of actinopterygians), to which increments are added marginally throughout the life of the organism.

The earliest Devonian dipnoans (*Dipnorhynchus, Dipterus, Uranolophus*) had cosmine. Other Devonian genera (e.g., *Fleurantia, Holodipterus*) did not possess cosmine, a characteristic that they share with all post-Devonian dipnoans (Westoll, '49). In contrast to cosmine of porolepiform and osteolepiform rhipidistians, dipnoan cosmine is organized into zones separated by narrow exposed zones of bone called Westoll lines. These lines were first described by Westoll ('36) as regions of resorption that separated older (inner) from younger (outer) areas of cosmine. Ørvig ('69) and Thomson ('75) have since proposed that Westoll lines represent areas where cosmine never formed and that such lines are the boundaries of separate growth episodes. Thus, the lines show evidence of the earlier ontogeny of the structure even though the cosmine itself would have been deposited at a single time interval.

Uranolophus wyomingensis, one of the oldest lungfish from the Lower Devonian, had cosmine on both dermal bones and scales. Resorption was quite extensive in the dermal bones, but not as widespread on the scales (Denison, '68). Several specimens that I examined (e.g., FMNH3792, #3868) had no cosmine or showed patches of cosmine on the

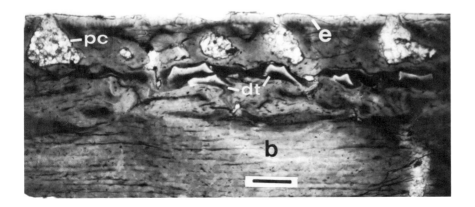

Fig. 1. Photograph of thin ground section, showing cosmine morphology of *Uranolophus wyomingensis* (FMNH 5089) overlying denticles (dt). pc, pore-canals; e, enameloid; b, bone. Scale = 100 μm.

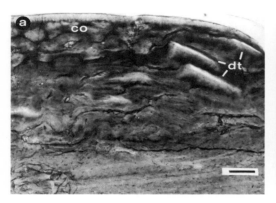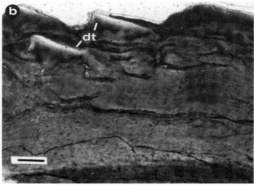

Fig. 2. Thin ground sections of *Uranolophus wyomingensis* scale (FMNH 5096). a) Section in posterior region of scale showing cosmine (co) overlying denticles (dt), some of which have been partly resorbed. Scale = 100 μm. b). Section in anterior region of scale (directly adjacent to 2a) with denticles (dt) at the surface. Scale = 100 μm

skull roof with a gradual transition to a dermal ornament of low ridges or tubercles/denticles. This arrangement indicates that denticle formation was sometimes contemporaneous with cosmine deposition. Such denticles also must have been periodically resorbed, as there is only occasional evidence of their preservation beneath a new layer of cosmine. Denison ('68) did describe a growth series of three opercular bones that showed an ontogenetic transition from small denticles to a stage with only cosmine. Exposed denticles were also fairly common on scales, especially anteriorly (Fig. 2b), and thin sections show that scale denticles were often buried beneath a superficial sheet of cosmine (Fig. 2a) without being resorbed. In *Uranolophus*, cosmine boundaries tended to follow dermal bone sutures (e.g., FMNH 3816, Fig. 3a). Such Westoll lines were also marked by linear arrangements of enlarged pores, opening into the pore-canal system. Westoll lines on scales often show an interesting variation; the lines form where an outer zone of cosmine slightly overlaps an inner area, leaving no bone exposed.

Dipnorhynchus sussmilchi, an Early to Middle Devonian lungfish from Europe, had dermal bones and scales covered with cosmine (Thomson and Compbell, '71). Bones of the skull roof occasionally showed Westoll lines. In the snout region, cosmine merged into an enameloid/dentine layer on the upper lip that differed from cosmine only in lacking the pore-canal system. Similarly, dermal bones of the mandible are cosmine-covered

except for the dentary, which demonstrates a simple enameloid/dentine layer in the region of the lower lip, and the medial surface of the surangular, which exhibits numerous closely packed flattened denticles. The thick rhombic scales are cosmine-covered with Westoll lines, and Thomson and Campbell ('71) detected several generations of denticles overlain by the cosmine layer. Anterior covered areas of the scales are ornamented with flattened denticles reported to be composed of dentine (Thomson and Campbell, '71), but the preservation of the material was not good enough to examine histology in detail.

One of the best-known fossil lungfishes, *Dipterus*, has well-developed cosmine with distinct Westoll lines on the dermal skull and scales (Forster-Cooper, '37; Fig. 3b). Small individuals especially show extensive resorption of cosmine (Westoll, '36; Forster-Cooper, '37); however, White ('65) suggested that cosmine did not appear at all in small forms. Posterior exposed areas of scales bear cosmine, but the anterior regions have only bony ridges. Thin sections of scales reveal patches of cosmine with varying degrees of relief separated by Westoll lines (Gross, '56). Cosmine on scales was apparently deposited repeatedly and over successively larger areas as the fish grew, because cosmine occurs over re-

Fig. 3. a) Dorsal surface view of *Uranolophus wyomingensis* dermal bone (FMNH 497) showing Westoll lines (wl). Scale = 100 μm. b) Dorsal surface view of Dipterus sp. (WU950053) posterior skull roof showing Westoll lines (wl). Scale = 100 μm.

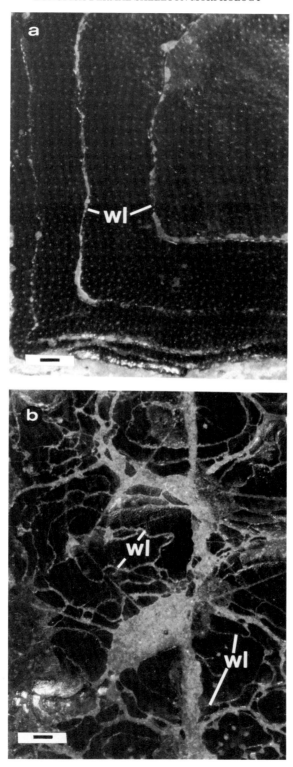

gions that had previously exposed bony ridges (Fig. 4).

Both *Rhinodipterus secans* and *Ganorhyncus splendens* possessed cosmine, the latter known only from several preserved snouts. Thin sections figured by Gross ('56, Figs. 76, 77) show very large pore-canals with enameloid linings, although the dorsal surface of the snout lacked enameloid. Dermal bones and scales of *Rhinodipterus* exhibit Westoll lines of exposed bone and also Westoll lines created by zones of slight overlap between cosmine sheets. Gross ('56) identified some boundaries that represented completed depositional events, but he also recognized areas of cosmine resorption, both within patches of cosmine and along the Westoll line boundaries of cosmine units. Gross ('56, Fig. 62) noted several instances where resorption of one cosmine patch was occurring while another area retained a "finished" boundary (e.g., a cosmine blister) and was apparently quiescent. Similar blisters have been described in several osteolepiforms (Jarvik, '48, '50; Thomson, '75) and have been interpreted by Thomson ('75) as examples of the loss of synchronization that normally characterized cosmine resorption and redeposition. Occasional loss of synchronization could be the result of wound-healing, but when common in some taxa it may reflect a normal developmental phenomenon (e.g., Thomson, '75).

Of the three genera of dipnoans from the Gogo Formation in Western Australia examined histologically by Smith ('77), *Chirodipterus australis* is the only form with cosmine. Miles ('77) originally reported that specimens of *Chirodipterus* show Westoll lines on the skull and only occasional evidence of resorption. Smith's ('77) work indicated that superpositional growth of cosmine occurred, shown by some overlap of cosmine layers. Cosmine extended to the anterior part of the snout in *Chirodipterus*, then changed to a smooth enameloid/dentine layer lacking the pore-canal system on the anterior and ventral snout surface (i.e., the upper lip). This change is marked by a slight ridge and small areas of resorption (Smith, '77).

Holodipterus gogoensis and *Griphognathus whitei* show superpositional growth and resorption of enameloid and dentine denticles, but have no cosmine (Smith, '77). These genera also exhibit a continuous enameloid/dentine cover in the snout region and anterior mandible, but it is not cosmine because it does not contain a pore-canal system. Smith ('77) described the microstructure of this region as dentine, arranged in parallel units perpendicular to the surface, and clearly viewed it as an adaptation to biting with this "lip." She observed openings that she called sensory pores but did not interpret them as pore-canal openings. Smith ('77) also described many areas in the snout region as resorbing surfaces. Schultze's ('69) description of *Griphognathus sculpta* from Bergisch Gladbach made a passing reference to cosmine patches on scales near the ventral mid-

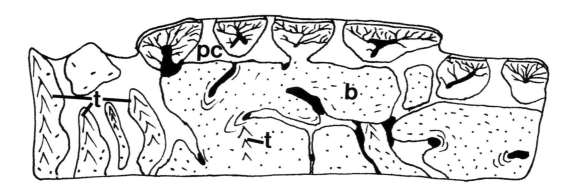

Fig. 4. Diagram of thin section of *Dipterus* sp. scale (after Gross, '56). Cosmine is superficial to bony tubercles (t), which are also exposed anteriorly (left of figure). pc, pore-canal; b,bone.

line, but he described most of the scales as ornamented only with bony ridges.

Finally, Ørvig ('69) identified cosmine on some articulated body scales (gen. et sp. indet.) of Dipnoi from the Devonian of Germany and he used the material to describe the mechanism of cosmine growth. Ørvig ('69) proposed that cosmine growth began on anterior ventral scales and spread posteriorly and dorsally during subsequent depositional events. Successive waves of growth were marked on the earliest-formed scales by concentric zones of cosmine separated by Westoll lines. The latest-formed scales, however, were covered with a single sheet of cosmine, recording only the latest episode of cosmine formation.

Other Devonian dipnoans already show the reduction in the dermal skeleton that is characteristic of all post-Devonian taxa (Westoll, '49). Scales and dermal bones became thinner and came to consist primarily of bone tissue; they certainly do not exhibit cosmine and in many cases they do not even show denticles of enameloid and dentine. The notable exceptions to this trend of reduction in the dermal skeleton are the structurally and ontogenetically complex toothplates of many forms.

In summary, the dermal skeleton of dipnoans has several important features. The primitive condition for lungfishes is the presence of cosmine, although in taxa that also possessed denticles the latter represent an earlier ontogenetic stage. A few taxa possess denticles only, while post-Devonian forms are restricted to bone tissue. In cosmine-bearing dipnoans, the cosmine is arranged differently than in osteolepiforms. It does not cover the sutures between dermal bones; instead the cosmine is divided into narrow concentric zones more or less following the outlines of dermal bones. These Westoll lines are likely to represent areas where cosmine was not laid down. Interestingly, these boundary zones are also sometimes formed by slight overlap of two cosmine layers. Some dipnoans (e.g., *Dipnorhynchus, Chirodipterus, Griphognathus*) exhibit a continuous dentine/enameloid layer on the snout and anterior mandible. However, there is no pore-canal system enclosed and I would not strictly define it as cosmine even though it may undergo periods of resorption, particularly to permit growth of the mosaic of small dermal bones on the snout.

ONTOGENY OF THE DERMAL SKELETON IN LUNGFISHES

Developmental pathways followed to produce the variety of morphologies in the dermal skeleton of fossil dipnoans may be at least partially reconstructed because in many cases the ontogeny of the skeleton is preserved. Because of the considerable variation in cosmine morphology and the occurrence of denticles at some (or all) ontogenetic stages in different forms, it seems appropriate to speculate on developmental pathways that would have produced these morphologies.

A proposal for the development of the skeletal tissues themselves (in both cosmine-bearing and denticle-bearing fishes) is summarized below:

1. Vascular and lamellar bone form in the dermis as the result of differentiation of osteoblasts from neural crest/ectomesenchyme. There has been no conclusive work on the neural crest derivation of dermal bones and scales in fishes. Indirect evidence for such an origin of bones and scales comes from work on the craniofacial skeleton of birds and mammals (LeDouarin, '82; Noden, '83), which has shown direct neural crest contributions to upper and lower jaws, hyoid arch components, and facial parts of the skull. Earlier work on amphibians (particularly Stone, '29; see also Hörstadius, '50) also supports a neural crest origin for cranial dermal bones. Hall ('75, '78, '83) has studied this problem for years and has concluded that developmental pathways leading to the different skeletal tissues have been very conservative through time; therefore, one may assume that skeletal tissues in fishes do have a neural crest origin. This is clearly an area where research is needed on fishes, particularly in view of the many controversies that continue to arise over the relationship between dermal bones and the lateral line system.

2. In a more superficial location (in fact, specifically associated with the epitheliomesenchymal interface), and at a somewhat later time, dentine and enameloid form, independently of the underlying bone tissue. A set of inductive interactions leads to differentiation of odontoblasts from neural crest, formation of dental epithelial cells from undifferentiated epithelium and production of

extracellular matrices. Again, information on the origin of odontoblasts from neural crest comes from studies of amphibians (Chibon, '66; Hörstadius and Sellman, '46; Raven, '35) and is inferred for fishes. There is very little evidence so far of any neural crest contribution to postcranial skeletal structures, except that Raven ('31, '36) has shown neural crest participation in formation of the amphibian dorsal fin. Studies on scale development in fishes are sorely needed to confirm this point.

3. The deeper bone and superficial dentine and enameloid grow together from opposite directions, leaving no evidence of their independent origins. This point will achieve greater importance in the upcoming section on the relationship of cosmine to the dermal skeletons of other fishes. The developmental pathways described above are best known from the study of teeth (e.g., Grady, '70; Kerr, '60; Meinke, '82b); however, they are widely considered to apply to development of other structures (dermal bones, scales) in many groups of fishes (see e.g., Schaeffer, '77; Meinke, 82a).

As described in the preceding section, lungfishes exhibit diverse arrangements of the skeletal tissues that approach conditions found in other bony fishes. These range from single sheets of dentine and enameloid on bone (characteristic of cosmine but also found in the snout of some dipnoans) to denticles of dentine and enameloid, often arranged in several layers. These differences in form may be attributed to differences in the area of epithelio-mesenchymal interacions that produce dental tissues. As yet, the mechanism for controlling the area of tissue interactions is not understood, but Lumsden (personal communication) is approaching this problem through his attempts to understand patterning of mammalian dentitions.

The unique feature of cosmine is the pore-canal network enclosed in the skeletal tissues. Therefore, one may legitimately ask what the developmental relationship is between the pore-canal network and the skeletal tissues and how that relationship can change through ontogeny to produce different morphologies. To this end, I will examine recent ideas on the function and ontogeny of the pore-canal system. Because pore-canal systems are only found in certain fossil groups (osteostracans, acanthodians, rhipidistians, and extinct dipnoans), our understanding and interpretation of these systems

of course depend on comparisons with analogous systems in extant fishes and to this extent, the comments below are rather speculative.

Pore-canal systems are generally assumed to have had a sensory function. Denison ('66) suggested that pore-canals were primitively linked to the lateral line system in fishes, based on physical connections seen in thin sections of *Tremataspis*, a Silurian agnathan (Denison, '47). Denison also believed that the presence of a pore-canal system was primitive for vertebrates, with the lateral line being a specialized derivative. Thomson ('77) assigned an electroreceptive function to the pore-canal network in lobe-finned fishes. He based his hypothesis on the similarities between individual pore openings and ampullary organs in living fishes. In his opinion, however, the pore-canals of osteostracans and acanthodians primarily housed mechanoreceptors and electroreception was only a secondary function if it occurred at all.

There is an increasing body of evidence that most primitive living fishes have ampullary organs that act as electyroreceptors (Bodznick and Northcutt, '81). Bemis and Hetherington ('82) have recently shown that the rostral organ in *Latimeria* is probably electroreceptive as well. A notable feature of these ampullary organs is that they are single structures (except in *Latimeria* where there are three openings to the exterior) and do not communicate directly with one another. Also, they are normally restricted to the head, especially the rostrum. Northcutt (personal communication), however, has found electroreceptors covering the entire body in living lungfishes, though not arrayed as a network. In summary then, there is strong evidence that pore-canal systems and ampullary organs are in some way related and that electroreception forms an important component of their function.

The ontogeny of ampullary organs has apparently not been well investigated, even in elasmobranchs where there is considerable information on their function. Bennett ('71) asserted that all electroreceptors are modified lateral line organs, implying that they are ontogenetically similar as well. Direct links between the lateral line and pore-canal systems have been observed in osteostracans, (Denison, '47), osteolepids, and dipnoans (Gross, '56). One may reasonably assume then that there are underlying developmental similarities among ampullary organs, pore-canal networks, and lateral line canals.

Thomson ('75) proposed a pathway for development of the pore-canal network in the osteolepid *Ectosteorhachis nitidus* that relied on analogies with the broad outlines of lateral line development. The ontogenetic sequence for pore-canal development that Thomson suggested is outlined as follows:

1. Migration of neuromast precursors, either from cranial neural crest or from epidermal placodes, resulting in their uniform distribution over head and trunk.

2. Development of free neuromast organs by the sinking of neuromast precursors, forming shallow depressions in the dermis.

3. Further development of the free neuromasts into flask-shaped structures and formation of lateral canals connecting porecavities. As Thomson ('75, '77) showed, porecanal morphology is similar enough between osteolepids and dipnoans that the same developmental pathways may be presumed for each.

Thomson's overall hypothesis for the ontogeny of cosmine includes an assertion that the pore-canal system and skeletal tissues share a morphogenetic relationship with one another, i.e., that one system has a causal or inductive effect on the positioning and manifestation of the other. Thomson ('75) demonstrated that the presence of the pore-canal system strongly influenced the microstructure of the dentine layer, by specifying directions of movement of odontoblasts (away from pore-canals and toward pulp cavities located equidistant from the pore-canals). In order to produce the observed morphology, he proposed that preodontoblasts would have been arrayed in a single layer immediately below the epithelio-mesenchymal interface, a layer that would have deformed as neuromast organs settled into the dermis (Fig. 5). However, there is very little known about the initial patterning process that results in the localization of dermal structures such as teeth, scales, and dermal bones. Some experimental work with the mouse (Kollar and Lumsden, '79) indicates that the innervation is responsible for patterning the dentition but the nature of this influence is unclear.

The above scenario for the development of cosmine seems reasonable for those fishes that developed cosmine initially in the dermal skeleton. However, in view of the variation in dermal skeleton morphology in lobe-finned fishes generally and dipnoans in particular, it may be more appropriate to consider the pore-canal network and skeletal tissues as systems that could vary independently of one another during ontogeny (see also Meinke, '84). One could say then that, when present, the pore-canal system induces development of skeletal tissues; however, in its absence skeletal tissues still form, induced by another unknown agent. A brief discussion of a related problem, that of lateral line/dermal bone relationships, will further illustrate this point.

The lateral line system was originally believed to induce the development of dermal bones (e.g., Allis, 1898). However, experimental work on trout (Moy-Thomas, '41) showed that bones will still develop even in the absence of their normal lateral line. Also, of course, the existence of dermal bones with no lateral line component (anamestics) shows that the laterosensory system is not essential for dermal bone formation. In addition, the laterosensory system in some groups is so superficial that it does not appear to influence bone development (Devillers, '47).

The ability of the lateral lines and dermal bones to shift their positions relative to one another has created many difficulties in homologizing dermal bones between groups of fishes. Graham-Smith ('78) has explored this problem recently in his study on the formation of dermal bone patterns in crossopterygians and dipnoans. He concluded that the laterosensory and dermal skeletal systems are essentially independent in development and that their influences upon one another may change according to the timing of the systems' development. Although a few experiments have been performed on lateral line development in fishes (Merrilees, '75; Merrilees and Crossman, '73), there is no current work that has clarified this problematic relationship between lateral lines and dermal bones. Pehrson's ('49) study of the dipnoan lateral line system is simply a description of the system and the order in which its parts appear during ontogeny, but it would form a base from which to perform experimental studies on lateral line development in extant lungfishes.

To return to the problem at hand, in my view the best explanation for the variation in dermal skeleton morphology in dipnoans lies in treating the pore-canal network and

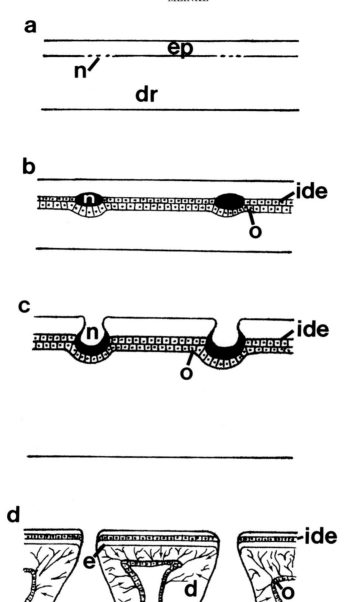

Fig. 5.   Diagram of stages in development of the pore-canal system (after Thomson, '75). a) Neuromast precursors (n) migrate to the epithelio-mesenchymal interface. ep, epidermis; dr, dermis. b) Migration of neural crest to dermis and initial differentiation of epithelial (ide) and odontoblast (o) cells. c) Neuromasts begin to develop and sink into the dermis carrying differentiating odontoblasts with them. d) Pore-cavities containing neuromasts are fully developed and have formed lateral connections with other pore-cavities as dentine (d) and enameloid (e) are deposited.

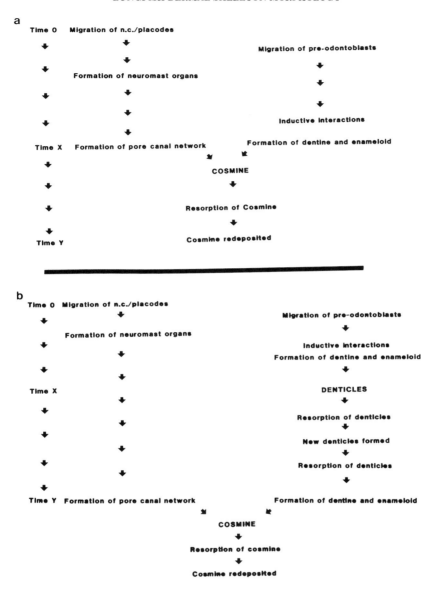

Fig. 6. Hypothesized sequence of developmental events in the dermal skeleton of cosmine-bearing fishes. a) Direct development of cosmine. b) Development of cosmine following initial formation of denticles. If pore-canal development is permanently arrested, only denticles will form (e.g., in some dipnoans and primitive actinopterygians).

skeletal tissues as independently varying systems. Then, changes in timing of hard tissue and pore-canal development would have produced different cosmine morphologies and complexes of tissues that have normally been viewed as entirely unrelated to cosmine (see Fig. 6). Determining the direction of heterochronic change is a difficult problem when one's phylogeny is also uncertain; nevertheless, the presence of cosmine seems to be a primitive character for adult lobe-finned fishes. Figure 6a shows one set of developmental pathways with relative time markers (Time O, X, and Y) in which the development of pore-canals and production of dentine and enameloid occurred at the same time (Time X) and yielded the set of tissues that are conventionally defined as cosmine. Such a sequence of events accounts for the morphology seen in lungfishes such as *Dipterus* and *Chirodipterus*.

In some lungfishes (e.g., *Dipnorhynchus, Uranolophus*), however, there was an ontogenetic shift from an initial covering of dentine and enameloid denticles to cosmine. Figure 6b shows how this might have been accomplished in developmental terms. In this case, at Time X when dentine and enameloid were first being deposited, there must not have been a pore-canal network developed to influence the morphology of the skeletal tissues. I hypothesize that the electroreceptive sensory system was confined to a free neuromast stage, which later (at Time Y) underwent further development to form a pore-canal network. Also at Time Y, a new generation of skeletal tissues was probably forming and their morphology would necessarily have been constrained by the newly developed pore-canal network. Any further generations of skeletal tissues would also have experienced this same morphological constraint. It is possible that a pore-canal network was fully developed but lodged in soft tissues between denticles, but this seems unlikely for several reasons. First, if the pore-canal network were developing simultaneously with differentiating odontoblasts, it is difficult to understand how it did *not* affect the distribution and movement of odontoblasts as suggested by Thomson ('75) for *Ectosteorhachis*. Furthermore, Thomson ('75) thought that the pore-canal network required encasement by hard tissues (at least at key points like the centers of dermal bones and scales) in order for the system to function free from distortion. The free neuromast stage would be a likely stage for arrested development (and not an earlier point) because neuromast precursors would surely migrate to their destinations early in ontogeny. Much later, formation of skeletal tissues would commence if the behavior of epidermal placodes and neural crest cells in skeletal formation of living organisms is representative of processes in these extinct animals (LeLièvre,'78). Further support for the free

neuromast hypothesis comes from living lungfishes, which have electroreceptors covering the whole body. These are arrayed as single shallow structures and are not developed into an integrated pore-canal network (Northcutt, personal communication). Fossil lungfishes that bore only denticles (e.g., *Holodipterus*) would then show permanent arrest of the pore-canal system, perhaps analogous to the condition in living lungfishes. It is also likely then that reduction of the dermal skeleton in some Devonian and all post-Devonian lungfishes was the result of a separate event, inhibition of the tissue interactions necessary to produce dentine and enameloid.

In summary then, there is considerable indirect evidence to suggest that the skeletal tissues and pore-canal network varied independently of one another to produce a wide spectrum of dermal skeleton morphologies in lungfishes. Unfortunately, much of the evidence concerning the patterning and control of developmental pathways leading to the skeletal system comes not from fishes but from birds and mammals (LeLievre, '82). New research is needed on fishes to establish the role of the neural crest in postcranial skeletal development. Nevertheless, Hall ('75, '78) makes a very good case for the essential conservatism of the developmental processes leading to the skeletal tissues, with most evolution occurring by rearrangement of the components. Ontogeny of the pore-canal network has also been the subject of speculation in this paper, based largely on present understanding of lateral line development. There is little doubt that the pore-canal system did represent some kind of sensory apparatus, probably electroreceptive. Evidence for electroreceptive organs in most primitive extant fishes continues to accumulate (e.g., Bodznick and Northcutt, '81); future study of their function and ontogeny will clarify their relationship to the laterosensory system and make comparisons to pore-canals more fruitful.

RELATIONSHIPS TO THE DERMAL SKELETON IN OTHER FISHES

Variations in dermal skeleton morphology in dipnoans share a number of similarities with conditions found in other groups of fishes, especially bony fishes (Table 2). Most importantly, the arrangement and structure of dentine and enameloid denticles in dipnoans are highly reminiscent of those ob-

TABLE 2. Comparison of dermal skeletal characters among teleostomes

Character	Actinopterygian	Osteolepiform	Porolepiform	Coelacanth	Dipnoan	Acanthodian
Pore-canal system	Absent	Present	Present (late ontogeny)	Absent	Present	Present
Denticles	Present	Absent	Present (early ontogeny)	Present	Present (early ontogeny)	Absent
Resorption	Present	Present	Absent	Present	Present	Absent
Concentric growth	Present (ganoid scale)	Absent (except *Megalichthys*)	Absent	Absent	Present (Westoll-lines)	Present

served in coelacanths, actinopterygians, and early ontogeny of porolepiforms (also ?*Poracanthodes* shows early dentine tubercles overlain by a pore-canal system; Gross, '56, Fig. 103A). Such denticles often occur in several layers, showing superpositional growth. Furthermore, denticles in many taxa show evidence of resorption prior to deposition of new tissues, a process that is apparently quite primitive. (Indeed, it is this same process of resorption that is fundamental to the process of tooth replacement in gnathostomes.) Actinopterygians that have ganoid scales are specialized in having suppressed resorption, although both *Polypterus* and *Lepisosteus* apparently retain this ability early in ontogeny until denticles are replaced by sheets of enameloid (Nickerson, 1893). In cosmine-bearing lobe-finned fishes, the resorption process was elaborated in such a way that the entire cosmine unit was removed and then replaced, often as a more extensive sheet to cover a larger fish. This process would have been necessary to allow growth of the fish, but would also have been useful physiologically to mobilize calcium, perhaps for reproduction (Thomson, '75). Presumably, however, the physiological function of resorption was also used by denticle-bearing fishes even though not in the extreme way that cosmine-bearing fishes required.

A second way in which dipnoans resemble actinopterygians is the acquisition of a concentric growth pattern in the cosmine as well as in the underlying bone unit. Such a pattern is shown by the Westoll lines that are arranged concentrically on dermal bones and scales. They represent separation of cosmine into zones and reflect the ontogenetic history of the structure as also discussed by Ørvig ('69) and Thomson ('75). Typically, these lines are areas of naked bone but they may also be formed by zones of slight overlap between cosmine units, which were nevertheless pre-sumably deposited during a single episode of cosmine formation. One type may merge directly with another, indicating that their mode of development is virtually the same. Finally, Westoll lines can appear as linear arrangements of enlarged pore-canal openings although the cosmine unit itself is continuous across this boundary. The appearance of Westoll lines in dipnoan cosmine parallels development of the ganoid scale in actinopterygians and also concentric growth seen in the *Acanthodes* type of acanthodian scale. The difference between them, however, lies in the synchronous resorption of cosmine and subsequent deposition over a larger area once the new episode of bone formation is complete.

The observation that cosmine normally exhibits synchronous resorption and redeposition over a large area, while the underlying bone shows incremental growth, shows that the cosmine and bone units are under differing developmental controls. As discussed above, this independence seems to have been lost in dipnoans because they have developed Westoll lines that do reflect an incremental growth pattern. This characteristic is not unique to fishes with cosmine, however. In many groups of fishes these two components of the dermal skeleton also show considerable independence. Many actinopterygians have enameloid and dentine denticles as superficial ornamentation of the dermal skeleton instead of the derived ganoid scales. In *Polypterus*, such denticles develop after the initial bone rudiment and physically separate from it, after which the two parts grow together and fuse (Meinke, '82a). The development of teeth and the tooth replacement process in gnathostomes is further evidence for the primitive nature of this dermal skeleton characteristic.

It is also pertinent at this point to discuss whether cosmine is homologous in the major groups of fishes that possess it. Different groups of fishes show various combinations of dermal skeletal characters (see Table 2), some of which fall into the category of cosmine. Northcutt and Gans ('83; see also Gans and Northcutt, '83) have argued that electroreception was one of the earliest of the special senses to develop in vertebrates; indeed, the widespread occurrence of ampullary electroreceptors in Recent primitive fishes does suggest that this sensory apparatus is very ancient. The presence of a pore-canal network is well established for cephalaspid osteostracans (Denison, '51). In addition, Denison ('64) proposed that the intercostal grooves of the dermal skeleton of cyathaspid heterostracans housed a pore-canal system as well; thus both groups of fossil agnathans may show this type of sensory system. The structure of the pore-canal network in agnathans varies considerably from that in lobe-finned fishes, causing Thomson ('77) to question its role as an electroreceptive system in the former. However, Bodznick and Northcutt ('81) have recently shown that lampreys have electroreceptive capabilities. The evidence therefore suggests that electroreception using a network of pore-canals is a primitive vertebrate character.

Northcutt and Gans ('83) further suggest (supported by other workers, e.g., Ørvig, '77) that dentine and enameloid were the first skeletal tissues to evolve and that they were originally adaptive in shielding electroreceptors. Their hypothesis involves a functional shift from a filter-feeding larva to predaceous adult vertebrate, for which electroreceptors and the accompanying dermal skeleton would have been highly adaptive. As a primitive feature of adult vertebrates then, the pore-canal component of cosmine would be homologous among all groups. It also seems likely that this system would have followed the same broad outlines in its ontogenetic development (despite resulting differences in morphology and perhaps function) in all groups.

The timing of pore-canal development then would have affected dermal skeleton morphology in other groups of fishes in the same ways as proposed for dipnoans (see Fig. 6). Even if the development of dentine and enameloid were primitively linked to the developing pore-canal system, this close relationship could have been uncoupled ontogentically to yield different dermal skeleton morphologies. For example, a delay in the formation of the pore-canal network (or acceleration of skeletal development) could account for the appearance of dentine tubercles located beneath later-formed cosmine in ?*Poracanthodes* (Gross, '56, Fig. 103A). Complete arrest of pore-canal development (and perhaps restriction of electroreceptors to the rostrum) would have allowed the formation of simple denticles. Interplay between timing and rate of resorption and growth of the skeletal tissues adds a further level of complexity to the ontogenetic processes at work in the dermal skeleton — at one extreme yielding cosmine (resorbed completely and redeposited during a single time interval), to the other of superpositional growth of dentine and enameloid tissues that show little or no reworking through ontogeny.

In essence then, the dermal skeleton of lungfishes is unique in showing a particular combination of processes (Table 2). Likewise, dermal skeletons in other groups of fishes are characterized by other combinations of these same processes. The developmental processes involved are: 1) inductive tissue interactions between epithelium and mesenchyme to yield dentine and enameloid; 2) formation of an electroreceptive pore-canal network from shallow free neuromasts, and 3) resorption and renewed deposition of skeletal tissues, including superpositional growth and concentric growth.

THE DERMAL SKELETON IN LIVING LUNGFISHES (EXCLUDING TOOTHPLATES)

The most notable feature of the dermal skeleton in living lungfishes is its considerable reduction from the primitive dipnoan condition of thick cosmine-covered scales and dermal bones. The dermal bones of the skull are reduced in number and lie rather deep within the dermis. They consist only of bone tissue and show no cosmine or denticles of enameloid and dentine.

Scales are also very reduced, but of the three extant dipnoans, the scales of *Neoceratodus* are the most complex in many respects. According to Kerr ('55), the cycloid scales of *Neoceratodus*, *Protopterus*, and *Lepidosiren* are contained completely within the dermis and have no connection with the epithelium. The scales themselves are very thin and consist of two layers. The upper layer is made up of separate poorly calcified plates ornamented with ridges on the exposed portion of the scale and spinules on the anterior covered portion of the scales. The two types of ornamentation are formed in the same way and one can be regarded as a continuation of the other. The tiny spines do not contain a pulp cavity (also true of these structures in *Protopterus* and *Lepidosiren*, Bemis, '82). They grow upward from the bony plates; thus they cannot be regarded as homologues of denticles in more primitive dipnoan scales. Kerr ('55) proposed that these plates represent highly modified remnants of the vascular bone of cosmoid scales. He further suggests that the inner region of unmineralized collagenous laminae was not equivalent to lamellar bone, but instead represented the addition of dermal connective tissue to the scale itself (a similar process occurs in teleost scales as well).

Many specimens of *Protopterus* exhibit more highly mineralized, irregularly shaped concretions on the scales that are developmentally independent of the underlying plates (Bemis, '82). Bemis ('82) proposed that these concretions represent vestiges of the cosmine found in primitive dipnoans, noting that their calcospheritic structure is similar to dentine, that there is evidence that they contain dentine tubules, and that their ontogenetic independence from the plates is reminiscent of cosmine deposition. In the absence of evidence for such structures on the scales of related fossil dipnoans (e.g., *Ceratodus*), I hesitate to designate these concretions as dentinous remnants of cosmine. Perhaps they are neomorphs equivalent to the bone of attachment that forms the base of denticles and also forms the connection of the cosmine unit to underlying vascular bone. Also, a major feature of dentine is its formation in association with the epithelio-mesenchymal interface following a specific set of inductive tissue–interactions. Nevertheless, these unusual structures do indicate that genetic information to form the more superficial tissues (of which cosmine is one manifestation) is available for re-expression in the living lungfishes.

There are several identifiable developmental changes that account for the reduction of dermal structures in living lungfishes (and also for many of their extinct counterparts). The electroreceptive sensory system is reduced to single structures rather than an interconnecting network. These ampullary electroreceptors are most prominent in the rostrum but may be scattered over the entire body surface (see Northcutt, this volume). Second, there must not be inductive interactions between epithelium and mesenchyme to produce differentiated odontoblasts associated with scale ornamentation; thus, the area of such activity is confined to the oral cavity and production of the toothplates. Further work on the scales of *Protopterus* may necessitate modification of the latter statement. Finally, the activity of osteoblasts is quite reduced so that they produce very little mineral as part of the bone's extracellular matrix. Bemis ('84) has examined numerous characters of lungfishes and concluded that paedomorphosis has played a significant role in dipnoan evolution. Certainly the characters discussed in the present contribution show that heterochronic changes in the dipnoan dermal skeleton have occurred repeatedly and that results of such changes have yielded a dermal skeleton that is juvenilized with respect to the primitive condition. In detailing the types of heterochronic changes that have taken place within dipnoan phylogeny, it is also evident that several distinct developmental pathways have been altered rather than a single morphogenetic event.

SUMMARY

The primitive condition of the dipnoan dermal skeleton is the presence of cosmine, which has unusual structural features and biological properties that easily distinguish it from other forms of the dermal skeleton in fishes. The only unique feature of cosmine is the sensory pore-canal network. However, there is increasing evidence that this type of sensory system was a primitive feature of vertebrates; thus, its simple presence will be useless as a synapomorphy for relating groups of fishes. Perhaps, however, the differences in pore-canal morphology between rhipidistians/dipnoans and agnathans/acanthodians (which may also reflect functional differences, e.g., Thomson, '77) will still hold systematic significance. It is important to be able to make this distinction rather than simply noting presence or absence of cosmine.

Another unusual feature of cosmine is the extreme development of mechanisms of resorption and redeposition of skeletal issues so that in many cosmine-bearing fishes only a single layer of dentine/enameloid tissues persists through the ontogeny of the individual. The process of resorption is widespread in primitive fishes, although it rarely achieves the synchronization found in many cosmine-bearing fishes. Many fossil dipnoans show a dermal skeleton with discrete enameloid/dentine denticles or such denticles overlain by cosmine. I have proposed that these conditions arise from a decoupling of pore-canal from skeletal development so that the pore-canal system is delayed (relatively) or permanently arrested at the free neuromast stage. Skeletal tissue morphology and distribution are thus unaffected and the appearance of the dermal skeleton closely resembles that in actinopterygians and coelacanths. Differences in the distribution of skeletal tissues through ontogeny and phylogeny in all of these groups are likely to have been dependent on changes in the area of tissue interactions between epithelium and mesenchyme. Further reductions in skeletal development in post-Devonian to Recent lungfishes would have resulted from turning off such interactions, but the neomorph concretions on scales of *Protopterus* and complex toothplates of all living genera show that genetic information to form such tissues is retained.

ACKNOWLEDGMENTS

This paper was originally presented at the 1984 American Society of Zoologists, Symposium on the Morphology and Evolution of Lungfishes. I thank William Bemis for organizing the symposium and for inviting me to participate. I thank two anonymous reviewers for suggesting improvements in the manuscript.

LITERATURE CITED

Allis, A.P. (1898) On the morphology of certain bones of the cheek and snout of *Amia calva*. J. Morphol. *14*:425–466.

Bemis, W.E. (1982) Studies on the functional and evolutionary morphology of lepidosirenid lungfish. Ph.D. Dissertation, University of California, Berkeley.

Bemis, W.E. (1984) Paedomorphosis and the evolution of the Dipnoi. Paleobiology *10*:293–307.

Bemis, W.E., and T.E. Hetherington (1982) The rostral organ of *Latimeria chalumnae*: Morphological evidence of an electroreceptive function. Copeia *1982*:467–471.

Bennett, M.V.L. (1971) Electroreception. In W.S. Hoar and D.J. Randall (eds): Fish Physiology, Vol. 5. New York: Elsevier, pp. 493–574.

Bodznick, D., and R.G. Norethcutt (1981) Electroreception in lampreys: Evidence that the earliest vertebrates were electroreceptive. Science *212*:465–467.

Chibon, P. (1966) Analyse expérimentale de la regionalisation et des capacités morphogénétiques de la crête neural chez l' Amphibien Urodéle *Pleurodeles waltii* Michah. Mem. Soc. Fr. Zool. *36*:1–107.

Dension, R.H. (1947) The exoskeleton of *Tremataspis*. Am. J. Sci. *245*:337–365.

Denison, R.H. (1951) Evolution and classification of the Osteostraci. The exoskeleton of early Osteostraci. Fieldiana Geol. *11*:157–218.

Denison, R.H. (1964) The Cyathaspidae: A family of Silurian and Devonian jawless vertebrates. Fieldiana Geol. *13*:309–473.

Denison, R.H. (1966) The origin of the lateral-line sensory system. Am. Sool. *6*:369–370.

Denison, R.H. (1968) Early Devonian lungfishes from Wyoming, Utah, and Idaho. Fieldiana Geol. *17*:353–413.

Devillers, C. (1947) Recherches sur le crâne dermique des téléostéens. Annl. Palaont. *33*:1–94.

Forster-Cooper, C. (1937) The Middle Devonian fish fauna of Achanarras. Trans. R. Soc. Edinburgh *59*:223–239.

Gans, C., and R.G. Northcutt (1983) Neural crest and the origin of vertebrates: A new head. Science *220*:268–274.

Grady, J.E. (1970) Tooth development in sharks. Arch. Oral Biol. *15*:613–619.

Graham-Smith, W. (1978) On the lateral lines and dermal bones in the parietal region of some crossopterygian and dipnoan fishes. Phil. Trans. R. Soc. Lond. (B) *282*:1–39.

Gross, W. (1956) Über Crossopterygier und Dipnoer aus dem baltischen Oberdevon in Zusammenhang einer vergleichenden Untersuchung des Porenkanalsystems paläozoischer Agnathen und Fische. K. Svenska Vetensk. Handl. *5*:1–140.

Hall, B.K. (1975) Evolutionary consequences of skeletal development. Am. Zool. *15*:329–350.

Hall, B.K. (1978) Developmental and Cellular Skeletal Biology. New York: Academic Press.

Hall, B.K. (1983) Epigenetic control in development and evolution. In B.C. Goodwin (ed): Development and Evolution. Cambridge: Cambridge University Press, pp. 353–379.

.Hörstadius, S. (1950) The Neural Crest: Its Properties and Derivatives in the Light of Experimental Research. London: Oxford University Press.

Hörstadius, S., and S. Sellman (1946) Experimentelle Untersuchungen über die Determination des knorpeligen Kopfskeletts bei Urodelen. Nova Acta Soc. Scient. Uppsaliensis, Ser. 4, *13*:1–170.

Jarvik, E. (1948) On the morphology and taxonomy of the Middle Devonian osteolepid fishes of Scotland. K. Svenska Vetensk. Handl. *25*:1–301.

Jarvik, E. (1950) Middle Devonian vertebrates from Canning Land and Wegeners Halvo (East Greenland). 2. Crossopterygii. Meddelser øm Gronland *96*:1–132.

Kerr, T. (1955) The scales of modern lungfish. Proc. Zool. Soc. Lond. *125*:335–345.

Kerr, T. (1960) Development and structure of some actinopterygian and urodele teeth. Proc. Zool. Soc. Lond. *133*:401–422.

Kollar, E.J., and A.G. Lumsden (1979) Tooth morphogenesis: The role of the innervation during induction and pattern formation. J. Biol. Bucc. *7*:49–60.

LeLièvre, C.S. (1978) Participation of neural crest derived cells in the genesis of the skull in birds. J. Embryol. Exp. Morphol. *66*:175–190.

Maderson, P.F.A. (1975) Embryonic tissue interactions as the basis for morphological change in evolution. Am. Zool. *15*:315–328.

Meinke, D.K. (1982a) A light and scanning electron microscope study of microstructure, growth, and development of the dermal skeleton of *Polypterus* (Pisces, Actinopterygii). J. Zool. (Lond.) *197*:355–382.

Meinke, D.K. (1982b) A histological and histochemical study of developing teeth in *Polypterus* (Pisces, Actinopterygii). Arch. Oral Biol. *27*:197–206.

Meinke, D.K. (1984) A review of cosmine: Its structure, development, and relationship to other forms of the dermal skeleton in osteichthyans. J. Vert. Paleontol *4*:457–470.

Merrilees, M.J. (1975) Tissue interaction: Morphogenesis of the lateral-line system and labyrinth of vertebrates. J. Exp. Zool. *192:*113–118.

Merrilees, M.J., and E.J. Crossman (1973) Surface pits in the family Esocidae. II. Epidermal dermal interaction and evidence of aplasia of the lateral line sensory system. J. Morphol. *144:*321–332.

Miles, R.S. (1977) Dipnoan (lungfish) skulls and the relationships of the group: A study based on new species from the Devonian of Autralia. Zool. J. Linn. Soc. Lond. *61:*1–328.

Moy-Thomas, J.A. (1941) Development of the frontal bones of the trout. Nature *147:*681–682.

Nickerson, W.S. (1893) Development of the scales of *Lepisosteus.* Bull. Mus. Comp. Zool. *24:*115–139.

Noden, D.M. (1983) The role of the neural crest in patterning of avian cranial skeletal, connective, and muscle tissues. Dev. Biol. *96:*144–165.

Northcutt, R.G., and C. Gans (1983) The genesis of neural crest and epidermal placodes: Reinterpretation of vertebrate origins. Q. Rev. Biol. *58:*1–28.

Ørvig, T. (1967) Phylogeny of tooth tissues: Evolution of some calcified tissues in early vertebrates. In A.E.W. Miles (ed): Structural and Chemical Organization of Teeth, Vol. 1. New York: Academic Press, pp. 45–110.

Ørvig, T. (1969) Cosmine and cosmine growth. Lethaia *2:*241–260.

Ørvig, T. (1976) Palaeohistological notes 4: The interpretation of osteodentine, with remarks on the dentition in the Devonian dipnoan *Griphognathus.* Zool Scr. *5:*79–96.

Ørvig, T. (1977) A survey of odotodes ("dermal teeth") from developmental, structural, functional, and phyletic points of view. In S.M. Andrews, R.S. Miles, and A.D. Walker (eds): Problems in Vertebrate Exolution. London: Academic Press, pp. 53–76.

Pehrson, T. (1949) The ontogeny of the lateral line system of the head of dipnoans. Acta Zool. Scand. *30:*153–182.

Raven, C.P. (1931) Zur Entwicklung der Ganglienleiste. I. Die Kinematik der Ganglienleistenentwicklung bei den Urodelen. W. Roux Arch. Entw.-mech. Org. *125:*210–292.

Raven, C.P. (1935) Zur Entwicklung der Ganglienleiste. IV. Untersuchungen über Zeitpunkt und Verlauf der "materiellen Determination" des präsumptiven Kopfganglienleistenmaterials der Urodelen. W. Roux, Arch. Entw.-mech. Org. *132:*509–575.

Raven, C.P. (1936) Zur Entwicklung der Ganglienleiste. V. Über die Differenzierung des Rumpfganglienleisten materials. W. Roux Arch. Entw.-mech. Org. *134:*122–145.

Rosen, D.E., P.L. Forey, B.G. Gardiner, and C. Patterson (1981) Lungfishes, tetrapods, paleontology, and plesiomorphy. Bull. Am. Mus. Nat. Hist. *167:*159–276.

Schaeffer, B. (1977) The dermal skeleton in fishes. In S.M. Andrews, R.S. Miles, and A.G. Walker (eds): Problems in Vertebrate Evolution. London: Academic Press, pp. 25–52.

Schultze, H.-P. (1969) *Griphognathus* Gross, ein langschnauziger Dipnoer aus dem Überdevon von Bergisch-Gladbach (Rheinisches Schiefergebirge) und von Littland. Geol. Paleontol. (Marburg) *3:*21–79.

Shellis, R.P., and A.E.W. Miles (1974) Autoradiographic study of the formation of enameloid and dentine matrices in teleost fishes using tritiated amino acids. Proc. R. Soc. Lond. (B) *185:*51–72.

Smith, M.M. (1977) The microstructure of the dentition and dermal ornament of three dipnoans from the Devonian of Western Australia: A contribution towards dipnoan interrelations and morphogenesis, growth, and adaptation of the skeletal tissues. Phil. Trans. R. Soc. Lond. (B) *281:*29–72.

Smith, M.M. (1979) Structure and histogenesis of toothplates in *Sagenodus inaequalis* Owen considered in relation to the phylogeny of post-Dovonian dipnoans. Proc. R. Soc. Lond. (B) *204:*15–39.

Smith, M.M. (1984) Petrodentine in extant and fossil dipnoan dentitions: Microstructure, histogenesis and growth. Proc. Linn. Soc. N.S.W. *107:*367–407.

Stone, L.S. (1929) Experiments showing the role of migrating neural crest (mesectoderm) in the formation of head skeleton and loose connective tissue in *Rana palustria.* W. Roux Arch. Entw.-mech. Org. *118:*40–77.

Thomson, K.S. (1975) On the biology of cosmine. Peabody Mus. Nat. His. Bull. *40:*1–59.

Thomson, K.S. (1977) On the individual history of cosmine and possible electroreceptive function of the porecanal system in fossil fishes. In S.M. Andrews, R.S. Miles, and A.D. Walker (eds): Problems in Vertebrate Evolution. London: Academic Press, pp. 247–270.

Thomson, K.S., and K.S.W. Campbell (1971) The structure and relationships of the primitive dipnoan lungfish-*Dipnorhynchus sussmilchi* (Etheridge). Peabody Mus. Nat. Hist. Bull. *38:*1–109.

Westoll, T.S. (1936) On the structure of the dermal ethmoid shield of *Osteolepis.* Geol. Mag. *73:*157–171.

Westoll, T.S. (1949) On the evolution of the Dipnoi. In G.L. Jepsen, E. Mayr, and G.G Simpson (eds): Genetics, Palaeontology and Evolution. Princeton, University Press, pp. 121–184.

White, E.I. (1965) The head of *Dipterus valenciennesi* Sedgwick and Murchison. Bull. Br. Mus. Nat. Hist. (Geol.) *11:*1–45.

JOURNAL OF MORPHOLOGY SUPPLEMENT 1:151–162 (1986)

Lungfish: Phylogeny and Parsimony

CHARLES R. MARSHALL
Department of Zoology, Australian National University, Canberra, A.C.T. 2601, Australia

ABSTRACT   Miles ('77) has produced the only comprehensive cladistic analysis of the Dipnoi. His phylogeny involves both definitely and uncertainly placed genera. An analysis of the data for the definitely placed genera, using a Wagner routine, showed that his phylogeny is similar to two of eight equally parsimonious cladograms. Analysis of the data for all the genera of Miles's phylogeny produced sixteen equally parsimonious cladograms. They have a wide range of topologies, none of which corresponds to Miles's phylogeny. It is shown that Miles employed some character weighting to obtain his phylogeny. A cladogram is presented based on Campbell and Barwick's ('83, '84) study of early dipnoan dentitions. The phylogenetic conclusions drawn from Campbell and Barwick's work are dependent on stratigraphic and functional data. The resulting cladogram differs from all the trees produced by the re-analysis of Miles's complete phylogeny; it is less parsimonious and requires that the type of dentition consisting of a shagreen of small denticles that are shed during growth is an advanced dipnoan feature rather than a primitive one. Campbell and Barwick's ('83) phylogeny is favored since, for theoretical and practical reasons, parsimony is not a good criterion for choosing between the possible phylogenies for dipnoans. Campbell and Barwick's ('83) phylogenetic conclusions are based on a richer empirical base and are more consistent with observed functional trends. A new phylogeny of the Dipnoi is presented, with the basic structure being defined by the conclusions drawn from Campbell and Barwick's ('83) work, namely, that patterns of dentition characterized by expanding growth and fusion of denticles or of the development of organized tooth plates each arose only once in evolution. The addition of Miles's ('77) characters, using the principle of parsimony, gives the fine structure of the phylogeny.

The Dipnoi are thought to be a monophyletic group of fishes. They first appeared in the geologic record in the Early Devonian and persist to the present (Moy-Thomas and Miles, '71). Many Paleozoic genera are known from relatively complete cranial material. About 50 extinct genera are represented by some 120 species, although some genera and species may not be valid. Three extant genera contain six species. A summary of the extant species and fossil record of the Dipnoi can be found in Marshall (this volume).

There are only three reasonably comprehensive studies of relationships within the Dipnoi, those of Bertmar ('68), Thomson and Campbell ('71), and Miles ('77). Of these, the paper by Miles provides the only cladistic analysis and the only clear statements about

the supposed relationships of the dipnoans. Consequently it is the best phylogeny to date. In reality it presents a "levels of organization" or "grade" diagram more than a phylogeny (Miles, '77:307). Many of the genera are uncertainly placed (see Fig. 1), and Miles intended it as a "first step towards a more thoroughgoing phylogeny of the dipnoans" ('77:307). He used the principle of parsimony to establish the phylogeny, although he does not indicate how he arrived at the topology shown in Figure 1. In the first section of this paper, I provide a quantitative re-analysis of the data Miles used to construct his phylo-

Mr. Marshall's present address is Department of Geophysical Sciences, University of Chicago, 5734 S. Ellis Avenue, Chicago, Illinois 60637.

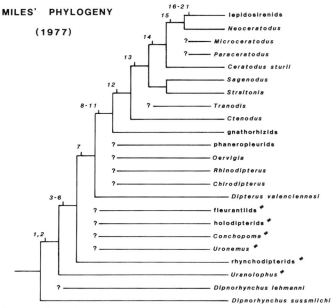

Fig. 1. Miles's phylogeny of the dipnoans (redrawn from Miles, '77:306). The numbers indicate the acquisition of derived characteristics and are explained in Table 1. Genera with denticulated dentitions are marked with the symbol "#." In the phylogeny, lepidosirenids = *Lepidosiren* and *Protopterus*; gnathorhizids = *Gnathorhiza* and *Monongahela*; phaneropleurids = *Phaneropleuron*, *Scaumenacia* and *Pentlandia*; fleurantiids = *Fleurantia* and *Jarvikia*; holodipterids = *Holodipterus* and *Devonosteus*; rhynchodipterids = *Rhynchodipterus*, *Soederberghia* and *Griphognathus*.

geny. A number of equally parsimonious trees were produced.

Campbell and Barwick ('83) presented new phylogenetic hypotheses of the relationships among dipnoans based on the study of their dentitions. Their hypotheses were not presented in the form of a cladogram. Stratigraphic data and functional inferences are crucial to their arguments. In the second section of this paper I summarize the evidence Campbell and Barwick ('83) use for their arguments and present their conclusions in the form of a cladogram.

The cladogram derived from Campbell and Barwick's ('83) data has many unparsimonious features and differs considerably from any of the cladograms produced by the re-analysis of Miles's ('77) data. In the final section of the paper I consider the unparsimonious consequences resulting from Campbell and Barwick's phylogenetic conclusions and attempt to weigh these against the functional and stratigraphic evidence supporting their conclusions. I conclude that the functional and stratigraphic data are stronger than the requirements of parsimony (the

simple counting of character changes required by different cladograms). A new phylogeny of the Dipnoi is presented with the basic structure being defined by the conclusions of Campbell and Barwick's work ('83, '84), namely, 1) that a dentition formed by the addition to the margins of a growth area and subsequent thickening is primitive for the Dipnoi and only arose once, and 2) that dentitions formed by denticles and ridges that grow by periodic resorption and replacement are characteristic of another natural group. The addition of some of Miles's characters, using the principle of parsimony, gives the fine structure of the phylogeny.

RE-ANALYSIS OF MILES'S DATA

Miles's ('77) phylogeny is reproduced in Figure 1. Note that many of the genera are given only tentative positions. The numbers indicate the acquisition of derived characters, which are listed in Table 1. The last three characters were not placed on the phylogeny by Miles, but were discussed by him when he considered the unparsimonious features of his phylogeny (Miles, '77:307–308).

TABLE 1. Key to derived characters used in
phylogenetic analysis[1]

1. The pineal foramen is closed.
2. D is a single medial bone.
3. K is situated more anteriorly than X.
4. An anastomosis is developed between the supraorbital and infraorbital sensory lines.
5. A and B are in contact and they separate the I's.
6. The parasphenoid has a posterior stalk.
7. Highly organized entopterygoid and prearticular tooth-plates are present.
8. A is not present as an independent bone.
9. The supraoccipital commisure passes through B.
10. Z is integrated in the skull roof.
11. The entopterygoid and prearticular tooth-plates have large pulp-chambers.
12. The buccal face of the parasphenoid is formed as a raised lozenge, and this bone has an anterior process.
13. C is not present as an independent bone.
14. An ascending process of the entopterygoid articulates with the skull-roof.
15. D is not present as an independent bone.
16. B is situated below the adductor muscles and has spread over the dorsal face of the neurocranium.
17. The posterior part of the internasal septum is reduced, in association with the development of large entopterygoid tooth-plates.
18. The entopterygoid and prearticular tooth-plates have columns of petrodentine surrounded by trabecular dentine.
19. The subnasal cartilage is attached to the nasal capsule.
20. The vomer is reduced to a small, conical tooth.
21. The outer dermal series of the lower jaw is reduced to a single bone (angular) and there is extensive development of the meckelian cartilage on the lateral and mesial face of the prearticular.
22. Cosmine is largely absent from the dermal bones.
23. The buccohypophysial canal is closed.
24. The vomers are reduced to a single median bone.

[1]Based on Miles ('77).

Presumably he omitted them because he believed that these characters would be highly homoplasious in any phylogenetic scheme. The main analytical tool used by Miles in constructing the phylogeny was parsimony (Miles, '77:300). However, he also employed some character weighting, which influenced his results, as will be shown below.

Techniques of analysis

The re-analysis was done in two parts. The first used only the data for the genera that are definitely linked in Miles's phylogeny. These data will be referred to as the Small Data Set. The second stage of the analysis includes all genera studied by Miles; this set will be referred to as the Complete Data Set. The first 23 characters listed in Table 1 were used for both analyses. The last character, the status of the vomer, was omitted due to insufficient information for most genera. The

Small Data Set is given in Table 2(a), the Complete Data Set by Table 2(a+b). Where, due to poor preservation, a character could not be observed for a genus, the character was coded on the basis of that genus' position on Miles's phylogeny. For example, of those genera for which character 7 could not be observed, those lying above *Dipterus* in Figure 1 were assigned a "1" and those below a "0" for that character. In "reconstructing" incompletely preserved genera this way, the possibility of reproducing Miles's phylogeny was maximized. "Reconstruction" was necessary because the computer routines used to search for the most parsimonious tree did not accept missing values. The coding for *Dipnorhynchus lehmanni* was based on *Speonesydrion*, recently described from well-preserved material and considered to be congeneric with *Dipnorhynchus lehmanni* (Campbell and Barwick, '83, '84).

Both data sets were analyzed by using a Wagner routine (Farris algorithm, written by Don Colless). The routine starts its search for shortest trees with a pair of genera. In some cases the trees found depend on the particular pair selected. To avoid this problem the routine was run once for each of all the possible starting pairs of genera. The shortest trees produced were then subjected to a global pair-wise branch swapping routine to search for further shortest trees (written by Colless). A number of shortest trees were generated. Consensus trees, which provide summaries of the shortest trees, were produced by using an algorithm written by Swofford and modified by Colless. All computer programs were run on a PDP 11 computer by Don Colless. In each analysis I followed Miles ('77) in taking *Dipnorhynchus sussmilchi* as the outgroup.

The Small Data Set

Eight different shortest trees, each 26 steps long, were produced. The strict consensus tree (SCT), a summary of the monophyletic groups held in common by all the shortest trees, is given in Figure 2A. It is identical with the majority consensus tree (for information on majority consensus trees, see Margush and McMorris, '81; Rohlf, '82). Miles's phylogeny, with the uncertainly placed genera removed for ease of comparison, is shown in Figure 2B and is fully consistent with the SCT. Nodes that lead to three or more branches in Figure 2A indicate places of difference between the eight trees. There are

TABLE 2. Small (a) and Complete (a+b) Data Sets[1]

Lungfish	Character no.																						
	1	2	3	4	5	6	7	8	9	10	11	12	13	14	15	16	17	18	19	20	21	22	23
(a)																							
Ceratodus sturii	1	1	1	1	1	1	1	1	1	1	1	0	1	1	0	0	0	0	0	0	0	1	1
Ctenodus	1	1	1	1	1	1	1	1	1	1	1	1	1	0	0	0	0	0	0	0	0	1	1
Dipnorhynchus	0	0	0	0	0	0	0	0	0	0	0	0	0	0	0	0	0	0	0	0	0	0	0
Dipterus valenciennesi	1	1	1	1	1	1	1	0	0	0	0	0	0	0	0	0	0	0	0	0	0	0	0
gnathorhizids	1	1	1	1	1	1	1	1	1	1	1	0	0	0	0	0	0	0	0	0	0	1	1
lepidosirenids	1	1	1	1	1	1	1	1	1	1	1	0	1	1	1	1	1	1	1	1	1	1	1
Neoceratodus	1	1	1	1	1	1	1	1	1	1	1	0	1	1	1	0	0	0	0	0	0	1	1
rhynchodipterids	1	1	1	1	1	1	0	0	0	0	0	0	0	0	0	0	0	0	0	0	0	1	1
Sagenodus	1	1	1	1	1	1	1	1	1	1	1	1	1	0	0	0	0	0	0	0	0	1	1
Straitonia	1	1	1	1	1	1	1	1	1	1	1	0	1	0	0	0	0	0	0	0	0	1	1
Uranolophus	1	1	0	0	0	0	0	0	0	0	0	0	0	0	0	0	0	0	0	0	0	0	1
(b)																							
Chirodipterus	1	1	1	1	1	1	1	0	0	0	0	0	0	0	0	0	0	0	0	0	0	0	1
Conchopoma	1	1	1	1	1	1	0	0	0	1	0	0	0	0	0	0	0	0	0	0	0	1	1
Fleurantia	1	1	1	1	1	1	0	0	0	0	0	0	0	0	0	0	0	0	0	0	0	1	1
holodipterids	1	1	1	1	1	1	0	0	0	0	0	0	0	0	0	0	0	0	0	0	0	1	1
Jarvikia	1	1	1	1	1	1	0	0	1	0	0	0	0	0	0	0	0	0	0	0	0	1	1
Microceratodus	1	1	1	1	1	1	1	1	1	1	1	0	1	1	0	0	0	0	0	0	0	1	1
Oervigia	1	1	1	1	1	1	1	0	0	0	0	0	0	0	0	0	0	0	0	0	0	1	1
Paraceratodus	1	1	1	1	1	1	1	1	1	1	1	0	1	1	0	0	0	0	0	0	0	1	1
phaneropleurids	1	1	1	1	1	1	1	0	0	0	0	0	0	0	0	0	0	0	0	0	0	1	1
Rhinodipterus	1	1	1	1	1	1	1	0	0	0	0	0	0	0	0	0	0	0	0	0	0	0	1
Speonesydrion	0	0	0	0	0	0	0	0	0	0	0	0	0	0	0	0	0	0	0	0	0	0	0
Tranodis	1	1	1	1	1	1	1	1	1	1	1	0	0	0	0	0	0	0	0	0	0	1	1
Uronemus	1	1	1	1	1	1	0	1	1	1	0	0	0	0	0	0	0	0	0	0	0	1	1

[1]Presence of a derived character designated by "1", or of a presumably primitive character by "0".

two such nodes, labelled I and II, in Figure 2A. The low resolution at node I is accounted for by characters 7 (organized tooth plates present) and 22 (the loss of cosmine); either one or the other of these characters must be homoplasious. Figure 3 shows the effect each homoplasious character has on the topology of the SCT. The topologies shown in Figure 3 are not dependent on whether the homoplasious character underwent a reversal or was acquired twice. The low resolution at node II is due to either a reversal or independent acquisition of character 12 (special parasphenoid characteristics of *Ctenodus* and *Sagenodus*), or to a reversal or independent acquisition of character 13 (loss of C as an independent bone). The effect each of these four possibilities has on the topology of the SCT is shown in Figure 4. The two-fold topological variation of Figure 3 combined with the four-fold variation of Figure 4 accounts for the eight shortest trees. For all characters, except character 23 (closure of the buccohypophysial canal), the "0" state corresponds with the supposed primitive state. Character 23 may have either the "0" or "1" state as the primitive condition. Outgroup comparison suggests that the "0" state is primitive, and this is the way the character has been marked in Figure 3.

The shortest trees with node I of the SCT resolved as in Figure 3A, and node II resolved as Figure 4A and 4B, are the closest of the eight trees to Miles's phylogeny. Both differ in only one minor feature. On the tree with node II resolved as in Figure 4A, *Sagenodus* and *Straitonia* are resolved; these genera are unresolved on Figure 2B despite appearances to the contrary. Although Miles placed *Sagenodus* and *Straitonia* on a separate branch, he gave no character for the clade. On the tree with node II resolved as in Figure 4B the gnathorhizids and *Ctenodus* are not resolved; the gnathorhizids appear before *Ctenodus* on Figure 2B.

The choice of Figure 3A for the resolution of node I amounts to the weighting of a homoplasious loss of cosmine (and the definition of a monophyletic group for all tooth-plate-bearing forms) over a homoplasious evolution of tooth plates (and the definition of a monophyletic group for genera without cosmine). Miles ignored character 22 (loss of cosmine) and by weighting the characters in this way precluded the possibility of his parsimony analysis producing trees with a topology seen in Figure 3B. Limiting the analysis to the characters Miles used in his analysis (the first 21 characters in Table 1) results in disappearance of the two-fold variation at

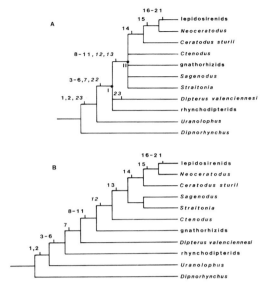

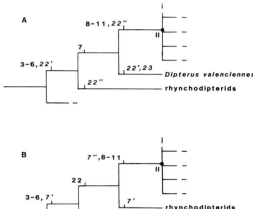

Fig. 2. A) Strict consensus tree derived from the parsimony analysis of the Small Data Set (data for the genera definitely linked in Miles's, '77, phylogeny). The numbers correspond to characters listed in Table 1. Characters in italics (7, 12, 13, 22, 23) are homoplasious. The incomplete resolution of Node I involves characters 7 and 22, and is fully resolved in Figure 3A and 3B. Characters 12 and 13 are involved in the incomplete resolution of Node II, which is fully resolved in Figure 4A–D. B) Miles's phylogeny with the uncertainly-placed genera omitted. It is fully consistent with Figure 2A.

Fig. 3. The two possible resolutions of Node I of the strict consensus tree resulting from the parsimony analysis of the Small Data Set (Fig. 2). Italicized characters (7, 22, 23) are homoplasious. A) The resolution of the node if character 22 were homoplasious, and the character either underwent a reversal (22') or evolved twice (22''). B) The resolution if character 7 were homoplasious, and the character either underwent a reversal (7'), or evolved twice (7'').

node I, but the four-fold variation at node II is still produced. None of the four topologies corresponds exactly to Miles's ('77) phylogeny. The two trees that his phylogeny most closely resembles involve a homoplasious evolution of character 12 (node II resolved as in Figure 4A and 4B). In favoring these two trees over those with node II resolved as in Figure 4C and 4D (character 13 homoplasious), Miles has weighted character 13 over character 12.

Miles has employed parsimony and character weighting, both in the selection of characters and choosing between character conflicts, to construct his phylogeny. Thus it is over-resolved. Using the principle of parsimony for choosing between character conflicts, the SCT (Fig. 2A), with two nodes of low resolution, yields the best phylogeny of the Dipnoi based on the Small Data Set.

The Complete Data Set

Sixteen different shortest trees, each of length 28, were produced by the computer analysis. The strict consensus tree, which has

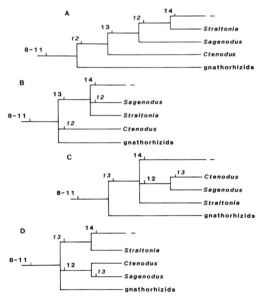

Fig. 4. Four possible resolutions of Node II of the strict consensus trees resulting from the analyses of the Small (Fig. 2) and Complete (Fig. 5) Data Sets. Italicized characters (12, 13) are homoplasious. A) The resolution of the node if character 12 underwent a reversal. B) The resolution if character 12 evolved twice. C) The resolution if character 13 underwent a reversal. D) The resolution if character 13 evolved twice.

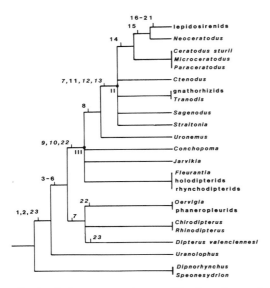

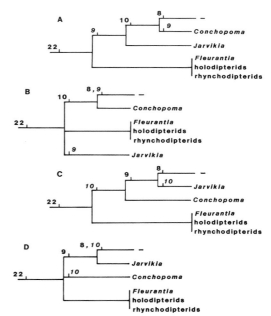

Fig. 5. Strict consensus tree resulting from the parsimony analysis of the Complete Data Set (data for all the genera of Miles's , '77, phylogeny). The numbers correspond to the derived characters listed in Table 1. Characters in italics (7, 9, 10, 12, 13, 22, 23) are homoplasious. The incomplete resolution of Node III involves characters 9 and 10 and is fully resolved in Figure 6A–D. Characters 12 and 13 are involved in the incomplete resolution of Node II, which is fully resolved in Figure 4A–D.

Fig. 6. Four possible resolutions of Node III of the strict consensus tree resulting from the parsimony analysis of the Complete Data Set (Fig. 5). Italicized characters (9, 10) are homoplasious. A) The resolution of the node if character 9 underwent a reversal. B) The resolution if character 9 evolved twice. C) The resolution if character 10 underwent a reversal. D) The resolution if character 10 evolved twice.

the same topology as the majority consensus tree, is given in Figure 5. Of particular interest is the fact that both characters 7 (tooth plates present) and 22 (loss of cosmine) are homoplasious on all the shortest trees. This is in contrast to the result with the Small Data Set, where either one or the other was homoplasious. The primitive character states are the same as in the analysis of the Small Data Set.

The SCT for the Complete Data Set has two nodes, labelled II and III, of low resolution. The low resolution at node II is due to the same four-fold variation involving characters 12 and 13 as discussed for node II of the SCT for the Small Data Set (Fig. 3) and is resolved into the topologies shown in Figure 4. The low resolution at node III is due either to a reversal or independent acquisition of character 9 (the supraoccipital commissure passes through B), or a reversal or independent acquisition of character 10 (Z integrated in the skull roof). The effect that each of these four possibilities has on the SCT is shown in Figure 6. The four topologies of Figure 4 in conjunction with the four-

fold variation of Figure 6 account for the sixteen trees produced.

None of these sixteen trees corresponds to Miles's phylogeny (Fig. 1). The principal difference between the SCT and Figure 1 is that on the SCT, of the Complete Data Set, all the Devonian forms that bear tooth plates are located between *Uranolophus* and the other forms with denticulate dentitions (viz., rhynchodipterids to *Uronemus*). Thus, the analysis implies the existence of two monophyletic groups, each defined by the presence of organized tooth plates. This fundamental difference remains even if the data set is restricted to the characters Miles used on his phylogeny, i.e., if characters 22 and 23 are omitted from the analysis. To form a single monophyletic group for the tooth plate bearing forms, as in Figure 1, would introduce two extra steps. Characters 8–10 would arise twice—once among the post-Lower Devonian forms with denticulated dentitions (united at node III, Fig. 5) and again among the post-Devonian tooth-plate-bearing forms (united at node II, Fig. 5). These three additional character changes are offset by one, since character 7 (the presence of tooth plates) would now only arise once. Miles cannot have both a most parsimonious phylogeny and tooth-plate-bearing dipnoans comprising a monophyletic group!

Using parsimony as the criterion for choosing between character conflicts, Figure 5 is the best phylogeny based on the Complete Data Set.

CAMPBELL AND BARWICK AND DIPNOAN DENTITIONS

Campbell and Barwick ('83) recognize two distinct forms of dipnoan dentitions:

(i) Dentitions with large dentine-covered surfaces that are added to during growth. In their conception, "Growth of the dentine layer took place by the development of small enamel covered denticles which expanded in area as they grew up from the underlying bone until they fused at their bases to form a continuous sheet" (Campbell and Barwick, '83:47). The two Lower Devonian genera *Dipnorhynchus* and *Speonesydrion* are the earliest known forms of this dental type. All forms with organized tooth plates also belong to the group.

(ii) Dentitions with a shagreen of small denticles that are shed during growth. *Uranolophus*, from the Lower Devonian, is the earliest known representative. The members of this group are indicated by the symbol "#" in Figure 1.

Campbell and Barwick argue that "No adequate reason has yet been given for the belief that any species has transgressed the boundary between these groups since the Dipnoi first appeared in the fossil record" ('83:23). By characterizing the dentitions by their mode of growth rather than by purely morphological similarity, Campbell and Barwick's study leads directly to the following statements of phylogenetic significance:

1. That forms with organized tooth plates constitute a monophyletic group.
2. That *Speonesydrion* and *Dipnorhynchus* must be phylogenetically related to the forms with organized tooth plates in such a way that the type (i) dentition, growth by addition, arises only once [note: Miles simply treats *Dipnorhynchus* as having a unique specialized dentition ('77:298)].

Further work on *Speonesydrion* by Campbell and Barwick ('84) suggests a third phylogenetic conclusion:

3. That *Speonesydrion* and the forms with organized tooth plates constitute a monophyletic group. This conclusion is based on the presence of rudimentary tooth rows in *Speonesydrion*.

Figure 7 is a cladogram based solely on the basis of these three statements. The crucial difference between it and any of the cladograms discussed above is that forms with a type (ii) dentition are shown as a monophyletic group, with the implication that a shagreen of denticles in dipnoans is a neomorphic rather than a primitive character. The dentitions of *Microceratodus*, *Paraceratodus*, *Straitonia*, and *Jarvikia* are unknown; thus these genera could not be placed on Figure 7.

Figure 8 shows the effect of adding Miles's ('77) characters (numbers 1–21 in Table 1), using parsimony, to the phylogeny presented in Figure 7.

The evidence that denticle shedding is a specialized dipnoan feature is supported by two functional arguments. First, Campbell and Barwick ('83) establish that *Griphognathus*, a denticle-shedding rhynchodipterid, has a highly specialized and derived (for a dipnoan) feeding mechanism in which denticles play an integral part. They suggest that a denticulate dentition in other forms indicates the same style of specialized feeding. As this feeding mechanism and its associated morphologies are unique to dipnoans, those sharing this dental morphology form a monophyletic group. Second, although the stratigraphic record does not directly show which type of dentition was primitive (since both types of dentition were present in the Lower Devonian, the epoch of the earliest known dipnoans), the record can be used indirectly to infer the primitive dipnoan dentition. All the stratigraphically oldest dipnoans had a massive bite. This is indicated by the high vault, upright quadrate, thick dermal bones, large Meckelian fossae, massive mandible, and other features of *Dipnorhynchus*, *Speonesydrion*, and *Uranolophus* (Campbell and Barwick, '83). Based on this stratigraphic data it is inferred that the primitive dipnoan had a massive bite. To establish the probable primitive dipnoan dentition, Campbell and Barwick ('83) argue that the massive bite is

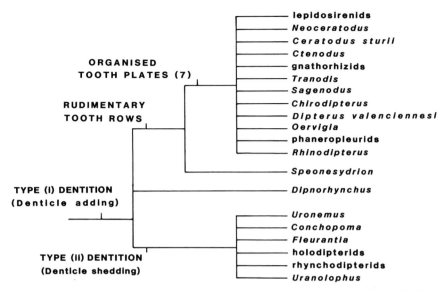

Fig. 7. A phylogeny of the dipnoans based on Campbell and Barwick's ('83, '84) study of the dentition. The character "organised tooth plates" is equivalent to Miles's ('77) character "7."

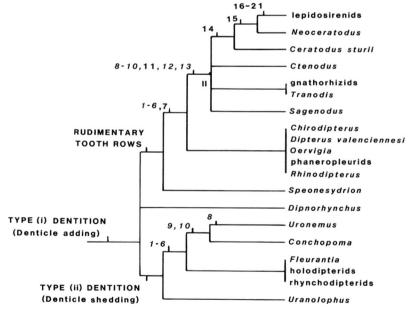

Fig. 8. A new phylogeny of the Dipnoi, derived from Campbell and Barwick's ('83, '84) study of the dentition and Miles's ('77) characters. See text for details of construction.

functionally more consistent with a type (i) dentition because this mode of growth leads to the formation of large crushing and grinding surfaces. In contrast, they argue that the type (ii) denitition would seem to suit a lighter mode of feeding. Thus the primitive

dipnoan dentition is inferred to have been a type (i) dentition (dentine adding), and denticle shedding (type ii) a secondary feature.

Dermal denticles occur primitively in the mouth cavity of gnathostomes (Nelson, '70) and, presumably, were present in the ancestors of the Dipnoi. As discussed above, the first dipnoans probably had a dentition consisting of large continuous dentine sheets (associated with a massive bite), rather than separate denticles. At a later stage in Dipnoan evolution, there arose a specialized feeding mechanism, best known in *Griphognathus*, that involved a re-evolution of a denticulated dentition. This dentition remodelled its surface by shedding denticles. Since the primitive dipnoan dentition did not consist of separate denticles, the denticulated dentition seen in some advanced dipnoans cannot be regarded as being homologous with the dermal denticles seen in primitive gnathostomes. The unusual mode of growth of the denticulated dentitions seen in dipnoans adds support to this conclusion.

DISCUSSION

Campbell and Barwick's ('83) phylogenetic conclusion that type (ii) dentition, a shagreen of small denticles that are shed during growth, is neomorphic within Dipnoi appears to conflict with the results of outgroup comparison which suggest that type (ii) dentition is primitive for the Dipnoi (Miles, '77). However, as discussed above, the type (ii) dentition cannot be considered homologous with the primitive gnathostome dentition. In fact, none of the dentitions seen in dipnoans have homologues in other gnathostomes; thus outgroup comparison cannot be appropriately applied to the problem of determining the primitive dipnoan dentition.

The cladogram in Figure 8 leads to a less parsimonious distribution of Miles's characters than does the SCT produced from the Complete Data Set (Fig. 5), which suggests that the SCT should be favored. Is the requirement of choosing the cladogram with the most parsimonious distribution of characters strong enough to outweigh the implications of the functional and stratigraphic data in this case?

Cladistics provides a method for making explicit statements about the characters used to support phylogenetic hypotheses. The making of such explicit statements highlights the perennial problem of phylogenetic reconstruction—different characters imply different relationships. Cladists employ the principle of parsimony as the criterion for selecting the "best" cladogram (Eldredge and Cracraft, '80) in cases of character conflict. However, the cladistic use of parsimony to choose between alternate cladograms has epistomological status, but not ontological status (Johnson, '82). The most parsimonious cladogram for a given data set is merely the simplest description of the character distribution among the taxa, and as such, carries no *special* significance when the actual relationships between taxa are being assessed. In accordance with this view, Wiley ('75:236) suggests that evaluation of a phylogenetic hypothesis "be done under the rule of parsimony, *not because nature is parsimonious* (my italics), but because only parsimonious hypotheses can be defended by the investigator without resorting to authoritarianism or apriorism." Different and independent information from that used in an initial cladistic analysis is required if phylogenetic histories are to be elucidated (Dullemeijer, '80). If there is decisive independent evidence that a parsimonious cladogram is mistaken, then parsimony should be ignored (Sober, '83).

I consider Campbell and Barwick's ('83) use of information independent of simple character distributions, viz., the mode of growth of the dentition, functional, and stratigraphic data, decisive enough to favor the phylogeny in Figure 8 over the more parsimonious SCT (Fig. 5). There are four reasons for making this choice.

First, if the SCT is favored, then we are left with the difficult task of explaining away Campbell and Barwick's ('83) supporting morphological, functional, and stratigraphic evidence.

Second, further functional considerations provide evidence for rejecting the SCT in Figure 5. Functional studies indicate that once the type (i) dentition (growth by addition) had been established there was a trend toward a more efficient crushing and grinding mode of feeding. The trend involves a sophistication of the tooth plates by the development of petrodentine and a sub-dental cavity, a more orderly distribution of pulp-canals, and the formation of a better defined radial tooth ridge pattern (Denison, '74; Kemp, '77, '79; Smith, '77, '79; Campbell and Barwick, '83). The functional trend is also highly correlated with the stratigraphic sequence of fossil forms. The trend in tooth plate development counts against the polyphyletic origin of tooth plates required by the SCT, as the SCT splits the trend in two; the trend arises and develops within the clade beginning at node III in Figure 5 and is terminated with the extinction of that lineage in the Upper Devonian, only to resume, *without antecedents*, in the Carboniferous with the clade beginning at node II!

Third, a choice between the phylogenies can be made by assessing which one involves the most probable set of homoplasies. As discussed above, Figure 8 involves eight homoplasious characters that are not homoplasious on the SCT derived from the Complete Data Set. These primarily involve the skull roof bone and lateral line patterns. In contrast, the SCT involves the homoplasious evolution of organized tooth plates. Thus the choice between the two can be reduced to whether tooth plates are more or less likely to have evolved homoplasiously than the skull roof bone and lateral line patterns. If more likely, the SCT is to be favored; if less likely, then Figure 8 is to be chosen. Tooth plates probably have greater functional constraints on them than do the skull roof bone and lateral line patterns; they are certainly more complex, and appear less variable (both inter- and intra-specifically), than do the skull roof bones. Evaluated intuitively, tooth plates seem less likely to have evolved homoplasiously than do the skull roof characters, an opinion that gives Figure 8 a certain amount of emotional appeal.

Finally, Campbell and Barwick (this volume) have found additional features supportive of the proposed early dichotomy in the evolution of the Dipnoi. These include the dentine types present, the form of the ceratohyals and ceratobranchials, palatal shape, presence or absence of a basibranchial/basihyal tooth plates, nature of the jaw articulation, and features of the pectoral girdle. These, and other features, are discussed more fully in Campbell and Barwick (this volume).

Even if these four arguments are ignored, there is still a problem in favoring the SCT in Figure 5 over the phylogeny in Figure 8 simply on the grounds that it is more parsimonious. The problem arises from the difficulty in defining, and thus counting, characters. We cannot be sure that we have selected the most parsimonious cladogram. For example, consider the SCT resulting from the analysis of the Complete Data Set (Fig. 5). It has two monophyletic groups defined by the presence of organized tooth plates. To form a single monophyletic group of all the organized tooth-bearing forms requires two extra steps (characters 8–10 would arise twice and character 7 would now arise only once). Or does it? Characters 8–10 are all associated with a decrease in the ossification at the posterior margin of the skull roof and thus could be regarded as one "character." If characters 8–10 are treated in this way, a monophyletic origin of tooth plates would be equally parsimonious with a polyphyletic origin of tooth plates. Moreover, the tooth plate character could be broken down into a number of separate characters: structure of pulp canals, size of subdental cavity, type of dentine present, form of tooth rows, etc. If this were done, then a monophyletic origin of tooth plates would be more parsimonious than their polyphyletic origin as required by the SCT in Figure 5. Deciding which is the most parsimonious of a number of cladograms is not necessarily straightforward.

The same difficulty in choosing the most parsimonious cladogram occurs when Figure 8 is compared with the SCT in Figure 5. As Miles's characters stand, Figure 8 is seven steps longer than the SCT. However, six of these steps involve skull roof characters, all of which are associated with the decrease in the ossification of the skull roof. Thus they could be treated as one character. This approach would render the SCT only marginally more parsimonious than Figure 8. Support for treating these skull roof characters as one character comes from Bemis ('84), who suggests that paedomorphosis may have played an extensive role in the evolution of the Dipnoi. The reduction of the ossification in the skull roof may be due to a single underlying paedomorphic process. Further, if the tooth plate character is treated as several characters, as discussed above, then Figure 8 may be regarded as being more parsimonious than the SCT in Figure 5. If the use of parsimony as a criterion for choosing between phylogenies is accepted, the SCT derived from the Complete Data Set cannot be considered a better phylogeny than Figure 8 since a case can be made for favoring either of the two phylogenies depending on how the characters are defined.

SUMMARY AND CONCLUSIONS

A re-analysis of an enlarged set of characters based on Miles ('77), using computer routines to search for most parsimonious trees, produced sixteen equally parsimonious cladograms. Their structures are summarized by a strict consensus tree (Fig. 5). None of the trees correspond to Miles's cladogram (Fig. 1). The re-analysis shows that the topology of Miles's phylogeny results both from parsimony and from character weighting, which is employed in the selection of characters and the favoring of certain characters in some cases of character conflict.

Campbell and Barwick ('83, '84) presented new phylogenetic conclusions concerning the evolution of the Dipnoi based on a study of the dentition and functional and stratigraphic arguments. Figure 7 summarizes their conclusions in the form of a cladogram, though it is important to realize that they did not employ cladistic techniques to arrive at these conclusions. Figure 8 shows a more fully resolved phylogeny, with a basic structure defined by Figure 7. The finer resolution was achieved by adding the first 21 characters in Table 1 to this basic structure, using parsimony. As thus constructed, the phylogeny should be regarded as provisional.

Figures 5 and 8 are quite different, the strict consensus tree (Fig. 5) being the more parsimonious with respect to Miles's ('77) characters. On the basis of available evidence—the theoretical difficulties encountered when using the principle of parsimony to reconstruct evolutionary histories, the strength of Campbell and Barwick's ('83) functional and stratigraphic arguments, the higher probability that the skull roof and lateral line characters rather than the dentition characters evolved homoplasiously, and the practical difficulties in defining (and thus counting) characters—I favor the phylogeny based on the dental characters of Campbell and Barwick's study ('83, '84, this volume) shown in Figure 8, even though it is less parsimonious than that of Figure 5.

A greater understanding is needed of the functional inter-relatedness of the characters used for phylogenetic studies and the search for new features to test the proposed phylogeny.

ACKNOWLEDGMENTS

I thank Don Colless, Division of Entomology, Commonwealth Scientific and Industrial Research Organisation, Canberra, Australia, for providing and running the computer programs. The paper stemmed from my honors thesis, written at the Australian National University, and I thank all involved, especially my supervisor, R.E. Barwick, the staff of the Zoology Department, and K.S.W. Campbell. I thank R.E. Barwick, W.E. Bemis, Chris Bryant, Don Colless, Dan Faith, Peter Forey, John Long, David Raup, Gavin Young, and an anonymous reviewer for assistance in preparation of this manuscript. K.S.W. Campbell assisted throughout, providing access to fossil material, many hours of fruitful discussion, and much encouragement. Finally, a special thanks to R.E. Barwick and family, without whom this paper would not have been written.

NOTE ADDED IN PROOF

Recent work by Smith, Smithson, and Campbell (in press) has shown that the marginal ridges in *Uronemus* are reduced tooth plates and not periodically shed structures. The palatal and mandibular denticles were secondarily developed. Thus, in Figures 7 and 8 *Uronemus* should be removed from the clade characterized by a type (ii) dentition and placed in the clade characterized by organized tooth plates (character 7).

LITERATURE CITED

Bemis, W.E. (1984) Paedomorphosis and the evolution of the Dipnoi. Paleobiology *10:*293–307.

Bertmar, G. (1968) Phylogeny and evolution in lungfishes. Acta Zool. *49:*189–201.

Campbell, K.S.W., and R.E. Barwick (1983) Early evolution of dipnoan dentitions and a new genus *Speonesydrion*. Mem. Assoc. Australas. Palaeontol. *1:*17–49.

Campbell, K.S.W., and R.E. Barwick (1984) *Speonesydrion*, an early Devonian dipnoan with primitive tooth plates. Palaeo Ichthyol. *2:*1–48.

Denison, R.H. (1974) The structure and evolution of teeth in lungfishes. Fieldiana Geol. *17:*353–413.

Dullemeijer, P. (1980) Functional morphology and evolutionary biology. Acta Biotheoretica *29:*151–250.

Eldredge, N., and J. Cracraft (1980) Phylogenetic Patterns and the Evolutionary Process. New York: Columbia University Press.

Johnson, R. (1982) Parsimony principles in phylogenetic systematics: A critical reappraisal. Evol. Theory *6:* 79–90.

Kemp, A. (1977) The pattern of tooth plate formation in the Australian lungfish, *Neoceratodus forsteri* Krefft. Zool. J. Linn. Soc. Lond. *60:*223–258.

Kemp, A. (1979) The histology of tooth plate formation in the Australian lungfish, *Neoceratodus forsteri* Krefft. Zool. J. Linn. Soc. Lond. *66:*251–287.

Margush, T., and F.R. McMorris (1981) Consensus *n*-trees. Bull. Math. Biol. *43:*239–244.

Miles, R.S. (1977) Dipnoan (lungfish) skulls and the relationships of the group: A study based on new species from the Devonian of Australia. Zool. J. Linn. Soc. Lond. *61:*1–328.

Moy-Thomas, J.A., and R.S. Miles (1971) Palaeozoic Fishes. 2nd Ed. Philadelphia: W.D. Saunders Co., pp. 140–160.

Nelson, G.J. (1970) Pharyngeal denticles (placoid scales) of sharks, with notes on the dermal skeleton of vertebrates. Am. Mus. Novit. *2415:*1–26.

Rohlf, F.J. (1982) Consensus indices for comparing classifications. Math. Biosci. *59:*131–144.

Smith, M.M. (1977) The microstructure of the dentition and dermal ornament of three dipnoans from the Devonian of Western Australia: A contribution towards dipnoan interrelationships, and morphogenesis, growth and adaptation of the skeletal tissues. Phil. Trans. R. Soc. Lond., Ser. B. *281(979):*29–72.

Smith, M.M. (1979) Structure and histogenesis of tooth plates in *Sagenodus inaequalis* Owen considered in relation to the phylogeny of post-Devonian dipnoans. Proc. R. Soc., Ser. B. *204:*15–39.

Smith, M.M., T.R. Smithson, and K.S.W. Campbell (in press) The relationships of *Uronemus*—a Carboniferous dipnoan with highly modified tooth plates. Phil. Trans. R. Soc. Lond.

Sober, E. (1983) Parsimony in systematics: Philosophical issues. Ann. Rev. Ecol. Syst. *14:*335–357.

Thomson, K.S., and K.S.W. Campbell (1971) The structure and relationships of the primitive Devonian lungfish—*Dipnorhynchus sussmilchi* (Etheridge). Bull. Peabody Mus. Nat. Hist. *38:*1–109.

Wiley, E.O. (1975) Karl R. Popper, systematics, and classification: A reply to Walter Bock and other evolutionary taxonomists. Syst. Zool. *24:*233–243.

Wiley, E.O. (1981) Phylogenetics: The Theory and Practice of Phylogenetic Systematics. New York: John Wiley and Sons.

JOURNAL OF MORPHOLOGY SUPPLEMENT 1:163-179 (1986)

The Natural History of African Lungfishes

P. HUMPHRY GREENWOOD
Department of Zoology, British Museum of Natural History, London SW7 5BD, England, U.K.

ABSTRACT   Remarkably little is known about the biology of the four *Protopterus* species, apart from certain detailed studies on their nesting behavior and estivating habits. What information we do have indicates that the species are essentially omnivorous carnivores (especially as predators on molluscs) and that they occupy a wide variety of habitats both lentic and lotic. As obligatory air-breathers able to survive temporary and sometimes extended desiccation of a habitat, lungfishes are often permanent residents in areas from which most actinopterygian fishes are excluded.

All four species are able to survive prolonged dry periods. The methods they employ in so doing are varied, and include the secretion of subterranean cocoons, lying-up in water-filled subsurface burrows, or simply burrowing into moist regions of the substrate. Some populations of at least two species live in permanent water and so do not estivate, although they apparently retain the ability to do so.

Three of the four species spawn in some form of seemingly constructed or prepared nest. The architecture of these nests shows marked inter- and intraspecific variability and is likely to be determined largely by various environmental factors. All three species show some type of parental care. The breeding biology of the fourth species, *P. amphibius*, is still unknown.

Other aspects of the breeding biology and behavior of *Protopterus* require a great deal more investigation, as does the biology of the young.

It is now almost 150 years since the capture in west Africa of *Protopterus annectens*, the first African dipnoan to be discovered. Yet, its field-biology, and that of its three congeners, is still very incompletely known (see Johnels and Svensson, '54; Thomson, '69), a situation contrasting strongly with the considerable amount of research already devoted to the anatomy and physiology of these animals (Thomson, '69). Perhaps that imbalance is not surprising when one considers the generally inhospitable habitats occupied by lungfishes, the particular interest which these animals have for students of evolution and vertebrate phylogeny (Rosen et al., '81), and the attractions offered to physiologists and biochemists by air-breathing and estivating fishes (see Burggren and Johansen, this volume; Fishman et al., this volume).

Taken in sum, the distribution of the four species extends across a large part of Africa (Fig. 1). Two species, *P. annectens* (Owen) and *P. dolloi* Blgr are essentially west African taxa. The other two, *P. aethiopicus* Heckel and *P. amphibius* (Peters), are essentially east African, but with *P. aethiopicus* also occurring in the Zaire basin, and *P. annectens* extending eastwards into the middle and lower Zambezi systems and the Limpopo system (for detailed locality records, see Gosse, '84).

The variety of habitats occupied by these species is noteworthy and, in broad terms, could be classified as both lentic (standing water) and lotic (running water), including as it does a wide variety of swamp localities, all the Rift Valley lakes, except Lake Malawi, a number of habitats therein, and the major river systems of tropical Africa.

Adults in three of the species are amongst some of the largest African freshwater fishes; *P. aethiopicus* reaches a total length of 1,800 mm, *P. dolloi* 1,300 mm, and *P. annectens* 820 mm, but the largest known adult of *P. amphibius* has a total length of only 443 mm. In many areas of east and west Africa, *Protopterus* are important food-fishes and in some places specialized fishing techniques have evolved for their capture, especially during those periods when the fishes are es-

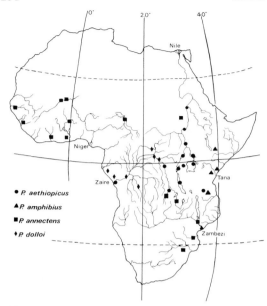

Fig. 1. Distribution map of *Protopterus* species. (Based on Bemis, unpublished; Gosse, '84; Pienaar, '81).

tivating (Johnels and Svensson, '54; Brien et al., '59; Wasawo, '59). Most *Protopterus aethiopicus* females in Lake Victoria reach sexual maturity at a length between 650 and 700 mm; the largest mature female examined was 980 mm long, the smallest 610 mm. Adult males reach a greater length (1,800 mm) than do females, but the size at which maturity is first attained is unknown (Greenwood, '58, '66). Data are not available for the size at which individuals of the three other species first reach maturity.

The four *Protopterus* species are much alike in their gross morphology, the taxa being defined principally on morphometric differences in body and head proportions, and on various meristic features of the skeletal system (Trewavas, '54). In its general appearance, except for the longer paired fins, *Protopterus* closely resembles the monotypic genus *Lepidosiren paradoxa* of South America, but unlike that species no *Protopterus* is known to develop the highly vascular pelvic fins that occur in sexually active male *L. paradoxa*.

There is a moderate degree of intraspecific variation within *Protopterus*, especially in coloration, scale size, and certain morphometric features. On the basis of these differences Poll ('61) recognizes four subspecies of *P. aethiopicus* and two of *P. annectens*; currently *P. dolloi* and *P. amphibius* are considered monotypic.

In higher level classifications *Protopterus* is either grouped with the closely similar *Lepidosiren* in the family Lepidosirenidae (order Lepidosireniformes), or is placed in a separate family, Protopteridae, of the same order. This difference in ranking seemingly depends on the taxonomic school to which the investigator belongs, and thus on the significance attached to the few differences existing between the genera (see Miles, '77). To date no scheme of intrageneric relationships has been proposed for *Protopterus*; Trewavas ('54) considers *P. amphibius* to be the most generalized African species and suggests that *Lepidosiren paradoxa* is the most derived member of a lineage comprising it and the *Protopterus* species (see also Wake, this volume).

ESTIVATION

Although the subterranean dry-season cocoon of *P. annectens* has now become the usual textbook example of estivation among lungfishes, it is by no means the only way in which at least three of the species can overcome temporary, seasonal desiccation of their habitats.

The estivation of *P. annectens* was first described by Jardine (1841), but large-scale field and laboratory investigation of estivation in this species was not carried out until a century later in the classical work of Johnels and Svensson ('54). This remains the most complete and comparative study of lungfish natural history available to date.

With the onset of the dry seasons and the consequent fall in water-level of the Gambian swamps, *Protopterus annectens* of 40-mm length and over begin to excavate a vertical burrow into the soft and still submerged mud of the swamp floor (Johnels and Svensson, '54). Excavation is carried out mostly by the fish biting its way into the soil, the mouthfuls of mud and water then being expelled through the branchial openings; body movement may also contribute to the burrowing process. The final depth of the burrow is between 30 and 250 mm below the mud-water interface and is positively correlated with the fish's length; the diameter is usually a little greater than that of the fish's body. Having excavated to the appropriate depth for its size, the fish then turns 180° on its long axis, coming to rest with the snout pointing upwards. In making that turn, the fish widens the base of the tube into a bulb-shaped chamber whose maximum diameter is approximately twice the width of the body.

Once the chamber is formed, the fish makes visits to the mouth of the tube in order to breathe. Once a breath is taken, the fish sinks back into the chamber, tail first, coming to rest in a curled position (See Johnels and Svensson, '54). The frequency of these breathing excursions gradually diminishes as the water level in the swamp, and later in the mud, falls. Once the water table in the mud falls below the snout-level of the fish, respiratory journeys cease and the fish remains coiled, almost double, in the chamber.

During the interval between the formation of the chamber and the last visit to the surface, the fish secretes large quantities of mucus into the water filling the chamber. It is this mucus that, as the water dries up, also dries and gives rise to the closely fitting cocoon surrounding the now dormant lungfish (Fig. 2).

Johnels and Svensson ('54) give a detailed and well-illustrated description of the cocoon and the so-called sleeping nest, that is, the chamber and its associated tube-like entrance shaft, which ultimately serves as the airway to the dormant fish. The shaft is usually almost vertical, but it may slope at a slight angle, and on occasion it may bifurcate. Mud ejected during the tube's excavation tends to collect around its surface opening, and when dried out forms a friable cap covering the entrance to the shaft.

The cocoon itself is very thin (ca. 50–60 μm); its top is perforated by a small hole leading into a funnel-like depression that enters the fish's mouth and through which air is drawn into the bucco-pharynx. The cocoon adheres closely to the walls of the sleeping chamber and to the body of the occupant.

There is some variation in the tightness with which the estivating fish is curled and in the intimacy with which the cocoon adheres to the body, variation apparently correlated with the humidity and/or the nature of the soil. A "classical" cocoon is seemingly produced in soils of high clay and low moisture content (Johnels and Svensson, '54). Under certain conditions cocoons may not be formed, a phenomenon apparently correlated with a short and wet "dry" season. Under those conditions P. annectens simply burrows into the still-moist levels of the swamp soil and spends the dry season with ". . . the body stretched out in the caves and without any trace of cocoon" (Johnels and Svensson, '54:143). It is not clear what is meant by "caves;" that is, are these natural burrows in the soil, or part of the burrow made by the lungfishes?

Judging from Johnels and Svensson's ('54) observations, the sleeping nests of P. annectens are located in both the formerly deep and shallow parts of a dried-out swamp, but they are commonest in the deeper regions, which are also the areas where the highest number of small individuals estivate. Sleeping nest densities are often as high as five per square meter.

In the opinion of Johnels and Svensson, P. annectens in the Gambian swamps make no

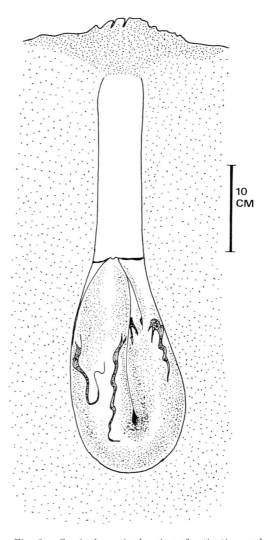

Fig. 2. Semi-schematic drawing of estivating and cocooned *Protopterus annectens*, as viewed from the ventral side of the fish. The loose cap covering the entrance to the tube is densely stippled, and the cap of the cocoon is shown as a thick, transverse line. (Modified after Johnels and Svensson, '54).

attempt to leave those areas when water levels begin to fall at the onset of the dry season. Indeed, unlike the other fishes, which enter the swamps when these are innundated and leave as the water level drops, the lungfishes are effectively permanent residents. Of particular interest in that context is Johnels and Svensson's ('54) observation that in swamps located near rivers, small lungfishes (spawned during the rainy season) develop a markedly positive rheotaxis and swim against the flow of the receding water; the other fishes on the contrary, ". . . seem inclined to follow the current" (Johnels and Svensson, '54:135) and leave the swamps for the permanent water. Perhaps significantly with regard to habitat preferences, *P. annectens* is less common in swamps having direct contact with the river and commonest in those that are effectively isolated from permanent water (Johnels and Svensson, '54).

In nature, *P. annectens* estivates for about seven or eight months, the period depending on the length of the dry season. No information is available on the temperatures reached within the cocoon or the sleeping nest of naturally estivating individuals during that time, nor are there data available on lethal temperature limits for either artificially or naturally estivated individuals (but see pages below).

On the basis of observations on *P. annectens* kept in aquaria for several years, Johnels and Svensson ('54) suggested that there is an endogenous rhythm of annual lethargy, manifest by a refusal to feed, by reduced activity, and a lowered rate of air breathing. Such periods of lethargy may last for a few weeks or for as much as 2 or 3 months. Since these specimens were unable to estivate, Johnels and Svensson suggested that the lethargic period might be explained as ". . . a substitute for true aestivation." No further work has been done on that idea, and it must for the moment remain only a suggestion (see also Blanc et al., '56; Fishman et al., this volume; also Godet and Pieri, '61 and Swan et al., '68, on attempts to isolate biochemical substances controlling estivation; and comments by Brien et al., '59).

In the essentially east African species *P. aethiopicus*, unlike its western counterpart *P. annectens*, cocoon formation appears to be a rare event. Poll ('38) records a single cocoon collected at Kande (Luapula drainage), while Brien et al. ('59) describe cocoons collected from the Umpuelo River in Angola; the latter authors described the cocoons as being comparable with those of *P. annectens*. Inter-

estingly, both these localities lie within the distributional area of *P. annectens* (Gosse, '84) but the authors refer the cocooned fishes to *P. aethiopicus*.

Apart from those records and Wasawo's ('59) discovery of a very dissimilar sleeping nest in Uganda (see below), there are no confirmed accounts of estivating *P. aethiopicus* anywhere within its extensive range (see Greenwood, '66; Curry-Lindahl, '59). This absence of estivation should probably be associated with the types of habitats occupied by *P. aethiopicus*. These include large lakes (Victoria, Edward, Tanganyika), smaller but permanent lakes (e.g., Lakes George, Nabugabo and Kyoga), and a major river system (the upper and middle Nile and their tributaries), none of which is affected by marked seasonal changes in water-level as are the usual habitats of *P. annectens*. *Protopterus aethiopicus* does, of course, enter swampy areas, some of which do dry out, but few of which are not in direct contact with permanent water throughout the drying-out phase. It is perhaps significant that it is in just such isolated areas that the cocoons of presumed *P. aethiopicus* were found (see above) and are those from which unsubstantiated reports of cocoons emanated; it is here, too, that the apparently estivating fishes recorded by Wasawo ('59) were located. In a temporary grass-swamp in northern Lake Victoria I have seen small specimens (ca. 350 mm long) stranded by rapidly receding flood waters. These fishes were not, however, making any attempt to burrow but were moving randomly across the damp but rapidly drying mud. That none was attempting to burrow could be attributable to several factors. The mud may have been unsuitable for the method of digging-burrowing used by *Protopterus*; under laboratory conditions artificially induced cocoon formation is possible only if the substrate is structurally suitable and is not too moist (see Smith, '31; Marlier, '57). The high ambient temperature and bright sunlight in the swamp might also have been inhibitory factors, while the manner and rate at which the water level in the swamp fell could have been unsuitable for cocoon formation.

The dry season burrows of *P. aethiopicus* described by Wasawo ('59) are in no way like the sleeping nests attributed to this species but do resemble the combined dry-season and breeding nests of *P. dolloi* (see below). Parenthetically it can be added that the dry-season burrows of *P. aethiopicus* closely resemble those described for the South American lungfish *Lepidosiren paradoxa* (see Carter and Beadle, '30).

The burrows of *P. aethiopicus* were located in a seasonal grass-swamp in the Teso district of Uganda, north of Lake Kyoga (Wasawo, '59). At the time of their discovery the swamp had not dried out completely and pools of water, some permanent, were present. One such pool lay beneath the horizontal entrance to the burrow, an opening about 150 mm wide formed in a soil bank underlying a road crossing the swamp. From the entrance a tunnel continued into the bank for a distance of about 1,200 mm, then turned sharply downwards, ran at an angle of approximately 45° for a distance of 3,300 mm, and ended blindly. Most of the diagonal part was filled with water, the surface level of which was estimated to be at the same level as the water in the pool (Fig. 3). A single large lungfish, about 700 mm long, was removed from each of the burrows. One of the fishes was described as "... lethargic as compared with normal lungfishes ... the body appeared to have more mucus covering it, and was decidedly paler"; it had, however, been wounded during capture. Wasawo ('59) based his comparisons on "... normal lungfishes seen under similar conditions" but does not clarify what he meant by "similar conditions."

Judging from the equipment used by a local fisherman to extract the burrow's occupants, these dry-season refuges must be well-known and regularly fished (Wasawo, '59).

Wasawo ('59) does not speculate on how the burrows were formed, but from my knowledge of the habitat it seems unlikely that the fishes had taken over natural subterranean cavities or burrows made by some other animal (including man). It seems more probable that either the burrows were excavated by the lungfishes, or were developed by the fishes from some smaller excavation or natural subsidence.

Under laboratory conditions, *Protopterus aethiopicus* has been induced to estivate (see Marlier, '57; Lüling, '61; Fishman et al., this volume). The resulting sleeping-nests and cocoons (see above) differ little from those produced naturally or under artificial conditions by *P. annectens*. As in that species, the nature of the sleeping chamber, its associated channels, and the cocoon itself are strongly influenced by the nature and physical properties of the substrate, especially the amount of moisture it retains. Smith ('31) found that, after artificially induced estivation, *P. aethiopicus* could be kept alive in their cocoons

for 6 to 15 months, and Coates ('37) found that individuals induced to estivate in a similar fashion could survive for up to 4 years (The specific identity of Coates' specimens is not clearly indicated, but by implication it seems that these were *P. aethiopicus* supplied to him by Smith).

Smith ('31) records that his cocooned fishes could survive, "without injury," temperatures of 40°C for a week and temperatures of 31.7°C for 18 days. He also suggests, on the assumption that *P. aethiopicus* may form cocoons in nature, that since "... the sun temperature ... may reach 65°C during the dry season ..." it would be likely that "... the nest with its open burrow leading to the surface, may reach temperatures of 37°C or more for short periods of time, even when 12 to 18 inches underground." It must be stressed that Smith's estimates have never been checked in the field.

The temperature of the water in the burrows investigated by Wasawo ('59) was 29° and 29.5°C; water temperatures in the open pools nearby were 27.5° and 30°C respectively, and the air temperature in direct sunlight was 36°C; the time of day was not recorded.

Protopterus dolloi, at least in the region of Stanley Pool (Zaire River) has developed another method (albeit one not dissimilar to that of *P. aethiopicus*) for surviving the dry season (Brien et al., '59). During the rainy season these populations of *P. dolloi* occupy the marginal swampy areas of Stanley Pool. The swamps are unusual in that they float; thus during the dry season the entire area is underlain by water in direct contact with the lake-like Pool (Brien et al., '59). The compacted, raft-like substrate of the swamp is of varying thickness, from less than a meter to more than two meters. Although the substrate is relatively hard near its surface, it becomes progressively softer as it approaches the underlying water.

With the onset of the dry season, and the departure of the water lying above the "raft," adult male *P. dolloi* that had invaded the swamps during the rains, or had emerged from their dry season nests, begin to burrow into the "raft" or to re-occupy existing burrows excavated in previous dry seasons. Each burrow begins as a vertical shaft that then becomes a gently sloping tunnel running downwards to open into the permanent water-body below the raft. Part of the tunnel near the vertical shaft is enlarged to form a cave-like chamber (Fig. 4). The tunnel, chamber, and a great part of the vertical shaft are

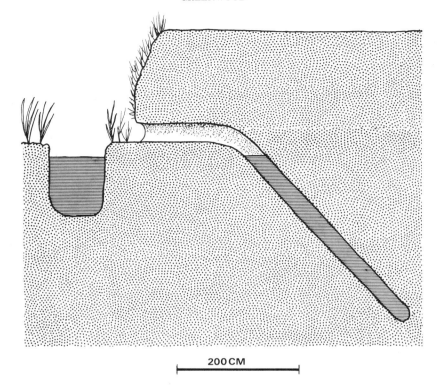

200 CM

Fig. 3.   Dry season burrow (semi-schematic) of *Protopterus aethiopicus*. Water in the permanent pool below the entrance to the burrow, and in the burrow itself, is indicated by horizontal hatching. (Modified after Wasawo, '59).

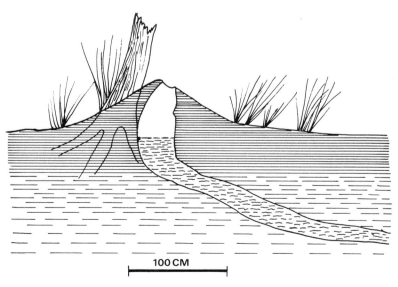

100 CM

Fig. 4.   Combined dry season burrow and wet season breeding nest of *Protopterus dolloi*. Dry soil indicated by close and continuous horizontal hatching, moister region by interrupted horizontal hatching. Water in the nest is shown by broken and sinuous horizontal lines. (Modified after Brien et al., '59).

filled with water, presumably by seepage from the surface as well as directly from the water below the raft. Water in the nest has a pH between 4.7 and 6.5, is rich in organic matter, and has a high CO_2 and a low O_2 content (see Brien et al., '59).

Much remains to be learned about the manner in which these burrows are excavated and whether or not both sexes are involved in their construction. Field observations by Brien et al. ('59) indicate that unlike P. annectens, P. dolloi excavates by using anguilliform body movements to burrow into the still moist soil. The entrance shaft has at the surface a molehill-like collar of dry soil, 300 mm or more in height, which strongly suggests that at some stage in the nest's construction (or renovation) the fish is pushing up soil from below.

During the dry season the nests are occupied only by males. Females leave the swamps as these begin to dry out and spend the dry season in the open water areas of Stanley Pool. It seems likely that small and presumably immature males also leave the drying swamps and spend the dry period in the same places as the females (see Brien et al., '59). Such sexual and age segregation during the dry season is unknown for P. annectens, in which adults and juveniles of both sexes estivate in the same areas, albeit with smaller fishes tending to congregate in the regions of formerly deep water. It is not known whether P. aethiopicus estivating in the burrows described by Wasawo ('59) are sexually segregated, since only two shelters were described and the sex of the single occupant in each was not determined.

Male P. dolloi occupying nests during the dry season are not dormant and make frequent journeys into the vertical shaft in order to breathe at the surface of the water accumulated there. These fishes remain in the nests as the swamps refill with the next rains, and spawning takes place in the enlarged part of the gallery (see below). The use of a single nest for both estivation and breeding is apparently a unique feature of P. dolloi.

Although estivating P. dolloi are not known to secrete a cocoon in nature, this species, like P. aethiopicus, can be induced to form a cocoon under laboratory conditions. As in P. aethiopicus, the form of the sleeping nest and the nature of the cocoon in P. dolloi are determined by the physical conditions of the substrate into which the individual burrows (Brien et al., '59; Lüling, '61).

Very little is known about the dry-season behavior of P. amphibius. A specimen in a cocoon has been collected near Mombasa, Kenya, but no details are available about the form and nature of the cocoon. Another specimen was found in the moist sand of a dry water-course north of the Lorian swamp (Eusso Nyiro Basin, northern Kenya). No cocoon had been formed, but other details about its condition are unavailable (Trewavas, '54). From these records it would seem that P. amphibius, like P. annectens, employs different methods of estivation depending on the nature of the substrate and on the extent to which the substrate is dried out.

That conclusion would, in general, seem to apply to all four species of Protopterus, namely, that general or particular environmental factors determine the precise nature of the actions taken to avoid desiccation. It would also seem that the "classical" pattern of cocoon formation is by no means the modal one for the genus and can probably be considered the usual one only in a single species, P. annectens. This conclusion, however, must be a very tentative one, since it is drawn from observations made in only a few of the several habitats known to be occupied by the various species. All four species do, nevertheless, have the ability to form cocoons, and all can exhibit the behavioral responses that lead up to cocoon formation in a drying environment. Whether or not any of the species regularly pass through an annual period of lethargy irrespective of environmental conditions (a suggestion made by Johnels and Svensson, '54), remains debatable, with little evidence from field studies to support it.

BREEDING BIOLOGY
Sex ratios

Catch records over a 22-month period in northern Lake Victoria indicate that in the mostly open-water habitats sampled, more adult female than adult male P. aethiopicus were caught, the ratio being 96:29; the number of immature females in these areas was also greater (Greenwood, '58). Since the samples were not made in marginal swampy areas, in papyrus-swamps, nor in water over 10 m in depth, it is not known if these figures represent a natural adult sex ratio or a sexual difference in the habitat preferences of non-breeding adults.

Breeding seasons

Protopterus annectens, P. aethiopicus, and P. dolloi spawn during periods when local rainfall is heavy and protracted, periods that usually have a well-defined and predictable seasonality. The breeding season of *P. amphibius* is unknown.

Protopterus aethiopicus inhabiting the northern region of Lake Victoria spawn from November through April, with peak activity in November-December and, especially, March-April. In addition, breeding may occur during periods of heavy but unseasonal rainfall (Greenwood, '58).

For Gambian populations of *P. annectens*, too, breeding is closely associated with heavy rainfall and, in this instance, the inundation of swamp lands both by direct precipitation and by lateral flooding from rivers. Spawning takes place within a month or 6 weeks after the emergence of the fishes from estivation, i.e., during August and September; the period of most intense breeding activity extends over approximately a month (Johnels and Svensson, '54).

The breeding season of *Protopterus dolloi* in the Stanley Pool region of Zaire is also correlated with the flooding of swamp lands and is confined to the wet season (Brien et al., '59).

Nests and parental behavior

That *Protopterus annectens* practiced some form of parental care by guarding its young in a nest-like hole, was known as far back as 1899 (Budgett, 1899; '01), and supposed nests of *P. aethiopicus* were described by Jackson ('16). Knowledge of the diversity of nests produced by *P. annectens*, and more details on the parental care exercised by nest guarding males, resulted from the field work of Johnels and Svensson ('54).

In its commonest form the breeding nest of *P. annectens* is a broadly U-shaped tunnel extending at its deepest point some 400 mm into the substrate, with the two openings about 500 mm apart (Fig. 5A). Between the vertical arms of the U there is an enlarged chamber in which the eggs are deposited and where the nestlings spend the greater part of their time. The openings to the nest are generally submerged, but if the water level in the swamp falls both may come to open directly to the air.

A variant of this nest type is one in which a third tunnel enters into the base of the U and extends away from it at approximately right angles (Fig. 5C). Since the opening of this tunnel is always submerged, it may be a later addition to an originally simple U-shaped nest, made by the parent fish in order to gain access when falling water levels re-

sult in other openings becoming exposed above water level. It should be noted, however, that fish have been seen entering nests along very shallow gutters made through the barely flooded surface of the swamp, exposing a large part of the body in so doing.

Other types of *P. annectens* nests are simpler structures (Fig. 5B) resembling, but smaller than, the dry season burrow of *P. aethiopicus* described by Wasawo ('59) or they may be even shorter tunnels excavated into the partly submerged earth banks separating rice fields.

There is no information on how the breeding nests are made, or on the sex of the individual responsible for their construction. Even the smallest nests are much larger and often more complicated excavations than those prepared for estivation. It seems possible that lungfishes may enlarge and modify pits and holes resulting from natural subsidence or erosion, or from the activity of other animals. It is also unknown whether the nests can be considered as permanent structures, which, like the nests of *P. dolloi*, are used for several years in succession (see above).

The breeding nests of *P. dolloi* are the same structures used by adult males as dry-season refuges. The eggs are deposited in the cave-like chamber in the main tunnel; it is here too, that the greatest concentration of young is subsequently found, although older nestlings make frequent excursions into the vertical part of the nest in order to breathe air at the water surface (Brien et al., '59).

Nests of *P. aethiopicus* in Lake Victoria, like those of *P. annectens* in Gambia, show some diversity in form. One kind, however, is basically like that of one *P. annectens* type, but differs from it in its environmental location since it was found in a permanent papyrus-swamp and not in a temporary grass-swamp. This nest—which will be referred to below as the "pit nest"—consisted of a deep hole in the matted papyrus roots at a distance some 400 mm from the swamp's margin with a narrow creek extending into the swamp from the water-lily zone of the main lake (see Greenwood, '58). It resembles the presumed nest of *P. aethiopicus* described by Poll ('39) from a marginal grass-swamp bordering Lake Edward.

At its deepest point the nest was 850 mm below the surface water level, which varied during the period of observation from 100 to 150 mm below the surface of the papyrus mat. The opening was oval with a greatest diameter of 680 mm. Only one submerged

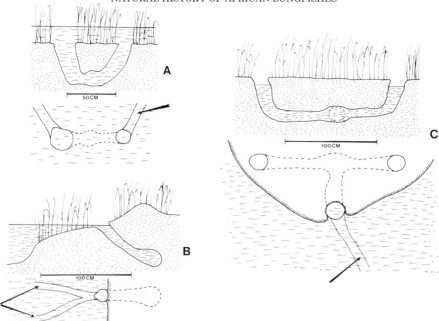

Fig. 5. Semi-schematic drawings of various types of breeding nests of *P. annectens*, each shown in section (above) and plan (below) views. In plan view, the entrance channel is indicated by an arrow, the subterra-nean part of the nest by dashed lines, and the openings to the nest by a near-circular continuous line. (Modified after Johnels and Svensson, '54).

passage into the nest was located, but neither its course nor its lakeward opening was discovered; it entered the nest at a depth of about 600 mm.

Papyrus stems surrounded the surface opening, forming a high, domed roof over it; on the lakeward side these stems were much less dense, and a distinct swathe of flattended vegetation and smoothed mud linked the nest with the creek (Fig. 6A). This area had the appearance of a "run-way," but at no time was it used by the parent; all entrances and exits were made through the submerged passageway.

Two other kinds of nests of *P. aethiopicus*, quite unlike the first but closely resembling one another, were discovered on a low-lying, tree covered island in a bay of Lake Victoria near Jinja (Greenwood, '58). One was located about 50 m from the open lake, at the end of a broad, shallow creek. It lay under an irregular mound of soil covering the roots and lower trunk of a partly up-rooted ambatch tree (*Herminiera elaphroxylon*). One side of the mound had collapsed, creating a hole some 200 mm in diameter. The surface of the nest was about 500 mm square, and was partly concealed on one side by the cave-like

mound of soil and plant debris (Fig. 6B). Water depth in the nest was between 180 and 250 mm, and there was a single entrance channel, 100–150 mm deep, running through the densely vegetated creek; the adult fish broke surface whenever it entered the nest.

The second nest on this island was about 30 m distant and closely resembled the nest described above. It differed, however, in having no obvious surface opening. There was a submerged chamber approximately 800 mm deep and 250 mm in diameter formed in the coarse sand and gravel lying against a fallen and partly submerged trunk of an ambatch tree; the completely subaquatic entrance channel ran below and along the length of the trunk and connected with a nearby creek.

The fourth type of nest was the simplest, consisting of a shallow clearing amongst water lilies and swamp-grass about 7 m offshore and in about 200 mm of water. This "scoop nest" was little more than a near-circular area, a meter in diameter, cleared of plants, and slightly sunken into the sandy substrate (Greenwood, '58). In most respects it resembled closely the presumed breeding nest described from Lake Victoria by Jackson ('16).

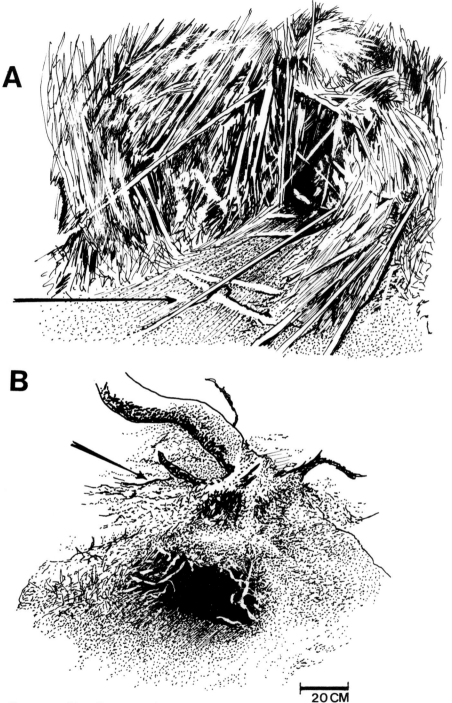

⊢——⊣	
20 CM	

Fig. 6.   Two types of breeding nests of *Protopterus aethiopicus* found in Lake Victoria. A) Surface view of the deep, pit-like nest near Jinja, Uganda. An arrow indicates the runway-like region in front of the nest. B) Surface view of a nest formed below the roots and asso- ciated soil and debris of an uprooted tree. The surface of the nest (black) is visible in the foreground, and the arrow indicates part of the shallow entrance channel leading to a nearby creek. (Drawn by Gordon Howes from photographs taken by the author).

Despite the diversity of *P. aethiopicus* nests known from Lake Victoria, all share one common feature, namely, a surface relatively protected from wind action; this feature is also shared with the nests of *P. annectens* and *P. dolloi*. Such protection could be of importance during the protracted stage of larval life history when the young are capable of air-breathing and frequently visit the surface for that purpose (see Greenwood, '58). In nature, nestling *P. aethiopicus* only project the snout one or two mm above the water when breathing. Wind ruffling an unsheltered surface might well reduce the opportunities for aerial respiration by small individuals.

Johnels and Svensson ('54) suggest that the shallowness of the nests of *P. annectens* also may be connected with the air breathing requirements of the young. Three of the four known types of *P. aethiopicus* nests are as shallow as those described for *P. annectens*; the fourth, the deep pit-like structure in the papyrus mat (see above), is considerably deeper. In that nest, many larvae were seen resting on the roots which traversed it near the surface, and when the nest was explored with a dip-net and a suction pump (see Greenwood, '58), the greatest concentration of nestlings was found in a narrow gallery some 300 mm below the surface. Those observations were made during daylight hours. From what is known of diel activity patterns in larval *P. aethiopicus* and *P. annectens* kept in aquaria (see Johnels and Svensson, '54; Greenwood, '58), their distribution within the nest may well differ at night when the larvae are most active.

Environmental conditions within the pit nest of *P. aethiopicus* are detailed in Greenwood ('58). Oxygen concentrations (as ppm), measured over a 14-day period between 1015 and 1615 hrs, ranged from 1.01 to 1.71 at the surface, and from 0.98 to 2.66 at the bottom of the nest. All readings were lower than those taken at comparable depths in the neighboring creek. During the same period, the minimum surface and bottom temperatures in the nest were 10.1°C and 17.8°C respectively, and the maximum was 25°C at both depths. Using a maximum and minimum thermometer suspended in the nest at about its mid-depth, the least diurnal temperature variation was 0.5°C, and the greatest 3.6°C; at all times the nest surface water temperature was 3°C cooler than at the surface of the creek, but the bottom of the nest was always isothermal with that in the creek.

A parent fish was sometimes present in three of the four nests studied. In two of these the fish's sex could not be determined definitely, but judging from the size of the individuals and from their broad pectoral fins and broad snouts, both were probably males. The adult in the third nest was a male. The fish (of undetermined sex) occupying the deep pit-like nest in the papyrus swamp guarded the young with vigor on some occasions, rising to the surface and snapping at any objects that fell or were introduced into the water, even attacking the observer's shadow when it fell across the surface. On other occasions, however, it left the nest on the observer's approach and remained absent for as long as half an hour. The same individual also showed the tail-lashing behavior at and just below the surface of the nest that was first described by Budgett ('01) for *P. annectens* and that is interpreted as a means of oxygenating at least the upper water of the nest.

Apart from the presumed (but probable) nest seen by Poll ('39) in Lake Edward, nests of *P. aethiopicus* have not been described from other parts of the species' extensive range.

Nothing is known of the nests or breeding biology of *Protopterus amphibius* of eastern and north-eastern Africa.

As with the dry-season nests of *Protopterus*, it would seem that the diversity of form and structure of breeding nests is dictated, to a large extent, by various physical parameters of the environment. Much less is known about the way in which the breeding nests are constructed. For the three species whose nesting habits are known, there are no direct observations on the way in which the parent fish (presumed to be the male) sets about building the nest. In the case of *P. dolloi*, however, there is circumstantial evidence that the male, by using anguilliform body movements, actively burrows into the soft substrate. Some of the simpler nests, like the saucer-shaped clearings in grass and water-lily swamps, could be achieved by a combination of biting and body movement. Others, like the deep papyrus-swamp pit, might involve the modification of preexisting holes in the papyrus mat (possibly made by hippopotami), again by combining body movements and biting. Those nests of *P. aethiopicus* associated with uprooted trees would definitely seem to involve the use, with modification by the parent, of preexisting sheltered sites.

Fecundity and brood-fractioning

Of the three *Protopterus* species whose breeding biology has been investigated, *P. aethiopicus* is seemingly the most fecund (Greenwood, '58; Brien et al., '59), but the data are very inadequate. In part the information stems from counts of ovulated eggs, and eggs near ovulation, in two ripe *P. aethiopicus* (Greenwood, '58); in part from estimates of the number of embryos and of young found in *P. aethiopicus* and *P. annectens* nests (Budgett, '01; Johnels and Svensson, '54; Greenwood, '58); and also from the estimated number of embryos in *P. dolloi* nests (Brien et al., '59).

Determinations of fecundity based on embryos and young in nests are likely to be imprecise and equivocal. Apart from the difficulty of ensuring that all the embryos or young are collected, there is a possibility that either more than one female spawns in a nest, or that a single female may spawn over a period of some days (Johnels and Svensson, '54; Greenwood, '58). This uncertainty stems from the occurrence of embryos and young at more than one developmental stage in a single nest, that is, brood fractioning. As many as three stages have been recorded in a nest of *P. aethiopicus* (Greenwood, '58), the modes being fairly clear-cut, with relatively few intermediate stadia represented; a similar phenomenon was noticed by Johnels and Svensson ('54). Direct evidence of polygamy is weak and rests on a single observation of three adult *P. aethiopicus* in one nest from which developmentally fractioned embryos and young were later recovered (Greenwood, '58). Some evidence relating to both fecundity and the cause of brood fractioning can be derived from egg counts in ripe female *P. aethiopicus*, but only two specimens have been examined (Greenwood, '58). One of these specimens (900 mm total length) had a total of ca. 2,200 ova free in the oviducts (a minimal count since a large number of eggs was shed when the fish was captured); many advanced but unovulated ova were present in the ovaries. The other female (910 mm long) yielded 1,760 free ova; a volumetric count of the large (ca. 4 mm) but unshed ova in one ovary gave a minimum count of 2,300 eggs near ovulation. It is estimated that either of these females could have shed between 5,000 and 6,000 ova within a short period of time. Those estimates must be related to the count of 5,192 young recovered from the deep pit-nest in the papyrus swamp and the incomplete sample of over 2,000 young collected in the shallow scoop-nest from which many were seen to escape (Greenwood, '58). If either of these fishes had spawned in a single nest and ovulated twice over a period of not more than 72 hours, each could have produced sufficient ova to account for the numbers of embryos or young recorded, and for the brood fractioning observed.

Some laboratory observations on developmental fractioning in embryos and young taken from a single *P. aethiopicus* nest and then raised *in vitro* seem to suggest that even if there are slight differences in fertilization times, those differences are reinforced by individual variation in the rate of ontogeny (Greenwood, '58).

No figures are available on the number of embryos or young in the nests of *Protopterus annectens*, beyond an estimate of "several thousands" or "considerably less" given by Johnels and Svensson ('54:155). Egg size is smaller than in *P. aethiopicus*, the greatest egg diameter being in the ranges of 3.5–4.0 mm and 4.5–5.0 mm for *P. annectens* and *P. aethiopicus*, respectively. Counts of ovulated or near-ovulated eggs are not available for *P. annectens*.

There is no reported evidence of brood fractioning in *P. dolloi*. Mature ova in this species are larger than in *P. annectens* or *P. aethiopicus*, but no measurements have been published (only the indication that the eggs are about the size of "petits pois"); certainly fewer embryos are found in the nests of *P. dolloi* ("quelques centaines") than in those of the other two species (see Brien et al., '59; Bouillon, '61).

Biology of nestling and immediate post-nestling young

Embryos of *Protopterus aethiopicus* hatch 11 to 15 days after fertilization (Greenwood, '58), those of *P. annectens* after about 8 days (Budgett, '01). These differences are probably associated with the larger egg size in *P. aethiopicus* and the lower water temperatures obtaining during the breeding season of this species (18°–25°C compared with 25°–30°C for *P. annectens*). Once hatched, the young (here referred to as nestlings) of *P. aethiopicus* are at first relatively inactive and, in the pit nest, are concentrated either near the bottom or attached by the well-developed thoracic sucker to the walls of the nest some 20–30 cm below the surface (Greenwood, '58).

In nature, nestling *P. aethiopicus* begin air-breathing at a length of between 23 and 27 mm (and those raised *in vitro* at a length of

25 mm); at these lengths the external gills are still well-developed (Greenwood, '58). Experimental evidence indicates that when the volume of water is large relative to the number of nestlings, *P. aethiopicus* of length 23–28 mm are not obligate air-breathers and can survive (at 23°C) for over a month without access to the surface (Greenwood, '58). Johnels and Svensson ('54) apparently did not observe *P. annectens* young taking air at the surface of the nest, since no mention of this activity is made in their paper; Budgett ('01) states that he did not observe air-breathing by nestling *P. annectens*.

On the basis of nestling growth rates it is estimated that in Lake Victoria young *P. aethiopicus* remain in the nest for 50–55 days after fertilization; it is thought that they leave the nest when at a length of about 34 mm, the entire brood doing so in a matter of hours (Greenwood '58). Budgett ('01) believed that *P. annectens* left the nest about 20 days after the eggs were fertilized; that figure was extended to a month by Johnels and Svensson ('54), who also estimated the young to have reached a length of 30–35 mm by that time.

It would seem that in both *P. aethiopicus* and *P. annectens* the yolk supply is exhausted just before the young leave the nest, or very shortly afterwards (Greenwood, '58; Johnels and Svensson, '54).

Virtually nothing is known about the biology of either young *P. annectens* or *P. aethiopicus* for some time after they have left the nest. For *P. aethiopicus* in Lake Victoria it seems probable that some months are spent living within the matted papyrus roots or amongst the root systems of semi-aquatic grass in marginal swamps (Graham, '29). Young, 35–40 mm in length, are fairly common seasonally in such habitats and specimens up to 300 mm occur there throughout the year (Greenwood, '58).

Considering the small size at which *Protopterus* leave the nest it is likely that their immediate habitat is determined largely by the locality of the nest. There is no evidence to support Graham's ('29) contention that, because young *P. aethiopicus* in Lake Victoria do not encounter conditions necessitating estivation, they ". . . bury themselves in the papyrus sod and pass the corresponding time in a quiescent condition." Small lungfishes living in that habitat, or amongst grass roots, are in fact extremely active (personal observations).

Even less is known about the early life history of post-nestling *P. annectens* and *P.*

dolloi (see Johnels and Svensson, '54; Brien et al., '59). Johnels and Svensson note that individuals of the former species under 30 mm in length do not dig into the mud as the swamp begins to dry and are thus incapable of estivation. Whether these very small fishes survive the dry season is not recorded, nor is it known at precisely what size they are capable of forming a cocoon, but cocoons containing specimens 40–50 mm long do occur (Johnels and Svensson, '54). *Protopterus annectens* 30–35 mm long are known from riverine habitats, but whether these were young from the swamps or were spawned in nests immediately adjacent to the river could not be determined. By implication, post-nestling *P. dolloi* leave their subterranean nest and pass the first wet season in the swamps; they then escape, together with the females, to permanent water as the swamp habitat dries out (Brien et al., '59).

During the wet season, small *P. amphibius* were collected with adults, in streams and water holes (Percy et al., '53).

OTHER ASPECTS OF THE NATURAL HISTORY
OF *PROTOPTERUS*

As was mentioned earlier, far less is known about other aspects of the natural history of *Protopterus* than about its breeding and estivating habits.

Habitats

In general it could be said that the four *Protopterus* species inhabit shallow water (Johnels and Svensson, '54; Curry-Lindahl, '56; Poll, '53; Greenwood, '66) although at least in Lake Victoria *P. aethiopicus* occurs some distance off-shore as well as in water over 20 m deep. It is not known to what depths it descends, but bottom trawls fished at over 30 m have yielded specimens. A trawl, however, can catch fish at intermediate depths when it is being hauled to the surface, and some doubt may be attached to these records. If the fishes do live at such depths then, since they are obligate air-breathers, they must surface to breathe, a total journey of some 60 m, and one involving not only a long transit time but marked pressure changes as well.

Little is known about the off-shore distribution of *P. aethiopicus* in the other major lakes, but in all, including Lake Victoria, the species is a prominent element of the inshore fauna occupying marginal grass- and water lily-swamps, and even papyrus-swamps (Poll, '53; Curry-Lindahl, '56; Greenwood, '66; personal observations).

Riverine populations of *Protopterus* seem to be associated more closely with swampy areas (either seasonal flood-swamps or the shallow, slow-flowing and well-vegetated margins of rivers) than with the faster flowing stretches.

Airbreathing and other behavior patterns

Post-nestling young of all four *Protopterus* species are obligate air-breathers, but this capability would not seem to be a prerequisite for life in many of the habitats they occupy. In other habitats, such as papyrus-swamps and shallow grass-swamps, air-breathing may be a necessity unless, as is the case with certain gill-breathing actinopterygian fishes, use is made of the thin, highly oxygenated surface film of water, a habit that imposes severe size limitations on the fishes that practice it. Air-breathing is, of course, a prerequisite for the type of nesting behavior found amongst lungfishes and for the various forms of estivation and other dry-season survival techniques employed by these animals.

Johnels and Svensson ('54) believe that in general *P. annectens* is more active by day than by night, a view also held by Curry-Lindahl ('56) for *P. aethiopicus*, but again there are few field observations. Certainly captive nestlings of *P. annectens* and *P. aethiopicus* are most active nocturnally (Johnels and Svensson, '54; Greenwood, '58). It must be remembered, however, that the obligate air-breathing of all *Protopterus* requires some activity, perhaps as frequently as once every 20 minutes, throughout the day (personal observations on captive adult and nestling *P. aethiopicus*).

The occupation and defense of a nesting site can be considered as a display of territoriality. Curry-Lindahl's ('56) extensive field observations on *P. aethiopicus* in the Lake Edward region also suggest that some degree of territorality may be displayed outside the breeding season.

Adult male and female *P. dolloi* occupy different habitats during the dry season, the males staying in the dried out swamps and the females returning to the permanent waters from whence they return when the swamp areas are again flooded (Brien et al., '59).

Food and feeding

There is a general belief, based on field and laboratory observations, that *Protopterus* locate their prey by olfaction, supplemented by taste buds on the paired fins, especially the pectorals (Johnels and Svensson, '54; Curry-Lindahl, '56; Thomson, '69). Electroreception is another distinct possibility (see Northcutt, this volume). There is apparently no experimental evidence to support the idea of prey location by olfaction, but Johnels and Svensson note, presumably on the basis of their own histological investigations, that in *P. annectens* "Large numbers of taste buds are distributed over the epithelial surface of the pectoral fins . . . and also of the pelvics, and the neuro-epithelial cells in these buds are the same type as those forming buds in the mouth cavity."

Feeding methods have been described in detail for both *P. annectens* and *P. aethiopicus* (Johnels and Svensson, '54; Curry-Lindahl, '56; personal observations). There are no anatomical or dental grounds for considering that this might differ in the other two species. Bemis and Lauder ('86; also see Bemis, this volume) describe the kinematics and electromyography in *Lepidosiren paradoxa*, which is broadly similar to that in *Protopterus*.

Ingestion involves a slow chewing of the food during which it is frequently spat out and sucked back into the mouth until, finally, it has undergone very complete maceration. In contrast, initial food intake is very rapid, and is effected by a powerful suction generated through depression of the hyoid apparatus by the massive recti cervicis muscles. Food is usually taken from the substrate, but can also be taken from the surface (personal observations).

Although there are many scattered records of the gut contents from the three better studied *Protopterus* species (especially *P. aethiopicus* and *P. annectens*; see Poll, '53; Johnels and Svensson, '54; Curry-Lindahl, '56; and Greenwood, '66), only one detailed analysis has been published, that by Corbet ('61) for *P. aethiopicus* in Lake Victoria.

From these various sources *P. annectens* and *P. aethiopicus* can be categorized as omnivorous carnivores, at least as adults. A wide variety of prey is consumed, especially invertebrates such as molluscs, crustaceans, and larval insects, with a probable emphasis on molluscs. Vertebrates, especially fishes, are consumed to a lesser extent. The slow stalking approach employed by *Protopterus* when feeding, or the alternative method, lying in wait for the prey to come within sucking range, may account for the relative infrequency with which fishes are taken. Johnels and Svensson ('54) suggest, however, that in the period immediately following their release from the estivation cocoon, larger *P. annectens* subsist cannibalistically on smaller individuals.

Young *P. aethiopicus* less than 100 mm long living in the papyrus mat appear to feed mainly on ostracods and small molluscs.

Plant material occurs quite frequently in the guts of *Protopterus*, but there is uncertainty as to whether this is actively sought as an item of diet or is ingested accidentally when the animal is burrowing or taking other food from the bottom (see discussions in Johnels and Svensson, '54; Curry-Lindahl, '56).

Predation

The only detailed consideration of possible predators (other than man) is that provided by Curry-Lindahl ('56) and is based on his observations of *P. aethiopicus* living in the swamp areas of Lake Edward and in the Ruzizi river (Tanzania). Curry-Lindahl's ('56) conclusions are not particularly clear-cut and seem to be derived mainly from circumstantial evidence. He implicates leopards, serval cats, and hyaenas as important nocturnal predators. The greatest predation on *Protopterus* in Lake Edward according to Curry-Lindahl ('56) is by fishes, though no quantitative data are given to substantiate these ideas. Judging from the predatory fishes listed, few *Protopterus* over 150 mm long are likely to be taken. Personal observations on the diet of several fish species in Lake Victoria certainly do not suggest that lungfishes are a common prey item in their diet. In that lake, *Protopterus* of a large size are eaten by otters, and, at least in the past were taken by crocodiles (personal observations).

Locomotion

Protopterus employs two principal methods of locomotion, namely, anguilliform swimming, and crawling with the paired fins (Johnels and Svensson, '54; Rosen et al., '81; personal observations). The anguilliform mode can be considered the usual one and is used whenever the animal is swimming above the bottom in open water; it is employed when moving to breathe at the surface in water of greater depth than the fish's length. When moving in this fashion, the paired fins trail loosely against the body.

Despite their flimsy, boot-lace-like appearance, the paired fins are employed when the fish is moving along the bottom, and often to support the body when at rest. When used in locomotion the fins are moved antero-posteriorly in a side-to-side alternating diagonal

pattern; that is, for example, when the left fore and right hind fins are moved anteriorly, the right fore and left hind fins are swung posteriorly, a pattern like that seen in the limb movements of lower tetrapods (Rosen et al., '81; personal observations). When crawling in this fashion, the body is raised above the substrate and supported by the fins. A considerable length of each fin is closely applied to the bottom, thus providing the necessary frictional resistance. Crawling in this manner is commonly seen in small (less than 60-mm) individuals kept in aquaria, but it is not uncommon in much larger individuals. There are few field observations of lungfishes using this form of progression (Curry-Lindahl, '56), but it is frequently used by nestlings 25–30 mm long (Greenwood, '58).

The pectoral fins are sometimes used to raise and support the anterior part of the body when the fish is at rest, and the pelvic fins are used as anchors and fulcra when, in shallow water, the trunk is arched upwards in order to bring the mouth above the surface for breathing (Fig. 7).

There are no explicit accounts of any *Protopterus* species making directional or seemingly purposeful excursions on land as, for instance, observed for eels (*Anguilla*). Certainly *Protopterus* can move, in an anguilliform manner, over dry land when, for example, they escape from a beached seine net, but the movement is seemingly a random one. Similar random movements were seen in lungfishes stranded on damp mud when a temporary grass-swamp was drying out (personal observations).

CONCLUSIONS

As more information on the natural history of *Protopterus* becomes available, it is apparent that the various species show a considerable range of both interspecific and intraspecific variability in a number of features. That variability is clearly seen in their breeding biology, especially nest architecture, and in their responses to seasonal desiccation. To a large extent, however, this variability seems to be environmentally determined, or at least strongly influenced by the environment. The environmental influences can be as general as climatic factors, or can be more narrowly circumscribed ones such as the physical features of the habitat occupied by different populations or even individuals of a species.

Protopterus species are not confined to swamps and marshes, but also occupy a variety of other habitats and niches. Some habi-

Fig. 7.   A specimen of *Protopterus* using the pelvic fins as anchors and fulcra when raising the forepart of the body toward the surface, while breathing in shallow water. (Drawn by Gordon Howes from a photograph published by P. Brien ('67) in African Wild Life *21*:214).

tats are occupied throughout the year, others during only part of the year; some are lentic, some lotic, and others are only temporary. There are several characteristics of the African lungfishes that have enabled them to enter, as permanent residents, a number of habitats unavailable or only temporarily available to actinopterygian fishes. Especially important in this respect are their body form and modes of locomotion. These allow lungfish to move through dense aquatic vegetation, to burrow, and even to move across barely flooded land. Their ability to breathe atmospheric air so effectively has permitted lungfishes to use poorly oxygenated or even completely deoxygenated habitats (see Burggren and Johansen, this volume). That facility, coupled with the burrowing habits, have allowed the evolution of a very effective means of estivation (see Fishman et al., this volume), a type of estivation apparently dependent on the urotelic excretory system and the ability of lungfishes to metabolize body proteins under certain conditions (see Janssens and Cohen, '66). Perhaps the only African fishes approaching *Protopterus* in their ability to occupy such a range of habitats are air-breathing catfishes of the genus *Clarias*. Although *Clarias* does not estivate as effectively as does *Protopterus* (for example, no cocoon is formed), and it does not build nests either for estivation or breeding, it could be considered a partial but close ecological analog of *Protopterus* with which it coexists in many parts of Africa (see Greenwood, '66).

Much has still to be learned about the biology of *Protopterus* and its sister taxon *Lep-*

idosiren of South America; both genera provide a very profitable area for future research into their natural history, research whose results could also be of considerable value in the wider field of evolutionary biology, especially that relating to the origin of the tetrapods.

ACKNOWLEDGMENTS

I am most grateful to my colleagues Gordon Howes and Bernice Brewster for the help they have given me in preparing this paper. In particular I would like to thank Gordon Howes for the skill and care he has taken in preparing the figures. My thanks also go to Dr. William Bemis for allowing me to use his unpublished distribution map for *Protopterus*.

LITERATURE CITED

Bemis, W.E., and G.V. Lauder (1986) Morphology and function of the feeding apparatus of the lungfish, *Lepidosiren paradoxa* (Dipnoi). J. Morphol. *187*:81–108.
Blanc, M., F. D'Aubenton, and Y. Plessis (1956) Étude de l'enkystement de *Protopterus annectens* (Owen, 1839). Bull I.F.A.N. A *18*:834–854.
Bouillon, J. (1961) The lungfish of Africa. Nat. Hist. *70*:62–70.
Brien, P., M. Poll, and J. Bouillon (1959) Ethologie de la reproduction de *Protopterus dolloi* Blgr. Ann. R. Belg. Sér. 8 *71*:3–21.
Budgett, J.S. (1899) Observations on *Polypterus* and *Protopterus*. Proc. Cambridge Phil. Soc. Biol. Sci. *10*:236–240.
Budgett, J.S. (1901) On the breeding habits of some West African fishes, with an account of the external features in the development of *Protopterus annectens* and a description of the larva of *Polypterus laparadei*. Trans. Zool. Soc. London. *16*:115–136.

Carter, G.S., and L.C. Beadle (1930) Note on the habits and development of *Lepidosiren paradoxa*. J. Linn. Soc. Zool. *37*:197–203.

Coates, C.W. (1937) Slowly the lungfish gives up its secrets. Bull. N.Y. Zool. Soc. *40*:25–34.

Corbet, P.S. (1961) The food of non-cichlid fishes in the Lake Victoria basin, with remarks on their evolution and adaptation to lacustrine conditions. Proc. Zool. Soc. Lond. *136*:1–101.

Curry-Lindahl, K. (1956) On the ecology, feeding behaviour and territoriality of the African lungfish, *Protopterus aethiopicus* Heckel. Ark. Zool. *9*:479–497.

Godet, R., and F. Pieri (1961) Effet hypothermisant sur le Rat d'un extrait du réserves lipidiques de Protoptère. C.R.S. Acad. Sci. Paris *252*:2600–2602.

Gosse, J.-P. (1984) Protopteridae. In J. Daget, J.-P. Gosse and D.F.E. Thys van den Audenaerde (eds): Check-list of the Freshwater Fishes of Africa. Paris: ORSTOM, pp. 8–17.

Graham, M. (1929) The Victoria Nyanza and its Fisheries. London: Crown Agents for the Colonies.

Greenwood, P.H. (1958) Reproduction in the east African lung-fish *Protopterus aethiopicus* Heckel. Proc. Zool. Soc. Lond. *130*:547–567.

Greenwood, P.H. (1966) The Fishes of Uganda. 2nd ed. Kampala: Uganda Society.

Jackson, R.J. (1916) African lung fish. J.E. Afr. Uganda Nat. Hist. Soc. *5*:3–4.

Janssens, P.A., and P.P. Cohen (1966) Ornithine-urea cycle enzymes in the African lungfish *Protopterus aethiopicus*. Science *152*:358–359.

Jardine, W. (1841) Remarks on the structure and habits of *Lepidosiren annectens*. Ann. Mag. Nat. Hist. *7*:21–26.

Johnels, A.G., and G.S.O. Svensson (1954) On the biology of *Protopterus annectens* (Owen). Ark. Zool. *7*:131–164.

Lüling, K.H. (1961) Untersuchungen an Lungenfischen, inbesondere an afrikanischen Protopteriden. Bonn. Zool. Beitr. *12*:87–112.

Marlier, G. (1957) L'enkystement du *Protopterus aethiop-*

icus Heckel. Ann. Soc. R. Zool. Belg. *87*:211–216.

Miles, R.S. 91977) Dipnoan (lungfish) skulls and the relationships of the group: A study based on new species from the Devonian of Australia. Zool. J. Linn. Soc. *61*:1–328.

Percy, R.C., H.E. Percy, and M.W. Ridley (1953) The water holes at Ijara, Northern Province, Kenya. J.E. Afr. Nat. Hist. Soc. *22*:2–14.

Pienaar, V. De V. (1981) Another important ichthyological find in the Kruger National Park (*Protopterus annectens brieni*). Koedoe *24*:189–191.

Poll, M. (1938) Poissons du Katanga (bassin du Congo) récoltés par le professeur Paul Brien. Rev. Zool. Bot. Afr. *30*:389–423.

Poll, M. (1939) Poissons—Exploration du Parc National Albert. Institute des Parcs Nationaux du Congo Belge, Brussels. Mission H. Damas (1935–1936) *6*:1–73.

Poll, M. (1953) Poissons non Cichlidae. Rés. Scient. Explor. Hydrobiol. Lac Tanganyika (1946–47) *35*A:1–251.

Poll, M. (1961) Revision systématic et raciation geographique des Protopteridae de l'Afrique centrale. Ann. Mus. R. Congo Belge, Ser. 8 Zool. *103*:3–50.

Rosen, D.E., P.L. Forey, B.G. Gardiner, and C. Patterson (1981) Lungfishes, tetrapods, paleontology and plesiomorphy. Bull. Am. Mus. Nat. Hist. *167*:159–276.

Smith, H.W. (1931) Observations of the African lungfish, *Protopterus aethiopicus*, and on evolution from water to land environments. Ecology *12*:164–181.

Swan, H., D. Jenkins, and K. Knox (1968) Anti-metabolic extract from the brain of *Protopterus aethiopicus*. Nature *127*:671.

Thomson, K.S. (1969) The biology of the lobe-finned fishes. Biol. Rev. *44*:91–154.

Trewavas, E. (1954) The presence in Africa east of the Rift Valleys of two species of *Protopterus*, *P. annectens* and *P. amphibius*. Ann. Mus. R. Congo Belg. (N.S.) 4to Zool. *1*:83–100.

Wasawo, D.P.S. (1959) A dry season burrow of *Protopterus aethiopicus* Heckel. Rev. Zool. Bot. Afr. *60*:65–70.

JOURNAL OF MORPHOLOGY SUPPLEMENT 1:181–198 (1986)

The Biology of the Australian Lungfish, *Neoceratodus forsteri* (Krefft 1870)

A. KEMP
Queensland Museum, Brisbane, Queensland, 4101, Australia

ABSTRACT   The literature on the biology of the Australian lungfish, *Neoceratodus forsteri* (Krefft, 1870), over the past 115 years is reviewed. Relevant unpublished information on the habits, environment, and distribution of the lungfish is included. Topics covered are the discovery and taxonomic position of the species, the appearance and habits of adults and juveniles, their environment and distribution (historical and modern), their oviposition and development, and their diet and catching methods. It is concluded that, despite locally abundant populations of lungfish in rivers of southeast Queensland, the species is still at risk of extinction from a number of natural or artificial causes.

The Australian lungfish, *Neoceratodus forsteri* (Krefft, 1870), is the sole survivor of the extensive lungfish fauna (family Ceratodontidae) of Australia that existed in the Triassic, Cretaceous, and Tertiary. The species is known from the Cretaceous in Australia (Kemp and Molnar, '81) and possibly in South America (Pascual and Bondesio, '76), and the genus is known from the Triassic of Russia (Obruchev, '76) and Australia (Woodward, '06, '08; Kemp, unpublished).

When Krefft (1870) originally described the Australian lungfish he thought it was an amphibian, "allied to the genus *Lepidosiren*," but he also recognized the similarity of the dentition to the fossil tooth plates described by Agassiz (1844) as sharks. Agassiz gave his fossils the generic name *Ceratodus*, which means "horned tooth." Krefft's (1870) newly discovered fish was accordingly *Ceratodus forsteri*. The species was named after William Forster, Minister for Lands in the New South Wales Government, and a landowner in the Wide Bay district of South East Queensland. As Whitley wrote in 1929, Forster tantalized Krefft for years with his stories of "fresh water salmon" and finally sent Krefft two specimens (Whitley, 1929). Krefft added the following postscript to his scientific description:

It is strange that a curious creature like this, which was well known to the early settlers at Wide Bay and other Queensland districts, should so long have escaped the eyes of those interested in natural history. I remember that Mr William Forster mentioned a 'fish' with cartilaginous backbone years ago, and that I expressed an opinion that he must be mistaken . . . . the northern squatters have named it the Burnett or Dawson Salmon, from its habits and from the rivers in which it is principally found. The poor bush cooks could have made a small fortune, had they preserved the heads and sent them to Sydney.

Günther, who published the first anatomical treatise on the Queensland lungfish in 1871, was scornful about the amphibian determination, and placed the new discovery firmly with the fishes, where it has remained ever since except for a digression back to the Amphibia (Kesteven, '44), which has been largely ignored by other researchers. Günther (1871) was adamant that there were no grounds for separating the fossil forms from the recent genus:

. . . there is not the slightest evidence that the recent and fossil ceratodonts differed from each other. It is true we have only the teeth for our guidance; but these are so well marked by peculiar characters, and the recent teeth so similar to those of certain extinct species, that we should be better justified in making generic distinctions among the fossil forms, than in separating the living from the extinct.

Günther's views have been echoed by subsequent authors (Stromer and Peyer, '17; Pascual and Bondesio, '76). However, a different view was given by Teller (1891) when he described a fossil calvarium, associated with typical ceratodont tooth plates. This skull differs significantly from the skull of the recent fish, and Teller (1891) accordingly reserved *Ceratodus* for the fossil forms and gave the recent genus a new name, *Epiceratodus*. However, in 1876 a living lungfish from Australia was described (de Castelnau, 1876a). De Castelnau claimed that the new species came from the Fitzroy River and was often to be seen in the Rockhampton market, a locality many miles distant from the Burnett River, where Krefft's fish were found. De Castelnau's (1876a) specimen was only 61 cm long with body proportions differing from those of *Ceratodus forsteri* and, apparently, having different teeth. De Castelnau (1876a) assigned this animal to a new genus and species, *Neoceratodus blanchardi*. Within a year he retracted (de Castelnau, 1876b), admitting that his specimen was a young *Ceratodus forsteri*, that the body proportions were juvenile and the teeth—once the mouth was properly cut open—no different from those of *C. forsteri*. But, if the generic name of the living form is to be different from that of the fossil, the laws of priority state that it has to be *Neoceratodus*. It is unfortunate that a generic name resulting from a mistake should take precedence over Teller's (1891) carefully reasoned argument.

APPEARANCE

Australian lungfish are often said to be "over six feet" or "at least six feet" in size (180 cm) (Krefft, 1870; Spencer, 1892; Longman, '28). This is rarely the case. O'Connor (1896) reports a range of 82.5–112.5 cm for 109 fish that he caught in the Mary River.

Adult Australian lungfish have a wide flat head, a thick heavy body, a diphycercal tail, and paddle-shaped fins (Fig. 1A). Except for the anterior part of the head, the fish is covered in scales, which are large over the body grading to small on the fins. Each scale is enclosed in an epithelial pocket, and the extensive overlapping of the scales ensures that vulnerable areas are protected by a thickness of at least four scales. The back of the head,

where the calvarium is thin, is covered by two unusually large and thick interlocking scales. The mouth is small and sub-terminal in position; the anterior naris is partly outside the upper lip, partly within; the posterior naris is inside the mouth cavity. The snout is covered in pores; the sensory lines on the head show as a series of pits connected by a canal below the skin, as does the lateral line of the body, which perforates the overlying scales at intervals. The eyes are small, bluish or dark brown in color—vision does not seem to be important to the animal. The color of the body blends in well with the environment—dark brown or olive brown dorsally and muddy salmon pink below. The pink color is much brighter in the breeding season (Dean '12), especially in males; otherwise there are no obvious distinguishing sexual characteristics. The yellow lines around the pectoral fin noted in some specimens (Dean, '12) do not necessarily mean that the fish is male (Bancroft, personal papers). Often there are patches of intense dark pigment on the body, and the position of these varies according to the individual.

Juvenile lungfish have different body proportions than those of the adults—the head is rounder, the fins relatively smaller and the trunk more slender (Fig. 1B). The mouth is initially terminal, but shifts back as the fish grows. The dorsal fin reaches to the back of the head in young juveniles and gradually moves caudally until it extends only mid-dorsally in the adult. Juveniles are distinctly mottled with a ground color of gold or olive brown. There are also patches of intense dark pigment, which persist long after the mottling has disappeared. The belly of a small Australian lungfish is a muddy pink color. Young juveniles are capable of a color change in response to light, but this ability is gradually lost as the pigment becomes denser.

MOVEMENTS

Adult Australian lungfish are quiet, unresponsive fish by day (except in the breeding season) but become more active in the late afternoon and evening when they move around feeding. They are also active at night (Grigg, '65a). Movements are usually slow and sinuous, using the tail with or without fins. If alarmed or excited they can move fast, using the tail only (Ramsay, 1876). Fins are important during feeding, when they are used to brace the body against the substrate (Dean, '06)—a habit displayed by lungfish less

Fig. 1. A) A living specimen of *Neoceratodus forsteri* photographed in an aquarium as it was about to rise to the surface. Pores of the lateral line system are visible on the head and body. Scale bar = 1 cm. B) Two living juveniles of *N. forsteri*, showing body proportions differing from those of the adult—rounder heads, relatively smaller pelvic fins, and a dorsal fin reaching further forward. Scale bar = 1 cm.

than an inch long. Lungfish are also able to slither through wet grass—with the assistance of a downhill slope—but are much too heavy to support the body on the fins without additional support from the water (Illidge, 1894). Dean ('06, '12) discusses the movements of Australian lungfish in considerable detail.

RESPIRATION

To breathe air the lungfish may rise to the surface, exhale through the mouth, inhale, and dive forwards, or rise to the surface, breathe, and reverse back into the water. They do not breathe air very often; the Australian lungfish, unlike the African or South American lungfish, is not an obligate aerobe, and under normal circumstances, breathes air only rarely. Bancroft ('18) considers that if *N. forsteri* is breathing air regularly, as described by Semon (1899) and Dean ('06) the fish are sick or experiencing unusual physiological stress. Spencer (1892) considers that the lung is of most use to the animal when the river is in flood and the water full of suspended sand and mud. Grigg ('65a) found experimentally that more frequent air breathing was correlated with periods of greater activity at night, and then the lung is useful as a supplementary organ of respiration. However, Thomson ('69) argues that the lung functions more as a hydrostatic organ. Burggren and Johansen (this volume) present more information on the comparative physiology of dipnoan respiration.

Like adult Australian lungfish, juveniles do not need to breathe air. Facultative air breathing develops at stage 52 (25 mm long) (Kemp, '82b). Young African and South American lungfish begin to breathe air at much the same size as young Australian lungfish (Johnels and Svensson, '55; Greenwood, '58; Kerr, 1900). Bancroft ('13) considered that young lungfish reared in captivity required a slope to rest on with the mouth out of the water, but, in fact, they develop normally without a slope (Kemp, '81). Small lungfish maintain a current of water, presumably respiratory, over the body surface, using well-developed ciliated cells (Whiting and Bone, '80). Cilia develop much earlier than these authors found and last much longer. Neurulae of stage 23 (Fig. 5A) have cilia and they are still present in juveniles of stage 52 (Fig. 7B), the oldest so far examined (Kemp, unpublished). Skin respiration may be very important in juvenile lungfish.

SURVIVAL UNDER ADVERSE CONDITIONS

Neoceratodus forsteri has been credited with a considerable ability to survive adverse conditions. It is true that they can survive for long periods wrapped in damp moss or water weeds. O'Connor (1898) records that lungfish he sent to London in 1898 arrived in good condition after a voyage of 8 weeks, presumably using the method that he had found effective for transferring lungfish by Queensland Railways (O'Connor, '09). He placed the fish in narrow wooden compartments, wrapped them in water weeds, and sprinkled them with water at intervals. The Australian lungfish can also survive for some months under natural conditions in a dried out pond provided that some damp leaves, water weeds, and mud are still present (Kemp, unpublished). In the environment that most Australian lungfish normally inhabit, such events are rare. Their ability to withstand desiccation is vastly inferior to that of the African lungfish, which can survive in a cocoon of mucus and dry mud (Owen, 1841; see Greenwood, this volume; Fishman et al., this volume). Nor does it equal the achievements of *Lepidosiren paradoxa*, which can survive for months in a burrow of mud and mucus (Kerr, 1900). When water levels in the pond or river are low, air breathing may become more important for *N. forsteri* (see Burggren and Johansen, this volume). However, if the rivers are polluted, e.g., with sugar mill effluent, the lungfish

succumb as quickly as any other creature that is unable to leave the water.

ENVIRONMENT AND DISTRIBUTION

There is some confusion about the original distribution of the Australian lungfish and the environment in which they live. In fact, few of the environments actually occupied by *Neoceratodus forsteri* today conform either to the popular image of Australian rivers—stagnant pools only occasionally interconnected to make a river—or to "quiet water bodies that are often poorly oxygenated" (Campbell and Barwick, '84). *N. forsteri* occupies diverse environments, some of which are described below.

Enoggera Reservoir is a large, man-made reservoir created by convict labor in 1868 by building a dam across a valley in the hills outside Brisbane (Fig. 2A). It is a permanent body of water, approximately 60 hectares in area, filled by springs in the D'Aguillar Ranges, and overflowing into Enoggera Creek, which ultimately drains into the estuary of the Brisbane River. The water level drops significantly only in a very dry summer. The reservoir is up to 60 feet deep, with steeply sloping sides. The substrate has a high clay content and a few metamorphic rocks. The bottom is covered thickly with detritus from water lilies and eucalypt leaves, and the water, clear but stained brown by tannin, has a pH of 5.

Except for occasional algal blooms, plants survive only at the edges and consist mainly of para grass (*Brachiaria mutica*) and numerous species of aquatic weeds, among which live small fish, prawns, and several species of snail. Para grass grows out from the bank in water up to 8 feet deep and forms a loosely woven mat floating on the surface of the water. This makes excellent cover for the adult lungfish, which move around in it leaving trails one fish wide (cf. *L. paradoxa*, Kerr, 1900), but it is not used for spawning.

Enoggera Reservoir is a relatively poor environment for lungfish. Eggs have not been found in the lake since water hyacinth (*Eichornia crassipes*) was effectively controlled in 1974. Before this, the breeding season in the lake was short—usually a month or less, compared with 3 months or more in the environment of the Brisbane River (Kemp, '84). Attempts to catch juveniles in 1981 by electrofishing, a method known to be successful in the Brisbane River, produced only adults—large adults with every sign of advanced

Fig. 2. A. Enoggera Reservoir, near Brisbane, southeast Queensland, built in 1868. *Neoceratodus forsteri* were introduced into the reservoir in 1898 by O'Connor. It is a comparatively poor environment for lungfish, and recruitment to the population is currently low. B) The Brisbane River, near Fernvale, southeast Queensland. This is a typical locality for Australian lungfish, richer than Enoggera Reservoir. The upper reaches of the Brisbane River system have now been completely converted into two large reservoirs, Somerset and Wivenhoe Dams, below which are smooth flowing stretches of river. Five *Neoceratodus forsteri* were introduced in 1898 by O'Connor into "a dam near Cressbrook, which communicates with the Brisbane River in times of flood," but it is unlikely that these were responsible for the present population of lungfish in the Brisbane River.

age—and no juveniles at all. Apparently, there has been no recruitment of young fish to the Enoggera population in the last few years.

By contrast, the Brisbane River system (Fig. 2B) is a rich environment for lungfish. This was a large meandering system but is now mostly converted into two reservoirs, Somerset and Wivenhoe Dams. Both have large populations of Australian lungfish. The Brisbane River system is also a permanent environment for lungfish; it floods several times a year, but never runs dry. Below the dams the river is still in a condition approaching the original—wide, mostly slow-flowing, with some reaches of fast water over rocks. The maximum depth is about fifteen feet. The river bottle brush, *Callistemon saligna* and a species of *Casuarina*, both trees of medium height, grow on the water's edge with their root masses in the water. Underwater vegetation is dense. The substrate varies from fine sand through to gravel or rocks, rarely mud, and there is little detritus. Fauna used as food by the lungfish include freshwater prawns, e.g. *Macrobrachia* sp., insect larvae, bivalve molluscs like *Corbiculina* sp., and snails like *Plotiopsis* sp., both very common, and small fish (Kemp et al., '81).

The water is normally clear, although it may be turbid after rain, has a pH close to 8 and a high oxygen content (Kemp, '84). The temperature fluctuates more or less independently of season; the Brisbane River system is a major water storage source for the city of Brisbane and water is released as needed from the bottom of the two large dams across the upper reaches of the river. Water in these impoundments is deep and cold, and, it is quite possible to be collecting eggs in spring in water of 16–17°C when the air temperature is 24°C (Kemp, '84). Shallow areas will reach 24–26°C or more in mid-summer, but the deeper parts of the river are cold.

The Mary River a little further north (Fig. 3) is similar to the Brisbane River system although it flows more slowly, is less extensive, and in places is narrow enough to stop with a bucket. Only in a severe drought—every seven years or so—does it fulfill the classic description of "dries out to a chain of waterholes." The Burnett River, the type locality for *N. forsteri*, further west than the Mary (Fig. 3), is supposed to be more like a chain of waterholes in the dry season (Semon, 1899). However, Spencer (1892) in the following quotation pointed out that the wa-

terholes inhabited by lungfish in dry periods are more than a mile long and a perfectly adequate environment for lungfish:

It is always to be met with in the deep pools, and not in the shallow waters, and it is important to notice that these pools are many of them of considerable extent—some more than a mile long. In the hottest summer they contain a good supply of water and thus, though occasionally a Ceratodus may, of course, find its way into a shallow pool which gets dried up, normally no such thing happens and the animal passes its whole life in water.

The Fitzroy River system is larger than the Brisbane, Burnett, and Mary River systems (Fig. 3), with many tributaries (e.g., the Dawson River). It lies northwest of the Burnett. There are occasional reports of lungfish from this area—an early name of *Neoceratodus forsteri* was "Dawson River Salmon" though this also applies to the barramundi, *Scleropages leichardtii* (Whitley, '27). The lungfish described by de Castelnau (1876a) was apparently caught in the Fitzroy River. Despite this, the Fitzroy River system is not thought to be part of the original range of the lungfish, a distinction reserved for the Mary and Burnett Rivers (Semon 1899; Bancroft, '11). The Fitzroy River was not one of the rivers to which Australian lungfish were introduced by O'Connor in 1898. O'Connor believed that the Australian lungfish was about to become extinct, although he was able to catch 98 lungfish (plus 11 that escaped) from a small area of the Mary River near Miva (O'Connor, '02). With the help of the Royal Society of Queensland, he transplanted the 69 survivors to rivers and reservoirs further south [e.g., 18 to Enoggera Reservoir, 16 to the Coomera River, three to the North Pine River, 21 to the Condamine, which is part of the Murray Basin (Fig. 3), four in a lagoon near the Albert River, and five to a dam at Cressbrook, which communicates with the upper reaches of the Brisbane River in time of flood (O'Connor, '02]. The latter five fish are supposed to be responsible for the whole of the lungfish population of the Brisbane River system (Welsby, '05). I think that this is unlikely for several reasons. Lungfish were involved in a fish kill in the upper Brisbane River only a few years after they were placed in the dam at Cressbrook (Welsby, '05). For this to happen without an existing fish pop-

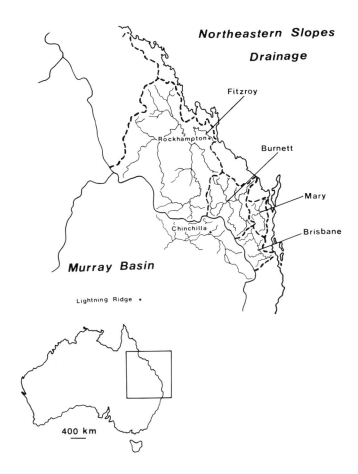

Fig. 3. Map of northeastern Australia, showing present day drainage systems and details of the Fitzroy, Burnett, Mary, Brisbane, and adjacent river systems. Fossil *N. forsteri* localities at Lightning Ridge and Chin-chilla, both within the drainage of the Murray River, are included. Chinchilla is situated on the Condamine River.

ulation in the River, that is, from the five Cressbrook fish, they would have had to escape from the dam and the population would have had to build up to a level sufficient to include some members in a fish kill. This is not consistent with historical (Bancroft, '11, '13, '18, '28, '33) or recent views of the breeding ability of lungfish (Kemp, '84; Kemp, unpublished). The Australian lungfish is not known to migrate and in my experience is reluctant to leave dams even in times of flood. It is much more likely that lungfish were already in the Brisbane River System, and this applies also to the North Pine River,

whose present population was supposedly established with the three transplanted fish!

The historical view that lungfish were confined to the Mary and Burnett River systems (Fig. 3) is untenable for several further reasons. Australia prior to 1895 was wild and not easy to explore. It is unlikely that every possible river system had been thoroughly checked for the presence of lungfish prior to O'Connor's distribution. Lungfish are cryptic, difficult to observe in the wild, and often impossible to catch using conventional methods (Bancroft, '11). Failure to catch an animal in a particular environment is not evidence for absence of the animal. Lungfish are adaptable—able to survive in environments as diverse as Enoggera Reservoir and the Burnett River—and cosmopolitan in their diet. If they were restricted to the Mary and Burnett Rivers, it was not because they could only live in these two systems. The fossil distribution was much wider; *N. forsteri* is known from Cretaceous deposits at Lightning Ridge (Kemp and Molnar, '81) and from Pleistocene sediments near Chinchilla on the Darling Downs (Kemp, '82a). *Neoceratodus forsteri* was widely distributed before the present coastal rivers and mountain ranges were formed. Further, there were persistent reports in letters to the Queensland Museum, before and after O'Connor's time, of lungfish from rivers into which he did not introduce fish. It is unlikely that the historical view of lungfish distribution is correct, but, thanks to the well-intentioned but premature activities of O'Connor, this can never be proved.

SPAWNING

Australian lungfish may spawn from August to December throughout the range, and eggs are found most abundantly in September and October. Folklore about lungfish spawning abounds. For example, the nests reported by Macleay (1884) belong to some other fish, not to the lungfish. Eggs of *N. forsteri* were not found until 1884 when Caldwell discovered some in the Burnett River (Caldwell, 1884) and the external features of the embryology were not described until Semon made collections in 1892 and 1893 (Semon, 1893). Aside from water flow and availability of suitable species of weed (Kemp, '84), and factors as yet unknown (Kemp, unpublished) stimulus for oviposition seems to be increasing photo-period (Kemp, '84). Spawning usually starts within 6–8 weeks of the winter solstice (Kemp, '84). Temperature, rainfall, and oxygen tension are not apparently important (Kemp, '84). Lungfish lay eggs in water at any temperature between 16° and 26°C (Kemp, '84). The breeding season usually starts before any spring rain and is over before the heavy rains of January and February, and the occasional rain periods of September and October are not related to the finding of new eggs (Kemp, '84). Oxygen tension is always high during the day in the spawning grounds, because of abundant plants, and there are no detectable fluctuations correlated with oviposition (Kemp, '84).

Lungfish are specific in their choice of spawning site. Weeds that they could use for spawning occur all along the river bank, but the choice of the actual site is governed by unknown factors. Eggs are found on weeds rooted in sand or in gravel in slow or fast flowing water. Eggs are found on submerged weed that is shaded or in full sun, on clean weed (without attached algae) and on dirty weed (with masses of attached algae). They are never found in stagnant water, or on weeds infested with slimy algae, or if there is loose debris on the water surface. The species of plant used is specific too. They spawn on plants that form dense masses, or on plants situated against a bank, like *Vallisneria spiralis* or the roots of *Callistemon saligna* trees (Kemp, '84).

Lungfish go through a complex courtship behavior, the full sequence of which has not been reported from observations in the wild. *Neoceratodus forsteri* does not need to breathe air under normal circumstances, but as spawning time approaches it breathes air more frequently, and usually noisily. This may reflect no more than an increased physiological requirement for oxygen, or it may be a sort of mating call, as Kesteven ('44) states. Illidge (1894) claims that the noise is made below the water surface or above. Bancroft ('11, '13', '18, '23, '28, '33), who studied the lungfish of the Burnett River extensively for many years, does not mention noisy breathing associated with the spawning season; Spencer (1891) merely notes that it occurs in the evening. This behavior has been observed in Enoggera Reservoir on two occasions, in 1973 and 1976, but never in the Brisbane River (Kemp, '84). Enoggera Reservoir, landlocked and filled by shallow slow-flowing creeks, is consistently warmer than the Brisbane River, which receives an influx of cold water several times a week. The lungfish seem to do their noisy breathing in concert, close to but not in the areas where eggs are actually laid. The two occasions on which noisy breathing was observed were on very hot days and no new eggs were found immediately afterwards.

Grigg ('65b) has described part of the courtship of lungfish when he observed a pair near a weed bank and found eggs in the weeds next day. Other accounts indicate that the fish circle rapidly in pairs, at the surface of the water (Kemp, '84). Such behavior is common in the breeding season. When they actually lay eggs, the fish are intertwined, lying on their sides; the eggs are usually deposited singly, occasionally in pairs, and very rarely in clusters (Kemp, '84). The male fertilizes each egg as it emerges, and the eggs have the appearance of being carefully placed, in weeds with the right sort of micro-environment (dense cover and plenty of food) for the young fish when it hatches. The jelly coat is sticky when first laid, and eggs are usually attached to the weeds. For fish normally of crepuscular or nocturnal habits, they are surprisingly cosmopolitan about egg laying. Any time of the day or night will do, to judge by the ages of the eggs collected. They lay eggs in mid-morning and at such times they are slow to move away when disturbed (Kemp, '84).

Neoceratodus forsteri does not make a nest, and there is no parental care once the eggs are laid (Kemp, '84). It is possible that the male has a territory—often it looks as though there are two or more clutches of eggs, of different ages, as if the male was visited by females at intervals. Each female has a huge ovary and the potential to lay many eggs, but in practice she lays only 50-100 at a time (Kemp, '84).

DEVELOPMENT

The newly laid egg is delicate, heavily yolked, hemispherical in shape, and enclosed in a single vitelline and triple jelly envelope (Kemp, '82b; Kemp, unpublished). The egg itself is about 3 mm across, with the jelly, 1 cm across. About 5% of eggs in the wild are unfertilized, and most of the fertilized eggs will reach hatching if left in the river. This is not the case if the eggs are brought into the laboratory where they are susceptible to bacterial and fungal infections and not easy to rear.

There is considerable variation among individuals in the times taken to complete each stage of development, and some stages last much longer than others (Kemp, '81). Cleavage (Fig. 4A–D) is rapid, each taking 4–7 hours. A large-celled blastula (stage 8) will be a day and a half old. It takes a further 18 hours to reach the stage of development described as a small-celled blastula (stage 10, Fig. 4E) and eggs will now be between 3.5 and 4.5 days old. Formation of stage 11, a blastula preparing to invaginate, is often delayed by further cell division and the formation of a large fluid-filled blastocoel, and eggs will be 5–7 days old. The stages of gastrulation that follow (12–16) are usually completed within a day, and neurulae (Figs. 4F, 5A) develop to stage 23 in the next 2 days. Head structures (stages 26–34, Fig. 5B,C,D) form in the next 4–6 days and pigment starts to appear at stage 36 by day 17. Fish of stage 40 are up to 23 days old, and under certain circumstances hatching may occur at this stage (depending partly on an alkaline pH in the water). Eggs from Enoggera Reservoir hatch much later, at about stage 44, when they are about 30 days old.

Despite alterations in the shape of the embryo (Fig. 4,5), there is little change in size in the early stages of development, and it fits within the innermost vitelline membrane. At about stage 28 the head starts to extend forwards. Though capable of movement when removed from the membrane, the embryo lies inert in the capsule with the head bent round to the tail. The vitelline space does not begin to expand until the embryo is at stage 32, when it becomes more active. Large cracks appear in the inner albumen and the vitelline membranes, and soon they break down completely and lie in pieces within the capsule. The middle jelly membrane is dissolved away from within, thus gradually expanding the capsule in which the young fish lives (Kemp, '82b). The outer jelly membrane persists for many weeks, long after the young fish emerges from a hole in the side. In fact, the hatchling is capable of slipping back into the capsule for some weeks after it has hatched. This has been observed in the laboratory and in the field (Kemp, unpublished).

Small Australian lungfish show a gradual change in body form as they develop (Figs. 5,6,7). There is no externally detectable metamorphosis, and no obvious point at which they can be called adult as opposed to larval. The head grows forwards, nares and mouth form, eyes appear and become pigmented, the pronephros becomes prominent for a short period, the ductus endolymphaticus and the thin-roofed hind brain can be seen before stage 39 (Fig. 6A) when they become obscured by pigment, dark and red chromatophores appear, and the lateral line system develops. A pre-anal fin grows and is resorbed. The position of the mouth and the dorsal fin changes; body proportions alter. The yolk is used up, a spiral valve develops in the intestine and the fish starts to feed. The animal's habits also change slowly; on hatching, the young fish is a supine creature, hiding in the weeds, moving only when stimulated (Illidge, 1894; Bancroft, '11) and not

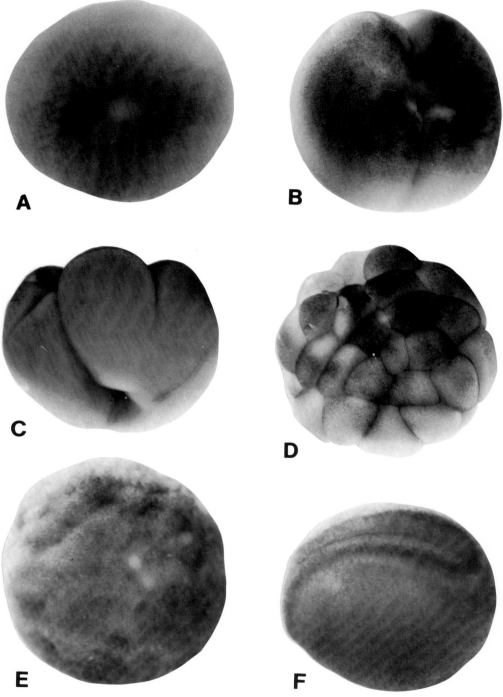

Fig. 4. A) Photograph of the animal pole of a fertilized uncleaved egg showing the pigment distribution and the pale area. B) Photograph of the animal pole of an egg at stage 2, showing the first cleavage furrow and partition of the pigment and pale area. C) An egg between stages 3–4, photographed from the side to show the unpigmented vegetal pole and the cleavage furrows. D) An egg at stage 6 (late cleavage) showing the pigmented cells of the animal pole. The pale area has disappeared. E) An egg at stage 10 (large-celled blastula), showing the many small pigmented cells of the animal pole. Pronounced dimpling of the surface appears after fixation. F) View of the developing neural plate of an embryo of stage 18. Egg pigment is concentrated within the presumptive neural folds. All eggs were fixed in Karnovsky's fixative and removed intact from the membranes. Scale bar = 1 mm.

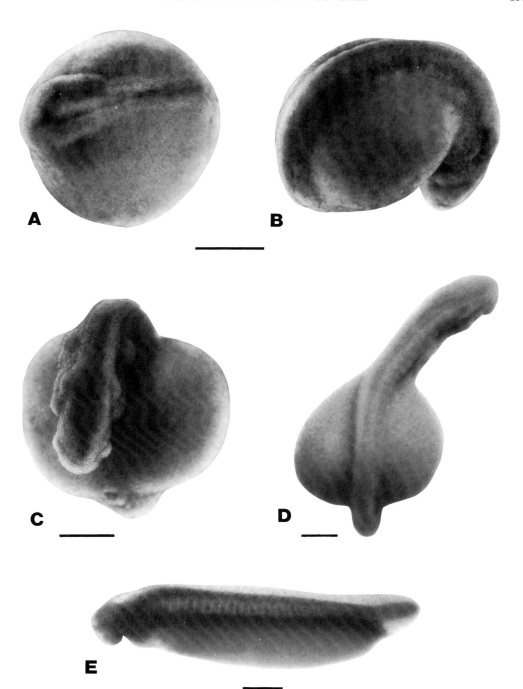

Fig. 5. A) An embryo of stage 23 showing the presumptive fore-, mid- and hind-brain regions. Pigment lies within the neural folds. B) An embryo of stage 26 in lateral view showing early development of head structures and myotomes. C) An embryo of stage 30 showing development of head structures, prominent pronephros, anus, tail bud, and rounded yolk laden endoderm. D) An embryo of stage 34 showing head structures, pronephros, myotomes, tail bud, and lengthening of the region of yolky endoderm. E) An embryo of stage 37 showing melanophores in the dorsal skin and around the eye, development of the cardiac region and myotomes, and growth of the tail bud. The embryos shown in A and B were fixed in Karnovsky's fixative and removed intact from the membranes; those in C, D, and E were living decapsulated embryos. Scale bars = 1 mm.

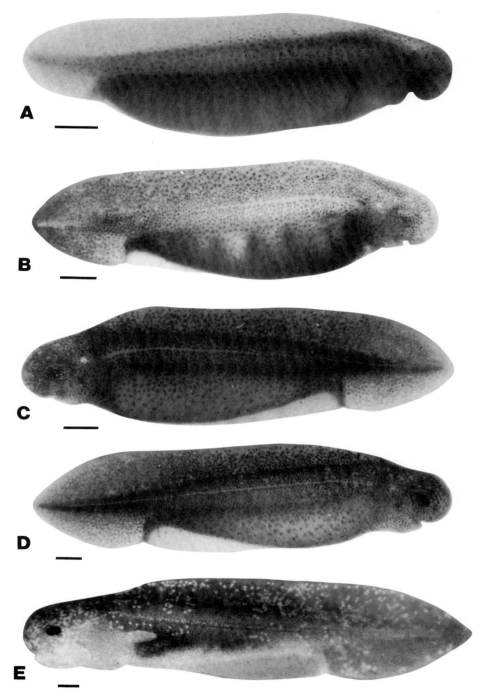

Fig. 6. A series of living decapsulated embryos and hatched fish showing the gradual change in body form as the animal develops. A) An embryo of stage 39 showing the developing pigmentation, moulding of the endodermal region, and appearance of the ventral pre-anal fin. B) An embryo between stages 41–42 showing the primordium of the pectoral fin, increase in size of the ventral pre-anal fin, and lateral line extending half way down the trunk. Cells containing red pigment are present in the skin as well as melanophores. C) An embryo of stage 43 showing the sub-terminal mouth and lateral line extending all the way along the trunk. Primordia of the sensory lines of the head are visible. D) A hatchling between stages 45–46 showing the dorsal fin reaching as far forward as the back of the head, pigment cells that include erythrophores as well as melanophores, extension of the pre-anal ventral fin, and reduction in the amount of yolk in the gut endoderm. E) A hatchling of stage 48 showing fin development, pigmentation, and the lateral line system. Yolk has nearly disappeared. Scale bars = 1 mm.

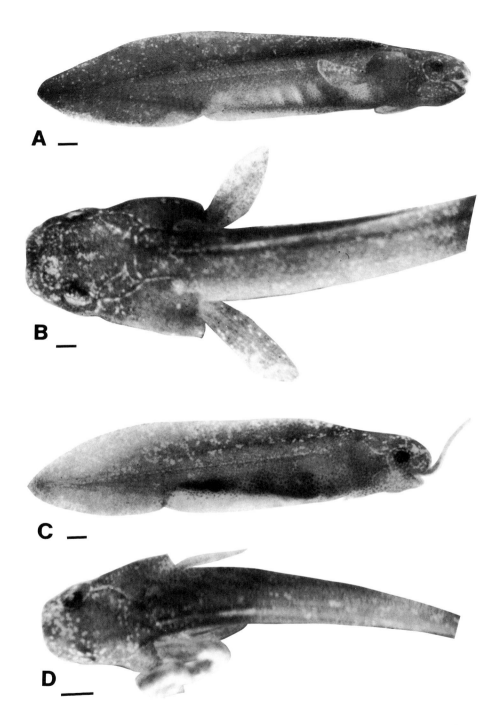

Fig. 7. A) A living fish of stage 49 showing the terminal mouth and the spiral valve of the intestine. B) Dorsal view of the head of the live fish of stage 52 showing development of the sensory canals of the head. C,D) Ingestion of a prey item (C) and its escape through a gill slit (D). Feeding owes more to enthusiasm than to efficiency. Scale bars = 1 mm.

feeding for 2–3 weeks while yolk is still present (Kemp, '82b). Gradually it becomes more venturesome and soon is feeding voraciously (Fig. 7C,D). At this stage of the life cycle, the young fish are vulnerable to predators like insect larvae or shrimps (Illidge, 1894) or jewfish (*Tandanus tandanus*) and wood duck (Bancroft, '28).

JUVENILES

One of the mysteries about *Neoceratodus forsteri* was the apparent lack of juvenile fish. Adults could be caught, but no small fish were found. Illidge (1894) complained that he had never seen nor heard of a lungfish less than 4 lbs in weight in 6 years of fishing the Burnett. Bancroft ('11) made exhaustive searches, using nets, lime, and dynamite, or scooping up weeds and debris, or dredging in places where spawn had been plentiful a short time before, and found no small lungfish, though the young of several other species of fish could be collected. Bancroft ('11) felt that the lungfishes were nearing extinction, and that in a normal year no newly hatched fish survived their many natural enemies. The other explanation was that the young lungfish buried into the mud and did not emerge for 3 years. However, a glance through the records of the Queensland Museum and the literature (Table 1) shows that a few juveniles have been found over the last 110 years—de Castelnau's specimen of 61 cm in 1876, Semon's of 2.5 cm in 1892, sporadic occurrences mainly from the Burnett River between 1894 and 1918, and then some juveniles from Enoggera (Longman, '28). Eight were found in February and March 1928 (I4436–4438; 4441–4445) and eight more (I4470–4477) later in the year. More isolated specimens turned up between 1929 and 1937; then none appeared until six (weighing 27.0–50 gm) were recovered from Mount Crosby Water Treatment plant on the Brisbane River in 1961 (Grigg, '65c). No more were caught from this source until 1982, when some more (eight live fish, Table 1) turned up in the filters. At the same time (in 1981 and 1982) numerous juveniles were caught, using electrofishing methods in the Mary and Brisbane Rivers, but none from Enoggera Reservoir (Johnson, personal communication). In the parts of the Brisbane Rivers where juvenile lungfish have been found, the substrate is of sand or gravel and the fish were caught near weed banks, hence it is not true that the young lungfish always spend their first 3 years in the mud, as some authors have claimed (Welsby, '05).

The lack of juveniles between 1876–1928, 1929–1961, and 1961–1981 may owe more to inadequate catching methods and the uncanny ability of small lungfish to get away from nets than to an actual lack of little fish. However, Bancroft's methods of liming and dynamiting should have produced juveniles, unless they had left the area in which they were spawned. Therefore the disturbing possibility arises that few juveniles do in fact survive their natural enemies, and that the peaks of small lungfish in 1928, 1965, and 1981–1982 suggest peaks of breeding and recruitment in cycles of twenty or so years. The peaks of juveniles in 1981–1982 follow prolific and extensive spawning in the same areas in 1979 and 1980.

An alternative explanation for the paucity of small specimens could also be that the growth rate of young fish in the wild is fast. In the laboratory, it is usually notoriously slow, a fish of 10–12.5 cm being up to 2 years old (Illidge, 1894; Kemp, '81; Bancroft; '18, '33). However, it is possible for a young Australian lungfish in captivity to grow very fast, on the order of one inch per month, depending on the conditions under which they are kept (McMahon, personal communication). It is possible that this is the case in the wild. Fish caught by Longman in February were 9.6–15 cm long and fish caught 6 months later were 21–25 cm long, under the conditions in Enoggera Reservoir (Longman, '28).

DIET

The diet of lungfish changes as the animal develops, and this can be correlated with a change in the dentition (Kemp, '77). At stage 48, when feeding on worms or small crustacea begins, the dentition consists of sharp cones, a "hold and catch" dentition, and the preferred food is live animals—*Tubifex, Daphnia*, and brine shrimp, supplemented sometimes with filamentous algae (Fig. 7C) (Kemp, '77, '81). Australian lungfish of this age cannot be maintained on microscopic algae alone. "Infusoria and conferva" are not a suitable diet for lungfish, as Bancroft discovered ('28). They will in fact tackle live food as big as themselves, but not always very efficiently, as the prey items may escape between the gill slits (Fig. 7D). Digestion is often ineffective, and live worms may even leave through the anus.

TABLE 1. *Occurrence of small lungfish (61-cm length or less, 2-kg weight or less) in Queensland between 1876 and 1982*

Specimen No. or source of data	Month, year of capture	Place of capture	Length in cm; weight in gm
de Castelnau, 1876a	Not known, 1876	Rockhampton market	61.0 cm
Semon, 1899	January, 1892	In weeds, Boyne River	2.5 cm
Illidge (cit. by Welsby, 1905)	Not known	Burnett River	37.5 cm
Welsby, 1905	Not known	Mary River	52.5 cm
O'Connor, 1909	"Dry season," 1909	From mud, Burnett River	35.0, ca. 30 cm
Ogilby, 1912	Not known, 1912	Quay St., Bundaberg[1]	36.7 cm
I2528	November, 1915	Burnett River	32.1 cm
Bancroft, 1918	May, 1914	Mullet net, Burnett River	50.0 cm; 906 gm
Johnston and Bancroft, 1915	April, 1915	Dynamite, Burnett River	41.25 cm; 680 gm
Longman, 1928	September, 1918	Coomera River	49.5 cm
I4436–4438	March, 1928	In hyacinth on bywash, Enoggera Reservoir	15.0, 14.6, 11.0 cm
I4441–4445	March, 1928	In hyacinth on bywash, Enoggera Reservoir	14.8, 15.0, 14.5, 9.6, 13.4 cm
I4470–4477	September, 1928	In hyacinth on bywash, Enoggera Reservoir	21.25, 24.37, 24.37, 25.0 23.75, 24.06 24.37, 25.0 cm
I4511	January, 1929	Upper reaches, Enoggera Creek	15.0 cm
I4867	February, 1932	Enoggera Reservoir	12.0 cm
I4944	June, 1932	Enoggera Reservoir	18.0 cm
I5972	July, 1937	Enoggera Reservoir	25.0 cm
Grigg, 1965	"Cold history"[2], 1961	Mount Crosby Water Treatment Plant (Brisbane River)	27.0, 28.0, 29.0, 33.0, 44.0, 50.0 gm
Live fish, Queensland Museum	February, 1982	Mount Crosby Water Treatment Plant (Brisbane River)	28 cm; 250 gm 32 cm; 300 gm 32 cm; 300 gm 33 cm; 300 gm 33 cm; 350 gm 35 cm; 400 gm 37 cm; 400 gm 41 cm; 500 gm

[1]During a flood in the Burnett River.
[2]Grigg's wording, presumably meaning winter.

As the sharp cones grow out and wear down into tooth plates, the diet begins to change to include snails and other molluscs, and they will also take prepared food or algae (stage 52–53). They are still mostly carnivorous and prefer live food.

Adults have the crushing molariform tooth plates characteristic of Ceratodontidae. In captivity they will eat a wide range of food—fish, insect larvae, crustaceans, molluscs, worms, tadpoles, meat, offal, egg yolk, dried dog or poultry food, *Vallisneria spiralis, Hydrilla verticillata*, filamentous algae, water hyacinth rootlets, and dead toads (Kemp et al., '81). Examination of faecal samples from adults taken from Enoggera Reservoir reveals black slime and *H. verticillata* leaves in keeping with the poverty of the enviroment (Kemp et al, '81); and from adults caught in the river, plants (*V. spiralis, H. verticillata* and filamentous algae) and molluscs (*Corbiculina* sp. and *Plotiopsis balennensis*) with a few prawns (Kemp et al., '81). River fish also ingest sand, possibly unintentionally (Kemp et al., '81). As Semon (1899) notes, quantities of ingested vegetable material pass out apparently undigested, and it is likely that this was eaten for the sake of the minute animal food attached to it.

Prehension of food ranges from suctorial

(dried food, filamentous algae, or water hyacinth rootlets) as in *Lepidosiren paradoxa* (Bemis and Lauder, '86) to a more active capture (snails, worms). Jaw movements are usually of the crushing variety (Longman, '28) but vary depending on the sort of food being eaten. Worms and plants seem to be partially crushed with a few quick bites and swallowed, and the plants, at least, emerge in the faeces in identifiable condition. The fish have more difficulty with snails; these are often pushed out and pulled back in several times. It is not unusual for particles of food to escape from the operculum, even in adults. The potential for grinding or rotating movements of the jaw exists (Perkins, '72), but its importance varies, as an examination of the tooth wear of a sample of specimens reveals.

COLLECTING LUNGFISH

Seine netting, cast netting, and gill netting are useless for catching juvenile Australian lungfish (Kemp, unpublished). Gill netting works for adults if a feeding channel is completely blocked (Kemp, unpublished), or if explosive charges are dropped in the water on one side of the net (Kelly, personal communication), although this often damages or kills the fish. The best method of catching lungfish in an undamaged condition is electrofishing (Johnson, personal communication). All lungfish within 20–30 feet of the positive electrode are stunned and rise to the surface, from which they can be scooped out of the water and into the boat. The effect of the electric charge lasts long enough to measure the fish, take faecal samples, and slip them in a sack or put them back in the water. Since the lungfish is totally protected, collecting activities are carefully controlled by the Queensland Government, and since it is regarded as an endangered species, the Federal Government prohibits export without special justification. Unfortunately, these measures do not prevent a thriving illegal trade in lungfish.

CONCLUSIONS

Bancroft believed firmly that *Neocerotadus* was in danger of becoming extinct and was one of the people responsible for the Queensland State Government law that specifically protects this species (The Fish and Oyster Act, 1914). Some of his premises were false: lungfish do breed successfully more often than twice in a century, contrary to his belief

(Bancroft, '11), and they are not excessively long lived, certainly not to the 1,000 years claimed in a letter to the Brisbane Courier (Bancroft, '23). A lungfish 20 inches long is more likely to be 20 months old than 20 years, as he claims (Bancroft, '18). It is true that the newly hatched fish is very vulnerable to numerous natural enemies (Bancroft, '11). Further, the environment is now under threat from water conservation schemes, fertilizer contamination from surrounding cultivation, and clearing of the natural or introduced aquatic weeds where lungfish like to live and breed. A further disturbing possibility is that deficient breeding over several years (Kemp, unpublished) may mean cycles of spawning by the lungfish and therefore less recruitment. Addition of this factor to the many natural enemies of the young fish and to man-made environmental disturbance would place the lungfish at risk.

Better that we should share Bancroft's ('33) amusement and indignation when he received the following message in a letter from a correspondent overseas—"We have all the stages of *Ceratodus* so it does not matter now if the animal becomes extinct"—than that we should witness the extinction of this ancient and intriguing fish.

ACKNOWLEDGMENTS

Dr. D.H. Kemp of the Commonwealth Scientific and Industrial Research Organisation, Meiers Road, Indooroopilly, Queensland, 4068, kindly read and commented on the text, and assisted with photography. Mr. D. Knowles of the Queensland Museum, Fortitude Valley, Brisbane, Queensland, 4006, took the photographs reproduced in Figure 1. Their help is warmly appreciated. Unpublished information on *N. forsteri* was made available to me by Mr. B. McMahon, Queensland Institute of Technology, George Street, Brisbane, Queensland, 4000 and Mr. O. Kelly and Mr. I. Johnson, both of the Department of Zoology, University of Queensland, St Lucia, Brisbane, Queensland, 4067.

LITERATURE CITED

Agassiz, L. (1844) Recherches sur les Poissons Fossiles. Du Genre *Ceratodus*. Vol. III. Neuchâtel: Imprimerie de Petitpierre, pp. 129–136.

Bancroft, T.L. (1911) On a weak point in the life history of *Neoceratodus forsteri* Krefft. Proc. R. Soc. Qd. 23:251–256.

Bancroft, T.L. (1913) On an easy and certain method of hatching *Ceratodus* ova. Proc. R. Soc. Qd. 25:1–3.

Bancroft, T.L. (1918) Some further notes on the life history of *Ceratodus* (*Neoceratodus*) *forsteri*. Proc. R. Soc. Qd. *30*:91–94.

Bancroft, T.L. (1923) The Ceratodus. Letter to the editor, Brisbane Courier, 5th Nov., 1923.

Bancroft, T.L. (1928) On the life history of *Ceratodus*. Proc. Linn. Soc. N.S.W. *53*:315–317.

Bancroft, T.L. (1933) Some further observations on the rearing of *Ceratodus*. Proc. Linn. Soc. N.S.W. *58*:467–469.

Bemis, W.E., and G.V. Lauder (1986) Morphology and function of the feeding apparatus of the lungfish, *Lepidosiren paradoxa* (Dipnoi). J. Morphol. *187*:1–28.

Caldwell, W.H. (1884) On the development of the monotremes and *Ceratodus*. J. Proc. R. Soc. N.S.W. *18*:117–122.

Campbell, K.S.W., and R.E. Barwick (1984) The choanae, maxillae, premaxillae and anterior palatal bones of early dipnoans. Proc. Linn. Soc. N.S.W. *107*:147–170.

de Castelnau, F. (1876a) Mémoire sur les poissons appelés barramundi par les aborigènes du Nord-Est de l'Australie. J. Zool. *5*:129–136.

de Castelnau, F. (1876b) Remarques au sujet du genre *Neoceratodus*. J. Zool. *5*:342–343.

Dean, B. (1906) Notes on the living specimens of the Australian lungfish, *Ceratodus forsteri*, in the Zoological Society's collection. Proc. Zool. Soc. Lond. *1906*:168–178.

Dean, B. (1912) Additional notes on the living specimens of the Australian lungfish (*Ceratodus forsteri*) in the collection of the Zoological Society of London. Proc. Zool. Soc. Lond. *1912*:607–612.

Greenwood, P.H. (1958) Reproduction in the East African Lungfish, *Protopterus aethiopicus* Heckel. Proc. Zool. Soc. Lond. *130*:547–567.

Grigg, G.C. (1965a) Studies on the Queensland lungfish, *Neoceratodus forsteri* (Krefft). III. Aerial respiration in relation to habits. Aust. J. Zool. *13*:413–421.

Grigg, G.C. (1965b) Spawning behaviour in the Queensland lungfish, *Neoceratodus forsteri*. Aust. Nat. Hist. *15*:75.

Grigg, G.C. (1965c) Studies on the Queensland lungfish, *Neoceratodus forsteri* (Krefft) II. Thermal acclimation. Aust. J. Zool. *13*:407–411.

Günther, A. (1871) Description of *Ceratodus*, a genus of ganoid fishes recently discovered in rivers of Queensland, Australia. Philos. Trans. R. Soc. Lond. (Biol.) *161*:511–571.

Illidge, T. (1984) On *Ceratodus forsteri*. Proc. R. Soc. Qd. *10*:40–44.

Johnels, A.G., and G.S.O. Svensson (1955) On the biology of *Protopterus annectens* (Owen). Arkiv Zoologi *7*:131–164.

Johnston, T.H., and T.L. Bancroft (1915) Notes on an exhibit of specimens of *Ceratodus*. Proc. R. Soc. Qd. *27*:58–59.

Kemp, A. (1977) The pattern of tooth plate formation in the Australian lungfish, *Neoceratodus forsteri*, Krefft. Zool. J. Linn. Soc. Lond. *60*:223–258.

Kemp, A. (1981) Rearing of embryos and larvae of the Australian lungfish, *Neoceratodus forsteri* under laboratory conditions. Copeia *1981*:776–784.

Kemp, A. (1982a) Australian Mesozoic and Cenozoic lungfish. In P.V. Rich and E.M. Thompson (eds): The Fossil Vertebrate Record of Australia, Clayton, Australia: Monash University, pp. 133–144.

Kemp, A. (1982b) The embryological development of the Queensland lungfish, *Neoceratodus forsteri* (Krefft). Mem. Qd. Mus. *20*:553–597.

Kemp, A. (1984) Spawning of the Australian lungfish, *Neoceratodus forsteri* (Krefft) in the Brisbane River and in Enoggera Reservoir, Queensland. Mem. Qd.

Mus. *21*:391–399.

Kemp, A. and R.E. Molnar (1981) *Neoceratodus forsteri* from the lower Cretaceous of New South Wales, Australia. J. Palaeontol. *55*:211–217.

Kemp, A., T. Anderson, A. Tomley, and I. Johnson (1981) The use of the Australian lungfish (*Neoceratodus forsteri*) for the control of submerged aquatic weeds. 5th International Conference on Weed Control. Melbourne: C.S.I.R.O., pp. 155–158.

Kerr, J.G. (1900) The external features in the development of *Lepidosiren paradoxa*, Fitz. Philos. Trans. R. Soc. Lond. (Biol.) *182*:299–330.

Kesteven, H.L. (1944) The evolution of the skull and the cephalic muscles. Part II. The Amphibia. Mem. Aust. Mus. *8*:133–236.

Krefft, G. (1870) Description of a giant amphibian allied to the genus *Lepidosiren* from the Wide Bay district, Queensland. Proc. Zool. Soc. Lond. *1870*:221–224.

Longman, H. (1928) Discovery of juvenile lungfishes with notes on *Epiceratodus*. Mem. Qd. Mus. *9*:161–173.

Macleay, W. (1884) Notes on a collection of fishes from the Burdekin and Mary Rivers, Queensland. Proc. Linn. Soc. N.S.W. *8*:199–213.

Obruchev, D.V. (ed) (1976) Fundamentals of Palaeontology, Vol. XI. Moscow: Izdatelstvo Nauka.

O'Connor, D. (1896) Letter to the President and Council of the Royal Society of Queensland. Proc. R. Soc. Qd. *11*:xxi.

O'Connor, D. (1898) On *Ceratodus*. Proc. Zool. Soc. *1898*:493.

O'Connor, D. (1902) Letter to the editor, Brisbane Courier, June 1902. (Quoted in full by Welsby, '05).

O'Connor, D. (1909) Notes on the *Ceratodus*. Report to the Australian Association for the Advancement of Science *12*:383–384.

Ogilby, J.D. (1912) On some Queensland fishes. Mem. Qd. Mus. *1*:26–65.

Owen, R. (1841) Description of the *Lepidosiren annectens*. Trans. Linn. Soc. Lond. *18*:327–361.

Pascual, R., and Bondesia, Y.P. (1976) Notas sobre vertebrados de la frontera Certaceo-Terciaria. Actas Sexto Congr. Geol. Arg. *1*:565–577.

Perkins, P.L. (1972) Mandibular Mechanics and Feeding Groups in the Dipnoi. PhD Dissertation, Yale University, New Haven, Connecticut.

Ramsay, E.P. (1876) On the habits of *Ceratodus*. Proc. Zool. Soc. Lond. *1876*:698–699.

Semon, R. (1899) In the Australian Bush. London: Macmillan and Company.

Semon, R. (1893) Die aüssere Entwickelung des *Ceratodus forsteri*, Denkschr. Med.-Naturwiss. Ges. Jena. *4*:29–50.

Spencer, W.B. (1891) Notes on the habits of *Ceratodus forsteri*. Proc. R. Soc. Vict. *4*:81–84.

Spencer, W.B. (1892) A trip to Queensland in search of *Ceratodus*. Vict. Nat. *9*:16–32.

Stromer, E., and B. Peyer (1917) Über rezente und triassische Gebisse von Ceratodontidae. Das Gebiss von *Epiceratodus forsteri*. Z. Deutsch. Geol. Gesellschaft *1917*:1–84.

Teller, F. (1891) Über den Schädel eines fossilen Dipnoers *Ceratodus sturii*. Geol. Reichsanst. Wien, Abh. *15*:1–38.

Thomson, K.S. (1969) Gill and lung function in the evolution of the lungfishes (Dipnoi): An hypothesis. Forma et Functio *1*:250–262.

Welsby, T. (1905) Schnappering and Fishing. Brisbane: Outridge Printing Company.

Whiting, H.P., and Bone, Q. (1980) Ciliary cells in the epidermis of the larval Australian dipnoan, *Neoceratodus*. Zool. J. Linn. Soc. Lond. *68*:125–137.

Whitley, G.P. (1927) The Queensland lungfish. Aust. Mus. Mag. *3:*50–52.

Whitley, G.P. (1929) The discovery of the Queensland lungfish. Aust. Mus. Mag. *3:*363–364.

Woodward, A.S. (1906) On a tooth of *Ceratodus* and a dinosaurian claw from the Lower Jurassic of Victoria, Australia. Ann. Mag. Nat. Hist. *(17)18:*1–3.

Woodward, A.S. (1908) The fossil fishes of the Hawkesbury series at St. Peters. Mem. Geol. Survey N.S.W. Palaeontology *10:*1–30.

JOURNAL OF MORPHOLOGY SUPPLEMENT 1:199–216 (1986)

Urogenital Morphology of Dipnoans, With Comparisons to Other Fishes and to Amphibians

MARVALEE H. WAKE
Department of Zoology and Museum of Vertebrate Zoology,
University of California, Berkeley, California 94720

ABSTRACT   The morphology of the urogenital system of extant dipnoans is compared among the three genera, and to that of other fishes and amphibians. Analysis is based on dissections, sectioned material, and the literature. Urogenital system morphology provides no support for the hypothesis of a sister-group relationship between dipnoans and amphibians, for virtually all shared characters are primitive, and most characters shared with other fishes are also primitive. Urogenital morphology is useful at the familial level of analysis, however, and synapomorphies support the inclusion of *Lepidosiren* and *Protopterus* in the family Lepidosirenidae separate from *Neoceratodus* of the family Ceratodontidae.

Analysis of relationships of the Dipnoi to other fishes and to tetrapods have largely been based on the morphology of hard tissues—the skeleton, tooth plates, and scales. Several studies of other systems are available in the literature, but most are descriptive and few are comparative, at least in considering all three genera of living lungfish. Soft-tissue systems have had limited evaluation in terms of assessing evolution and relationships.

Several current hypotheses of the relationships of the Dipnoi exist. These include the proposal by Romer ('66) that dipnoans are the sister group to actinistians and rhipidistians; that of Miles ('77) classifying dipnoans as the sister group of rhipidistians only; and that of Rosen et al. ('81) in which dipnoans are the sister group of tetrapods, with actinistians the outgroup and rhipidistians (porolepiforms) in an unresolved cladistic position. Within the Recent Dipnoi, *Neoceratodus* (one species: *forsteri*) is placed in the family Ceratodontidae; *Lepidosiren* (one species: *paradoxa*) and *Protopterus* (four species: *amphibius, aethiopicus, annectens,* and *dolloi*) are placed in the Lepidosirenidae. Soft-tissue morphology, because of the extreme paucity of extinct forms, can offer virtually nothing to our understanding of the relationships of dipnoans to rhipidistians, and little to the association of dipnoans with actinistians (*Latimeria* not necessarily being "representative"). However, soft-tissue morphology can contribute to information about dipnoan-tetrapod relationships (Rosen et al., '81, utilized muscle characters, for example) and to generic and familial relationships.

This survey and review of urogenital morphology of the three genera of extant dipnoans and of the literature is undertaken with the following objectives: 1) to provide information from a direct comparison of representatives of all three extant genera; 2) to see if the urogenital system offers support for any of the current hypotheses of dipnoan relationships; and 3) to determine whether or not the urogenital system offers additional characters for the familial allocation of the genera. Urogenital morphology and physiology have received little consideration in these contexts (see, for example, Thomson, '69; Rosen et al. '81). In this paper I review the morphology of the components of the urogenital system in dipnoans, adding new information where possible, and I compare the morphology of these components among dipnoan species as well as with the urogenital structures of other fishes and amphibians. For each component I discuss the implications of the morphology for assessment of relationships and suggest directions for further research.

MATERIALS AND METHODS

Urogenital organs from five specimens of *Lepidosiren paradoxa* (220–300 mm standard length) from Laguna Oca, Rio Paraguay, Formosa, Argentina, six of *Protopterus aethiopicus* (230–320 mm standard length) from Kusa Beach, Lake Victoria, near Kisumu, Kenya, and four of *Neoceratodus forsteri* (520–560 mm standard length) from the Brisbane River system, Queensland, Australia, were dissected. Specimens had been fixed in 10% formalin and stored in 70% ethanol. Males and females including immature specimens of each species were examined; several mature males and females were in breeding condition, with active spermatogenesis in the former and well-yolked eggs in the latter. Parts of each urogenital structure were excised and prepared for histological examination. Twenty histological preparations of the kidneys, gonads, ducts, and cloacas of each species were made by embedding in paraffin, cutting at 10 μm, and staining with hematoxylin-eosin.

The nomenclatorial format for the morphological comparisons is as follows: The generic epithet only is used in situations in which morphological descriptions are 1) appropriate to all species of a genus, 2) obviously my work on the species listed above, 3) relate to the single species in the genera *Neoceratodus* and *Lepidosiren*, or, 4) if an author did not identify species. If the morphology is species-specific, or if inter-specific variation is questionable or unknown, the *Protopterus* species examined is identified.

DESCRIPTION AND ANALYSIS
The kidney and the gonads

Kidney

Considerable attention has been paid to kidney structure, especially its development, in considering vertebrate relationships. In fact, few vertebrate organs have so extensive a developmental and morphological data base. Those data have been treated in terms of physiological and ecological correlates, and in terms of evolutionary relationships, including the origins of major vertebrate groups. Several decades of pertinent literature on vertebrates in general are summarized by Goodrich ('30) and Fraser ('50), and by Gerard ('54) and Hickman and Trump ('69) for fishes specifically. Fox ('60, '61, '62, '63) made significant contributions to understanding both dipnoan and amphibian kidney development. (He emphasized the similarities between those two groups, but seems not to have considered teleosts; see below.) Torrey ('65) reviewed the morphogenesis of the vertebrate kidney. Jesperson ('69) examined kidney structure of *Neoceratodus* with reference to the testicular network and summarized much of the literature produced during the 1930s on lungfish nephron structure.

Gross morphology. Lungfish kidneys are paired, somewhat lobed, elongate, highly pigmented retroperitoneal structures (Fig. 1). As illustrated by Kerr ('01) and confirmed in my material (Fig. 1B,E), the kidneys of *Lepidosiren* are nearly as long as the testes and are closely bound to the testes, some testicular tissue invading the kidney posteriorly. The kidneys of *Protopterus* (*annectens*; Kerr, '01; *aethiopicus*, this work) are shorter but stouter, lying more posteriorly in the body cavity (Fig. 1A,D). *Neoceratodus* (Fig. 1C,F) also has short, stout, posteriorly situated kidneys, more lobular than those of other genera. Kerr ('01) distinguished the genital or vesicular posterior portion of the kidney from the anterior urinary part, the latter recognizable in part by reduced pigment, especially in *Protopterus*. Jesperson ('69) was not able to distinguish two such regions in *Neoceratodus* grossly or in section, nor can I in my material.

Histology. Several workers have examined nephron structure in both the anterior and "vesicular" parts of the kidney. Hickman and Trump ('69) summarize research on *Protopterus* and *Lepidosiren* and describe the regions of the nephron—a typical corpuscle and glomerulus, a ciliated neck segment, a proximal tubule of two components, a ciliated intermediate segment, a distal segment, and a collecting duct system. Jesperson ('69) added information on *Neoceratodus* and compared its nephron cytology to that of *Lepidosiren* and *Protopterus dolloi* and *P. aethiopicus*. My observations agree with these reports (Fig. 2). The structure of the urinary nephrons approaches uniformity among the three genera. Hickman and Trump ('69) conclude that the cytological features of the nephron of lungfishes are similar in all aspects to those of a number of "typical" freshwater teleosts.

The nephrons in the vesicular portion of the kidney have all of the components described above, including a well-developed glomerulus (as in Kerr's, '01, Figs. 50 and 51 of *Lepidosiren*). Kerr ('01) did not find capsules and glomeruli in *P. annectens*, but I find them in the posterior kidney in the specimens of *P. aethiopicus* I examined (Fig. 1A). They differ little from anterior nephrons but have greater tubular diameters, as Jesperson ('69) noted. Anterior nephric tubules have outer diameters of approximately 0.1 mm (Fig. 2B), while posterior tubules have outer diameters of 0.15–0.3 mm. Capsules are approximately 0.13 mm wide and 0.15–0.2 mm high in both regions of the kidney. The tubule dilation may be due to the recent presence of sperm, for capsule and tubule may be packed with sperm at breeding season (Fig.

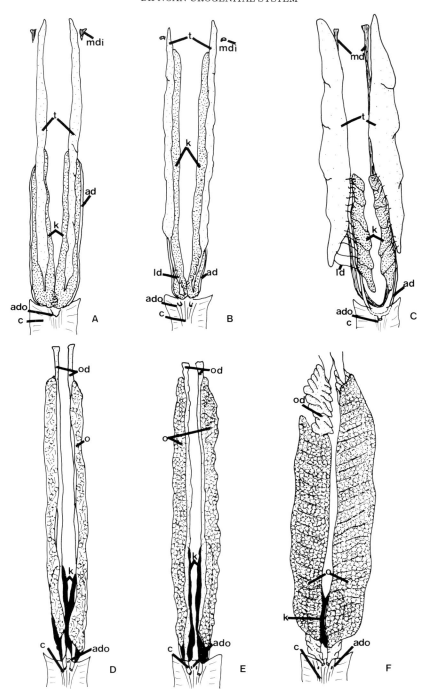

Fig. 1. Urogenital morphology of dipnoans. A) Male *Protopterus aethiopicus* (dissection, and after Kerr, '01). B) Male *Lepidosiren paradoxa* (dissection, and after Kerr, '01). C) Male *Neoceratodus forsteri* (dissection, and after Jesperson, '69). D) Female *Protopterus aethiopicus* (dissection). E) Female *Lepidosiren paradoxa* (dissection). F) Female *Neoceratodus forsteri* (dissection). Ventral view. Abbreviations: ad, archinephric duct; ado, archinephric duct orifice; b, bladder; c, cloaca; k, kidney; ld, lateral duct; md, Müllerian duct; mdi, Müllerian duct infundibulum; o, ovary; od, oviduct; t, testis. Not drawn to scale.

6D). The morphology suggests that the posterior nephrons are capable of urinary function. It is not known specifically whether they are functional at any time, nor is it known whether lungfish urine would inhibit sperm in any way. Smith ('30) found that *P. aethiopicus* urine is very dilute (16.5–18.8 mOsm/l) and contains 5 mEq/l of Na^+ and 3.5 mEq/l of $NH4^+$.

The modification of the kidney for sperm transport is distinctly different in dipnoans when compared with amphibians, which seems not to have been noted previously. In dipnoans the posterior kidney is involved in sperm transport, and the nephrons are essentially unmodified from typical urinary structures. In amphibians the *anterior* mesonephros is utilized for sperm transport if the kidney is used reproductively. In gymnophiones the nephrons are unmodified; in anurans and urodeles the nephrons are altered for sperm transport, usually lacking a capsule and glomerulus (see Wake, '70).

Development. Several workers have drawn attention to the similarity of dipnoan and amphibian pronephric development. In particular, Semon ('01), working on *Neoceratodus*, Kerr ('19) examining *Lepidosiren* and *P. annectens*, Kindahl ('37) and especially Fox, from work on *Neoceratodus* ('60, '61) and numerous urodeles (summarized in '63), indicated marked similarities of pattern. These similarities include: 1) A reduced number of pronephric units is present in larval dipnoans, urodeles, and anurans; 2) the pronephroi in these groups are related positionally to the anteriormost spinal nerves; and 3) the pronephric (archinephric) duct is similarly induced.

The pattern of development is indeed very similar, but the conclusion that ontogenetic similarity suggests an evolutionary relationship between dipnoans and amphibians is faulty. First, the similarity in number of functional nephrostomal units (two in larvae of all three dipnoan genera, two in a number of urodeles, and three in anurans) is a property of *derived* amphibian (and fish) taxa. In fact, the more primitive urodeles have up to five nephrostomial units (Fox, '63). The only gymnophione amphibian examined, *Hypogeophis rostratus*, has nine functional units (Brauer, '02), and the greater number is thought to represent the primitive condition. Many authors note that greater numbers of pronephric units develop in all of these taxa, but that many are eliminated or are nonfunctional. There is slight variation among

dipnoans and amphibians in the body segment from which the functional pronephric units are derived (Fox, '63). Very few amphibians of each of the orders have actually been examined, and therefore there is inadequate information to permit generalizations on variation or patterns of change.

Pronephric development of few osteichthyans has been examined, and the available data are crucial to consideration of relationships. Fraser ('27) rigorously analyzed kidney development in the sturgeon *Acipenser* and Maschowzeff ('34–'35) examined *Salmo*, as well as the sturgeon, a frog, and a salamander. Fraser ('27) also carefully compared development among fishes and amphibians. She found that *Acipenser* has six nephrostomic units in the pronephros, derived from somites four through nine. This pattern also occurs in *Salmo*; it has three functional pronephric units which must be assumed to be the primitive actinopterygian condition. It seems logical that the pronephric units arise from the anterior-most body segments as a property of cephalized development. Fraser ('27) summarized her own work and the literature, with the following conclusions:

1. The pronephric chamber is segmented early on in cyclostomes, *Polypterus*, and gymnophione amphibians, but slightly later in chondrosteans (her "ganoids") and dipnoans. The pronephric chamber is recognizable as segmental only in terms of numbers of tubules in anurans and urodeles and is a single, never metameric chamber in teleosts.

2. In gymnophiones the pronephric nephrostomal units remain serial; in cyclostomes, chrondrosteans, *Polypterus*, and dipnoans the walls of the units break down, a limited occurrence in anurans and urodeles.

3. In cyclostomes, *Polypterus*, amphibians, and dipnoans the units open into the coelomic space; in chondrosteans only anterior units are open (the units of dipnoans close developmentally like those of chondrosteans); and the pronephric units of teleosts are closed off from the coelom. Goodrich ('30) also presented a useful summary of pronephric development. *Polypterus* (Kerr, '02) has two functional tubules, *Lepisosteus* three, *Amia* (Jungersten, 1900) three or four. The number varies among teleosts and includes retention of a functional pronephros in adults of some species. Elasmobranchs have three to seven functional units (Goodrich, '30).

It therefore seems apparent that chondrosteans, holostean neopterygians, amphibians, dipnoans, elasmobranchs, and even cyclostomes share a primitive pattern of pronephric development and structure. Reduction in number of pronephric units is a general derived state in *each* lineage. Teleosts show a similar pattern but with a greater diversity of derived states. In addition, mesonephric development shows considerable diversity among cyclostomes, elasmobranchs, primitive osteichthyans, dipnoans, teleosts, and amphibians. Therefore there are no shared derived states that support the hypothesis of a sister-group relationship between amphibians and dipnoans, unless one were to assume that gymnophiones are ancestral to sharks, osteichthyans, and other amphibians, and are a sister group to cyclostomes. The pattern is one of convergence in reduction of numbers of pronephric units in *all* vertebrate lineages. It seems that workers who saw the similarity in the pattern: 1) selected *among* amphibians to find data to support the hypothesis; 2) ignored the work on osteichthyans or chose not to compare them to dipnoans and amphibians; and 3) did not recognize that shared primitive character states and patterns of convergence do not provide evidence of relationship except at the most general level.

Gonads

The testis. The testes of dipnoans also have been described extensively. Günther (1871), Ballantyne ('28), and Jesperson ('69) have examined *Neoceratodus*, and Kerr ('01) has described *Lepidosiren* and *P. annectens*. I have examined material representing all three genera (one of the surprisingly few such examinations) and can largely corroborate earlier descriptions, while putting the patterns of development and of spermatogenesis in a more current context.

Dipnoan testes are elongate structures (Fig. 1A–C), bound to kidney and dorsal body wall by mesenteries, and overlain by fat, especially before the dry season, as Kerr ('01) noted. The testes are stout medially, tapering laterally. In *Protopterus* and *Lepidosiren* the posterior part of the testis is not spermatogenic, but is "vesicular" (Kerr, '01). The vesicular testis invades kidney tissue (Fig. 3C). *Neoceratodus* lacks a vesicular posterior region (Jesperson, '69; confirmed by my dissections). The vesicular region is described by Kerr ('01) as spongy, trabecular, and lacking spermatogenic tubules; this too is confirmed by the present study (Fig. 4B). During the breeding season the spermatogenic part of the testis is filled with tubules containing mature sperm (Figs. 3A,B; 4A). The tubules are enlarged and have nests of primary spermatogonia peripherally, secondary spermatogonia somewhat more medially, and spermatids in the lumen (Figs. 3A,B; 4A). Tubules open into a longitudinal testis duct that extends posteriorly to a series of lateral ducts, the "vasa efferentia," which carry sperm to the nephrons as described below and illustrated by Jesperson ('69), Kerr ('01), and Goodrich ('30).

The regressed testis has much stromatous tissue. Tubules are reduced and few spermatogonia are stained, although a few mature sperm are still present (Fig. 3C).

Grier et al. ('80) reevaluated testicular morphology in several orders of teleosts and found two different tubular types. Salmoniform, perciform, and cypriniform fishes have spermatogonia distributed the length of the tubule; atheriniform fishes have spermatogonia only in the distal end of the tubule. My observations indicate that all three genera of dipnoans have a spermatogonial distribution identical to the salmoniform, perciform, and cypriniform type. Lungfish therefore share the primitive osteichthyan pattern with many teleosts and are unlike amphibians (reviewed in Wake, '79).

My material did not allow spermatogenesis to be traced. However, spermatogenesis and the fine structure of sperm have been examined by several workers. Agar ('11) described spermatogenesis in *Lepidosiren*, as did Boisson ('61, '63), and Boisson et al. ('67) in *P. annectens*. Jesperson ('71) described the fine structure of the sperm of *Neoceratodus*, and Boisson and Mattei ('65) and Purkerson et al. ('74) described spermatozoa of *P. aethiopicus*. Sperm of *Protopterus* have a long tapering head, a short middle piece, and two flagella each about twice the length of the head. The head piece of *Neoceratodus* is similar to that of *Protopterus*, but sperm of *Neoceratodus* have a single flagellum about three times the length of the head. Agar ('11) did not describe mature sperm of *Lepidosiren*. In my material the head pieces of *Lepidosiren* sperm are similar to those of other dipnoans, but the tail could not be distinguished. Purkerson et al. ('74) note that biflagellate sperm occur normally in diverse species of fishes. This appears to be a convergence, assuming that the monoflagellate state is primitive, and as such allows no evaluation of relationship.

The ovary. Very little attention has been paid to the morphology of the female urogen-

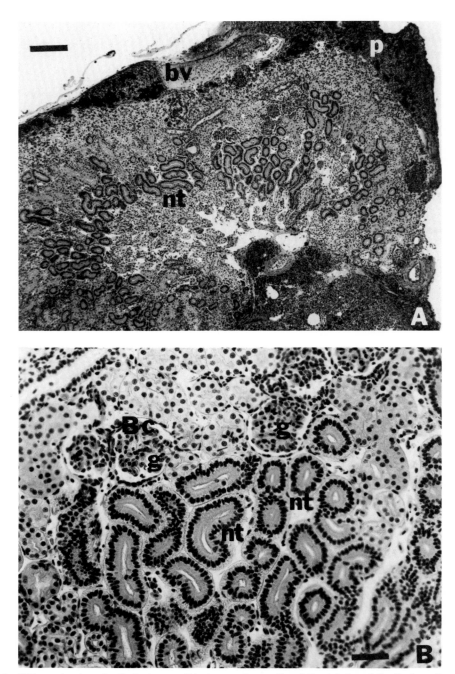

Fig. 2. Kidney structure in *Protopterus aethiopicus.* A) Posterior "vesicular" part of the kidney. Note the pigmented periphery, the orientation of tubules, and the large diameter of the nephric tubules. B) Anterior region of the kidney, illustrating large Bowman's capsules and glomeruli and the tubules of the "urinary" part of the kidney. Abbreviations: Bc, Bowman's capsule; bv, blood vessel; g, glomerulus; nt, nephric tubule; p, pigmented region. Scale bar in A, 0.4 mm; in B, 50 μm.

Fig. 3. Testis morphology of *Protopterus aethiopicus.* A) Spermatogenic tubules in transverse section. B) Tubules in longitudinal section. Note primary spermatogonia peripherally the length of the tubule, secondary spermatogonia somewhat more medially, and spermatids projecting into the lumen of the tubule. C) Vesicular part of the testis. Note absence of spermatozoa and invasion of testicular tubules into kidney tissue. Abbreviations: k, kidney; s, spermatids; t, spermatogenic tubule; 1, primary spermatogonia; 2, secondary spermatogonia. Scale bar, 50 μm.

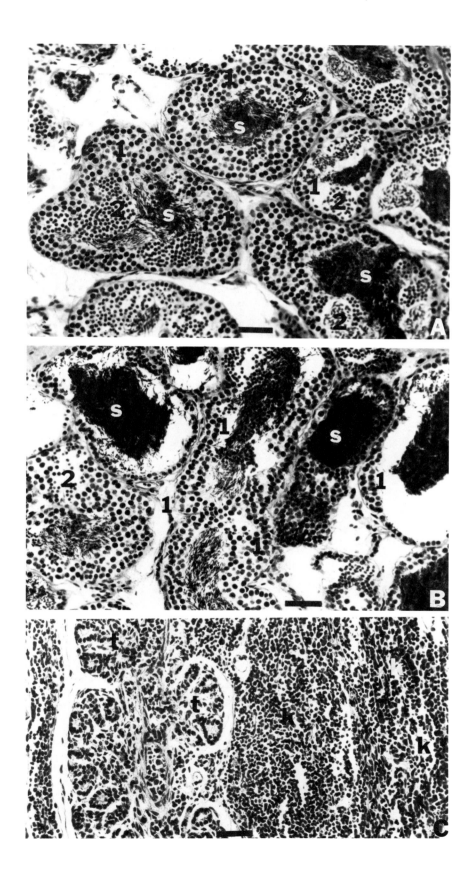

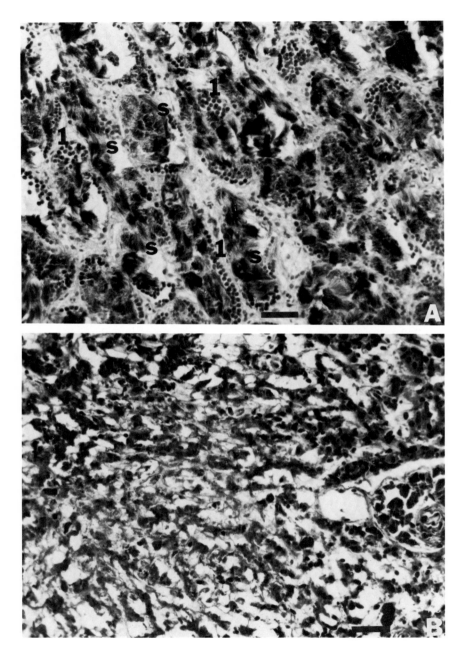

Fig. 4. Testis morphology of *Neoceratodus forsteri* and *Lepidosiren paradoxa.* A) Spermatogenesis in *Neocerato-dus.* Tubules are elongate and lined with primary spermatogonia. Spermatids in the lumen are in small, sworled masses in contrast to the large amorphous mass of *Protopterus.* The tubules of *Neoceratodus* are smaller in diameter than those of *Protopterus;* both are large adult specimens. B) The vesicular region of the testis of *Lepidosiren.* It is "spongy" and virtually atubular. Abbreviations: s, spermatids; 1, primary spermatogonia; 2, secondary spermatogonia. Scale bar, 50 μm.

ital systems, perhaps because it presents a "typical vertebrate" pattern. Only the early descriptive work of Owen (1841), Ayers (1885), and Parker (1892) on *P. annectens*, and Günther (1871) on *Neoceratodus* contain substantive information, most of which has simply been restated by others. By dissecting adult females of each of the living genera and examining the female urogenital structures histologically, I corroborate their descriptions, 100 years later.

The ovaries are large, elongate structures that extend from near the heart to the posterior end of the kidneys (Fig. 1D–F). They are paired, and held to the dorsal body wall by a stout mesovarium. The ovaries are also tightly bound to the oviducts by a mesentery, as illustrated by Goodrich ('30).

Approximately 5,000 large mature oocytes ("ova") may be present in each ovary (extrapolated from my count of 46/cm^3 of a mature *Neoceratodus* ovary 350-mm long, 40-mm wide most of its length, and 8 mm deep; the female was 560 mm standard length). Greenwood ('58; this volume) found more than 5,000 larvae in one *P. aethiopicus* nest and more than 2,000 in another and noted that the latter was an incomplete sample. Communal nesting is not likely. Ovaries of the females of the three genera that I examined all contained oocytes of three sizes and maturation (state of vitellogenesis) classes (Fig. 5). None appeared recently spent of mature ova. I have been unable to find data on size of mature ova. Ovarian oocytes of the largest size class in a large *Neoceratodus* are 3.0 mm in diameter (Fig. 5C). This probably represents full development, for Kemp ('81) illustrates a fertilized ovum beginning second cleavage at 3 mm diameter, which should reflect the size of eggs just laid and before any embryonic growth would have occurred. Kerr (1900) noted that the laid egg of *Lepidosiren* is very large (6.5–7.0 mm diameter) and surrounded by a capsule that is thick and jelly-like before fertilization but "thin and horny" after. The mature egg is unpigmented. Division is similar to that of large yolky eggs in diverse fish and amphibians (Kemp, '81; '82; this volume). Egg structure and vitellogenesis were described 100 years ago by Beddard (1886a,b). His description of ovum maturation in all three genera is basically accurate, though the terminology must be updated. His "germinal vesicle" is the unfertilized nucleus; the "vesicular dots" are nucleoli; plate 29 in Beddard (1886a) sug-

gests the true vesicle, or enlarged, diplotene nucleus but does not label it. My histological examination of the ovaries of each of the three genera confirms Beddard's basic description, including staining characteristics of oocytes. In vitellogenic oocytes the yolk stains differently medially and peripherally. The nucleoli at that stage are adjacent to the nuclear envelope, and are numerous. Beddard (1886a) did not comment on the pigmentation of the ovary. Melanocytes are present in ovaries of all three genera; they are few and largely peripheral in *Protopterus* and *Lepidosiren*, whereas they are very numerous and distributed throughout the ovarian stroma as well as densely in the periphery of the ovary in *Neoceratodus* (see Fig. 4).

Beddard (1886a,b) paid much attention to what he called "multinuclear bodies" or "multinuclear ova" in the ovaries of the three genera. He described these as multicellular structures that coalesced, modified the follicular layer, and acquired yolk. At maturity, they were fully yolked and the equivalent of ova that had undergone the standard pattern of vitellogenesis. He constructed a sequence of development based on stages observed in his sections but of course could not trace a particular oocyte through development. I interpret his multicellular bodies rather differently. I consider that they are simply atretic follicles and that Beddard (1886a,b) construed their place in the sequence of development backward. I suggest that the bodies observed to have some yolk, multicellular invasion of the center of the follicle, and a modified follicle wall are early in atresia; those that lack yolk and have a fully cellular center and virtually no follicle wall are late in atresia and are being resorbed. I note numerous red blood cells in the cellular mesh of such bodies, which suggests capillary invasion during resorption (Fig. 5B), but Beddard made no mention of the presence of blood cells.

Ovarian structure and pattern of ovum development in dipnoans shed no light on dipnoan relationships. The pattern is a primitive one, shared with most osteichthyans and many amphibians, particularly frogs. Grodzinski's ('72) work on yolk structure in *Neoceratodus* indicates closest similarity to that of *Latimeria*. The yolk spheres are structurally the same, though much smaller in *Neoceratodus*. There is also some resemblance to elasmobranch yolk granules, particularly in boundary organization, but less similarity to

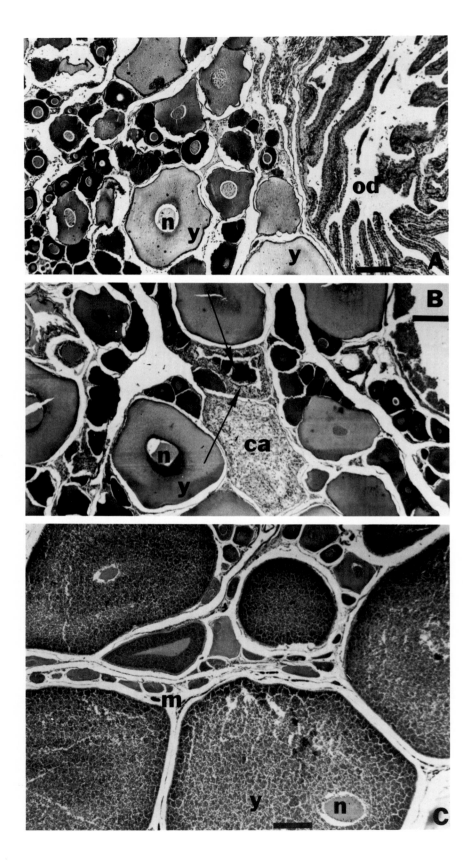

those of chondrosteans and holosteans which lack the peripheral organization of the yolk spheres.

The urogenital ducts and the cloaca
The urinary ducts

In development and function, the archinephric (mesonephric, Wolffian) ducts of female dipnoans are typical of female vertebrates in general, except teleosts. The archinephric duct transports urine from the adult mesonephric kidney to the cloaca. The ducts in all three genera are separate, rather than fused, as they enter the cloaca, according to Ayer's (1885) and Parker's (1892) figures and my observations (Fig. 1D–F).

Much more attention has been paid to the ducts of males, for the archinephric duct transports both urine and sperm. The lengthy literature is summarized by Jesperson ('69), and his own work on *Neoceratodus* sheds considerable light on the male system. In all three genera of lungfish, the archinephric duct drains the elongate kidney (Fig. 1A–C). In *Neoceratodus* 11–13 "vasa efferentia" (lateral ducts) connect the longitudinal testis duct to nephrons over the entire length of the kidney. The testis does not have discrete sperm-producing and vesicular components. Thus the archinephric duct evacuates urine, and also sperm during the breeding season, from the entire extent of the kidney. Sperm packing the nephrons and the archinephric duct are shown in Figure 6A,C,D. *Lepidosiren* has sperm transported from a tubular longitudinal testis duct extending through the vesicular part of the testis, where 5–6 lateral ducts lead to nephrons of the posterior part of the kidney (Fig. 1; Kerr, '01, '02). *Protopterus* had a reduced "testicular net" in which a single lateral duct extends from the longitudinal testis duct to several posterior nephrons (Fig. 1; Parker, 1892; Kerr, '01, '02).

The dipnoan situation differs significantly from that in amphibians. In gymnophiones the archinephric duct transports both sperm and urine and lateral ducts conduct sperm from the longitudinal testis duct to the mesonephrons, which lead to collecting ducts and then to the archinephric duct (Wake, '68, '70). The gymnophione testis is essentially unmodified for sperm transport. In urodeles the anterior part of the kidney is reduced, and in anurans it is reduced or lost; in dipnoans, as noted, the posterior part of the kidney is modified. The trend is for the archinephric duct to bear sperm from reduced anterior mesonephric tubules (received by lateral ducts from the longitudinal testis duct) and to bear a limited quantity of urine from the medial part of the kidney. A further trend in urodeles, and especially in anurans, is for the development *de novo* of a variable (by taxa) number of accessory ducts that evacuate urine to the cloaca from the posterior or urinary part of the kidney. Such accessory ducts do not occur in dipnoans. Jesperson ('69) notes that in *Polypterus* the testis duct opens into the distal part of the archinephric duct. He commented that *Lepisosteus* and *Acipenser* resemble *Neoceratodus*, with several lateral ducts leading from the short testes to the kidney. *Amia* (Jungersen, 1900) has numerous vasa efferentia that conduct sperm from the testis duct to a longitudinal kidney canal, then to the nephrons, and finally to the archinephric duct and the cloaca. Jesperson ('69) concluded that *Neoceratodus*, at least, showed a primitive osteichthyan pattern similar to that of primitive actinopterigians. Clearly, sperm transport in dipnoans differs significantly from that of amphibians, probably due to the constraint of the pattern of mesonephric reduction as noted above.

The oviducts

The oviducts are Müllerian duct derivatives that extend from near the heart to their entrance in to the cloaca dorsal to the urinary caecum. The full sequence of development has not yet been traced for any dipnoan, though Semon ('01) described several stages. Members of all three genera that I examined have slightly dilated infundibula (Fig. 1D–F). In all genera examined, adult females with yolky ovarian ova have ducts that are highly convoluted, hyperemic, and lined with a multi-layered secretory epithelium (Fig. 7B,C). The regressed duct of a specimen with very few large ova has a luminal epithelium without secretory cells and a much reduced diameter.

The primitive vertebrate state has the embryonic Müllerian ducts becoming the adult oviducts. Among osteichthyans, this pattern is retained by dipnoans, actinistians, chondrosteans, and some holostean neopterygi-

---

Fig. 5. Dipnoan ovaries. A) *Protopterus aethiopicus*. Ovary closely adheres to oviduct. Note stages of ovum development. Nuclei have numerous peripheral nucleoli. B) *Lepidosiren paradoxa*. Note ova in two different stages of atresia. The upper one (arrows) still contains some yolk; the lower is multicellular and the follicle is nearly disintegrated. C) *Neoceratodus forsteri*. Note large, yolky, (postvitellogenic) ova, a second class of vitellogenic ova, and a third class of slightly-yolked ova. Abbreviations: ca, corpus atretecum; m, melanocyte; n, nucleus; od, oviduct; y, yolk. Scale bar, 50 μm.

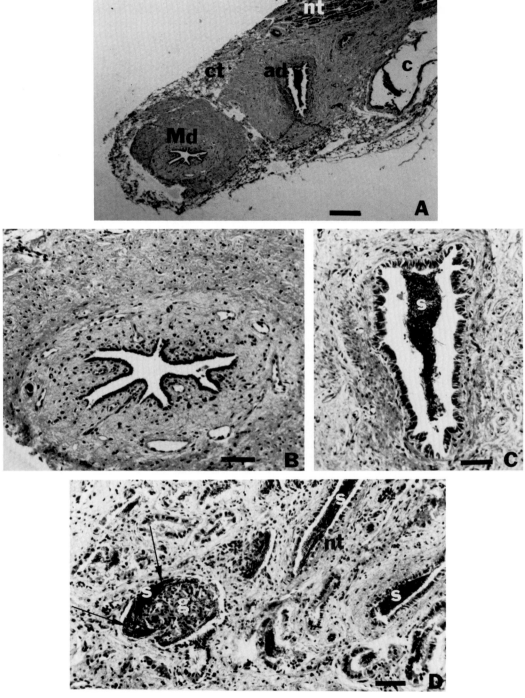

Fig. 6. Cloaca, archinephric duct, Müllerian duct, and posterior kidney of a male *Neoceratodus forsteri.* A) Transverse section of periphery of cloaca with ducts bound to cloaca by connective tissue. Section taken just above juncture of ducts with cloaca. B) Müllerian duct. Epithelium of lumen is not secretory. C) Archinephric duct. Note mass of sperm in lumen. D) Posterior kidney. Note glomerulus and tubules packed with sperm (arrows). Abbreviations; ad, archinephric duct; c, cloaca; ct, connective tissue; g, glomerulus; md, Müllerian duct; nt, nephric tubule; s and arrow, sperm. Scale bar in A, 0.4 mm; in B,C,D, 50 μm.

ans. The condition in which most neopterygians do not develop Müllerian ducts (their "oviducts" are therefore not homologous to those of other vertebrates) is a derived state (see Wake, '85). The presence of the oviducts of dipnoans therefore gives no positive support to hypotheses of relationship using presence of Müllerian duct derivatives as a character. The abdominal pores of *Protopterus* opening by a single aperture was likened by Goodrich ('30) to the condition in "primitive osteichthyans," but this conclusion seems very tenuous.

The male Müllerian ducts

Males of all three genera of lungfish retain Müllerian ducts, at least to some extent. Those of *Neoceratodus* extend from the anterior end of the testis to the cloaca, where they fuse. They do not open to the cloaca (Jesperson, '69), as confirmed in my dissections (Fig. 1C) but *contra* Gunther (1871). Jesperson's ('69) Figure 4 shows the duct with a dilated infundibulum; I did not find such a dilation. The ducts are thin, non-functional, connective tissue strips.

In *Protopterus*, adult males retain vestiges of the infundibulum at the anterior end of the kidney, and a few millimeters of each duct posteriorly. The ducts unite in the wall of the cloaca. My dissection of *P. aethiopicus* revealed a condition similar to that described by Kerr ('01) for *P. annectens*, but the ducts do not reach the urogenital papilla in my specimen (Fig. 1A). The ducts are even more reduced in males of *Lepidosiren* (Fig. 1B). Only the anterior infundibula are present (the funnels of Kerr, '01). Kerr ('01) reported that additional vestiges of the ducts were present in a second-year male.

In amphibians, if Müllerian ducts are retained at all by males, they are represented only by connective tissue strips of varying lengths beside the kidneys or, as in gymnophiones, by connective tissue strips anteriorly followed by several millimeters of glandular tissue posteriorly. The lumen of the glandular portion opens into the cloaca. Wake ('81) suggested that this secretory activity in the male Müllerian duct of amphibians is correlated with internal fertilization and terrestriality. I find no indication of secretory cells in the posterior ducts of *Neoceratodus* (Fig. 5B) and *P. aethiopicus*. The retention of anterior components and the lack of effective association with the cloaca by lungfish is distinctly different from the situation in amphibians that retain the ducts.

Abdominal pores

Despite the reports of a single abdominal pore in *Lepidosiren* (Owen, 1841) and paired pores in *Neoceratodus* (Gunther, 1871), it seems reasonable that the large numbers of mature ova of all genera are borne to the cloaca via the convoluted, glandular oviducts and extruded via the vent. The pores are located at the vent opening just beyond the cloaca (but may be variable according to Owen, 1841), and the oviducts open into the cloaca anteriorly. Bles (1898) noted that *Lepidosiren* lacks pores, in contradiction to Owen's 1841 report. The abdominal pores are therefore likely not associated with ovum transport as Goodrich ('30) also stated. Bles (1898) argued that the abdominal pores are excretory, alluding to data on kidney-gonad development that are unclear to me. They may be vestigial, or involved in other fluid flow, as Goodrich ('30) suggested.

The cloaca

All three genera of dipnoans retain a simple cloaca (Fig. 1) with the urinary ducts opening by a single aperture (Jesperson, '69, *Neoceratodus*; Kerr, '01, *Lepidosiren* and *P. annectens*). All three genera have a urinary caecum or bladder. Kerr ('01) considered the caecum to be an anteriorly projecting dilation of the fused urinary ducts, or the urogenital sinus. The amphibian bladder is an outpocketing of the cloaca. In males the archinephric (testis) ducts open separately on the dorsal wall of the cloacal caecum at its juncture with the cloaca proper (Fig. 1A–C). Kerr ('01) noted that each aperture is marked by a prominent papilla during the breeding season in *P. annectens* and *Lepidosiren*. I observed slight prominences at the openings in spermatogenic specimens of *Lepidosiren*, *P. aethiopicus*, and *Neoceratodus*, but I do not know if these were in breeding condition. Goodrich ('30) illustrates genital and urinary papillae in a female *P. annectens*. My dissections of females of all three genera of dipnoans revealed slight rings of tissue at these apertures but not pronounced papillae. The rectal portion of the intestine is dilated and narrows slightly at its juncture with the cloaca. The vent opens to the left of the tail fin in the specimens I examined.

Lagios and McCosker ('77) report the presence of a cloacal gland in *P. aethiopicus* and *P. dolloi*, and its absence in *Neoceratodus* and *Lepidosiren*. The gland is dorsal and posterior to the urinary caecum and opens into the cloaca at the juncture of the caecum with

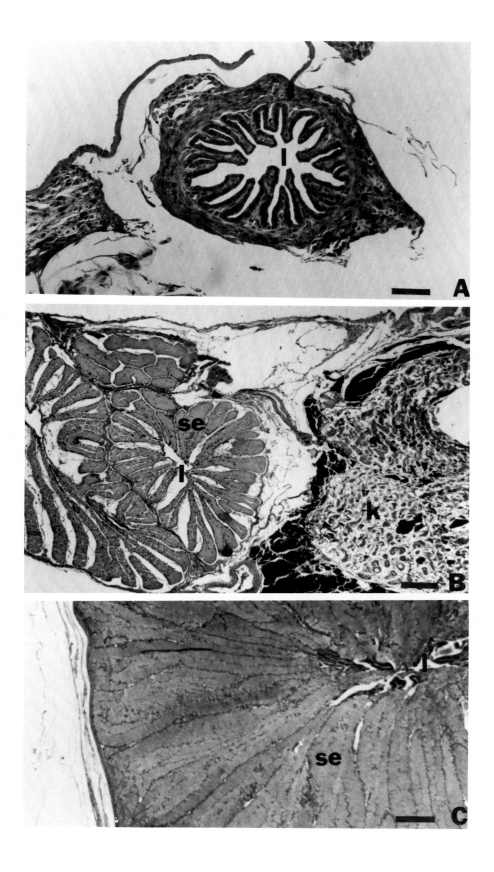

the cloaca. Lagios and McCosker ('77) suggest that the gland may be cation-secreting, functionally similar to the rectal glands of elasmobranchs, holocephalans, and *Latimeria*, though the anatomical relationship differs from that of the latter groups. The sizes of Lagios and McCosker's ('77) specimens were not indicated; I cannot determine whether they looked for age or sex differences in the morphology of the gland.

Presence of a cloaca is of course the primitive vertebrate pattern, and all bony fish that lack a cloaca are derived.

The "adrenal"

Several workers have cited the "amphibian characteristics" of the interrenal or adrenocortical homolog tissue of dipnoans (Chester Jones and Mosley, '80; Janssens et al., '65; Call and Janssens, '75). Such tissue has been identified in *Protopterus* (Gerard, '54; Janssens et al., '65) (species not listed) and in *Neoceratodus* (Call and Janssens, '75) based on morphology and histochemistry. Cord-like cell groups located on the postcardinal veins and their tributaries between renal and perirenal tissue converted progesterone to corticosterone when tested *in vitro*, and tested positively for cholesterol (Call and Janssens, '75). No chromaffin tissue was found in either genus (Call and Janssens, '75). The position and histochemical characteristics of the interrenal tissue in *Protopterus* and *Neoceratodus* were considered to be very similar to those of interrenal tissue in adult *Pleurodeles* (Certain, '61), a urodele, and the larvae of certain frogs (Chester Jones and Mosley, '80).

An examination of the position and cellular characteristics suggests that the similarity of dipnoan and amphibian interrenals is a tenuous one. The interrenal of *Latimeria* has a large number of corpuscles in the walls and along the extent of the postcardinals and their tributaries in the kidney (Lagios and

Stasko-Concannon, quoted in Chester Jones and Mosley, '80). *Acipenser* has a similar interrenal distribution along the cardinals and their tributaries beside and within the kidney (Youson and Butler, '76a); corpuscles are found throughout the kidney, but primarily in the reduced anterior two-thirds of the kidney. Corpuscles lie in the anterior two-thirds of the kidney of the brachiopterygian *Polypterus* (Youson and Butler, '85). A similar situation obtains in *Polyodon* (Lagios and Stasko-Concannon, quoted in Chester Jones and Mosley, '80) and in the neopterygian "holostean" *Amia* (Youson and Butler, '76b). In the neopterygian *Lepisosteus*, corpuscles are in the anterior half of the kidney (Bhattacharyya et al., '81). As Youson and Butler ('85) point out, the distribution of adrenocortical corpuscles offers little to support (or negate) current hypotheses of the taxonomic status of the "primitive" osteichthyans. Among teleosts, interrenal tissue is confined to the head kidney, so far as is known, which is largely lymphoid and hemopoietic tissue. I found no information about the interrenal tissue of teleosts that: 1) lack a head kidney (*sensu* Nandi, '62); or 2) retain a functional pronephros throughout life, as do some teleosts (*Zoarces*, for example). When one examines the data on interrenal tissue for amphibians, one quickly realizes that there is no common amphibian pattern, despite assertions in the literature. Dittus ('36) considered the gymnophione condition primitive for amphibians. The interrenal tissue starts anterior to the kidney and is associated with the aorta. Masses of interrenal tissue extend posteriorly in the entire extent of the kidney associated with post-cardinal and renal vessels. Tissue may also lie medial to the kidneys or embedded in the medial kidney tissue, especially ventrally (see also Gabe, '71). Urodele interrenal tissue shows considerable variation, from association with blood vessels only in *Siren*, to being embedded in the kidney along the renal vessels in *Amphiuma*, and embedded and concentrated anteriorly in *Necturus* (Hartman and Brownell, '49) and several other diverse species (Hanke, '78). Anurans usually have interrenal tissue concentrated as a longitudinal mass on the ventral side of each kidney associated with branches of the renal vein.

The literature is contradictory with regard to dipnoans. Chester Jones and Mosley ('80:422) state that "the adrenocortical homologue consists of small cells closely associated with the post-cardinal veins and their

Fig. 7. Dipnoan oviducts. A) Regressed duct in *Protopterus aethiopicus*. The ovary of the specimen lacked large yolky ova; thus I infer that it is post-breeding. B) *Lepidosiren paradoxa* oviduct bound to posterior part of the kidney. The epithelium of the lumen is proliferated and secretory. C) *Neoceratodus forsteri* oviduct in a hyperemic, secretory state. The ovary contained large ova; thus I infer that ovulation is imminent, and the oviduct ready to transport ova. Little appears to be known of endocrine regulation of breeding in dipnoans. Abbreviations: k, kidney; l, lumen of oviduct; se, secretory epithelium. Note that all three specimens are photographed to the same scale. Bar, 50 μm.

tributaries where these vessels pass through the kidneys." Balment et al. ('80:529) claim that "jawed fish, teleosts and elasmobranchs" share a common association with the cardinal vein and pronephric-mesonephric units, but they state that dipnoans have an amphibian-type interrenal associated with kidney tissue. Hanke ('78) defines the amphibian characteristic as a "close association [of interrenal tissue] with kidney cells, separated from the tubules only by a basement membrane and a thin layer of connective tissue." The "amphibian characteristic" does *not* obtain for many amphibians and appears to be a derived state among some urodeles and most frogs. This is probably a convergence within amphibians, since some frogs show a more primitive condition. It appears then that urodeles and anurans (and gymnophiones) followed independent evolutionary courses to their particular states, although it should be noted that information is available only for primitive gymnophiones (Dittus, '36). The interrenal morphology of *Protopterus* (see Janssens et al., '65) approaches the "amphibian characteristic" less closely than does *Neoceratodus* (see Call and Janssens, '75) and is clearly associated with postcardinal and renal veins. Dipnoan interrenals, while resembling those of *selected* amphibians, also resemble to some degree those of chondrosteans and *Latimeria*. Chester Jones ('57) suggested teleost and crossopterygian affinities before he emphasized the "amphibian" features.

I concur with Lagios and Stasko-Concannon (in Chester Jones and Mosley, '80) that the diffuse distribution of interrenal tissue along the cardinal veins and their branches is a primitive condition in vertebrates. A number of lineages often have modified that pattern in different ways, apparently independently. There are no shared derived characters of the interrenals that ally dipnoans with amphibians as a group, or with urodeles in particular. There are, however, some convergences among derived genera in several fish and amphibian lineages.

CONCLUSIONS

It is apparent that analysis of the comparative biology and evolution of the dipnoan urogenital system is incomplete for several reasons: 1) lack of direct comparison of members of all three genera; 2) lack of information for many primitive osteichthyans and for an effective representation of the diversity of teleosts; 3) lack of any attempt to compare dipnoans with other fish taxa for

which information is available; and 4) an almost dogmatic assumption that amphibian morphology provides information crucial to understanding dipnoan biology. Some very general but similar aspects of dipnoan and amphibian biology suggest that bases for similarity should be explored, but that exploration has rarely been done on an appropriate scale. Further, comparisons with amphibians have usually been made with highly selected species, not considering whether the species were primitive and representative of the entire amphibian grade, or exhibiting states derived for particular lineages and therefore indicative of convergence if "shared" by dipnoans and one or more amphibian species. As indicated above, analysis of urogenital morphology almost invariably indicates one of three conclusions: 1) Dipnoans share a primitive vertebrate pattern with fishes and with amphibians; 2) dipnoans share general features with many osteichthyans, and various teleostean lineages are derived; and 3) the derived features shared by dipnoans and *some* amphibian species are not those of the order, let alone the class, and often not even the family of amphibians being compared. Therefore, convergence, not relationship, must be inferred. In general, the data do not support hypotheses of dipnoans being the sister group of tetrapods. Urogenital system morphology is more similar to that of actinistians, chondrosteans, and primitive teleosts, but there are few shared derived characters of the urogenital system to ally even these groups (Fraser, '27, lists some). This is not to say definitively that dipnoans are not the sister group of tetrapods, but that support for that hypothesis (and most others) must come from other systems.

Urogenital morphology does, however, provide support for the familial allocation of dipnoans, in agreement with osteology (Marshall, this volume), myology (Bemis, this volume), and numerous other features (Goodrich, '30). *Lepidosiren* and *Protopterus* have four synapomorphies; *Protopterus* and *Neoceratodus* each have an autapomorphy (see Fig. 8). These data support the inclusion of *Lepidosiren* and *Protopterus* in a family separate from *Neoceratodus*. Even these data are incomplete. For example, *Neoceratodus* has uniflagellate sperm and *Protopterus* biflagellate, as noted above. However, there is no comparable information about the sperm of *Lepidosiren*; thus the difference between *Lepidosiren* and *Neoceratodus* is not a useful character.

Examples of paucity of complete information for most aspects of urogenital morphology have been indicated in several instances above. Therefore my first goal, that of providing a direct comparison of all three genera of dipnoans, is not yet completely fulfilled. First, more basic data on structure and development of the urogenital system of dipnoans, non-teleostean osteichthyans, various teleosts, and a greater diversity of amphibians of all three orders are needed. These should be provided systematically, using modern technology. Second, an objective cross-comparison of *many* taxa must be undertaken. Third, hypotheses of relationship must be structured rigorously, and alternative hypotheses also considered. Identification of character states should be done according to current methods, with assessment of polarities and analysis of grades and clades, not by comparisons of just randomly (or worse, subjectively) chosen species. With these three criteria met, analysis of the urogenital system should provide insight into the functional biology of the system and its pattern of diversification, thereby giving clues to the evolutionary relationships of dipnoans to other vertebrates.

ACKNOWLEDGMENTS

I thank William E. Bemis for insisting that I undertake this survey, and for providing specimens and the Annotated Bibliography compiled by Elizabeth Conant. I am grateful to Dr. Conant for compiling that extremely helpful list. I thank Stuart Poss for the loan of *Lepidosiren* and *Neoceratodus* from the California Academy of Sciences and Kristen Nygren for sectioning the material. I am pleased to acknowledge the research support of the National Science Foundation (BSR 83-05771).

LITERATURE CITED

Agar, W.E. (1911) The spermatogenesis of *Lepidosiren paradoxa*. Q. J. Microsc. Sci. *57*:1–44.

Ayers, H. (1885) Beiträge zur Anatomie und Physiologie der Dipnoer. Z. Naturwiss. Jena *18*:479–527.

Ballantyne, F.M. (1928) Note on the male genito-urinary organs of *Ceratodus forsteri*. Proc. Zool. Soc. Lond. *1928*:697–698.

Balment, R.J., I.W. Henderson, and I. Chester Jones (1980) The adrenal cortex and its homologues in vertebrates; evolutionary comparisons. In I. Chester Jones and I.W. Henderson (eds): General, Comparative and Clinical Endocrinology of the Adrenal Cortex. London: Academic Press, pp. 525–562.

Beddard, F.E. (1886a) Observations on the ovarian ovum of *Lepidosiren* (*Protopterus*). Proc. Zool. Soc. Lond. *1886*:272–292.

Beddard, F.E. (1886b) Observations on the development and structure of the ovum in the Dipnoi. Proc. Zool. Soc. Lond. *1886*:502–527.

Bhattacharyya, T. K., D. G. Butler, and J. H. Youson (1981) Distribution and structure of the adrenocortical homolog in the garpike. Am. J. Anat. *160*:231–246.

Bles, E. J. (1898) The correlated distribution of abdominal pores and nephrostomes in fishes. J. Anat. Physiol. *32*:484–512.

Boisson, D. (1961) La spermatogénèse de *Protopterus annectens* (Dipneuste) du Sénégal. Ann. Fac. Sci. univ. Dakar *6*:133–144.

Boisson, C. (1963) La spermiogénèse de *Protopterus annectens* (Dipneuste) du Sénégal étudiée au microscope optique et quelques détails au microscope électronique. Ann. Fac. Sci. Univ. Dakar *10*:43–72.

Boisson, C., and X. Mattei (1965) A propos de l'acrosome des spermatozoïdes du Dipneuste *Protopterus annectens* Owen. C. R. Soc. Biol. Paris *159*:2247–2249.

Boisson, C., C. Mattei, and X. Mattei (1967) Troisième note sur la spermiogénèse de *Protopterus annectens* (Dipneuste) de Sénégal. Bull. Inst. Fondam. Afr. Noire Ser. A. Sci. Nat. *29*:1097–1121.

Brauer, A. (1902) Beitrag zur Kenntnis der Entwicklung und Anatomie der Gymnophionen. III. Entwicklung der Excretionsorgane. Zool. Jl. Anat. *3*:1–176.

Call, R. N., and P. A. Janssens (1975) Histochemical studies of the adrenocortical homologue in the kidney of the Australian lungfish, *Neoceratodus forsteri*. Cell Tissue Res. *156*:533–538.

Certain, P. (1961) Organogénèse des formations interrénales chez le bactracien urodèle *Pleurodeles waltlii*. Mich. Bull. Biol. France-Belgique *95*:134–148.

Chester Jones, I. (1957) The Adrenal Cortex. London: Cambridge University Press.

Chester Jones, I., and W. Mosley (1980) The interrenal gland in Pisces. In I. Chester Jones and I. W. Henderson (eds): General, Comparative and Clinical Endocrinology of the Adrenal Cortex. New York: Academic Press, pp. 395–472.

Dittus, P. (1936) Interrenalsystem und chromaffine Zellen im Lebenslauf von *Ichthyophis glutinosus*. Z. Wiss. Zool. *147*:459–512.

Fox, H. (1960) Early pronephric growth in *Neoceratodus* larvae. Proc. Zool. Soc. Lond. *134*:659–663.

Fox, H. (1961) The segmentation of components in the hind region of the head of *Neoceratodus* and their relation to the pronephric tubules. Acta Anat. *47*:156–163.

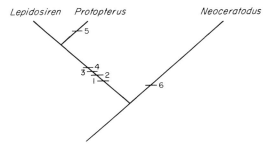

Fig. 8. Cladogram of dipnoan interrelationships based on urogenital morphology. Many symplesiomorphies ally the two groups of genera. Synapomorphies of *Protopterus* and *Lepidosiren* are: kidney divided into urinary and "vesicular" regions (1); testis divided into spermatogenic and vesicular regions (2); reduced number of "vasa efferentia" (3); reduced male Müllerian duct (4). The *Protopterus* autapomorphy (5) is the presence of the cloacal gland, that of *Neoceratodus* (6) is the invasive pigmentation of the ovary.

Fox, H. (1962) A study of the evolution of the amphibian and dipnoan pronephros by an analysis of its relationship with anterior spinal nerves. Proc. Zool. Soc. Lond. *138*:225–256.

Fox, H. (1963) The amphibian pronephros. Q. Rev. Biol. *38*:1–25.

Fraser, E. A. (1927) Observations on the development of the pronephros of sturgeon, *Acipenser rubicundus*. Q. J. Microsc. Sci. *71*:75–112.

Fraser, E. A. (1950) The development of the vertebrate excretory system. Biol. Rev. *25*:159–187.

Gabe, M. (1971) Données histologiques sur la glande surrénale d'*Ichthyophis glutinosus*. Arch. Biol. (Liège) *82*:1–23.

Gerard, P. (1954) Organes uro-génitaux. In P. P. Grasse (ed): Traité de Zoologie. Vol. 12. Paris: Masson Publ., pp. 974–1043.

Goodrich, E. S. (1930) Studies on the Structure and Development of Vertebrates. (Republished by Dover Publications, Inc., New York, 1958)

Greenwood, P. H. (1958) Reproduction in the East African lung-fish *Protopterus aethiopicus* Heckel. Proc. Zool. Soc. Lond. *130*:547–567.

Grier, H. J., J. R. Linton, Q. F. Leatherland, and V. L. de Vlaming (1980) Structural evidence for two different testicular types in teleost fishes. Am. J. Anat. *159*:331–345.

Grodzinski, Z. (1972) The yolk of *Neoceratodus forsteri* Krefft (Dipnoi-Pisces). Acta Biol. Cracov. Ser. Zool. *15*:193–199.

Günther, A. (1871) Description of *Ceratodus*, a genus of ganoid fishes, recently discovered in rivers of Queensland, Australia. Trans. R. Soc. Lond. *161*:511–571.

Hanke, W. (1978) The adrenal cortex of Amphibia. In I. Chester Jones and I. W. Henderson (eds): General, Comparative and Clinical Endrocrinology of the Adrenal Cortex. Vol. 2. London: Academic Press, pp. 419–495.

Hartman, F. A., and K. A. Brownell (1949) The Adrenal Gland. Philadelphia: Lea and Febiger.

Hickman, C.P., Jr., and B. F. Trump (1969) The Kidney. In W. S. Hoar, and D. J. Randall (eds): Fish Physiology. Vol. 1. New York: Academic Press, pp. 91–239.

Janssens, P. A., G. P. Vinson, I. Chester Jones, and W. Mosely (1965) Amphibian characteristics of the adrenal cortex of the African lungfish (*Protopterus* sp.). J. Endocrinol. *32*:373–382.

Jesperson, A. (1969) On the male urogenital organs of *Neoceratodus forsteri*. Biol. Skr. Dan. Vidensk. Selsk. *16*:1–11.

Jesperson, A. (1971) Fine structure of the spermatozoon of the Australian lungfish *Neoceratodus forsteri* (Krefft). J. Ultrastruct. Res. *37*:178–185.

Jungersen, H. F. E. (1900) Ueber die Urogenital-organe von *Polypterus* and *Amia*. Zool. Anz. *23*:328–334.

Kemp, A. (1981) Rearing of embryos and larvae of the Australian lungfish, *Neoceratodus forsteri*, under laboratory conditions. Copeia *1981*:776–784.

Kemp, A. (1982) The embryological development of the Queensland lungfish, *Neoceratodus forsteri* (Krefft). Mem. Qd. Mus. *20*:553–597.

Kerr, J. G. (1900) The external features in the development of *Lepidosiren paradoxa*. Trans. R. Soc. Lond. *192*:299–330.

Kerr, J. G. (1901) On the male genito-urinary organs of the *Lepidosiren* and *Protopterus*. Proc. Zool. Soc. Lond. *1901*:484–498.

Kerr, J. G. (1902) The genito-urinary organs of dipnoan fishes. Proc. Cambridge Philos. Soc. *11*:329–333.

Kerr, J.G. (1919) Textbook of Embryology. Vol. II. Vertebrata. London: MacMillan and Co.

Kindahl, M. (1937) Zur Entwicklung der Exkretionsorgane von Dipnoern und Amphibien. Acta. Zool. (Stockh.) *19*:1–190.

Lagios, M.D., and J.E. McCosker (1977) A cloacal excretory gland in the lungfish *Protopterus*. Copeia *1977*:176–178.

Maschkowzeff, A. (1934–1935) Zur Phylogenie der Geschlechtsdrüsen und der Geschlechts-ausführgange bei den Vertebrata auf Grund von Forschungen betreffend die Entwicklung des Mesonephros und der Geschlechtsorgane bei den Acipenseridae, Salmoniden und Amphibien. Zool. Jb. Anat. *59*:1–68, 201–276.

Miles, R.S. (1977) Dipnoan (lungfish) skulls and the relationships of the group: A study based on new species from the Devonian of Australia. Zool. J. Linn. Soc. *61*:1–328.

Nandi, J. (1962) The structure of the interrenal gland in teleost fishes. Univ. Calif. Publ. Zool. *65*:129–212.

Owen, R. (1841) Description of the *Lepidosiren annectens*. Trans. Linn. Soc. Lond. *18*:327–361.

Parker, W.N. (1892) On the anatomy and physiology of *Protopterus annectens*. Trans. R. Irish Acad. *30*:109–216.

Purkerson, M.L., J.U.M. Jarvis, S.A. Luse, and E.W. Dempsey (1974) Analysis coupled with scanning and electron microscopic observations of spermatozoa of the African lungfish, *Protopterus aethiopicus*. J. Zool. (Lond.) *172*:1–12.

Romer, A.S. (1966) Vertebrate Paleontology. Chicago: University of Chicago Press.

Rosen, D.E., P.L. Forey, B.G. Gardiner, and C. Patterson (1981) Lungfishes, tetrapods, paleontology, and plesiomorphy. Bull. Am. Mus. Nat. Hist. *167*:159–276.

Semon, R. (1901) Zur Entwicklungsgeschichte des Urogenitalsystems der Dipnoer. Zool. Anz. *24*:131–135.

Smith, H.W. (1930) Metabolism of the lungfish, *Protopterus aethiopicus*. J. Biol. Chem. *88*:97–130.

Thomson, K.S. (1969) The biology of the lobe-finned fishes. Biol. Rev. (Cambridge) *44*:91–154.

Torrey, T.W. (1965) Morphogenesis of the vertebrate kidney. In R.L. DeHaan and R. Ursprung (eds): Organogenesis. New York: Holt, Rinehart and Winston, pp. 559–579.

Wake, M.H. (1968) Evolutionary morphology of the caecilian urogenital system. Part I. The gonads and fat bodies. J. Morphol. *126*:291–332.

Wake, M.H. (1970) Evolutionary morphology of the caecilian urogenital system. Part II. The kidneys and the urogenital ducts. Acta Anat. *75*:321–358.

Wake, M.H. (1979) The comparative anatomy of the urogenital system. In M.H. Wake (ed): Hyman's Comparative Vertebrate Anatomy. 3rd Ed. Chicago: University of Chicago Press, pp. 555–614.

Wake, M.H. (1981) Structure and function of the male Müllerian gland in caecilians (Amphibia: Gymnophiona), with comments on its evolutionary significance. J. Herpet. *15*:17–22.

Wake, M.H. (1985) Oviduct structure and function in non-mammalian vertebrates. In H.-R. Duncker and G. Fleischer (eds): Functional Morphology of Vertebrates. Fortschr., Zool., *30*:427–435.

Youson, J.H., and D.G. Butler (1976a) The adrenocortical homolog in the Lake Sturgeon, *Acipenser fulvescens*. Rafinesque. Am. J. Anat. *145*:207–224.

Youson, J.H., and D.G. Butler (1976b) Fine structure of the adrenocortical homolog and the corpuscles of Stannius of *Amia calva* L. Acta Zool. (Stockh.) *57*:217–230.

Youson, J.H., and D.G. Butler (1985) Distribution and structure of the adrenocortical homolog in *Polypterus palmas* Ayres. Acta Zool. (Stockh.) *66*:131–143.

JOURNAL OF MORPHOLOGY SUPPLEMENT 1:217-236 (1986)

Circulation and Respiration in Lungfishes (Dipnoi)

WARREN W. BURGGREN AND KJELL JOHANSEN
*Department of Zoology, University of Massachusetts, Amherst,
Massachusetts 01003-0027 (W.B.) and Department of Zoophysiology,
University of Aarhus, Aarhus, DK-8000C, Denmark (K.J.)*

ABSTRACT This paper reviews the cardiorespiratory morphology and physiology of the living lungfishes, in the special context of their highly effective use of both air and water for gas exchange. Particular emphasis is placed on describing those features of the circulatory and respiratory systems that distinguish *Neoceratodus* from the Lepidosirenidae (*Protopterus, Lepidosiren*), and which, in turn, distinguish lungfishes from other aquatic vertebrates. Morphological and physiological characters that represent the plesiomorphic condition for the living Dipnoi are indicated (e.g., separate atrial chambers, vertical septum in ventricle, pulmonary veins, conal valves, twisting of bulbus cordis), as are those characters that may be shared derived features of the Lepidosirenidae (e.g., paired lungs, reduced anterior gill arches, well-developed spiral valve in conus). Morphological and physiological comparisons and contrasts with tetrapods are made to elucidate systematic relationships of the Dipnoi with other vertebrates.

The appearance of aerial respiration in ancestral fishes was a pivotal development in the evolution of terrestrial vertebrates (Johansen, '70; Gans, '70a; Johansen and Burggren, '80; Randall et al., '81; Little, '83). Since extremely little information on this respiratory transformation can be gleaned from the fossil record, physiologists interested in the evolution of aerial respiration must be content with the study of extant animals occupying a transitional position between an aquatic and terrestrial lifestyle. While these animals represent but a poor pseudophyletic progression (cf. Gans, '70a), investigation of the morphological and physiological adaptations for air breathing shown by these animals has, nonetheless, contributed greatly to our perception of how aerial respiration must have arisen in ancestors of the tetrapods.

The purpose of this review is to describe the cardiorespiratory adaptations for aerial respiration of extant lungfishes and to place these adaptations in the context of other vertebrates. Although the Dipnoi are a relict group only remotely related to other air-breathing fishes and separate from the amphibians by hundred of millions of years of independent evolution (Forey, this volume), we contend that ancestors of the tetrapods were probably very similar *physiologically* to the modern lungfishes.

AIR BREATHING IN FISHES—DIVERSE "SOLUTIONS" TO A COMMON PROBLEM

The unique morphological and physiological features for aerial respiration of lungfish are best appreciated when compared with those of other living fishes that breathe air. Aerial respiration has arisen independently numerous times in the evolutionary history of fishes, frequently (but not always) as a response to aquatic hypoxia (Bertin, '58; Gans, '70a; Munshi, '76; Graham, '76; Randall et al., '81); yet it is not a common evolutionary response to this environmental stress, since fewer than 70 of the more than 4000 genera of living fishes contain species that can actually breathe air (see Gans, '70b). While the vast majority of air-breathing fishes are tropical freshwater teleosts (see Gans, '70a; Dehadrai and Tripathi, '76), aerial gas exchange is remarkably prevalent amongst phyletically ancient gnathostome fishes (Burggren et al., '86), perhaps attesting to the value for survival of this innovative respiratory process. Whatever their evolutionary history, however, air-breathing fishes use a diverse range of structures to exchange respiratory gases with air. Organs

---

Address reprint requests to Warren W. Burggren, Department of Zoology, University of Massachusetts, Amherst, MA 01003-0027.

for air breathing (arising both *de novo* and as adaptations of existing structures serving other functions) include the skin, the alimentary canal, the gills and structures derived from them, and diverticula of the branchial and buccal chambers, pharynx, and esophagus (for reviews, see Johansen; '70; Munshi, '76; Randall et al., '81). Virtually all air-breathing fishes still retain gills and gas-permeable skin functional in aquatic gas exchange. Thus, many air-breathing fish are so-called "facultative" air breathers, able to subsist entirely on aquatic gas exchange, but using the air-breathing organ (ABO) to facilitate respiration. Other fish are regarded as "obligatory" air breathers that will eventually drown if denied access to air. However, increasing metabolic rate or decreasing water O_2 availability, for example, can make air breathing obligatory for survival in fishes that under different conditions would be only facultative air breathers (Rahn et al., '71; Johansen et al., '70; McMahon and Burggren, '86).

In spite of considerable morphological and physiological diversity of air-breathing organs in fishes, these structural adaptations for air breathing are conceptually rather simple and not particularly effective by the standards of gas-exchange organs of tetrapods. The "effectiveness" of a particular respiratory system such as a gas bladder or lung depends greatly upon the source (and therefore gas content) of blood perfusing it and the consequent fate of blood draining it. In crocodilians, birds, and mammals, for example, the lungs are perfused exclusively by systemic venous blood that is relatively deoxygenated and high in carbon dioxide. In almost all nondipnoan fishes that breathe air, however, the blood supply to the ABO consists only partially of deoxygenated blood draining from the systemic tissues, with the remainder (and sometimes the major portion) consisting of blood that has most recently passed through a gas-exchange organ rather than the systemic tissues (Fig. 1). This situation can arise either when the ABO is downstream and in series with the gills (Fig. 1D,E) or in parallel with the gills (Fig. 1B,C). In either situation, some proportion of the circulation of blood to the ABO is "wasted," because little additional respiratory gas transport can be achieved by that proportion of oxygenated blood that has been shunted directly back into the afferent circulation to the ABO.

Why does the ABO (and for that matter the gills) of many air-breathing fish (e.g., Fig. 1B,D,E,F) receive blood that has already been partially oxygenated? In essence, the venous circulation of the ABO of most fishes is arranged just as that of any other systemic vascular bed, with the anatomical confluence of the efferent vessel from the air-breathing organ and the central systemic veins occurring well before the heart. This leads to substantial, if not complete, admixture of oxygenated blood from the ABO with deoxygenated blood from the systemic vascular beds on the venous side *before* the heart in almost all nondipnoan fishes.

As a direct consequence of the heart receiving a homogeneous venous input, in most air-breathing fishes there has been little selection for specializations leading to separate blood streams within the atrium and ventricle. Only with the evolution of an ABO with completely separate venous drainage directly to the atrium will any subsequent adaptation involving division of the heart or central arterial circulation confer any selective advantage to respiration. When preferential distribution of oxygenated blood to the tissues and deoxygenated blood to the ABO is facilitated by central cardiovascular division, gas exchange becomes more effective and can more readily be matched to changing internal and external conditions (see reviews in Johansen and Burggren, '85).

In considering the general phylogenetic progression in living vertebrates, there is a clear *physiological* progression toward a divided circulation with a separate, independently perfused circuit for gas exchange (Johansen, '85). The value is recognizing such a physiological progression, albeit in phylogenetically distant vertebrate lineages, is that it is strongly suggestive of the physiological transformations that we believe must have occurred in the actual ancestors of particular vertebrate lines as they evolved into terrestrial, air-breathing animals. In this context, the lungfishes are of vital importance, for they display morphological and physiological characters for respiration and circulation that were almost surely shared by the ancestral tetrapods going onto land.

The pulmonary circulation and the lung itself are crucial components of cardiorespiratory design in which the lungfishes appear both highly derived compared with other fishes and more closely affiliated with characters found in modern tetrapods. The follow-

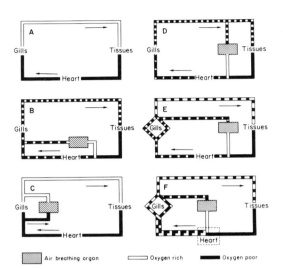

Fig. 1. Schematic representation of the flow of oxygenated (white) and deoxygenated (black) blood through the circulation of various air-breathing fishes. A. General arrangement of typical strictly aquatic fish breathing with gills. B. Air-breathing organ (ABO) derived from pharyngeal or opercular mucosa—e.g., *Monopterus, Ophiocephalus, Electrophorus, Amphipnous, Periophthalmus, Anabas.* C. Gills, buccal mucosa, or chambers extending from the opercular cavity serving as ABO—e.g., *Clarias, Saccobranchus.* D. Intestinal tract used as ABO—e.g., *Hoplosternum, Plecostomus, Ancistrus, Misgurnus.* E. Air bladder serving as ABO—e.g., *Polypterus, Calamoichthys, Amia, Lepisosteus.* F. A lung homologous to that of tetrapods serving as ABO—e.g., *Neoceratodus, Lepidosiren, Protopterus.* (From Johansen, '70.)

ing discussion deals with both the morphology and physiology of gas exchange in the Dipnoi.

THE CARDIORESPIRATORY INNOVATIONS OF THE LUNGFISHES

With respect to circulatory and respiratory characters, *Neoceratodus* appears less highly derived from the plesiomorphic condition for lungfishes than either *Lepidosiren* or *Protopterus.* The Lepidosirenidae have many characters in common with tetrapods, in most instances likely representing convergence. This relationship appears to hold not only for morphological characters but also for what we presume to be the much more evolutionarily labile physiological processes.

The pulmonary venous circulation

The site of entry of oxygenated blood from the ABO into the central venous circulation is of crucial importance, for it portends further cardiovascular specialization. In *Neoceratodus,* the pulmonary vein from the single lung joins the systemic venous circulation prior to the heart at the level of the sinus venosus (Fox, '65) or left ductus Cuvieri (Satchell, '76). This shows a clear tendency for a more central termination of the pulmonary vein than of the veins draining the ABO of any phyletically ancient fish or teleost. Interestingly, a very similar arrangement of venous drainage from the gas bladder occurs in *Amia,* while in *Polypterus* and *Calamoichthys* the pulmonary vein enters the systemic circulation slightly more distally at the level of the hepatic vein (Purser, '26).

The greatest degree of separation of venous blood from the ABO and systemic blood from the tissues in any living fish is evident in *Protopterus* and *Lepidosiren.* In these genera the paired pulmonary veins draining the lungs fuse to form a single pulmonary vein lying dorsal and slightly lateral to the large vena cava. After passing anteriorly in the dorsal wall of the sinus venosus, the pulmonary vein empties *directly* into the left side of the atrium, rather than into the central systemic veins as in other fishes. Consequently, in *Lepidosiren* and *Protopterus,* oxygenated pulmonary blood and deoxygenated systemic blood are kept completely separate during passage to the heart. Thus, in comparison with *Neoceratodus* and other fishes, the central venous circulation of *Protopterus* and *Neoceratodus* much more closely resembles the condition in all tetrapods, where the pulmonary vein drains directly into a distinct left atrium.

Although beyond the scope of this paper, it is interesting to note that the systemic veins of the Dipnoi also show characters absent in other fishes (except *Latimeria*—Rosen et al., '81) but present in tetrapods, most notable being the prominent posterior vena cava and large sinus venosus (Goodrich, '30).

The heart and pericardium

Detailed accounts of the cardiac morphology of the Dipnoi have been given by Lankester (1878), Spencer (1898), Robertson ('13), Goodrich ('30), Bugge ('61), and Johansen et al. ('68). Generally, the hearts of living lung-

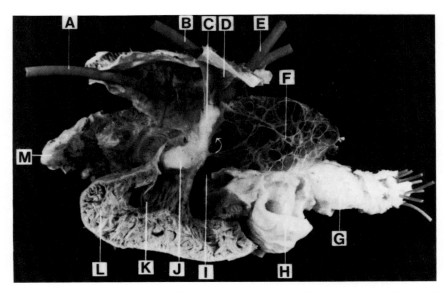

Fig. 2. Sagittal section through the heart of *Protopterus aethiopicus*. The arrow shows where the vena pulmonalis ends behind the pulmonalis fold. A. Probe in vena cava posterior; B. Probe in vena pulmonalis; C. Pulmonalis fold; D. Oblique fold separating the apertures of the two ducti Cuvieri; E. Probe in the right ductus Cuvieri; F. Anterior unpaired part of the atrium; G. Distal section of the bulbus cordis; H. Spiral fold in the transverse section of the bulbus cordis, which has been opened; I. Atrioventricular aperture; J. Atrioventricular plug; K. Ventricular septum; L. Ventricular apex; M. Left auricular lobe. (From Bugge, '61.)

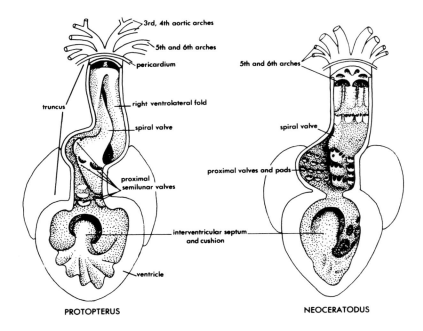

Fig. 3. Schematic sagittal sections through the heart of *Protopterus* and *Neoceratodus*. Hearts are shown from a ventral aspect. (From Jollie, '73, after Goodrich, '30.)

fishes are much more complex than the typical piscine heart, which functions only to propel deoxygenated systemic venous blood to the gills (Fig. 1A). The most notable specializations of the dipnoan heart are its more extensive S-folding, giving it an external appearance much more like that of a urodele amphibian, and the extensive internal septation, tending to subdivide the atrial and ventricular chambers.

In all three genera of lungfishes, the single atrium is partially divided into a larger right and smaller left side by a partial septum termed the pulmonalis fold, which arises from a deformation of the atrial wall caused by the overlying pulmonary vein, and by a unique structure termed the atrioventricular "cushion" (Goodrich, '30) or atrioventricular "plug" (Bugge, '61). The sinus venosus, conveying systemic venous blood, enters the atrium on its right side via a valved sinoatrial aperture. The pulmonary veins enter the atrium to the left of the pulmonalis fold, with this opening guarded by a tissue fold purportedly serving a valving function. Of the living lungfishes, *Lepidosiren* shows the greatest degree of atrial subdivision, possessing an almost complete interatrial septum. The atrioventricular orifice is not valved as in other fishes or in amphibians, but rather is guarded by the atrioventricular plug (Figs. 2, 3). This plug is raised out of the a-v orifice during atrial systole and lowered into it during atrial diastole, and thus it serves a valving function preventing regurgitation of blood into the atrium from the ventricle.

The dipnoan ventricle typically is composed of spongy, highly trabeculate myocardium (Fig. 2), resembling the construction of the ventricular walls of amphibians. In all three genera of lungfishes, a vertical septum arising from the dorsal and ventral walls of the ventricle anatomically divides much of the ventricular lumen, particularly toward the apex of the heart (Figs. 2, 3). Once again, *Lepidosiren* shows the greatest degree of ventricular septation, while *Neoceratodus* shows the least (Johansen et al., '68). In all three genera, the arrangement of the ventricular septum with respect to the pulmonalis fold and atrioventricular plug is such that oxygenated blood on the left side of the atrium will tend preferentially to flow into and to collect in the left side of the ventricle prior to ejection into the bulbus cordis. Deoxygenated blood from the right side of the atrium will flow toward the right side of the ventricle. In

amphibians, there is during diastole a heterogeneous distribution of atrial blood within the ventricle (which, with the exception of the ventricle of *Siren*, lacks any septation). The ventricular walls are highly trabeculate and act to trap and immobilize blood during ventricular filling. Together, these features minimize intraventricular mixing of oxygenated and deoxygenated blood prior to systolic ejection (Shelton, '76). Effective separation of blood in passage through the heart occurs in *Protopterus*, *Lepidosiren*, and, to a lesser extent, *Neoceratodus* (see below), a condition doubtlessly aided by mechanisms comparable to those operating in amphibians.

In all lungfishes the heart is surrounded by a tough, semi-rigid pericardium through which the central veins enter and the bulbus cordis exits. Although teleost fishes lack a stiff pericardium, it is a highly characteristic feature of all elasmobranchs, and its integrity is essential for normal cardiovascular function in sharks (Johansen, '65; Shabetai et al., '85). The condition of the pericardium in most actinopterygians is unknown.

The bulbus cordis

Separation of systemic and pulmonary blood streams passing through the heart will not assist preferential channelling of oxygenated and deoxygenated blood distally in the arterial tree unless laminar streaming of discrete blood flows can be maintained in the proximal arterial circulation. In this respect, the complex architecture of the bulbus cordis (or "truncus") plays a highly important role.

The bulbus cordis extends from the undivided anterior end of the ventricle, generally to the left of the ventricular midline (Fig. 3). Its walls are invested with cardiac muscle for the first third of its length. In *Neoceratodus*, there are several proximal rows of small conal valves (Lankester, 1878; Spencer, 1898; Goodrich, '09). These valves are reminiscent of the selachian conus, suggesting that this is a primitive character of gnathostomes. The lumen of the proximal region of the bulbus cordis is quite wide, and Satchell's ('76) interpretation is that these valves could prevent regurgitation of blood into the ventricle only during systole of the bulbus cordis when the valves are brought into apposition. Blood pressure in the bulbus cordis of *Neoceratodus* remains briefly elevated after pressure in the ventricle has fallen toward diastolic levels (Johansen et al., '68), suggesting that func-

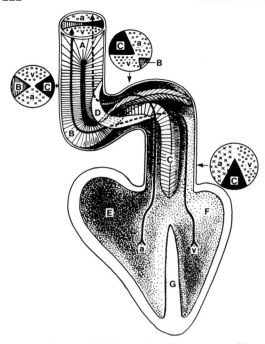

Fig. 4. Heart and bulbus cordis of *Protopterus aethiopicus* showing the structure of the ventricle and the bulbus cordis seen from the dorsal side. The arrows indicate the course of the arterial (a) and the venous (v) blood flow. A. The anteriorly joined part of the folds; B. The short left fold; C. The spiral fold; D. Cut surface where the spiral fold has been attached to the transverse section of the bulbus cordis; E. Left half of the ventricle; F. Right half of the ventricle; G. Vertical septum. (From Bugge, '61.)

tional valving at the base of the bulbus cordis does occur. The proximal base of the bulbus cordis of *Protopterus* and *Lepidosiren* contains a row of small "pocket valves" (Lankester, 1879; Boas, 1880; Robertson, '13; Bugge, '61), though these are considered largely "vestigial" (Johansen et al., '68). As discussed in detail by Satchell ('76), the hemodynamic function of the valves in the dipnoan bulbus cordis remains obscure and would be highly worthy of further anatomical and physiological investigation.

After leaving the heart, the bulbus cordis is sharply folded and twisted in all three genera (Fig. 3). This condition appears unique to lungfishes. However, a similar rotation of the truncus arteriosus occurs about its long axis in amphibians but is much more exaggerated in the lungfish, approximating 270°. In *Lepidosiren* and *Protopterus*, the lumen of the proximal region of the bulbus cordis is partially divided by the bulbar or spiral fold,

a fold of tissue arising from the ventral row of conal valves (Boas, 1880). This spiral fold continues down the length of the bulbus cordis, rotating 270° along with the bulbus cordis itself. In *Lepidosiren*, there is a spherical thickening of the distal end of the spiral valve that may serve a distal valving function (Robertson, '13). More distally, in *Lepidosiren* and *Protopterus*, a second smaller tissue fold arises from the inner bulbar wall directly opposite the spiral fold. The free edges of these two folds are nearly in apposition, thus partially dividing the lumen of the bulbus cordis into two outflow channels. In the most distal region of the bulbus cordis, the two folds fuse to form a horizontal septum that completely divides the lumen into dorsal and ventral channels. The ventral channel at the distal end of the bulbus cordis conveys primarily oxygenated blood that originates from the left side of the heart (Fig. 4). Comparatively dexoygenated blood from the right side of the heart is preferentially directed into the dorsal channel at the termination of the bulbus cordis.

Neoceratodus appears to show a less derived condition compared to other lungfishes, in that the bulbus cordis lacks a well-developed spiral valve (Fig. 3). Proximally, the spiral valve is evident, but within the bulbus cordis the distal pathway occupied by the spiral valve in the other lungfishes is instead marked by large semilunar valves in *Neoceratodus*. Distally, the spiral valve is increasingly prominent in *Neoceratodus*, dividing the bulbus cordis into a discrete dorsal and ventral channel as in the Lepidosirenidae.

Branchial and pulmonary arterial circulation

The aortic arch distribution of the Dipnoi shows the greatest modification from the basic piscine pattern of any living fish. In all lungfishes, the ventral aorta is virtually nonexistent, with the afferent branchial arteries arising almost directly from the distal end of the bulbus cordis (Fig. 3). In *Neoceratodus*, all four branchial afferents perfuse corresponding holobranchs of the branchial arches (Fig. 5). These arches bear numerous gill filaments and constitute a major site for respiratory gas exchange (Laurent, '84). There are no hemibranchs on the hyoid arch of *Neoceratodus*, which distinguishes this genus from *Lepidosiren* and *Protopterus* where the hyoid arch does bear a hemibranch. In these two genera, the two anterior-most holobranches

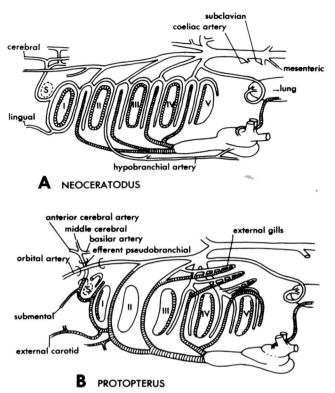

Fig. 5. Highly diagrammatic lateral view of the central circulatory morphology of *Neocera-todus* (A) and *Protopterus* (B). (Modified from Jollie, '73, after Goodrich, '30.)

are devoid of gill filaments (Johansen et al., '68; Laurent, '84). The afferent blood supply for these degenerate arches is derived from the ventral (oxygenated) channel of the bulbus cordis (as in *Neoceratodus*). The branchial efferents from these two anterior arches pass directly into the dorsal aorta. In essence, these two arches are nonrespiratory conduits shunting oxygenated blood from the left side of the heart directly into the dorsal aorta and on to the systemic tissues. In *Protopterus*, the two posterior-most arches possess highly modified gill filaments bearing secondary lamallae (Johansen et al., '68; Laurent et al., '78; Laurent, '85). Unlike the two anterior arches, these posterior arches can thus serve as respiratory surfaces. In *Lepidosiren*, however, the gill filaments on the two posterior arches are very sparse and coarse, and their respiratory role is equivocal (Fullarton, '31; Johansen and Lenfant, '67; Laurent et al., '78). Interestingly, equally well-developed gill filaments occur on all of

the branchial arches of the fossil lungfish *Griphognathus*, suggesting that the condition in *Lepidosiren* and *Protopterus* is derived rather than primitive (Campbell and Barwick, this volume).

In all three genera, the afferent blood supply to the posterior arches is derived from the dorsal channel of the bulbus cordis, which conveys relatively deoxygenated blood derived from the right side of the heart.

The course of the efferent vessels of the posterior arches of the Dipnoi is complex, particularly since many vessels merge and arise in a confined area dorsal to the gill arches (Fig. 5). Of the two posterior branchial arches, the third arch flows most directly into the dorsal aorta. The efferent vessel of the fourth branchial arch (embryonic arch VI) gives rise to the pulmonary artery in all three lungfish genera. This vessel is thus homologous with the pulmonary artery of tetrapods. In addition, however, efferent blood from this arch can bypass the lungs and flow directly into the dorsal aorta via a highly specialized vascular segment variously termed the "ductus" (Fishman et al., '85) or "ductus arteriosus" (Laurent, '85). This structure has been considered analogous rather than homologous to the ductus arteriosus of mammals (Fishman et al., '85). Both the proximal pulmonary artery and the ductus are highly vasoactive and provide a mechanism by which blood draining the fourth gill arch can be preferentially directed into either the pulmonary or systemic circuits (see below).

In addition to the four branchial arches confined within the branchial cavity, all larval lepidosirenids possess external gills. *Neoceratodus* never has external gills as larva or adult (Kerr, '19). Some species of *Protopterus* retain external gills throughout the life cycle. These external gills are located downstream and in series with the three posterior gill arches (Fig. 5). Trewavas ('54) summarizes observations of many workers on the external gills of *Protopterus*. *Protopterus annectens*, *P. amphibius*, and *P. aethiopicus* all show external gills or their vestiges at even relatively advanced stages of development (e.g., 0.6-meter body length for *P. annectens*), although they are lost earliest in *P. aethiopicus*. However, the size of both these external gills and of the specimens bearing them is highly variable, and is an equivocal character on which to base species identification (Trewavas, '54).

The pulmonary circulation and lung structure

Many air-breathing fish carry out aerial respiration using a gas bladder connected via a pneumatic duct to the esophagus (Wilmer, '34; Johansen, '70; Randall et al., '81). In many species, these gas bladders are not just hollow bags but are structurally rather complex. Indeed, in fishes such as *Calamoichthys* or *Polypterus* the air-breathing organ should be regarded as a lung, in that 1) the pneumatic duct originates from a ventral evagination of the esophagus, and 2) its blood supply is derived from the sixth branchial arch, both conditions very similar to those of tetrapods (Goodrich, '30). Yet, amongst all air-breathing fishes, only in the Dipnoi does the structure of the lung so closely resemble that of extant amphibians and reptiles.

Neoceratodus possesses only a single lung, unlike both *Lepidosiren* and *Protopterus*, which have paired lungs. However, a small vestige of a left pulmonary lobe has been described in the embryo of *Neoceratodus* (Neumayer, '04; Ballantyne, '27), suggesting that the adult condition of a single lung in *Neoceratodus* is a derived feature. In *Lepidosiren* and *Protopterus*, the lungs are fused anteriorly to form a common penumatic duct that opens into the posterior region of the pharynx at the glottis. The pneumatic duct, which bears little resemblance to the tracheal-bronchiolar system of terrestrial vertebrates, is heavily invested with smooth muscle (Johansen et al., '68). This smooth muscle, as well as the considerable smooth muscle in the lung parenchyma, is probably important to the mechanics of lung ventilation and internal gas distribution (Grigg, '65; Johansen and Reite, '67).

Detailed accounts of the morphology of dipnoan lungs are given by Owen (1840), Hyrtl (1845), Gunther (1871), Parker (1892), Poll ('62), Grigg ('65), and Hughes and Weibel ('76). Internal septa, ridges, and pillars partition the lung into smaller lateral compartments opening into a central cavity (Fig. 6), similar to the arrangement in many amphibians and reptiles. The smallest pulmonary compartments in Dipnoi are approximately 1 mm in diameter, with the least degree of septation evident in *Neoceratodus* (Spencer, 1898; Poll, '62; Grigg, '65; Hughes and Weibel, '76). Although this degree of pulmonary septation exceeds that of some amphibians, Hughes and Weibel ('76) have estimated that *Lepidosiren*, for example, has a total pulmonary respiratory surface area only about one-tenth of that anticipated for a "typical" amphibian of similar body mass. However, mass-specific respiratory surface area of dipnoan lungs does considerably surpass that of the ABOs of many nondipnoan fishes (Munshi, '76). Diffusion distance between gas and blood in the lung capillaries of dipnoans is approximately 0.5–1.0 μm (Klika and Lelek, '67), which approaches the diffusion distance in mammal lungs.

The ventral surfaces of the lung(s) are perfused by the left pulmonary artery, which bifurcates about one-third of the way back from the cranial end of the lungs. The dorsal surfaces of the lung are perfused by the right pulmonary artery (Goodrich, '30).

GAS EXCHANGE IN LUNGFISHES

The preceding discussion has shown that extant lungfish show many cardiorespiratory morphological characters that distinguish

(A)

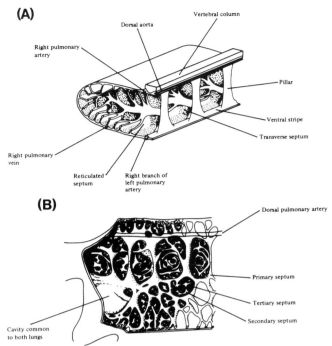

(B)

Fig. 6.   Lung structure in Dipnoi. A. Reconstruction of a section of the right half of the single lung of *Neoceratodus forsteri*. (From Little, '83, after Grigg, '65.) B. Septa in the anterior region of one of the paired lungs of *Protopterus*. (From Little, '83, after Poll, '62.)

them from other air-breathing fishes and align them much more closely with tetrapods. While some of these characters clearly represent convergent evolution, others apparently are shared derived characters. What physiological advantages, if any, do these characters provide to the lungfishes, and what differences may exist among extant genera? To attempt to answer this question, it is necessary to examine how the cardiovascular and respiratory systems of lungfishes perform *physiologically*.

Mechanics of gill and lung ventilation

In spite of some structural differences (e.g., reduction of opercular and hyoid bones in *Protopterus* relative to *Neoceratodus*), the mechanics of both gill and lung ventilation are qualitatively the same in *Lepidosiren* (Bishop and Foxon, '68), *Neoceratodus* (Grigg, '65), and *Protopterus* (McMahon, '69). The most extensive account of the ventilatory mechanics of a dipnoan has been provided for *Protopterus aethiopicus* by McMahon ('69), who used X-ray cinematography, electromyography, and pressure recording to describe

the mechanics of both air and water breathing. Ventilation of the gills with water occurs through the action of a positive pressure buccal pump anterior to the gills and an opercular suction pump posterior to the gills. These pumps operate in concert to generate a nearly continuous water pressure gradient favoring water flow in the mouth, through the gills, and out the opercular opening (Fig. 7). Such a ventilatory system is widely shared amongst aquatic vertebrates, occurring in phyletically ancient fishes, highly derived teleosts, and is even preserved somewhat in larval and adult amphibians (Shelton, '70; Gans, '70a; Randall et al., '81; Burggren et al., '86).

Ventilation of the lungs with air in *Protopterus* is achieved by action of the same musculoskeletal elements involved in aquatic ventilation (Fig. 7). In essence, a single aquatic ventilatory cycle irrigating the branchial chamber is replaced by a modified cycle that generates a single air breath. The single-breathing cycle occurs immediately after the snout has been thrust above the water surface into the air. The glottis, which has

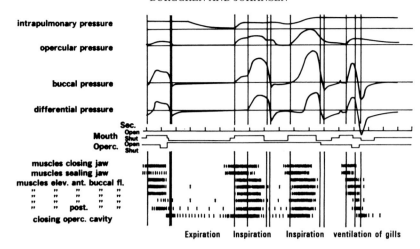

intrapulmonary pressure

opercular pressure

buccal pressure

differential pressure

Sec.
Mouth   Open
        Shut
Operc. Open
        Shut

muscles closing jaw
muscles sealing jaw
muscles elev. ant. buccal fl.
  ,,   ,,   ,,   ,,   ,,
  ,,   ,,   ,,   ,,   ,,
  ,,   ,,   post. ,,   ,,
closing operc. cavity

Expiration   Inspiration   Inspiration   ventilation of gills

Fig. 7. Respiratory muscle activity and corresponding pressure changes during water- and air-breathing cycles in *Protopterus aethiopicus*. (From McMahon, '69.)

been tightly closed during water-breathing cycles, is opened, and pressure in the lungs decreases as expiration occurs. There follows a particularly tight closure of the opercular flaps, brought about by extended activity of the constrictor hyoideus muscle, and an exaggerated depression of the buccal floor drawing a large volume of fresh air through the opened mouth into the buccal activity. The mouth is then closed, and the head reimmersed in water. A subsequent strong elevation of the buccal floor increases buccal pressure to approximately 20 mmHg, which is much higher than during a normal aquatic ventilatory cycle. This elevated buccal pressure drives inspired air past the open glottis into the lungs, completing the air-breathing cycle. The aquatic ventilatory cycles both preceding and following the cycle in which the lungs are ventilated show different patterns of muscle activation and the corresponding motor responses (Fig. 7). Lungfishes usually ventilate their lungs with a single air breath followed by a period of apnea of variable length, though under some experimental conditions tightly-grouped multiple breaths may occur (Bishop and Foxon, '68; McMahon, '69; Delaney and Fishman, '77). Estivation also causes changes in patterns and mechanics of lung ventilation (see Delaney and Fishman, '77; Fishman et al., this volume).

Lung ventilation in the Dipnoi thus incorporates a buccal force pump mechanism. Although several workers have suggested that aspiration breathing involving rib movements for generation of subambient pleural pressures may occur in lungfish (Lomholt et al., '75) and other air-breathing fishes (Farrell and Randall, '78), these claims have not been substantiated (Greenwood and Liem, '84). It is most likely that the lung ventilatory mechanism seen in extant Dipnoi is similar to that of the earliest tetrapods, and that aspiration ventilation of the lung replaced buccal force ventilation only later as ribs took on increasing structural importance in fully terrestrial vertebrates (McMahon, '70).

Ventilatory patterns and oxygen uptake

As could be predicted from its elaborate and more typically piscine gill structure, *Neoceratodus* is an obligatory water breather. Laboratory observations indicate buccal/opercular movements at a frequency of about 30 cycles per min at room temperature (Johansen et al., '67). Observations of captive laboratory specimens at rest indicate that ventilation of the lung with air is comparatively rare when the fish is in oxygenated water. Thus, nearly 100% of both oxygen uptake and carbon dioxide elimination is aquatic via gills and skin (Table 1; Fig. 8). During prolonged swimming activity, when metabolic rate increases, air breathing becomes frequent and regular (Grigg, '65). Field observations of *Neoceratodus* (Kemp, this volume) indicate that air breathing may oc-

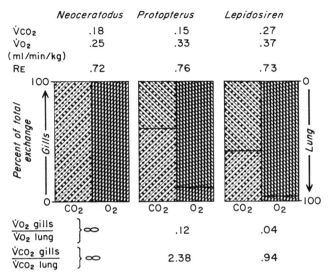

Fig. 8. Relative contributions of aquatic and aerial breathing to total gas exchange at 20°C in the three living genera of lungfishes. (From Lenfant et al., '70.)

cur more commonly during the breeding season, perhaps related to increased activity levels.

Although the respiratory surface of the gills of *Protopterus* is considerably reduced compared to *Neoceratodus*, the former nonetheless ventilates the gills with water, using slow, rhythmic buccal/opercular movements at a frequency of 0.5–10 cycles per min at 20–24°C (Lenfant and Johansen, '68; McMahon, '69, '70). Branchial respiratory movements in resting *Lepidosiren* are very shallow and almost imperceptible at rest, also varying widely between 1 and 20 breaths per min (Johansen and Lenfant, '67). Air-breathing frequencies in both genera range from 2–30 breaths hr^{-1} at water temperatures of 20–24°C (Johansen and Lenfant, '67, '68; McMahon, '69,'70). Both *Protopterus* and *Lepidosiren* in postjuvenile stages are obligatory air breathers at normal environmental temperatures, and will drown if denied access to air. In adult *Protopterus* and *Lepidosiren*, 90% or more of total O_2 uptake occurs via the lungs, while a lower but still substantial proportion of CO_2 elimination occurs via this route (Table 1). This partitioning of O_2 and CO_2 exchange between air and water is also typical of larval amphibians that are similarly equipped with gills, permeable skin, and lungs (Burggren, '84).

While most experimental data have been collected from adult lungfishes, a limited but compelling number of observations indicate that developmental stage exerts a strong influence on patterns of gas exchange in lungfishes. In *Protopterus amphibius*, for example, the dependence upon aerial respiration increases dramatically as body mass increases (Fig. 9), and a similar trend appears to exist for *Lepidosiren* (Table 1). The influence of development on both cardiorespiratory morphology and physiology is one of the most neglected yet promising fields for future research.

At rest, *Neoceratodus* is clearly much less dependent upon aerial respiration than *Protopterus* or *Lepidosiren* (Table 1). What if more severe respiratory demands occur? A comparison of the ability to use aerial respiration can be assessed in more detail by comparing the respective abilities of lungfishes to survive brief periods of complete air exposure. Although this experiment is ecologically irrelevant for *Neoceratodus*, which, unlike *Protopterus* and *Lepidosiren*, does not estivate, laboratory air exposure makes specific and equivalent respiratory demands of all three lungfishes. The physiological responses to these demands will reveal the existence of mechanisms crucial to the evolution of a terrestrial capability. Figure

TABLE 1. Oxygen uptake, carbon dioxide elimination, and the gas exchange ratio in Dipnoi[1]

Species	Temperature (°C)	Oxygen uptake (ml O_2 g^{-1} h^{-1})			Carbon dioxide elimination (ml O_2 g^{-1} h^{-1})			Gas exchange ratio			References
		Aquatic (%)	Aerial (%)	Total	Aquatic (%)	Aerial (%)	Total	Aquatic	Aerial	Total	
Neoceratodus forsteri	18	15.0 (100)	0 (0)	15.0	18.6 (100)	0 (0)	18.6	1.24	—	1.24	Lenfant et al., '67
Lepidosiren paradoxa (juvenile, 150 gm)	18	54.0 (64)	30.6 (30)	84.6	72.6 (77)	22.2 (23)	94.8	1.34	0.73	1.12	Johansen and Lenfant, '67
Lepidosiren paradoxa (adult)	20	1.8 (4)	40.2 (96)	42.0	—	—	—	—	—	—	Sawaya, '46
Lepidosiren paradoxa	20	0.7 (3)	21.5 (97)	22.2	6.7 (41)	9.5 (59)	16.2	9.57	0.44	0.73	Lenfant et al., '70
Protopterus aethiopicus	20			52.2							Smith, '30
Protopterus aethiopicus	24	5.0 (8)	57.5 (92)	62.5	31.8	15.6	47.4	5.40	0.27	0.73	McMahon, '70
Protopterus aethiopicus	20	1.3 (11)	10.1 (89)	11.4	6.1 (70)	2.6 (30)	8.7	4.69	0.26	0.76	Lenfant and Johansen, '68

[1]All values recorded at the indicated temperature in air-saturated water with free access to air.

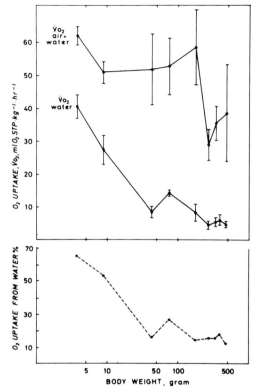

Fig. 9. Mass-specific oxygen uptake in *Protopterus amphibius*, expressed in absolute amount (top) and as a percentage of total O_2 uptake (bottom). (From Johansen and Lomholt, '76.)

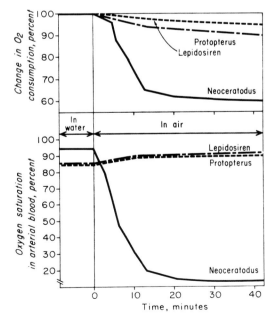

10 compares total O_2 consumption and ability to saturate systemic arterial blood with oxygen in *Neoceratodus*, *Lepidosiren*, and *Protopterus* before and during 40 min of complete air exposure. When removed from water, all three genera of lungfishes show highly elevated rates of lung ventilation. Both *Protopterus* and *Lepidosiren* can maintain blood O_2 saturation and total O_2 uptake by shifting entirely to pulmonary gas exchange. *Neoceratodus*, in contrast, shows a serious insufficiency in blood gas transport within just 5–10 min of air exposure, reaffirming the much more aquatic nature of the Australian lungfish.

Neoceratodus can be further distinguished from *Protopterus* and *Lepidosiren* on the basis of its respiratory responses to environmental O_2 availability. When exposed to moderately hypoxic water, *Neoceratodus* responds with an immediate and large increase in rate of gill ventilation (Johansen et al., '67). Air breathing is initiated and progressively increases in frequency, though the onset of lung hyperventilation is much later than that of increased gill ventilation. Given that *Neoceratodus* has elaborate gills and depends heavily on aquatic exchange under normoxic conditions (Table 1), it is not surprising that this lungfish should show responses to aquatic hypoxia very reminiscent of strictly aquatic fishes (see Shelton '70). Adult *Protopterus*, on the other hand, shows virtually no branchial ventilatory response to aquatic hypoxia (Johansen and Lenfant, '68). This is consistent with the almost total lack of reliance on water for O_2 uptake shown by this fish (Table 1; Fig. 8). Exposure to aerial hypoxia, however, induces rapid increases in air-breathing frequency, indicating that *Protopterus* does, in fact, have chemoreceptors sensitive to changes in internal O_2 levels. Interestingly, juvenile *Protopterus* respond to exposure to hypoxic water by increasing rates of both water and air breathing (Jesse et al., '67). Juvenile *Protopterus* are more dependent on aquatic gas exchange (Johansen and Lefant, '68; Johansen et al., '76a; Fig. 9), and a ventilatory response to hypoxic water in these less mature lungfish is more appropriate.

Fig. 10. Effect of air exposure upon O_2 uptake and O_2 saturation of arterial blood in *Neoceratodus*, *Lepidosiren*, and *Protopterus*. (From Lenfant et al., '70.)

Blood respiratory properties

Blood and its circulation represent an indispensable link in the transport of respiratory gases between the ambient environment and the metabolizing cells. The most important respiratory properties of vertebrate bloods are the O_2 affinity of the blood, expressed as the partial pressure of O_2 at which the blood is half saturated with O_2 (the P_{50}), O_2 capacity, which is the maximum possible amount of O_2 contained per unit of blood, and the influence of blood pH on the O_2 affinity (commonly referred to as the "Bohr shift"). Blood is also important in CO_2 transport and in acid-base balance of the body fluids.

The respiratory properties of blood show a remarkable evolutionary plasticity or adaptability to environmental and behavioral situations in lower vertebrates. In regard to air-breathing fishes breathing bimodally with gills and/or an air-breathing organ, blood O_2 affinity tends to decline with increased dependence on aerial breathing (Johansen and Lenfant, '71). Since atmospheric air has a stable and high concentration of O_2, blood in the air-breathing organ can become fully O_2 saturated even in the face of a reduced blood O_2 affinity. Yet, at the level of the body tissues, the lower O_2 affinity will enhance unloading of oxygen from the blood (Johansen and Lenfant, '71). In air-breathing fishes that depend predominantly on aquatic breathing for oxygen uptake, there is an equally clear tendency for blood O_2 affinity to be increased, *particularly if the species lives in oxygen deficient water*. Thus, even though the major respiratory medium is oxygen deficient, blood of a higher O_2 affinity may still become O_2 saturated before leaving the gills or skin. The blood O_2 affinity of fishes thus appears to show evolutionary adaptation to the O_2 availability of the external medium most important to respiration. However, it is important to emphasize that an adaptation that may assist O_2 unloading at the tissues may be maladaptive with respect to loading in the gas-exchange organ, and *vice versa* (see Johansen and Lenfant, '71). Thus, each species in each environmental condition has to be examined individually to assess whether changes in blood properties are assisting blood oxygen transport.

A comparison of blood respiratory properties in lungfishes is difficult, primarily due to a shortage of data and to the different techniques used to measure blood O_2 affinity. Johansen and Lenfant ('67) found a very high

blood O_2 affinity in juvenile *Lepidosiren*. Using different techniques, Johansen et al. ('78) studied blood from mature *Lepidosiren* and obtained similar high affinities (P_{50}-8 mmHg at pH 7.4, 29°C). *Neoceratodus* shows a lower blood O_2 affinity than *Lepidosiren* or *Protopterus* if compared at similar blood pH to take into account the Bohr shift. However, when compared at the values for pH occurring in vivo in arterial blood, *Neoceratodus* has a higher affinity for O_2 than the obligate air breathers *Lepidosiren* and *Protopterus* (Lenfant et al., '67). The blood of *Neoceratodus* also shows a larger CO_2 combining power and buffer capacity than the blood of either *Lepidosiren* or *Protopterus*. However, there appears to be little difference in blood oxygen capacity between lungfish genera (Johansen and Lenfant, '71).

Protopterus shows a low O_2 affinity expressed by a P_{50} of 33 mmHg at pH 7.5 and 26°C (Johansen et al., '76b). Blood O_2 affinity of estivating *Protopterus* shows a dramatic increase to 9 mmHg when measured at the same temperature and pH as typical for an active, hydrated lungfish. However, since the blood pH of the estivating fish is much lower, the very large difference in blood oxygen affinity will be diminished by the Bohr shift when considering the in vivo situation. No satisfactory explanation has been advanced to explain the marked increases in O_2 affinity with estivation. Its mechanism, however, is clearly related to a large reduction in the red cell organic phosphates GTP and ATP, both of which act as important cofactors (or competing ligands) for the O_2 binding to hemoglobin. A higher Bohr factor in *Neoceratodus* than the other lungfishes must also be considered adaptive as long as this species maintains a much higher blood pH than the other lungfishes.

Much additional research on the blood respiratory properties of lungfishes is required to understand fully to what extent the differences in blood properties between genera represent important adaptive changes to differing demands on blood gas transport.

Cardiorespiratory regulation

A fundamental requirement of effective gas exchange is that the O_2 capacitance and other respiratory properties of blood on one side of the gas-exchange membranes should at all times be closely matched with the oxygen capacitance of the respiratory medium on the other side of the membrane (Piiper

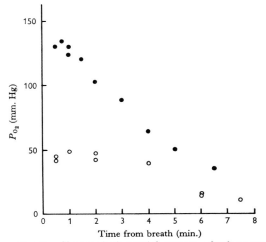

Fig. 11. Changes in O_2 partial pressure of pulmonary venous blood (open circles) and pulmonary gas (solid circles) following a spontaneous breath in *Lepidosiren paradoxa*. (From Johansen and Lenfant, '67.)

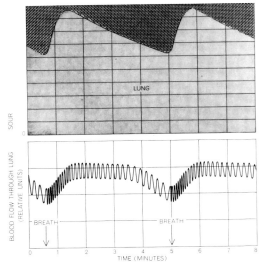

Fig. 12. Influence of voluntary, intermittent breathing upon source of systemic arterial blood (top) and upon pulmonary blood flow and heart rate (bottom) in *Protopterus aethiopicus*. (From Johansen, '68.)

and Scheid, '84). Stated differently, the ability of the blood to convey O_2 away from the gas-exchange organ should ideally equal the ability of the ventilatory pump to supply O_2 to that organ. Thus, hyperventilation of a gas-exchange organ with respiratory medium will achieve little increased gas exchange *unless there is a corresponding increase in blood flow* to that organ.

This concept of "ventilation-perfusion" matching takes on particular importance in

animals in which the ABO is ventilated intermittently rather than continuously. In animals such as the Dipnoi, the partial pressure of O_2 (PO_2) in pulmonary gas is typically high during and immediately after an air breath, but then falls progressively during breath holding until a subsequent breath renews the gas in the ABO (Fig. 11). Thus, both the total O_2 stores of the lungs *and* the gas partial pressure gradient driving O_2 from the gas into blood in the pulmonary capillaries are greatest in the early moments of breath holding. For most effective gas exchange, perfusion of the lungs with blood should be highest during this period when the potential for pulmonary gas exchange is highest, and should then diminish as breath holding progresses.

Physiological investigations of the last two decades have revealed that lungfishes possess effective mechanisms for matching blood perfusion of the lung to the intermittent pattern of lung ventilation. The most extensive hemodynamic studies have been performed on *Protopterus*, with limited observations on *Neoceratodus* and *Lepidosiren* (for reviews see Johansen, '70; Johansen and Burggren, '80; Johansen, '85; Fishman et al., '85; Burggren et al., '86). These experiments, often performed on intact, unanesthetized lungfish, have combined radiographic studies, direct measurement of blood flows and pressures, and estimations of cardiac output distribution based on O_2 concentrations of blood sampled from indwelling catheters located at various sites in the circulation. During the early minutes following an air breath in *Protopterus aethiopicus*, heart rate and cardiac output increase (Fig. 12). Blood leaving the two posterior-most gill arches is directed primarily into the pulmonary artery rather than the ductus arteriosus, and so pulmonary blood flow rises considerably. Since the PO_2 of lung gas is highest at this time, there is a major transfer of O_2 from lung gas to pulmonary venous blood. However, as breath holding progresses and the gas exchange potential of the lung decreases, then heart rate, cardiac output, and total lung blood flow decrease.

Clearly, *Protopterus* regulates cardiovascular function to match lung perfusion to lung ventilation. For several reasons, however, simply increasing pulmonary blood flow when lung PO_2 is highest is not sufficient for effective gas exchange. It must be emphasized that those gills that bear filaments and

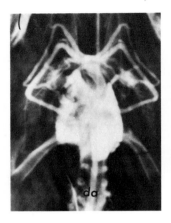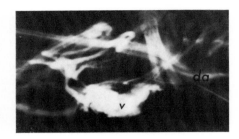

Fig. 13. Ventro-dorsal (left) and lateral view of the passage of radio-opaque dye injected into the pulmonary vein. da. dorsal aorta; v. ventricle. (From Johansen and Hol, '68.)

secondary lamellae can be a site of O_2 *loss* as well as gain. Since lungfishes may encounter water with low O_2 levels (see Greenwood, Kemp, both in this volume), there is a very real potential that O_2 transferred from lung gas into pulmonary venous blood may be lost immediately back to hypoxic water flowing over the gills. Such a reversal of O_2 flow has been well documented for both air-breathing fish (Burggren, '79) and larval amphibians (West and Burggren, '82). Thus, it is essential for lungfish that, at least immediately following an air breath, oxygenated pulmonary venous blood en route to the systemic tissues not come into contact with branchial water. This separation can be achieved in one of two ways. In *Protopterus aethiopicus*, each secondary lamella of the gills has, in addition to the distal blood channels exposed to water, a thick-walled and muscular basal blood channel that directly connects afferent and efferent branchial arterial vessels (Laurent, '85). A decrease in the vasomotor tone of this basal channel (which has yet to be experimentally established) would, at the level of each secondary lamellae, shunt blood around rather than through the respiratory membranes (Fishman et al., '85; Laurent, '85). A second mechanism preventing oxygenated blood from contacting branchial water potentially low in O_2 involves a preferential distribution of pulmonary venous blood into the two anterior-most branchial arches bearing few (*Lepidosiren*) or no (*Protopterus*) secondary lamellae. Perfusion of the anterior arches with primarily pulmonary

venous blood will achieve a functional bypass of the respiratory membranes of the gills. Importantly, it will also prevent oxygenated blood from being needlessly recirculated back to the lungs before perfusing systemic tissues.

While the anatomical basis for channelling of systemic and venous blood during its passage through the central circulation has long been appreciated (see discussion above), physiological evidence for this separation has been provided only in the last few decades. As indicated in Figure 12, immediately following an air breath nearly 100% of the blood perfusing the anterior arches (and thus passing directly into the dorsal aorta without exposure to branchial water) is derived from the pulmonary vein. The extent of separation can be seen quite clearly in Figure 13, which shows the course of radio-opaque dye directed via an indwelling catheter into the pulmonary vein of *Protopterus aethiopicus*. As breath holding progresses, the partial pressure of O_2 in pulmonary venous blood decreases (Fig. 11) and approaches that of systemic venous blood. Under this condition, separation of pulmonary and systemic venous blood becomes less important and could even become detrimental if there is an energetic cost associated with maintaining this separation (see Burggren, '87). In fact, as breath holding continues, the proportion of pulmonary blood perfusing the anterior branches diminishes (Fig. 12), while the proportion perfusing the posterior, gill-bearing branches increases.

The actual mechanisms by which these labile and constantly changing patterns of gill and lung perfusion are achieved has been investigated in some detail, once again primarily for *Protopterus aethiopicus* (see Fishman et al., '85). Pharmacological investigations employing cholinergic and adrenergic agonists and antagonists have revealed that the ductus and the extrinsic segment of the pulmonary artery are highly vasoactive. Interestingly, vasoactivity in the extrinsic segment of the pulmonary artery is characteristic of amphibians (De Saint-Aubain and Wingstrand, '79; Malvin, '85) and is retained in some reptiles (Burggren, '77; Milsom et al., '77). Importantly, in *Protopterus* the pharmacological responses of the ductus are somewhat opposed to those of the extrinsic pulmonary artery. For example, perfusion of isolated arterial segments with dilute acetylcholine solutions induces vasodilation of the ductus but vasoconstriction of the pulmonary artery (Fishman et al., '85). Norepinephrine, on the other hand, induces intense vasoconstriction of the ductus but has no effect on the extrinsic segment of the pulmonary artery. How might these mechanisms operate in vivo? An increase in catecholamines circulating in blood plasma will cause vasodilation of the ductus relative to the pulmonary artery, favoring a pulmonary bypass in which blood from the fourth branchial arch flows through the ductus into the dorsal aorta, rather than into the pulmonary artery (Fig. 5). Parasympathetic activity, on the other hand, will cause vasoconstriction of the ductus and vasodilation of the extrinsic pulmonary artery, tending to direct blood draining the fourth branchial arch preferentially into the pulmonary rather than the systemic circuit.

As evident from the above discussion, the mechanisms by which perfusion is matched to intermittent lung ventilation, where they have been determined, are known primarily for *Protopterus*. Although *Neoceratodus* increases lung ventilation during exposure to hypoxic water (Johansen et al., '67; Lenfant et al., '67), very little is known about how cardiac output is redistributed and how oxygenated blood circumvents the branchial respiratory membranes.

PHYLOGENETIC CONSIDERATIONS

As abundantly evident from other presentations in this volume, most considerations of the systematics of lungfishes have been based on characters of dentition, cranial structure, etc. The major reason for this is not that these characters are inherently "more reliable" than soft tissues, but rather that the fossil record contains more evidence of such structural elements of phylogenetically primitive lungfishes, allowing direct comparisons with the surviving genera.

Although somewhat beyond the scope of this paper, it is important to emphasize that characters based on cardiorespiratory morphology (and the physiological processes which these structures support) may be of great value in describing systematic relationships of living fishes, including the Dipnoi. To give but a few examples, *Neoceratodus*, with less septate lungs, more fully developed gills, and a less partitioned central circulation, appears considerably less derived from what is generally interpreted to be the plesiomorphic condition for lungfishes. *Lepidosiren* and *Protopterus*, with cardiorespiratory structures more heavily modified for aerial respiration and terrestrial survival, possess many structures comparable to those of the tetrapods. At the same time, *Lepidosiren* and *Protopterus* also exhibit a number of differences in cardiorespiratory characters, such as the degree of anatomical and functional atrial and ventricular division, branchial structure, and persistence of external gills.

It is important to emphasize that any phylogenetic analysis of morphological or physiological characters should include not only consideration of characters for the ingroup in question (in this instance, the Dipnoi), but also in more primitive fish taxa. Such a cladistic analysis of lungfish systematics based on respiration and cardiovascular characters is currently being attempted.

CONCLUSIONS

Perhaps no vertebrates so recently discovered, with so few living representatives, and with such remote distributions, have received so much attention from so many biologists as have lungfishes. While many contributions in this volume attest to the fascinating morphology and systematics of the Dipnoi, we wish to emphasize that, after all, they were named LUNGfish! Their successful exploitation of aerial respiration, culminating in the ability to tolerate months or years of air exposure during estivation, surely ranks among the most remarkable features of vertebrates.

In our attempt to present a coherent overview of the cardiorespiratory physiology of living lungfishes, we have made many generalizations. Perhaps most notable of these is our position that *Neoceratodus* is less highly derived from the plesiomorphic condition for lungfishes than either *Lepidosiren* or *Protopterus*, which have many morphological and physiological features similar to those of tetrapods. However, it is important to indicate that, just as the fossil record of lungfishes has gaps, so too does the "morphological and physiological record" pertaining to circulation and respiration in living lungfishes. Particularly important areas of lungfish cardiorespiratory physiology that require much additional investigation include:

1) effects of embryonic and larval development and maturation

2) environmental/ecological influences

3) mechanisms for reflex regulation

4) more intensive investigation of *Lepidosiren*, which is poorly represented in the physiological literature

5) influence of estivation on metabolism

Finally, it is somewhat ironic that, in attempting to better our understanding of the cardiorespiratory morphology and physiology of lungfishes relative to other air-breathing fishes and amphibians, in some instances we now know more about lungfishes than the animals to which we compare them. Only by thoroughly understanding the general processes by which aquatic organisms came to exploit the aerial/terrestrial environment will we be able to use the Dipnoi to help us interpret the evolutionary transition from fishes to tetrapods.

ACKNOWLEDGMENTS

The authors acknowledge grant support from the National Science Foundation (WB) and the Danish Research Council (KJ). Drs. W. Bemis and D. Klingener provided many useful comments during the preparation of the text, and Jacqueline Fay provided skilled assistance in preparation of the figures.

LITERATURE CITED

Ballantyne, F.M. (1927) Air-bladder and lungs. Trans. R. Soc. Edinburgh 55:371–394.

Bertin, L. (1958) Organes de la respiration aerienne. In P.D. Grasse (ed): Traité de Zoologie 13:1363–1398.

Bishop, I.R., and G.E.H. Foxon (1968) The mechanism of breathing in the South American lungfish, *Lepidosiren paradoxa*; a radiological study. J. Zool. London 154:263–271.

Boas, J.E.V. (1880) Ueber Herz und Arterienbogen bei *Ceratodus* und *Protopterus*. Morph. Jahrb. 6:321–354.

Bugge, J. (1961) The heart of the African lung fish, *Protopterus*. Vidensk. Medd. Dansk Naturh. Foren. Kjobenhavn 123:193–210.

Burggren, W. (1977) The pulmonary circulation of the chelonian reptile: morphology, haemodynamics and pharmacology. J. Comp. Physiol. 116:303–324.

Burggren, W. (1979) Bimodal gas exchange during variation in environmental oxygen and carbon dioxide in the air breathing fish *Trichogaster trichopterus*. J. Exp. Biol. 82:197–214.

Burggren, W. (1984) Transition of respiratory processes during amphibian metamorphosis: from egg to adult. In R.S. Seymour (ed): Respiration and Metabolism of Embryonic Vertebrates. Dordrecht: Junk, pp. 31–53.

Burggren, W. (1985) Hemodynamics and regulation of central cardiovascular shunts in reptiles. In K. Johansen and W. Burggren (eds): Cardiovascular Shunts; Phylogenetic, Ontogenetic and Clinical Aspects. Copenhagen: Munksgaard, pp. 121–136.

Burggren, W. (1987) Form and function in reptilian circulations. Am. Zool. (In press).

Burggren, W., K. Johansen, and B.R. McMahon (1986) Respiration in primitive fishes. In R. Foreman, R. Fange, and A. Gorbmen (eds): The Biology of Primitive Fishes. New York: Plenum Press. (In press).

Dehadrai, P., and S. Tripathi (1976) Environment and ecology of freshwater air-breathing teleosts. In G.M. Hughes (ed): Respiration in Amphibious Vertebrates. New York: Academic Press, pp. 39–72.

DeLaney, R.G., and A.M. Fishman (1977) Analysis of lung ventilation in the aestivating lungfish *Protopterus aethiopicus*. Am. J. Physiol. 233:R181–R187.

De Saint-Aubain, M.L., and K. Wingstrand (1979) A sphincter in the pulmonary artery of the frog *Rana temporaria* and its influence on blood flow in skin and lungs. Acta Zool. Stockh. 60:163–172.

Farrell, A., and D. Randall (1978) Air-breathing mechanics in two Amazonian teleosts, *Arapaima gigas* and *Hoplerythrinus unitaeniatus*. Can. J. Zool. 56:939–945.

Fishman, A.P., R.G. DeLaney, P. Laurent, and J.P. Szidon (1985) Blood shunting in lungfish and humans. In K. Johansen and W. Burggren (eds): Cardiovascular Shunts; Phylogenetic, Ontogenetic and Clinical Aspects. Copenhagen: Munksgaard, pp. 88–95.

Fox, H. (1965) Early development of the head and pharynx of *Neoceratodus* with a consideration of its phylogeny. J. Zool. Lond. 146:470–554.

Fullarton, M.H. (1931) Notes on the respiration of *Lepidosiren*. Proc. Zool. Soc. London 99:1301–1306.

Gans, C. (1970a) Respiration in early tetrapods—the frog is a red herring. Evolution 24:723–734.

Gans, C. (1970b) Strategy and sequence in the evolution of the external gas exchangers of ectothermal vertebrates. Forma et Functio 3:61–104.

Goodrich, E.S. (1909) Vertebrata craniata. In R. Lankester (ed): A Treatise on Zoology. London: Adam and Black.

Goodrich, E.S. (1930) Studies on the Structure and Development of Vertebrates. London: Macmillan.

Graham, J.B. (1976) Respiratory adaptations of marine air-breathing fishes. In G.M. Hughes (ed): Respiration of Amphibious Vertebrates. New York: Academic Press, pp. 165–187.

Greenwood, P.H., and K.F. Liem (1984) Aspiratory respiration in *Arapaima gigas* (Teleostei, Osteoglossomorpha) a reappraisal. J. Zool. London 203:411–425.

Grigg, G. (1965) Studies on the Queensland lungfish *Neoceratodus forsteri* (Krefft). I. Anatomy, histology, and functioning of the lung. Aust. J. Zool. 13:243–253.

Gunther, A. (1871) Description of *Ceratodus*, a genus of ganoid fishes, recently discovered in rivers of Queensland, Australia. Trans. R. Soc. London 161:511–792.

Hughes, G.M., and E.R. Weibel (1976) Morphometry of fish lungs. In G.M. Hughes (ed): Respiration of Amphibious Vertebrates. New York: Academic Press, pp. 213–232.

Hyrtl, J. (1845) Monographie von Lepidosiren paradoxa. Abhandlungen Bohmischen Gesellschaft der Wissenschaften. Prague 3:605–668.

Jesse, M.J., C. Shub, and A.P. Fishman (1967) Lung and gill ventilation of the African lungfish. Respir. Physiol. 3:267–287.

Johansen, K. (1965) Dynamics of venous return in elasmobranch fishes. Hvalradets Skrifter 48:94–100.

Johansen, K. (1968) Air-breathing fishes. Sci. Amer. 219:102–111.

Johansen, K. (1970) Air breathing in fishes. In W.S. Hoar and D.J. Randall (eds): Fish Physiology 4. New York: Academic Press, pp. 361–411.

Johansen, K. (1985) A phylogenetic overview of cardiovascular shunts. In K. Johansen and W. Burggren (eds): Cardiovascular Shunts; Phylogenetic, Ontogenetic and Clinical Aspects. Copenhagen: Munksgaard, pp. 17–32.

Johansen, K., and W. Burggren (1980) Cardiovascular function in lower vertebrates. In G. H. Bourne (ed): Hearts and Heart-like Organs. New York: Academic Press, pp. 61–117.

Johansen, K., and W. Burggren (1985) Cardiovascular Shunts; Phylogenetic, Ontogenetic and Clinical Aspects. Copenhagen: Munksgaard.

Johansen, K., and R. Hol (1968) A radiological study of the central circulation in the lungfish, Protopterus aethiopicus. J. Morphol. 126:333–348.

Johansen, K., and C. Lenfant (1967) Respiratory function in the South American lungfish, Lepidosiren paradoxa (Fitz). J. Exp. Biol. 46:205–218.

Johansen, K., and C. Lenfant (1968) Respiration in the African lungfish, Protopterus aethiopicus. II. Control of breathing. J. Exp. Biol. 49:453–468.

Johansen, K., and C. Lenfant (1971) A comparative approach to the adaptability of O₂-Hb affinity. Proceedings of the Alfred Benzon Foundation, 4: Copenhagen: Munksgaard, pp. 750–780.

Johansen, K., and O. Reite (1967) Effects of acetylcholine and biogenic amines on pulmonary smooth muscle in the African lungfish, Protopterus aethiopicus. Acta Physiol. Scand. 71:248–252.

Johansen, K., C. Lenfant, and G.C. Grigg (1967) Respiratory control in the lungfish, Neoceratodus forsteri. Comp. Biochem. Physiol. 20:835–854.

Johansen, L., C. Lenfant, and D. Hanson (1968) Cardiovascular dynamics in the lungfishes. Z. Vergl. Physiol. 59:157–186.

Johansen, K., D. Hanson, and C. Lenfant (1970) Respiration in a primitive air breather, Amia calva. Respir. Physiol. 9:162–174.

Johansen, K., J.P. Lomholt, and G.M.O. Maloiy (1976a) Importance of air and water breathing in relation to size of the African lungfish Protopterus amphibius Peters. J. Exp. Biol. 65:395–399.

Johansen, K., G. Lykkeboe, R.E. Weber, and G.M.O. Maloiy (1976b) Respiratory properties of blood in awake and estivating lungfish, Protopterus amphibius. Respir. Physiol. 27:335–345.

Johansen, K., C.P. Magnum, and G. Lykkeboe (1978) Respiratory properties of the blood of Amazon fishes. Can. J. Zool. 56:898–906.

Jollie, M. (1973) Chordate Morphology. Huntington: Krieger.

Kerr, J.G. (1919) Textbook of Embryology, Vol. 2. Vertebrata. London: Macmillan.

Klika, E., and A. Lelek (1967) A contribution to the study of the lungs of Protopterus annectens and Polyp-

terus senegalensis. Folia Morphol. Prague 15:168–175.

Lankester, E.R. (1878) On the hearts of Ceratodus, Protopterus, and Chimaera with an account of undescribed pocket valves in the conus arteriosus of Ceratodus and Protopterus. Trans. Zool. Soc. London 10:493–505.

Laurent, P. (1984) Internal morphology of the gill. In W.S. Hoar and D.J. Randall (eds): Fish Physiology, Vol. 10A. New York: Academic Press, pp. 73–183.

Laurent, P. (1985) Organization and control of the respiratory vasculature in lower vertebrates; Are there anatomical gill shunts? In K. Johansen and W. Burggren (eds): Cardiovascular Shunts; Phylogenetic, Ontogenetic and Clinical Aspects. Copenhagen: Munksgaard, pp. 57–67.

Laurent, P., R.G. DeLaney, and A.P. Fishman (1978) The vasculature of the gills in the aquatic and aestivating lungfish (Protopterus aethiopicus). J. Morphol. 156:173–208.

Lenfant, C., and K. Johansen (1968) Respiration in the African lungfish, Propterus aethiopicus. I. Respiratory properties of blood and normal patterns of breathing and gas exchange. J. Exp. Biol. 49:437–452.

Lenfant, C., K. Johansen, and G.C. Grigg (1967) Respiratory properties of blood and patterns of gas exchange in the lungfish Neoceratodus forsteri (Krefft). Respir. Physiol. 2:1–12.

Lenfant, C., K. Johansen, and D. Hanson (1970) Bimodal gas exchange and ventilation-perfusion relationships in lower vertebrates. Fed. Proc. 29:1124–1129.

Little, C. (1983) The Colonization of Land: Origins and Adaptations of Terrestrial Animals. Cambridge: Cambridge University Press.

Lomholt, J.P., K. Johansen, and G.M.O. Maloiy (1975) Is the aestivating lungfish the first vertebrate with suctional breathing? Nature 257:787–788.

Malvin, G.M. (1985) Cardiovascular shunting during amphibian metamorphosis. In K. Johansen and W. Burggren (eds): Cardiovascular Shunts; Phylogenetic, Ontogenetic and Clinical Aspects. Copenhagen: Munksgaard, pp. 163–172.

McMahon, B. (1969) A functional analysis of the aquatic and aerial respiratory movements of an African lungfish Protopterus aethiopicus, with reference to the evolution of the lung-ventilation mechanism in vertebrates. J. Exp. Biol. 51:407–430.

McMahon, B. (1970) The relative efficiency of gaseous exchange across the lungs and gills of an African lungfish Protopterus aethiopicus. J. Exp. Biol. 52:1–15.

McMahon, B.R., and W.W. Burggren (1987) Respiratory physiology of intestinal air breathing in the teleost Misgurnus anguillicaudatus. J. Exp. Biol. (In press).

Milsom, W.K., L.B. Langille, and D.R. Jones (1977) Vagal control of pulmonary vascular resistance in the turtle Chrysemys scripta. Can. J. Zool. 55:359–367.

Munshi, J.S.D. (1976) Gross and fine structure of the respiratory organs of air-breathing fishes. In G.M. Hughes (ed): Respiration of Amphibious Vertebrates. New York: Academic Press, pp. 73–104.

Neumayer, L. (1904) Die Entwickelung des Darmkanales von Lunge, Leber, Milz und Pankreas bei Ceratodus forsteri. Denkschr. Med. Naturwiss. Ges. Jena 4:377–422.

Owen, R. (1840) Description of the Lepidosiren annectens. Trans. Linn. Soc. London 18:327–361.

Parker, W.N. (1982) On the anatomy and physiology of Protopterus annectens. Trans. R. Irish Acad. 30:109–230.

Piiper, J., and P. Scheid (1984) Respiratory gas transport system: Similarities between avian embryos and lungless salamanders. In R.S. Seymour (ed): Respiration and Metabolism of Embryonic Vertebrates. Dordrecht: Junk, pp. 181–191.

Poll, M. (1962) Etude sur la structure adulte et la formation des sacs pulmonaires des Protoptères. Ann. Mus. R. Afr. Cent. Ser. Quarto Zool. *108:*129–172.

Purser, G.L. (1926) *Calamoichthys calabaricys* J.A. Smith. Part I. The alimentary and respiratory system. Trans. R. Soc. Edinburgh *54:*767–784.

Rahn, H., K.B. Rahn, B.J. Howell, C. Gans, and S.M. Tenney (1971) Air breathing of the garfish, *Lepisosteus osseus*. Respir. Physiol. *11:*285–307.

Randall, D.J., W.W. Burggren, A.P. Farrell, and M.S. Haswell (1981) The Evolution of Air Breathing in Vertebrates. Cambridge: Cambridge University Press.

Robertson, J.I. (1913) The development of the heart and vascular system of *Lepidosiren paradoxa*. Quart. J. Microsc. Sci. *59:*53–132.

Rosen, D.E., P.L. Forey, B.G. Gardiner, and C. Patterson (1981) Lungfishes, tetrapods, paleontology, and plesiomorphy. Bull. Am. Mus. Nat. Hist. *167:*159–275.

Satchell, G.H. (1976) The circulatory system of air-breathing fish. In G.M. Hughes (ed): Respiration of Amphibious Vertebrates. New York: Academic Press, pp. 105–124.

Sawaya, P. (1946) Sobre a biologia de alguns peixes de respiracao aerea (*Lepidosiren paradoxa* Fitz e *Arapaima gigas* Cuvier). Bol. Fac. Filos Cienc. Letras Univ. Sao Paulo Ser. Zool. *11:*255–285.

Shabetai, R., D.C. Abel, J.B. Graham, V. Bhargava, R.S. Keyes, and K. Witztum (1985) Function of the pericardium and pericardioperitoneal canal in elasmobranch fishes. Am. J. Physiol. *248:*H198–H207.

Shelton, G. (1970) The regulation of breathing. In W.S. Hoar and D.J. Randall (eds): Fish Physiology, Vol. 4. New York: Academic Press, pp. 293–359.

Shelton, G. (1976) Gas exchange, pulmonary blood supply, and the partially divided amphibian heart. Perspec. Exp. Biol. *1:*247–259.

Smith, H.W. (1930) Metabolism of the lungfish, *Protopterus aethiopicus*. J. Biol. Chem. *88:*97–130.

Spencer, W.B. (1898) Der Bau der Lungen von *Ceratodus* und *Protopterus*. Denkschr. Med. Naturwiss. Ges. Jena *4:*51–58.

Trewavas, E. (1954) The presence in Africa east of the rift valley of two species of *Protopterus, P. annectens* and *P. amphibius*. Ann. Mus. Congo Belge Ser. Quarto Zool. *1:*83–100.

West, N.H., and W.W. Burggren (1982) Gill and lung ventilatory responses to steady-state aquatic hypoxia and hyperoxia in the bullfrog tadpole (*Rana catesbeiana*). Respir. Physiol. *47:*165–176.

Wilmer, E.N. (1934) Some observations on the respiration of certain tropical fresh-water fishes. J. Exp. Biol. *11:*283–306.

JOURNAL OF MORPHOLOGY SUPPLEMENT 1:237–248 (1986)

Estivation in *Protopterus*

ALFRED P. FISHMAN, ALLAN I. PACK, RICHARD G. DELANEY, AND RAYMOND J. GALANTE
Cardiovascular-Pulmonary Division, Department of Medicine, University of Pennsylvania School of Medicine, Philadelphia, Pennsylvania 19104

ABSTRACT   Estivation in *Protopterus* is an episodic event characterized by elaboration of a cocoon as ambient water is withdrawn, a state of torpor, and distinctive cardiorespiratory and metabolic changes. Among the more striking of these features is a decrease in oxygen consumption, a complete reliance on air breathing to satisfy metabolic need, a slowing of the heart rate, and a drop in blood pressure. The initiating mechanism for these dramatic changes is not known. As yet, specific "estivating factors" have not been identified. However, the pattern of decrease in oxygen uptake during estivation and starvation are quite similar, suggesting that a common factor may be involved in both. Attempts to implicate suppression of thyroid function in the onset of estivation have been unconvincing. Although initiating mechanisms for estivation in *Protopterus* remain uncertain, once estivation sets in a variety of adaptive changes occur that enable the estivating lungfish to survive for months to years without ingesting food or water. Among these are oliguria and a shift in metabolic pathways. Although estivation in *Protopterus* has been characterized with respect to cardiorespiratory and metabolic parameters, no attempt is made to extrapolate from the biologic processes in *Protopterus* to other lepidosirenid lungfish or to other genera.

"Estivation" is a loose term that signifies little more than summer torpor as a mechanism for surviving torrid ambient conditions. The term has been used to describe the listless state of ground squirrels as well as the existence of the cactus mouse during its life in a burrow at the height of summer heat (MacMillen, '65). It has also been applied to Amphibia which make a cocoon that encases them for weeks to more than a year during "summer sleep" (Lee and Mercer, '67; Reno et al., '72). Estivation in the African lungfish (genus *Protopterus*) resembles that of the amphibian, *Siren intermedia*. Analogies are often drawn between hibernation and estivation, but too few comparable data are available for valid comparison of the two states even though they do have features in common.

For many years, prompted by the observations of Homer W. Smith ('30, '31, '35a,b), who was primarily concerned with the evolution of the mammalian kidney, we have investigated the cardiorespiratory adjustments that enable African lungfish to use, as the occasion demands, various combinations of gills and lungs for breathing, and how these adjustments change during estivation. To facilitate our studies we have developed an experimental approach that allows us to induce estivation at will in the laboratory. Before substituting artificial estivation for natural estivation, we demonstrated that estivation under controlled conditions in the laboratory provides almost a physiologic facsimile of natural estivation as observed by us and previously described by others in lungfish transported from Africa in cocoons (Smith, '30; Johansen et al., '76). This presentation is confined to estivation in the African lungfish and no attempt is made to extrapolate our findings to *Lepidosiren*.

MATERIALS AND METHODS

The great majority of our studies were done on *Protopterus aethiopicus* (2–6 kg). For the first decade of our research, lungfish were obtained from Lake Victoria near Kampala,

Address reprint requests to Alfred P. Fishman, Cardiovascular Pulmonary Division, Department of Medicine, University of Pennsylvania School of Medicine, Philadelphia, PA 19104.

Uganda; more recently, we have used *Protopterus aethiopicus* from Ghana. They were transported to Philadelphia by air freight, in plastic bags partially filled with water. The travel time varied from 1–3 days. After arrival, lungfish were maintained in individual tanks filled with dechlorinated tap water at 21–25°C. Dechlorinated tap water was used throughout. While in the tanks, the fish were fed Purina Trout Developer (Ralston Purina Company, St. Louis, Missouri) ad libitum, every other day. All had eaten well, seemed to be thriving, and had been in the laboratory for at least one month before use in the estivation studies.

For implantations of electrodes and vascular cannulae, general anesthesia was induced by submersing the fish in 0.5% tricaine methanesulfonate (Ayerst Labortories, Inc., New York, New York).

Details of procedures and instrumentation can be found elsewhere (DeLaney et al., '74). In brief, sampling of arterial blood and monitoring of blood pressure was performed via polyethylene tubing placed in the artery of the third branchial arch. Strain-gauge transducers (Statham) were used to monitor blood pressure. For recording an electrocardiogram, using bipolar ECG electrodes, the indifferent electrode was sutured to the cartilaginous portion of the right subopercular bone and the other electrode was placed at the level of the heart in the vicinity of the pericardium. The electrocardiogram not only provided a measure of the heart rate but also produced electrical artifacts that allowed timing of air breaths. The air breaths also produced characteristic distortions of the blood pressure record. Buccal pressures were determined with a strain-gauge transducer, using a water-filled polyethylene catheter (PE 160) placed in the buccal cavity via the operculum. Blood gases were determined at 25°C, using microelectrodes (Radiometer BMS-3).

Estivation in the laboratory

Estivation experiments were done on lungfish living either in mud or in cloth sacks. The only difference between the two methods is that our technique for estivation in cloth seems to promote more rapid evaportion of surface water, leading thereby to more rapid and intense dehydration, than does estivation in mud (DeLaney et al., '77).

Mud

In the studies using mud, the fish was placed on the surface of semiliquid mud contained either in a large oil drum or styrofoam box. The fish then remained quietly on the surface, breathing rapidly at a rate of 30–60 breaths per hour (compared with its usual rate of 2–10 breaths per hour while in water) for a period that lasted from 5 min to 2 hr. Without warning, it began to burrow and, within a few minutes, disappeared in the mud. Shortly thereafter its head reappeared via a fresh opening, it immediately gulped several breaths of air and then settled back into the mud beneath the surface. Subsequently, it continued to surface periodically for breaths of air, gradually retreating into its burrow during the ensuing days to weeks as the mud dried. Within a month, when the surface of the mud had crusted, the lungfish was lodged in its cocoon, connected to the surface by a thin breathing channel that was about 15 cm long and 1–2 cm wide.

It proved exceedingly difficult to maintain patency of the arterial cannulae in fish that estivated in mud. Moreover, the sites of insertion of the cannulae tended to become infected despite the use of antibiotics. Because of the technical difficulties and the high mortality associated with burrowing in mud, a technique was developed for inducing estivation in cloth bags, using a modification of the method devised by Godet and Pieri ('61) and developed by Janssens and Cohen ('68).

Cloth bags

The technique of inducing estivation in cloth sacks (Fig. 1) involved placing the lightly anesthetized fish in a muslin sack so that its body formed a "U" with its head toward the top of the sack, the normal position for a fish estivating in mud (Johnells and Svensson, '54). Recording leads and cannulae were exteriorized through a small hole in the side of the bag. To initiate the estivation process, the sack was suspended inside a tank filled with water. The tank was then allowed to drain slowly over a period of 5–15 days until the sack became completely dry. Through a small opening at the top of the sack, formation of the cocoon was observed. The cannulae and wires were connected as necessary to external recording devices for periodic sampling and tracings.

Using this system, oxygen consumption was monitored, using two types of apparatus.

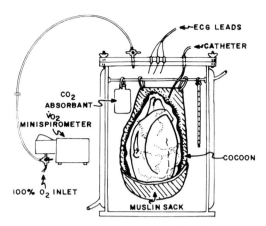

Fig. 1. Schematic representation of lungfish aestivating in a cloth sack. The estivating fish is shown within a metabolic chamber for determining oxygen consumption. At the same time, the electrocardiogram is recorded, blood can be sampled as needed and blood pressures can be recorded at will through indwelling vascular catheters.

In the initial studies, oxygen consumption was measured by connecting a spirometer filled with 100% oxygen to the tank (cylindrical Plexiglas chamber) containing the fish (Fig. 1) (DeLaney et al., '74). Currently oxygen consumption is measured in a constant pressure volumetric apparatus (Asplund, '70).

As indicated above, the results obtained during estivation in mud and estivation in a cloth sack were similar. Consequently, they will be considered together in the discussion that follows.

RESULTS AND DISCUSSION
The cocoon

During estivation, African lungfish form a cocoon (also see Greenwood, this volume). This cocoon is formed from a pearly, slimy, tenacious mucus that dries in earth or in the cloth sack to envelop the entire body up to the mouth. However, outpouring of this mucus does not necessarily presage the formation of a cocoon. We have witnessed elaboration of mucus in extraordinary quantities, without formation of a cocoon, in lungfish kept in tanks from which the water had been drained rather than in mud or a sack. Although there was no layer of water in the tank, the air surrounding the fish was fairly moist. In two fish treated in this way, the white undersurfaces grew extremely flushed

and became intensely congested as mucus poured from the surface, but the mucus did not harden because of the moist environment. After 20 hours, we transferred one such fish to the top of a container of moist mud. It soon burrowed into the mud and proceeded to form a cocoon in which it lived for the next 6 weeks of observation. In contrast, the second fish, which was kept moist and undisturbed in its tank after elaborating mucus, continued to secrete the white tenacious material for 3 days without forming a cocoon. Thus, the fish stressed on the floor of the tank without access to water or mud (but kept moist) responded, as did the fish entering estivation in mud, by the outpouring of material which, under proper environmental conditions, could harden to form a cocoon.

Circulatory and respiratory changes

Protopterus, as well as *Lepidosiren*, is an obligatory air breather, equipped with both gills and lungs for external gas exchange (also see Burggren and Johansen, this volume). In their dependence on air breathing, these species differ from *Neoceratodus*, an obligatory water breather, which soon dies if forced to rely on air breathing (Lenfant et al., '70). During the stage of their life cycle that is spent in water, lungfish rely primarily on their gills to eliminate carbon dioxide; an occasional breath of air suffices for about 90% of the oxygen supply. In contrast, during life in the cocoon, full responsibility for both oxygen and carbon dioxide exchange falls upon the lungs (Lahiri et al., '70).

While in water, the ratio of gill to lung breathing in the unanesthetized lungfish is about 30:1 (Jesse et al, '67); the heart rate is of the order of 20–25 per min. During the first few weeks in the cocoon, the frequency of lung breaths (respiratory frequency) increases, whereas oxygen consumption and heart rate decrease (Fig. 2). Respiratory frequency slows gradually so that within 1 to 2 months, respiratory frequency and heart rate are at their nadirs. The respiration and circulation of *Protopterus* stabilize gradually after the start of estivation (Fig. 3). The gradual cardiorespiratory adjustments of *Protopterus* differ sharply from those of ground squirrels entering into hibernation in which the nadirs of cardiovascular, respiratory, and metabolic performance are reached in 5 to 10 hr (Lyman and Dawe, '60).

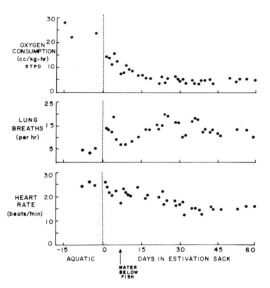

Fig. 2. Sequential changes in oxygen consumption, frequency of lung breaths, and heart rate during the first 2 months of estivation (DeLaney et al., '74).

Circulation

Upon entering into estivation, the circulation of the gills is bypassed so that the pattern of blood flow switches from that of a highly modified piscine single circulation to a circulation resembling that of the adult amphibian (Johansen and Reite, '68; Szidon et al., '69). Involved in these readjustments are peripheral vasoconstriction, the redirection of blood flow within the heart, and the rerouting of blood by the closed ductus to the dilated pulmonary vasomotor segment and pulmonary arteries (Fig. 4). The complicated interplay among heart, pulmonary arteries, ductus, and gills that optimizes blood flow for the sake of air breathing has been described elsewhere (Laurent et al., '78; Fishman et al., '85a,b; reviewed by Burggren and Johanson, this volume). Presumably, as in the turtle (Johansen et al., '77), the vagus nerves are intimately involved in these rearrangements, which could serve to direct blood flow to the lungs as they inflate.

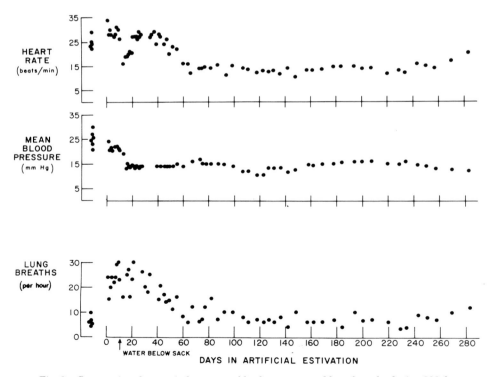

Fig. 3. Consecutive changes in heart rate, blood pressure, and lung breaths during 283 days of estivation. (Modified after DeLaney et al., '74).

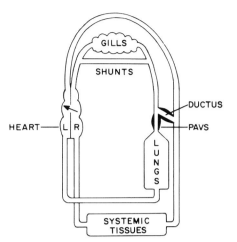

Fig. 4. Schematic representation of circulation in *Protopterus* indicating the sites involved in rerouting blood flow from the gills to the lungs during estivation.

Respiration

The lungs in both *Protopterus* and *Lepidosiren* extend as paired, long hollow sacs along the dorsal portion of the abdominal cavity from the pectoral to the pelvic girdle. The dorsal surface of each lung is fixed to the body wall beneath the ribs so that expansion of the lungs during breathing takes place primarily in the ventral (nonfixed) portions. Cephalad, the two sacs merge to form a common chamber that is connected to the glottic sphincter of the pharynx by a short pneumatic duct. Each lung is innervated by a branch of the ramus intestinalis from the vagus nerve. The right lung is innervated by the pulmonary branch of the left ramus intestinalis; the left lung is innervated by the corresponding branch of the right ramus intestinalis.

During estivation, the breathing pattern consists of alternating periods of rapid breathing and arrested breathing. The pattern is similar to that used to ventilate the lungs during life in water except that a burst of rapid shallow inspirations and expirations follows the first large expiration. This pattern differs from the usual aquatic pattern of a single breath followed by a prolonged apnea. The large expiration that seems to trigger the tachypneic phase seems to correspond to the single expiration during air breathing while the fish is in water. Minute ventilation increases during the bouts of tachypnea because of the rapid frequency, even though

tidal volumes decrease (DeLaney and Fishman, '77).

In water, the mechanical process of lung breathing begins when the lungfish surfaces and the mouth opens. Expiration involves the release of gas from the lungs from behind the closed glottis; until the glottis opens, this gas is under a positive pressure that originates partly from the hydrostatic pressure of the surrounding water and partly from contraction of smooth muscle intrinsic to the lungs; inspiration of air is by a buccal force-pump mechanism similar to that prevalent among anurans (McMahon, '69; DeLaney et al., '77; Johansen et al., '76; Wood and Lenfant, '76). This pattern also applies during estivation (DeLaney et al., '77). Although the buccal force-pump mechanism resembles that used by anurans, it is pertinent that toads can resort to adominal aspiratory breathing when prevented from using the buccopharyngeal mechanism (Bentley and Shield, '73). The coexistence of this dual breathing mechanism in toads suggests that the evolution of respiratory mechanisms in lung breathers may have included the buccopharyngeal pump as an intermediate step en route to aspiration breathing (McMahon, '69; Lomholt et al., '75; Gans, '70; Randall et al., '81).

As the lungfish settles into its estivation nest and the cocoon begins to form, the lungs become the principal organ for CO_2 elimination. However, the efficiency of CO_2 elimination is compromised not only by the loss of the gills as sites for aquatic CO_2 exchange but also by the increase in respiratory dead space produced by extension of the burrow to the surface and the decrease in tidal volume. As a result, the arterial PCO_2 increases even though respiratory frequency and minute ventilation increase and oxygen consumption decreases (Fig. 5). These respiratory effects on acid-base balance and the electrolyte composition of blood are accompanied by a fall in bicarbonate concentration produced by the accumulation of fixed acid as food and water intake stop, excretory functions are reduced, and metabolic pathways and endocrine functions are rearranged.

Little is known about the control of breathing during estivation. However, during air breathing in the aquatic phase, *Protopterus* increases the frequency of lung breaths during induced hypoxia and decreases the frequency of lung breaths during hyperoxia (Jesse et al., '67). In contrast, increasing concentrations of PCO_2 in inspired air elicit a

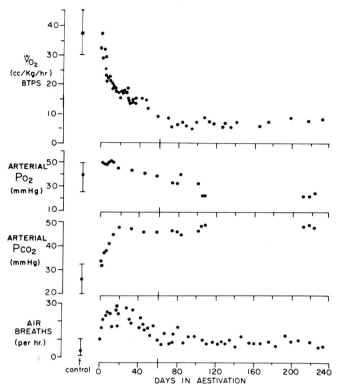

Fig. 5. Blood gas composition during estivation gradually adjusts at lower levels of arterial PO_2 and higher values for arterial PCO_2 than existed prior to estivation. Control values are shown as mean $\pm$ 1 S.D.

biphasic response: low levels of CO_2 (0.5%) increase lung breaths and gill frequency, whereas higher levels (1–5%) depress both. The depressive effect is more marked on the gills (Jesse et al., '67). Although gills and lungs respond qualitatively in a similar fashion to the individual test, i.e., both lung and gill ventilation change in the same direction, the combination of moderate hypoxia and hypercapnia increases lung frequency but depresses gill frequency. Chemoreceptors, widely distributed on the gill arches, but predominantly located on the first three arches, mediate the ventilatory response to hypoxia. The response to hypoxia is abolished by sectioning the nerves to the arches (Lahiri et al., '70). Although chemoreceptors on the gill arches—predominantly on the first three— are believed to be responsible for the ventilatory response to hypoxia in the aquatic lungfish, receptor cells on these arches have not been identified despite an intensive histological search. The relative contribution of

chemical stimuli in the blood to breathing in the estivating lungfish has not been assessed.

Early observations had suggested that a reflex, similar to the Hering-Breuer inflation reflex elicited in anesthetized amphibians and mammals may exist in the lungs of the lungfish (Smith, '31; DeLaney et al., '74). In the anesthetized cat, maintained distention of the lungs decreases the frequency of the inspiratory effort or elicits a transient arrest of breathing. The stimulus for this reflex is pulmonary inflation, the sensors are stretch receptors (proprioceptors) within the smooth muscle of the airways, and the afferent pathway is via large myelinated fibers in the vagus. More recently, pulmonary mechanoreceptors that behave physiologically like the proprioceptors of the frog lung but unlike those of the swim bladder of teleosts (Taglietti and Casella, '66) have been identified in *Protopterus* and *Lepidosiren* (DeLaney et al., '83). These consist of both slowly adapting receptors and rapidly adapting receptors.

The fact that these fish possess mechanoreceptors that represent a transition from aquatic to aerial breathing raises the possibility that, instead of operating initially to adjust the switch from inspiration to expiration during air breathing, the original Hering-Breuer reflex was primarily concerned with monitoring the volume of air contained in the lungs during submersion for the sake of buoyancy. Moreover, the control of pulmonary smooth muscle tone by the vagus nerves suggests that an important element in adjusting buoyancy is by way of a vasovagal reflex loop (DeLaney et al., '83). Another possibility is that pulmonary stretch receptors in the lungfish, as in the turtle (Johansen et al., '77), modulate pulmonary blood flow in response to changes in lung volume. Thus, the lungfish is provided with mechanisms that provide afferent information concerning the mechanical state of the lungs. These mechanisms have properties similar to those of higher vertebrates and operate similarly in the control of breathing.

The blood

During estivation, the concentration of erythrocytes, the hematocrit, oxygen capacity, and hemoglobin concentration increase progressively with time (Lenfant and Johansen, '68; Johansen et al., '76). These increases are attributable to a decrease in plasma volume rather than to an increase in red cell formation (DeLaney et al., '76). Presumably, the hemoconcentration is a consequence of dehydration and is consistent with the progressive increase in the concentration of plasma electrolytes that occurs during estivation in mud as well as in the cloth sack. An erythropoietic stimulus to red cell proliferation does not develop because the drop in oxygen consumption sustains arterial oxygenation at about the same levels as during life in water. Accompanying the increase in red cell concentration are rearrangements in the proportions of the four electrophoretically distinct hemoglobin fractions. The physiological implications of these rearrangements are unclear.

During the first month of estivation, *Protopterus* also develops an increase in circulating neutrophils (DeLaney et al., '76). However, this neutrophilia is transient and subsides within the next 60 days. This sequence is consistent with the idea of stress or local inflammation at the start of estivation. Emergence from estivation is also associated with a considerable leukocytosis that subsides within a few days.

Comparisons of the O_2 affinities of blood from different fishes is complicated by the facts that they live at different temperatures, that many undergo O_2 affinity changes with the season, and that their levels of activity and natural habitats vary so widely. *Protopterus* blood manifests a Bohr effect (O_2-releasing effect of CO_2 on hemoglobin) but lacks a root effect (pronounced effect of acid seen in some fish, that prevents full oxygenation of hemoglobin at low pH no matter how high the PO_2). Each of these effects is attributable to a different hemoglobin species (Gillen and Riggs, '73). A Haldane effect (increased ability of hemoglobin to transport CO_2 during deoxygenation), if it does exist, is modest (Lahiri et al., '70; Johansen et al., '76). Indeed, in its overall properties, the O_2 dissociation curves for *Protopterus* can be likened to those of human blood when appropriate allowances are made for blood pH and temperature (e.g., aquatic lungfish: pH = 7.65, temp. = 25 °C; human: pH = 7.40, temp. = 37 °C). Although it might be anticipated that transition from aquatic to aerial gas exchange would be accompanied by a reduction in Bohr effect, this generalization has not withstood experimental scrutiny in lungfish. The Bohr effect is larger in *Neoceratodus* than in *Lepidosiren* and that of *Protopterus* falls between (Lenfant et al., '66; Lenfant and Johansen, '68). Oxygen stores in the tissues are modest and could satisfy the O_2 need of a 5-kg lungfish for about 100 min if it were denied all access to ambient O_2 (Lahiri et al., '70).

An unexpected finding is the striking increase in the O_2-Hb affinity of the blood during estivation in *Protopterus aethiopicus*. This characteristic has been attributed to a reduction in the red cell concentration of guanosine triphosphate (Johansen et al., '76). Although, as a rule, the blood of fishes that rely heavily on air breathing favors O_2 unloading in the tissues, the P_{50} during estivation in *Protopterus aethiopicus* seems to favor O_2 loading of blood by atmospheric oxygen. This distinctive feature, coupled with its natural positive pressure breathing throughout the respiratory cycle, can be rationalized as an adaptation to abnormal mechanics of ventilation in the upright fish out of water and by the stagnant air surrounding a fish trapped in soil. The handicap to unloading O_2 in *Protopterus* may be partially compensated by an increase in Bohr effect. However, other

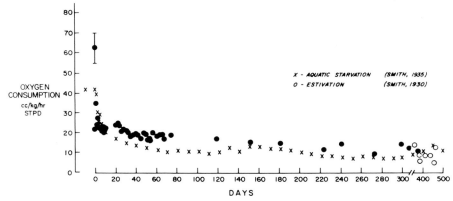

Fig. 6.　Oxygen consumption during estivation and starvation. (Redrawn after Smith, '30).

observations on the respiratory functions of the blood, based on arterial PO_2 in *Protopterus aethiopicus* estivating in cloth sacks, are inconsistent with the proposition that the blood in *Protopterus* favors O_2 loading (De-Laney et al., '74). The adaptive role of the respiratory functions of the blood in the estivating lungfish remains a fertile field for future study.

Oxygen consumption

During estivation, *Protopterus* lives for months to years without food or water. Ever since the origial observations by H.W. Smith ('30), it has been agreed that oxygen consumption falls to remarkably low levels during estivation (Swan, '69). Smith ('30) believed that the decline in metabolism during estivation was due to progressive starvation and emaciation (Fig. 6). *Protopterus* living in water can survive for many months without food (Smith, '35a; Janssens, '64). Our initial observations on the changes in oxygen consumption in *P. aethiopicus* early in estivation were in accord with Smith's view ('35a). However, comparisons were complicated by differences in the size of the fish and in caloric intake in the two studies and by variability in the preestivation feeding of our fish.

More recently, we have controlled food intake in captive lungfish (Fig. 7). Our preliminary observations confirm that starvation produces a decrease in oxygen uptake. A similar pattern of decrease occurs in *P. aethiopicus*, in *P. annectens* and in *Lepidosiren*. However, considerable variability has been observed in the rate of decrease, not due to species differences but to the amount of food

consumed, the duration of the feeding period before starvation began, and the size of the fish. During starvation, a single feeding prompts a burst in oxygen uptake to virtually the same level as before the start of starvation: Oxygen uptake then decreases rapidly as starvation is continued. This type of observation suggests that an important determinant of the oxygen consumption is due to the specific dynamic action of the ingested food. The metabolic effect of previously ingested food seems to exert a continuing effect for 4–7 days after feeding. Whether the pattern of drop in oxygen uptake during prolonged estivation mimics that of prolonged starvation is currently being reexamined in our laboratory, using fishes that are comparable in size and much more rigid control of antecedent food intake than has been practiced previously (Smith, '35a,b).

Life in the cocoon

The behavior of the fish in the cocoon provides some insight into the degree of torpor associated with estivation. A sudden noise in the laboratory exaggerates the bradycardia of the fish in the cocoon; in one fish, heart rate slowed from about 15 to 6 per min and a premature lung breath was stimulated. As the disturbance continued, the heart rate returned toward the original 15 beats per min while the breathing pattern resumed the characteristic pattern of the undisturbed, estivating lungfish.

Arterial blood pressure begins to plateau at a lower level within a few days after the cocoon is formed (Fig. 3). Part of the decrease in blood pressure during estivation seems attributable to dehydration. Another contrib-

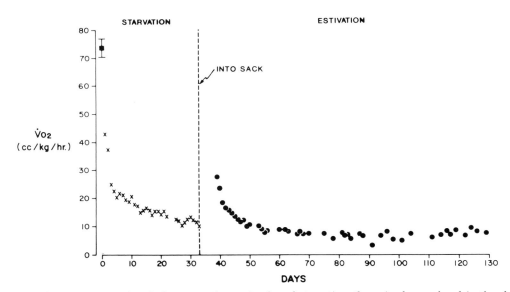

Fig. 7. Oxygen consumption during starvation and estivation. Before starvation, oxygen consumption averaged about 74 cc/kg/hr. Starvation in water caused a hyperbolic decline in oxygen consumption. On the 33rd day of starvation, the animal was placed in the cloth sack for estivation. During estivation, oxygen consumption fell to about the same level as during starvation in water.

uting factor is probably venous pooling resulting from the fixed upright position of the lungfish in its cocoon. But probably more important than either of these is autonomic nervous activity. Unfortunately, little is known about autonomic nervous regulation in the lungfish. Although the fish has distinct vagal innervation, the countervailing sympathetic nervous system is poorly defined structurally and functionally (Abrahamsson et al., '79; Fishman et al., '85b).

The unavailability of water by mouth and the continued elimination of small quantities of water by the lungs implies progressive desiccation during estivation. To a large extent, oliguria (marked reduction in urine formation) coupled with the waterproofing effect of the cocoon protects against insufferable water loss. However, a penalty is paid for the oliguria and desiccation in the form of accumulated metabolic wastes (Smith, '30; Janssens, '64). The role played by these metabolic materials in propagating the state of estivation is unclear.

The trigger for estivation appears to be related either to the torrid ambience, to starvation, or to desiccation. Most popular among the three theories is torrid ambience, which by drying of the skin could provide a signal for the start of estivation. This belief underlies our experimental approach to inducing

estivation by surrounding the fish in a cloth sack. However, although the technique does work, confidence in this hypothesis was shaken by: 1) the demonstration that the ingredients of a cocoon are elaborated when the fish is out of water (but kept moist) and denied opportunity either to burrow in mud or curl up in a cloth sack, and 2) the observation that the fish is clearly agitated as it either burrows in mud or assumes its position in the sack. These observations suggested the possibility that stress, rather than drying of the skin, is responsible for triggering the start of estivation; as indicated above, stress can lead to an outpouring of mucus. If the setting is right for dessication of the mucus, a cocoon replaces the slime. Whether subsequent dehydration contributes to the ultimate composition of the cocoon remains unsettled.

Acid-base balance and plasma composition

The partial pressure CO_2 (PCO_2) in the arterial blood of *P. aethiopicus* living in water under natural condition is higher (of the order of 26 mmHg) than in fish that rely solely on gills for breathing (arterial $PCO_2 < 5$ mmHg) (Fig. 5). Because of the limitations of CO_2 exchange imposed by the sparse gill filaments and the slower gill ventilation of *Protopterus*, only 60% of metabolic CO_2 is exchanged across the gills. In the aquatic lungfish at 25°C, arterial pH is around 7.6 and the plasma bicarbonate about 31 mEq/l. Accordingly, the arterial pH at 25°C is within the pH range expected for other water breathing fish (Rahn and Baumgardner, '72).

Upon entering into estivation, *Protopterus aethiopicus* develops an acute respiratory acidosis. The time course of acid-base changes during estivation has two distinct phases: initially, an uncompensated respiratory acidosis develops as the exchange of CO_2 across gill and skin decreases; in a subsequent phase, one of compensation, plasma bicarbonate increases slowly along the course of the isopleth of arterial $PCO_2 = 50$ mmHg, reaching a new buffer line that is 6–8 mEq/l above the preestivation *in vivo* buffer line for the same pH. It is noteworthy that the time course of the increase in plasma bicarbonate is relatively slow, taking over 2 months to reach the maximum level. Moreover, the plasma bicarbonate does not increase enough to compensate completely for the decrease in arterial pH that accompanies the increase in arterial PCO_2. In a fish estivating for 7 months, arterial pH is in the range of 7.40 to 7.44, arterial PCO_2 is about 50–55 mmHg and the concentration of bicarbonate in plasma is about 39 mEq/l.

Because of the decrease in oxygen consumption during estivation, the metabolic acidosis is modest. Thus, the decrease in metabolic rate contributes to the acid-base balance both by decreasing CO_2 production and by minimizing the need for anaerobic metabolism. However, the renal secretion of hydrogen ions is assumed to be greatly reduced during the oliguria of estivation so that the low production of hydrogen ions may limit the increase in plasma bicarbonate. Because of the cessation of water intake from the start of estivation and the resulting hemoconcentration, the concentrations of most plasma constituents increase progressively during estivation. The increase in urea concentration becomes disproportionately high for the degree of dehydration and constitutes an increasing fraction of total plasma osmolality. Acid-base and electrolyte balances do not reach a new equilibrium during one year in the cocoon.

Neurohumoral and/or metabolic factors

Whether neurohumoral or metabolic factors are involved in intitiating and continuing estivation has long intrigued investigators. "Estivation factors" have been sought in "brown fat" taken from the tail region of estivating *P. annectens* (Godet and Pieri, '61) and from the brain (Swan et al., '68; Swan, '74). The endpoints were a decrease in body temperature and in oxygen consumption; for expediency, and despite the enormous evolutionary gulf, rats were used as the test animals. Also, because of similarities in the patterns of decrease in oxygen uptake during estivation and starvation, a common "factor" hs been sought to account for both (Swan et al., '68). However, whether estivation factors do exist is still uncertain. An alternative approach to account for the decrease in oxygen consumption during estivation has been a search for changes in thyroid function (Dupé, '68). However, because of the surgical manipulations involved in these experiments and uncertainties about the feeding schedules of the fish under study, the role of the thyroid in the process of estivation also remains unsettled.

Theories of estivation

In attempting to account for the process of estivation, sharp distinction has to be made between intitiating and perpetuating mechanisms. Clearly, these need not be the same. Also, because of the episodic nature of the event, it is unreal to picture estivation as part of a chronobiological rhythm. Instead, it seems to be an episodic event requiring an initiating stimulus, such as those considered above.

Although it is possible to draw schematic representations of the various factors that might be involved in initiating and maintaining estivation in *Protopterus*, the picture is apt to be misleading in that features are misinterpreted for mechanisms. Some features of estivation are shown in Figure 8. None of these has been singled out as the initiating mechanism for the syndrome of estivation. However, the figure does take into account that estivation in *Protopterus* is characterized by elaboration of a cocoon as insulation against a threatening torrid environment, a state of torpor, and distinctive cardiorespiratory and metabolic changes.

Several avenues are currently being explored to identify initiating and perpetuating mechanisms. As indicated above, one is the possible role of starvation in effecting the metabolic, circulatory, and respiratory changes. Another is the possible role of the central nervous system and neurohumoral

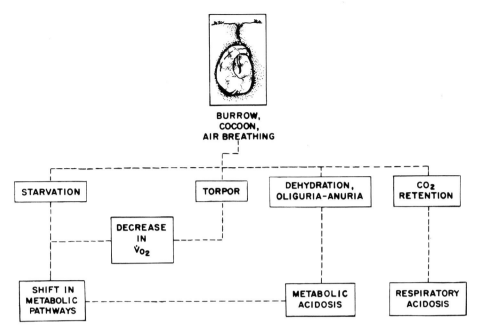

Fig. 8. Factors involved in estivation. Four basic results of burrowing and cocoon formation are starvation, torpor, dehydration, and CO_2 retention. These factors in turn produce a series of metabolic and respiratory consequences. See text for further description.

mediators. A third is the role of the thyroid gland. How stress and desiccation relate to the overall process is still a mystery for future investigation.

SUMMARY

In this paper, certain aspects of the process of estivation have been considered, using as a point of departure our prolonged laboratory experience with artificial estivation that closely stimulates the natural state. Although many of the distinctive features of estivation can be readily defined, neither initiating mechanisms nor perpetuating factors are understood. One current line of research is the exploration of the role of neurohumoral mechanisms in starting the estivation process. Another is the role of starvation. An important caveat in these studies is the recognition that the designation "estivation" is a cloak for biologic processes that have not yet been shown to be the same from genus to genus, even among the lepidosirenid lungfish. Consequently, caution is required in extrapolating initiating and propagating mechanisms from one genus to another.

ACKNOWLEDGMENTS

The research summarized in this report has been uninterruptedly supported by Program Project Grants (HL-08805) from the National Heart, Lung and Blood Institute, National Institutes of Health.

LITERATURE CITED

Abrahamsson T., S. Holmgren, S. Nilsson, and K. Pettersson (1979) Adrenergic and cholinergic effects on the heart, the lung and the spleen of the African lungfish, *Protopterus aethiopicus*. Acta Physiol. Scand. *107*:141–147.

Asplund, K.K. (1970) Metabolic scope and body temperatures of whiptail lizards (*Cnemidophorus*). Herpetologica *26*:403–411.

Bentley, P.J., and J.W. Shield (1973) Ventilation of toad lungs in the absence of the buccopharyngeal pump. Nature *243*:538–539.

DeLaney, R.G., and A.P. Fishman (1977) Analysis of lung ventilation in the aestivating lungfish *Protopterus aethiopicus*. Am. J. Physiol. *233*:R181–R187.

DeLaney, R.G., S. Lahiri, and A.P. Fishman (1974) Aestivation of the African lungfish, *Protopterus aethiopicus*: Cardiovascular and respiratory functions. J. Exp. Biol. *61*:111–128.

DeLaney, R.G., C. Shub, and A.P. Fishman (1976) Hematologic observations on the aquatic and aestivating African lungfish, *Protopterus aethiopicus*. Copeia *1976*:423–434.

DeLaney, R.G., S. Lahiri, B. Hamilton, and A.P. Fishman (1977) Acid-base balance and plasma composition in the aestivating lungfish (*Protopterus*). Am. J. Physiol. *232:*R10–R17.

DeLaney, R.G., P. Laurent, R. Galante, A.I. Pack, and A.P. Fishman (1983) Pulmonary mechanoreceptors in the dipnoi lungfish *Protopterus* and *Lepidosiren*. Am. J. Physiol. *244:*R418–R428.

Dupé M. (1968) Essai d'Interprétation Physiologique due Cycle Annuel de *Protopterus annectans Owen*. Ph.D. Thesis. University of Aix-Marseille, France.

Fishman, A.P., R.G. DeLaney, P.Laurent, and J.P. Szidon (1985a) Blood shunting in lungfish and humans. In K. Johansen and W. Burggren (eds): Cardiovascular Shunts. Phylogenetic, Ontogenetic and Clinical Aspects (Proc. Alfred Benzon Symposium No. 21). Copenhagen: Munksgaard, pp. 88–96.

Fishman, A.P., DeLaney, R.G., and P. Laurent (1985b) Circulatory adaptation to bimodal respiration in the dipnoan lungfish. J. Appl. Physiol. *59:*285–294.

Gans, C. (1970) Respiration in early tetrapods—the frog is a red herring. Evolution *24:*723–734.

Gillen, R.G., and Riggs, A. (1973) Structure and function of the isolated hemoglobins of American eel, *Anguilla rostrata*. J. Biol. Chem. *248:*1961–1969.

Godet, R., and F. Pieri (1961) Hyperthermic effect on the rat of an extract from the lipid reserves of *Protopterus* (dipnoan fish). C.R. Acad. Sci. (Paris) *252:*2600–2602.

Janssens, P.A. (1964) The metabolism of the aestivating African lungfish. Comp. Biochem. Physiol. *11:*105–117.

Janssens, P.A., and P.P. Cohen (1968) Nitrogen metabolism in the African lungfish. Comp. Biochem. Physiol. *24:*879–886.

Jesse, M.J., C. Shub, and A.P. Fishman (1967) Lung and gill ventilation of the African lungfish. Resp. Physiol. *3:*267–287.

Johansen, K., W. Burggren, and M. Glass (1977) Pulmonary stretch receptors regulate heart rate and pulmonary blood flow in the turtle, *Pseudemys scripta*. Comp. Biochem. Physiol. *A 58:*185–191.

Johansen, K., G. Lykkeboe, R.E. Weber, and G.M.O. Maloiy (1976) Respiratory properties of blood in awake and estivating lungfish, *Protopterus amphibius*. Respir. Physiol. *27:*335–345.

Johansen, K., and O.B. Reite (1968) Influence of acetylcholine and biogenic amines on branchial, pulmonary and systemic vascular resistance in the African lungfish, *Protopterus aethiopicus*. Acta Physiol. Scand. *74:*465–471.

Johnells, A.G., and G.S.O. Svensson (1954) On the biology of *Protopterus annectens Owen*. Arkiv. Zool. *7:*131–158.

Lahiri, S., J.P. Szidon, and A.P. Fishman (1970) Potential respiratory and circulatory adjustments to hypoxia in the African lungfish. Fed. Proc. *29:*1141–1148.

Laurent, P., R.G. DeLaney, and A.P. Fishman (1978) The vasculature of the gills in the aquatic and aestivating lungfish (*Protopterus aethiopicus*). J. Morphol. *156:*173–208.

Lee, A.K., and E.H. Mercer (1967) Cocoon surrounding desert-dwelling frogs. Science *157:*87–88.

Lenfant, C., and K. Johansen (1968) Respiration in the African lungfish *P. aethiopicus*. I. Respiratory properties of blood and normal patterns of breathing in gas exchange. J. Exp. Biol. *49:*437–452.

Lenfant, C., K. Johansen, and G.C. Grigg (1966) Respiratory properties of blood and pattern of gas exchange in the lungfish *Neoceratodus forsteri (Krefft)*. Resp. Physiol. *2:*1–21.

Lenfant, C., K. Johansen, and D. Hanson (1970) Bimodal gas exchange and ventilation-perfusion relationships in lower vertebrates. Fed. Proc. *29:*1124–1129.

Lomholt, J.P., K. Johansen, and G.M.O. Maloiy (1975) Is the lungfish the first vertebrate with suctional breathing? Nature *257:*787–788.

Lyman, C.P., and A.R. Dawe (eds) (1960) Mammalian Hibernation. Proc. 1st Int. Symp. Nat. Mammal. Hibernation. Bull. Mus. Comp. Zool. Harvard College, No. 124. Boston: Harvard University Press, 547 p.

MacMillen, R.E. (1965) Aestivation in the cactus mouse, *Peromyscus eremicus*. Comp. Biochem. Physiol. *16:*227–248.

McMahon, B.R. (1969) A functional analysis of the aquatic and aerial respiratory movements of an African lungfish, *Protopterus aethiopicus*, with reference to the evolution of the lung-ventilation mechanism in vertebrates. J. Exp. Biol. *51:*407–430.

Rahn, H., and F.W. Baumgardner (1972) Temperature and acid-base regulation in fish. Respir. Physiol. *14:*171–182.

Randall, D.J., W.W. Burggren, A.P. Farrell, and M.S. Haswell (1981) The Evolution of Air Breathing in Vertebrates. Cambridge: Cambridge University Press, p. 133.

Reno, H.W., F.R. Gehlbach, and T.A. Turner (1972) Skin and aestivational cocoon of the aquatic amphibian, *Siren intermedia*. Copeia *1972:*625–631.

Smith, H.W. (1930) Metabolism of the lungfish, *Protopterus aethiopicus*. J. Biol. Chem. *88:*97–130.

Smith, H.W. (1931) Observations in the African lungfish, *Protopterus aethiopicus*, and on evolution from water to land environments. Ecology *12:*164–181.

Smith, H.W. (1935a) The metabolism of the lungfish. I. General considerations of the fasting metabolism inactive fish. J. Cell Comp. Physiol. *6:*43–67.

Smith, H.W. (1935b) The metabolism of the lungfish. II. Effect of feeding meat on metabolic rate. J. Cell Comp. Physiol. *6:*335–349.

Swan, H. (1969) Metabolic torpor in *Protopterus aethiopicus*: An anti-metabolic agent from the brain. Am. Naturalist *103:*247–258.

Swan, H. (1974) Thermoregulation and Bioenergetics. New York: American Elsevier Publishing Co.

Swan, H., D. Jenkins, and K. Knox (1968) Anti-metabolic extract from the brain of *Protopterus aethiopicus*. Nature *217:*671.

Szidon, J.P., S. Lahiri, M. Lev, and A.P. Fishman (1969) Heart and circulation of the African lungfish. Circ. Res. *25:*23–28.

Taglietti, V., and C. Casella (1966) Stretch receptors stimulation in frog's lungs. Pflueger's Arch. *292:*297–308.

Wood, S.C., and C. Lenfant (1976) Physiology of fish lungs. In G.M. Hughes (ed): Respiration of Amphibious Vertebrates. New York: Academic Press, pp. 257–270.

JOURNAL OF MORPHOLOGY SUPPLEMENT 1:249–275 (1986)

Feeding Systems of Living Dipnoi: Anatomy and Function

WILLIAM E. BEMIS
*Department of Zoology, University of Massachusetts, Amherst,
Massachusetts 01003-0027*

ABSTRACT   Living lungfishes capture prey by means of suction and then use a simple "hydraulic" transport system to position it for processing between the tooth plates. Three major morphological features—an autostylic jaw suspension, tooth plates, and a reduced but highly mobile branchial apparatus—largely determine the special cranial morphology of living dipnoans and are directly related to these feeding functions. Within Dipnoi, however, there are many striking and functionally significant differences between *Neoceratodus* and the lepidosirenid genera. These include the structure of the tooth plates, lower jaw, jaw articulation, skull roof, tongue, lips, and jaw closing and opening muscles. For example, the rami of the lower jaw of *Neoceratodus* flex slightly at the symphysis, and the jaw joint is "unrestrictive." As a result, the upper and lower tooth plates can be ground against each other in a fashion distinct from the precise and restricted occlusion of lepidosirenids. Understanding the anatomy and function of these features will ultimately aid in interpreting the evolution of dipnoan feeding systems.

The unique cranial organization of lungfishes has been appreciated for more than 100 years (Owen, 1841; Bischoff, 1840; Günther, 1871; Huxley, 1876). The major cranial structures play a role in both feeding and respiration. The former draws attention because so much of what typifies dipnoans involves the feeding apparatus (Denison, '74). All living and most fossil lungfishes share characteristic features such as tooth plates, an autostylic jaw suspension, a short lower jaw, and a stout braincase. Living Dipnoi show many additional unusual cranial features such as: 1) a poorly differentiated hyoid apparatus; 2) a simple jaw adductor musculature covered by either a thin or "emarginated" skull roof; 3) a muscular opercular flap supported by small opercular bones; and 4) cranial ribs.

Descriptive anatomical and paleontological studies of the dipnoan head are now bolstered by functional morphological studies of the respiratory and feeding systems (Bishop and Foxon, '68; McMahon, '69; Thomson, '69; Perkins, '72; Bemis, '82; Bemis and Lauder, '86). Also, there is a growing body of comparative information on these systems in other vertebrates (e.g., Hildebrand et al., '85).

Although the dipnoan fossil record is among the best available for any major lineage of vertebrates, there have been problems in interpreting the evolution of the suite of cranial anatomical features characteristic of living genera. Skulls and tooth plates of *Lepidosiren* and *Protopterus* differ greatly from those of *Neoceratodus*. As a result, some authors have suggested that lepidosirenids are more closely related to late Paleozoic gnathorhizids than to *Neoceratodus* (Romer and Smith, '34; Carlson, '68). Yet despite the fact that many of the anatomical differences among living Dipnoi are well-known, their functional significance remains largely unexplored.

This paper reviews cranial anatomy and functional data on the feeding of *Neoceratodus* and lepidosirenids as a first step toward interpreting the evolution of dipnoan feeding systems. There are large gaps in our knowledge and one function of this review is to indicate where further work should be concentrated. As a general observation, far more information is currently available for lepidosirenids than for *Neoceratodus*. Due to the sheer volume of literature it is impractical to review every aspect of dipnoan feeding. Topics such as the effect of diet on metabolic rate and estivation (e.g., Smith, '35a,b; Fishman et al., this volume) are omitted, as are the anatomy and physiology of the digestive system (e.g., Rafn and Wingstrand, '81). Emphasis is on the anatomy and function of the feeding aparatus. Many important components of the feeding system are touched on only briefly here, but my attempt to provide a broad, synthetic account is warranted because structures do not function in isolation, nor do they necessarily perform in only one activity (Gans, '74). For example, the tongue and hyoid apparatus, which produce suction during olfaction, prey capture, and respiration, also serve to transport food items during processing of prey.

COMPARISONS AND PHYLOGENETIC RELATIONSHIPS

Phylogenetic relationships among Sarcopterygii (Actinistia, Dipnoi, and "Rhipidistia") recently have been among the most debated problems in vertebrate systematics (Løvtrup, '77; Compagno, '79; Gaffney, '79; Jarvik, '80; Lagios, '79; Rosen et al., '81; Gardiner, '83; Holmes, '85; Forey, this volume; Campbell and Barwick, this volume; Schultze, '81, this volume; Schultze and Campbell, this volume). It is not an objective of this paper to revise or test proposed hypotheses of sarcopterygian relationships; however, these represent a prerequisite to comparative analysis.

Figure 1A diagrams the relationships of living gnathostomes. There are two major points:

1. The Dipnoi are Osteichthyes rather than "Plagiostomi." Support for this view comes from a great many studies, including Miles ('77), Rosen et al. ('81), and Schultze (this volume); however, Jarvik ('80) disagrees.

2. The Dipnoi are the *living* sister group of tetrapods. Although this view comes originally from the last century (e.g., Huxley, 1876), it has recently been restated by Miles ('77), Wiley ('79), and Rosen et al. ('81). Further analysis of this phylogeny is presented in Bemis ('84b).

Figure 1B focuses on fossil and living Dipnoi. This diagram also relates to two problem areas:

1. There are two main lineages of Paleozoic dipnoans, referred to as "tooth-plated" vs. "denticulated" (Campbell and Barwick, '84, this volume). Periodic resorption and shedding of sheets of dentine is interpreted to be a synapomorphy of the denticulated lineage (Marshall, this volume). Marshall's phylogenetic interpretation is presented in Figure 1B as an advance over that of Miles ('77).

2. *Neoceratodus* is the sister group of *Lepidosiren* + *Protopterus*. Several authors have proposed that lepidosirenids may be more closely related to the late Paleozoic genera *Gnathorhiza* and *Monongahela* than to the Mesozoic and Cenozoic "ceratodont" line (e.g., Romer and Smith, '34; Carlson, '68; Olson and Daly, '72). That interpretation has been criticized by Berman ('68, '76) and by Miles ('77), who lists synapomorphies of lepidosirenids and *Neoceratodus*.

The Lepidosirenidae constitute a monophyletic lineage. Synapomorphies include: features of cranial osteology, such as the pattern of blades in the tooth plates (Martin, '82) and the absence of postsplenial bones (Miles, '77); features of soft anatomy, such as the presence of two lungs (Goodrich, '30); features from ontogeny, such as cement glands (Kerr, '19; Fox, '65); and features of the nervous

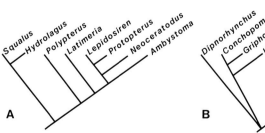
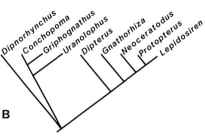

Fig. 1. Phylogenetic relationships of living Dipnoi. A) Relationships of Dipnoi to major lineages of living gnathosomes as illustrated by representative genera: *Squalus* [Elasmobranchii], *Hydrolagus* [Holocephali], *Polypterus* [Actinopterygii], *Latimeria* [Actinistia], *Neoceratodus, Lepidosiren, Protopterus* [Dipnoi] and *Ambystoma* [Tetrapoda]. B) Relationships among fossil and living Dipnoi as illustrated by representative genera. There are two lineages of Paleozoic dipnoans, one characterized by a shagreen dentition that is periodically shed (illustrated by *Griphognathus, Conchopoma,* and *Uranolophus*), and one by tooth plates see Campbell and Barwick ('84; this volume) and Marshall (this volume).

Abbreviations

A,	Articular region of Meckel's cartilage
AM,	Adductor mandibulae
AN,	Angular
ANP,	Antorbital process
BB,	Basibranchial element
BC,	Buccal cavity
CH,	Ceratohyal
ConH,	Constrictor hyoideus
DE,	Dermal ethmoid
DM,	Depressor mandibulae
E,	Ethmoid portion of chondrocranium
EO,	Exoccipital bone or region of the chondrocranium
EP,	Epaxialis
F,	Frontoparietal
GC,	Gill cavity
GCr,	Geniocoracoideus
GT,	Geniothoracicus
H,	Heart and pericardial cavity
HH,	Hypohyal
HSL,	Hyoid suspensory ligament
IH,	Interhyoideus
IM,	Intermandibularis
L,	Lower lip
LC,	Loose connective tissue ventral to the hyoid apparatus
LF,	Lingual furrow
LH,	Levator hyoideus
LTP,	Lower tooth plate

M,	Meckel's cartilage
MHL,	Mandibulohyoid ligament
NC,	Nasal capsule
NE,	Excurrent naris
NI,	Incurrent naris
O,	Otic region of chondrocranium
OP,	Opercular
P,	Pad between blades of tooth plates
PG,	Pectoral girdle
PR,	Prearticular
PS,	Parasphenoid
PSP,	Presplenial
PT,	Pterygoid
Q,	Quadrate
RAO,	Retractor angulae oris
RC,	Rectus cervicis
S,	Supraorbital
SO,	Subopercular
SQ,	Squamosal
SY,	Mandibular symphysis
T,	Tongue
TC,	Tegmen cranii
TP.	Chondroid tongue pad
TPB,	Tooth plate blades
TR,	Trabecular region of chondrocranium
U,	Upper lip
ULC,	Upper lip cartilage
UTP,	Upper (=pterygoid) tooth plate
V,	Vomerine tooth plate

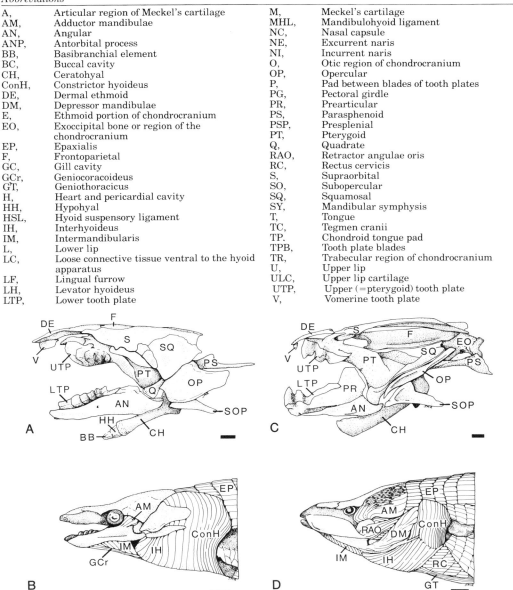

Fig. 2. General cranial anatomy of *Neoceratodus* and *Protopterus*, I: cranial osteology and superficial myology. A) Lateral view of the skull of *N. forsteri* (MCZ 54386). Circumorbital and preopercular canal bones, posterior gill arches, pectoral girdle, and cranial ribs omitted for clarity. The hyoid arch has separate hypohyal (HH) and basibranchial (BB) elements as well as a hyomandibula (not shown; see text). The skull roof covers the adductor fossa, and there is no coronoid process on the lower jaw. B) Superficial cranial muscles of *Neoceratodus* (MCZ 33115). The extensive constrictor hyoideus sheet is divisible into interhyoideus (IH) and constrictor hyoideus (ConH) portions. Drawing is of right side, reversed for ease of interpretation. C) Skull of *Protopterus aethiopicus* (AMNH 55220). Posterior gill arches, pectoral girdle, and cranial ribs omitted for clarity. The quadrate remains cartilaginous but is associated with the squamosal bone (SQ). Note the pocket defined between the opercular (OP) and subopercular (SOP) bones for the depressor mandibulae. D) Superficial cranial muscles of *Protopterus*. Note in particular the depressor mandibulae muscle (DM), coronoid process of the lower jaw, and the reduced skull roof. The large adductor mandibulae complex (AM) is readily visible from the side of the head. All scale bars = 10 mm.

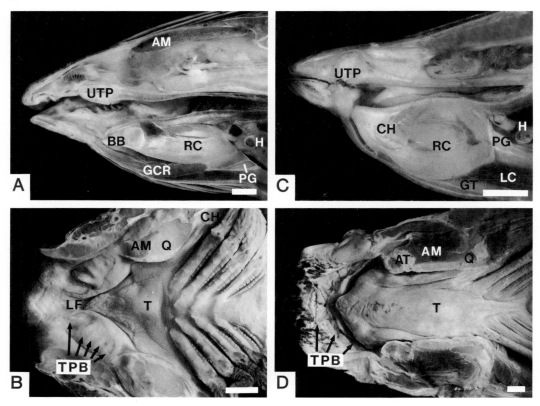

Fig. 3. General cranial anatomy of *Neoceratodus* and *Protopterus*, II: mid-sagittal views of the oral cavity and frontal views of the tongue. A) Mid-sagittal cut through the oral cavity of *Neoceratodus forsteri*, showing upper and lower tooth plates with respect to the lips, oral cavity, and tongue. Basibranchial (BB) and hypohyal elements support the tongue. The rectus cervicis (RC) muscles insert on the hyoid arch, acting to depress it during respiration, suction feeding, or food transport. The adductor musculature (AM) originates from the surface of the braincase beneath a thin skull roof. B) Dorsal aspect of the tongue, lower jaws, and gills of *Neoceratodus*. There are five blades (TPB) on the lower tooth plates of this specimen. The right and left tooth plates do meet in the midline but are separated by the lingual furrow (LF) in which lies the anterior portion of the tongue. C) Mid-sagittal cut through the head of *Protopterus aethiopicus*. The hyoid arch of *Protopterus* and *Lepidosiren* lacks basibranchial and hypobranchial cartilages. The tongue is supported by a chondroid connective tissue pad. The rectus cervicis muscles (RC) of lepidosirenids are larger than in *Neoceratodus*, but the belly of the geniothoracicus muscle is posterior to and smaller than its homologue in *Neoceratodus*. Ventral and posterior to the tongue is an area of loose-connective tissue (LC). D) Dorsal view of the tongue, oral cavity, and gill arches of *Protopterus*. The oral cavity of lepidosirenids is narrow and elongate in comparison to that of *Neoceratodus*. Lepidosirenids have three blades in the tooth plates and lack a lingual furrow. All scale bars = 10 mm.

system, such as neurocranial endolymphatic sacs (Northcutt, this volume).

ANALYSIS OF DIPNOAN FEEDING SYSTEMS

General anatomy

The cranial anatomy of living lungfishes has been intensively studied since the 1830s (see Conant, this volume). Most accounts emphasize homology rather than function. This account emphasizes function. It is built around a series of illustrations. Figures 2 and 3 illustrate the general anatomy of the head of *Neoceratodus forsteri* and *Protopterus aethiopicus* in drawings and photographs. Figures 4 and 5 present additional details of the skull, jaw joint, and chondrocranium of *Protopterus*. Figure 6 shows surface views of tooth plates and cranial bones. Figure 7 presents histological sections through the major joints and ligaments. Features of the lips, tongue, and tooth plate pads are shown in Figure 8. For information concerning specimens and histological methods, see Bemis

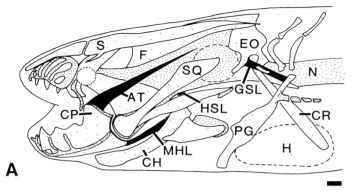

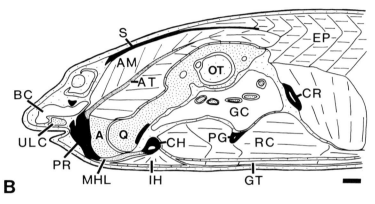

Fig. 4. Cranial ligaments, cartilages and associated connective tissues of *Protopterus*. A) Tracing of a cleared and double-stained *Protopterus aethiopicus*. Gill arches II–V ommitted for clarity. Positions of the eye and ear shown by dotted outlines. The pectoral girdle (PG) is attached to the occipital region of the skull by a girdle suspensory ligament (GSL), in which lies the small ossification of the anocleithrum. Passing posteriorly beneath the girdle is the cranial rib (CR). The frontoparietal bone of *Protopterus* does not ensheath the dorsal surface of the chondrocranium as in *Lepidosiren*, and the braincase is visible laterally. The adductor tendon (AT) inserts on the medial side of the coronoid process. There are two major ligaments associated with the hyoid arch. The hyoid suspensory ligament (HSL) runs from the ventral surface of the suspensorial region to the expanded posterior tip of the ceratohyal. The mandibulohyoid ligament (MHL) runs from the ceratohyal to the posteroventral corner of the lower jaw. B) Parasagittal section through the head of *Protopterus aethiopicus* showing jaw articulation and gill cavity. The quadrate process of the chondrocranium (Q) projects forward at about a 30° angle to the long axis of the body. A large muscle is associated with the posterior surface of the cranial rib. The adductor mandibulae originates in part from the surface of the braincase and in part from the strut-like supraorbital bone (S). Scale bars = 1 mm.

('82, '84a,b), Bemis and Lauder ('86), and Thomas ('83). Where not specified, descriptions apply to all three genera.

Tooth plates, osteology, joints, and ligaments

Terminology. The naming of dipnoan cranial bones is highly controversial (Bridge 1898; Goodrich, '25; Edgeworth, '35; de Beer, '37; Holmgren and Stensiö, '36; Holmgren, '49; Forster-Cooper, '37; Westoll, '49; Parrington, '67; Jarvik, '67, '80; Miles, '75). Efforts to derive a uniform and satisfactory terminology are confounded by the complex-

ity of the skull in fossil dipnoans. Because recognition of homologues in the skull roofs of dipnoans and other fishes is problematic, Forster-Cooper ('37) proposed an independent numbering scheme for these bones. In his study of the Gogo dipnoans, Miles ('77) used the teleostome terminology for all but the bones of the skull roof. He discussed the problems caused by application of the standard teleostome names to the bones of the dipnoan skull roof and advocated instead an updated version of the Forster-Cooper ('37) nomenclature (Miles, '77:220). However, functional morphologists have usually retained the te-

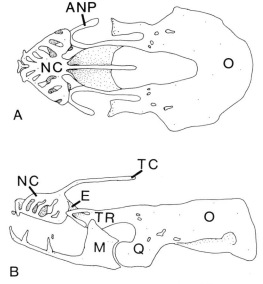

Fig. 5. Chondrocranium and lower jaw of *Protopterus*, redrawn from Winslow (1898). The chondrocranium unites the pterygoids, parasphenoids, frontoparietal, squamosal, and other dermal bones of the skull.

leostome designations for the cranial roofing bones of lepidosirenids (e.g., Bishop and Foxon, '68; McMahon, '69; Bemis and Lauder, '86). Because the present paper is concerned with comparative functional anatomy of *Neoceratodus* and lepidosirenids, I continue this tradition. A related issue concerns terminology of the mandibular bones. Jarvik ('67, '80) devised a scheme for designating these elements. Again, I follow other functional morphologists in using the teleostome terminology for lower jaw bones. To aid in communication, however, I provide an abbreviated tabular summary of terms and synonyms for the cranial bones of living Dipnoi (Table 1).

Tooth plates. Tooth plates are perhaps the most striking derived feature of the lineage that includes the living genera, and they have been the subject of many studies since their first desciption by Agassiz (1833). Comparative descriptions of the histology and development of the tooth plates include Denison ('74), Kemp ('77, '79), Kerr ('19), Lison ('41), Ørvig ('67, '76), Peyer ('69), Schmidt and Keil ('71), and Smith ('79, '84). The dentition develops by the fusion of isolated denticles (Lison, '41; Kemp, '77, '79). The main upper (UTP) and lower (LTP) tooth plates are supported by the pterygoid and prearticular

bones (Figs. 2–4, 6, 7A). Anterior to the pterygoid tooth plates lie the vomerine teeth (V). Their bases are supported by ethmoid cartilage.

Tooth plates of *Neoceratodus* and lepidosirenids differ strikingly in gross anatomy, specifically in the degree of "heterodonty" along the tooth plate and the shapes of the blades (Figs. 2A,C, 3B,D, and 5). Starting from a single cusp in larvae, the tooth plates of *Neoceratodus* add cusps and ridges and eventually consist of a series of blades radiating from the central crushing surface (Kemp, '77). Blades continue to develop to a maximum of seven in this species (Kemp, '77). Left and right main tooth plates do not meet at either the pterygoid or prearticular symphyses. Except for slight differences in size, the blades are generally similar to each other. Opposing upper and lower blades slide past one another at occlusion, forming a series of shearing surfaces and wearing deep furrows in the opposing plate. The structure of the jaw joint and symphysis permits the crushing surfaces to grind against each other (below). The vomerine teeth of *Neoceratodus* are long and ridge-like and their mesial surfaces approach one another in the midline. Worked against the fleshy lower lip, the vomerine teeth form a cropping surface at the front of the mouth.

The main tooth plates of lepidosirenids bear only three blades. Four regions can be distinguished: cropping and stabbing surfaces anteriorly, a central region with pounding surfaces, and a slicing blade in the rear. Because the left and right tooth plates contact

Fig. 6. Tooth plates and cranial bones. A) Pterygoid and vomerine tooth plates of *Neoceratodus forsteri*. Note the multiple blades and medial grinding surfaces (UTP). Right and left tooth plates do not meet in the midline. The vomerine tooth plates (V) are blade-like. B) Pterygoid and vomerine tooth plates of *Protopterus aethiopicus*. The three blades in the tooth plates of *Protopterus* meet in the midline and show distinct stabbing, crushing, and cutting surfaces. The vomerine tooth plates are conical. C) Prearticular tooth plate and mandibular symphysis of *Neoceratodus*. The symphysis is flexible. D) Ventral view of symphysial region of *Neoceratodus* to show postsplenial bones. Three separate postsplenials (two on the left, one on the right) are present in this specimen. E) Prearticular tooth plate and mandibular symphysis of *Lepidosiren paradoxa*. Note the stout and immobile symphysis and worn surface of the tooth plate. F) Lateral view of coronoid process of *Protopterus aethiopicus*. Trabeculae of the bone are oriented with the line of action of the adductor tendon. G, H) Dorsal views of frontoparietal bones of *Lepidosiren paradoxa* and *Protopterus aethiopicus* respectively. All scale bars = 10 mm.

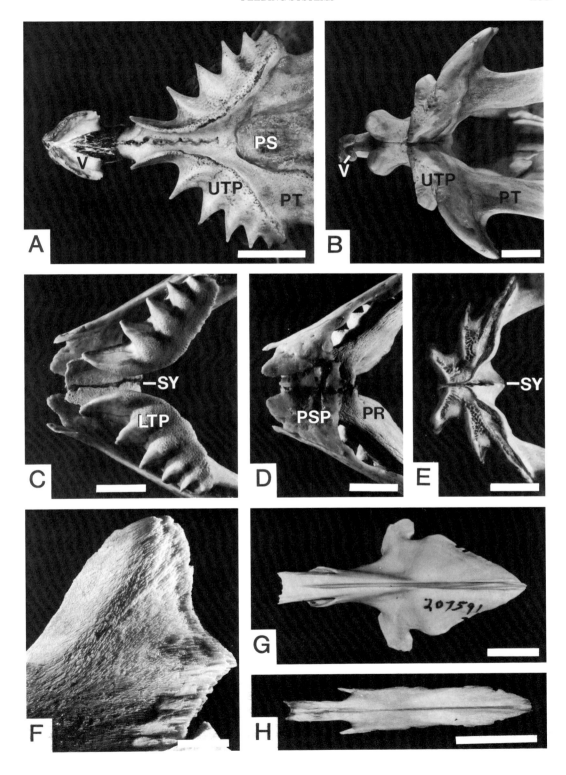

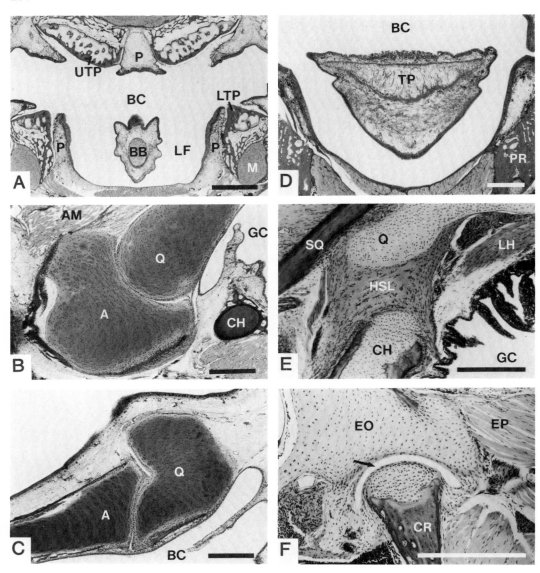

Fig. 7. Cranial joints and ligaments of *Neoceratodus* and *Protopterus*. Sections and photographs prepared using methods of Thomas ('83) and Bemis ('84a). A) Cross section through the buccal cavity (BC), tooth plates (UTP, LTP), and lingual furrow (LF) of *Neoceratodus*. The tongue lies in the lingual furrow, where it is supported by the basibranchial (BB) and hypohyal cartilages. The blades of the tooth plates are surrounded by pads (P). B,C) Para-sagittal and frontal views of the jaw joint of *Neoceratodus*. The joint is not as restrictive of lower jaw motion as is the joint of lepidosirenids, D) Cross section through the buccal cavity and tongue of *Protopterus*, showing the tongue pad (TP) made of chondroid tissue. E) Parasaggital section through the hyoid suspensory ligament of *Protopterus*, showing relations to the squamosal (SQ) and quadrate (Q) above and posterior wing of the ceratohyal (CH) below. F) Parasagittal section through the joint between the cranial rib and exoccipital region of the braincase in *Protopterus aethiopicus*. All scale bars = 1 mm.

each other in the midline, the anterior blades form a nipping surface. Lepidosirenids have cone-shaped vomerine teeth that form an additional stabbing surface at the front of the mouth. Regional differentiation along the length of the tooth plates is achieved by the continuous growth and wear of differentially placed hard petrodentine and softer trabecular dentine. Wear of exposed surfaces keeps the cutting edges sharp and promotes re-

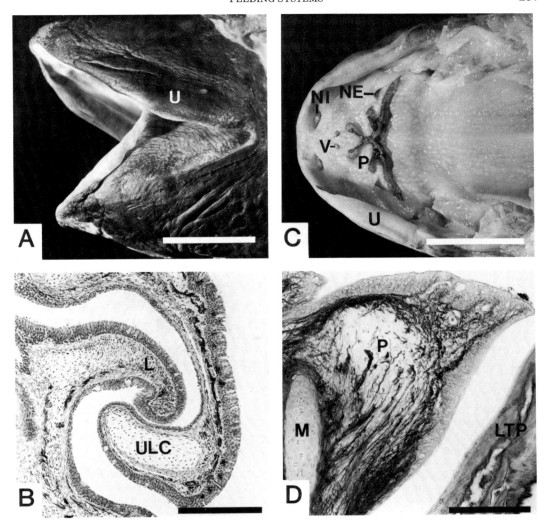

Fig. 8. Lips, palate and tooth plate pad. A) Lateral view of the lips of *Lepidosiren paradoxa* showing the upper lip (U) folding around the lower lip. Scale bar = 10 mm. B) Cross-section view of the lips in *Protopterus aethiopicus*, showing the elastic cartilage (ULC) that supports the upper lip. The interlocking between the upper and lower lip folds is tight, and presumably functions to prevent water influx through the side of the mouth during suction feeding. Scale bar = 0.5 mm. C) Palate of *Protopterus aethiopicus*, showing incurrent and excurrent narial openings, blades of the tooth plates, and pads (P) between the tooth plate blades. Scale bar = 10 mm. D) Cross-section through the chondroid tissue of the tooth plate pad in *Lepididsiren paradoxa*. This pad lies lateral to the lower tooth plate (LTP) and is supported by one of the small cartilages extending dorsally from Meckel's cartilage. Scale bar = 0.05 mm.

gional differentiation during growth (Bemis, '84a).

Lower jaw. Lower jaws of dipnoans have been described by Jarvik ('67, '80), Miles ('77), and Campbell and Barwick ('83, this volume). The lower jaw of *Neoceratodus* includes three types of ossifications (Figs. 2A, 6C,D). The prearticular (PR) is the largest element. It bears the tooth plates and serves as the insertion site for the adductor mandibulae. In comparison to lepidosirenids, *Neoceratodus* lacks a coronoid process. Right and left prearticular bones meet in the horizontal plane at the symphysis, which is thin in dorso-ventral section and permits limited independent movement of the rami (Figs. 3A, 6C). Flat postsplenial bones (PSP, Fig. 6D) lie ventral to the prearticular bones near the

TABLE 1. List and partial synonomy of cranial bones of living Dipnoi[1]

Name used here	Present in *Neoceratodus*	Present in lepidosirenids	Synonyms
Lower jaw			
Angular[2,3]	X	X	Articular[4], surangular[5], MdE[6]
Prearticular[3,7]	X	X	Dentary[4], splenial[2], coronoid[5,8], MdI[6]
Postsplenial[3]	X		MdMc[6]
Upper jaw and braincase			
Pterygoid[8,9]	X	X	Entopterygoid[3], maxillopterygoid[4], palatopterygoid[2,5], pterygopalatine[7]
Parasphenoid[2,3,5,7,9]	X	X	Basisphenoid/basioccipital[4]
Vomerine teeth[2,3,7]	X	X	Intermaxillary teeth[4], prevomer[5]
Quadrate (ossified)[5]	X		
Exoccipital[5]	X	X	
Skull roof and opercular series			
Dermal ethmoid[2,7]	X	X	F[3], intermaxillary bone[4], postrostral[5,8]
Supraorbital[8,9]	X	X	K-M[3], frontal[5,7], posterior frontal[4], dermal ectethmoid[2]
Frontoparietal[2,9]	X	X	B[3], parietal[4,8], medial parietal[5]
Squamosal[2,9]	X	X	Y1+Y2[3], tympanic[4], intertemporal[5], supratemporal/intertemporal[7]
Dermosphenotic[8]	X		X[3]
Extrascapular[8]	X		I[3]
Opercular	X	X	Preopercular[4]
Subopercular[7,8,9]	X	X	Interopercular[2,5], stylohyoid[4]

[1]Excluding smaller canal bones, visceral skeleton and pectoral girdle.
[2]Bridge, 1898.
[3]Miles, '77.
[4]Owen, 1841.
[5]de Beer, '37.
[6]Jarvik, '80.
[7]Bertmar, '66.
[8]Holmgren, '49.
[9]Edgeworth, '35.

mandibular symphysis. As in other canal bones of the head, these show some variation. The specimen shown has two elements on the left, one on the right. The postsplenials are thin, do not cross the symphysis, and do not prevent mobility of the rami. The angular bone covers the lateral surface of each ramus (AN, Fig. 2A). Midway along its length, the lower jaw of *Neoceratodus* has a nearly circular cross-section with the gap between the prearticular and angular bones largely filled by Meckel's cartilage. The symphysial plate extends forward, supporting the lower lip to provide a surface against which the vomerine teeth can cut.

The lower jaw of lepidosirenids is distinctive (Fig. 2C). Each ramus contains a prearticular and angular, but there is no trace of postsplenial bones. The prearticular is solid, heavily ossified, and has a tall coronoid process (Figs. 2C, 4A, 6F). Two shallow fossae for Meckel's cartilage are present on the me-

dial surface of the coronoid process. In small skulls of lepidosirenids these fossae are smooth, but in large *Protopterus* a set of strong horizontal ridges increase the surface area for attachment between Meckel's cartilage and prearticular. Bony trabeculae on the lateral face of the coronoid parallel the line of action of the adductor tendon (Fig. 6F); however, these are unrelated to the actual insertion of the tendon on the anterior and medial surface of the coronoid process. Anteriorly, the prearticular bones meet in a completely immobile symphysis (Bemis, '84a). Meckel's cartilage is most extensive at the articulation (Figs. 4, 5). In *Protopterus*, it tapers anteriorly to form a thin rod that passes along the outer ventral margin of the jaw to meet its opposite anterior to the symphysis. At the point of fusion, the cartilage forms a forwardly projecting symphysial plate. The rod-like portion of the cartilage has three attached or sometimes floating vertical processes between the blades of the tooth plate (Figs. 4A, 5B). The symphysial plate and the vertical processes support connective tissue pads between the blades of the tooth plates (described below).

Jaw joint. The jaw joint of *Neoceratodus* differs from that of lepidosirenids (Perkins, '72). Here, I refer to it as "unrestrictive" in that it allows rotation of the rami. Parasagittal sections show the loose fit between the quadrate and articular cartilages (Q,A Fig. 7B). The medial condyle of the joint is supported by the adjacent pterygoid bone and the lateral condyle is supported by the quadrate ossification. Thus, two separate condyles meet the articular cartilage (Fig. 7C). Perkins ('72) concluded that this shape forces the rami of the lower jaw to rotate outwards during adduction, producing two distinct phases during chew: a slicing phase in which the blades of the tooth plates occlude with each other, and a grinding phase in which food is ground by the central crushing surface of the tooth plate. Perkins's ('72) analysis was supported by tracings from an X-ray film of a chew in *Neoceratodus*, and from fresh specimens he estimated rotation of the rami to be about 5°. My study of fresh specimens confirms this mobility at the jaw joint. However, it seems unlikely that the shape of the joint by itself could force the tooth plates to occlude with these two distinct phases, and activity of the intermandibular muscles is predicted to be necessary. Additional X-ray cinematography and electromyography are needed to resolve this.

In contrast, lepidosirenids have a very close fit between the quadrate and articular cartilages. The joint is "restrictive" in that it limits the lower jaw to an up-and-down hinge motion (Figs. 4, 5). Together with the immobile symphysis, it eliminates any possibility that the lower jaw might rotate at the joint (Bemis, '84a).

Pterygoid, parasphenoid, braincase, quadrate, and cranial rib. The pterygoids and parasphenoid form the upper jaw and palate. In such Devonian genera as *Holodipterus* these elements are so firmly fused together that no suture can be detected between them (Miles, '77). Whereas this is not the case in living Dipnoi, the pterygoids and parasphenoid bones are closely apposed and fixed in position by the chondrocranium.

Because the pterygoids are generally similar in the living genera, a single description will suffice. Anteriorly, the right and left pterygoids meet in a broad and solid symphysis (Fig. 6A,B). Short lateral processes of the pterygoid support the blades of the tooth plates. Dorsal to the tooth plates, the ascending process of each pterygoid engages the skull roof. The posterior surfaces of the pterygoid wings meet the dorsal surface of the parasphenoid. Between the wing of the pterygoid and the tooth plate, the bone forms a solid arch that must bear the force of the occluding tooth plate.

The comparative anatomy of the dipnoan parasphenoid has received special attention from Miles ('77). In *Neoceratodus* the parasphenoid forms a complete bony support for the palate (Fig. 6A). In contrast, lepidosirenids have a gap between the pterygoid symphysis and the anterior edge of the parasphenoid, which is partially filled by the chondrocranium (Fig. 6B). The parasphenoid is thin along its anterior and lateral borders but is thicker in the otic region. In *Neoceratodus*, the parasphenoid continues posteriorly along the notochord with an elongate tab (Fig. 2A). In lepidosirenids, the parasphenoid broadens at its attachment to the notochord. The lateral crests of this surface extend up to support the exoccipitals and first neural arch (Fig. 2C).

The braincase of dipnoans is short and undivided. Chondrocranial anatomy and embryology has been well-studied in living and fossil Dipnoi (Winslow, 1898; Agar, '06; de Beer, '37; Edgeworth, '35; Säve-Söderbergh, '52; Fox, '65; Bertmar, '66; Miles, '77; Campbell and Barwick, '82). In the living genera, it is large and closely associated with the pterygoids, parasphenoid, and exoccipital bones. Though not evolutionarily part of the chondrocranium, the quadrate is continuous with the braincase. The chondrocranium forms a major structural unit by connecting these elements and providing the suspension for the lower jaw (Fig. 5).

The following description focuses on *Protopterus*; see Miles ('77) for a recent treatment of *Neoceratodus*. Anteriorly, the nasal capsules have fenestrated lateral surfaces (Fig. 5A). Details of the cartilages in this region are presented by Jarvik ('42, '80), Thomson ('65), Bertmar ('66), and Miles ('77). Portions of the anterior and lateral walls of the nasal capsule play a role in supporting the lips (see below) as well as in protecting the olfactory tracts. The capsules are united in the midline by the ethmoid plate, more of a solid mass of cartilage than a true plate.

The ethmoid plate lies adjacent to the dermal ethmoid bone and bears the two vomerine teeth. The ethmoid region connects to the trabecular plate dorsal to the pterygoid symphysis.

In lepidosirenids, the chondrocranium forms a portion of the roof of the mouth anterior to the parasphenoid. Posterior to the pterygoids the antorbital processes branch off (Figs. 4B, 5). Each antorbital process runs anteriorly and laterally from the trabeculae, adjacent to the ascending process of the pterygoid. They support the posterior corner of the upper lip and fuse with the rod of connective tissue that supports the upper lip (see lips, below).

There are important differences between the quadrate of *Neoceratodus* and that of lepidosirenids (Fig. 2A,C). In *Neoceratodus*, the shaft of the quadrate undergoes partial perichondral ossification. In lepidosirenids, however, the quadrate does not ossify. It lies between the ventrolateral wing of the pterygoid and the medial ventral edge of the squamosal ($= Y1 + Y2$). The portion of the squamosal that underlies the lateral condyle of the jaw is flattened in a vertical plane, where it stands with a ragged, nearly circular condylar process and provides most of the support for the jaw articulation. Autostyly arises very early in lepidosirenid development: the quadrate is fused to the braincase in the earliest embryos in which it can be detected (Agar, '06).

The suspensorial region of the lepidosirenid chondrocranium is open ventrally, so that the brain sits in a trough defined by ridges on the dorsal surface of the parasphenoid. Posteriorly, the two sides reunite to form the floor of the otic region (Fig. 5A). The dorsal portion of the otic region is expanded laterally, where it serves as the origin for portions of the adductor mandibulae muscle in *Protopterus*; in *Lepidosiren*, this region is covered by the expanded frontoparietal bone (see below). The only portions of the braincase to ossify are the exoccipitals, which are buried in the cartilage of the otic region dorsal to the cranial rib (Fig. 4).

The shaft of the cranial or occipital rib is ossified perichondrally. In *Neoceratodus* the cranial rib is only moderately larger than ribs of the trunk: In lepidosirenids, however, it is greatly enlarged. The well-developed synovial articulation with the chondrocranium in lepidosirenids (Fig. 7F) allows the rib to move in an antero-posterior plane.

Visceral skeleton, opercular, and subopercular bones. The visceral skeleton of Dipnoi is generally reduced relative to other gnathostomes (Miles, '77) and is greatly reduced in the lepidosirenids. Several studies have focused on the structure and homologies of the hyoid arch components (Ridewood, 1894; Edgeworth, '25; Fox, '63). In Recent genera, the perichondrally ossified ceratohyals are the only bony elements of the gill arch skeleton. The shafts of the ceratohyals provide the origin for the interhyoideus and are the insertion site for the rectus cervicis. The proximal end of the ceratohyal is laterally compressed and serves as the site of attachment for two important ligaments. The fibrocartilaginous hyoid suspensory ligament (HSL, Figs. 4A, 7E) allows the ceratohyal to swing ventrally during suction feeding or respiration. The mandibulohyoid ligament (MHL, Fig. 4) runs from the posterodorsal border of the ceratohyal to the angular process of the lower jaw. The ligament leaves a prominent scar, probably the same feature as the lateral area of the ceratohyal described by Miles ('77) in *Chirodipterus* (see also Campbell and Barwick, this volume). This ligament transmits the mechanical movements of the hyoid to the lower jaw.

In *Neoceratodus*, the hyoid suspensory ligament originates from the hyosuspensory eminence of the quadrate (Miles, '77). A separate hyomandibular cartilage lies just posterior to the ligament. A separate accessory element ("symplectic") is variably present in *Neoceratodus* (see discussion in Miles, '77: 284). Distal to the shaft of the ceratohyal in *Neoceratodus* are paired, cartilaginous hypohyals and the median basibranchial (Fig. 2A). The basibranchial extends forward to support the anterior tip of the tongue (Figs. 3A, 7A). Because the anterior cartilaginous elements are bound together by connective tissue, independent movement of the ceratohyals is limited.

The hyoid arch of lepidosirenids is reduced in comparison to that of *Neoceratodus*, and consists solely of the ceratohyal: no discrete structures homologous to the hyomandibula, hypohyal, or basibranchial appear to be present. The hyoid suspensory ligament originates from the quadrate cartilage ventral to the squamosal (Fig. 7E) and not the parasphenoid as stated by Miles ('77). At their anterior ends, the ceratohyals are bound together by ligaments and the chondroid tongue pad (Fig. 3C).

The remaining visceral arches are small, cartilaginous, and "simple," being divided only into epibranchial and ceratobranchial elements. They support reduced gill filaments, the reduction being correlated with the predominance of lung breathing in lepidosirenids (Burggren and Johansen, this volume). In *Neoceratodus*, a small second basibranchial cartilage lies in the ventral midline. Lepidosirenids lack such an element.

Figure 2 shows the shapes of the external faces of the opercular and subopercular bones. In *Neoceratodus*, both lie just deep to the dermis and present their slightly convex surfaces toward the exterior. The opercular bones of lepidosirenids are smaller than those of *Neoceratodus* and their shape defines the fossa in which lies the depressor mandibulae muscle. The external faces of the opercular elements are not exposed in *Lepidosiren* and *Protopterus* but are buried beneath the muscle (Fig. 2D). Small, variably developed opercular and subopercular cartilages are associated with the posterior margins of these bones (Fig. 4A). Bridge (1898) hypothesized that these cartilages represent vestigial hyoidean rays. Whatever their homologies, their role in supporting the fleshy gill cover and defining the gill opening of lepidosirenids is significant because films of feeding show the gill cover being forcefully sucked onto the opening during hyoid depression.

Skull roof. The median anterior element in the skull roof is the dermal ethmoid (= F bone or postrostral). In *Neoceratodus*, it is thin and variably shaped. Its lateral margins meet the adjacent cartilage of the nasal capsule. Posteriorly it has a sutural connection to the frontoparietal. In lepidosirenids the dermal ethmoid is flat, triangular, and truncated at the tip. The joint with the supraorbitals is akinetic (Bemis and Lauder, '86). The lack of kinesis is noteworthy because were it to be mobile, this would offer a means of moving the vomerine teeth (see Berman, '79).

The remaining elements of the skull roof are strikingly different in *Neoceratodus* and lepidosirenids. Relative to *Neoceratodus*, the skull roof of lepidosirenids demonstrates a condition I will refer to as "emarginated" because the adductor muscles are incompletely covered by bone. Posterior to the dermal ethmoid are the paired supraorbitals (= K-M) and a median frontoparietal (= B). In *Neoceratodus*, these elements together with one or more dermosphenotics (X) and extra-

scapulars (I) form a thin roof over the adductor fossa. This roof is supported by the ascending processes of the pterygoid bones.

Neither dermosphenotics nor extrascapulars are present in the skull roof of lepidosirenids. The frontoparietal lies buried beneath the adductor muscles, and only the thin strut-like supraorbital bone covers a portion of the adductor fossa (Figs. 2C,D, 4). As a result, the jaw adductor muscles are free to bulge outwards during their contraction. The supraorbitals meet in the midline anteriorly, where they are bound together by a stout sheet of connective tissue. They are supported by the ascending process of the pterygoid; ligamentous sheets bind them to each other and to the sagittal crest of the frontoparietal. The supraorbitals and the tensile sheets of connective tissue that they support are an important site of origin for the adductor mandibulae. A flange on the ventral surface of the supraorbitals gives them a "T" cross-section, which may be interpreted as a means of stiffening the bone to resist excessive bending during contraction of the adductor muscles.

The frontoparietal is quite differently shaped in *Lepidosiren* and *Protopterus* (Fig. 6F,G). In *Protopterus*, the bone is narrow. In *Lepidosiren*, the bone spreads broadly over the otic and suspensorial regions, contacting the quadrate and squamosal, and its sagittal crest is better developed than in *Protopterus*. Perhaps the bony frontoparietal of *Lepidosiren* is well-suited for bearing the large forces associated with jaw muscle contraction, although this has not been demonstrated.

Pectoral girdle. The anatomy of dipnoan pectoral girdles has been discussed by Jarvik ('80), Rosen et al. ('81), and Campbell and Barwick (this volume). The girdle provides the origin of the rectus cervicis muscles (Fig. 5). The girdle of *Neoceratodus* includes a separate clavicle, cleithrum, and anocleithrum (Jarvik, '80). A ligament joins the anocleithrum to the otic region of the skull. In *Neoceratodus*, right and left halves of the girdle are joined by cartilage, and independent motion of the two halves of the girdle is prevented. The anocleithrum is small in *Protopterus* (Fig. 4A) and absent in *Lepidosiren* (Rosen et al., '81). Embedded in the hypaxial musculature and suspended from the skull by the girdle suspensory ligament, the girdle of *Lepidosiren* is capable of undergoing large anterior and posterior movements as documented by cine-radiography (Bishop and Foxon, '68).

Connective tissue binds the cranial rib and pectoral girdle to the adjacent thickened wall of the pericardial cavity.

Musculature

Dipnoan cranial muscles are well known (e.g., Bridge, 1898; Luther, '13; Edgeworth, '23, '26, '35; Säve-Söderbergh, '44; Fox, '65; McMahon, '69; Wiley, '79; Jollie '82; Bemis and Lauder, '86), although studies of muscle fiber architecture and histochemistry are needed. In the following brief description, the focus is on muscles that move the lower jaw and hyoid arch. Smaller muscles, such as those of the larynx or the branchial apparatus, are omitted.

For the convenience of functional analysis, the muscles are grouped in five categories (Table 2): jaw closing; jaw opening; hyoid depressing; hyoid raising; head raising (Bemis and Lauder, '86).

The components of the adductor mandibulae complex arise from two condensations in the mesenchyme. The resulting pinnate muscle has a single, stout tendon (AT, Figs. 3, 4). Fibers originate from the periosteum of the skull roofing bones, the chondrocranium, and the fascia covering the skull in lepidosirenids. In *Neoceratodus*, the adductor tendon inserts just posterior to the tooth plate. In lepidosirenids, the tendon runs to the anterior medial side of the coronoid process.

The lip retractor muscles of *Lepidosiren* and *Protopterus* are derived embryologically from the adductor muscle mass (Edgeworth, '35). *Lepidosiren* has two slips of this musculature; *Protopterus* has only one (Fig. 2D). These muscles are active during jaw adduction (McMahon, '69) and also serve to draw the upper lip closed when feeding on large prey items (Bemis and Lauder, '86).

Several muscles are potentially important in jaw opening. The geniothoracicus (GT) of lepidosirenids is homologous to the geniocoracoideus (GCr) of *Neoceratodus*. These muscles are small and strap-like in lepidosirenids but are larger in *Neoceratodus* (Fig. 3B,D). The massive rectus cervicis (RC) originates from the pectoral girdle and inserts on the ceratohyals beneath the tongue pad (Figs. 2, 3). In lepidosirenids, the depressor manidulae (DM) originates from the subopercular and opercular bones and inserts on the ventral margin of the angular process of the prearticular (Fig. 2D). Embryologically the depressor mandibulae is derived from the middle portion of the hyoid constrictor sheet

(Edgeworth, '26, '35). The muscle in *Protopterus* is pinnate, originates primarily from the operculum, and passes via a stout tendon to the retroarticular process of the lower jaw. Throughout its length, the tendon is lateral to and distinct from the mandibulohyoid ligament. Although Fox ('65) and Perkins ('72) suggested otherwise, this muscle is present only in lepidosirenids and not in *Neoceratodus* (Edgeworth, '26; Luther, '13, '38; Bemis, unpublished investigation). As noted above, each cranial rib has a joint that allows movement in the vertical plane. This joint is stabilized by the "posterior muscle of the cranial rib" (McMahon, '69). The "anterior muscle of the cranial rib" inserts on the pectoral girdle. McMahon ('69) suggested that this arrangement stabilizes the origin of the pectoral girdle during suction movements.

The intermandibularis (IM) and constrictor portion of the interhyoideus (ConH) are the principal constricting muscles according to the classification in Table 2. The intermandibularis spans between the medial surfaces of the rami, taking its origin in lepidosirenids from prominent flanges on the ventral surface of the mandible. The intermandibular muscles meet in the ventral midline, covering the course of the geniothoracicus in lepidosirenids. The intermandibular muscles of *Neoceratodus* are large and are probably important in rotating the mandible during grinding of foods. The hyoid constrictor of

TABLE 2. *Functional classification of cranial muscles*

Functional group	Principal muscles
1. Jaw closing	Adductor mandibulae
	Retractor angulae oris superficialis[1]
	Retractor angulae oris profundus[1,2]
2. Jaw opening	Geniothoracicus[1]
	Geniocoracoideus[3]
	Rectus cervicis
	Depressor mandibulae[1]
3. Jaw and hyoid raising	Intermandibularis
	Interhyoideus
	Levator hyoideus
4. Hyoid depressing	Rectus cervicis
	Other hypaxialis[4]
5. Head raising	Epaxialis

[1]Not present in *Neoceratodus*.
[2]Not present in *Protopterus*.
[3]Not present in Lepidosirenidae.
[4]Anterior and posterior muscles of the cranial rib.

Neoceratodus consists of an interhyoid portion (IH) that originates from the ceratohyal bones and a posterior constrictor portion (ConH) originating from the fascia overlying the skull roof and epaxial muscles and lying in the opercular flap. The muscular sheet is interrupted by the opercular bones and does not cover them. These muscles act to return the ceratohyals and tongue to the pre-suction position, compress food in the oral cavity, and to control valving and water flow in the opercular cavity (e.g., Dean '06, '12). As in *Neoceratodus*, the hyoid constrictor musculature of *Protopterus aethiopicus* consists of a constricting sheet (ConH) in the opercular fold and an interhyoideus portion (IH) between the ceratohyals (Fig. 2D).

The levator hyoideus originates on the ventral surface of the chondrocranium and passes ventrally to its insertion on the expanded proximal portion of the ceratohyal (Fig. 7E). Owing to its insertion on the posterior margin of the ceratohyal, the levator hyoideus acts to rotate the ceratohyal ventrally. In *Protopterus*, the levator hyoideus has a deep red color, relative to other cranial muscles, suggesting that its fibers are aerobic. Such a physiological profile would agree with a role in regular periodic ventilation of the gills and olfactory epithelium.

Epaxial muscles of *Neoceratodus* extend forward from the trunk to insert on the dorsal surface of the skull (Fig. 2B). Those of lepidosirenids cover the posterior portion of the jaw adductor muscles.

Lips, oral cavity, tongue, and gills

Importance of chondroid tissue. Non-skeletal connective tissues largely define the shapes of such functionally important components as the tongue and palatal surface. These tissues can only be studied in sections and have been neglected in most accounts of dipnoan cranial anatomy (although see Parker, 1892). The tissue referred to here as chondroid is intermediate between cartilage and a dense connective tissue. Its cells are similar to fibroblasts seen in other areas. As in cartilage, however, the ground substance of chondroid shows a positive reaction to Alcian blue at pH 1.0. Patches are walled off from surrounding connective tissues by a tough, fibrous coat; thick bundles of collagen fibers course through these tissues (TP, Fig. 7D; P, Fig. 8D).

Lips. The lips of dipnoans, particularly *Neoceratodus*, have been described and illustrated by Allis ('19), Jarvik ('42), Thomson ('65), Bertmar ('66), Panchen ('67), and Rosen et al. ('81) among others. Most of these studies are related to the problem of choanal homology. The position of the internal and external nares relative to the lips was discussed by Allis ('19, '32). Allis distinguished primary, secondary, and tertiary lips among various groups of fishes, considering the lips of Dipnoi to be "tertiary" and unique because they pass aboral to both narial openings. The possible significance of these observations would seem to be confounded by the absence of premaxillae and maxillae in most (if not all) Dipnoi (see Schultze and Campbell, this volume; Forey, this volume), and the lips have not offered real insight into the choana problem.

Despite attention to the homologies of the lips, there has been little attention paid to the functional significance of their structure. There are major differences between *Neoceratodus* and the lepidosirenids. The mouth of *Neoceratodus* has an oval opening; in lepidosirenids, it is approximately circular. *Neoceratodus* lacks both intrinsic and extrinsic labial musculature, whereas lepidosirenids have extrinsic lip retractor muscles (above).

An even more striking difference concerns the interlocking of upper and lower lips. In lepidosirenids, the margin of the upper lip curls laterally around that of the lower along more than three-quarters of its length. This "zip-lock seal" prevents lateral influx of water during suction feeding. The arrangement in lepidosirenids is anatomically more complex than the flaps at the angles of the mouth in *Neoceratodus*, *Polypterus* (Lauder, '80b) or salamander larvae (Özeti and Wake, '69; Shaffer and Lauder, '85). The upper lip is supported by a rod of chondroid tissue (ULC), which gives the curl its shape. Bertmar ('66) homologized this rod with the upper labial cartilage (although see Miles, '77, for another view). At the angle of the mouth, the rod meets and fuses with the antorbital process. Anteriorly, the rod ends at the level of the anterior nasal opening, where it merges with dense connective tissue. In addition to collagen fiber bundles, the chondroid tissue of the upper lip has numerous long, branched fibers. On the basis of their staining reaction with Verhoeff's iodine stain, these are probably elastic fibers (Bemis, '82).

The lower lip does not contain a comparable support bar, although its medial edge is well-defined, with a slight curl that mates with that of the upper lip. The significance of this arrangement for focusing suction and increasing the velocity of the water stream is probably great, but their design also allows the grasping of larger prey items, with the subsequent dislocaton of the upper and lower lip folds. Such dislocation is easily observed as specimens feed on large prey items. The elastic fibers presumbly aid in recovering the closed position.

Oral cavity, tongue, and sublingual region. In cross section, the oral cavity of *Neoceratodus* is broad, whereas that of lepidosirenids is an elongate, inverted U. The epithelial lining of the mouth forms ridges and folds running along the axis of the head, with many small papillae scattered over the palatal and lingual surfaces. The palate is supported by the parasphenoid bone (*Neoceratodus*) or by the parasphenoid together with portions of the chondrocranium and adjacent dense connective tissues (lepidosirenids). The sides of the cavity are rigidly supported by the ventral wings of the pterygoid bones.

In *Neoceratodus*, the tongue is broadest at its base (Fig. 3B). It narrows as it extends forward in the lingual furrow between the right and left rami of the jaw (Figs. 3A,B, 7A). Only at its base does it contact the sides of the oral cavity, and there is an extensive free margin. The tongue of *Neoceratodus* is supported by the ceratohyals and by the hypo- and basi-branchial elements. There is a chondroid "tongue pad," but it is not as extensive as in lepidosirenids.

Lepidosirenids have large, rectangular tongues that are stiffened by the tongue pad (TP, Fig. 7D). The tongue of *Protopterus* was described by Parker (1892). In dorsal view, it is stubby and U-shaped with crests along its lateral margins (Fig. 3C,D). At its anterior end, the tongue fits snugly against the posterior surfaces of the prearticular tooth plates. The tongue pad is most extensive in the region anterior and lateral to the ceratohyals and rectus cervicis muscles but extends posteriorly to support the lateral crests of the tongue. A section through the tongue pad shows numerous collagen fiber bundles connecting its outer fibrous coats (Fig. 7D). When fresh, the tongue pad is springy and resilient, and it forces the lateral crests of the tongue to seal against the walls of the oral cavity. The tongue presses so closely against the roof and sides of the cavity that it leaves only a small amount of dead space in the mouth.

The structure of the sublingual region allows rapid ventral movement of the tongue and hyoid. Ventral and posterior to the tongue in the living genera is an area of sublingual loose connective tissue (LC, Fig. 3A,C) that provides a space into which the tongue can move as the ceratohyals rotate ventrally (Bemis and Lauder, '86). The skin also accommodates depression of the hyoid. In *Neoceratodus*, the intermandibular scales are smaller in size than those of the throat region. In lepidosirenids, the skin between the rami of the jaws lacks scales altogether (Fig. 8A). This culminates the reduction in gular plates and scalation that has occurred during dipnoan evolution (Westoll, '49).

Tooth plate pads. In life, the blades of the tooth plates are surrounded by pads (Parker, 1892; Röse, 1892; Bridge, 1898). In surface view, only the apical ridges of the plate project from the surface of the surrounding tissues in both the lower jaw (Figs. 3B,D, 7A) and palate (Fig. 8C). The extent of the pads can be appreciated by comparing the tooth plates in Figure 6 with the lower jaws in Figure 3. The epithelium covering the pads has taste buds and many goblet cells. It is supported by underlying chondroid tissue. The chondroid is very densely fibered (Fig. 8D) yet, when fresh, the pads are easily deformed when pressed upon. The pads are interpreted as important in holding food when it is not completely engaged by the tooth plates.

Gills. In most fish, gills provide a resistance to flow between the buccal and opercular cavities that keeps the buccal and opercular pressure peaks out of phase (Lauder, '83). Relative to *Neoceratodus*, lepidosirenids show a great reduction of the gill rakers (Fig. 3B,D). Due to the larger gaps, the buccal and opercular cavities are in relatively open communication. Support for this comes from films showing that strong suction movements in the buccal cavity also suck the opercular flap against the opercular opening. However, McMahon ('69) documented differential pressures in the buccal and opercular cavities during some phases of the respiratory cycle of *Protopterus*.

Ecological information

Dipnoan tooth plates are usually regarded as adaptations for feeding on "small molluscs and other invertebrates" (Romer, '66:76). Available ecological data generally support this interpretation, although the emphasis should probably be on the small size of the food rather than its hardness. Field data show that a great diversity of foods is eaten, including plants and scavenged food items; living lungfishes are usually classified as omnivores (Johnels and Svensson, '54; Curry-Lindahl, '56; Thomson, '69).

The diet of *Protopterus aethiopicus* is most completely known. Corbet ('61) examined stomach and spiral valve contents of a large series (N = 335, 90.1% of which had identifiable remains in the digestive tract) from Lake Victoria and the Uganda Nile. His study of the Lake Victoria population documented an ontogenetic shift toward preference for molluscs. The small specimens were taken in marginal swamps of the lake; larger specimens came from open water. An abbreviated summary of his detailed breakdown of gut contents for fishes collected in three habitats is included in Table 3. Small individuals ate a variety of hard and soft food items, including insects, scavenged fish, and some plant material, whereas larger individuals ate a large number of molluscs (Table 3). The largest individuals had fed almost entirely on large pelecypods: "Records suggest that lungfishes of 70 cm and over may eat more pelecypods than those below this size. If this is so, it may be a simple expression of the size of the mouth and the strength of the jaws, which are used to crush the molluscs it eats. It is possible that the largest pelecypods, such as *Mutela*, may become increasingly important to very large *Protopterus* which are not well represented in my sample." (Corbet, '61:17; also Greenwood, this volume).

Young *Lepidosiren* readily eat soft food items in captivity, and such prey items as worms and insect larvae are probably important in the wild (Carter and Beadle, '30), although adult *Lepidosiren* do eat the hard-shelled snail, *Ampullaria* (Lankester, 1896). *Neoceratodus* eats large amounts of plant material in addition to small snails and other foods (Kemp, this volume).

Behavior and functional morphology of feeding

Overview

In all three genera food items are brought into the mouth by suction and then masticated before being swallowed (Thomson, '69). These basic feeding behaviors in lepidosirenids were described soon after living specimens reached Europe in the 1850s: "I have seen an active little minnow, an inch and a half or two inches from the mouth of the *Lepidosiren* [=*Protopterus annectens*], suddenly sucked in . . .The prey is drawn into the mouth with immense rapidity, by depressing the hyoid bone, and making a gulp rather than a snap." (McDonnell, 1860:97); "In feeding, this creature masticates the food much, frequently putting it forward almost quite out of its mouth and then gradually chewing it back again . . ." (Grey, 1856:347, citing a letter from A.D. Bartlett). Dean ('06, '12) briefly described feeding in captive *Neoceratodus*, noting that the fish take food "blunderingly" ('06:172). Additional descriptions of feeding behavior including field observations are provided in several accounts (e.g., *Lepidosiren*, Carter and Beadle, '30; *Protopterus*, Curry-Lindahl, '56; Johnels and Svensson, '54; *Neoceratodus*, Kemp, this volume).

Although there are several relevant studies of the functional morphology of the living genera, we still lack cinematographic and electromyographic studies for *Neoceratodus* and *Protopterus* and a complete cine-radiographic study of feeding in any species. Per-

TABLE 3. *Body size and percentage occurrence of different food types of* Protopterus aethiopicus *in Lake Victoria*[1]

	Habitat type		
	Marginal swamp	Mixed lake bottom	Hard lake bottom
Range in body size (N)	3–32 mm (52)	43–118 mm (145)	49–130 mm (83)
Percentage of food types			
Arthropods	14	—	—
Insects	83	20.0	10
Gastropods	8	91.7	92
Pelecypods	2	83.4	70
Fishes	4	30.3	16
Plants	22	2.0	7

[1]Modified from Corbet, '61.

Fig. 9. Prey capture by *Protopterus*. A) When hunting for prey on the bottom of aquaria, *Protopterus* and *Lepidosiren* typically arch the anterior portion of the trunk. B) Having located the prey, the hyoid is rapidly de-

pressed, drawing the food into the mouth. Elapsed time 400 milliseconds (not representative of the amount of time required to produce suction).

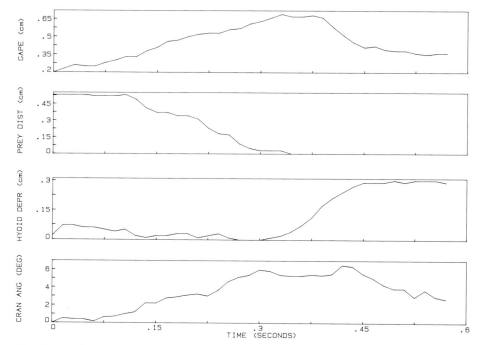

Fig. 10. Kinematics of a successful prey capture by *Lepidosiren* feeding on a worm traced from a film taken at 200 frames per second (from Bemis and Lauder, '86). Mouth opening as indicated by the gape profile steadily increases as the food moves steadily into the mouth.

Although there is a slight initial depression of the hyoid apparatus, hyoid depression does not peak until after peak gape. Head raising at the cranio-vertebral joint occurs during mouth opening.

kins' ('72) broad study of the feeding system included anatomy, some motion analysis and cine-radiography, with the goal of interpreting the cranial anatomy of fossil dipnoans. Studies of lepidosirenid respiratory mechanics employing cinematography and radiogra-

phy (Bishop and Foxon, '68) and cine-radiography and electromyography (McMahon, '69) have provided insight into cranial function. Bemis and Lauder ('86) used cinematography and electromyography to study feeding in small *Lepidosiren paradoxa*.

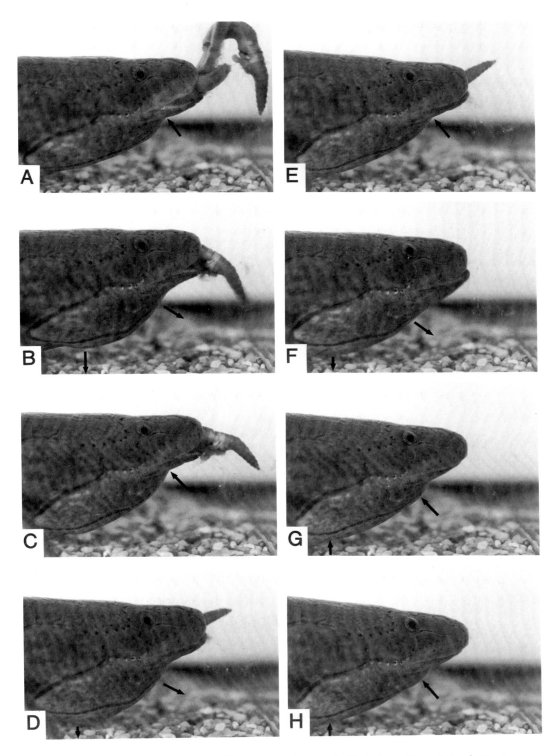

Fig. 11. A series of chews and food transport phases in *Protopterus*. Elapsed time between frames is 250 milliseconds. A) Chew. B) Inward transport; note expansion and contraction of hyoid region. C) Chew. D) Inward transport. E) Chew. F) Inward transport. G,H) Constriction.

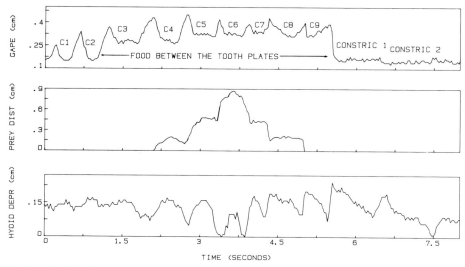

Fig. 12. Records of a chewing bout by *Lepidosiren*, traced from a film taken at 100 frames per second (modified from Bemis and Lauder, '86). The nine chews in this bout each consist of an adduction phase, during which the gape was minimal, and a transport phase, during which the mouth was opened and the food was transported. The prey was partially expelled from the mouth during chewing. During the transport phases, raising the hyoid transported the food forward; depression of the hyoid transported it back into the mouth. In the two constrictions that followed, the food was squeezed between the tongue and palate, after which it was swallowed.

A complete feeding event includes five behaviors: 1) food detection; 2) food intake; 3) chewing-adduction; 4) chewing-transport; and 5) constriction. Each of these is discussed in series, using Figures 9–14. Due to the absence of published information for *Neoceratodus*, the focus is on *Protopterus* and *Lepidosiren*. For additional details see Bemis and Lauder ('86).

The events of feeding

Food detection in captive *Protopterus* can occur very rapidly, and trained specimens will capture prey dropped into the open water column. Small *Lepidosiren* have been observed to feed on food floating on the surface. More typically, however, food is taken from the bottom. Olfaction appears to be the main method of food location. *Protopterus* irrigates the olfactory epithelium by depressing the hyoid while the mouth is closed, forcing water through the nasal sacs. These olfactory cycles are temporally unrelated to respiratory activity, and their frequency increases during the search for food (Derivot et al., '79).

In a typical prey capture from the bottom, the trunk is arched and the head is held at an angle to the bottom (Fig. 9). The mouth is opened, the hyoid region is depressed rapidly, and the prey item is sucked into the mouth. Cine-radiography of respiratory movements of *Lepidosiren* (Bishop and Foxon, '68) showed that after peak hyoid depression, the pectoral girdle moves ventrally and posteriorly to draw air into the posterior part of the buccal cavity. Films of feeding suggest that comparable movement of the girdle also occurs during food capture and transport phases, although this should be confirmed with X-ray cinematography. Figure 10 shows the kinematics of a typical prey capture in *Lepidosiren*. Although there is inter- and intra-individual variation in the speed of the strike and in the gape profile, food intake in *Lepidosiren* permits two important generalizations: 1) the start of mouth opening involves slight depression of the hyoid, although *peak* hyoid depression occurs after the peak gape; and 2) mouth opening is achieved by elevation of the head as well as depression of the lower jaw (Bemis and Lauder, '86).

Once food has been taken into the mouth, a variable period of time may pass before the start of the first chewing bout (Fig. 13). Each bout comprises a variable number of adduction cycles or chews (Fig. 13), each of which consists of alternating adduction and transport phases. In the adduction phase, food is

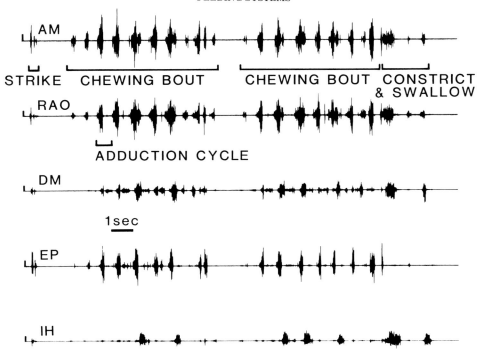

Fig. 13. Electromyographic records of a complete feeding sequence in *Lepidosiren* (from Bemis and Lauder, '86). Each chewing bout includes a series of adduction cycles each of which has an adduction phase and a transport phase. See text for further description.

crushed between the tooth plates, and strong activity is recorded from the jaw adductor musculature. During the transport phase the lower jaw is depressed, and food is transported either forward in the buccal cavity to a position between the tooth plates or drawn back into the buccal cavity. Forward transport is accomplished by raising the hyoid apparatus. The open mouth permits a forward flow of water and food. Posterior transport is caused by depressing the hyoid (Fig. 11). Typically, forward transport occurs early in a given chewing bout (e.g., chewing cycles 4–6 in Fig. 12). After several successive chews and forward transports, the prey item is drawn back into the buccal cavity (e.g., chewing cycles 7–9 in Fig. 12).

A chewing bout is usually followed by a constriction, during which the jaws are tightly closed and the hyoid region is compressed; this compacts the prey item against the palate (Figs. 11, 13). *Lepidosiren* usually engages in additional chewing bouts but these are eventually followed by a strong final constriction and swallowing.

Of the three muscles that could open the lower jaw in *Lepidosiren* (Table 2), electro-

myography confirms that the depressor mandibulae is consistently active during jaw depression in both suction and chewing-transport; it may be the most important jaw opening muscle (Bemis and Lauder, '86). In McMahon's ('69) study of *Protopterus* ventilation, however, the depressor was found to be active only during maximal movements of the jaw. Activity in the depressor likely relates to the speed of jaw opening. During slow suction feeding, the electromyographic activity in the depressor mandibulae is reduced, whereas greater activity is recorded during more rapid suctions or a series of chews (Bemis and Lauder, '86).

COMMENTS ON THE EVOLUTION OF DIPNOAN FEEDING SYSTEMS

Denison ('74:31) provided a succinct description of autostyly and tooth plates in the evolution of dipnoan feeding systems:

The most distinctive characteristics of Dipnoi, present even in the earliest members of the group, are modifications of the skull and jaws that are related presumably to a particular manner of feeding. The cranium is sol-

A. SUCTION

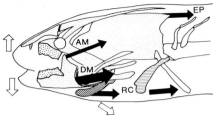

B. CHEWING - ADDUCTION

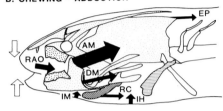

C. CHEWING - TRANSPORT

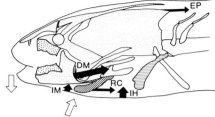

D. CONSTRICTION

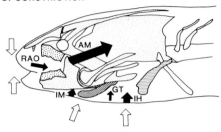

Fig. 14. Summary of the kinematic and electromyographic events for *Lepidosiren* feeding on earthworms (from Bemis and Lauder, '86). External movements are indicated by white arrows; lines of action and relative levels of electromyographic activity of the muscles are shown with black arrows. During suction, the mouth is opened by the depressor mandibulae (DM) and rectus cervicis (RC) muscles. The former muscle acts directly on the lower jaw while the latter acts via the hyoid and mandibulohyoid ligament. Anatomically, the geniothoracicus (GT) muscle could also function in jaw opening; however, electromyography shows it to be relatively inactive during this period. In the adduction phase of chewing, both the adductor mandibulae anterior and posterior (AM) and the retractor angulae oris (RAO) are strongly active. Food transport occurs by opening the mouth and then raising (interhyoideus, IH, and intermandibularis, IM) or lowering (rectus cervicis, RC) the hyoid apparatus. During a constriction, all of the muscles that close the mouth and raise the hyoid are active.

idly constructed with a completely fused, holostylic [= autostylic] jaw suspension. The lower jaws are short and articulate far forward, resulting in a small gape and a powerful bite. The marginal jaw bones and teeth are reduced or lost, and paired tooth plates with radiating ridges and grooves are commonly developed on the pterygoids and prearticulars. All of these characters are clearly related to an adaptation for powerful jaw action, often for crushing food, though not necessarily hard food as is sometimes assumed.

The skulls and tooth plates of fossil lungfishes are of great systematic importance, but there has been much disagreement about primitive characters of the feeding system. The recognition of the plesiomorphic condition of the skull in Dipnoi is treated in several recent papers (Miles, '77; Rosen et al., '81; Schultze and Campbell, this volume; Campbell and Barwick, this volume). It is now widely held that dipnoans evolved from a non-autostylic ancestor. Embryology suggests that autostyly is distinct in holocephal-

ans, tetrapods, and dipnoans (Schultze, this volume). However, this view is not universally accepted (Jarvik, '80).

A second debate centers on the inferred dentition of the earliest dipnoans. Dipnoans with tooth plates are almost certainly monophyletic. Examples of this lineage include genera such as *Dipterus*, *Gnathorhiza*, *Neoceratodus*, *Lepidosiren*, and *Protopterus* (Fig. 1). The basic phylogenetic problem stems from the fact that many Devonian lungfishes have neither tooth plates nor discrete teeth and have instead a series of bulbous crushing surfaces on the palate (e.g., *Dipnorhynchus sussmilchi*) or a shagreen of scattered denticles on the palate, as well as denticle-bearing basibranchial elements (e.g., *Griphognathus whitei*). Miles ('77) argued that the shagreen of denticles was plesiomorphic for dipnoans. Evidence favoring this interpretation comes from outgroup comparison, specifically observations on the palatal denticles of elasmobranchs reported by Nelson ('70).

In contrast, Campbell and Barwick ('83, this volume) and Marshall (this volume) argue that the bulbous crushing surfaces of *Dipnorhynchus sussmilchi* are primitive, and that the forms with denticulated palates form a distinct lineage, termed "denticulated" or "denticle shedding." Central to their phylogenetic interpretion is the function of the feeding system in such Devonian genera as *Griphognathus*. According to their model, *Griphognathus* processed food by rasping it between the denticulated basibranchial tooth plate and the palate. To accommodate growth, it was necessary to shed and replace large sheets of denticles.

Despite the important differences between tooth-plated and denticulated dipnoans there are four primitive features of the feeding system of living lungfishes that likely apply to all Dipnoi. These are: 1) Food intake occurs by suction feeding with a unidirectional flow of water; 2) elevation of the head is caused by the epaxial muscles during the mouth opening phase; 3) the hyoid apparatus produces the suction, and together with the mandibulohyoid ligament, offers one means for depressing the lower jaw; 4) peak hyoid depression occurs after peak gape (Bemis and Lauder, '86). All four of these features are present in primitive actinopterygians and are probably plesiomorphic at the teleostome level (Lauder, '80b). Comparable studies of the feeding system of aquatic ambystomatid salamanders (Shaffer and Lauder, '85) confirm that tetrapods retain these features.

In addition to these four primitive features, feeding systems of living dipnoans have many specializations, generally of unknown hierarchical level. The cranial ribs are particularly intriguing. There is a surprisingly small literature on the ribs. My interpretation, derived largely from the X-ray cinematography of Bishop and Foxon ('68) and McMahon ('69), is that the ribs of lepidosirenids are stabilized in a variety of positions relative to the skull where they provide an anchor for the pectoral girdle during strong hyoid depression. However, experimental verification of this idea is needed. Cranial ribs are also present in fossil Dipnoi (e.g., *Scaumenacia*, Goodrich, '09). *Polypterus* and *Latimeria* lack cranial ribs, and no tetrapod has this specialization. It is therefore likely that they evolved within Dipnoi. Hypertrophy of the cranial ribs in lepidosirenids is correlated with reduction of the pectoral girdle. Their assistance in anchoring the girdle may allow it to support an enlarged hyoid depressing musculature.

There are many unanswered questions about the functional morphology of feeding in *Neoceratodus*, but there is no doubt that the most important difference between lepidosirenids and *Neoceratodus* concerns the ability of the latter to grind food between the tooth plates (Perkins, '72). In lepidosirenids, the tooth plates and lower jaw are used only in cutting and crushing of food. No grinding of the upper and lower tooth plates is possible in lepidosirenids because of the restrictive jaw joint and solid symphysis. Rotation of the rami of the mandible about their long axes is believed by Perkins ('72) to yield the grinding mode in *Neoceratodus*. Primitively, however, the mandibular symphysis of dipnoans was solid and would not have permitted such axial rotation. Wear patterns on the tooth plates of plesiomorphic genera such as *Speonesydrion* suggest that retraction of the mandible produced grinding (Campbell and Barwick, '84). In this case, Campbell and Barwick ('84) model grinding as having occurred by the unilateral activity of the jaw adductors, to rotate the entire mandible (rather than the individual rami) approximately 4°. In future work on the evolution of dipnoan feeding, it will be particularly important to document feeding function in *Neoceratodus* for comparisons to fossil taxa.

The emarginated skull roof of lepidosirenids poses some intriguing questions. As in tetrapods that crush food items (e.g., skinks, Gans, de Vree and Carrier, '85), lepidosirenids have extremely powerful jaw closing muscles. Films of lepidosirenid feeding show that during adduction, strong bulging of jaw muscles occurs. Much of the adductor musculature originates on the supraorbital or the stout aponeurosis which attaches to its lateral and medial borders. The stiffened "T" cross-section of the supraorbital allows it to function as a beam from which the tensile elements that support the large adductor muscles are suspended. The functional role and evolution of fenestration or emargination of the skull roof have long been of interest to vertebrate anatomists (e.g., Zangerl, '48). Models to explain the loss of bone in the temporal region of tetrapods often emphasize the importance of "jaw muscle bulging" as an adaptive aspect of cranial fenestration (Gregory and Adams, '15; Frazzetta, '68). There are alternative models to explain the loss of bone in the temporal region, including the suggestion that not making unnecessary bone conserves energy (Fox, '64) and the hypothesis that fenestrations allow stronger attachments between bones and tendons (Frazzetta, '68). Oxnard ('71) suggested that in situations where net tensile forces are developed normal to the surface of a skeletal element, the bone will be replaced by a fibrous sheet. It is difficult to test these hypotheses, and the original adaptive value of fenestration (if, in fact, there is only one explanation) remains uncertain. However, the arrangement of the supraorbital in lepidosirenids does permit very large adductors that undergo extensive bulging. Once an open skull roof first appeared, the potential existed for further expansion and overgrowth of the adductors to cover the posterior surface of the skull, as in the salamander, *Amphiuma*. Another variant on the problem of situating large jaw adductors is seen in the caecilian *Dermophis*. *Dermophis* retains a solid skull roof over a small adductor fossa, but uses a portion of the hyoid arch musculature located behind the skull to provided additional jaw closing action (Bemis et al., '83).

Mastication requires not only powerful jaw adductors but also a means for transporting and positioning food directly between the tooth plates. Tetrapods that masticate use the tongue and cheeks to transport and place food (e.g., Gans et al., '78; Hiiemae and Crompton, '85). As the tongue lacks intrinsic musculature, lungfishes are limited to an imprecise transport system; they move food hydraulically by motions of the entire hyoid apparatus (Bemis and Lauder, '86).

The size and origin of the depressor mandibulae suggest that it is a synapomorphy of *Lepidosiren* and *Protopterus*. *Neoceratodus* lacks the muscle (Edgeworth, '26; Bemis, unpublished investigation). Two lines of evidence suggest that *Neoceratodus* retains the plesiomorphic condition for dipnoans: 1) Outgroup forms such as *Polypterus*, *Lepisosteus*, and *Latimeria* lack the muscle; and 2) the fossil record shows that the opercular bones underwent both reductions and losses during dipnoan evolution (Westoll, '49). The four opercular and gular elements of *Uranolophus* and other Devonian lungfishes form a bony opercular cover, similar to that of other plesiomorphic osteichthyans. In *Uranolophus*, these bones are covered with dermal ornamentation (Denison, '68), suggesting that the hyoid constrictor musculature did not overlie these bony elements. Thus, phylogenetically primitive lungfishes were similar to *Neoceratodus* in lacking a depressor mandibulae.

A system mediated by the mandibulohyoid ligament is the only means of lower jaw depression in *Polypterus*, *Lepisosteus*, and *Latimeria*. Presumably, the primitive gnathostome jaw-opening system consisted of strap muscles that inserted on the lower jaw and hyoid (Lauder, '80a,b, '85). *Neoceratodus* presumably depresses the mandible by such a mechanism, and it is interesting that the geniothoracicus of *Neoceratodus* is larger than that of lepidosirenids (Fig. 3).

Specializations of hyoid arch musculature for depressing the lower jaw have arisen independently several times in vertebrate evolution. The levator operculi of teleosts, which develops from the dorsal portion of the hyoid constrictor sheet (Edgeworth, '35), moves the elements of the opercular chain system to produce mouth opening (Liem, '70). The topographically and functionally comparable depressor mandibulae of salamanders develops during ontogeny by the shift of the insertion of the levator hyoideus (Edgeworth, '26, '35). The digastricus of mammals involves mandibular and hyoid arch components, both of which are used in jaw opening (e.g., Gorniak, '85).

Finally, the presence of an autostylic jaw suspension has had major functional consequences, some of which have greatly constrained subsequent evolution of the dipnoan head. This is most obvious in the case of lepidosirenids. Apart from its obvious role in supporting the upper jaw, autostyly restricts the possible degrees of freedom at the jaw joint and effectively eliminates the possibility that the oral volume might be increased by flaring of the suspensorium (as in teleosts). Evolution of a more powerful suction feeding system is thus restricted to a path of increasing the mobility of the hyoid apparatus. As in actinopterygians (Schaeffer and Rosen, '61; Lauder, '82), the "freeing up" of skeletal components during dipnoan evolution has been important in this. Several factor together produce the powerful and highly specialized suction system of lepidosirenids: 1) The distensibility of the hyoid region is increased by the loss of scales; 2) simplification of the hyoid apparatus and elongation of the ceratohyal increases the hyoid's ventral travel; and 3) loss of the bony attachment of the pectoral girdle to the skull and use of the cranial rib to draw the entire hyoid apparatus caudally further increase the working distance of the hyoid.

CONCLUSIONS

The major components of the feeding system of living dipnoans are autostyly and tooth plates. Together, these features largely determine the special cranial morphology of dipnoans because they require a suite of related characters. Over and above these features, however, *Neoceratodus* and the lepidosirenids show many important differences in cranial anatomy and function. Key points are: 1) Dipnoans evolved from a non-autostylic ancestor; 2) dipnoans with tooth plates are monophyletic; 3) the skeleton of the hyoid arch was reduced during dipnoan evolution but increased its possibilities for ventral excursion; 4) the cranial roofing bones and opercular series were reduced, with the consequence that lepidosirenids can have a depressor mandibulae muscle on the outside of the opercular bones and a large adductor mandibulae unrestricted by the skull roof; 5) cranial ribs are unique to dipnoans and probably enlarged to facilitate hyoid depression; 6) low jaw elements were lost and rotation of the rami became important in the lineage leading to *Neoceratodus*, whereas stabilization of the rami became important in lepidosirenids; and 7) lepidosirenids have a highly specialized feeding apparatus with respect to other dipnoans with tooth plates.

ACKNOWLEDGMENTS

This study was supported by a Healey Endowment Grant and Biological Research Support Grants (NIH RR07048-19) through the University of Massachusetts. James Ryan drew the figures. Carl Gans, Norman Kemp, David Klingener, Karel Liem, Glenn Northcutt, Eric Findeis, and Catherine Tannert provided discussions and helpful criticism. I am particularly grateful to Tom Bemis for help with many aspects of the work.

LITERATURE CITED

Agar, W.E. (1906) The development of the skull and visceral arches in *Lepidosiren* and *Protopterus*. Trans. R. Soc. Edinburgh *45*:49–64.

Agassiz, L. (1833) Recherches sur les Poisson Fossiles. Vol 3. Neuchâtel: Imprimerie de Petitpierre.

Allis, E.P. (1919) The lips and the narial appertures in the gnathostome fishes. J. Morphol. *32*:145–205.

Allis, E.P. (1932) Concerning the nasal apertures, the lachrymal canal and the bucco-pharyngeal upper lip. J. Anat. *66*:650–658.

de Beer, G.R. (1937) The Development of the Vertebrate Skull. London: Oxford University Press.

Bemis, W.E. (1982) Studies on the Evolutionary Morphology of Lepidosirenid Lungfish (Pisces: Dipnoi). Phd Dissertation, University of California, Berkeley.

Bemis, W.E. (1984a) Morphology and growth of lepidosirenid lungfish tooth plates (Pisces: Dipnoi). J. Morphol. *179*:73–93.

Bemis, W.E. (1984b) Paedomorphosis and the evolution of the Dipnoi. Paleobiology *10*:293–307.

Bemis, W.E., and G.V. Lauder (1986) Morphology and function of the feeding apparatus of the lungfish, *Lepidosiren* paradoxa (Dipnoi). J. Morphol. *187*:81–108.

Bemis, W.E., K. Schwenk, and M.H. Wake (1983) Morphology and function of the feeding apparatus in the caecilian, *Dermophis mexicanus* (Amphibia, Gymnophiona). Zool. J. Linn. Soc. *77*:75–96.

Berman, D.S. (1968) Lungfish from the Lueders formation (Lower Permian, Texas) and the *Gnathorhiza*-lepidosirenid ancestry questioned. J. Paleontol. *42*:827–835.

Berman, D.S. (1976) Cranial morphology of the Lower Permian lungfish *Gnathorhiza* (Osteichthyes: Dipnoi). J. Paleontol. *50*:1020–1033.

Berman, D.S. (1979) *Gnathorhiza bothrotreta* from the Lower Permian Abo Formation of New Mexico. Ann. Carnegie Mus. *48*:211–230.

Bertmar, G. (1966) The development of the skeleton, blood-vessels and nerves in the dipnoan snout, with a discussion on the homology of the dipnoan posterior nostrils. Acta Zool. Stockh. *47*:82–150.

Bischoff, T.L.W. (1840) *Lepidosiren paradoxa*. Anatomisch Untersucht und Beschrieben. Leipzig: Leopold Voss.

Bishop, I.R., and G.E.H. Foxon (1968) The mechanism of breathing in the South American lungfish, *Lepidosiren paradoxa*: A radiological study. J. Zool. Lond. *154*:263–271.

Bridge, T.W. (1898) On the morphology of the skull in the Paraguayan *Lepidosiren* and in other dipnoids. Trans. Zool. Soc. Lond. *14*:325–376.

Campbell, K.S.W., and R.E. Barwick (1982) The neurocranium of the primitive dipnoan *Dipnorhynchus sussmilichi* (Etheridge). J. Vert. Paleontol. *2*:286–327.

Campbell, K.S.W., and R.E. Barwick (1983) Early evolution of dipnoan dentitions and a new genus *Speonesydrion*. Mem. Ass. Australas. Paleontols. *1*:17–49.

Campbell, K.S.W., and R.E. Barwick (1984) The choana, maxillae, premaxillae, and anterior palatal bones of early dipnoans. Proc. Linn. Soc. N.S.W. *107*:147–170.

Carlson, K.J. (1968) The skull morphology and estivation burrows of the Permian lungfish, *Gnathorhiza serrata*. J. Geol. *76*:641–663.

Carter, G.S., and L.C. Beadle (1930) Notes on the habits and development of *Lepidosiren paradoxa*. J. Linn. Soc. Lond. (Zool.) *37*:197–203.

Compagno, L.J.V. (1979) Coelacanths: Shark relatives or bony fishes? Occ. Pap. Calif. Acad. Sci. *134*:45–52.

Corbet, P.S. (1961) The food of non-cichlid fishes in the Lake Victoria basin, with remarks on their evolution and adaptation to lacustrine conditions. J. Linn. Soc. Lond. (Zool.) *37*:197–203.

Curry-Lindahl, K. (1956) On the ecology, feeding behavior and territoriality of the African lungfish, *Protopterus aethiopicus* Heckel. Ark. Zool. *9*:479–497.

Dean, B. (1906) Notes on the living specimens of the Australian lungfish, *Ceratodus fosteri* in the Zoological Society's collection. Proc. Zool. Soc. Lond. *1906*:168–178.

Dean, B. (1912) Additional notes on the living specimens of the Australian lungfish (*Ceratodus forsteri*) in the collection of the Zoological Society of London. Proc. Zool. Soc. Lond. *1912*:607–612.

Denison, R.H. (1968) Early Devonian lungfishes from Wyoming, Utah and Idaho. Fieldiana (Geology) *17*:353–413.

Denison, R.H. (1974) The structure and evolution of teeth in lungfishes. Fieldiana Geol. *33*:31–59.

Derivot, J.H., M. Dupé, and R. Godet (1979) Anatomie

functionelle de l'organe olfactif de *Protopterus annectens* Owen (Dipneustes): Contribution à la connaisance du méchanisme d'irrigation de l'organe olfactif. Acta Zool. Stockh. *60*:251–257.

Edgeworth, F.H. (1923) On the development of the hypobranchial, branchial, and laryngeal muscles of *Ceratodus*. With a note on the development of the quadrate and epihyal. Q. J. Microsc. Sci. *67*:325–368.

Edgeworth, F.H. (1925) On the hyomandibula of Selachii, Teleostomi and *Ceratodus*. J. Anat. Lond. *60*:173–193.

Edgeworth, F.H. (1926) On the development of the cranial muscles in *Protopterus* and *Lepidosiren*. Trans. R. Soc. Edinburgh *54*:719–734.

Edgeworth, F.H. (1935) The Cranial Muscles of Vertebrates. Cambridge: Cambridge University Press.

Forster-Cooper, C. (1937) The Middle Devonian fish fauna of Achanarras. Trans. R. Soc. Edinburgh *59*:223–239.

Fox. H. (1963) The hyoid of *Neoceratodus* and a consideration of its homology in urodele amphibians. Proc. Zool. Soc. Lond. *141*:803–810.

Fox, H. (1965) Early development of the head and pharynx of *Neoceratodus* with a consideration of its phylogeny. J. Zool. Lond. *146*:470–554.

Fox, R.C. (1964) The adductor muscles of the jaw in some primitive reptiles. Univ. Kansas Mus. Nat. Hist. *12*:657–680.

Frazzetta, T.H. (1968) Adaptive problems and possibilities in the temporal fenestration of tetrapod skulls J. Morphol. *125*:145–158.

Gaffney, E.S. (1979) Tetrapod monophyly: A phylogenetic analysis. Bull. Carnegie Mus. Nat. Hist. *13*:92–105.

Gans, C. (1974) Biomechanics: An Approach to Vertebrate Biology. Philadelphia: Lippincott.

Gans, C., F. De Vree, and G. Gorniak (1978) Analysis of mammalian masticatory mechanisms: Progress and problems. Anat. Histol. Embriol. *7*:226–244.

Gans, C., F. De Vree, and D. Carrier (1985) Usage pattern of the complex masticatory muscles in the shingleback lizard, *Trachydosaurus rugosus:* A model for muscle placement. Am. J. Anat. *173*:219–240.

Gardiner, B.G. (1983) Gnathostome vertebrae and the classification of the Amphibia. Zool. J. Linn. Soc. *79*:1–59.

Goodrich, E.S. (1909) Vertebrata Craniata, 1st Fasicle: Cyclostomes and Fishes. In E.R. Lankester (ed.): A Treatise on Zoology, Part IX. London: Black.

Goodrich, E.S. (1925) On the cranial roofing bones in the Dipnoi. J. Linn. Soc. Lond. (Zool.) *36*:78–86.

Goodrich, E.S. (1930) Studies on the Structure and Development of Vertebrates. London: Macmillan.

Gorniak, G.C. (1985) Trends in the action of mammalian masticatory muscles. Am. Zool. *25*:331–337.

Gray, J.E. (1856) Observations on a living African *Lepidosiren* in the Crystal Palace. Proc. Zool. Soc. Lond. *24*:342–348.

Gregory, W.K., and L.A. Adams (1915) The temporal fossae of vertebrates in relation to the jaw muscles. Science *41*:763–765.

Günther, A. (1871) Description of *Ceratodus*, a genus of ganoid fishes recently discovered in rivers of Queensland, Australia. Phil. Trans. R. Soc. *B161*:511–571.

Hiiemae, K.M., and A.W. Crompton (1985) Mastication, food transport, and swallowing. In M. Hildebrand, D.M. Bramble, K. Liem, and D.B. Wake (eds): Functional Vertebrate Morphology. Cambridge: Harvard University Press.

Hildebrand, M., D.M. Bramble, K. Liem, and D.B. Wake (eds.) (1985) Functional Vertebrate Morphology. Cambridge: Harvard University Press.

Holmes, B. (1985) Are lungfishes the sister group of tetrapods? Biol. J. Linn. Soc. *25*:379–397.

Holmgren, N. (1949) Contributions to the question of the origin of the tetrapods. Acta Zool. Stockh. *30*:459–484.

Holmgren, N., and E.A. Stensiö (1936) Kranium und Visceralskelett der Akranier, Cyclostomen und Fische. In L. Bolk, E. Göppert, E. Kallius, and W. Lubosch (eds): Handbuch der vergleichenden Anatomie *4*. Berlin und Wien: Urban und Schwarzenberg, pp. 435–500.

Huxley, T.H. (1876) Contributions to morphology. Ichthyopsida. No. 1: On *Ceratodus fosteri*, with observations on the classification of fishes. Proc. Zool. Soc. Lond. *1876*:24–59.

Jarvik, E. (1942) On the structure of the snout of crossopterygians and lower gnathostomes in general. Zool. Biddr. Uppsala *21*:235–675.

Jarvik, E. (1967) On the structure of the lower jaw in dipnoans: With a description of an early Devonian dipnoan from Canada, *Melanognathus canadensis* gen. et spec. nov. J. Linn. Soc. Lond. (Zool.) *47*:155–183.

Jarvik, E. (1980) Basic Structure and Evolution of Vertebrates. London: Academic Press.

Johnels, A.G., and G.S.O. Svensson (1954) On the biology of *Protopterus annectens*. Ark. Zool. *7*:131–164.

Jollie, M. (1982) Ventral branchial musculature and synapomorphies questioned. Zool. J. Linn. Soc. *74*:35–47.

Kemp, A. (1977) The pattern of tooth plate formation in the Australian lungfish *Neoceratodus fosteri* (Krefft). J. Linn. Soc. Lond. (Zool.) *60*:223–258.

Kemp, A. (1979) The histology of tooth formation in the Australian lungfish *Neoceratodus forsteri* (Krefft). Zool. J. Linn. Soc. *66*:251–287.

Kerr, J.G. (1919) Text-book of Embryology, Vol. 2. Vertebrata. London: Macmillan.

Lagois, M.D. (1979) The coelacanth and chondrichthyes as sister groups: A review of shared apomorph characters and a cladistic analysis and reinterpretation. Occ. Pap. Calif. Acad. Sci. *134*:25–44.

Lankester, E.R. (1896) On the *Lepidosiren* of Paraguay and on the external characters of *Lepidosiren* and *Protopterus*. Trans. Zool. Soc. Lond. *14*:11–24.

Lauder, G.V. (1980a) The role of the hyoid apparatus in the feeding mechanism of the coelacanth *Latimeria chalumnae*. Copeia *1979*:1–9.

Lauder, G.V. (1980b) Evolution of the feeding mechanism in primitive actinopterygian fishes: A functional anatomical analysis of *Polypterus, Lepisosteus,* and *Amia*. J. Morphol. *163*:283–317.

Lauder, G.V. (1982) Patterns of evolution in the feeding mechanism of actinopterygian fishes. Am. Zool. *22*:275–285.

Lauder, G.V. (1983) Prey capture hydrodynamics in fishes: Experimental tests of two models. J. Exp. Biol. *104*:1–14.

Lauder, G.V. (1985) Aquatic feeding in lower vertebrates. In M. Hildebrand, D.M. Bramble, K. Liem, and D.B. Wake (eds): Functional Vertebrate Morphology, Cambridge: Harvard University Press pp. 210–229.

Liem, K.F. (1970) Comparative functional morphology of the Nandidae. Fieldiana Zool. *56*:1–166.

Lison, L. (1941) Recherches sur la structure et l'histogenèse des dents des poissons Dipneustes. Arch. Biol. *52*:279–320.

Løvtrup, S. (1977) The Phylogeny of Vertebrata. New York: John Wiley and Sons.

Luther, A. (1913) Über die vom N. trigeminus versorgte Muskulatur der Ganoiden und Dipneusten. Acta Soc. Sci. Fennicae, Helsingfors. *41*:3–72.

Luther, A. (1938) Die Visceralmuskulatur der Acranier, Cyclostomen, und Fische. In L. Bolk, E. Göppert, E. Kallius, und W. Lubosch, (eds): Handbuch der vergleichenden Anatomie der Wirbeltiere *5*. Wien: Urban und Schwarzenberg, pp. 468–542.

Martin, M. (1982) Nouvelles données sur la phylogénie et la systématique des Dipneustes postpaléozoiques. C.

R. Acad. Sci. Paris *294*:413–416.

McDonnell, R. (1860) Observations on the habits and anatomy of the *Lepidosiren annectens*. Nat. Hist. Rev. 7:93–112.

McMahon, B.R. (1969) A functional analysis of the aquatic and aerial respiratory movements of an African lungfish, *Protopterus aethiopicus*, with reference to the evolution of lung ventilation movements in vertebrates. J. Exp. Biol. *51*:407–430.

Miles, R.S. (1975) The relationships of the Dipnoi. Colloq. Intl. C.N.R.S. *218*:133–148.

Miles, R.S. (1977) Dipnoan (lungfish) skulls and the relationships of the group: A study based on new species from the Devonian of Australia. J. Linn. Soc. Lond. (Zool.) *61*:1–328.

Nelson, G. (1970) Pharyngeal denticles (placoid scales) of sharks, with notes on the dermal skeleton of vertebrates. Am. Mus. Novitates *2415*:1–26.

Olson, E.C., and E. Daly (1972) Notes on *Gnathorhiza* (Osteichthyes, Dipnoi). J. Paleontol. *46*:371–376.

Ørvig, T. (1967) Phylogeny of tooth tissues: Evolution of some calcified tissues in early vertebrates. In A.E.W. Miles (ed): Structural and Chemical Organization of Teeth. London:Academic Press, pp. 45–110.

Ørvig, T. (1976) Palaeohistological notes. 4. The interpretation of osteodentine, with remarks on the dentition in the Devonian dipnoan *Griphognathus*. Zool. Scripta. 5:79–96.

Owen, R. (1841) Description of the *Lepidosiren annectens*. Trans. Linn. Soc. *18*:327–361.

Oxnard, C.E. (1971) Tensile forces in skeletal structures. J. Morphol. *134*:425–436.

Özeti, N., and D.B. Wake (1969) The morphology and evolution of the tongue and associated structures in salamanders and newts (family Salamandridae). Copeia *1969*:91–123.

Panchen, A.L. (1967) The nostrils of choanate fishes and early tetrapods. Biol. Rev. *42*:374–420.

Parker, W.K. (1892) On the anatomy and physiology of *Protopterus annectens*. Trans. R. Irish Acad. *30*:109–230.

Parrington, F.R. (1967) The identification of the dermal bones of the head. J. Linn. Soc. Lond. (Zool.) *47*:231–239.

Perkins, P.L. (1972) Mandibular Mechanics and Feeding Groups in the Dipnoi. PhD Dissertation, Yale University, New Haven, Connecticut.

Peyer, B. (1969) Comparative Odontology. Translated and edited by R. Zangerl. Chicago: University of Chicago Press.

Rafn, S., and K.G. Wingstrand (1981) Structure of intestine, pancreas and spleen of the Australian lungfish, *Neoceratodus forsteri* (Krefft). Zool. Scripta *10*:223–240.

Ridewood, W.G. (1894) On the hyoid arch of *Ceratodus*. Proc. Zool. Soc. Lond. *1894*:632–640.

Romer, A.S. (1966) Vertebrate Paleontology. Chicago: University of Chicago Press.

Romer, A.S., and H.S. Smith (1934) American Carboniferous dipnoans. J. Geol. *42*:700–719.

Rosen, D.E., P.L. Forey, B.G. Gardiner, and C. Patterson (1981) Lungfishes, tetrapods, paleontology, and plesiomorphy. Bull. Am. Mus. Nat. Hist *167*:159–275.

Röse, C. (1892) Über Zahnbau und Zahnwechsel der Dipnoer. Anat. Anz. 7:821–839.

Säve-Söderbergh, G. (1944) Notes on the trigeminal musculature in non-mammalian tetrapods. Nova Acta Reg. Sci. Uppsaliensis *13*:5–59.

Säve-Söderbergh, G. (1952) On the skull of *Chirodipterus wildungenesis* Gross, an Upper Devonian dipnoan from Wildungen. Kgl. Svenska Vetenskapsakad. Handl. *3*:5–29.

Schaffer, B., and D.E. Rosen (1961) Major adaptive levels in the evolution of the actinopterygian feeding mechanism. Am. Zool. *1*:187–204.

Schmidt, M.J., and A. Keil (1971) Polarizing Microscopy of Dental Tissues. Translated by D.F. Poole and A.I. Darling. New York: Pergamon.

Schultze, H.-P. (1981) Hennig und der Ursprung der Tetrapoda. Palaontol. Z. *55*:1–86.

Shaffer, H.B., and G.V. Lauder (1985) Aquatic prey capture in ambystomatid salamanders: patterns of variation in muscle activity. J. Morphol. *183*:273–284.

Smith, H.W. (1935a) The metabolism of the lungfish. I. General considerations of the fasting metabolism in active fish. J. Cell Comp. Physiol. *6*:43–67.

Smith, H.W. (1935b) The metabolism of the lungfish. II. Effect of feeding meat on metabolic rate. J. Cell. Comp. Physiol. *6*:335–349.

Smith, M.M. (1979) SEM of the enamel layer in the teeth of fossil and extant crossopterygian and dipnoan fishes. Scanning Elect. Microsc. *1979*:483-490.

Smith, M.M. (1984) Petrodentine in extant and fossil dipnoan dentitions: Microstructure, histogenesis, and growth. Proc. Linn. Soc. N.S.W. *107*:367–407.

Thomas, K. (1983) A nitrocellulose embedding technique for vertebrate morphologists. Herp. Rev. *14*:80–81.

Thomson, K.S. (1965) The nasal apparatus in Dipnoi, with special reference to *Protopterus*. Proc. Zool. Soc. Lond. *145*:207–238.

Thomson, K.S. (1969) The biology of the lobe-finned fishes. Biol. Rev. *44*:91–154.

Westoll, T.S. (1949) On the evolution of the Dipnoi. In G.G. Simpson, and E. Mayr (eds): Genetics, Paleontology, and Evolution. Princeton: Princeton University Press, pp. 121–184.

Wiley, E.O. (1979) Ventral gill arch muscles and the interrelationships of gnathostomes, with a new classification of the Vertebrata. Zool. J. Linn. Soc. *67*:149–179.

Winslow, G.M. (1898) The chondrocranium in the Ichthyopsida. Tufts College Studies 5:147–200.

Zangerl, R. (1948) The methods of comparative anatomy and its contributions to the study of evolution. Evolution 2:351–374.

JOURNAL OF MORPHOLOGY SUPPLEMENT 1:277–297 (1986)

Lungfish Neural Characters and Their Bearing on Sarcopterygian Phylogeny

R. GLENN NORTHCUTT
*Division of Biological Sciences, University of Michigan,
Ann Arbor, Michigan 48109-1048*

ABSTRACT   The phylogenetic affinity of lungfishes has been disputed since their discovery, and they have variously been considered the sister group of actinistians, the sister group of amphibians, or equally related to actinopterygians and crossopterygians. Previous discussions of these hypotheses have considered neural characters, but there has been no general survey of the nervous systems of sarcopterygians that examines the bearing of neural characters on these hypotheses in the context of a cladistic analysis. Such a survey of representatives of all living sarcopterygian groups reveals at least twenty-three characters that are possible apomorphies at some hierarchical level among sarcopterygians. Neural synapomorphies corroborate the phylogenetic hypotheses that actinistians, amphibians, and dipnoans are each monophyletic taxa. The hypothesis that *Latimeria* is the sister group of amphibians is the least corroborated, as only a single possible synapomorphy, presence of cervical and lumbar enlargements of the spinal cord, supports this hypothesis. The hypothesis that lungfishes are the sister group of amphibians is supported by two possible synapomorphies: loss of a saccus vasculosus and the presence of neurocranial endolymphatic sacs. The hypothesis that actinistians are the sister group of lungfishes is the most corroborated, based on five possible synapomorphies: presence of a superficial isthmal nucleus, a laminated dorsal thalamus with marked protrusion into the third ventricle, olfactory peduncles, evaginated cerebral hemispheres with pronounced septum ependymale, and electroreceptive rostral organs. However, all five characters may be plesiomorphic for bony fishes. The nervous systems of *Latimeria* and *Neoceratodus* are very similar to each other, as are the nervous systems of lepidosirenid lungfishes, caecilians, and salamanders. If *Neoceratodus* is the most plesiomorphic species of living lungfishes, then lepidosirenid apomorphies may have arisen by paedomorphosis. Our inability to examine the neural characters of a relevant outgroup (rhipidistians) may result in many sarcopterygian plesiomorphic characters being interpreted as apomorphic characters, due to the wide distribution of paedomorphic characters among living sarcopterygians and their possible resemblance to plesiomorphic characters present in living outgroups that can be examined.

The phylogenetic affinity of lungfishes has been disputed since their discovery in the nineteenth century (see also Conant, this volume). Both lepidosirenid (Fitzinger, 1837; Natterer, 1837) and neoceratodontid (Krefft, 1870) lungfishes were initially described as amphibians. During the next thirty years, many zoologists came to realize that dipnoans were bony fishes and that they were closely allied to fossil fishes such as *Dipterus*, but their affinities with other fishes were still disputed (Owen, 1841; Günther, 1871;

Dr. Northcutt's present address is Department of Neurosciences, A-001, University of California, San Diego, La Jolla, CA 92093.

Huxley, 1876; Cope 1887; Dollo, 1896). By the turn of the century, similarities noted between lungfishes and amphibians led most zoologists to believe that lungfishes gave rise to amphibians (Huxley, 1876; Cope, 1884; Haeckel, 1889; Goodrich, '24; Kerr, '32). In 1892 Cope revised his position and argued that amphibians must have arisen from rhipidistian crossopterygians rather than lungfishes. This viewpoint gained support during the first half of this century (Gregory, '15; Romer, '33; Säve-Söderberg, '35) and was almost universally accepted until Rosen et al. ('81) revived the idea that lungfishes and tetrapods are sister groups.

The neuroanatomical literature, like much of the biological literature, reflects these changing views regarding dipnoan affinities. In most anatomical descriptions of the brains of lungfishes (Beauregard, 1881; Fulliquet, 1886; Wilder, 1887; Sanders, 1889; Burckhardt, 1892; Kerr, '02; Bing and Burckhardt, '04; Elliot Smith, '08; Kuhlenbeck, '24; Holmgren and van der Horst, '25; Gerlach, '33; Rudebeck, '44, '45; Schnitzlein and Crosby, '67, '68; Clairambault and Capanna, '73; Clairambault et al., '74; Thors and Nieuwenhuys, '79) similarities of dipnoan and amphibian brains have been noted, and researchers have frequently assumed that the neural characters exhibited by lungfishes were the characters present in fishes that gave rise to amphibians. With the discovery of a living crossopterygian, *Latimeria chalumnae*, attention focused on this species (Millot and Anthony, '56, '65, '67; Millot et al., '64; Nieuwenhuys, '65; Lemire, '71; Nieuwenhuys et al., '77; Northcutt et al., '78; Kremers and Nieuwenhuys, '79; Kremers, '81) with the expectation that its brain would reveal many of the primitive neural characters of the crossopterygians. Nieuwenhuys et al. ('77) concluded that *Latimeria* exhibits neural characters common to the brains of cartilaginous, dipnoan, and ray-finned fishes, but they noted no special structural similarities to the brains of amphibians. Northcutt et al. ('78) noted that the relative size of many of the brain components in *Latimeria* is more similar to that in amphibians than to that in other fishes, but lungfishes were not included in this analysis. Kremers ('81) analyzed various neural characters of *Latimeria* in a cladistic context in an attempt to determine the polarity of these characters. His analysis supports the hypothesis that dipnoans and *Latimeria* are sister groups and

that tetrapods are, in turn, the sister group of lungfishes and *Latimeria*. Kremers ('81) did not examine the brains of amphibians or lungfishes for additional shared derived (synapomorphic) characters but appears to have relied on published accounts of these brains. Similarly, Rosen et al. ('81) included a number of neural characters in their cladistic analysis of sarcopterygian relationships, but they also appear to have relied on the earlier literature rather than examining the nervous systems of these taxa to evaluate presumed synapomorphies or discover potential new ones.

The present study surveys the nervous system in representatives of all living sarcopterygian groups in order to assess previously claimed neural synapomorphies and to search for possible new ones. Further, these synapomorphies are applied in evaluating the following hypotheses of relationships among living sarcopterygians: 1) Actinistians are the sister group of amphibians, and dipnoans are, in turn, their sister group (Fig. 1A); 2) Amphibians are the sister group of dipnoans, and actinistians are, in turn, their sister group (Fig 1B); 3) Actinistians are the sister group of dipnoans, and amphibians are in turn, their sister group (Fig. 1C); 4) Actinistians, amphibians, and dipnoans are equally related. Like that of Rosen et al. ('81), this analysis is based on a number of assumptions: 1) Tetrapods are monophyletic (Gaffney, '79); 2) sarcopterygians (actinistians, dipnoans, and tetrapods), as defined by Rosen et al. ('81), are monophyletic; 3) osteichthyans are monophyletic, and their sister group is the chondrichthyans; 4) actinopterygians are monophyletic and include the chondrosteans and neopterygians; 5) the cladistians (*Erpetoichthys* and *Polypterus*) and actinistians are each monophyletic taxa; 6) comparisons among primitive (plesiomorphous) members of each group (*Neoceratodus* among dipnoans and salamanders among amphibians) should be emphasized (Rosen et al., '81); 7) ray-finned and cartilaginous fishes are considered the relevant outgroups.

MATERIALS AND METHODS

Perfused brains, or whole heads in the case of smaller specimens, of the species listed in Table 1 were embedded in wax, and serial sections (15 μm) were cut in the transverse plane. Sections were subsequently stained with a Nissl stain, cresyl violet, to demonstrate neural somata and/or a modification of

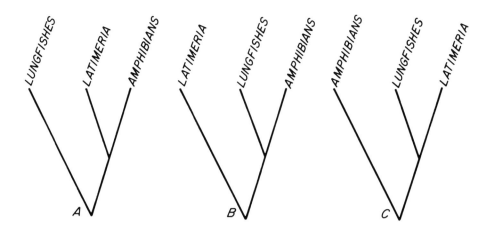

Fig. 1. Three of the four hypotheses regarding the interrelationships of living sarcopterygians. The fourth hypothesis is that the three taxa are equally related.

TABLE 1. Brain and head series examined

Chondrichthyes	Sarcopterygii (continued)
Heterodontus francisci	Dipnoi
Hydrolagus colliei	*Lepidosiren paradoxa*
Mustelus canis	*Neoceratodus forsteri*
Notorynchus maculatus	*Protopterus aethiopicus*
Platyrhinoidis triseriata	*Protopterus annectens*
Squalus acanthias	Tetrapoda
Squatina dumerili	*Ambystoma tigrinum*
Osteichthyes	*Amphiuma means*
Actinopterygii	*Ascaphus truei*
Amia calva	*Cryptobranchus*
Erpetoichthys calabaricus	*alleganiensis*
Lepisosteus osseus	*Hyla crucifer*
Polypterus palmas	*Ichthyophis glutinosus*
Salmo gairdneri	*Nectocaecilia haydee*
Scaphirhynchus	*Necturus maculosus*
platorynchus	*Notophthalmus*
Sarcopterygii	*viridescens*
Actinistia	*Rana catesbeiana*
Latimeria chalumnae	

the Bodian protargol method to demonstrate fiber pathways and peripheral nerves.

Three brains from adult specimens of *Latimeria* were cut in the transverse plane and stained by variations of the Bodian or Klüver and Barrera methods. Details regarding the collection and preparation of these specimens were reported by Northcutt et al. ('78).

Three brains from adult *Neoceratodus* were also available for this study. The first specimen (6.1 kg), obtained from Dr. S. J. Zottoli and the Research Institute of Alcoholism, Buffalo, New York, was perfused with a mixture of 1% glutaraldehyde and 2.5% paraformaldehyde, embedded in paraffin and cut in the transverse plane. Sections from this specimen were stained with cresyl violet. The second and third specimens (gravid females, 8.9 kg and 10 kg, respectively) were perfused with AFA (80% ethanol: 100% formalin:

glacial acetic acid, 90:5:5) by Dr. W. E. Bemis; permit and collecting arrangements were made by Drs. J. M. Thomson and Anne Kemp of the Department of Zoology, University of Queensland. The brain of the second specimen was sectioned in the transverse plane, and the third brain was retained whole as a reference specimen. The sections were divided into two sets and stained by the Bodian or Klüver and Barrera methods.

The dorsal views of the brains illustrated in Figures 2–4 were prepared with a Wild M4 dissecting microscope and attached drawing tube. Details of each final drawing were checked against serial sections from that brain before inking was completed.

RESULTS

A survey of the nervous system in representatives of all living sarcopterygian groups reveals at least twenty-three characters that are possible apomorphies at some hierarchical level among sarcopterygians. The analysis is complicated in part because the brains of living sarcopterygians constitute two phenetic sets. The brain of the Australian lungfish, *Neoceratodus* (Fig. 3), is far more similar to that of *Latimeria* (Fig. 2) than to the brains of the lepidosirenid lungfishes, while the brains of lepidosirenid lungfishes (Fig. 4A), caecilians, and salamanders (Fig. 4B) are

more similar to each other than they are to the brains of *Neoceratodus* and *Latimeria*.

The brains of *Latimeria* and *Neoceratodus* are characterized by an extensive cerebellum divided into a central corpus (Figs. 2, 3) and laterally paired auricles; lepidosirenids and all amphibians possess brains that are characterized by a small cerebellum (Fig. 4) in which the auricle can be distinguished from the corpus only histologically. Similarly, the midbrain roof in *Latimeria* and *Neoceratodus* is relatively large and composed of cellular laminae, whereas the midbrain roof in lepidosirenids, caecilians, and salamanders is relatively small and nonlaminated (Northcutt, et al., '78; Kremers, '81). The overall proportions of the telencephalon, however, are more similar among the lungfishes than between any one dipnoan genus and *Latimeria* or amphibians.

Dipnoan neural synapomorphies

The neural similarities between *Latimeria* and *Neoceratodus* might suggest that these genera constitute a natural taxon and that dipnoans are paraphyletic. This does not appear to be the case, however, as the living dipnoan genera share four apomorphic neural characters that are not seen in any other group of gnathostomes. The olfactory bulbs in all dipnoans (Figs. 5A,B, 6C) consist

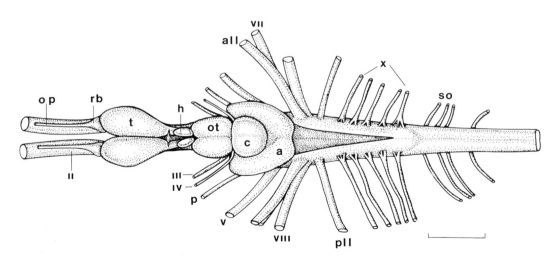

Fig. 2. Dorsal view of the brain of *Latimeria chalumnae*. Olfactory bulbs of the telencephalon are far anterior and are not pictured. a, auricle of the cerebellum; all, anterior lateral line nerve; c, corpus of the cerebellum; h, habenula; op, olfactory peduncle or tract; ot, optic tectum; p, profundus nerve; pll, posterior lateral line nerve; rb, rostral body; so, spino-occipital (hypoglossal) nerves; t, telencephalic hemispheres; II, optic nerve; III, oculomotor nerve; IV, trochlear nerve; V, trigeminal nerve; VII, facial nerve; VIII, octaval nerve; X, vagus nerve. Bar scale equals 1 cm.

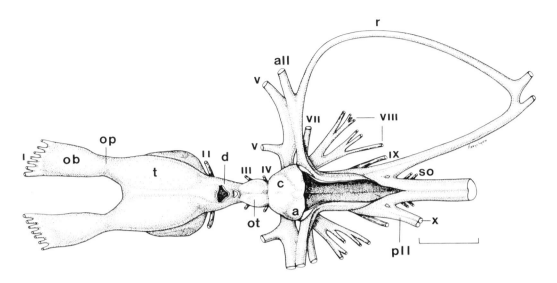

Fig. 3. Dorsal view of the brain of *Neoceratodus forsteri*. a, auricle of the cerebellum; all, anterior lateral line nerve; c, corpus of the cerebellum; d, diencephalon; ob, olfactory bulb; op, olfactory peduncle; ot, optic tectum; pll, posterior lateral line nerve; r, recurrent ramus of anterior lateral line nerve; so, spino-occipital nerves; t, telencephalic hemisphere; I, olfactory nerve; II, optic nerve; III, oculomotor nerve; IV, trochlear nerve; V, trigeminal complex; VII, facial nerve; VIII, octaval nerve; IX, glossopharyngeal nerve; X, vagus nerve. Bar scale equals 1 cm.

of a number of concentric layers in the following centripetal order: 1) primary olfactory nerve fibers, 2) glomerular layer, 3) secondary olfactory fibers, 4) internal cellular layer, 5) subependymal fiber plexus, and 6) the ependyma. The subependymal fiber plexus (Fig. 5B) occurs in all dipnoans and in no other known group of gnathostomes. Nothing is known about the nature or functional significance of these fibers in dipnoans.

All dipnoans possess a recurrent ramus of the anterior lateral line nerve (Fig. 3). This ramus courses caudally to run with fibers of the posterior lateral line nerve that distribute to the skin areas around the dorsal, main, and ventral lateral lines of the trunk. The fibers of the recurrent ramus in lungfishes innervate only trunk electroreceptors (Northcutt, '83). Neither *Latimeria* nor any known amphibian possesses a recurrent ramus of the anterior lateral line nerve, and this character is apparently shared only by lampreys and gymnotoid teleosts. The course and distribution of the recurrent ramus in lungfishes, and an outgroup analysis of this character suggest that it may have been a plesiomorphic character of the earliest vertebrates that was lost with the origin of gnathostomes and reevolved independently in dipnoans and gymnotids (Northcutt, '85).

All lungfishes are characterized by a distinctly expanded ventral telencephalic floor (Figs. 3, 4A) whose neurons form distinct clusters or islands (Fig. 5C). Traditionally, this region of the telencephalic floor has been considered homologous to the olfactory tubercle in other sarcopterygians. However, recent experimental and immunohistochemical studies indicate that this region in lungfishes does not receive secondary olfactory fibers but does contain fibers and neurons that are comparable to the basal ganglia in other sarcopterygians (Northcutt and Reiner, '85).

All dipnoan genera possess a pair of large neurons, termed Mauthner cells (Fig. 5D), that are located in the reticular formation adjacent to the entry of the octaval nerves into the medulla. In most anamniotes, these cells are characterized by extensive laterally and ventrally directed dendrites and an axon that decussates and courses caudally into the spinal cord as one component of the medial longitudinal fasciculus. Mauthner cell axons in most anamniotes are heavily myelinated and can be traced caudally as a large isolated

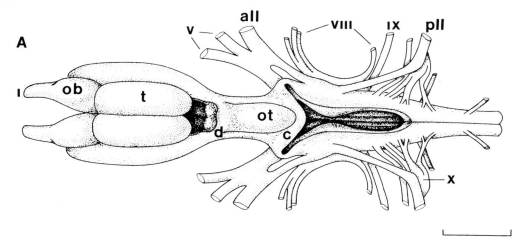

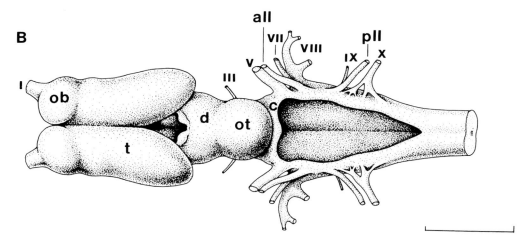

Fig. 4. Dorsal views of the brains of *Protopterus annectens* (A) and *Ambystoma tigrinum* (B). all, anterior lateral line nerve; c, cerebellum; d, diencephalon; ob, olfactory bulb; ot, optic tectum; pll, posterior lateral line nerve; t, telencephalic hemisphere; I, olfactory nerve; III, oculomotor nerve; V, trigeminal complex; VII, facial nerve; VIII, octaval nerve; IX, glossopharyngeal nerve; X, vagus nerve. Bar scales equal 5 mm (A) and 3 mm (B).

fiber. In lungfishes, however, the axon is unmyelinated initially and is closely associated with several axons of additional reticular neurons. The axons of these reticular cells, as well as the axon of the Mauthner cell, are subsequently ensheathed as a single complex (Zottoli, '78). A comparable Mauthner axonal complex has not been described in any other group.

Neural autapomorphic characters of *Latimeria*

A survey of the nervous system of *Latimeria* reveals at least two autapomorphic characters. The telencephalic hemispheres of

this species are characterized by a pair of rostrally located lobes termed the rostral bodies (Nieuwenhuys, '65). These are not the olfactory bulbs, which are located immedi-

Fig. 5. Photomicrographs of transverse sections through the olfactory bulb (A and B) of *Protopterus*; the caudal telencephalon (C) of *Protopterus*, and the medulla (D) at the level of entry of the octaval nerve in *Lepidosiren*. In all sections, dorsal and lateral are to the top and left of the figure, respectively. M, matrix zone of "standby" cells; Ma, Mauthner neuron; PM, pars medialis of the olfactory bulb; SP, subependymal fiber plexus. Arrows in C mark neuronal islands of basal ganglia. Magnification of A and C is identical, as is B and D. Bar scales for B and C equal 20 μm and 50 μm, respectively.

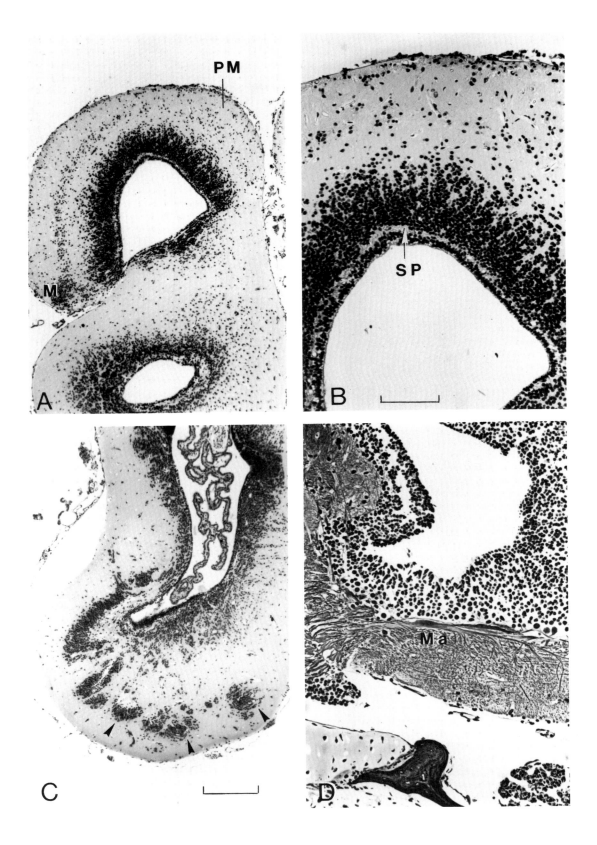

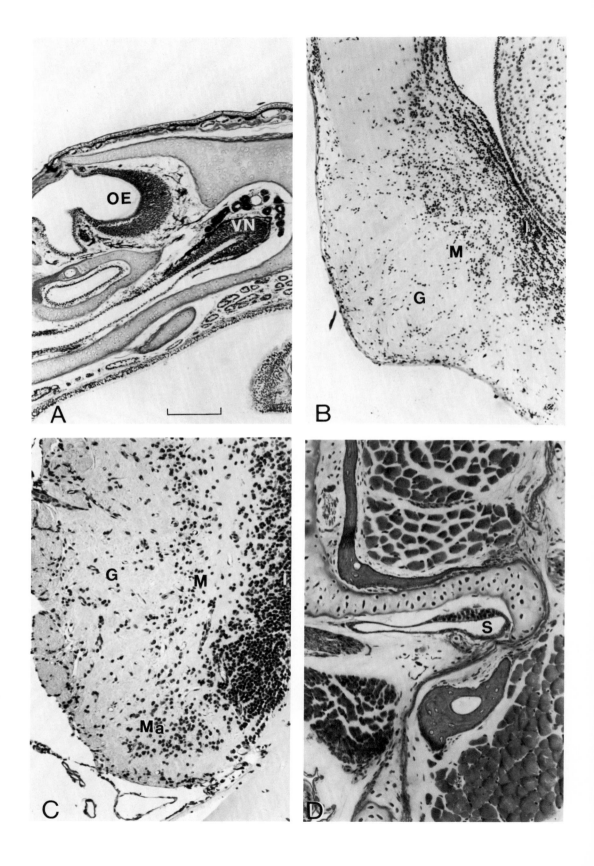

ately adjacent to the olfactory organs, but rostral subdivisions of the cerebral hemispheres (Fig. 2) that appear to receive fibers from the olfactory bulbs via the olfactory peduncles or tracts. The rostral bodies in *Latimeria* may be homologous to the retrobulbar nuclei in many ray-finned fishes (Kremers, '81); regardless, they constitute a gross anatomical feature of the telencephalon that is unique to *Latimeria*.

The absence of Mauthner neurons in *Latimeria* constitutes a second autapomorphy. These neurons are present in adult lampreys, holocephalians, chondrosteans, many neopterygians, cladistians, dipnoans, and larval as well as many adult amphibians (Ariëns Kappers et al., '36; Zottoli, '78) but apparently do not exist in *Latimeria* (Kremers and Nieuwenhuys, '79; Kremers, '81). Zottoli ('78) claims that Mauthner cells do exist in *Latimeria*, based on axon identification, but I have not been able to confirm their existence in my own histological preparations.

Amphibian neural synapomorphies

The olfactory organs in most amphibians (Fig. 6A) are divided into a dorsal main olfactory epithelium and a more ventral sensory epithelium termed a vomeronasal or Jacobson's organ. The vomeronasal organ arises embryonically (Schmalhausen, '68) as a ventrolateral (salamanders) or ventromedial (anurans and caecilians) blind diverticulum that opens directly into a main chamber of the olfactory organ in the adult. The receptors of the epithelium of the main olfactory organ and those of the vomeronasal organ give rise to axons collectively termed the olfactory and vomeronasal nerves, respectively, which terminate in the ipsilateral main and accessory olfactory bulbs, respectively (Northcutt and Kicliter, '80). The accessory olfactory bulbs in amphibians (Fig. 6B) are located caudolateral to the main olfactory bulbs and are similarly organized in concentric layers in the following centripetal order: 1) primary

nerve fibers, 2) glomerular layer, 3) mitral cell layer, 4) secondary fiber layer, 5) internal cellular layer, and 6) the ependyma. The primary targets of fibers leaving the main and accessory olfactory bulbs are the lateral pallium and the lateral division of the amygdala, respectively (Northcutt and Royce, '75; Northcutt and Kicliter, '80). Thus the main olfactory and vomeronasal chemoreceptive systems in amphibians maintain separate and parallel pathways within the telencephalon. The vomeronasal system can be recognized peripherally as a distinct ventral diverticulum of the main olfactory organ; centrally, a distinct laterally situated accessory olfactory bulb is present, as is a nucleus in the caudal telencephalon that receives input only from the accessory olfactory bulb.

A distinct vomeronasal system has been recognized in representatives of all three extant orders of amphibians (Northcutt and Kicliter, '80) and in many reptiles and mammals but has not been seen in birds (Ariëns Kappers et al., '36; Northcutt, '81). The peripheral olfactory organs and their neural centers in *Latimeria* exhibit no features of a vomeronasal system (Millot and Anthony, '65; Nieuwenhuys, '65; Kremers, '81). However, Kerr ('02), Fullarton ('33), and Bertmar ('65) described a "lateral" diverticulum in the embryonic nasal sac of lepidosirenid lungfishes, which led to claims that these fishes possess a vomeronasal organ (Rudebeck, '44; Rosen et al., '81). The "lateral" diverticulum of the embryonic nasal sac is, in fact, a caudal diverticulum and, in any case, is not topographically comparable to the rostroventral diverticulum that gives rise to the vomeronasal organ in amphibians. The caudal diverticulum in lepidosirenid lungfishes is only one of several transitory diverticuli that occur in embryonic and larval lepidosirenids (Rudebeck, '44), and examination of juvenile and adult specimens of all three dipnoan genera reveal no trace of any diverticuli associated with the olfactory organ. In their study of the telencephalon of *Protopterus*, Schnitzlein and Crosby ('67) labeled a rostromedial portion of the olfactory organ as a vomeronasal organ. Again, however, my own examination of at least fifty specimens of *Protopterus* during several experimental studies of the nervous system in this genus has revealed no anatomical specialization within any part of the olfactory sac.

Two distinctly different telencephalic cell groups in lungfishes have been claimed to be homologous to the accessory olfactory bulbs

Fig. 6. Photomicrographs of transverse sections through the nasal region (A) in *Hyla*, the accessory olfactory bulb (B) in *Rana*, the ventrolateral portion of the olfactory bulb (C) in *Protopterus*, and the hyoid pouch (D) in *Protopterus*. Lateral is toward the left (B,C) and right (A,D) of the figure and dorsal toward the top. G, glomerular layer of the accessory (B) or main (C) olfactory bulb; I, internal cellular layer of the accessory (B) or main (C) olfactory bulb; M, mitral cell layer of the accessory (B) or main (C) olfactory bulb; Ma, matrix zone of olfactory bulb; OE, olfactory organ; S, spiracular organ; VM, vomeronasal organ. Magnification of A through D is identical; bar scale equals 20 μm.

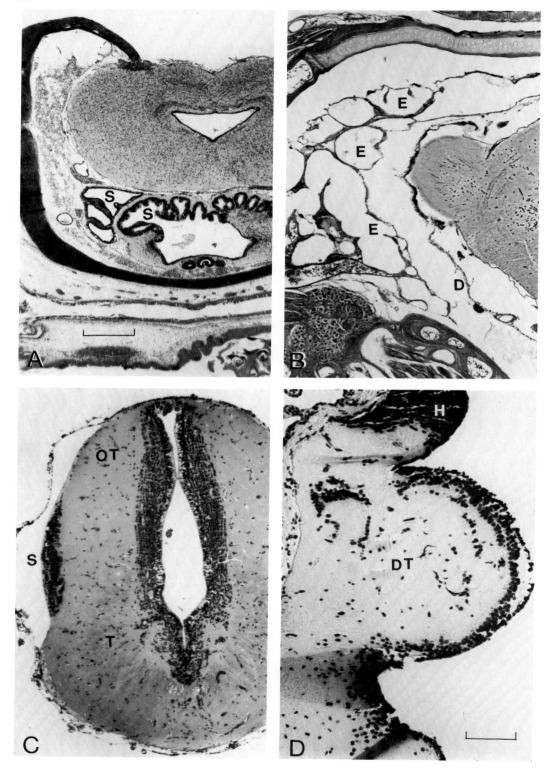

in amphibians. Rudebeck ('44) and Schnitzlein and Crosby ('67) described supracortical neurons (Fig. 5A) immediately beneath the pial surface of the telencephalon in lepidosirenid lungfishes as an accessory olfactory bulb; Clairambault and Capanna ('73) described a ventrolateral spherical cell group (Figs. 5A, 6C) in *Protopterus* as an accessory olfactory bulb. In both *Lepidosiren* and *Protopterus* the olfactory nerve divides into lateral and medial fascicles as it forms the implantation cone of the olfactory bulb, and the olfactory axons terminate in distinct lateral and medial glomerular zones (Derivot, '84a). It is this medial zone of the olfactory bulb, or the dorsal pallium immediately caudal to it, that has been termed an accessory olfactory bulb (Rudebeck, '44; Schnitzlein and Crosby, '67). The existence of an accessory olfactory bulb so described would require that the entire medial half of the olfactory nerve and its target be interpreted as a vomeronasal system, whereas the vomeronasal system in amphibians is a distinctly separate nerve that runs ventrolaterally to the olfactory nerve and terminates in a lateral region of the cerebral hemisphere. Finally, experimentally determined efferents of the pars medialis and lateralis of the olfactory bulb in *Protopterus* exhibit overlap (unpublished observations), which should not be the case if either division were comparable to the accessory olfactory bulb in amphibians.

Clairambault and Capanna ('73) interpreted a rostrolateral group of granulelike cells in the olfactory bulb of *Protopterus* as an accessory olfactory bulb. However, this cell group does not have any of the internal organization of the accessory olfactory bulb in amphibians, and Derivot ('84b) has recently argued that these cells constitute an embryonic matrix zone composed of "standby" cells that give rise to additional neuronal populations as the olfactory bulb continues to grow throughout life. Thus there

is no evidence that lungfishes possess a vomeronasal organ or nerve, nor is there any indication centrally of an accessory olfactory bulb. These observations support the interpretation that a vomeronasal system is a synapomorphy of amphibians.

Paired spiracular organs (Fig. 6D) occur as diverticulae of the hyoid pouches in many nontetrapod gnathostomes. These sensory organs are neuromastlike, are innervated by a ramus of the anterior lateral line nerve, and appear to be mechanoreceptors of unknown specific function (Barry and Boord, '84). Spiracular organs occur in dipnoans, cladistians, chondrosteans, and nonteleost neopterygians (Agar, '06; Norris and Hughes, '20). *Latimeria* possesses a spiracular chamber, but a spiracular organ was not described in the most complete reports on the anatomy of this animal (Millot and Anthony, '58; '65). It is not clear, however, that the spiracular chamber was specifically examined for the presence of a spiracular organ. Spiracular organs have not been seen in larval or adult amphibians (Noble, '31; Schmalhausen, '68; Jarvik, '80). If *Latimeria* does possess a spiracular organ, its loss in amphibians should be viewed as an amphibian synapomorphy; if *Latimeria* does not possess a spiracular organ, its loss in *Latimeria* and amphibians could be viewed as a synapomorphy linking these two groups.

Possible neural synapomorphies linking two of the three sarcopterygian taxa

Examination of the nervous systems of living sarcopterygians reveals only a single possible synapomorphy to support the hypothesis that *Latimeria* is the sister taxon of amphibians (Fig. 1A). In most amphibians and other tetrapods the spinal cord shows enlargements in the cervical and lumbar regions that are associated with innervation of the paired limbs. Similar spinal enlargements associated with the paired fins have been described in *Latimeria* (Millot and Anthony, '65). Lepidosirenid lungfishes do not exhibit spinal enlargements; to my knowledge, however, the spinal cord of *Neoceratodus* has not been examined for this character. Thus if *Neoceratodus* does not exhibit cervical and lumbar enlargements, this pattern could be interpreted as a synapomorphy linking *Latimeria* and amphibians. However, if such spinal enlargements occur in *Neoceratodus*, this character should be viewed as a synapomorphy for all sarcopterygian taxa.

Fig. 7. Photomicrographs of transverse sections through the optic tectum and caudal diencephalon (A) of *Platyrhinoidis*, the otic capsule and midbrain (B) of *Hyla*, the midbrain (C) of *Protopterus*, and diencephalon (D) of *Neoceratodus*. In all sections dorsal and lateral are toward the top and left of the figure, respectively. D, dura mater; DT, dorsal thalamus; E, endolymphatic sac; H, habenular nucleus; OT, optic tectum; S, superficial isthmal nucleus; I, midbrain tegmentum. Magnification of A and C is identical, as is B and D. Bar scales for A and D equal 50 μm and 20 μm, respectively.

There are at least two possible neural synapomorphies to support the hypothesis that lungfishes are the sister group of amphibians (Fig. 1B): the loss of the diencephalic saccus vasculosus and the presence of an expanded endolymphatic sac containing calcareous crystals associated with the inner ear.

In most cartilaginous and ray-finned fishes, the ependyma of the caudal wall of the posterior tuberculum has an extremely thin evagination termed the saccus vasculosus (Fig. 7A). The saccus, like the pituitary, is closely associated with an extensive vascular system and is suspected to have hormonal functions, but its exact biological role(s) is presently unknown. A saccus vasculosus, albeit rather reduced relative to that in most ray-finned fishes, has been described in *Latimeria* (Lagios, '75). However, neither dipnoans nor any tetrapods possess a recognizable saccus vasculosus.

In most amphibians, the roof of the otic organ or inner ear exhibits a short duct, termed the endolymphatic duct, a remnant of the embryonic connection of the inner ear with the overlying ectoderm. In lepidosirenid lungfishes and amphibians, the endolymphatic ducts are not rudimentary but expand dorsally and medially to fill much of the neurocranial cavity overlying the midbrain and medulla (Fig. 7B). In some cases these endolymphatic sacs are so extensive that they invade the neural canal of the vertebrae (Dempster, '30; Whiteside, '22). Although these sacs are extremely thin, they are easily recognized by their content of dense calcareous endolymph, and it is possible that they consitute a mechanism to aid sound localization (W. Wilczynski, personal communication). Endolymphatic sacs that invade the neurocranium do not occur in *Neoceratodus* (Burne, '13) and have not been reported in *Latimeria* (Millot and Anthony, '65). Thus, although large calcareous-containing endolymphatic sacs of the inner ear may be synapomorphic for lungfishes and amphibians, their absence in *Neoceratodus*, the most plesiomorphous living dipnoan, suggests that their presence in lepidosirenids and amphibians may be due to parallel homoplasy.

There are five possible neural synapomorphies to support the hypothesis that *Latimeria* and lungfishes are sister groups (Fig. 1C): 1) the presence of a superficial isthmal nucleus, 2) the ventricular protrusion of a laminated dorsal thalamus, 3) pedunculated olfactory bulbs, 4) evaginated cerebral hemispheres with an extensive septum ependymale, 5) an electroreceptive rostral organ.

In *Latimeria* (Kremers and Nieuwenhuys, '79) and in all three genera of living lungfishes (Northcutt, '77, '80; Thors and Nieuwenhuys, '79), the rostral isthmus is characterized by a superficial nucleus of small, darkly staining granular cells that lie immediately beneath the pia (Fig. 7C). This superficial isthmal nucleus has been described as the lateral optic cells (Burckhardt, 1892), the isthmal ganglion (Holmgren and van der Horst, '25), and superficial isthmal and mesencephalic grey (Kremers and Nieuwenhuys, '79; Thors and Nieuwenhuys, '79). Although a single similarly situated nucleus does not occur in any other craniate, it is possible that the superficial isthmal nucleus of *Latimeria* and lungfishes is a field homologue of the tegmental optic nucleus and nucleus isthmi in other vertebrates, as the rostral segment of the superficial isthmal nucleus in lungfishes receives direct retinal input (Clairambault and Flood, '75; Northcutt, '77, '80). This interpretation would be supported if it could be demonstrated experimentally that the caudal segment of the superficial isthmal nucleus in lungfishes has reciprocal connections with the optic tectum. Basal or tegmental optic nuclei in amphibians and teleosts occur at the level of the oculomotor nucleus, whereas nucleus isthmi in amphibians and teleosts occupy a transitional zone in the caudal mesencephalon. Thus the topography of these nuclei in amphibians and teleosts is distinctly different from that of the potential field homologue in lungfishes and *Latimeria*. If the position of these nuclei in amphibians and teleosts is interpreted as the plesiomorphic condition for sarcopterygians, then the presence of a single superficial nucleus in *Latimeria* and lungfishes could be interpreted as a synapomorphy.

The dorsal thalamus in lungfishes (Figs. 7D, 9A) and *Latimeria* (Fig. 8C) exhibits a number of similarities. In each of these taxa the dorsal thalamus protrudes extensively into the third ventricle and is delimited by distinct dorsal and ventral sulci. In each case the periventricular cell bodies of the dorsal thalamus are arranged into distinct laminae, a pattern particularly pronounced in *Latimeria* (Fig. 8C) and *Neoceratodus* (Fig. 7D). A dorsal thalamus characterized by a periventricular plate of cells, sometimes laminated, occurs in amphibians (Fig. 9B), as well

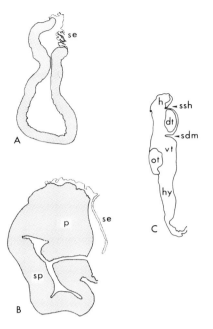

Fig. 8. Diagrams of transverse sections through the cerebral hemisphere (A) in *Neoceratodus*, and the cerebral hemisphere (B) and diencephalon (C) in *Latimeria*. Dt, dorsal thalamus; h, habenular nuclei; hy, hypothalamus; ot, optic tract; p, pallium; sdm, sulcus diencephalicus medius; se, septum ependymale; sp, subpallium; ssh, sulcus subhabenularis or diencephalicus dorsalis; vt, ventral thalamus.

as cladistians, squalomorph sharks, and lampreys, and is thus the probable plesiomorphic condition for vertebrates. However, in no other vertebrate group does the dorsal thalamus protrude into the third ventricle to the same extent as in *Latimeria* and lungfishes.

In amphibians and lepidosirenid lungfishes the olfactory bulbs are sessile (i.e., in direct continuity with the cerebral hemispheres, Fig. 4). However, in *Latimeria* (Fig. 2) and *Neoceratodus* (Fig. 3) the olfactory bulbs are pedunculated (i.e., located more rostrally in the neurocranium and connected to the hemispheres by distinct olfactory tracts or peduncles). A survey of other living anamniotes reveals sessile olfactory bulbs in hagfishes, lampreys, holocephalians, and all ray-finned fishes except some teleosts. Sessile olfactory bulbs thus appear to be the plesiomorphic pattern and pedunculated bulbs the apomorphic pattern for anamniotes. If the pedunculated olfactory bulbs of *Neoceratodus* are interpreted as the plesiomorphic condition for lungfishes, their occurrence in *Latimeria* and these lungfishes would be interpreted as a synapomorphy.

The cerebral hemispheres in *Neoceratodus* (Fig. 8A) and *Latimeria* (Fig. 8B), like those in other sarcopterygians (Fig. 9D) arise embryonically by evagination of the rostrolateral walls of the prosencephalon. In lepidosirenid lungfishes and amphibians the development of the evaginated hemispheres is also marked by an extensive inversion of the dorsomedial roof. This is not the case in *Latimeria* or *Neoceratodus*; the hemispheres in these taxa are characterized by an extensive nonneural septum ependymale (Nieuwenhuys and Hickey, '65). The presence of evaginated cerebral hemispheres with an extensive median septum ependymale in *Latimeria* and *Neoceratodus* could be interpreted as a synapomorphy. Ray-finned fishes also possess an extensive septum ependymale, but their hemispheres develop by eversion rather than evagination. Evaginated cerebral hemispheres without a septum ependymale occur in all other living vertebrates and are thus most likely the plesiomorphic condition for vertebrates. However, a septum ependymale may be a synapomorphy of osteichthyans, rather than dipnoans and actinistians, as a reduced spetum ependymale also occurs in the caudal hemispheres in salamanders (Nieuwenhuys, '69).

The snouts of *Latimeria* and *Neoceratodus* are characterized by invaginated epithelial sacs, termed the rostral organs and labial cavities, respectively, that may be synapomorphic electroreceptive organs. The rostral organs in *Latimeria* are extensive mucosal sacs whose epithelium is folded into numerous crypts that are remarkably similar (Bemis and Hetherington, '82) to the electroreceptive ampullary organs in other nonteleost anamniotes. The labial cavities or sacs in *Neoceratodus* (Günther, 1871; Rosen et al., '81) occupy a site topographically similar to that of the rostral organs in *Latimeria*, and the sacs in both taxa appear to be innervated by branches of the anterior lateral line nerve. Unfortunately, nothing is known about the histology of the mucosa of the labial sacs in *Neoceratodus*. If this mucosa is shown to contain ampullary organs, this would suppport the interpretation that the labial sacs and rostral organs are synapomorphies. Similarly, the tentacular organ in caecilians and the nasolacrimal duct in salamanders should be reexamined, as all of these structures may be homologous among sarcopterygians.

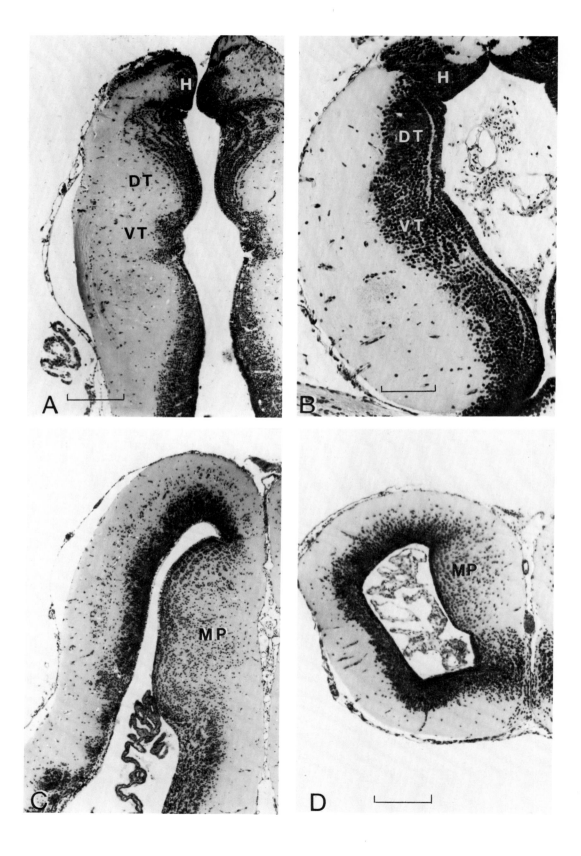

Additional neural apomorphic characters among sarcopterygians.

The optic tectum in lepidosirenid lungfishes (Fig. 7A), as well as in caecilians and salamanders (Fig. 7B), is relatively small compared to that in *Latimeria* (Fig. 2), *Neoceratodus* (Fig. 3), and anurans. Not only is the tectum relatively small in lepidosirenid lungfishes and non-anuran amphibians, most if not all of its constituent cell bodies are restricted to a periventricular zone rather than being distributed throughout the tectal roof in distinct laminae (Northcutt, '77; Thors and Nieuwenhuys, '79). The tectum in *Latimeria* (Northcutt and Neary, '75; Kremers, '81) and *Neoceratodus* (Northcutt, '80) is relatively larger, distinctly bilobed, and well laminated, as it is in all other craniates. Thus, although a reduced, nonlaminated optic tectum is an apomorphic character of lepidosirenid lungfishes and amphibians, tectal reduction appears to have occurred independently in these sarcopterygian taxa.

Similarly, the cerebellar corpus in lepidosirenid lungfishes (Fig. 4a) and in all amphibians is relatively small compared to that in *Latimeria* (Fig. 2), *Neoceratodus* (Fig. 3), and other gnathostomes. The cerebellar corpus in amphibians and, most likely, lepidosirenid lungfishes appears to represent one of the most striking reductions of a major brain division in any vertebrate (Northcutt et al., '78). Thus a reduced cerebellar corpus in lepidosirenid lungfishes and amphibians is an apomorphic character but appears to have occurred independently.

In all gnathostome vertebrates the cerebellum is divided into a median corpus and laterally paired vertibulolateralis lobes or auricles. In *Latimeria* (Fig. 2) and *Neoceratodus* (Fig. 3) the extensive vestibulolateralis lobes are divided into distinct upper and lower leaves, separated by sizable lateral recesses of the fourth ventricle. Similarly organized vestibulateralis lobes occur in cartilaginous and chondrostean fishes (Larsell, '67) and appear to be the plesiomorphic

condition for gnathostomes. The vestibulolateralis lobes in lepidosirenid lungfishes (Fig. 4A) and all amphibian taxa (Fig. 4B) are distinctly different. In these forms the lobes and lateral recesses of the fourth ventricle are barely recognizable, and a distinct ventral leaf can be identified only with difficulty. Thus, while a reduced vestibulolateralis lobe could be interpreted as a synapomorphy for lepidosirenid lungfishes and amphibians, the presence of extensive lobes in *Neoceratodus* and other gnathostomes suggests that reduction of the vestibulolateralis lobes has occurred independently in lepidosirenid lungfishes and amphibians.

There are at least two distinctly different patterns of organization for the branchiomeric motor nuclei among vertebrates. In all vertebrates the trigeminal motor nucleus is recognizable as a separate nucleus at the rostral end of the branchiomeric motor column. In cartilaginous fishes, however, the remaining branchiomeric motor neurons, whose axons consititute the facial, glossopharyngeal, and vagal nerves, form a single motor column (Smeets et al., '83). A single continuous branchiomeric motor column for neurons of the facial-vagal complex appears to be apomorphic for cartilaginous fishes, as other vertebrates exhibit separate branchiomeric motor nuclei associated with each of these cranial nerves (Nieuwenhuys, '77; Kremers and Nieuwenhuys, '79; Thors and Nieuwenhuys, '79; Nieuwenhuys and Pouwels, '83). Holmgren and van der Horst ('25) claimed that two separate facial motor nuclei (a pars rostralis and pars caudalis) occur in *Neoceratodus*. However, Gerlach ('33) and Thors and Nieuwenhuys ('79) reported only a single facial motor nucleus in *Protopterus* and *Lepidosiren*, respectively. It is possible that some lungfishes, and perhaps other sarcopterygians, exhibit a facial motor pattern different from that in other gnathostomes. However, it is extremely difficult to determine whether a motor nerve arises from one or more nuclei without experimental tracing studies, and resolution of this question will definitely require such investigation.

The roof or pallium of most, if not all, craniates can be divided into lateral, dorsal, and medial components (Northcutt, '81). The medial pallium in lepidosirenid lungfishes (Fig. 9C) and amphibians (Fig. 9D) forms a distinct ventricularly directed ridge that is characterized by extensive migration of neuronal cell bodies away from the periventri-

Fig. 9. Photomicrographs of transverse sections through the thalamus in *Protopterus* (A) and *Ambystoma* (B) and the telencephalon in *Protopterus* (C) and *Ambystoma* (D). In all sections, dorsal and lateral are toward the top and left of the figure, respectively. DT, dorsal thalamus; H, habenular nuclei; MP, medial pallium; VT, ventral thalamus. Magnification of A and C are identical. Bar scales equal 50 μm (A), 20 μm (B), and 40 μm (D).

cular zone (Northcutt and Kicliter, '80; Northcutt and Reiner, '85). The telencephalon in *Neoceratodus* (Fig. 8A) is not characterized by a similarly developed medial pallium (Nieuwenhuys and Hickey, '65). Holmgren and van der Horst ('25) recognized a medial pallial division in *Neoceratodus* as that portion of the pallium immediately lateral to the dorsal attachment of the septum ependymale, but Nieuwenhuys and Hickey ('65), while noting the same differential thickness of the periventricular zone, concluded that it was due solely to the mechanical effect of the inversion of the hemispheric wall. The existence or absence of a medial pallial component in *Neoceratodus* will clearly require immunohistochemical or experimental connectional studies for determination. However, it is clear that a distinct medial pallial field, characterized by migrated cell bodies, does not exist in *Neoceratodus*.

Recognition of a medial pallium in *Latimeria* is similarly complicated, as the pallium constitutes an expanded solid body protruding into the ventricular cavity (Fig. 8B). In the caudal portion of this body, distinct lateral, dorsomedial, and ventromedial cellular fields have been recognized (Kremers, '81). If the ventromedial pallial field in *Latimeria* were demonstrated to be homologous to the medial pallium in other vertebrates, one could argue that a distinctly enlarged medial pallium with migrated cell bodies is a synapomorphy for actinistians and amphibians. If the pallial condition in *Neoceratodus* is interpreted as the plesiomorphic condition for lungfishes, then a medial pallium with migrated cells in lepidosirenid lungfishes would be considered an independently evolved apomorphic character for lepidosirenids. However, a similarly organized medial pallium also occurs in squalomorph sharks, which suggests that this condition is a symplesiomorphic character for gnathostomes and its absence in *Neoceratodus* is apomorphic.

In most anamniotic gnathostomes, many of the mechanoreceptive neuromasts of the ordinary lateral line system are housed in canals on the head and trunk (Northcutt, '86). In lepidosirenid lungfishes and amphibians, neuromasts occur in rows or lines that are in the same topographical positions as the canals in other anamniotes. The lateral line system in *Lepidosiren* and living amphibians is totally devoid of canals, and only a short

canal occurs along part of the infra- and supraorbital lines in *Protopterus*. However, well-developed lateral line canals occur in *Latimeria* (Millot and Anthony, '65) and in *Neoceratodus* (Pehrson, '49). Thus reduction or loss of canals associated with lateral line neuromasts appears to have occurred independently as an apomorphic character in lepidosirenid lungfishes and amphibians.

Examination of transverse sections through various levels of the spinal cord in sarcopterygians reveals two basic patterns. The neural cell bodies forming the gray matter of the spinal cords in lepidosirenids, caecilians, and salamanders are distributed around the central canal in an oval pattern with indistinct dorsal and ventral horns. The central gray in *Latimeria* (Millot and Anthony, '65) and *Neoceratodus* (Keenan, '28), as well as in anuran amphibians and most other tetrapods, is organized in the well-known H-pattern with distinct dorsal and ventral horns. The dorsal gray columns are further pronounced in that they are bordered medially and dorsally by an extensive dorsal funiculus. Spinal gray columns with distinct dorsal horns appear to be the plesiomorphic condition for gnathostomes, as this pattern occurs in cartilaginous and ray-finned fishes (Keenan, '28), although the dorsal horns may be fused medially and the dorsal funiculus weakly developed. Thus the presence of distinct dorsal horns and extensive dorsal funiculi in sarcopterygians are symplesiomorphic and synapomorphic characters, respectively. However, reduced or indistinct dorsal horns in lepidosirenids, caecilians, and salamanders are likely an apomorphic character state that has evolved independently.

DISCUSSION

The present survey of neural characters in living sarcopterygians reveals possible synapomorphies that could corroborate each of the phylogenetic hypotheses illustrated in Figure 10.

The hypothesis that *Latimeria* is the sister group of amphibians (Fig. 10A) is the least corroborated, as the presence of cervical and lumbar enlargements of the spinal cord is the only possible synapomorphy identified, and it is not clear that the spinal cord of *Neoceratodus* does not exhibit this character. If spinal enlargements are found to occur in *Neoceratodus*, the character should be interpreted as a sarcopterygian synapomorphy. The absence of cervical and lumbar enlargements of the spinal cord in lepidosirenid lungfishes may well be apomorphic, as this character is correlated with well-developed lateral limbs. The lack of spinal enlargements, the lack of distinct horns of the spinal gray, and filamentous pectoral and pelvic fins without extensive muscles may represent a paedomorphic suite of characters in lepidosirenid lungfishes, caecilians, and many salamanders.

The hypothesis that lungfishes are the sister group of amphibians (Fig. 10B) is supported by two possible synapomorphies: the loss of a saccus vasculosus, and the presence of neurocranial endolymphatic sacs. A saccus vasculosus is a distinct structure that is easily identified, and it is unlikely that there have been errors made in recognizing this character and determining its phylogenetic distribution. The presence of neurocranial endolymphatic sacs is more problematic. While *Neoceratodus* does possess endolymphatic sacs, they are restricted to the otic capsules (Burne, '13) and do not extend into the neurocranium. Throughout this analysis, I have emphasized comparisons among plesiomorphous taxa; one could therefore conclude that neurocranial endolymphatic sacs

have evolved independently in lepidosirenid lungfishes and amphibians. However, the distribution of this character among living sarcopterygians could have resulted from one of three phylogenetic sequences (two independent gains, two independent losses, or one gain and one loss), depending on which phylogenetic hypothesis is valid. Thus it is equally possible that neurocranial endolymphatic sacs in lungfishes and amphibians are synapomorphic or that they are the result of parallel homoplasy. The brain and surrounding tissues of *Eusthenopteron*, a Devonian rhipidistian, have been reconstructed to show extensive neurocranial endolymphatic sacs (Jarvik, '80). If Jarvik's reconstruction is valid, and if *Eusthenopteron* is considered a terminal taxon in any phylogenetic hypothesis of sarcopterygian relationships in which lungfishes are not the sister group of all other sarcopterygians, an outgroup analysis leads to the conclusion that neurocranial endolymphatic sacs are a synapomorphic character for sarcopterygians and have been lost in *Latimeria* and *Neoceratodus*. Clearly the possible synapomorphy of neurocranial endolymphtaic sacs between lungfishes and amphibians must be viewed with caution.

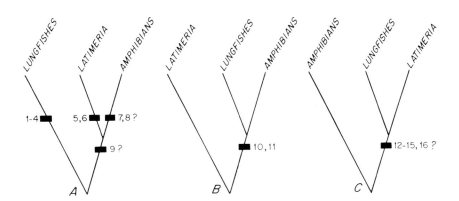

Fig. 10. Cladograms illustrating the three hypotheses of sarcopterygian interrelationships supported by neural characters. The various characters (black bars) interpreted as autapomorphies or possible synapomorphies are indicated at the appropriate level. 1, presence of a subependymal fiber plexus within the olfactory bulb; 2, presence of a recurrent ramus of the anterior lateral line nerve; 3, presence of a Mauthner axon ensheathed with reticular axons; 4, presence of cellular islands in the caudal telencephalic floor; 5, presence of distinct rostral bodies of the telencephalon; 6, loss of Mauthner neurons; 7, presence of a vomeronasal system; 8, loss of spiracular organ; 9, presence of cervical and lumbar enlargements of the spinal cord; 10, saccus vasculosus lost; 11, presence of neurocranial endolymphatic sacs; 12, presence of a superficial isthmal nucleus; 13, presence of a laminated dorsal thalamus with marked protrusion into ventricle; 14, presence of olfactory peduncles; 15, evaginated cerebral hemispheres with pronounced septum ependymale; 16, presence of an electroreceptive rostral organ. Question marks denote characters whose distribution is uncertain.

So far in this analysis, I have considered neural characters only among living sarcopterygians, but it is clear that examination of fossil taxa can be critical, particularly when a very important outgroup (Rhipidistia) is extinct. The problem is particularly vexing if one or more relevant outgroups are extinct and paedomorphic characters are widely distributed in the extant groups, as is evident in considering possible synapomorphies for *Latimeria* and lungfishes.

The hypothesis that *Latimeria* is the sister group of lungfish (Fig. 10C) is the most corroborated. However, there are also problems with the interpretation of the characters that constitute their possible synapomorphies.

Determining the polarity of pedunculated versus sessile olfactory bulbs is particularly troublesome. Two phyletic transformations (two gains or two losses) could account for the distribution of these characters, regardless of the actual phylogeny. Emphasis on *Neoceratodus* as a plesiomorphic taxon would suggest that pedunculated bulbs are a synapomorphy for *Latimeria* and lungfishes and that sessile bulbs are the plesiomorphic condition for sarcopterygians. Outgroup analysis and ontogenetic precedence would also support this conclusion. However, the brains of *Eusthenopteron* (Jarvik, '80) and *Megalichthys* (Romer, '37), Devonian and Carboniferous rhipidistians, respectively, have been reconstructed to show pedunculated olfactory bulbs similar to those of *Neoceratodus*. While there is considerable risk of error in interpreting brain shape from endocranial casts, the possible presence of pedunculated olfactory bulbs in rhipidistians strongly suggests that this condition is plesiomorphic for sarcopterygians, particularly if additional characters corroborate the hypothesis that rhipidistians are the sister group of amphibians. In this context, the presence of pedunculated olfactory bulbs in *Latimeria* and *Neoceratodus* would be interpreted as the retention of a plesiomorphic sarcopterygian trait.

Comparable problems of interpretation plague determination of the polarity of the superficial isthmal nucleus, a laminated dorsal thalamus protruding into the third ventricle, and evaginated hemispheres with a pronounced septum ependymale. While it is extremely probable that these characters are homologous in *Latimeria* and *Neoceratodus*, they may be either symplesiomorphies or synapomorphies.

The most obvious conclusion reached after examining the nervous system of living sarcopterygians is that the nervous system of *Latimeria* and *Neoceratodus* are very similar to each other, as are the nervous systems of lepidosirenid lungfishes, caecilians, and salamanders. If *Neoceratodus* is considered the most plesiomorphic species among living lungfishes, then most lepidosirenid apomorphies have apparently arisen by paedomorphosis (see Bemis, '84 for evidence that many derived characters among living lungfishes are paedomorphic). It is possible that our inability to examine the neural characters of a relevant outgroup (rhipidistians) that does not exhibit extensive paedomorphic characters leads us to interpret many sarcopterygian plesiomorphic characters as apomorphic characters, due to the fact that the most widely distributed characters among living sarcopterygians are paedomorphic and resemble plesiomorphic characters present in living outgroups that can be examined. Thus a superficial isthmal nucleus, a laminated dorsal thalamus, and evaginated cerebral hemispheres exhibiting a septum ependymale may be plesiomorphic characters for bony fishes that have been retained in *Latimeria* and *Neoceratodus*. These considerations suggest that cladistic analyses of soft tissue characters in living groups that exhibit pronounced paedomorphosis are of limited value. Where extensive paedomorphosis exists in extant groups, a cladistic analysis must rely heavily on hard tissue characters whose polarity can be determined by examining fossil taxa.

The possible synapomorphy of the rostral organs of *Latimeria* and the labial sacs of *Neoceratodus* is presently very tenuous. While the rostral organs of *Latimeria* are almost certainly electroreceptive organs (Bemis and Hetherington, '82), the innervation and function(s) of the labial sacs of *Neoceratodus* are unknown. In this context, the possible homology of these organs to the tentacular organs of apodans and the nasolacrimal ducts of salamanders is based primarily on topography and only suggests a fruitful area of research.

Finally, Kremers ('81) listed two additional possible synapomorphies linking *Latimeria* and lungfishes, neither of which appears to be valid: the lack of a bilaterally lobed optic tectum and the presence of an evaginated thin-walled subpallium of the cerebral hemispheres. The optic tectum of *Neoceratodus* is clearly bilobed (Holmgren and van der Horst, '25; Northcutt, '80), and an evaginated thin-walled subpallium is probably a plesiomorphic character of gnathostomes, as it also occurs among cartilaginous fishes.

In summary, a survey of neural characters among living sarcopterygians supports the hypotheses that actinistians, dipnoans, and amphibians are each monophyletic taxa. However, further analysis is complicated by a high frequency of paedomorphic characters in lepidosirenid lungfishes and amphibians. Such characters make it difficult to determine the polarity of the homologies. Most of the neural characters that could constitute synapomorphies for any two of the three living sarcopterygian groups could also be symplesiomorphies for all sarcopterygians, unrecognized as such because of our inability to examine the relevant neural characters in extinct groups. On the basis of neural characters alone, it appears impossible to determine whether amphibians or lungfishes are the sister group of actinistians; such determination must rely on characters for which there is a substantial fossil record.

ACKNOWLEDGMENTS

I am grateful to Patricia Kay for untiring tenacity in retrieving the literature referenced herein. William L. Fink, Richard L. Puzdrowski, Georg F. Striedter, and Mario Wullimann kindly read the manuscript and have offered insightful and provocative comments in our discussions. Mary Sue Northcutt assisted in many phases of my own research and in the preparation of this paper. The research was supported by NIH grants NS11006 and EY02485.

LITERATURE CITED

Agar, W. E. (1906) The spiracular gill cleft in *Lepidosiren* and *Protopterus*. Anat. Anz. *28*:298–304.

Ariëns Kappers, C. U., G. C. Huber, and E. C. Crosby (1936) The Comparative Anatomy of the Nervous System of Vertebrates, Including Man. New York: Hafner.

Barry, M. A., and R. L. Boord (1984) The spiracular organ of sharks and skates: Anatomical evidence indicating a mechanoreceptive role. Science *226*:990–992.

Beauregard, D. H. (1881) Encéphale et nerfs craniens du *Ceratodus forsteri*. J. Anat. Physiol. *17*:1–13.

Bemis, W. E. (1984) Paedomorphosis and the evolution of the Dipnoi. Paleobiol. *10*:293–307.

Bemis, W. E., and T. E. Hetherington (1982) The rostral organ of *Latimeria chalumnae*: Morphological evidence of an electroreceptive function. Copeia *1982*:467–471.

Bertmar, G. (1965) The olfactory organ and upper lips in Dipnoi, an embryological study. Acta Zool. Stockholm *46*:1–10.

Bing, R., and R. Burckhardt (1904) Das Zentralnervensystem von *Ceratodus forsteri*. Anat. Anz. *25*:588–599.

Burckhardt, R. (1892) Das Centralnervensystem von *Protopterus annectens*. Berlin: Verlag v. Friedländer & Sohn.

Burne, R. H. (1913) Note on the membranous labyrinth of *Neoceratodus forsteri*. Anat. Anz. *43*:396–400.

Clairambault, P., and E. Capanna (1973) Suggestions for a revison of the cytoarchitectonics of the telencephalon of Protopterus, *Protopterus annectens* (Owen). Boll. Zool. *40*:149–171.

Clairambault, P., E. Capanna, M. Chanconie, and G. Pinganaud (1974) Architectural pattern of the diencephalon and mesencephalon of the African lungfish *Protopterus dolloi*. Boll. Zool. *41*:107–122.

Clairambault, P., and C. Flood (1975) Les centres visuels primaires de *Protopterus dolloi* Boulenger. J. Hirnforsch. *16*:497–509.

Cope, E. D. (1884) Note on the phylogeny of the Vertebrata. Am. Nat. *18*:1255–1257.

Cope, E. D. (1887) Geology and palaeontology. Am. Nat. *21*:1014–1019.

Cope, E. D. (1892) On the phylogeny of the Vertebrata. Proc. Am. Phil. Soc. *30*:278–281.

Dempster, W. T. (1930) The morphology of the amphibian endolymphatic organ. J. Morphol. *50*:71–126.

Derivot, J. H. (1984a) Functional anatomy of the peripheral olfactory system of the African lungfish *Protopterus annectens* Owen: macroscopic, microscopic, and morphometric aspects. Am. J. Anat. *169*:177–192.

Derivot, J. H. (1984b) Functional anatomy of the peripheral olfactory system of the African lungfish *Protopterus annectens* Owen: development of the primary olfactory pathway during postembryonic growth. Am. J. Anat. *171*:15–23.

Dollo, L. (1896) Sur la phylogénie des dipneustes. Bull. Soc. Belge Geol. Paleontol. Hydrol. *9*:79–128.

Elliot Smith, G. (1908) The cerebral cortex in *Lepidosiren*, with comparative notes on the interpretation of certain features of the forebrain in other vertebrates. Anat. Anz. *33*:513–540.

Fitzinger, L. J. F. J. (1837) Vorläufiger Bericht über eine höchst interessante Entdeckung Dr. Natters in Brasil. Isis, Jena, pp. 379–390.

Fullarton, M. H. (1933) On the development of the olfactory organ in *Protopterus*. Proc. R. Soc. Edinburgh *53*:1–16.

Fulliquet, G. (1886) Recherches sur le cerveau de *Protopterus annectens*. Geneve. (cited by Elliot Smith, 1908).

Gaffney, E. S. (1979) Tetrapod monophyly: A phylogenetic analysis. Bull. Carnegie Mus. Nat. Hist. *13*:92–105.

Gerlach, J. (1933) Über das Gehirn von *Protopterus annectens*. Anat. Anz. *75*:310–406.

Goodrich, E. S. (1924) The origin of land vertebrates. Nature *114*:935–936.

Gregory, W. K. (1915) Present status of the problem of the origin of the Tetrapoda, with special reference to the skull and paired limbs. Ann. N.Y. Acad. Sci. *26*:317–383.

Günther, A. C. L. G. (1871) Description of *Ceratodus*, a genus of ganoid fishes, recently discovered in rivers of Queensland, Australia. Phil. Trans. R. Soc. London *161*:511–571.

Haeckel, E. (1889) Natürliche SchöpfungsGeschichte. Berlin: G. Reimer.

Holmgren, N., and C. J. van der Horst (1925) Contribution to the morphology of the brain of *Ceratodus*. Acta Zool. *6*:59–165.

Huxley, T. H. (1876) Contributions to morphology. Ichthyopsida No. 1. On *Ceratodus forsteri*, with observations on the classification of fishes. Proc. Zool. Soc. London pp. 24–59.

Jarvik, E. (1980) Basic Structure and Evolution of Vertebrates, Vol. 1. London: Academic Press.

Keenan, E. (1928) The phylogenetic development of the substantia gelatinosa Rolandi. Part I. Fishes. Proc. R.

Acad. Amsterdam *31:*837–854.

Kerr, J. G. (1902) The development of *Lepidosiren paradoxa.* Q. J. Mic. Sci. *46:*417–459.

Kerr, J. G. (1932) Archaic fishes—*Lepidosiren, Protopterus, Polypterus*—and their bearing upon problems of vertebrate morphology. Jena Z. Natur. *67:*419–433.

Krefft, J. (1870) Description of a gigantic amphibian allied to the genus *Lepidosiren*, from the Wide Bay District, Queensland. Proc. Zool. Soc. London pp. 221–224.

Kremers, J. W. P. M. (1981) The Brain of the Crossopterygian Fish *Latimeria chalumnae* Smith. Nijmegen: Stichting Studentenpers.

Kremers, J. W. P. M., and R. Nieuwenhuys (1979) Topological analysis of the brain stem of the crossopterygian fish *Latimeria chalumnae.* J. Comp. Neurol. *187:*613–638.

Kuhlenbeck, H. 1924 Über die Homologien der Zellmassen im Hemisphärenhirn der Wirbeltiere. 1924 Folia Anatomica Japonica *2:*325–364.

Lagios, M. D. (1975) The pituitary gland of the coelacanth *Latimeria chalumnae* Smith. Gen. Comp. Endocrinol. *25:*126–146.

Larsell, O. (1967) The Comparative Anatomy and Histology of the Cerebellum from Myxinoids through Birds. Minneapolis: University of Minnesota Press.

Lemire, M. (1971) Etude architectonique du rhombencéphale de *Latimeria chalumnae* Smith. Bull. Muséum Nat. D'Histoire Naturelle, sér. 3, no. 2, pp. 41–95.

Millot, J., and J. Anthony (1956) L'organe rostral de *Latimeria* (Coelacanthidae). Comptes Rendus Acad. Sci. Paris *239:*1241–1243.

Millot, J., and J. Anthony (1958) Anatomie de *Latimeria chalumnae.* Tome I., Squellete, Muscles et Formations de Soutien. Paris: Centre National Recherche Scientifique.

Millot, J., and J. Anthony (1965) Anatomie de *Latimeria chalumnae.* Tome II., Système Nerveux et Organes de Sens. Paris: Centre National Recherche Scientifique.

Millot, J., and J. Anthony (1967) L'Organisation générale du prosencephale de *Latimeria chalumnae* Smith (Poisson crossopterygien coelacanthide). In R. Hassler and H. Stephan (eds): Evolution of the Forebrain. New York: Plenum, pp. 50–60.

Millot, J., R. Nieuwenhuys, and J. Anthony (1964) Le diencéphale de *Latimeria chalumnae* Smith (Poisson Coelacanthidé). Comptes Rendus Acad. Sci. Paris *258:*5051–5055.

Natterer, J. (1837) *Lepidosiren paradoxa*, eine neue Gatung aus der Familie der fischähnlichen Reptilien. Ann. Naturhist. Mus. Wien *2:*165–170.

Nieuwenhuys, R. (1965) The forebrain of the crossopterygian *Latimeria chalumnae* Smith. J. Morphol. *117:*1–24.

Nieuwenhuys, R. (1969) A survey of the structure of the forebrain in higher bony fishes (Osteichthyes). Ann. N.Y. Acad. Sci. *167:*31–64.

Nieuwenhuys, R. (1977) The brain of the lamprey in a comparative perspective. Ann. N.Y. Acad. Sci. *299:*97–145.

Nieuwenhuys, R., and M. Hickey (1965) A survey of the forebrain of the Australian lungfish *Neoceratodus forsteri.* J. Hirnforsch. *7:*434–452.

Nieuwenhuys, R., J. P. M. Kremers, and C. van Huijzen (1977) The brain of the the the crossopterygian fish *Latimeria chalumnae:* A survey of its gross structure. Anat. Embryol. *151:*157–169.

Nieuwenhuys, R., and E. Pouwels (1983) The brain stem of actinopterygian fishes. In R. G. Northcutt and R. E. Davis (eds): Fish Neurobiology, Vol. 1 Ann Arbor: University of Michigan Press, pp. 25–87.

Noble, G. K. (1931) The Biology of the Amphibia. New York: McGraw-Hill. Republished, 1954, New York: Dover.

Norris, H. W., and S. P. Hughes (1920) The spiracular sense-organ in elasmobranchs, ganoids and dipnoans. Anat. Rec. *18:*205–209.

Northcutt, R. G. (1977) Retinofugal projections in the lepidosirenid lungfishes. J. Comp. Neurol. *174:*553–574.

Northcutt, R. G. (1980) Retinal projections in the Australian lungfish. Brain Res. *185:*85–90.

Northcutt, R. G. (1981) Evolution of the telencephalon in nonmammals. Ann. Rev. Neurosci. *4:*301–350.

Northcutt, R. G. (1983) The primary lateral line afferents in lepidosirenid lungfishes. Soc. Neurosci. Abstr. *9:*1167.

Northcutt, R. G. (1985) The brain and sense organs of the earliest vertebrates: Reconstruction of a morphotype. In R. E. Foreman, A. Gorbman, J. M. Dodd, and R. Olsson (eds): Evolutionary Biology of Primitive Fishes. New York: Plenum, pp. 81–112.

Northcutt, R. G. (1986) Electroreception in non-teleost bony fishes. In T. H. Bullock and W. Heiligenberg (eds): Electroreception. New York: Wiley, pp. 257–285.

Northcutt, R. G., and E. E. Kicliter (1980) Organization of the amphibian telencephalon. In S. O. E. Ebbesson (ed): Comparative Neurology of the Telencephalon. New York: Plenum, pp. 203–255.

Northcutt, R. G., and T. J. Neary (1975) Observations on the optic tectum of the coelacanth, *Latimeria chalumnae.* Am. Zool. *15:*806.

Northcutt, R. G., T. J. Neary, and D. G. Senn (1978) Observations on the brain of the coelacanth, *Latimeria chalumnae:* External anatomy and quantitative analysis. J. Morphol. *155:*181–192.

Northcutt, R. G., and A. Reiner (1985) An immunohistochemical study of the telencephalon of the African lungfish. Soc. Neurosci. Abstr. *11:*1310.

Northcutt, R. G., and G. J. Royce (1975) Olfactory bulb projections in the bullfrog *Rana catesbeina.* J. Morphol. *145:*251–267.

Owen, R. (1841) Description of the *Lepidosiren annectens.* Trans. Linnean Soc. London *18:*327–361.

Pehrson, T., (1949) The ontogeny of the lateral line system in the head of dipnoans. Acta Zool. *30:*153–182.

Romer, A. S. (1933) Vertebrate Paleontology, 1st ed. Chicago: University of Chicago Press.

Romer, A. S. (1937) The braincase of the Carboniferous crossopterygian *Megalichthys nitidus.* Bull. Mus. Comp. Zool. *82:*1–73.

Rosen, D. E., P. L. Forey, B. G. Gardiner, and C. Patterson (1981) Lungfishes, tetrapods, paleontology, and plesiomorphy. Bull. Am. Mus. Nat. Hist. *167:*163–275.

Rudebeck, B. (1944) Does an accessory olfactory bulb exist in Dipnoi? Acta Zool. *25:*89–96.

Rudebeck, B. (1945) Contributions to forebrain morphology in Dipnoi. Acta Zool. *26:*9–156.

Sanders, A. (1889) Contributions to the anatomy of the central nervous system in *Ceratodus forsteri.* Ann. Mag. Nat. Hist. *3:*157–188.

Säve-Söderbergh, G. (1935) On the dermal bones of the head in labyrinthodont stegocephalians and primitive Reptilia. Meddel. Grønland *98:*1–211.

Schmalhausen, I. I. (1968) The Origin of Terrestrial Vertebrates. New York: Academic Press.

Schnitzlein, H. N., and E. C. Crosby (1967) The telencephalon of the lungfish, *Protopterus.* J. Hirnforsch. *9:*105–149.

Schnitzlein, H. N., and E. C. Crosby (1968) The epithalamus and thalamus of the lungfish, *Protopterus.* J. Hirnforsch. *10:*351–371.

Smeets, W. J. A. J., R. Nieuwenhuys, and B. L. Roberts (1983) The Central Nervous System of Cartilaginous Fishes. Berlin: Springer-Verlag.

Thors, F., and R. Nieuwenhuys (1979) Topological analysis of the brain stem of the lungfish *Lepidosiren paradoxa*. J. Comp. Neurol. *187*:589–612.

Whiteside, B. (1922) The development of the saccus endolymphaticus in *Rana temporaria* Linné. Am. J. Anat. *30*:231–266.

Wilder, B. G. (1887) The dipnoan brain. Am. Nat. *21*:544–548.

Zottoli, S. J. (1978) Comparative morphology of the Mauthner cell in fish and amphibians. In D. S. Faber and H. Korn (eds): Neurobiology of the Mauthner Cell. New York: Raven Press, pp. 13–45.

JOURNAL OF MORPHOLOGY SUPPLEMENT 1:299–303 (1986)

The Biology of Lungfishes: An Epilogue

KAREL F. LIEM
Museum of Comparative Zoology Harvard University,
Cambridge, Massachusetts 02138

The present symposium shows convincingly how an interdisciplinary study may illuminate many important biological problems for such a seemingly specialized subject as the biology of lungfishes. Although the contributions to this volume seem highly diverse, all of them deal either directly or indirectly with evolution. The volume clearly reflects the end of the traditional era during which biologists could be classified as either functional biologists or evolutionary biologists (Mayr, '76:359). Functional biologists approached problems experimentally and asked the ever-repeated question, "How does something operate?", whereas evolutionary biologists asked the historical, "How has it come to work?" We can indeed analyze biological phenomena either by equilibrium or by historical analysis (Liem and Wake, '85). Equilibrium analysis considers organisms to be in complete equilibrium with their environment (extrinsic factors); it searches for present-day environmental correlates of structure. In contrast, historical analysis focuses on the evolutionary transformation of intrinsic organizational features (Lauder, '81). However, a complete explanation for the biology of lungfishes requires a synthetic blend of both equilibrium and historical analyses. This symposium represents such an integrative approach to the lungfishes, a group that holds important answers to key evolutionary questions surrounding the emergence of tetrapods.

SCOPE OF SYMPOSIUM
Literature on dipnoan biology

E.B. Conant provides us with a general overview of 150 years of research on dipnoan biology, basing this on 2,200 citations. The anatomy, physiology, ecology, and behavior is best known for *Protopterus*, whereas *Lepidosiren* is perhaps the least researched lungfish. Even this symposium does not include a discussion of the biology of *Lepidosiren*. Only Wake's paper on urogenital morphology, Burggren and Johansen's review on circulation and respiration, and Bemis' paper on feeding include *Lepidosiren* in the discus-

sions. This paucity of modern data on *Lepidosiren* may well be the result of the false assumption that most of the biology of *Lepidosiren* is virtually identical to that of *Protopterus*. It is clear that much more research is needed on *Lepidosiren* in order to gain a comprehensive comparative perspective of living dipnoans. Preliminary experimental studies in my laboratory have revealed differences between *Lepidosiren* and *Protopterus* in their mechanisms of ventilation and respiratory strategies that can be correlated with differences in their respective environments rather than with their morphological differences. Conant's overview also reveals that as new experimental approaches became available, physiology, biochemistry, functional morphology, and ultrastructure of the lungfishes underwent quantum progress. However, a rich historical literature grew as controversies surrounding the evolutionary relationships of lungfishes, rhipidistians, and tetrapods increased in number and intensity. It is evident from this symposium that the controversy that began 140 years ago has not yet subsided.

Historical analysis

C.R. Marshall furnishes an up-to-date list of the six extant species and 55 genera and 112 fossil species and their phylogeny. This comprehensive list allows one to decipher that the rate of morphological change was the greatest soon after the origin of the Dipnoi in the Devonian and became very low during the Carboniferous. Structural analysis of the Dipnoi has generated nested sets of unique derived structural features with which the dipnoan species can be ordered into clusters; these can be interpreted as a phylogeny. Marshall offers a critical re-examination of the phylogenetic relationships within the Dipnoi and presents a new phylogeny on a richer empirical base than was previously possible. He concludes that both dentitions added to during growth and organized tooth plates have arisen only once. His proposed phylogeny is the most robust hypothesis available and will form the basis for future workers interested in evolutionary questions on Dipnoi.

A thorough structural analysis of the head skeleton of the primitive dipnoans has enabled H.-P. Schultze and K.S.W. Campbell to define the fossil and extant dipnoans as a monophyletic group characterized by 21 shared derived characters.

K.S.W. Campbell and R.E. Barwick have made a landmark contribution on the basis of an elegant and detailed structural analysis of the primitive dipnoans *Griphognathus*, *Speonesydrion*, and *Holodipterus*. They have successfully interpreted the structural features of the skull, jaws, hyoid, and gill arches in functional terms. Thus they combine a historical analysis with an equilibrium analysis by giving the latter approach a time axis in that structural changes of the primitive dipnoans are described as adaptive transformations to changing environments. They postulate that early dipnoans were sluggish bottom-feeding animals of marine origin, which were not air-breathers. Finally, they caution that structural specializations of the heart and circulatory systems of modern lungfish related to air breathing must have been derived after the dipnoans became a separate group. Similarities in the respiratory and circulatory systems of modern lungfishes and amphibians would therefore be the result of convergent evolution.

Likewise, H.-P. Schultze offers an elegant and impressive anatomical analysis of numerous structures in a broad spectrum of sarcopterygian fishes and concludes that dipnoans are not the sister group of tetrapods. He and K.W.S. Campbell argue that characters of the soft and skeletal anatomy of advanced dipnoan genera should not be taken as representative of the whole of the Dipnoi in the absence of corroborative evidence.

An alternate hypothesis (Rosen et al., '81) is defended by P.L. Forey, who reviews the evidence that lungfishes and tetrapods are sister-groups and that coelacanths are the primitive sister-group to that combined group. Forey offers 15 synapomorphies including skeletal, ontogenetic, myological, cardiovascular, endocrinological, and lens protein features linking Dipnoi with tetrapods. Thus this symposium has not resolved the competing hypotheses on Dipnoi-Tetrapods relationships, a problem raised by Bischoff in 1840. The solution will most likely emerge when more shared derived characters are found and ordered into the most parsimonious nested set. It is very important

that this problem be resolved, as only a corroborated hypotheis of phylogeny will lead to testable generalizations about historical and ontogenetic changes of form (Fink, '82).

D.K. Meinke has demonstrated repeated heterochronic changes in the dipnoan dermal skeleton. Heterochronic changes have produced a dermal skeleton that is juvenilized in descendant dipnoan lineages with respect to the primitive condition. She also presents evidence that several distinct developmental pathways have been altered rather than that a single morphogenetic event occurred. It is important to stress that the general conclusions Meinke was able to draw on developmental patterns and pathways reflect the availability of the phylogenetic information and theories presented earlier in this symposium.

Ecology

Living lungfishes represent the legacy of more than 380 million years of dipnoan evolution. Yet remarkably little is known about their ecology aside from very general observations on their natural history as summarized by P.H. Greenwood for *Protopterus* and A. Kemp for *Neoceratodus*. As information on *Lepidosiren* is so limited, no account on the neotropical genus is given in this symposium. Ecologically, *Protopterus* appears eurytopic, inhabiting a great variety of habitats each of which is, in turn, subject to much periodic variation. It exploits a great variety of food resources, engages in parental care and requires specific breeding sites to maximize the survival of nestlings. However, no data are available on the relative proficiency with which *Protopterus* uses the different food resources under fluctuating environmental conditions. Contrary to common belief among biologists, A. Kemp's findings indicate that *Neoceratodus* is also eurytopic, occurring in diverse environments and feeding on a wide array of prey types. However, its spawning grounds are restricted to areas with abundant plant growth and high oxygen tensions. In contrast to *Protopterus* and *Lepidosiren*, *Neoceratodus* does not engage in parental care.

A. Kemp and P.H. Greenwood have provided us with an up-to-date foundation of the natural history of extant lungfishes. However, much ecological research is needed, including long-term field studies on population dynamics, reproductive strategies, and behavioral responses to stress. Occasional bottlenecks of intense selection during a small portion of the life history of lungfishes may reveal adaptive features that cannot be detected by short-term studies in the laboratory. There is no information on the behavioral ecology of larvae, nestlings, and postnestling juveniles. Intense selection may well be exerted on these vulnerable ontogenetic stages, during which aquatic respiration often depends on very specialized countercurrent flow mechanisms, as shown in *Neoceratodus* (Whiting and Bone, '80) and in *Monopterus,* a close ecological analog of *Protopterus* (Liem, '81).

Functional analysis

In finding present-day environmental correlates of physiological adaptations in lungfishes, experimental biologists hope to gain a better understanding of the various mechanisms that have played an important role in the emergence of tetrapods. The basic premise is that ancestors of the tetrapods were similar physiologically to the modern lungfishes. W. Burggren and K. Johansen demonstrate that modern lungfishes possess cardiorespiratory features that distinguish them from other air-breathing fishes and align them more closely with tetrapods. *Neoceratodus* is an obligatory water breather with less septate lungs, more fully developed gills, and a less partitioned central circulation. In sharp contrast, *Lepidosiren* and *Protopterus,* having cardio-respiratory structures and functions strongly modified for aerial respiration and terrestrial survival, possess many features comparable to those of the tetrapods. Burggren and Johansen postulate that the lung ventilatory mechanism seen in extant Dipnoi is similar to that of the earliest tetrapods and that aspiration ventilation of the lung replaced buccal force ventilation only later as ribs took on increasing structural importance. In *Protopterus* and *Lepidosiren,* dependence upon aerial respiration increases dramatically as body mass increases. Futhermore, the respiratory properties of blood show a remarkable adaptability to various environmental conditions. A.P. Fishman, A.I. Pack, R.G. Delaney, and R.J. Galante show that estivation in *Protopterus* is accompanied by a complete reliance on air breathing, a slowing of the heart rate, and a drop in oxygen consumption as well as blood pressure. Equipped with these adaptive features, *Protopterus* has entered a number of habitats that are unavailable or only temporarily available to actinopterygian fishes. It is argued that such a penetration of inhospit-

able areas is made possible by the physiological adaptability of the cardiovascular apparatus, the facility to burrow and estivate, oliguria, and a shift in metabolic pathways. Interesting physiological and ecological analogs of these phenomena in the actinopterygian fish *Synbranchus marmoratus* are being studied by Jeffrey Graham at the Scripps Institution of Oceanography. Fishman et al. emphasize that the initiating mechanisms for estivation in *Protopterus* remain unknown, but may be related to starvation. They made no attempt to extrapolate from their knowledge of estivation in *Protopterus* to *Lepidosiren,* an area that remains very poorly studied.

Functional morphology of the feeding systems of living lungfishes has yielded perhaps the broadest data base upon which general conclusions can be made on dipnoan evolution. W.E. Bemis has shown that all dipnoans possess a plesiomorphic feeding system that is retained in primitive tetrapods. The primitive feeding pattern is that of unidirectional suction with an elevated head and a lowered mandible followed by a depressed hyoid. Maximization of suction results from a greater excursion of the hyoid made possible by the reduced hyoid arch and, the well-differentiated cranial ribs that evolved in all dipnoans. Within the Dipnoi, *Neoceratodus* differs from lepidosirenids in its ability to grind food with the mobile rami of the mandible, which lost some elements, whereas *Lepidosiren* and *Protopterus* cut and crush their food—for which the rigidly stabilized rami of the mandible are well adapted. The mandible in lepidosirenids is operated by depressor mandibulae and large adductor mandibulae muscles that are accommodated by the reduction of roofing as well as opercular bones. Bemis's analysis shows convincingly how various structural elements are functionally integrated into major complexes that evolve in close unison rather than as individual independent entities.

The lungfish, the cow, and the salmon revisited

M.H. Wake and R.G. Northcutt re-examine existing hypotheses on the relationships of lungfishes, tetrapods, and primitive actinopterygian fishes by studying the comparative anatomy of, respectively, the urinogenital and nervous systems. Wake concludes that dipnoan urinogenital features are shared with many osteichthyans and show a primitive vertebrate pattern. Derived urinogenital features shared by dipnoans and some amphibian species are due to convergent evolution. Thus, comparative anatomy of the urinogenital system does not support the hypothesis that dipnoans and tetrapods are sister-groups. Northcutt concludes that it is impossible to determine whether amphibians or lungfishes are the sister-group of coelacanths (actinistians). On the basis of an impressive analysis of neural characters, Northcutt is unable to generate substantial support for the hypothesis that the Dipnoi is a sister-group of the tetrapods. Instead, neural features favor a sister-group relationship of lungfishes and coelacanths (actinistians). More importantly, Northcutt has discovered an unusually high frequency of paedomorphic neural characters in lepidosirenid lungfishes and amphibians making it difficult to determine the polarity of the character transformations.

CONCLUDING REMARKS

The present symposium shows that even though much progress has been made since Thomson's ('69) benchmark contribution on the biology of lobe-finned fishes, the analysis of this intriguing evolutionary transition from aquatic to terrestrial vertebrate life has only begun. Many important questions await future research workers. Obviously, studies of tetrapod origins are highly speculative and are likely to remain so. Nevertheless it should be possible to judge the various hypotheses of dipnoans and tetrapods on the basis of a rapidly expanding data base of both fossil and extant forms and the application of objective phylogenetic methods. Whether the Dipnoi and tetrapods are sister groups remains a tantalizing but elusive problem. A greater focus on embryology may produce some important clues to the polarity of evolutionary change. The phylogenetic significance of the presence of ciliated larvae in *Neoceratodus* and some amphibians (Whiting and Bone, '80) has not been evaluated in this symposium. Bemis ('84) has shown that paedomorphosis has played an important role in dipnoan evolution. Both Meinke and Northcutt have provided a substantial data base of dermal and neural paedomorphic characters in lepidosirenid lungfishes. Thus we have now very good evidence for postulating a paedomorphic origin of lepidosirenid dipnoans in which morphological plasticity of juvenile structures has been preserved by the linking of retarded somatic development with delayed maturation.

In order to understand the ecological aspects of the origins of tetrapods we must theorize from the known to the unknown. This symposium illuminates our inadequate knowledge of the ecology of extant dipnoans. We still do not know the mechanisms triggering estivation. There are no explicit accounts that any dipnoan species makes seemingly purposeful excursions on land. Do dipnoans feed on terrestrial invertebrates? What was the original function of overland excursions? The dipnoan nephron possesses a ciliated neck and an intermediate segment, indicating a basic adaptation to eliminate large volumes of water. How does the osmoregulatory apparatus reverse its function when a premium is put on water retention during terrestrial excursions or prior to estivation?

In general most biologists agree that exceptionally ancient fishes have escaped extinction because they may have unusual general adaptations. It appears that extant dipnoans are indeed broadly adapted. They live on a variety of foods and in diverse habitats, and environmental factors may fluctuate greatly without requiring any evolutionary change for survival. Lungfishes have apparently been bradytelic for perhaps 200 million years. A broadly-based comparative study of the biology of "living fossils" may shed light on the various factors contributing to the ability of particular animal groups to resist extinction without appreciable evolutionary change. From my perspective, the most general usage of the term lungfish-tetrapod relationship embodies the range of evolutionary questions presented in this volume. It is hoped that the volume will act as a semaphore to alert biologists to this set of unique opportunities to solve important biological problems.

ACKNOWLEDGMENTS

I thank Carl Gans for improving this manuscript and Karsten Hartel, Christine Fox, and Frances Irish for their help and comments. I am grateful for support from NSF Grant DCB 85-00585.

LITERATURE CITED

Bemis, W.E. (1984) Paedomorphosis and the evolution of the Dipnoi. Paleobiology *10*:293–307.
Bischoff, T.L.W. (1840) *Lepidosiren paradoxa* Anatomisch untersucht und beschrieben. Leipzig: Leopold Voss.
Fink, W. L. (1982) The conceptual relationship between ontogeny and phylogeny. Paleobiology 8:254–264.
Lauder, G. V. (1981) Form and function: Structural anal-

ysis in evolutionary morphology. Paleobiology 7:430–442.

Liem, K. F. (1981) Larvae of air-breathing fishes as countercurrent flow devices in hypoxic environments. Science *211*:1177–1179.

Liem, K. F., and D. B. Wake (1985) Morphology: Current approaches and concepts. In M. Hildebrand, D. Bramble, K.F. Liem, and D.B. Wake (eds): Functional Vertebrate Morphology. Cambridge: Belknap Press of Harvard University Press, pp. 366–377.

Mayr, E. (1976) Evolution and the diversity of life. Cambridge: Belknap Press of Harvard University Press.

Rosen, D.E., P.L. Forey, B.G. Gardiner, and C. Patterson (1981) Lungfishes, tetrapods, paleontology, and plesiomorphy. Bull. Am. Mus. Nat. Hist. *167*:159–276.

Thomson, K.S. (1969) The biology of the lobe-finned fishes. Biol Rev. *44*:91–154

Whiting, H.P., and Q. Bone (1980) Ciliary cells in the epidermis of the larval Australian dipnoan, *Neoceratodus*. Zool. J. Linn. Soc. *68*:125–137.

JOURNAL OF MORPHOLOGY SUPPLEMENT 1:305–373 (1986)

Bibliography of Lungfishes, 1811–1985

ELIZABETH BABBOT CONANT
Department of Biology, Canisius College, Buffalo, New York 14208

Code For Bibliography

P	*Protopterus*	1	Anatomy, including histology, cytology, and karyology
L	*Lepidosiren*		
N	*Neoceratodus (Epiceratodus, Ceratodus, Recent)*	2	Biochemistry, pharmacology, and general physiology
C	*Ceratodus* (Fossil)	3	Tegumentary system, including scales, color
D	Dipnoi	4	Skeletal system, including teeth
F	Fossil (used with other category: FD, FL, FP, FN)	5	Muscular system
		6	Nervous system
O	Other, i.e., not dipnoans exclusively	7	Sensory systems
G	Denotes General Information, e.g., G(1 10 11) (not indexed)	8	Endocrine system
		9	Respiratory system
		10	Air-breathing, including lungs
*	Signifies that paper was annotated from its abstract only	11	Circulation, including cardiology, immunology, lymphatics
+	Signifies that paper was annotated from its title only	12	Digestion (including coproliths, in conjunction with 'F')
( )	Signifies categories used comparatively, as descriptors	13	Excretory system
		14	Reproductive system
		15	Embryological development
O	Following genus (e.g., PO) signifies significant dipnoan material	16	Growth and regeneration
		17	Evolution, phylogenetic relationships
O	Preceding genus (e.g., OPL) signifies that the dipnoan material is embedded in a larger series or is less significant.	18	Natural history, zoogeography, ecology, location of fossil
		19	Behavior, excluding estivation and feeding
		20	Estivation
		21	Feeding
		22	Pathology, parasitism and predation
		23	Fishing and fisheries
		24	Fish and human culture

Ceratodus, **Anatomy:** 16, 66, 179–180, 207, 266, 282, 355, 357, 365, 371, 427–428, 431, 484, 652, 663, 1033–1034, 1185, 1235, 1239, 1257–1260, 1272, 1326–1327, 1329–1330, 1334–1335, 1357, 1386, 1389, 1433, 1505, 1607–1608, 1610, 1612–1613, 1669, 1681, 1832, 1882, 1943, 1978, 2001, 2077, 2079–2080, 2084, 2091, 2106, 2180–2181, 2205

Ceratodus, **Biochemistry, Pharmacology, and General Physiology:**

Ceratodus, **Tegumentary System:** 66, 370, 483, 663, 913, 1235, 1237, 1257, 1433, 2083, 2091, 2095

Ceratodus, **Skeletal System:** 16, 41, 42, 65, 66, 137, 179, 180, 207, 266, 274–275, 284, 291, 327, 345, 355, 357–358, 365, 371, 376, 390, 426–428, 431, 441, 483–484, 530, 539, 564–565, 648, 652, 663, 872, 904, 910, 963, 991, 1018, 1030, 1033, 1114, 1172, 1183, 1185, 1195, 1235, 1237–1239, 1258–1260, 1272, 1322, 1326–1330, 1332–1335, 1337–1338, 1357, 1386, 1387, 1389, 1418, 1492, 1505, 1526, 1566, 1607–1608, 1610–1613, 1634, 1669, 1681, 1713, 1751, 1832, 1866–1867, 1882, 1943, 1948, 1962, 1978–1979, 1983, 2001, 2009–2011, 2018, 2039, 2056, 2079–2080, 2083–2084, 2091, 2095, 2106, 2155, 2174, 2176–2177, 2180–2181, 2191–2192, 2203, 2205

Ceratodus, **Muscular System:** 663

Ceratodus, **Nervous System:** 663

Ceratodus, **Sensory Systems:** 663, 1235, 1330

Ceratodus, **Endocrine System:**

Ceratodus, **Respiratory System:** 66, 663

Ceratodus, **Air-Breathing:** 66, 1433, 1979

Ceratodus, **Circulatory System:**

Ceratodus, **Digestive System:** 327, 1034, 1433, 1505

Ceratodus, **Excretory System:**

Ceratodus, **Reproductive System:** 66

Ceratodus, **Embryological Development:** 66, 266, 663, 1612–1613

Ceratodus, **Growth and Regeneration:** 1257, 1607, 1943, 2083

Ceratodus, **Evolution, Phylogenetic Relationships:** 275, 285, 365, 486, 1337–1338, 1340, 1612, 1802, 2090, 2181

Ceratodus, **Natural History, Zoogeography, Ecology, Location of Fossil:** 19, 41–42, 65–66, 101, 137, 179, 207, 274–275, 282, 284–285, 292, 327, 345, 355–358, 365, 370–371, 376, 390, 426, 428, 431, 441–442, 483–486, 529–530, 539, 564–565, 595, 648, 652, 872, 904, 910, 913, 915, 991, 1018, 1033–1034, 1096, 1114, 1116, 1155, 1172, 1183, 1185, 1195, 1220, 1228, 1235, 1238, 1257–1260, 1271–1272, 1322, 1325–1326, 1328, 1330–1332, 1334, 1337–1338, 1357, 1386–1387, 1389, 1402, 1418, 1433, 1492, 1505, 1510, 1526, 1564, 1566, 1569, 1607–1608, 1611, 1613, 1628, 1634, 1669, 1681–1682, 1713, 1750–1751, 1803, 1840, 1866–1867, 1882, 1906, 1948, 1962, 1978–1979, 1983, 2001, 2007–2011, 2039, 2056, 2077, 2079–2080, 2083, 2084, 2090, 2095–2096, 2106, 2155, 2174, 2176–2177, 2179–2180, 2191–2193, 2203, 2205

Ceratodus, **Behavior:** 66

Ceratodus, **Estivation:** 66, 1235, 1433, 1510

Ceratodus, **Feeding:** 207, 1433, 1979

Ceratodus, **Pathology, Parasitism and Predation:**

Ceratodus, **Fishing and Fisheries:**

Ceratodus, **Fish and Human Culture:** 1183

Protopterus, Estivation: 11, 57, 66, 68, 80, 82, 124, 126, 132, 186, 189–190, 193, 203, 218, 226, 236, 248–249, 252–253, 255, 257, 260, 262–263, 312–313, 350, 378, 404, 409, 412, 415, 434, 447, 450, 459–460, 464, 478, 490–493, 506, 516, 532, 535, 537–538, 547–548, 550, 552, 557, 588–589, 601, 632, 712, 714–716, 720, 724–725, 727–729, 731–733, 735–739, 751, 781, 787, 814, 847, 858, 873, 883, 885, 900–901, 926, 937, 940, 962, 999, 1011, 1023, 1036–1037, 1040–1041, 1045, 1080, 1085, 1093, 1169, 1179, 1208, 1224, 1244, 1247, 1250, 1277, 1284–1285, 1319–1321, 1336, 1350, 1361–1362, 1371, 1384, 1406, 1410–1411, 1413–1414, 1420, 1458, 1516–1517, 1533, 1557–1558, 1561–1562, 1573, 1586, 1590, 1599–1600, 1602, 1631, 1637, 1639–1640, 1642, 1653–1656, 1701, 1705, 1720, 1746, 1754, 1765, 1830, 1871, 1883, 1892, 1912, 1914, 1923, 1925–1926, 1929, 1933–1934, 1964, 1980–1981, 1986–1992, 2004, 2028, 2061, 2100–2101, 2107, 2111, 2147–2148, 2195

Protopterus, Feeding: 75, 103, 140, 148, 163, 189–190, 198, 218, 226, 230, 238, 248, 256, 411, 414, 434, 436, 447, 450, 459, 478, 535, 566, 715, 738, 781, 787, 792, 809, 873, 883, 885, 937, 988, 1023, 1085, 1179, 1217, 1282, 1285, 1295, 1318, 1361–1362, 1367, 1422, 1444, 1470, 1558, 1590, 1592, 1597, 1599, 1632, 1640, 1642, 1650, 1695, 1746, 1833, 1838, 1914, 1930–1931, 1979–1981, 1991, 2028, 2147, 2184–2185

Protopterus, Pathology, Parasitism and Predation: 53, 121, 313, 323, 349, 411, 443, 457–459, 491, 517–520, 555, 615, 658, 848, 865–866, 883, 918, 971, 1156, 1217, 1349, 1444, 1456, 1469, 1635, 1980–1981, 2015, 2070, 2169

Protopterus, Fishing and Fisheries: 86, 142, 151–152, 193, 212, 260, 263, 326, 439, 440, 544, 567, 587, 687, 787, 933, 988, 1022, 1190–1191, 1323–1324, 1422, 1439, 1444, 1672–1673, 1720–1721, 1981, 2116, 2184

Protopterus, Fish and Human Culture: 37, 212, 238, 256, 349, 450, 556, 587, 711, 781, 883, 937, 1011, 1285, 1301, 1320–1321, 1353, 1586, 1602, 1640, 1642, 1701, 1721, 1746, 1981, 2121

---

1 Abrahamsson, Tommy, Susanne Holmgren, Stefan Nilsson, and Knut Pettersson (1978) Catecholamine content in blood plasma, heart and intercostal arteries of the African lungfish. Acta Physiol. Scand. *102*:33A–34A. (Abstract) P:1 2 8 11

2 Abrahamsson, Tommy, Susanne Holmgren, Stefan Nilsson, and Knut Pettersson (1979) On the chromaffin system of the African lungfish, *Protopterus aethiopicus.* Acta Physiol. Scand. *107*:135–139. P:1 2 8 11

3 Abrahamsson, Tommy, Susanne Holmgren, Stefan Nilsson, and Knut Pettersson (1979) Adrenergic and cholinergic effects on the heart, the lung and the spleen of the African lungfish, *Protopterus aethiopicus.* Acta Physiol. Scand. *107*:141–147. P:2 6 8 10 11

4 Abrahamsson, Tommy, Ann-Catherine Jönsson, and Stefan Nilsson (1979) Catecholamine synthesis in the chromaffin tissue of the African lungfish, *Protopterus aethiopicus.* Acta Physiol. Scand. *107*:149–151. P:2 6 8 11

5 Abrahamsson, Tommy (1980) On the peripheral adrenergic system in fish. Thesis, University of Göteborg. PO:2 8 11

6 Acher, Roger, Jacqueline Chauvet, and Marie-Thérèse Chauvet (1970) A tetrapod neurohypophysial hormone in African lungfishes. Nature (London) *227*:186–187. P:2 8 17

7 Acher, Roger, Jacqueline Chauvet, and Marie-Thérèse Chauvet (1970) Phylogeny of the neurohypophysial hormones. The avian active peptides. Eur. J. Biochem. *17*:509–513. O(P):2 8

8 Acher, Roger (1971) The neurohypophyseal hormones: an example of molecular evolution. IN Ernest Schofeniels (ed): Biochemical Evolution and the Origin of Life. New York: North-Holland Pub. Co., pp.43–51. OP:8 17

9 Adams, Leverett Allen (1919) A memoir on the phylogeny of the jaw muscles in recent and fossil vertebrates. Ann. New York Acad. Sci. *28*:51–166. (*Neoceratodus*:80–83). ON:1 4 5 6

10 Agar, Wilfred Eade (1906) The development of the skull and visceral arches in *Lepidosiren* and *Protopterus.* Trans. Roy. Soc. Edinburgh *45*:49–64. LP:1 4 15

11 Agar, Wilfred Eade (1906) The spiracular gill cleft in *Lepidosiren* and *Protopterus.* Anat. Anz. *28*:298–304. LP:4 6 7 11 20

12 Agar, Wilfred Eade (1907) The development of the anterior mesoderm, and paired fins with their nerves, in *Lepidosiren* and *Protopterus.* Trans. Roy. Soc. Edinburgh *45*:611–639. LP(N):1 4 5 6 15

13 Agar, Wilfred Eade (1908) On the appearance of vascular filaments on the pectoral fin of *Lepidosiren paradoxa.* Anat. Anz. *33*:27–30. L:1 9 11

14 Agar, Wilfred Eade (1911) The spermatogenesis of *Lepidosiren paradoxa.* Quart. J. Microsc. Sci. *57*:1–44. L:1 14

15 Agar, Wilfred Eade (1912) Transverse segmentation and internal differentiation of chromosomes. Quart. J. Microsc. Sci. *58*:285–298. L:1

16 Agassiz, Louis (1833) Recherches sur les Poissons Fossiles. Vol. II, III. Neuchâtel: Imprimerie de Petitpierre. (*Ceratodus:* 46, 129-136). 1833–1843 OC:1 4

16a Agassiz, Louis (1844-45) Monographie des poissons fossiles du vieux grès rouge ou système Dévonien (Old Red Sandstone) des Isles Britaniques et de Russie. Neuchâtel: Imprimerie de Petitpierre.

17 Agassiz, Louis (1870) Letter on 'synthetic types'. Nature *3*:166–167.N:4 17

18 Ahl, J., P. C. Schroeder, and John H. Larsen, Jr. (1984) Comparative ultrastructure of mature ovarian follicles of the Australian lungfish, *Neoceratodus forsteri* and amphibians. Amer. Zool. *24*:84A. (Abstract) N(O):1 14

19 Alberti, Friedrich von (1864) Überblick über die Trias. Stuttgart: J. G. Cottaschen Buchhandlung. (*Ceratodus*:205–207). OC:18

20 Albrecht, Paul (1886)Über eine in zwei Zipfel auslaufende, rechtsseitige Vorderflosse bei einem Exemplare von *Protopterus annectens* Ow. Stiz. Akad. Berlin *1886*:545–546. P:16

21 Ali, M. Athar (1971) Les reponses retinomotrices: caractères et mechanismes. Vision Res. *11*:1225–1288. ONPL:1 7 17 19

22 Ali, M. Athar and Michel Anctil (1973) Retina of

the South American lungfish, *Lepidosiren paradoxa* Fitzinger. Can. J. Zool. *51*:969–972. L:1 7

23 Allen, Grant (1885) Fish out of water. Pop. Sci. Monthly *28*:334–342. OP:G(9 10 18 20)

24 Allis, Edward Phelps, Jr. (1914) The pituitary fossa and trigemino-facialis chamber in *Ceratodus forsteri*. Anat. Anz. *46*:625–637. N:1 4 6

25 Allis, Edward Phelps, Jr. (1914) The pseudobranchial and carotid arteries in *Ceratodus forsteri*. Anat. Anz. *46*:638–648. N:1 5 11 15 17

26 Allis, Edward Phelps, Jr. (1915) The homologies of the hyomandibula of the gnathostome fishes. J. Morphol. *26*:563–624. (*Neoceratodus*:594–605). NO:1 4 6 11 15

27 Allis, Edward Phelps, Jr. (1919) The myodome and trigemino-facialis chamber of fishes and the corresponding cavities of higher vertebrates. J. Morphol. *32*:207–325. (*Neoceratodus*:281-284). NO:1 4 6 11 15

28 Allis, Edward Phelps, Jr. (1919) The lips and the nasal apertures in the gnathostome fishes. J. Morphol. *32*:145–205. (Dipnoi:178-183). NO:1 4 15

29 Allis, Edward Phelps, Jr. (1928) Concerning the pituitary fossa, the myodome and the trigemino-facialis chamber in recent gnathostome fishes. J. Anat. *63*:95–141. NO:1 4 15

30 Allis, Edward Phelps, Jr. (1929) Concerning the course of the efferent mandibular artery in *Ceratodus*: a correction. J. Anat. *63*:282. N:1 4 11 15

31 Allis, Edward Phelps, Jr. (1930) Concerning the subpituitary space and the antrum petrosum laterale in the Dipnoi, Amphibia and Reptilia. Acta Zool. (Stockholm) *11*:1–38. ON:1 4 5 11 15

32 Allis, Edward Phelps, Jr. (1932) The pre-oral gut, the buccal cavity and the bucco-pharyngeal opening in *Ceratodus*. J. Anat. *66*:659–668. N:1 4 12 15

33 Allis, Edward Phelps, Jr. (1932) Concerning the nasal apertures, the lachrymal canal and the bucco-pharyngeal upper lip. J. Anat. *66*:650–658. OD:1 4 15

34 Allis, Edward Phelps, Jr. (1934) Concerning the course of the latero-sensory canals in recent fishes, prefishes and *Necturus*. J. Anat. *68*:361–415. (Dipnoi:366–375). NPO:1 6 7 17

35 Allis, Edward Phelps, Jr. (1935) On a general pattern of arrangement of the cranial roofing bones in fishes. J. Anat. *69*:233–291. (Dipnoi:275–282). FDNLPO:1 3 4 5 7 17

36 Allis, Edward Phelps, Jr. (1936) Comparison of the latero-sensory lines, the snout and the cranial roofing bones of the Stegocephali with those in fishes. J. Anat. *70*:293–316. O(D):1 4 7 17

37 Alluaud, Charles (1904) Mission scientifique de Ch. Alluaud en Afrique orientale (Juin 1903-Mai 1904). Poissons. I. Hydrographie et procédés de pêche. Mem. Soc. Zool. Fr. *17*:167–174. OP:18 24

38 Altman, Philip L. and Dorothy S. Dittmer (1971) Respiration and Circulation Biology Handbooks, Fed. Amer. Soc. Exp. Biol., Bethesda, Md. ODNPL:1 2 9 11

39 Altner, Helmut (1968) Untersuchungen an Ependym und Ependymorganen im Zwischenhirn niederer Wirbeltiere (*Neoceratodus*, Urodelen, Anuren). Z. Zellforsch. Mikrosk. Anat. *84*:102–140. NO:1 6 11

40 Alvey, Clifford H. (1932) The epidermal "glands" of *Ceratodus* and *Protopterus*. Anat. Rec. *54*(suppl.):91. (Abstract) NP:1 3 7

41 Ameghino, Carlos (1916) Sobre "*Ceratodus Iheringi*" de la formación guaranitica de la Patagonia. Physis. Rev. Soc. Argent. Cienc. Natur. *2*:169. C:4 18

42 Ameghino, Florentino (1906) Les formations sédimentiares du Crétacé Supérieur et du Tertiare de Patagonie. Anal. Mus. Nac. Bs. Aires ser. 3, *8*:1–564. (*Ceratodus*: 19–20,71). OC:4 18

43 Amos, Bernie, Ian G. Anderson, Geoffrey A. D. Haslewood, and Laszlo Tökes (1977) Bile salts of the lungfishes *Lepidosiren*, *Neoceratodus* and *Protopterus* and those of the coelacanth *Latimeria chalumnae* Smith. Biochem. J. *161*:201–204. LNPO:2 12 17

44 Andrews, S. Mahala, Brian G. Gardiner, Roger S. Miles, and Colin Patterson (1967) Pisces. In W. B. Harland, C. H. Holland, M. R. House, N. F. Hughes et al. (eds): The Fossil Record: A Symposium with Documentation. London: Geol. Soc. London, pp.637–683. OFDLNP: 18

45 Andrews, S. Mahala (1977) The axial skeleton of the coelacanth *Latimeria*. In S. Mahala Andrews, Roger S. Miles and A. D. Walker (eds): Linnean Society Symposium Series #4: Problems in Vertebrate Evolution. New York: Academic Press, pp.271–288. O(NP): 4 15 17

46 Andrews, S. Mahala, Roger S. Miles, and A. D. Walker, eds. (1977) Problems in Vertebrate Evolution. Linnean Society Symposium Series #4. New York: Academic Press.

47 Angel, L. Madeline (1966) *Bancroftrema neoceratodi*, gen. et sp. n., a paramphistomatid trematode from the Australian lungfish. J. Parasitol. *52*:1058–1061. N:22

48 Anonymous (W. H. J.) (1923) The palatability of *Ceratodus*. Brisbane Courrier, Feb. 17. N:23

49 Anomymous (1923) *Ceratodus* caught in the Coomera River, with evidence of breeding. Brisbane Courrier, Feb. 3. N:15 18

50 Anonymous (1929) *Ceratodus* in Enoggera River. Brisbane Courrier, April 4. N:18

51 Anonymous (1929) *Ceratodus* fishing near Cressbrook, Brisbane River. Brisbane Courrier, April 25. N:18 23 24

52 Anonymous (1930) Waranbini: on Ompax. The Bulletin (Sydney), Aug. 6:21. O

53 Anonymous (1940) American Museum of Natural History. Upper Nile Diorama.OP:18 22

54 Anonymous (1950) The Queensland Lung-fish or *Ceratodus*. Mimeographed flyer, Fisheries Branch Library, Brisbane. N:G(18 24)

55 Anonymous (1959) The lung fish. Fish Culturist *38*:53. P:G(10 20)

56 Anonymous (1965) Giant perch exported, grass carp imported. Aust. Fish. Newsl. *24*:27. N:24

57 Anonymous (1969) The lungfish carries its own knock-out drops. New Sci. *44*:225. P:2 20

58 Anonymous (1972) Fossil lungfish from Australia. Nature (London) *236*:143. FD(N):4 17

59 Anonymous (1974) Lungfish for research. Freshwater Fisheries Newsl. #6:8. Fish. and Wildlife Div., Min. for Conserv., Victoria. N:G(10 18)

60 Anonymous (1975) What is a lungfish? Rep. Brit. Mus. Natur. Hist. *1972-4*:46-48. FDNPL:G(1 3 4 17 18)

61 Anonymous (1975) Lungfish: ins and outs and evolution. Sci. News *108*:310. P:G(10 17 20)

62 Anonymous (1981) The case of the selfish DNA. Discovery (June) #6:32–36. D:1

63 Anonymous (1982) Rare fish die in creek. Brisbane Courier-Mail, Jan. l2. N:18

64 Anthonioz, P., Tahsin Mohsen, and G. Jadoun (1978) Preuves histochimiques et ultrastructurales de l'innervation du coeur de Protopterus annectens (Poisson Dipneuste). C. R. Soc. Biol. Paris 172:208–211. P:1 6 11

65 Arambourg, Camille and L. Joleaud (1943) Vertébrés fossiles du Bassin du Niger. Bull. Direction Mines Afr. Occident. Fr. #7:31-84. (Ceratodus:45–48). OC:4 18

66 Arambourg, Camille and Jean Guibé (1958) Sousclasse des Dipneustes (Dipneusti). In Pierre-P. Grassé (ed): Traité de Zoologie. Paris: Masson et Cie, 13:2522–2540. PLNCFD:1 3 4 9 10 14 15 18 19 20

67 Arbel, Emanuel R., Richard Liberthson, Richard Langendorf, Alfred Pick, Maurice Lev, and Alfred P. Fishman (1977) Electrophysiological and anatomical observations on the heart of the African lungfish. Amer. J. Physiol. 232:H24–H34, or Amer. J. Physiol.: Heart Circ. Physiol. 1:H24–H34. P:1 2 11

68 Armstrong, Garner Ted (1966) The air-breathing fish. IN Some Fishey Stories About an Unproved Theory (Evolution). Pasadena: Ambassador College Press, pp.21-29. PO:10 17 20

69 Arvy, Lucie (1957) Les labrocytes chez Protopterus annectens Owen. C. R. Assoc. Anat. 44:100–106. P:1 11

70 Atthey, Thomas (1868) Notes on various species of Ctenodus obtained from the shales of the Northumberland Coal-field. Ann. Mag. Natur. Hist. Ser. 4, 1:77–87. FD:4

71 Atthey, Thomas (1875) On the articular bone and supposed vomerine teeth of Ctenodus obliquus; and on Palaeoniscus Hancocki, n. sp. from Low Main, Newsham, Northumberland. Ann. Mag. Natur. Hist. Ser. 4, 15:309–312. Response from L. C. Miall:436 FD(N):1 4

72 Atz, James W. (1952) Narial breathing in fishes and the evolution of internal nares. Quart. Rev. Biol. 27:366–377. PLNO:1 7 10 17 18 19

73 Atz, James W. (1956) In a way, the lungfish is a missing link. Anim. Kingdom 59:57-59. P:1 10 18

74 Atz, James W. (1973) Comparative endocrinology and systematics. Amer. Zool. 13:933–936. OPL:2 13

75 Ayers, Howard (1884) Beiträge zur Anatomie und Physiologie der Dipnoër. Z. Naturwiss. Jena 18:479–527. PLN:1 7 11 12 13 14 21

76 Ayers, Howard (1893) On the genera of the Dipnoi dipneumones. Amer. Natur. 27:919–932. PL:1 12 14

77 Babiker, M. Mekki (1973) The renal responses to neurohypophysial hormones of the freshwater (FWE) and seawater (SWE) adapted eel (Anguilla anguilla L.), the aglomerular anglerfish (Lophius piscatorius L.), and the African lungfish (Protopterus aethiopicus). Acta Endocrinol. suppl. 177:83. (Abstract) PO:8 13

78 Babiker, M. Mekki and J. C. Rankin (1975) Rationale for the use of ^{51}Cr EDTA for estimation of glomerular filtration rate in fish. Comp. Biochem. Physiol. 50A:177-179. PO:2 13

79 Babiker, M. Mekki (1979) Respiratory behaviour, oxygen consumption and relative dependence on aerial respiration in the African lungfish (Protopterus annectens, Owen) and an air-breathing teleost (Clarias lazera, C.). Hydrobiologia 65:177–187. PO:2 9 10 19

80 Babiker, M. Mekki and Obeid H. El-Hakeem (1979) Changes in blood characteristics and constituents associated with aestivation in the African lungfish Protopterus annectens Owen. Zool. Anz. 202:9–16. P:2 11 13 20

81 Babiker, M. Mekki and J. C. Rankin (1979) Renal and vascular effects of neurohypophysial hormones in the African lungfish Protopterus annectens (Owen). Gen. Comp. Endocrinol. 37:26–34. P:2 8 11 13

82 Babiker, M. Mekki (1984) Adaptive respiratory significance of organophosphates (ATP & GTP) in air-breathing fishes. Hydrobiologia 110:339–349. PO:2 11 15 18 20

83 Bachmann, Konrad, Olive B. Goin, and Coleman J. Goin (1972) Nuclear DNA amounts in vertebrates. In Harold Hill Smith (ed): Evolution of Genetic Systems. New York: Gordon and Breach, Brookhaven Symp. Biol. #23:419–450. OD:1 17

84 Baird, Donald (1978) Studies on Carboniferous freshwater fishes. Novit. Amer. Mus. #1641:1–22. OFD:4 18

85 Baird, Harley S. (1923) The occipital bones of the Dipnoi. Proc. Roy. Soc. Victoria 35(N.S.), Part II:115–116. NL:1 4 15

86 Baker, Samuel White (1869) The Albert N'yanza Great Basin of the Nile and Explorations of the Nile Sources. Philadelphia: J. B. Lippincott Co. (Protopterus:330–331) OP:1 18 23

87 Balfour, Francis Maitland (1875) On the origin and history of the urinogenital organs of vertebrates. J. Anat. Physiol. 10:17–48. O(N):13 14 15

88 Balfour, Francis Maitland (1881) On the development of the skeleton of the paired fins of Elasmobranchii, considered in relation to its bearings on the nature of the limbs of the Vertebrata. Proc. Zool. Soc. London 1881:656–671. ON:1 4 17

89 Balinsky, J. B., E. L. Choritz, C. G. L. Coe, and Gerda S. van der Schans (1967) Amino acid metabolism and urea synthesis in naturally aestivating Xenopus laevis. Comp. Biochem. Physiol. 22:59–68. O(P):2 20

90 Ballantyne, Frances M. (1925) The continuity of the vertebrate nervous system: studies on Lepidosiren paradoxa. Trans. Roy. Soc. Edinburgh 53:663–670. L:1 6 15

91 Ballantyne, Frances M. (1927) Air-bladder and lungs: a contribution to the morphology of the air-bladder of fish. Trans. Roy. Soc. Edinburgh 55:371–394. (Neoceratodus:373–377). NO:1 9 15 17

92 Ballantyne, Frances M. (1928) Note on the male genito-urinary organs of Ceratodus forsteri. Proc. Zool. Soc. London 1928:697–698. N(LP):1 13 14

93 Bancroft, Thomas Lane (1912) On a weak point in the life-history of Neoceratodus forsteri, Krefft. Proc. Roy. Soc. Queensland 23:251–256. N:14 15 18

94 Bancroft, Thomas Lane (1913) On an easy and certain method of hatching Ceratodus ova. Proc. Roy. Soc. Queensland 25:1–3. N:10 15 19

95 Bancroft, Thomas Lane (1918) Some further notes on the life-history of Ceratodus forsteri. Proc. Roy. Soc. Queensland 30:91–94. N:10 15 19

96 Bancroft, Thomas Lane (1923) On the taking of Ceratodus in the Coomera River. Brisbane Courrier, May 11. N:16 18 23 24

97 Bancroft, Thomas Lane (1924) A suggestion for a

biological laboratory on Stradbroke Island for the protection of *Ceratodus*. Proc. Roy. Soc. Queensland *36*:19–20. N:15 18

98 Bancroft, Thomas Lane (1928) On the life-history of *Ceratodus*. Proc. Linnean Soc. N.S.W. *53*:315–317. N:15 21

99 Bancroft, Thomas Lane (1933) Some further observations on the rearing of *Ceratodus*. Proc. Linn. Soc. N.S.W. *58*:467–469. N:1 15 21

100 Banister, Keith E. and Roland G. Bailey (1979) Fishes collected by the Zaïre River Expedition, 1974-75. Zool. J. Linn. Soc. *66*:205–249. OP:18

101 Banks, Max and Noel Kemp (1975) Fossils from Old Beach Road, Derwent, Tasmania. Austral. Cont. to Soc. Vert. Paleontol. News Bull. #104:1–2. CO:18

102 Barbosa Rodrigues, Joan (1892) Vellosia. Contribuições do Museu botanico do Amazonas. Vol. 2, 2nd edition. Rio de Janeiro: Imprensa Nacional. (*Lepidosiren*:59–60). OL:1 3 18 19 24

103 Barbour, Thomas (1941) Notes on two African fishes. Copeia *1941*:39–40. PO:1 16 19 21

104 Bardack, David (1974) A larval fish from the Pennsylvanian of Illinois. J. Paleontol. *48*:988–993. FD:1 4 7 9 15 18

105 Bardack, David (1978) The non-chondrichthyan fishes from the Mazon Creek nodules. Geol. Soc. Amer. Programs *10*:246. (Abstract) FD:3 18

106 Bargmann, Wolfgang (1934) Untersuchungen über Histologie und Histophysiologie der Fischniere. I. Dipnoer: *Lepidosiren paradoxa*. Z. Zellforsch. Mikrosk. Anat. *21*:388–411. L(P):1 11 13

107 Bargmann, Wolfgang (1939) Die Langerhansschen-Inseln des Pankreas. In Wilhelm von Möllendorff (ed): Handbuch der mikroskopischen Anatomie des Menschen. Berlin: Springer, 2:197–288. ONL:G(1 8 12)

108 Barker, David (1974) The morphology of muscle receptors. In Carlton C. Hunt (ed): Handbook of Sensory Physiology. New York: Springer-Verlag, 2:1–190. (*Protopterus*:134). OP:1 5 7

109 Barnett, Robert C., Jr. (1971) Fossil vertebrates of Ohio, with emphasis on north and north central regions. Earth Sci. *24*:188–190. FDO:4 18

110 Barr, W. A. and B. M. Hobson (1965) The gonadotrophin content of the pituitary gland of the lungfish, *Protopterus aethiopicus*, and of other vertebrate species. Gen. Comp. Endocrinol. *5*:664. (Abstract)PO:2 8 17

111 Barrington, Ernest James William (1960) Some problems of adenohypophysial relationships in cyclostomes and fish. Symp. Zool. Soc. London #2:69–85. OP:8

112 Barrington, Ernest James William (1964) Hormones and Evolution. London: The English Universities Press, Ltd. (*Protopterus*:106–107). OP:2 8

113 Barrington, Ernest James William (1971) Evolution of hormones. In Ernest Schoffeniels (ed): Biochemical Evolution and the Origin of Life. New York: North-Holland Pub. Co., pp.174–190. OP:8 17

114 Barrio, Avelino (1943) Observaciones sobre *Lepidosiren paradoxa* y fijacion de material argentino. Rev. Argent. Zoogeog. *3*:9–20. L:3 10 14 15 18 19 21 22

115 Bartlett, Grant R. (1977) Phosphate compounds in fish red cells. Amer. Zool. *17*:889. (Abstract) OL:2 11

116 Bartlett, Grant R. (1978) Phosphates in red cells of

two lungfish: the South American, *Lepidosiren paradoxa*, and the African, *Protopterus aethiopicus*. Can. J. Zool. *56*:882–886. LP:2 11

117 Bartlett, Grant R. (1980) Phosphate compounds in vertebrate red blood cells. Amer. Zool. *20*:103–114. OLP:2 11

118 Bates, Henry Walter (1863) On some insects collected in Madagascar by Mr. Caldwell. Proc. Zool. Soc. London *1863*:472–476. OPL:17 18

119 Bateson, W. (1890) The sense-organs and perception of fishes. J. Mar. Biol. Assoc. U.K. (Plymouth) *1*:225–256. OP:6 7 19

120 Baur, Georg (1887) Über *Lepidosiren paradoxa* Fitzinger. Zool. Jahrb. *2*:575–583. L(P):1 18

121 Baylis, Harry Arnold. (1915) A trematode from *Protopterus*. Ann. Mag. Natur. Hist. Ser. 8, *16*:85–96. P:22

122 Beadle, L. C. (1932) Scientific results of the Cambridge expedition to the East African lakes, 1930–1. 3. Observations on the bionomics of some East African swamps. J. Linnean Soc. London Zool. *38*:135–155. OP:18

123 Beard, John (1890) The inter-relationships of the Ichthyopsida. A contribution to the morphology of vertebrates (first of two papers). Anat. Anz. *5*:146–159. ODPN:1 6 13 14 15 17

124 Beard, John (1890) The inter-relationships of the Ichthyopsida. A contribution to the morphology of vertebrates (concluding article). Anat. Anz. *5*:179–188. ODP:8 10 17 20

125 Beauregard, Henri (1881) Encéphale et nerfs craniens du *Ceratodus forsteri*. J. Anat. Physiol. (Paris) *17*:230–242. N:1 6

126 Beauregard, Henri (1889) Note sur le Protoptère (*Protopterus annectens*). C. R. Mem. Soc. Biol. Paris *41*:556–558. P:9 10 20

127 Beddard, Frank E. (1886) Observations on the ovarian ovum of *Lepidosiren* (*Protopterus*). Proc. Zool. Soc. London *1886*:272–292. Also in Zool. Anz. *9*:373–375, 635-637. Summarized in J. Roy. Microscop. Soc. *1887*:44. P:1 14 15

128 Beddard, Frank E. (1886) Observations on the development and structure of the ovum in the Dipnoi. Proc. Zool. Soc. London *1886*:505–527. PN:1 14

129 Beer, Gavin R. de (1924) Studies on the vertebrate head. I. Fish. Quart. J. Microsc. Sci. *68*:288–341. (*Neoceratodus*:320–324). N:1 4 11 15

130 Beer, Gavin R. de (1926) Studies on the vertebrate head. II. The orbito-temporal region of the skull. Quart. J. Microsc. Sci. *70*:263–370. (Dipnoi:303–307). OPN:1 4 6 11 15

131 Beer, Gavin R. de (1937) The Development of the Vertebrate Skull. Oxford: Clarendon Press. (Dipnoi:168-176). ONPL:1 4 6 15

132 Begumya, Y. R. and M. J. Rice (1972) Cardiac acetylcholine content of three vertebrates. Comp. Gen. Pharmacol. *3*:315–318. PO:2 11 20

133 Behdad, Mehdy and Gordon M. Folger, Jr. (1972) Scimitar syndrome with anatomic variations. Amer. J. Cardiol. *29*:252–253. (Abstract) OD:1 11

134 Behrisch, Hans Werner and Peter W. Hochachka (1969) Unique regulatory properties of fish fructose diphosphatase. Fed. Proc. *28*:412. (Abstract) DO:2

135 Behrisch, Hans Werner and Peter W. Hochachka (1969) Temperature and the regulation of enzyme activity in poikilotherms. Properties of lungfish fructose

diphosphatase. Biochem. J. *112*:601–607. L:2 12 18

136 Behrisch, Hans Werner (1970) Temperature and the regulation of enzyme activity in poikilotherms: regulatory properties of fish fructose 1,6- diphosphatase. Diss. Abstr. Int. *31B*:443–444. (Abstract) LO:2

137 Beltan, Laurence (1968) La faune ichthyologique de l'Eotrias du N.W. de Madagascar: le neurocrâne. Cent. Nat. Rech. Sci. Paris:1–134. (Dipneustes:119-125). CO:4 18

138 Bemis, William E. and George V. Lauder (1986) Morphology and function of the feeding apparatus of the lungfish, *Lepidosiren paradoxa* (Dipnoi). J. Morphol. *187*:81–108. Amer. Zool. *23*:1010. [1983]. (Abstract) L:5 19 21

139 Bemis, William E. (1984) Morphology and growth of lepidosirenid lungfish tooth plates (Pisces: Dipnoi). J. Morphol. *179*:73–93. Amer. Zool. *22*:923. [1982]. (Abstract) PL:1 4 16

140 Bemis, William E. (1984) Studies on the evolutionary morphology of lepidosirenid lungfish (Pices: Dipnoi). Diss. Abstr. Int. *44*:2355-B. (Abstract) P:1 3 4 17 19 21

141 Bemis, William E. (1984) Paedomorphosis and the evolution of the Dipnoi. Paleobiology *10*:293–307. Amer. Zool. *20*:757. (Abstract) NPLFD:1 3 4 15 17

142 Benda, R.S. (1979) Analysis of catch data from 1968 to 1976 from nine fish landings in the Kenya waters of Lake Victoria. J. Fish. Biol. *15*:385–387. PO:23

143 Bendix-Almgreen, S. E. (1983) *Carcharodon megalodon* from the Upper Miocene of Denmark, with comments on elasmobranch tooth enameloid coronin. Bull. Geol. Soc. Den. *32*:1–32. OD*:4

144 Benl, Gerhard and Günther Sterba (1964) Über einen merkwürdigen Fall doppelseitiger, partieller Mehrfachbildung bei *Protopterus dolloi* Blgr. (Pisces, Dipnoi). Zool. Anz. *173*:360–363. P:1 16

145 Benl, Gerhard (1965) Seltsame Erscheinung an einem Lungenfisch. Aquarien Terrarien Z. *18*:142–144. P:16

146 Benninghoff, Alfred (1933) Herz. In Louis Bolk, Ernest Göppert, Erich Kallius, and Wilhelm Lubosch (eds): Handbuch der vergleichenden Anatomie der Wirbeltiere. Berlin und Wien: Urban und Schwarzenberg, *VI*:467-556. (Dipnoi:480–487). OPLN:1 5 6 11

147 Bentley, Peter J. (1971) Endocrines and Osmoregulation: A Comparative Account of the Regulation of Water and Salt in Vertebrates. New York: Springer-Verlag. OP:2 8 13

148 Benzien, Joachim (1958) Zum Kongo-Lungenfisch— *Protopterus dolloi*. Aquarien Terrarien Z. *11*:284. P:19 21

149 Berg, Leo S. (1940) Classification of Fishes both Recent and Fossil. Trudy Zool. Inst. Leningrad *5*:1–517. English edition by Dover Pub. Co., Ann Arbor, Mich. (1947). (Dipnoi:144–148). OFDNLP:1

150 Bergquist, Harry (1932) Zur Morphologie des Zwischenhirns bei niederen Wirbeltieren. Acta Zool. (Stockholm) *13*:57–303. (*Neoceratodus*:220–233). ON(PL):1 6 15

151 Bergstrand, Eva (1971) Ett fiskeriprojekt i Nyanzasjön. Zool. Revy *33*:3–16. OP:18 23

152 Bergstrand, Eva and Almo J. Cardone (1971) Exploratory bottom trawling in Lake Victoria. Afr. J. Trop. Hydrobiol. Fisheries *1*:13–23. PO:18 23

153 Berman, David S. (1968) Lungfish from the Lueders Formation (Lower Permian, Texas) and the *Gna-*

thorhiza—lepidosirenid ancestry questioned. J. Paleontol. *42*:827–835. FD(NLP):1 4 12 17 20 21

154 Berman, David S. (1976) Cranial morphology of the Lower Permian lungfish *Gnathorhiza* (Osteichthyes: Dipnoi). J. Paleontol. *50*:1020–1033. FD(N):1 4 18 20

155 Berman, David S. (1976) Occurrence of *Gnathorhiza* (Osteichthyes: Dipnoi) in estivation burrows in the Lower Permian of New Mexico with description of a new species. J. Paleontol. *50*:1034–1039. FD(LP):1 4 7 18 20

156 Berman, David S. (1979) *Gnathorhiza bothrotreta* (Osteichthyes: Dipnoi) from the Lower Permian Abo Formation of New Mexico. Ann. Carnegie Mus. *48*:211–230. FD(NPL):1 4 17

157 Berman, David S. and Robert R. Reisz (1980) A new species of *Trimerorhachis* (Amphibia, Temnospondyli) from the Lower Permian Abo Formation of New Mexico, with discussion of Permian faunal distributions in that State. Ann. Carnegie Mus. *49*:455–485. O(FD):18 20

158 Bern, Howard A. (1967) Hormones and endocrine glands of fishes. Science (Washington) *158*:455–462. OP:1 2 8

159 Bern, Howard A., Robert Gunther, Donald W. Johnson, and Richard S. Nishioka (1973) Occurrence of urotensin II (bladder-contracting activity) in the caudal spinal cord of anamniote vertebrates. Acta Zool. (Stockholm) *54*:15–19. OL:2 6 8

160 Bernacsek, Garry M. (1977) A lungfish cranium from the Middle Devonian of the Yukon Territory, Canada. Palaeontogr. Abt. A Palaozool. Stratigr. (Stuttgart) *157*:175–200. FD:1 4 5 6 7 11

161 Bernacsek, Garry M. and Robert L. Carroll (1981) Semicircular canal size in fossil fishes and amphibians. Can. J. Earth Sci. *18*:150–156. FPPFDO:1 7 17

162 Bert, J. and René Godet (1963) Réaction d'éveil télencéphalique d'un Dipneuste. C. R. Soc. Biol. Paris *157*:1787–1790. P:2 6 7

163 Bert, J., Mireille Dupé, and René Godet (1964) Potentiel évoqué visuel, à la surface du tectum mésencéphalique d'un Dipneuste. Importance des réponses "off". C. R. Soc. Biol. Paris *158*:788–790. P:2 6 7 19 21

164 Bertin, Leon (1940) Catalogue des types de poissons du Muséum National d' Histoire naturelle. II. Dipneustes, Chondrosteens, Holosteens, Isospondyles. Bull. Mus. Natl. Hist. Natur. Paris sér. 2, *12*:244–322. (*Neoceratodus*:246). ON

165a Bertin, Leon (1958) Appareil digestif. In Pierre-P. Grassé (ed): Traité de Zoologie. *13*:1248–1302. OPLN:1 9 10 11 12 15

165b Bertin, Leon (1958) Nidification. In Pierre-P. Grassé (ed): Traité de Zoologie. *13*:1653–1684. OPLN:1 9 10 11 12 15

165c Bertin, Leon (1958) Organes de la Respiration aerienne. IN Pierre-P. Grassé: Traité de Zoologie. *13*:1303–1341. OPLN:1 9 10 11 12 15

165d Bertin, Leon (1958) Appareil Circulatoire. In Pierre-P. Grassé: Traité de Zoologie. *13*:1399–1485. OPLN:1 9 10 11 12 15

166 Bertmar, Gunnar (1959) On the ontogeny of the chondral skull in Characidae, with a discussion on the chondrocranial base and the visceral chondrocranium in fishes. Acta Zool. (Stockholm) *40*:203–364. ONP:1 4 15 17

167 Bertmar, Gunnar (1961) Tungbensbågens skelett hos fiskarna. Zool. Revy *23*:45-60. PLNO: 4 15

168 Bertmar, Gunnar (1962) Homology of ear ossicles. Nature (London) *193*:393–394. NO:1 7 15 17

169 Bertmar, Gunnar (1963) The trigemino-facialis chamber, the cavum epiptericum and the cavum orbitonasale, three serially homologous extracranial spaces in fishes. Acta Zool. (Stockholm) *44*:329–344. NO:1 4 6 11 15

170 Bertmar, Gunnar (1963) Finns det kotor i huvudet? Zool. Revy *1963*:47–54. OD:4 15

171 Bertmar, Gunnar (1964) On the development of the jugular and cerebral veins in fishes. Proc. Zool. Soc. London *144*:87–130. NO:1 11 15

172 Bertmar, Gunnar (1965) The olfactory organ and upper lips in Dipnoi, an embryological study. Acta Zool. (Stockholm) *46*:1–40. NPL:1 7 15 17

173 Bertmar, Gunnar (1966) The development of skeleton, blood-vessels and nerves in the dipnoan snout, with a discussion on the homology of the dipnoan posterior nostrils. Acta Zool. (Stockholm) *47*:81–150. NPL:1 4 5 6 7 10 11 15

174 Bertmar, Gunnar (1968) Lungfish phylogeny. In Tor Ørvig (ed): Nobel Symposium 4: Current Problems of Lower Vertebrate Phylogeny. Stockholm: Almquist and Wicksell, pp. 258–284. ONPL:1 4 6 7 11 15 17

175 Bertmar, Gunnar (1968) Phylogeny and evolution in lungfishes. Acta Zool. (Stockholm) *49*:189–201. PLN:1 4 17

176 Bertmar, Gunnar (1969) The vertebrate nose, remarks on its structural and functional adaptation and evolution. Evolution *23*:131–152. NDO:1 7 15 17

177 Bertmar, Gunnar (1981) Evolution of vomeronasal organs in vertebrates. Evolution *35*:359–366. OP:1 7 17

178 Bertoni, A. de Winkelried (1939) Catalogos sistematicos de los vertebrados del Paraguay. Rev. Soc. Cient. Paraguay *4*:1–60. (*Lepidosiren*:51). OL:18

179 Beyrich, Ernst (1850) Über einige organische Reste der Lettenkohlenbildung in Thuringen. I. *Ceratodus*. Z. Dtsch. Geol. Ges. *2*:153–168. C:1 4 18

180 Bicknell, Edwin (1871) On the teeth of fishes. Proc. Boston Soc. Natur. Hist. *14*:189–190. C:1 4

181 Bing, Robert and Rudolf Burckhardt (1904) Das Zentralnervensystem von *Ceratodus forsteri*. Anat. Anz. *25*:588–599. N(LP):1 6 17

182 Bing, Robert and Rudolf Burckhardt (1905) Das Centralnervensystem von *Ceratodus forsteri*. Denkschr. Med.-Naturwiss. Ges. Jena *4*:511–584. N(P):1 6 7 11 15

183 Bischoff, Theodor Ludvig Wilhelm(1840) *Lepidosiren paradoxa*. Anatomisch untersucht und beschrieben. Leipzig: Leopold Voss, pp.1–34. Translation in Ann. Sci. Natur. *14*:116–159. L(P):1 3 4 5 6 7 13 14 17 18

184 Bishop, I. R. and G. E. H. Foxon (1965) A visit to the lower Amazon. Nature (London) *208*:114–117. O:18

185 Bishop, I. R. and G. E. H. Foxon (1968) The mechanism of breathing in the South American lungfish, *Lepidosiren paradoxa*; a radiological study. J. Zool. (London) *154*:263–271. L:4 10 19

186 Blache, J. (1964) Les poissons du bassin Tchad et du bassin adjacent du Mayo Kebbi. Mem. O.R.S.T.O.M. (Office Recherche Science Technical Outre-mer), Paris. (*Protopterus*:12, 15, 274–275, 477). PO:1 3 18 20

187 Blair-West, John R., J. P. Coghlan, D. A. Denton, Angela P. Gibson, Catherine J. Oddie, Wilbur H. Saw-yer, and B. A. Scoggins (1977) Plasma renin activity and blood corticosteroids in the Australian lungfish *Neoceratodus forsteri*. J. Endocrinol. *74*:137–142. N:2 8 11

188 Blanc, Maurice (1954) La répartition des poissons d'eau douce Africains. Bull. Inst. Fondam. Afr. Noire sér. A Sci. Natur. *16*:599–628. PO:18

189 Blanc, Maurice, François d'Aubenton, and Yves Plessis (1955) Note preliminaire sur l'enkystement de *Protopterus annectens* (Owen 1839). Bull. Mus. Natl. Hist. Natur. Paris sér. 2, *27*:193–195. P:3 18 19 20 21

190 Blanc, Maurice, François d'Aubenton, and Yves Plessis (1956) IV. Étude de enkystement de *Protopterus annectens* (Owen 1839). Bull. Inst. Fondam. Afr. Noire sér. A Sci. Natur. *18A*:843-854. P(LN):1 3 16 18 19 20 21

191 Blanchard, Raphaël (1894) Anomalie des nageoires chez le Protoptère. Bull. Soc. Zool. Fr. *19*:54–57. P:1 16

192 Bles, Edward J. (1898) The correlated distribution of abdominal pores and nephrostomes in fishes. J. Anat. Physiol. *32*:484–512. OP(LN):1 13

193 Bloss, J. F. E. (1945) The Sudanese angler. Sudan Notes Rec. *26*:257–281. OP:20 23

194 Bluntschli, Hans (1904) Eisenhämatoxylin und Biondipräparate der Leber von *Ceratodus forsteri* und *Acipenser ruthenus*. Anat. Anz. *23*:198–199. NO:1 11 12

195 Bluntschli, Hans (1904) Der feinere Bau der Leber von *Ceratodus forsteri*, zugleich ein Beitrag zur vergleichenden Histologie der Fischleber. Denkschr. Med.-Naturwiss. Ges. Jena *4*:333–375. N:1 11 12

196 Boas, Johan Erik Vesti (1880) Über Herz und Arterienbogen bei *Ceratodus* und *Protopterus*. Gegenbaurs Morphol. Jahrb. *6*:321-354. NP:1 9 11

197 Boas, Johan Erik Vesti (1890) Lehrbuch der Zoologie. Jena: Gustav Fischer, pp.1-578. (Dipnoi:402-403). ONPL:G(3 4 9 10 11 12)

198 Boaz, Noel Thomas and J. Hampel (1978) Strontium content of fossil tooth enamel and diet of early hominids. J. Paleontol. *52*:928-933. OP:4 21

199 Bodian, David (1942) Cytological aspects of synaptic function. Physiol. Rev. *22*:146-169. O(N):1 6

200 Bodznick, David and R. Glenn Northcutt (1980) Segregation of electro- and mechanoreceptive inputs to the elasmobranch medulla. Brain Res. *195*:313-321. O(D):2 6 7

201 Boeger, W. A. and V. E. Thatcher (1983) *Kalipharynx piramboae*, n.gen., n.sp., trematode (Fellodistomidae) parasite of the Amazonian lungfish *Lepidosiren paradoxa*. Acta Amazonica *13*:171-176. [in Portugese]. L*:18 22

202 Bohls, J. (1894) Mitteilungen über Fang und Lebensweise von *Lepidosiren* aus Paraguay. Nachr. Ges. Wiss. Göttingen *1894*:80-83. L:16 18 19 21 24

203 Boisson, Charles (1961) La spermatogénèse de *Protopterus annectens* (Dipneuste) du Sénégal. Ann. Fac. Sci. Univ. Dakar *6*:133-144. P:1 14 18 20

204 Boisson, Charles (1963) La spermiogenèse de *Protopterus annectens* (Dipneuste) du Sénégal, étudiée au microscope optique et quelques détails au microscope électronique. Ann. Fac. Sci. Univ. Dakar *10*:43-72. P+:1 14

205 Boisson, Charles and X. Mattei (1965) À propos de l'acrosome des spermatozoïdes du Dipneuste *Protopterus* annectens Owen. C. R. Soc. Biol. Paris *159*:2247-

2249. P:1 4 18

206 Boisson, Charles, C. Mattei, and X. Mattei (1967) Troisième note sur la spermiogenèse de *Protopterus annectens* [Dipneuste] du Sénégal. Bull. Inst. Fondam. Afr. Noire sér. A Sci. Natur. *29*:1097-1121. P:1 14

207 Böklen, Hermann (1887) Die Gattung *Ceratodus*. Jahresh. Vaterl. Ges. Naturkd. Württemberg *43*:76-81. FDC(NP):1 4 18 21

208 Bolau, Heinrich (1901) Lungenfisch, Stummel-schwanzeidechse und Rot-Albinos der Sumpfschnecke. Verh. Naturwiss. Ver. Hamburg Ser. 3 *9*:XLVIII. PO

209 Bolau, Heinrich (1910) Über lebende Schuppen-molche (*Lepidosiren annectens*) und die Familie der Lungenfische. Verh. Naturwiss. Ver. Hamburg *17*:LIV-LV. LP(N): G(1 3 4 9 10 18 19 20 24)

210 Bolk, Louis, Ernest Göppert, Erich Kallius, and Wilhelm Lubosch (1931) Handbuch der vergleichenden Anatomie der Wirbeltiere. Vol. I (1933), Vol. II (1934), Vol. III (1937), Vol. V (1938). Berlin and Wien: Urban und Schwarzenberg.

211 Bolognari, Fantin A. M., and F. Porcelli (1969) I tipi cellulari cutanei in *Protopterus dolloi*. Boll. Zool. *36*:425-426. P:1 3

212 Bon, J., K. H. Ibrahim, and F. G. de Ruijter de Wildt (1978) The African lung-fish (*Protopterus aethiopicus* Heckel), a good source of high quality protein of value in the cure of malnutrition in children. Voeding *37*:250-255. P:23 24

213 Bondesio, Pedro and Rosendo Pascual (1977) Restos de Lepidosirenidae (Osteichthyes, Dipnoi) del Grupo Honda (Mioceno Tardio) de Colombia. Sus denotaciones paleoambientales. Rev. Asoc. Geol. Argent. *32*:34-43. FL:4 18

214 Bone, Quentin (1964) Patterns of muscular innervation in lower chordates. Int. Rev. Neurobiol. *6*:99-147. (*Protopterus*:127-130). OP:1 5 6 7

215 Bone, Quentin (1978) Locomotor muscle. In William S. Hoar and David J. Randall (eds): Fish Physiology. New York: Academic Press, 7:361-424. (Dipnoi:415). OP:5 7

216 Borisov, I. N. (1970) Evolyutsiya istochnikov razvitiya konechnostei pozvonochnykh. (Evolution of limb development sources in vertebrates). Zh. Obshch. Biol. *31*:327-336. OD:5 15 17

217 Borkhvardt, V. G. (1969) Sootnoshenie khryashchevoi i kostnoi stadii v evolyutsii tel pozvonkov. (Relationship between the osseus and cartilaginous stages during evolution of corpus vertebrae). Arkh. Anat. Gistol. Embriol. *57*:111-118. D*:1 4 17

218 Bouillon, Jean (1961) The lungfish of Africa. Natur. Hist. *70*:62-71. P:9 10 14 15 18 19 20 21

219 Boulenger, George Albert (1891) On limb regeneration in *Protopterus*. Proc. Zool. Soc. London *1891*:147-148. P:16

220 Boulenger, George Albert (1897) On a collection of fishes from the Island of Marajo, Brazil. Ann. Mag. Natur. Hist. Ser. 6 *20*:294-299. OL:18

221 Boulenger, George Albert (1898) Report on the collection of fishes made by Mr. J. E. S. Moore in Lake Tanganyika during his expedition 1895-6. Trans. Zool. Soc. London *15*:1-26. OP:18

222 Boulenger, George Albert (1900) Matériaux pour la faune du Congo. Lepidosirenidae. Ann. Mus. Congo Belge sér. Quarto Zool. *1*:154-156. 1898-1900. P:1 16 18 19

223 Boulenger, George Albert (1900) List of the fishes collected by Mr. J. S. Budgett in the River Gambia. Proc. Zool. Soc. London *1900*:511-516. OP:18

224 Boulenger, George Albert (1900) Display of a type specimen of *Protopterus dolloi*. Proc. Zool. Soc. London *1900*:775. P(L):1

225 Boulenger, George Albert (1901) On a small collection of fishes from Lake Victoria made by order of Sir H. H. Johnson, K.C.B. Proc. Zool. Soc. London *1901*:158-162. PO:1 18

226 Boulenger, George Albert (1901) Poissons du Bassin du Congo. Ordre II. Dipneusti. Bruxelles: Publication de l'État Indépendant du Congo, pp.29-42. P(LN):1 3 15 16 18 19 20 21

227 Boulenger, George Albert (1902) Second account of the fishes collected by Dr. W. J. Ansorge in the Niger Delta. Proc. Zool. Soc. London *1902*:324-330. PO:1 18

228 Boulenger, George Albert (1905) The distribution of African fresh-water fishes. Nature (London) *72*:413-421. OP:18

229 Boulenger, George Albert (1905) A list of the fresh-water fishes of Africa. Ann. Mag. Natur. Hist. *16*:36-60. OP:18

230 Boulenger, George Albert (1906) Fourth contribution to the ichthyology of Lake Tanganyika—Report on the collection of fishes made by Dr. W. A. Cunnington during the Third Tanganyika Expedition, 1904-1905. Trans. Zool. Soc. London *17*:537-576.O P:1 18 21

231 Boulenger, George Albert (1909) Catalogue of the Fresh-water Fishes of Africa in the British Museum. London: British Museum. (Lepidosirenidae:19-23). 1909-1916. OP:1 18

232 Boulenger, George Albert (1913) Display of *Protopterus aethiopicus*. Proc. Zool. Soc. London *1913*:241. P

233 Boulenger, George Albert (1919) A list of the fresh-water fishes of Sierra Leone. Ann. Mag. Natur. Hist. Ser. 9 *4*:34-36. PO:18

234 Boulenger, George Albert (1920) Poissons recueillis au Congo Belge par l'expedition du Dr. C. Christy. Ann. Mus. Congo Belge sér. 1 Zool. *2*:1-38. OP:1 18

235 Boulenger, George Albert (1938) Obituary: see Max Poll, 1967 and Malcolm Smith, 1938. O

236 Boyer, Jacques (1913) Le Protoptère, curieux poisson aérien. Cosmos (Paris) *68*:514-516. P:1 10 19 20

237 Branagan, D. F. (1972) The Challenger Expedition and Australian science. Proc. Roy. Soc. Edinburgh *73B*:85-95. ON:18

238 Brandes, Gustav (1893) Biologisches vom afrikanischen Lungenfisch. Z. Naturwiss. Leipzig *66*:402-403. P:19 21 24

239 Bräunle, Eduard (1911) Die Lurch- oder Molchfische. Wochenschr. Aquar. Terrar.-Kd. *8*:546-547. PLN:G(1 4 14 18 19 20 21)

240 Braus, Hermann (1898) Über die Innervation der paarigen Extremitäten bei Selachiern, Holocephalen und Dipnoern. Z. Naturwiss. Jena *31*:239-468. NO:1 4 5 6 15 17

241 Braus, Hermann (1901) Die Muskeln und Nerven der Ceratodusflosse: ein Beitrag zur vergleichenden Morphologie der freien Gliedmaasse bei niederen Fischen und zur Archipterygiumtheorie. Denkschr. Med.-Naturwiss. Ges. Jena *4*:137-300. N: 1 4 5 6 19

242 Breder, Charles M., Jr. (1926) The locomotion of fishes. Zoologica (New York) *4*:159-297. (Dip-

neusti:273). OLN:19

243 Breder, Charles M., Jr. (1947) An analysis of the geometry of symmetry with especial reference to the squamation of fishes. Bull. Amer. Mus. Natur. Hist. *88*:325-412. (*Neoceratodus*:387-388). ON:1 3

244 Brehm, Alfred Edmund (1879) Die Lungenfische (Sirenoidei). Brehms Thierleben, 2:27-30. Leipzig: Bibliographischen Instituts.P:G(1 4 19 20 21)

245 Bricteux-Grégoire, S., R. Schyns, and Marcel Florkin (1974) N-terminal amino acid sequence of trypsinogen from the elephant seal *Mirounga leonina* L. (Carnivora). Biochim. Biophys. Acta *351*:87-91. O(P):2 12 17

246 Bridge, T. William (1879) Pori abdominales of vertebrata. J. Anat. Physiol. *14*:81-100. (Dipnoi:88-89). ONP:1

247 Bridge, T. William (1898) On the morphology of the skull in the Paraguayan *Lepidosiren* and in other Dipnoids. Trans. Zool. Soc. London *14*:325-376. Reported in Proc. Zool. Soc. London *1897*:602-603. L(PN):1 4 5 6 17

248 Bridge, T. William (1922) Chapter XIX: Dipneusti. IN The Cambridge Natural History. London: Macmillan and Co., Ltd. 7:505-520. FDNPL:1 3 10 14 15 16 17 18 19 20 21

249 Brien, Paul (1938) La plaine du Kamolondo. Son aspect natural - sa faune, ses feux de brousse. Ann. Soc. Roy. Zool. Belg. *69*:119-137. OP:15 18 19 20

250 Brien, Paul (1957) Présentation d'un mémoire en collaboration avec M. Poll et J. Bouillon, intitulé: Mission Zoologique Cemubac au Stanley-Pool. Bull. Acad. Roy. Sci. Colon. N.S. *3*:1343-1344. OP:18

251 Brien, Paul, Max Poll, and Jean Bouillon (1957) Éthologie de la reproduction d'un Dipneuste africain *Protopterus dolloï* (Boulenger). C. R. Acad. Sci. Paris *245*:1988-1990. P:14 19

252 Brien, Paul, Max Poll and Jean Bouillon (1958) Une mission zoologique CEMUBAC au Stanley Pool (1957). Acad. Roy. Sci. Colon. (Sci. Natur. Med.) N.S. 7:3-35. OP:1 14 15 18 19 20

253 Brien, Paul, Max Poll, and Jean Bouillon (1958) Éthologie de la reproduction du *Protopterus dolloï* (Boulenger). Proc. Int. Congr. Zool. *15*:76-78. P:14 15 18 19 20

254 Brien, Paul and Jean Bouillon (1959) Les sacs gazeux du Protoptère et la phylogénie des poumons. C. R. Acad. Sci. Paris *248*:2049-2051. P(NO):10 15 17

255 Brien, Paul (1959) Éthologie du *Protopterus dolloï* (Boulenger) et de ses larves. Signification des sacs pulmonaires des Dipneustes. Ann. Soc. Roy. Zool. Belg. *89*:9-48. P:1 3 9 10 11 14 15 18 19 20

256 Brien, Paul, Max Poll, and Jean Bouillon (1959) Éthologie de la reproduction de *Protopterus dolloï* Blgr. Ann. Mus. Congo Belge sér. Quarto Zool. *71*:3-21. P:1 14 15 18 19 21 24

257 Brien, Paul and Jean Bouillon (1959) Éthologie des larves de *Protopterus dolloï* Blgr. et étude de leurs organes respiratoires. Ann. Mus. Congo Belge sér. Quarto Zool. *71*:25-74. P:1 3 9 10 11 15 18 19 20

258 Brien, Paul (1962) Formation du cloaque urinaire et origine des sacs pulmonaires chez *Protopterus*. Ann. Mus. Roy. Afr. Cent. sér. Quarto Zool. *108*:1-51. P:1 9 12 13 14 15 17

259 Brien, Paul (1962) Étude de la formation, de la structure des écailles des Dipneustes actuels et de leur comparaison avec les autres types d'écailles des Poissons. Ann. Mus. Roy. Afr. Cent. sér. Quarto Zool. *108*:53-129. P(NO):1 3 9 1 5 17

260 Brien, Paul (1963) L'éthologie du Protoptère et sa signification dans l'histoire des Vertébrés. Publ. Univ. Elisabethville *6*:107-129. P:1 6 9 10 11 14 15 17 18 19 20 23

261 Brien, Paul (1964) Les sacs gazeux des Vertébrés primitifs. Ann. Soc. Belg. Méd. Trop. *44*:385-400. P(O):1 10 15 17

262 Brien, Paul (1964) Éthologie des Dipneustes en rapport avec les Vertébrés primitifs. Bull. Soc. Zool. Fr. *89*:271-310. PLN:1 3 9 10 14 15 17 18 19 20

263 Brien, Paul (1967) The African Protoptera: living fossils. Afr. Wildlife *21*:213-233. P:14 15 18 19 20 23

264 Brindley, H. H. (1900) Note on some abnormalities of the limbs and tail of dipnoan fishes. Proc. Camb. Philos. Soc. *10*:325-327. LP:1 4 16

265 Brinn, Jack E., Jr. (1973) The pancreatic islets of bony fishes. Amer. Zool. *13*:653-655. OP:1 2 8

266 Briquel, M. P. (1898) Les dents de *Ceratodus*. Bibliog. Anat. *1*:11-16. C(NLP):1 4 15

267 Brisson, A. (1973) Biosynthesis and iodination of thyroid proteins from some lower vertebrates. Existence of specific thyroglobulin differences. Bull. Mus. Natl. Hist. Natur. Sci. Phys.-Chim. *2*:108. OP+:2 8

268 Brisson, A., J. Marchelidon, and F. Lachiver (1974) Comparative studies on the amino acid composition of thyroglobulins from various lower and higher vertebrates: phylogenetic aspect. Comp. Biochem. Physiol. *49B*:51-63. PO:2 8 17

269 Brisson-Martin, A. and F. Lachiver (1970) Variations spécifiques du coefficient de sédimentation de la préthyroglobuline chez quelques Vertébrés inférieurs. C. R. Soc. Biol. Paris *164*:1922-1925. PO:2 8

270 Brisson-Martin, A. and F. Lachiver (1972) Influence de la température d'incubation sur la biosynthèse de la thyroglobuline dans la thyroïde de divers Poissons. Gen. Comp. Endocrinol. *18*:578. (Abstract) PO:2 8

271 Brocklehurst, Gordon (1979) The significance of the evolution of the cerebrospinal fluid system. Ann. Roy. Coll. Surg. Eng. *61*:349-356. DO:1 6 17

272 Broek, Arnold John Peter van den (1933) Urogenitalsystem. Zweiter Teil: Geschlechtsorgane. I. Gonaden und Ausführungsgänge. In Louis Bolk, Ernest Göppert, Erich Kallius, and Wilhelm Lubosch (eds): Handbuch der vergleichenden Anatomie der Wirbeltiere. Berlin and Wien: Urban and Schwarzenberg, *VI*:1-154. (Dipnoi:56-58). OLPN:1 13 14

273 Broek, Arnold John Peter van den, G. J. van Oordt, and G. C. Hirsch (1938) Urogenitalsystem. Erster Teil: Harnorgane. I. Allgemeine Morphologie der Harnorgane. In Louis Bolk, Ernest Göppert, Erich Kallius, and Wilhelm Lubosch (eds): Handbuch der vergleichenden Anatomie der Wirbeltiere. Berlin and Wien: Urban und Schwarzenberg, *V*:683-854. (Dipnoi:751-753, 839). OLPN:1 13

274 Broin, France de, Claude Grenot, and Roland Vernet (1971) Sur la découverte d'un nouveau gisement de Vertébrés dans le Continental Intercalaire saharien: la Gara Samani (Algérie). C. R. Acad. Sci. (D) Paris *272*:1219-1221. CO:4 18

275 Broin, France de, Eric Buffetaut, Jean-Claude Koeniguer, Jean-Claude Rage, Donald Russell, Phillipe Taquet, Collette Vergnaud-Grazzini, and Sylvie Wenz

(1974) La faune de Vertébrés continentaux du gisement d'In Beceten (Sénonien du Niger). C. R. Acad. Sci. (D) Paris 279:469-472. CFPO:4 17 18

276 Broman, Ivar (1905) Über die Entwickelung der Mesenterien, der Leberligamente und der Leberform bei den Lungenfischen. Denkschr. Med.-Naturwiss. Ges. Jena 4:585-640. NPL:1 11 12 15 17

277 Broman, Ivar (1937) B. Das Pankreas. I. Allgemeiner Teil. In Louis Bolk, Ernest Göppert, Erich Kallius, and Wilhelm Lubosch (eds): Handbuch der vergleichenden Anatomie der Wirbeltiere. Berlin and Wien: Urban und Schwarzenberg, III:775-796. OPN:1 12

278 Broman, Ivar (1937) Colom. I. Einleitung. In Louis Bolk, Ernest Göppert, Erich Kallius, and Wilhelm Lubosch (eds): Handbuch der vergleichenden Anatomie der Wirbeltiere. Berlin and Wien: Urban und Schwarzenberg, III:989-1018. (Dipnoi:997-998). ONPL:1 12

279 Broman, Ivar (1939) Passiert bei den Lungenfischen die Atemluft durch die Nasenhöhlen? Anat. Anz. 88:139-145. NP(L):10 19

280 Broman, Ivar (1939) Über die Entwicklung der Geruchsorgane bei den Lungenfischen. Gegenbaurs Morphol. Jahrb. 83:85-106. NPL:3 7 15

281 Bronchart-Lannoye, Marie and Georges Thinès (1975) Influence de quelques facteurs physiques sur le comportement des poissons à double système de respiration. Bull. Acad. Roy. Belg. 61:524-542. OP:9 10 19

282 Brongniart, Charles (1888) Sur un nouveau poisson fossile du terrain houillier de Commentry (Allier). C. R. Acad. Sci. Paris 106:1240-1242. C:1 18

283 Bronsshtein, A. A. (1976) Zakonomernosti ultrastrukturnoi organizatzii oboniatel'nykh retzeptorov v sravnitel'nom riadu pozvonochnykh. (Regularics of the ultrastructural organization of the olfactory receptors in the comparative line of vertebrates). Tsitologiya 18:535-548. OD:7 17

284 Broom, Robert (1908) The fossil fishes of the Upper Karroo Beds of South Africa. Ann. S. Afr. Mus. 7:251-269. CO:4 18

285 Brough, James (1931) On fossil fishes from the Karroo System, and some general considerations on the bony fishes of the Triassic Period. Proc. Zool. Soc. London 1931:235-296. OC:17 18

286 Broussy, J. and A. Serfaty (1959) Origine des cellules caliciformes de l'épithélium intestinal du Protoptère (Protopterus annectens). Bull. Soc. Hist. Natur. Toulouse 94:169-171. P:1 12

287 Brown, George W., Jr. (1965) Ornithine carbamoyltransferase in liver of the dipnoan Protopterus aethiopicus. Science (Washington) 149:1515. P:2 12 13

288 Brown, George W., Jr., Jesse James, Ralph J. Henderson, Walter N. Thomas, Robert O. Robinson, Arthur L. Thompson, Earlene Brown, and Susan G. Brown (1966) Uricolytic enzymes in liver of the dipnoan Protopterus aethiopicus. Science (Washington) 153:1653-1654. P:2 12 13

289 Brown, George W., Jr. and Susan G. Brown (1966) Intermediary nitrogen metabolism of the coelacanth, Latimeria chalumnae. Amer. Zool. 6:577. (Abstract) O(P):2 13

290 Brown, George W., Jr. and Susan G. Brown (1967) Urea and its formation in coelacanth liver. Science (Washington) 155:570-573. O(P):2 13

291 Brown, Roland W. (1938) Two fossils misidentified as shelf-fungi. J. Wash. Acad. Sci. 28:130-131. C:4

292 Browne, Montague (1893) On some vertebrate remains not hitherto recorded from the Rhaetic Beds of Britain. Rep. Brit. Assoc. Advan. Sci. 1893:748-749. CO:18

293 Brühl, Carl Bernhard (1847) Das Kopfskelet von Lepidosiren. Anfangsgründe der vergleichenden Anatomie, Sec. 72:216-221. PL:1 9

294 Brühl, Carl Bernhard (1875) Zootomie aller Thierklassen, für Lernende, nach Autopsien, skizzirt. Atlas. Wien: Alfred Holder. OPLN:1 4

295 Bruton, Michael N. (1979) The survival of habitat desiccation by air breathing clariid catfishes. Environ. Biol. Fish. 4:273-280. O(P):20

296 Bruyère, Henri (1901) Le Ceratodus. La Nature 1901:89-91. N(PL):G(1 3 5 10 19 21)

297 Bryce, Thomas H. (1903) The dividing cells of the embryo of Lepidosiren. J. Anat. Physiol. 38:lxx. L:1 15

298 Bryce, Thomas H. (1904) Histogenesis of blood in larval forms of Lepidosiren. Lancet 167:406. L:11 15

299 Bryce, Thomas H. (1905) The histology of the blood of the larva of Lepidosiren paradoxa. Part I. Structure of the resting and dividing corpuscles. Trans. Roy. Soc. Edinburgh 41:291-310. L:1 11 15

300 Bryce, Thomas H. (1905) On the histology of the blood of the larva of Lepidosiren paradoxa. Part II. Hematogenesis. Trans. Roy. Soc. Edinburgh 41:435-467. L:1 11 15

301 Bryce, Thomas H. (1905) Note on the development of the thymus gland in Lepidosiren paradoxa. J. Anat. Physiol. 40:91-99. L:1 11 15

302 Budgett, John Samuel (1899) General account of an expedition to the Gambia Colony and Protectorate in 1898-99. Proc. Zool. Soc. London 1899:931-937. OP:14 15 18

303 Budgett, John Samuel (1900) Observations on Polypterus and Protopterus. Proc. Camb. Philos. Soc. 10:236-240. PO:1 9 15 18 19

304 Budgett, John Samuel (1900) The breeding-habits of some West-African fishes, with an account of the external features in the development of Protopterus annectens, and a description of the larva of Polypterus lapradii. Proc. Zool. Soc. London 1900:835-836. PO(L):3 14 15 19

306 Budgett, John Samuel (1903) On a trip through East Africa. Proc. Zool. Soc. London 1903:2-10. OP:18

307 Budgett, John Samuel (1904) Notice of death. Obituary. Nature 69:278, 300-301. O(P):15

308 Buffetaut, Eric (1983) Mesozoic vertebrates from Thailand: a review. Acta Palaeontol. Pol. 28:43-54. OFD+:18

309 Buffetaut, Eric and Rucha Ingavat (1985) The Mesozoic vertebrates of Thailand. Sci. Amer., August, 1985:80-87. OFD:18

310 Bugge, Jørgen (1961) The heart of the African lungfish, Protopterus. Vidensk. Medd. Dansk Naturhist. Foren. Kjobenhavn 123:193-210. P:1 11

311 Bunge, Alexander von (1874) Über die Nachweisbarkeit eines biserialen Archipterygium bei Sela-

305 Budgett, John Samuel (1901) On the breeding-habits of some West-African fishes, with an account of the external features in the development of Protopterus annectens, and a description of the larva of Polypterus lapradei. Trans. Zool. Soc. London 16:115-136; Science, N.S., 12:1015. (Abstract) Summary in Proc. Camb. Philos. Soc. 11:102-104. PO(L):4 9 11 15 18 19

chiern und Dipnoern. Jenaisch. Z. Naturwiss. *8*:293-307. OLPN:1 4 17

312 Burckhardt, Karl Rudolf (1890) Mittheilung über *Protopterus annectens*. Sber. Ges. Naturforsch. Fr. Berlin *1890*:158. P:9 13 16 19 20

313 Burckhardt, Karl Rudolf (1891) Weitere Mittheilungen über *Protopterus annectens* und über einen in seiner Chorda Dorsalis vorkommenden Parasiten (*Amphistomum chordale*). Sber. Ges. Naturforsch. Fr. Berlin *1891*:62-64. P:4 20 22

314 Burckhardt, Karl Rudolf (1891) Die Zirbel von *Ichthyophis glutinosus* und *Protopterus annectens*. Anat. Anz. *6*:348-349. PO:1 6

315 Burckhardt, Karl Rudolf (1892) Über das Centralnervensystem der Dipnoer. Verh. Dtsch. Zool. Ges. Leipzig *2*:92-95. P(N):1 6 17

316 Burckhardt, Karl Rudolf (1892) Das Centralnervensystem von *Protopterus annectens*. Sber. Ges. Naturforsch. Fr. Berlin *1892*:23-25. P:1 6

317 Burckhardt, Karl Rudolf (1892) Das Centralnervensystem von *Protopterus annectens*. Berlin: Friedländer und Sohn, pp.8-64. Summary in J. Comp. Neurol. *2*:89-91. P:1 6

318 Burckhardt, Karl Rudolf (1905) Das Centralnervensystem von *Ceratodus forsteri*. C. R. Cong. Int. Zool. (Bern) *6*:314-315. (Abstract) N:1 6

319 Burdak, V. D. (1973) Tipy cheshui kak etapy istoricheskogo razvitija hidrodinamicheskoj funkcii kozhnogo pokrova ryb. (Types of scales as stages of evolution of the hydrodynamic function of cutaneous integument in fish). Zool. Zh. *52*:1208-1213. NPLO:3

320 Burne, R. H. (1894) On the aortic-arch system of *Saccobranchus fossilis*. J. Linnean Soc. London *25*:48-55. O(NPL):1 11

321 Burne, R. H. (1913) Note on the membranous labyrinth of *Neoceratodus forsteri*. Anat. Anz. *43*:396-400. N:1 7

322 Butler, David Gordon (1973) Structure and function of the adrenal gland of fishes. Amer. Zool. *13*:839-879. OPL:2 8

323 Buxton, L., J. Slater, and L. H. Brown (1978) The breeding behaviour of the shoebill or whale-headed stork *Balaeniceps rex* in the Bangweulu Swamps, Zambia. East Afr. Wildl. J. *16*:201-220. OP:22

324 Byczkowska-Smyk, Wanda (1973) Hepatic ultrastructure in the South American lungfish, *Lepidosiren paradoxa*. Folia Histochem. Cytochem. (Krakow) *11*:307-308. (Abstract) L:1 11 12

325 Byczkowska-Smyk, Wanda (1973) Observations on the ultrastructure and size of the hepatocytes of the lungfish *Lepidosiren paradoxa* (Dipnoi, Pisces). Acta Biol. Cracov, ser. Zool. *16*:247-255. L(P):1 11 12

326 Cadwallader, D. A. and J. Stoneman (1966) A review of the fisheries of the Uganda waters of Lake Albert. E.A.F.F.R.O. (East African Freshwater Fisheries Research Organization). Suppl. Pub. *3*:1-19. OP:23

327 Cahen, L., J. J. Ferrand, M. J. F. Haarsma, J. Lepersonne, and T. Verbeek (1959) Description du Sondage de Samba. Ann. Mus. Roy. Congo Belge sér. 8, Sci. Geol. *29*:1-210. (*Ceratodus*:29). OC:4 12 18

328 Caldwell, W. H. (1885) The eggs and larvae of *Ceratodus*. J. Proc. Roy. Soc. N.S.W. *18*:138. N:15

329 Caldwell, W. H. (1885) On the development of the Monotremes and *Ceratodus*. J. Proc. Roy. Soc. N.S.W. *18*:117-122. NO:14 15 18 22

330 Caldwell, W. H. (1887) The embryology of Monotremata and Marsupialia. Part I. Trans. Roy. Soc. London (B) *178*:463-486. NO:15 18

331 Caldwell, W. H. (1898) On the transportation of live *Ceratodus* from Queensland to London by Mr. O'Connor. Queensl. Agric. J. *3*:173 and 238. N

332 Call, R. N. and Peter A. Janssens (1975) Histochemical studies of the adrenocortical homologue in the kidney of the Australian lungfish, *Neoceratodus forsteri*. Cell Tissue Res. *156*:533-538. N:1 8 13

333 Campbell, Ken S. W. (1965) An almost complete skull roof and palate of the dipnoan *Dipnorhynchus sussmilchi* (Etheridge). Paleontol. *8*:634-637. FD:1 4 7 18 21

334 Campbell, Ken S. W. (1975) On new material of *Dipnorhynchus* from Wee Jasper. Preprint of Austral. Contrib. to the Soc. of Vert. Paleontol. News Bull. (104), June, 1975. FD:18

335 Campbell, Ken S. W. (1982) Lungfishes - alive and extinct. Field Mus. Natur. Hist. Bull. *52*:3-5. NFD:G(4 18 21)

336 Campbell, Ken S. W. and Richard E. Barwick (1982) A new species of the lungfish *Dipnorhynchus* from New South Wales. Paleontol. *25*:509-527. FD:1 4 7 18

337 Campbell, Ken S. W. and M. W. Bell (1982) *Soederberghia* (Dipnoi) from the Late Devonian of New South Wales. Alcheringa *6*:143-149. FD:1 4 18

338 Campbell, Ken S. W. and Richard E. Barwick (1982) The neurocranium of the primitive dipnoan *Dipnorhynchus sussmilchi* (Etheridge). J. Vert. Paleontol. *2*:286-327. FD:1 4 6 7 11 18

339 Campbell, Ken S. W. and Richard E. Barwick (1983) Early evolution of dipnoan dentitions and a new genus *Speonesydrion*. Mem. Assoc. Australas. Palaeontols *1*:17-49. FD(N):1 4 5 17 21

340 Campbell, Ken S. W. and Richard E. Barwick (1984) The choana, maxillae, premaxillae and anterior palatal bones of early dipnoans. Proc. Linn. Soc. N.S.W. *107*:147-170. FD:1 4 7 17

341 Capanna, Ernesto and S. Cataudella (1973) The chromosomes of *Calamoichthys calabaricus* (Pisces, Polypteriformes). Experientia (Basel) *29*:491-492. O(LP):1

342 Capanna, Ernesto and Pierre Clairambault (1974) Some considerations on the forebrain of the bipulmonate Dipnoi. Rend. Accad. Naz. Lincei *55*:603-610. P:1 6 17

343 Capanna, Ernesto and Pierre Clairambault (1974) Istologia e tipologia neuronale dell'Archipallio di *Protopterus dolloi* Boulenger. Rend. Accad. Naz. Lincei *57*:453-457. P:1 6

344 Caporiacco, Lodovico (1927) Pesci raccolti in Somalia nel 1924, dalla spedizione Stefanini e Puccioni. Monit. Zool. Ital. *38*:84-89. OP:1 3 16 18

345 Cappetta, H. (1972) Les poissons crétacés et tertiaires du Basin des Iullemmeden (République du Niger). Paleovert. *5*:179-251. (*Ceratodus*:229-230). OC:4 18

346 Carlisky, N. J. and A. Barrio (1972) Nitrogen metabolism of the South American lungfish *Lepidosiren paradoxa*. Comp. Biochem. Physiol. *41B*:857-873. Acta Cient. Venez. 22 (suppl. 2):R-23. [1971]. (Abstract) L:2 13 20

347 Carlson, Keith J. (1968) The skull morphology and estivation burrows of the Permian lungfish, *Gnathor-*

hiza serrata. J. Geol. *76*:641-663. Amer. Dissertation D. *11*:194. [1966]. (Abstract) FD(NLPC):1 4 17 18 19 20

348 Carlstrom, Diego (1963) A crystallographic study of vertebrate otoliths. Biol. Bull. (Woods Hole) *125*:441-463. PO(NL):1 7

349 Carpenter, G. D. Hale (1920) A Naturalist on Lake Victoria, with an Account of Sleeping-Sickness and the Tse-Tse Fly. New York: E.P. Dutton Co. OP:10 18 19 22 24

350 Carricaburu, P., René Godet, and R. Larmande (1962) Variations de l'impédance de la peau du Protoptère lors du passage de la phase sèche à la phase humide. C. R. Soc. Biol. Paris *156*:1333-1338. P:2 3 20

351 Carroll, Robert L. (1965) Lungfish burrows from the Michigan coal basin. Science (Washington) *148*:963-964. FD(PLN):1 18 20

352 Carter, George Stuart (1930) On the habits and development of *Lepidosiren paradoxa.* Proc. Linnean Soc. London *1928-29*:18-19. L:3 15 19 20

353 Carter, George Stuart and L. C. Beadle (1930) Notes on the habits and development of *Lepidosiren paradoxa.* J. Linnean Soc. London Zool. *37*:197-203. L:14 15 19 20 24

354 Carter, George Stuart and L. C. Beadle (1931) The fauna of the swamps of the Paraguayan Chaco in relation to its environment. II. Respiratory adaptations in the fishes. J. Linnean Soc. London Zool. *37*:327-368. OL:1 9 10 17 18

355 Case, Ermine Cowles (1901) The Vertebrates from the Permian bone bed of Vermilion County, Illinois. Cont. Walker Mus., Univ. Chicago *1*:1-29. (Dipnoi:8-12). CFDO:1 4 18

356 Case, Ermine Cowles (1915) The Permo-Carboniferous Red Beds of North America and their vertebrate fauna. Carnegie Inst. Wash. Pub. #207:1-176 OC:18

357 Case, Ermine Cowles (1921) A new species of *Ceratodus* from the Upper Triassic of western Texas. Occas. Pap. Mus. Zool. Univ. Mich. #101:1-2. C:1 4 18

358 Casier, E. (1961) Materiaux pour la faune ichthyologique eocretacique du Congo. Ann. Mus. Roy. Afr. Centr. (8) Geol. *39*:1-96. (*Ceratodus*:40-41). OC:4 18

359 Castelnau, Francis de (1855) Poissons. Animaux Nouveaux ou Rares dans l'Amerique du Sud. Paris: Bertrand. (*Lepidosiren*:104-106). OL:1 3 17 18 24

360 Castelnau, Francis de (1876) Mémoire sur les poissons appelés Barramundi par les aborigènes du nord-est de l'Australie. J. de Zool. *5*:129-136. N:1 3 18 19

361 Castelnau, Francis de (1876) Remarques au sujet du genre *Neoceratodus.* J. de Zool. *5*:342-343. N:1 3 19

362 Castelnau, Francis de (1876) Les Dipnés. C. R. Acad. Sci. Paris *82*:1034. N(LP):18

363 Castelnau, Francis de (1878) On a new Ganoid fish from Queensland. Proc. Linnean Soc. N.S.W. *3*:164-165. O:1

364 Castelnau, Francis de (1879) On Ompax. Zool. Rec. *16*:Pisces:4-5. O:1

365 Chabakov, Alexander V. (1931) Ob ostatkach guojakodyshashchich (Fam. Ceratodontidae) iz nizhnego triasa gory Bogdo. (Description des restes de Ceratodontidae, trouvé dans les calcaires triasiques du Mont Bogdo). Trav. Inst. Paleozool. Acad. Sci. URSS *1*:45-55. C:1 4 17 18

366 Chabaud, Alain G. (1959) Redescription d'*Amblyonema terdentatum* Linstow 1898. Nématode parasite

du Dipneuste australien *Neoceratodus.* Bull. Soc. Zool. Fr. *84*:188-194. N:22

367 Chadwick, A. (1966) Prolactin-like activity in the pituitary gland of fishes and amphibians? J. Endocrinol. *35*:75-81. OP:2 8

368 Champy, C. and J. Louvel (1939) Recherches sur l'hematopoièse chez *Protopterus annectens.* Arch. Anat. Microsc. *35*:243-281. P:1 11 15

369 Chang, Mee-Mann and Xiaobo Yu (1984) Structure and phylogenetic significance of *Diabolichthys speratus* gen. et sp. nov., a new dipnoan-like form from the Lower Devonian of eastern Yunnan, China. Proc. Linn. Soc. N.S.W. *107*:171-184. FD:1 4

370 Chapman, Frederick (1912) Report on Jurassic and Carboniferous fish-remains: Jurassic sandstone with *Ceratodus,* (Parish of Kirrak, S. Gippsland.) Rec. Geol. Surv. Victoria *3*:234-236. CO(N):3 18

371 Chapman, Frederick (1914) On a new species of *Ceratodus* from the Cretaceous of New South Wales. Proc. Roy. Soc. Victoria 27(N.S.):25-27. C:1 4 18

372 Chapman, Frederick (1914) Australasian Fossils. Melbourne: George Robertson and Co. (*Ceratodus*:265-267). OC:G(3 4)

373 Chardon, Michel (1961) Contribution a l'étude du système circulatoire lié à la respiration des Protopteridae. Ann. Mus. Roy. Afr. Cent. sér. Quarto Zool. #103:51-98. P:1 9 11 15

374 Charlton, H. H. (1932) Comparative studies on the nucleus preopticus pars magnocellularis and the nucleus lateralis tuberis in fishes. J. Comp. Neurol. *54*:237-275. ON:1 6

375 Chartrand, S. L. and Joanne Finstad (1971) A structurally unique immunoglobulin of the African lungfish. Fed. Proc. *30*:350. (Abstract) P:2 11 17

376 Chatterjee, S., Sohan L. Jain, T. S. Kutty, and T. K. Roy-Chowdhury (1969) On the discovery of Triassic cynodont reptiles from India. Sci. Cult. *35*:411-413. OC:4 18

377 Chaudhuri, S. K. (1964) On living lung-fishes. J. Bengal Natur. Hist. Soc. *32*:114-118. NPL:G(4 10 17 18 20)

378 Chauvet, Jacqueline, Marie Thérèse Chauvet, and Roger Acher (1971) Une éventuelle relation entre le taux d'urée dans le sang et la teneur en vasotocine de la neurohypophyse chez certains poissons. C. R. Acad. Sci. Paris *272*:1669-1671. PO:2 8 11 20

379 Chavin, Walter (1970) Brain-pituitary neurosecretory complex of the Australian lungfish, *Neoceratodus forsteri* Krefft. Amer. Zool. *10*:496. (Abstract) N(P):1 6 8 17

380 Chavin, Walter (1971) The hypothalamico-hypophyseal neurosecretory complex of *Neoceratodus forsteri* Krefft and its relation to the origin of the tetrapod neurosecretory apparatus. In Harold C. Mack and Alfred I. Sherman (eds): The Neuroendocrinology of Human Reproduction. Biological and Clinical Perspectives. Springfield: Charles C. Thomas, pp.23-59. N(PL):1 6 8 11 17

381 Chavin, Walter (1976) The thyroid of the sarcopterygian fishes (Dipnoi and Crossopterygii) and the origin of the tetrapod thyroid. Gen. Comp. Endocrinol. *30*:142-155. Amer. Zool. *12*:667. [1972]. (Abstract) NLPO:1 2 8 17

382 Cheeseman, Thomas Frederick (1879) Remarks on *Lepidosiren* and other fishes. Proc. New Zealand Inst. *12*:448. LO

383 Chester Jones, I. and J. G. Phillips (1960) Adreno-corticosteroids in fish. Symp. Zool. Soc. London #1:17-32. OP:2 8 17

384 Chester Jones, I. (1976) Evolutionary aspects of the adrenal cortex and its homologues. J. Endocrinol. *71*:3P-32P. OLD:1 2 8 17

385 Chester Jones, I. and W. Mosley (1980) The interrenal gland in Pisces. In I. Chester Jones and I. W. Henderson (eds): General Comparative and Clinical Endocrinology of the Adrenal Cortex. New York: Academic Press, pp.395-472. (Dipnoi:422). ONLP:2 8 13

386 Chiarelli, A. B. and Ernesto Capanna (1973) Checklist of fish chromosomes. In A. B. Chiarelli and Ernesto Capanna (eds): Cytotaxonomy and Vertebrate Evolution. London: Academic Press, pp.205-232. LPO:1

387 Chieffi, G. (1966) Occurrence of steroids in gonads of nonmammalian vertebrates and sites of their biosynthesis. Proc. Int. Congr. Hormon. Steroids *2*:1047-1057. OP:2 8 14

388 Chlupaty, Peter (1956) Lungenfische. Aquarien Terrarien Z. *9*:4-6. P(NL):G(9 14 15 16 18 19 20 21 24)

389 Chopard, Lucien (1957) Un poisson qui peut vivre sans eau: le Protoptère. Nature (Paris) #3261:30-34. P(LNFD):G(3 4 7 10 15 16 18 19 20 21)

390 Chorn, John (1977) Fossil lungfishes in Kansas. Trans. Kans. Acad. Sci. *79*:95-96. (Abstract) CFD:4 18

391 Chorn, John and Curtis D. Conley (1978) A late Pennsylvanian vertebrate assemblage from stromatolites in the Bern Limestone, northeastern Kansas. Trans. Kans. Acad. Sci. *81*:139. (Abstract) FDO:18

392 Christomanos, Anastasios A. and Friedrich Reinhard (1973) Das Hämoglobin des Lungenfisches *Protopterus aethiopicus*. I. Die elektrophoretische Trennung in seinen Komponenten. Folia Biochim. Biol. Graeca *10*:1-11. Also in Prakt. Akad. Athenon *48*:248-260. P:2 11 18

393 Christomanos, Anastasios A. and Friedrich Reinhard (1973) Die Aminosäurenzusammensetzung des Hämoglobins des Lungenfisches *Protopterus aethiopicus*. Folia Biochim. Biol. Graeca *10*:29-30. P:2 11

394 Christomanos, Anastasios A. (1973) Zur Konstitution des Hämoglobins des Lungenfisches *Protopterus aethiopicus*. III. Folia Biochim. Biol. Graeca *10*:84-88. P:2 11

395 Christomanos, Anastasios A. (1978) The problem of hemoglobin polymerization in the lungfish *Protopterus annectens*. Folia Biochim. Biol. Graeca *14* (special issue):1-10. P:2 11

396 Ciardi, John (1979) The lung fish. In For Instance. New York: W. W. Norton and Co., pp.54-55. P:G(11 20 24)

397 Clairambault, Pierre and Ernesto Capanna (1973) Suggestions for a revision of the cytoarchitectonics of the telencephalon of *Protopterus*, *Protopterus annectens* (Owen). Boll. Zool. *40*:149-171. P:1 6

398 Clairambault, Pierre, Ernesto Capanna, Marcelle Chanconie, and Gabrielle Pinganaud (1974) Tipologia neuronale del Septum telencefalico di un Dipnoo lepidosireniforme (*Protopterus dolloi* Boulenger). Rend. Accad. Naz. Lincei *56*:423-431. P:1 6

399 Clairambault, Pierre, Ernesto Capanna, Marcelle Chanconie, and Gabrielle Pinganaud (1974) Typologie neuronique du complexe Strio-amygdaloide de *Protopterus dolloi* (Boulenger). Rend. Accad. Naz. Lincei *56*:1017-1022. P:1 6

400 Clairambault, Pierre, Ernesto Capanna, Marcelle Chanconie, and Gabrielle Pinganaud (1974) Architectural pattern of the diencephalon and mesencephalon of the African lungfish *Protopterus dolloi*. Boll. Zool. *41*:107-122. P:1 6 7

401 Clairambault, Pierre (1975) The optic pathways of the lungfish *Protopterus*. Exp. Brain Res. *23*(suppl.):39. (Abstract) P:1 6 7

402 Clairambault, Pierre and C. Flood (1975) Les centres visuels primaires de *Protopterus dolloi* Boulenger. J. Hirnforsch. *16*:497-509. P:1 6 7

403 Clemens, P. (1895) Die äusseren Kiemen der Wirbeltiere. Anatomische Hefte *5*:65-155. In F. Merkel and R. Bonnet, (eds): Referate und Beiträge zur Anatomie und Entwickelungsgeschichte. Wiesbaden: J.F. Bergmann. (Dipnoi:67-77). PNO:1 3 4 5 6 9 11 16

404 Coates, Christopher W. (1937) Slowly the lungfish gives up its secrets. Bull. New York Zool. Soc. *40*:25-34. P:9 10 16 19 20

405 Cobbold, T. Spencer (1862) On the cranial bones of *Lepidosiren annectens*. Proc. Zool. Soc. London *1862*:129-132. P:1 4

406 Cockerell, Theodore Dru Alison (1911) The scales of the dipnoan fishes. Science N.S. *33*:831-832. NLP:1 3

407 Cockerell, Theodore Dru Alison (1911) Additional note on reticulated fish-scales. Science N.S. *34*:126-127. FD:3

408 Cohen, E. and F. J. Risso (1964) Observaciones preliminares sobre las proteínas sericas del dipnoo chaqueño (*Lepidosiren paradoxa*). Notas Biol. Fac. Cienc. Exactas Fis. Natur. Univ. Nac. Nordeste Corrientes *1964*:22-28. L:2 11 18

409 Conant, Elizabeth Babbott (1970) Regeneration in the African lungfish, *Protopterus*. I. Gross aspects. J. Exp. Zool. *174*:15-32. P:1 16 20

410 Conant, Elizabeth Babbott (1972) Regeneration in the African lungfish, *Protopterus*. II. Branching structures. J. Exp. Zool. *181*:353-364. P:1 16

411 Conant, Elizabeth Babbott (1973) Feeding behavior in the African lungfish, *Protopterus*. Va. J. Sci. *24*:132. (Abstract) P:1 4 5 19 21 22

412 Conant, Elizabeth Babbott (1973) Regeneration in the African lungfish, *Protopterus*. III. Regeneration during fasting and estivation. Biol. Bull. (Woods Hole) *144*:248-261. Va. J. Sci. *23*:109. (Abstract) P:1 16 20

413 Conant, Elizabeth Babbott (1975) Observations on cardiac and respiratory function in the African lungfish, *Protopterus*. Bios *46*:21-37. Va. J. Sci. *25*:61. (Abstract) P:2 9 10 11

414 Conant, Elizabeth Babbott and Hollon Meaders (1975) Studies on the tooth plates of the African lungfish, *Protopterus*. Va. J. Sci. *26*:53. (Abstract) P:1 4 21

415 Conant, Elizabeth Babbott (1976) Urea accumulation and other effects of estivation in the African lungfish, *Protopterus*. Va. J. Sci. *27*:42. (Abstract) P:1 2 4 13 20

416 Conant, Elizabeth Babbott and Susan F. Thomas (1976) Histological observations of the regenerating limb in the African lungfish *Protopterus*. Va. J. Sci. *27*:42. (Abstract) P:1 3 4 5 6 7 11 16

417 Conant, Elizabeth Babbott, James B. Patrick, and Sarah P. Lawrence (1976) Analysis of pigments in the bone of the lungfish *Protopterus* and the shelf fungus *Fomes igniareus*. Va. J. Sci. *27*:42. (Abstract) PO:2 4

418 Conant, Elizabeth Babbott (1977) Green color of bones and eggs in the African lungfish, *Protopterus annectens*, due to bile pigments. Amer. Zool. *17*:911. (Abstract) P:2 4 14

419 Conant, Elizabeth Babbott (1980) A lungfish bibliography: historical reflections. Amer. Zool. *20*:897. (Abstract) PLN

420 Conant, Elizabeth Babbott (1982) Johannes Natterer (1787-1843): forgotten naturalist. Amer. Zool. *22*:889. (Abstract) OL

421 Conant, Elizabeth Babbott (1983) John Samuel Budgett (1872-1904), embryologist/naturalist: in search of lungfish and *Polypterus* eggs. Proc. Rochester Acad. Sci. *14*:296. (Abstract) OLP

422 Conant, Elizabeth Babbott (1984) Lungfish: a singular embarrassment to taxonomists. Amer. Zool. *24*:84A. (Abstract) D

423 Cope, Edward Drinker (1871) Contribution to the ichthyology of the Lesser Antilles. Trans. Amer. Philos. Soc. N.S. *14*:445-483. ODL:1 4

424 Cope, Edward Drinker (1871) Observations on the systematic relations of the fishes. Amer. Natur. *5*:579-593. OD:1 4 17

425 Cope, Edward Drinker (1884) Note on the phylogeny of the Vertebrata. Amer. Natur. *18*:1255-1257. OD:17

426 Cope, Edward Drinker (1885) On fossil remains of Reptilia and fishes from Illinois. Proc. Acad. Sci. Phil. *1875*:404-411. OC:4 18

427 Cope, Edward Drinker (1876) Descriptions of some vertebrate remains from the Fort Union beds of Montana. Proc. Acad. Sci. Phil. *1876*:248-261. CO:1 4

428 Cope, Edward Drinker (1877) On the Vertebrata of the Bone Bed in Eastern Illinois. Proc. Amer. Philos. Soc. *17*:52-63. CO:1 4 18

429 Cope, Edward Drinker (1877) On the classification of the extinct fishes of the lower types. Proc. Amer. Assoc. *26*:292-299. DO

430 Cope, Edward Drinker (1884) Synopsis of the species of Oreodontidae. Proc. Amer. Philos. Soc. *21*:503-590. (Dipnoi:575, 577, 585). OPLN:1 4 17

431 Cope, Edward Drinker (1885) Fifth contribution to the knowledge of the fauna of the Permian Formation of Texas and the Indian Territory. Proc. Amer. Philos. Soc. *22*:28-47. CO:1 4 18

431a Cope, Edward Drinker (1887) Book review: Handbook der Paleontologie. Vol. 3, by Karl A. Zittel. Amer. Natur. *21*:1014-1019.

432 Cope, Edward Drinker (1890) The homologies of the fins of fishes. Amer. Natur.*24*:400-423. ND:1 4 17

433 Cope, Edward Drinker (1892) On the phylogeny of the vertebrata. Proc. Amer. Philos. Soc. *30*:278-281. OD:4 17

434 Copley, Hugh (1941) A short account of the fresh water fishes of Kenya. J. East Afr. Uganda Natur. Hist. Soc. *16*:1-24. OP:1 17 18 20 21

435 Corbel, M.J. (1975) The immune response in fish: a review. J. Fish Biol. *7*:539-564. OP:2 11

436 Corbet, Philip S. (1961) The food of non-cichlid fishes in the Lake Victoria basin, with remarks on their evolution and adaptation to lacustrine conditions. Proc. Zool. Soc. London *136*:1-101. (*Protopterus*:14-18). OP:16 18 21

437 Cordier, R. (1929) Le tube urinaire du Protoptère (Dipneuste). C. R. Assoc. Anat. *24*:157-165. P:1 13

438 Cordier, R. (1936) Les organes sensoriels cutanés du Protoptère. Bull. Acad. Roy. Belg. *22*:474-483. P:1 3 6 7

439 Cordone, Almo J. and Bill W. Kudhongania (1970) Stock evaluation and assessment. Rep. E. Afr. Freshw. Fish. Res. Org. *1970*:5-14. OP:18 23

440 Cordone, Almo J. and Bill W. Kudhongania (1972) Observations on the influences of codend mesh size on bottom trawl catches in Lake Victoria, with emphasis on the *Haplochromis* population. Afr. J. Trop. Hydrobiol. Fisheries *2*:1-19. OP:18 23

441 Corroy, Georges (1928) Les Vertébrés du Trias de Lorraine et le Trias Lorrain. Ann. Paleontol. *17*:1-136. (*Ceratodus*:97-98). OC:4 18

442 Cosgriff, J. William (1967) Triassic vertebrates from Western Australia. Diss. Abstr. Int. B Sci. Eng. *27*:2743. OC:18

443 Cott, Hugh B. (1954) The status of the Nile crocodile in Uganda. Uganda J. *18*:1-12. OP:22

444 Coujard, R. and Christiane Coujard-Champy (1947) Recherches sur l'épithélium intestinal du Protoptère et sur l'évolution des entérocytes chez les Vertébrés. Arch. Anat. Histol. Embryol. *30*:69-97. P:1 12

445 Coupin, Fernande (1922) Note sur les formations choroïdiennes et le sac auditif du *Protopterus annectens* O. Bull. Mus. Natl. Hist. Natur. Paris *28*:217-222. P:1 6 7 17

446 Craigie, E. Horne (1943) The architecture of the cerebral capillary bed in lungfishes. J. Comp. Neurol. *79*:19-31. Trans. Roy. Soc. Can. *37*:129. (Abstract) PLN:1 6 11 17

447 Crane, Agnes (1877) On certain genera of living fishes and their fossil affinities. Geol. Mag. (Decade II) *4*:209-219. PLNFDO:1 9 17 18 19 20 21

448 Crawford, Gerald Norman Cullen (1940) The evolution of the Haversian pattern in bone. J. Anat. *74*:284-299. PLO:1 4 17

449 Cserr, H. F., M. Bundgaard, J. K. Ashby, and M. Murray (1980) On the anatomic relation of choroid plexus to brain: a comparative study. Amer. J. Physiol. *238*:R76-R81. PLNO:1 2 6 10 11 17

450 Cuninghame, R. J. (1913) On the presentation of a live lung-fish to the Zoological Gardens, London. J. East Afr. Uganda Natur. Hist. Soc. *4*:82-84. PN:18 19 20 21 24

451 Cunningham, Joseph Thomas (1912) Fishes. In William Plane Pycraft (ed): Animal Life, an Evolutionary Natural History. London: Methuen and Co., Ltd., pp.299, 319-321, 384-386. PLN:G(1 10 11 18 19 20)

452 Cunningham, Joseph Thomas (1929) The vascular filaments on the pelvic limbs of *Lepidosiren*, their function and evolutionary significance. Proc. Roy. Soc. London *105*:484-493. Rep. Brit. Assoc. Advan. Sci. *1929*:330. (Abstract) L:1 9 11 18

453 Cunningham, Joseph Thomas (1931) The double lateral line of *Lepidosiren*. Nature (London) *128*:377. L:1 7

454 Cunningham, Joseph Thomas (1932) Experiments on the interchange of oxygen and carbon dioxide between the skin of *Lepidosiren* and the surrounding water, and the probable emission of oxygen by the male *Symbranchus*. Proc. Zool. Soc. London *1932*: 875-887. LO(P):2 3 9 11 18 19

455 Cunningham, Joseph Thomas and D. M. Reid (1932) Experimental researches on the emission of oxygen by the pelvic filaments of the male *Lepidosiren* with some experiments on *Symbranchus marmoratus*. Proc. Roy. Soc. London *110*:234-248. LO:2 3 9 11 18

456 Cunningham, Joseph Thomas and D. M. Reid (1933) Pelvic filaments of *Lepidosiren*. Nature (London) *131*:913. L:1 9 10 14 18 19

457 Cunnington, William A. (1913) Zoological results of the Third Tanganyika Expedition, conducted by W. A. Cunnington, 1904-1905. Report on the Branchiura. Proc. Zool. Soc. London *1913*:262-283. OP:18 22

458 Curry-Lindahl, Kai (1956) Ecological studies on mammals, birds, reptiles and amphibians in the eastern Belgian Congo. Ann. Mus. Roy. Congo Belge sér. Quarto Zool. *42*:7-77. OP:22

459 Curry-Lindahl, Kai (1956) On the ecology, feeding behavior and territoriality of the African lungfish, *Protopterus aethiopicus* Heckel. Ark. Zool. *9*:479-497. P:3 10 18 19 20 21 22

460 Daget, Jacques (1954) Poissons du Niger supérieur. Mem. Inst. Fondam. Afr. Noire sér. A. Sci. Natur. #36:40-44. PO:1 3 4 15 18 20

461 Daget, Jacques (1959) Les Poissons du Niger supérieur. (1re note complémentaire). Bull. Inst. Fondam. Afr. Noire *21*: sér. A Sci. Natur. #2:664-688. OP:1 14 18 19

462 Daget, Jacques (1960) La faune ichthyologique du bassin de la Gambie. Bull. Inst. Fondam. Afr. Noire Sci. Natur. *22*: sér. A #2:610-619. PO:18

463 Daget, Jacques (1962) Les Poissons du Fouta Dialon et de la Basse Guineé. Mem. Inst. Fondam. Afr. Noire sér. A Sci. Natur. #65:1-120. (*Protopterus*:48). OP:18

464 Daget, Jacques and A. Iltis (1965) Poissons de Côte d'Ivoire, eaux douces et saumâtres. Inst. Fondam. Afr. Noire, Dakar. (*Protopterus*:320-321). PO:1 10 18 20

465 Dakin, William J. (1931) The osmotic concentration of the blood of *Callorhynchus milli* and *Epiceratodus* (*Neoceratodus*) *forsteri* and the significance of the physico-chemical condition of the Holocephali and the Dipnoi. Proc. Zool. Soc. London *1931*:11-16. NO:2 11

466 Dalquest, Walter W. (1968) Lungfishes from the Permian of Texas. Copeia *1968*:194-197. FD(LP):1 4 18

467 Dalquest, Walter W. and Rose M. Carpenter (1975) A new discovery of fossil lungfish burrows. Texas J. Sci. *26*:611. FD:18 20

468 Damel (1875) Notizen uber *Ceratodus forsteri*. J. Mus. Godeffroy *8*:138. N:3 18 21 24

469 Dartevelle, Edmond and Edgard Casier (1949) Les Poissons fossiles du Bas-Congo et des régions voisines. Ann. Mus. Congo Belge A (Mineral.- Geol.-Paleo.) sér, 3 *2*:201-256. (*Protopterus*:205-207). FPO:4 12 18

470 Dasch, E. Julius and Ken S. W. Campbell (1970) Strontium-isotope evidence for marine or freshwater origin of fossil Dipnoans and Arthrodires. Nature (London) *227*:1159. OFD:17 18

471 Daugherty, Wayne F. Jr. (1966) Fish lactate dehydrogenase: ontogeny and phylogeny. Diss. Abstr. B *27*:2182-2183. (Abstract) OD:2 17

472 David, L. and Max Poll (1937) Contribution à la faune ichthyologique du Congo Belge. (Collections du Dr. H. Schoutenden (1924-26) et d' autres récolteurs). Ann. Mus. Congo Belge sér. 1 *3*:189-294. PO:18

473 Davidoff, M. von (1883) Beiträge zur vergleichen-den Anatomie der hinteren Gliedmasse der Fische. Dritter Theil: *Ceratodus*. Gegenbaurs Morphol. Jahrb. *9*:117-162. N:1 4 5 6

474 Davies, Arthur Morley and F. E. Eames (1971) Tertiary Faunas: A Text-book for Oil-field Palaeontologists and Students of Geology. Vol. 1: The Composition of Tertiary Faunas:488-491. New York: American Elsevier Inc. OFP:4

475 Dawson, Alden B. (1940) The pituitary body of the African lung-fish, *Protopterus aethiopicus*. Biol. Bull. (Woods Hole) *78*:275-283. Anat. Rec. *75*:124 [1939]. (Abstract) P:1 8

476 Day, Francis (1880) On the air-bladders of fish. Zoologist *4*:97-104. LPNO:9 10

477 Dean, Bashford (1895) Fishes, Living and Fossil. London: Macmillan and Co., Ltd. OP:G(1 4)

478 Dean, Bashford (1903) Obituary notice of a lungfish. Pop. Sci. Monthly *63*:33-39. P:1 3 16 19 20 21

479 Dean, Bashford (1906) Notes on the living specimens of the Australian lungfish, *Ceratodus forsteri*, in the Zoological Society's collection. Proc. Zool. Soc. London *1906*:168-178. N:7 9 10 19 21

480 Dean, Bashford (1912) A fish out of water. Amer. Mus. J. *12*:251-253. Reprinted in Sci. Amer. Suppl. *75*:52. [1913]. P:G(1 19 20)

481 Dean, Bashford (1912) Additional notes on the living specimens of the Australian lung-fish (*Ceratodus forsteri*) in the collection of the Zoological Society of London. Proc. Zool. Soc. London *1912*:607-612. N:3 9 10 16 21

482 Dean, F. D. and I. Chester Jones (1959) Sex steroids in the lungfish (*Protopterus annectens* Owen). J. Endocrinol. *18*:366-371. P:8 14

483 Dechaseaux, Colette (1948) Sur la présence du genre *Ceratodus* dans le Trias inférieur de Madagascar. Bull. Soc. Geol. Fr. *18*:157-158. C:3 4 18

484 Dechaseaux, Colette (1949) Paléontologie de Madagascar. XXVII. Contribution à l'étude du genre *Ceratodus*. Les *Ceratodus* de Madagascar. Ann. Paléontol. *35*:75-86. C:1 4 18

485 Deecke, Wilhelm (1926) Fossilium Catalogum. I. Animalia. *33* (Pisces triadici):1-201. Berlin: Junk, pp.1-201. (Dipnoi: 74-86). OFDC:18

486 Deecke, Wilhelm (1926) Über die Triasfische. Palaeontol. Z. *8*:184-198. OC:17 18

487 de Haën, Christoph and Arieh Gertler (1974) Isolation and amino-terminal sequence analysis of two dissimilar pancreatic proelastases from the African lungfish, *Protopterus aethiopicus*. Biochemistry *13*: 2673-2677. P:2 12 17

488 de Haën, Christoph, Hans Neurath, and David C. Teller (1975) The phylogeny of trypsin-related serine proteases and their zymogens. New methods for the investigation of distant evolutionary relationships. J. Mol. Biol. *92*:225-259. OP :2 11 12 17

489 de Haën, Christoph, Kenneth A. Walsh, and Hans Neurath (1977) Isolation and amino-terminal sequence analysis of a new pancreatic trypsinogen of the African lungfish *Protopterus aethiopicus*. Biochem *16*:4421-4425. P:2 12 17

490 DeLaney, Richard G., Sukhamay Lahiri, and Alfred P. Fishman (1974) Aestivation of the African lungfish *Protopterus aethiopicus*: cardiovascular and respiratory functions. J. Exp. Biol. *61*:111-128. Physiologist *15*:116. [1972]. (Abstract) P:2 9 10 11 20

491   DeLaney, Richard G., Clarence Shub, and Alfred P. Fishman (1976) Hematologic observations on the aquatic and estivating African lungfish, *Protopterus aethiopicus.* Copeia *1976*:423-434. P:1 11 20 22

492   DeLaney, Richard G., Sukhamay Lahiri, Richard Hamilton, and Alfred P. Fishman (1977) Acid-base balance and plasma composition in the aestivating lungfish (*Protopterus*). Amer. J. Physiol. *232*:R10-R17, or Amer. J. Physiol.: Regulatory Integrative Comp. Physiol. *1*:R10-R17. P:2 11 13 20

493   DeLaney, Richard G. and Alfred P. Fishman (1977) Analysis of lung ventilation in the aestivating lungfish *Protopterus aethiopicus.* Amer. J. Physiol. *233*: R181-R187. P:2 5 10 17 20

494   DeLaney, Richard G., Pierre Laurent, Raymond Galante, Allen I. Pack, and Alfred P. Fishman (1983) Pulmonary mechanoreceptors in the Dipnoi lungfish *Protopterus* and *Lepidosiren.* Amer. J. Physiol. *244*: R418-R428. PL:2 6 7 10

495   DeMar, Robert E. (1969) Pennsylvanian vertebrates from Illinois. Geol. Soc. Amer. *6*:10. (Abstract) OFD:18

496   Denison, Robert H. (1941) The soft anatomy of *Bothriolepis.* J. Paleontol. *15*:553-561. O(FD):1 9 10 18

496a   Denison, Robert H. (1951) Late Devonian freshwater fishes from the western United States. Fieldiana Geol. *11*:221-261. (Dipnoi: 237-240). FDO:4 8

497   Denison, Robert H. (1961) New fossil fishes from Wyoming. Bull. Chicago Natur. Hist. Mus. *32*:6-8. FDO(CLPN):3 4 17 18

498   Denison, Robert H. (1966) The origin of the lateral-line sensory system. Amer. Zool. *6*:369-370. OFD:7 17

499   Denison, Robert H. (1968) Early Devonian lungfishes from Wyoming, Utah, and Idaho. Fieldiana Geol. *17*:353-413. FD:3 17 18

500   Denison, Robert H. (1968) The evolutionary significance of the earliest known lungfish, *Uranolophus.* In Tor Ørvig (ed): Nobel Symposium 4: Current Problems of Lower Vertebrate Phylogeny. Stockholm: Almquist and Wicksell, pp.247-258. FD:1 3 4 17

501   Denison, Robert H. (1969) New Pennsylvanian lungfishes from Illinois. Fieldiana Geol. *12*:193-211. FD:1 3 4 17 18

502   Denison, Robert H. (1974) The structure and evolution of teeth in lungfishes. Fieldiana Geol. *33*:31-58. FD(NPL):1 4 17

503   Denton, T. E. and W. M. Howell (1973) Chromosomes of the African polypterid fishes, *Polypterus palmas* and *Calamoichthys calabaricus.* Experientia (Basel) *29*:122-124. O(PNL):1

504   Derivot, Jacques Henri, Mireille Dupé, and René Godet (1979) Anatomie fonctionnelle de l'organe olfactif de *Protopterus annectens* Owen (Dipneustes): contribution à la connaissance du mécanisme d'irrigation de l'organe olfactif. Acta Zool. (Stockholm) *60*:251-257. P:7 9 10 19

505   Derivot, Jacques Henri, Xavier Mattei, René Godet, and Mireille Dupé (1979) Étude ultrastructurale de la région apicale des cellules de l'épithélium olfactif de *Protopterus annectens* Owen (Dipneustes). J. Ultrastruct. Res. *66*:22-31. P:1 7

506   Derivot, Jacques Henri (1984) Functional anatomy of the peripheral olfactory system of the African lungfish, *Protopterus annectens* Owen: macroscopic, microscopic, and morphometric aspects. Amer. J. Anat. *169*:177-192. P(N):1 7 15 20

507   Derivot, Jacques Henri (1984) Functional anatomy of the peripheral olfactory system of the African lungfish *Protoperus annectens* Owen: development of the primary olfactory pathway during postembryonic growth. Amer. J. Anat. *171*:15-23. P:1 6 7 15 16

508   Devillers, C. (1958) Le système latéral. In Pierre-P. Grassé (ed): Traité de Zoologie. Paris: Masson et Cie, *13*:940-1032. (Dipnoi:1018-1023). ONP:1 7 15

509   Deyst, Katherine A. and Karel F. Liem (1985) The muscular basis of aerial ventilation of the primitive lung of *Amia calva.* Respir. Physiol. *59*:213-223. O(P):5 10 19

510   DiCaporiacco, Lodovico (1927) Pesci raccolti in Somalia nel 1924, dalla spedizione Stefanini e Puccioni. Monit. Zool. Ital. *38*:84-89. PO:1 3 16 18

511   Dingerkus, Guido (1984) Karotypic analysis of *Neoceratodus forsteri*, the Australian lungfish, and its influence on chordate cytogenetic interrelationships. Amer. Zool. *24*:83A. (Abstract) N(LP):1

512   Distèche, M. and H. Denis (1970) Spécificité des cistrons dirigeant la synthèse du RNA ribosomique chez les animaux, les plantes et les bactéries. Arch. Internat. Physiol. Biochim. *78*:584-586. OP:1 17

513   Ditmars, Raymond L. (1921) The lung fish. Zool. Soc. Bull. *24*:14-15. N:G(10 17 19 21 22)

514   Dodd, Ed and Tom Hill (1980) Mark Trail: the remarkable lungfish of South America. (comic strip) Courier Express, Buffalo, New York Jan. 13, 1980. L:G(18 20)

515   Dodd, J. M. and Thomas Kerr (1963) Comparative morphology and histology of the hypothalamo-neuro-hypophysial system. Symp. Zool. Soc. London #9:5-27. OP:1 6 8 17

516   Doflein, Franz (1914) Das Tier als Glied des Naturganzen. In Richard Hesse and Franz Doflein (eds): Tierbau und Tierleben in ihrem Zusammenhang betrachtet. Leipzig: Teubner, Vol. II. (Dipnoi:767-768, 779-781). OPL:18 20

517   Dollfus, Robert P. (1929) Contribution à l'étude de la faune du Cameroun. Helmintha. I. Trématoda et Acanthocephala. Faune Colonies Françaises *3*:73-114. OP*:18 22

518   Dollfus, Robert P. (1930) Metacercaire du Nephrocephala. Ann. Parisitol. Hum. Comp. *8*:216-217. OP+:22

519   Dollfus, Robert P. (1932) Mission saharienne Augieras-Draper, 1927-1928: Trématodes de Mammifieres, Oiseaux et Poissons. Bull. Mus. Natl. Hist. Natur. Paris sér. 2, *4*:555-603. OP+:22

520   Dollfus, Robert P. (1963) Hôtes et lieux récolte de quelques Trématodes digénétiques de Vertébrés de la collection du Musée royal de l'Afrique centrale. Rev. Zool. Bot. Afr. *68*:323-357. OP:22

521   Dollo, Louis (1895) La phylogénie des Dipneustes. Bull. Soc. Belg. Geol. Paleontol. Hydrol. *9*:79-128. Summary in Amer. Natur. *30*:479. [1896] PLNFD:1 4 17

522   Dollo, Louis (1906) Sur quelques points d'éthologie paléontologique relatifs aux poissons. Bull. Soc. Belg. Geol. Paléontol. Hydrol. *20*:135-138. OD

523   Dollo, Louis (1913) Sur un Dipneuste nouveau, de grandes dimensions, découvert dans le Dévonien Supérieur de la Belgique. Bull. Acad. Roy. Belg. *3*:15-17. FD:4 18

524   Donaldson, Edward M. (1973) Reproductive endocrinology of fishes. Amer. Zool. *13*:909-927. OP:1 2 8 14

525   Dorn, Emmi (1957) Das Zwischenhirn von *Protop-*

terus. Verh. Dtsch. Zool. Ges. Leipzig *1957*:226-230, or Zool. Anz. Suppl. *20*:226-230. P:1 6

526   Dorn, Emmi (1957) Über das Zwischenhirn - Hypophysensystem von *Protopterus annectens* (Zugleich ein Beitrag zum Problem des Saccus Vasculosus). Z. Zellforsch. Mikrosk. Anat. *46*:108-114. P(LN):1 6 8

527   Dorn, Emmi (1957) Über den Feinbau der Paraphyse von *Protopterus annectens*. Z. Zellforsch. Mikrosk. Anat. *46*:115-120. P:1 6 11

528   Dorn, Emmi and Friedrich Schaller (1968) Die Knochenzüngler — eine Besonderheit unter den Fischen. Umschau *14*:426-431. O(N):3 18

529   Douglas, J. G. and G. E. Wiliams (1982) Southern polar forests: the early Cretaceous floras of Victoria and their palaeoclimatic significance. Paleogr. Paleoclimatol. Paleoecol. *39*:171-185. OC:18

530   Dreyer, Dieter (1962) Zur Enstehung und Paläontologie der Bonebedlagen im Unteren Rät Thüringens. Freiberger Forschung. *125*:127-155. (*Ceratodus*:138). OC:4 18

531   Drzewina, Anna (1905) Contribution à l'étude du tissu lymphoïde des Ichthyopsidés. Arch. Zool. Exp. et Gen. sér. 4 *4*:145-338. OP:1 11 12 13 14

532   Dubois, Raphaël (1892) Contribution à l'étude du méchanisme respiratoire des Dipnoïques. Ann. Soc. Linn. Lyon *39*:65-72. Assoc. Français Advan. Sci. *20*:244. [1891]. (Abstract) P:6 9 10 19 20

533   Duchateau, Ghislaine, Marcel Florkin, and Gérard Frappez (1940) Enzymes du catabolisme des aminopurines présentes dans le foie d'un Dipneuste (*Protopterus annectens*). C. R. Soc. Biol. Paris *134*:115-116. P:2 12

534   Duméril, André Marie Constant and Gabriel Bibron (1854) Erpétologie Générale du Histoire Naturelles des Reptiles. *9*:208-213. Paris: Librairie Encyclopedique. OPL:1

535   Duméril, Auguste Henri André (1866) Observations sur des Lépidosiréniens (*Protopterus annectens*, Rich. Owen) qui ont vécu à la Menagerie des Reptiles du Muséum d'Histoire Naturelle et y ont formé leur cocon. C. R. Acad. Sci. Paris *72*:97-100. Summary in Ann. Mag. Natur. Hist. *17*:160. P:19 20 21

536   Duméril, Auguste Henri André (1870) Le *Lépidosiren* et le Protoptère. Ann. Soc. Linn. Maine-et-Loire Angers *12*:139-149. LP:1

537   Duméril, Auguste Henri André (1870) De la vessie natatoire des Ganoides et des Dipnés. Ann. Soc. Linn. Maine-et-Loire Angers *12*:150-169. PLO:1 9 20

538   Duméril, Auguste Henri André (1870) Histoire Naturelle des Poissons. Vol. II. III. Sous-Classe Dipnés, ou Dipnoi:427-472. Paris: Librairie Encyclopédique de Roret. PL:1 3 4 6 7 9 10 11 12 13 14 18 19 20

539   Dun, W. S. (1921) Exhibit of *Ceratodus* tooth from the Late Tertiary deposits at Wentworth. J. Proc. Roy. Soc. N.S.W. *55*:liv. C:4 18

540   Duncker, Hans-Rainer (1981) Stammesgeschichte der Structur- und Functionsprinzipien der Wirbeltierlungen. Verh. Anat. Ges. *75*:279-304. PLNO:1 4 5 10 17

541   Dunel, Suzanne and Pierre Laurent (1980) Functional organization of the gill vasculature in different classes of fish. In B. Lahlou (ed): Epithelial Transport in the Lower Vertebrates: Proceedings of the Memorial Symposium to Jean Maetz. New York: Cambridge Univ. Press, pp.37-58. OPL:1 9 11

542   Dunkerly, J. S. (1915) *Agarella gracilis*, a new genus and species of Myxosporidian, parasitic in *Lepidosiren paradoxa*. Proc. Roy. Phys. Soc. Edinburgh *19*:213-219. L:14 22

543   Dunkerly, J. S. (1925) The development and relationships of the Myxosporidia. Quart. J. Microsc. Sci. *69*:185-216. OL:14 22

544   Dunn, I. G. (1972) The commercial fishery of Lake George, Uganda (East Africa). J. Trop. Hydrobiol. Fish. *2*:109-120. PO:23

545   Dunn, Jeff F., William Davison, Geoffrey M. O. Maloiy, Peter W. Hochachka, and Michael Guppy (1981) An ultrastructural and histochemical study of the axial musculature in the African lungfish. Cell Tissue Res. *220*:599-609. P:1 5 11 19

546   Dunn, Jeff F., Peter W. Hochachka, William Davidson, and Michael Guppy (1983) Metabolic adjustments to diving and recovery in the African lungfish. Amer. J. Physiol. *245* (Regulatory Integrative Comp. Physiol. *14*):R651-R657. P:2 5 6 11 12

547   Dupé, Mireille (1967) Relation entre activité cholinestérasique et activité électrique du télencéphale, chez *Protopterus annectens* (Dipneuste). C. R. Acad. Sci. Paris *265*:1063-1066. P:2 6 20

548   Dupé, Mireille (1968) Essai d'interprétation physiologique du cycle annuel de *Protopterus annectens* Owen. Thesis, Univ. Aix-Marseille. Imprimer M. Bom (70-Vesoul - D.L. 1510.IV). 1-173. P:2 6 11 20

549   Dupé, Mireille and M. L. Bockelée-Morvan (1968) Mise en évidence d'une cholinestérase spécifique au niveau du système nerveux central et du système circulatoire chez un Dipneuste (*Protopterus annectens*). C. R. Soc. Biol. Paris *162*:823-829. P:2 6 11

550   Dupé, Mireille and M. L. Bockelée-Morvan (1969) Relation entre l'activité cholinesterasique centrale et l'évolution thermique annuelle et expérimentale chez un Dipneuste (*Protopterus annectens*). C. R. Soc. Biol. Paris *163*:263-267. P:6 8 18 19 20

551   Dupé, Mireille and René Godet (1969) Caractéristiques et variations de la réponse électrique induite par la stimulation de l'organe olfactif chez un Poisson Dipneuste (*Protopterus annectens* Owen). C. R. Soc. Biol. Paris *163*:267-270. P:6 7 19

552   Dupé, Mireille and René Godet (1969) Conditioning the responsiveness of the central nervous system in the life cycle of the lungfish (*Protopterus annectens*). Gen. Comp. Endocrinol. Suppl. 2, Jan. 1969:275-283. P:2 6 7 8 18 19 20

553   Dupé, Mireille and René Godet (1969) Variations de la réponse électrique d'origine olfactive sous l'effet d'un traitement thyroxinien. C. R. Acad. Sci. Paris *268*:1314-1317. P:2 6 7 8

554   Dupé, Mireille (1973) Factors conditioning the awakening reaction of olfactory origin in the lungfish (*Protopterus annectens*). Comp. Biochem. Physiol. *44A*:647-653. P:6 7 8

555   Dupont, Adolphe and Roger Vandaele (1959) Albinos *Protopterus annectens* Owen du Congo. Bull. Soc. Roy. Zool. Anvers #11:1-8. P:3 22

556   Duren, A. (1943) La pêche en eau douce au Congo belge. 111. Les Poissons d'eau douce les plus connus du Congo belge. Bull. Agric. Congo Belge *34*:133-148. PO:1 18 24

557   Dustin, Pierre, Jr. (1934) Recherches sur les organes hématopoïétiques du *Protopterus dolloi*. Arch. Biol. *45*:1-26. P:1 11 12 13 14 20

558 Dustin, Pierre, Jr. (1938) Les houses spléniques de Schweigger-Seidel. Étude d'histologie et d'histophysiologie comparées. Arch. Biol. 49:1-99. (Dipnoi:21-23). OP:1 11

559 Dutertre, A.-P. (1929) Découverte d'ossements de Poissons dans le Dévonien du Boulonnais. C. R. Acad. Sci. Paris 188:1116-1118. OFD:18

560 Duvernoy, Georges Louis (1846) Cours d'histoire naturelle des corps organisés. Rev. Zool. 1846:390-405. PLO:1 3 4 5 6 11 12 17

561 Duvernoy, Georges Louis (1847) Cours d'histoire naturelle des corps organisés. Rev. Zool. 1847:145-161. PLO:9 10 11

562 Dybowski, W. (1875) Die mit Lungen versehenen Fische. Sber. Naturforsch. Ges. Dorpat 4:225-228. PLN:G(1 10 21)

563 Dykhuizen, Daniel E., K. M. Harrison, and B. J. Richardson (1980) Evolutionary implications of ascorbic acid production in the Australian lungfish. Experientia (Basel) 36:945-946. N:2 17

564 Dziewa, Thomas John (1980) Note on a dipnoan fish from the Triassic of Antarctica. J. Paleontol. 54:488-490. C:4 18

565 Dziewa, Thomas John (1980) Early Triassic Osteichthyans from the Knocklofty Formation of Tasmania. Pap. Proc. Roy. Soc. Tasmania 114:145-160. OC:4 18

566 EAFFRO (1957) The age of a lungfish. E.A.F.F.R.O. (East African Freshwater Fisheries Research Org.) Ann. Report, 7/56-12/57:45. Jinja, Uganda. P:1 16 21

567 EAFFRO (1972) Comparative trawlhaul with Tilapia 220 and Ibis 264 1300 rpm. E.A.F.F.R.O. (East African Freshwater Fisheries Research Org.) File: 1972. OP:18 23

568 Eastman, Charles R. (1903) A peculiar modification amongst Permian Dipnoans. Amer. Natur. 37:493-495. FD:1 4 18

569 Eastman, Charles R. (1906) Dipnoan affinities of Arthrodires. Amer. J. Sci. 21:131-143. FDO:1 4 17

570 Eastman, Charles R. (1906) Devonic fishes of the New York Formations. Mem. New York State Mus. 10:1-235. FDO(CN):1 4

571 Eastoe, J. E. (1957) The amino acid composition of fish collagen and gelatin. Biochem. J. 65:363-368. NO:2

572 Eberth, David A. and David S. Berman (1983) Sedimentology and paleontology of Lower Permian fluvial red beds of north-central New Mexico - preliminary report. New Mexico Geol. 5:21-25. O(FD):18

573 Edgeworth, Francis H. (1911) On the morphology of the cranial muscles in some vertebrates. Quart. J. Microsc. Sci. 56:167-316. ON:1 4 5 6 15

574 Edgeworth, Francis H. (1923) On the development of the hypobranchial, branchial, and laryngeal muscles of Ceratodus. With a note on the development of the quadrate and epihyal. Quart. J. Microsc. Sci. 67:325-368. N(PL):1 4 5 6 15

575 Edgeworth, Francis H. (1925) On the autostylism of Dipnoi and Amphibia. J. Anat. 59:225-265. NPLO:1 4 5 15

576 Edgeworth, Francis H. (1926) On the hyomandibula of Selachii, Teleostomi, and Ceratodus. J. Anat. 60:173-193. NO:1 4 7

577 Edgeworth, Francis H. (1926) On the development of the cranial muscles in Protopterus and Lepidosiren.

Trans. Roy. Soc. Edinburgh 54:719-734. PL(N):1 4 5 6 15

578 Edgeworth, Francis H. (1935) The Cranial Muscles of Vertebrates. New York: Cambridge Univ. Press. NPLO:1 4 5 15

579 Edwards, J. Graham (1935) The epithelium of the renal tubule in bony fish. Anat. Rec. 63:263-280. (Protopterus:270). PO:1 13

580 Edwards, James L. (1977) The evolution of terrestrial locomotion. In Max K. Hecht, Peter Charles Goody, and Bessie M. Hecht (eds): Major Patterns in Vertebrate Evolution. New York: Plenum Press, pp.533-577. O(PLN):4 19

581 Ehlers, Ernst (1894) Über Lepidosiren. Verh. Dtsch. Zool. Ges. Leipzig 4:32-36. (Discussion by R. Semon). L(NP):4 14 15 18 19 21 24

582 Ehlers, Ernst (1894) Über Lepidosiren paradoxa Fitz. und articulata n. sp. aus Paraguay. Nachr. Ges. Wiss. Göttingen 1894:84-91. Translation in Ann. Mag. Natur. Hist. 14:1-8. L:1 3 4 7

583 Ehlers, Ernst (1895) Zur Kenntnis der Eingeweide von Lepidosiren. Nachr. Ges. Wiss. Göttingen 1895:34-50. L(N):1 9 11 12 13 14

584 Eichwald, Eduard von (1844) Über die Fische des devonischen Systems in der Gegend von Pawlowsk. Bull. Soc. Imper. Natur. Moscow 17:824-843. OFD:18

585 Eigenmann, Carl H. and Rosa S. Eigenmann (1891) A catalogue of the fresh-water fishes of South America. Proc. Natl. Mus. 14:1-81. OL:17 18

586 Eigenmann, Carl H. (1906) The fresh-water fishes of South and Middle America. Pop. Sci. Monthly 68:515-530. OL:G(17 18)

587 El-Hakeem, Obeid H. (1970) The occurrence of Protopterus annectens in Western Sudan. Rev. Zool. Bot. Afr. 82:271-279. P:1 4 18 23 24

588 El-Hakeem, Obeid H. (1979) A lungfish that survives over three and half years of starvation under aquatic conditions. Zool. Anz. 202:17-19. P:19 20

589 El-Hakeem, Obeid H. and M. Mekki Babiker (1983) Bioassay of insulin activity of pancreatic tissue in active and aestivated African lungfish, Protopterus annectens (Owen). J. Fish Biol. 23:277-282. P:2 8 20

590 Elliot, David K. and Anne C. Taber (1982) Mississippian vertebrates from Greer, West Virginia. Proc. W. Va. Acad. Sci. 53:73-80. OFD:4 18

591 Emery, Carl (1887) Über die Beziehungen des Cheiropterygiums zum Ichthyopterygium. Zool. Anz. 10:185-189. ON(PL):1 4 17

592 Epple, August and Jack E. Brinn, Jr. (1975) Islet histophysiology: evolutionary correlations. Gen. Comp. Endocrinol. 27:320-349. PLO:1 6 8 12 17

593 Escher, Konrad (1925) Das Verhalten der Seitenorgane der Wirbeltiere und ihrer Nerven beim Übergang zum Landleben. Acta Zool. 6:307-414. (Dipnoi:367-369). OFDNPL:1 7 18

594 Estes, Richard (1984) Fish, amphibians and reptiles from the Etadunna Formation, Miocene of South Australia. Aust. Zool. 21:335-343. FNO:4 18

595 Etheridge, Robert (1878) Catalogue of Australian Fossils, including Tasmania and the Island of Timor, stratigraphically and zoologically arranged. Cambridge: Cambridge Univ. Press, pp.1-232. (Ceratodus:204). OC:18

596 Fahrenholz, Curt (1929) Über die "Drüsen" und die Sinnesorgane in der Haut der Lungenfische. Jahrb. Morphol. Mikrosk. Anat. Abt. II., Gegenbaurs Morphol. Jahrb. *16*:55-74. And Z. Mikrosk.-Anat. Forsch. (Leipzig) *16*:175-212. LPN:1 3 7

597 Fange, Ragnar (1976) Gas exchange in the swimbladder. In George M. Hughes (ed): Respiration of Amphibious Vertebrates. New York: Academic Press, pp.189-211. (Dipnoi:192-193). O(P):2 5 6 8 11

598 Fange, Ragnar (1984) Lymphomyeloid tissues in fishes. Vidensk. Medd. Dan. Naturhist. Foren. *145*:143-162. OD*:1 11 12 17

599 Farmer, Martha (1979) The transition from water to air breathing: effects of CO_2 on hemoglobin function. Comp. Biochem. Physiol. *62A*:109-114. OL:2 10 11 17

600 Farmer, Martha, Hans Jorgen Fyhn, Unni E. H. Fyhn, and Robert W. Noble (1979) Occurrence of Root effect hemoglobins in Amazonian fishes. Comp. Biochem. Physiol. *62A*:115-124. LO:2 10 11 17

601 Farquharson, D. (1965) On an estivating lungfish, *Protopterus annectens*. News Bull., Zool. Soc. S. Afr. *6*:26. P:20

602 Felix, Walther and A. Bühler (1906) Entwickelung der Geschlechtsorgane der Myxinoiden, Teleostier, Selachier, Petromyzonten, Dipnoer. In Oscar Hertwig (ed): Handbuch der Entwickelungslehre der Wirbeltiere. Jena: Gustav Fischer, *2*:639-690, 742-750, 815-830. OLP:1 13 14 15

603 Fernandez, Jorge, Pedro Bondesio, and Rosendo Pascual (1973) Restos de *Lepidosiren paradoxa* (Osteichthyes, Dipnoi) de la Formación Lumbrera (Eogeno, ¿Eoceno?) de Jujuy. Consideraciones estratigráficas, paleoecologicas y paleozoogeograficas. Ameghiniana (Rev. Asoc. Paleontol. Argentina) *10*:152-172. FL(LP):1 4 18

604 Fernandez, Jorge (1976) Hallazgo de peces pulmonados fosiles en la Puna Jujeña. An. Soc. Cient. Argent. *201*:13-18. FL:18 20

605 Fink, B. Raymond (1978) Energy and the larynx. Ann. Otol. Rhinol. Laryngol. *87*:595-605. OP:1 4 10 12 17

606 Fink, William L. and Sarah V. Fink (1979) Central Amazonia and its fishes. Comp. Biochem. Physiol. *62A*:13-29. LO:18

607 Finstad, Connie, Gary W. Litman, and Joanne Finstad (1971) Natural antibodies to 2'4' dinitrophenol antigens. Fed. Proc. *30*:400. (Abstract) OD:2 11 17

608 Fish, G. R. (1956) Some aspects of the respiration of six species of fish from Uganda. J. Exp. Biol. *33*:186-195. PO:2 9 11 18

609 Fisher, Suzanne E. and Gregory S. Whitt (1978) Evolution of isozyme loci and their differential tissue expression. J. Mol. Evol. *12*:25-55. LO:2 17

610 Fisher, Suzanne E. and Gregory S. Whitt (1979) Evolution of the creatine kinase isozyme system in the primitive vertebrates. Occas. Pap. Calif. Acad. Sci. #134:142-159. LO:2 17

611 Fisher, Suzanne E. James B. Shaklee, Stephan D. Ferris and Gregory S. Whitt (1980) Evolution of five multilocus isozyme systems in the chordates. Genetica *52/53*:73-85. LO:2 17

612 Fishman, Alfred P., Jan P. Szidon, Sukhamay Lahiri, Maurice Lev, Richard G. DeLaney, Giuseppe Pietra, and Pierre Laurent (1984) Blood shunting in lungfish and man: adaptation and maladaptation. In Kjell Johansen and Warren W. Burggren (eds:) Cardiovascular Shunts: Phylogenetic, Ontogenetic and Clinical Aspects. Alfred Benzon Symposium #21:9. (Abstract) P:1 9 10 11

613 Fishman, Alfred P., Mary Jane Jesse, and Lawrence Shub (1968) The response of the African lungfish to varying gas tensions. In R. W. Torrance (ed): Arterial Chemoreceptors. Oxford: Blackwell Scientific Publications, pp.393-395. P:2 7 9 10

614 Fishman, Alfred P., Richard G. DeLaney, and Pierre Laurent (1985) Circulatory adaptation to bimodal respiration in the dipnoan lungfish. J. Appl. Physiol. *59*:285-294. PL:1 2 5 6 9 10 11

615 Fishman, Jay A., Ronald P. Daniele, and Giuseppe G. Pietra (1979) Lung defenses in the African lungfish: cellular responses to irritant stimuli. Res. J. Reticuloendothel. Soc. *25*:179-196. P:2 10 11 22

616 Fitzinger, Leopold Joseph(1837) Über *Lepidosiren*. Archiv Naturgesch. #2:232. L:1

617 Fitzinger, Leopold Joseph (1837) Vorläufiger Bericht über eine höchst interessante Entdeckung Dr. Natterers in Brasil. Isis *1837*:379-380. L:1 3 4 17

618 Fitzinger, Leopold Joseph (1843) Systema Reptilium. Vienna: Braumüller et Seidel. O(L)

619 Fleming, R. E. (1926) The origin of the vertebral and external carotid arteries in birds. Anat. Rec. *33*:183-199. O(N):1 11 15

620 Fletcher, Harold O. (1971) Catalogue of type specimens in the Australian Museum, Sydney. Mem. Aust. Mus. Sydney #13:1-167. (Pices:142-147). OFD:18

621 Fletcher, Joseph James (1906) The Hon. Sir William Macleay (1820-1891). In Joseph James Fletcher (ed.): Macleay Memorial Volume. Linnean Soc. N.S.W., pp.vii-li. O

622 Florkin, Marcel and Ghislaine Duchateau (1943) Les formes du système enzymatique de l'uricolyse et l'évolution du catabolisme purique chez les animaux. Arch. Int. Physiol. *53*:267-307. OP:2 13 17

623 Flower, Stanley Smyth (1925) Contributions to our knowledge of the duration of life in vertebrate animals. I. Fishes. Proc. Zool. Soc. London *1925*:247-289. OLPN:16

624 Flower, Stanley Smyth (1935) Further notes on the duration of life in animals. I. Fishes: as determined by otolith and scale-readings and direct observations on living individuals. Proc. Zool. Soc. London *1935*:265-304. ONLP:16

625 Follett, B. K. and Hans Heller (1962) The neurohypophysial hormones of the African lungfish (*Protopterus aethiopicus*). Gen. Comp. Endocrinol. *2*:606-607. (Abstract) P:2 8

626 Follett, B. K. and Hans Heller (1963) Pharmacological characteristics of neurohypophysial hormones in lungfish and amphibians. Nature (London) *199*:611-612. PNO:2 8

627 Follett, B. K. and Hans Heller (1964) The neurohypophysial hormones of lungfishes and amphibians. J. Physiol. (London) *172*:92-106. PNO:2 8 17

628 Fontaine, Maurice and Jacques Leloup (1957) Sur l'existence de différences spécifiques de perméabilité au radioiode des hématies de divers Poissons. J. Physiol. (Paris) *49*:164-169. OP:2 11

629 Fontaine, Maurice and Yves A. Fontaine (1962) Thyrotropic hormone (TSH) in lower vertebrates. Gen.

Comp. Endocrinol. Suppl. *1*:63-74. OP:2 8 17

630 Fontaine, Yves A., Jacques Daget, and Charles Roux (1961) Certaines différences qualitatives d'activité thyréotrope existant entre les hypophyses de Téléostéens d'une part, de Dipneuste et Mammifères d'autre part, ont-elles une signification adaptive ou phylogénenétique? Bull. Soc. Zool. Fr. #86:357-360. OP:2 8 17

631 Fontaine, Yves A. and N. Le Belle (1965) Comparaison des activités thyréotropes et hétérothyréotropes des hypophyses de différents vértebrés. Gen. Comp. Endocrinol. *5*:678-679. (Abstract) OP:2 8 17

632 Forster, Roy P. and Leon Goldstein (1966) Urea synthesis in the lungfish: relative importance of purine and ornithine cycle pathways. Science (Washington) *153*:1650-1652. P:2 13 20

633 Forster-Cooper, Clive (1937) The Middle Devonian fish fauna of Achanarras: *Dipterus*. Trans. Roy. Soc. Edinburgh *59*:223-240. FD(P):1 3 4 17 18

634 Fowler, Henry W. (1939) A collection of fishes obtained by Mr. William C. Morrow in the Ucayali River Basin, Peru. Proc. Acad. Natur. Sci. Phil. *91*:219-289. (*Lepidosiren*: 285). OL:18

635 Fowler, Henry W. (1945) Los Peces del Peru. Lima. (*Lepidosiren*: 20). OL:18

636 Fowler, Henry W. (1948) Os peixes de água doce do Brasil. Arq. Zool. Estado São Paulo *6*:1-204. (*Lepidosiren*:11-12). OL:18

637 Fox, Harold (1960) Early pronephric growth in *Neoceratodus* larvae. Proc. Zool. Soc. London *134*:659-663. N:1 13 15

638 Fox, Harold (1961) The segmentation of components in the hind region of the head of *Neoceratodus* and their relation to the pronephric tubules. Acta Anat. *47*:156-163. N:1 4 6 13 15

639 Fox, Harold (1962) A study of the evolution of the amphibian and dipnoan pronephros by an analysis of its relationship with anterior spinal nerves. Proc. Zool. Soc. London *138*:225-256. PNO:1 6 13 15 17

640 Fox, Harold (1963) Prootic arteries of larvae of Dipnoi and Amphibia. Acta Zool. (Stockholm) *44*:345-360. NPO:1 11 15

641 Fox, Harold (1963) Prootic anatomy of the *Neoceratodus* larva. Acta Anat. *52*:126-129. N:1 4 5 6 15

642 Fox, Harold (1963) The hyoid of *Neoceratodus* and a consideration of its homology in urodele Amphibia. Proc. Zool. Soc. London *141*:803-810. NO:1 4 15

643 Fox, Harold (1965) Early development of the head and pharynx of *Neoceratodus* with a consideration of its phylogeny. J. Zool. (London) *146*:470-554. N:1 4 5 6 11 15 17

644 Foxon, G. E. H. (1933) Pelvic fins of the *Lepidosiren*. Nature (London) *131*:732-733. L:1 9 14 18 19

645 Foxon, G. E. H. (1933) Pelvic filaments of *Lepidosiren*. Nature (London) *131*:913-914. L:1 9 14 18 19

646 Foxon, G. E. H. (1950) A description of the coronary arteries in dipnoan fishes and some remarks on their importance from the evolutionary standpoint. J. Anat. *84*:121-131. LP(N):1 9 11 15 17

647 Fraas, Eberhard (1889) Kopfstacheln von *Hybodus* und *Acrodus*, sog. *Ceratodus heteromorphus* Ag. Jahresh. Vaterl. Naturkd. Württemberg *45*:232-240. O(C):4

648 Fraas, Eberhard (1904) *Ceratodus priscus* E. Fraas aus dem Hauptbuntsandstein. Ber. Oberrhein. Geol.

Ver. *37*:30-32. C:4 18

649 Frankenberger, Zdenko (1926) Über die morphologische Bedeutung der Haftorgane bei den Larven einiger niederer Vertebraten. Zool. Anz. *69*:171-180. OPL:1 15

650 Franssen, J. and G. Nibaruta (1982) Utilisation de la technique d'électrophorèse dans la systématique des poissons. Hydrobiologica *88*:289-293. PO:2 11 17

651 Franz, Victor (1934) III. Höhere Sinnesorgane. In Louis Bolk, Ernest Göppert, Erich Kallius, and Wilhelm Lubosch (eds): Handbuch der vergleichenden Anatomie der Wirbeltiere. Berlin and Wien: Urban und Schwarzenberg, Vol. II. I., pp.989-1292. (Dipnoi: 1063-1064). PLNO:1 5 6 7 15

652 Frentzen, Kurt (1924) *Ceratodus palaeoruncinatus* n. sp. aus dem oberen Buntsandstein der Gegend von Durlach in Baden. Centralbl. Min. Geol. Geol. Paläontol. Stuttgart *1924*:216-220. C:1 4 18

653 Fritsch, Anton (1888) Fauna der Gaskohle und der Kalksteine der Permformation Bohems. Vol. *2*:65-92. FD(N):1 3 4 18

654 Fritzsch, Bernd and Ulrich Wahnschaffe (1983) The electroreceptive ampullary organs of urodeles. Cell Tissue Res. *229*:484-503. O(P):1 7 17

655 Frohriep, Ludwig Friedrich (1836) Über *Lepidosiren paradoxa* von Brasil. Notizen *1836*:90. L:1

656 Frohriep, Ludwig Friedrich (1847) Über den Minhocao von Goyaz. Notizen *1847*:198-200. L:1 18

657 Frommel, Dominique and Joanne Finstad (1970) Evolution of immunoglobulin structure and function. Fed. Proc. *29*:772. (Abstract) PO:2 11 17

657a Froriep, see Frohriep

658 Fryer, Geoffrey (1968) The parasitic Crustacea of African freshwater fishes; their biology and distribution. J. Zool. (London) *156*:45-95. OP:18 22

659 Fullarton, Margaret H. (1931) Notes on the respiration of *Lepidosiren*. Proc. Zool. Soc. London *1931*:1301-1306. L:1 2 9 10

660 Fullarton, Margaret H. (1932) On the development of the olfactory organ in *Protopterus*. Proc. Roy. Soc. Edinburgh *53*:1-6. P:1 6 7 15

661 Fulliquet, Georges (1886) Recherches sur le cerveau du *Protopterus annectens*. Rec. Zool. Suisse *3*:1-130. Arch. Sci. Phys. Natur. (Paris) *1886*:94-96. (Abstract) P(LN):1 6

662 Funkhouser, Deborah, Leon Goldstein and Roy P. Forster (1972) Urea biosynthesis in the South American lungfish, *Lepidosiren paradoxa*: relation to its ecology. Comp. Biochem. Physiol. *41A*:439-443. L:2 13 18 20

663 Fürbringer, Karl (1904) Beiträge zur Morphologie des Skeletes der Dipnoer, nebst Bemerkungen über Pleuracanthiden, Holocephalen und Squaliden. Denkschr. Med.-Naturwiss. Ges. Jena *4*:423-510. NPLC:1 3 4 5 6 7 9 15

664 Fürbringer, Karl (1904) Notiz über einige Beobachtungen am Dipnoerkopf. Anat. Anz. *24*:405-408. N:1 4 6 15

665 Fürbringer, Max (1878) Zur vergleichenden Anatomie und Entwickelungsgeschichte der Excretionsorgane der Vertebraten. Gegenbaurs Morphol. Jahrb. *4*:1-111. (Dipnoi:60-61). ONLP:1 13 14

666 Fürbringer, Max (1913) Schlussübersicht über den gesamten Inhalt von Professor Semon's Zoologischen

Forschungsreisen. Denkschr. Med.-Naturwiss. Ges. Jena *4*:1493-1554. NO(PL):G(3 4 5 6 8 9 10 11 12 15 18)

667 Fyhn, Unni E. H., Hans Jorgen Fyhn, Bonnie J. Davis, Dennis A. Powers, William L. Fink, and Robert L. Garlick (1979) Hemoglobin heterogeneity in Amazonian fishes. Comp. Biochem. Physiol. *62A*:39-66. LO:2 11

668 Gabe, Manfred (1957) Particularitiés histochimiques des cellules pigmentées du tissu périrénal chez le Protoptère (*Protopterus annectens* Owen). Ann. Histochim. *2*:215-224. P:1 11 13

669 Gabe, Manfred (1959) Données histochimiques sur le rein de *Protopterus annectens* Owen. Ann. Histochim. *4*:51-58. P:1 13

670 Gabe, Manfred (1961) Données histologiques sur les macrothyréocytes (cellules parafolliculaires) de quelques sauropsidés et anamniotes. Acta Anat. *47*:34-54. PO:1 8

671 Gabe, Manfred (1969) Données histologiques sur le pancréas endocrine de *Protopterus annectens* Owen. Arch. Anat. Microsc. Morphol. Exp. *58*:21-40. P:1 8 11

672 Gabe, Manfred (1973) Données histologiques sur les cellules endocrines intestinales de *Protopterus annectens* Owen. Bull. Biol. Fr. belg. *107*:3-20. P:1 8 12

673 Gadow, Hans (1882) Observations in comparative myology. J. Anat. Physiol. *16*:494-511. NO: 1 5 17

674 Gadow, Hans and E. C. Abbott (1895) On the evolution of the vertebral column of fishes. Phil. Trans. Roy. Soc. London *186*:163-221. (Dipnoi:198-200). ONP:1 4

675 Gaigher (1969) Aspekte m.b.t. die ekologie, geografie en taksonomie van varswatervisse in die Limpopoen Incomatiriviersisteem. Thesis, Randse Afrikaanse Universiteit, Blobufontein. PO*:18

676 Galli-Gallardo, Sara M., Peter K. T. Pang and Wilbur H. Sawyer (1977) Arginine-vasotocin actions on arterially perfused kidneys of bullfrogs, mudpuppies and South American lungfish. Fed. Proc. *36*:593. (Abstract) LO:2 8 13

677 Galvis-Vergara, Germán (1977) Notas sobre el esqueleto de los peces *Neoceratodus forsteri* y *Protopterus annectens*. (Notes on the skeleton of *Neoceratodus forsteri* and *Protopterus annectens*). Caldasia *12*:103-125. NP(FD):1 4 6

678 Gannon, B. J., David J. Randall, J. Browning, R. J. G. Lester and J. L. Rogers (1983) The microvascular organization of the gas exchange organs of the Australian lungfish, *Neoceratodus forsteri* (Krefft). Aust. J. Zool. *31*:651-676. N(PL):1 5 9 10 11 18

679 Gans, Carl (1970) Strategy and sequence in the evolution of the external gas exchangers of ectothermal vertebrates. Forma Functio *3*:61-104. PLNO:1 5 9 10 17 19

680 Gans, Carl (1970) Respiration in early tetrapods— the frog is a red herring. Evolution *24*:723-734. OP:1 5 9 10 18 19

681 Gardiner, Brian G. (1973) Interrelationships of teleostomes. In P. Humphry Greenwood, Roger S. Miles, and Colin Patterson (eds): Interrelationships of Fishes. pp.105-135. Also listed as Zool. J. Linn. Soc. *53* (suppl. 1):105-135. FDO(NLP):1 3 4 11 17

682 Gardiner, Brian G. and Roger S. Miles (1975) Devonian fishes of the Gogo Formation, Western Australia. Coll. Internat. Cent. Nat. Res. Sci. *218*:73-79. OFD:18

683 Gardiner, Brian G., Philippe Janvier, Colin Patterson, Peter L. Forey, P. Humphrey Greenwood, Roger S. Miles and R. P. S. Jefferies (1979) The salmon, the lungfish and the cow: a reply. Nature (London) *277*:175-176. [reply to L. B. Halstead] DO:17

684 Gardiner, Brian G. (1980) Tetrapod ancestry: a reappraisal. In A. L. Panchen (ed): The Terrestrial Environment and the Origin of Land Vertebrates. New York: Academic Press, pp.177-185. FDO:1 3 4 17

685 Gaudry, Albert (1881) Sur un nouveau genre de poisson primaire. C. R. Acad. Sci. *92*:752-754. O(C):3 4

686 Gaudry, Albert (1883) Les Enchainements du Monde Animal dans le Tempo Geologique. Vol. 3: Fossils primaires. Paris: P. Savoy. (Dipnoi:152-154). OLPNC:G(4 9 10 18 20)

687 Gee, J. M. (1967) Trawling operations on Lake Victoria. E.A.F.F.R.O. (East African Freshwater Fisheries Research Organization) Ann. Report *1967*:55-63. OP:18 23

688 Gegenbaur, Carl (1895) Das Flossenskelet der Crossopterygier und das Archipterygium der Fische. Gegenbaurs Morphol. Jahrb. *22*:119-160. ON:1 4 17

689 Gelderen, C. van (1926) Die Morphologie der Sinus durae matris. Z. Ges. Anat. Entwickl. *78*:339-489. (Dipnoi:365-367). ON:1 6 11

690 Gelderen, C. van (1927) Zur vergleichenden Anatomie der Vv. cardinales posteriores, der V. Cava inferior und der Vv. Azygos (vertebrales). Anat. Anz. *63*:49-72. OPN:1 11 13

691 Gelderen, C. van (1933) Venensystem, mit einem Anhang über den Dotter- und Plazentarkreislauf. In Louis Bolk, Ernest Göppert, Erich Kallius, and Wilhelm Lubosch (eds): Handbuch der vergleichenden Anatomie der Wirbeltiere. Berlin and Wien: Urban und Schwarzenberg, *VI*:685-744. (Dipnoi:705-707). ONP:1 11

692 Gerard, Pol (1931) Les sacs aériens des crossoptérygiens et les poumons des Dipneustes. Études anatomique et histologique. Arch. Biol. *42*:251-277. PO:1 5 10 11 15

693 Gerard, Pol (1951) Sur la cortico-surrénale du Protoptère (*Protopterus dolloi* Blgr.). Arch. Biol. *62*:371-377. P:1 8

694 Géraudie, Jacqueline and François-Jean Meunier (1982) Comparative fine structure of the Osteichthyan dermotricha. Anat. Rec. *202*:325-328. PO:1 4

695 Géraudie, Jacqueline and François-Jean Meunier (1984) Structure and comparative morphology of camptotrichia of lungfish fins. Tissue Cell *16*:217-136. PNFD:1 4 17

696 Géraudie, Jacqueline (1984) Fine structural comparative peculiarities of the developing dipnoan dermal skeleton in the fins of *Neoceratodus* larvae. Anat. Rec. *209*:115-123. N:1 4 15

697 Gerday, Charles, Bernard Joris, Nicole Gerardin-Otthiers, Serge Collin, and Gabriel Hamoir (1979) Parvalbumins from the lungfish (*Protopterus dolloi*). Biochimie *61*:589-599.P:2 5 6 13

698 Gerhardt, Ulrich (1933) Kloake und Begattungsorgane. In Louis Bolk, Ernest Göppert, Erich Kallius, and Wilhelm Lubosch (eds): Handbuch der vergleichenden Anatomie. Berlin and Wien: Urban und Schwarzenberg, *VI*:267-350. (Dipnoi: 270-271). OPN:1 12 13 14

699 Gerlach, Joachim (1933) Über das Gehirn von *Pro-*

topterus annectens. Anat. Anz. *75*:310-406. P(N):1 6

700 Gertler, Arieh (1975) Recent findings and theories on the evolution of serine proteinases. Isr. J. Med. Sci. *11*:1168. (Abstract) OD:2 17

701 Gervais, Paul (1876) À propos de *Ceratodus.* C. R. Acad. Sci. Paris *82*:1034. Reported in Ann. Mag. Natur. Hist. *17*:486. N(LP):G(18)

702 Geschwind, Irving I. (1967) Growth hormone activity in the lungfish pituitary. Gen. Comp. Endocrinol. *8*:82-83. P:2 4 8 17

703 Giacomini, Ercole (1906) Sulle capsule surrenali e sul simpatico dei Dipnoi. Ricerche in *Protopterus annectens.* Atti Reale Accad. Lincei (Roma) *15*:394-398. P:1 6 11 13

704 Giebel, Christoph Gottfried Andreas (1855) Odontographie. Leipzig: Ambrosius Abel, pp.1-129. (*Lepidosiren*:100). PLO:1 4

705 Giglioli, Henry H. (1887) *Lepidosiren paradoxa.* Nature (London) *35*:343. L:1 3 4 7 9

706 Giglioli, Henry H. (1888) On the capture of another *Lepidosiren.* Nature (London) *38*:102-103. L:18 24

707 Gilchrist, John Dow Fsher. and W. Wardlaw Thompson (1913) The freshwater fishes of South Africa. Ann. S. Afr. Mus. *11*:321-579. (*Protopterus*:321-323). OP:G(1 18 19 20)

708 Gill, Theodore (1861) Catalogue of the fishes of the eastern coast of North America from Greenland to Georgia. Proc. Acad. Natur. Sci. Philadelphia *13*:1-63. (Ganoidei:12-21). PLO:1 17

709 Gill, Theodore (1873) On the homologies of the shoulder-girdle of the Dipnoans and other fishes. Ann. Mag. Natur. Hist. *11*:173-178. PLNO:1 4 17

710 Gill, Theodore (1894) Lepidosirenids and Bdellostomids. Amer. Natur. *28*:581-584. PLO:1

711 Girgis, Sabet (1953) A list of common fish of the Upper Nile with their Shilluk, Dinka, and Nuer names. Sudan Notes Rec. *24*:1-7. PO:18 24

712 Gluski, Jacek (1973) Dewoński zabytek. (Devonian relics). Kontynenty *5*:40. PLN:1 7 10 18 20

713 Godet, Paul (1881) Les Dipneustes. Bull. Soc. Sci. Natur. Neuchâtel *12*:334-335. NPL:1 3 4 9 18

714 Godet, René (1959) Hypophyse et pigmentation chez le Protoptère (Poisson Dipneuste). C. R. Soc. Biol. Paris *153*:1432-1434. P:3 8 20

715 Godet, René (1959) Le rôle de la posthypophyse dans le passage de la phase aquatique à la phase terrestre chez le Protoptère du Sénégal (Poisson Dipneuste). C. R. Soc. Biol. Paris *153*:691-693. P:3 8 11 19 20 21

716 Godet, René (1959) Contribution à la physiologie du Protoptère du Cap Vert (Poisson Dipneuste). Ann. Fac. Sci. Univ. Dakar *4*:85-87. P:2 3 6 8 9 11 13 18 19 20

717 Godet, René and Tahsin Mohsen (1959) Action de la thyroxine sur la consommation d'oxygène du Protoptère (Dipneuste). C. R. Soc. Biol. Paris *153*:1430-1432. P:8 9

718 Godet, René (1960) Essai d'interprétation des structures urogénitales chez les Vertébrés. I. Dynamique du canal de Wolff. Ann. Fac. Sci. Univ. Dakar *5*:119-128. P:1 8 13 14 15

719 Godet, René (1960) Action du propionate de testostérone sur le tube urinaire du Protoptère. C. R. Soc. Biol. Paris *154*:758-760. P:1 8 13

720 Godet, René (1960) Evolution des substances posthypophysaires colorables à la fuchsine paraldéhyde chez le Protoptère. C. R. Soc. Biol. Paris *154*:1580-1581. P:8 20

721 Godet, René (1961) Étude expérimentale des relations intrahypophysaires chez le Protoptère. C. R. Soc. Biol. Paris *155*:578-580. P:1 8 11

722 Godet, René (1961) La livrée pigmentaire du Protoptère et le problème des antagonisms intra-hypophysaires. C. R. Acad. Sci. Paris *252*:2148-2150. P:2 3 8

723 Godet, René (1961) Étude expérimentale des relations intra-hypophysaires de nature nerveuse et vasculaire chez le Protoptère. C. R. Acad. Sci. Paris *252*:2308-2309. P:1 6 8 11

724 Godet, René (1961) Étude expérimentale de la formation de mucus tégumentaire et de la réalisation du cocon chez le Protoptère. C. R. Acad. Sci. Paris *252*:2451-2452. P:2 3 8 20

725 Godet, René and François Pieri (1961) Effet hypothermisant sur le rat d'un extrait des réserves lipidiques de Protoptère (Poisson Dipneuste). C. R. Acad. Sci. Paris *252*:2600-2602. P:2 20

726 Godet, René (1961) Un cas d'hermaphrodisme chez le Protoptère (Poisson Dipneuste). Ann. Fac. Sci. Univ. Dakar *6*:145-149. P:1 13 14 15

727 Godet, René (1961) Le problème hydrique et son controle hypophysaire chez le Protoptère. Ann. Fac. Sci. Univ. Dakar *6*:183-201. P:3 6 8 13 18 19 20

728 Godet, René (1962) Evolution de la pars intermedia hypophysaire chez le Protoptère au cours de l'épreuve de déshydration. C. R. Soc. Biol. Paris *156*:148-150. P:3 6 8 19 20

729 Godet, René and Mireille Dupé (1962) La fonction thyroïdienne à l'aide de ^{131}I chez le Protoptère. C. R. Acad. Sci. Paris *254*:4514-4515. P:2 8 20

730 Godet, René (1963) Interdépendance intrahypophysaire et développement de la pars intermedia. C. R. Soc. Biol. Paris *157*:598-599. PO:2 8

731 Godet, René (1963) Contribution à la physiologie du Poisson Dipneuste *Protopterus.* Proc. Int. Congr. Zool. *16*:276. P:2 3 6 8 19 20

732 Godet, René, J. Bert, and H. Collomb (1964) Apparition de la réaction d'éveil télencéphalique chez *Protopterus annectens* et cycle biologique. C. R. Soc. Biol. Paris *158*:146-149. P:2 6 7 19 20

733 Godet, René, Raymond Michel, and Mireille Dupé (1964) Métabolisme d'[131]I chez le Protoptère (*Protopterus annectens* Owen) en phase sèche (cocon expérimental). C. R. Soc. Biol. Paris *158*:1236-1241. P:1 2 8 20

734 Godet, René, Mireille Dupé, and J. Bert (1964) Action de la chlorpromazine et de la psilocybine sur la réaction d'éveil télencéphalique d'un Dipneuste. C. R. Soc. Biol. Paris *158*:1385-1388. P:2 6 7

735 Godet, René and Mireille Dupé (1965) Quelques aspects des relations neuro-endocriniennes chez *Protopterus annectens* (Poisson Dipneuste). Arch. Anat. Microsc. Morphol. Exp. *54*:319-330. P:2 6 7 8 19 20

736 Godet, René and Mireille Dupé (1965) Thyroxine et activité électrique spontanée sur le télencéphale du Protoptère. C. R. Soc. Biol. Paris *159*:220-223. P:6 8 20

737 Godet, René and Mireille Dupé (1965) Activité cardiaque chez le Poisson Dipneuste. C. R. Soc. Biol. Paris *159*:1195-1197. P:2 8 10 11 20

738 Godet, René (1968) Comparaison suggestive entre

la maladie de la malnutrition tropicale (Kwashiorkor) et l'état particulier du Protoptère en preénkystement. Additif to Thesis by Mireille Dupé, 1968. P:2 6 8 12 19 20 21

739   Godet, René and Tahsin Mohsen (1974) Variations de l'activité cardiaque en rapport avec le cycle biologique chez *Protopterus annectens* (Owen). Bull. Inst. Fondam. Afr. Noire sér. A Sci. Natur. *36*:937-951. P:2 8 11 20

740   Goeldi, Emil August (1895) Instrucções praticas sobre o modo de colligir productos da natureza para o Museu Paraense de Historia Natural e Ethnographia. Cap. Quarto: Peixes. Bol. Mus. Paraense *1*:239-256. (Lepidosiren: 239-243). OL(PN):1 3 18

741   Goeldi, Emil August (1896) Johannes von Natterer. Bol. Mus. Paraense *1*:189-217. OL:18

742   Goeldi, Emil August (1896) A *Lepidosiren paradoxa* descoberta na Ilha de Marajó. Bol. Mus. Paraense *1*:438-443. L:1 3 4 18

743   Goeldi, Emil August (1897) Miscellaneas menores: *Lepidosiren paradoxa*. Bol. Mus. Paraense *2*:247-250. L(PN):1 9 11 17 18

744   Goeldi, Emil August (1897) Communication concerning *Lepidosiren paradoxa*. Proc. Zool. Soc. London *1897*:921. L:1 3 7 9 10 18 19

745   Goeldi, Emil August (1898) On the *Lepidosiren* of the Amazons; being notes on five specimens obtained between 1895-97, and remarks upon an example living in the Pará Museum. Trans. Zool. Soc. London *14*:413-420. L:1 9 10 16 18 19 20 21 24

746   Goeldi, Emil August (1898) Further notes on the Amazonian *Lepidosiren*. Proc. Zool. Soc. London *1898*:852-857. L(P):1 9 16 18

747   Goeldi, Emil August (1898) Primeira contribuição para o conhecimento dos Peixes do valle do Amazonas e das Guyanas. Bol. Mus. Paraense *2*:443-488. OL:G(18 24)

748   Goeldi, Emil August (1904) On the rare rodent *Dinomys branickii* Peters. Proc. Zool. Soc. London *1904*:158-162. O(L)

749   Goin, Olive B. and Coleman J. Goin (1968) DNA and the evolution of the vertebrates. Amer. Midland Natur. *80*:289-298. OPN:1 17

750   Goldstein, Leon, Peter A. Janssens, and Roy P. Forster (1967) Lungfish *Neoceratodus forsteri*: activities of ornithine-urea cycle and enzymes. Science (Washington) *157*:316-317. N:2 13

751   Goldstein, Leon (1968) Comparative physiology of ammonia excretion. Proc. Int. Union Physiol. Sci. VI:2pp. OPN:2 13 20

752   Goldstein, Leon, Susan Harley-DeWitt, and Roy P. Forster (1973) Activities of ornithine-urea cycle enzymes and of trimethylamine oxidase in the coelacanth, *Latimeria chalumnae*. Comp. Biochem. Physiol. *44B*:357-362. O(P):2 11 12 17

753   Golshani, Farrokh, Philippe Janvier, Denise Brice, and Albert F. de Lapparent (1973) Sur la paléogéographie et la paléobiologie du Dévonien dans la région de Kerman, en Iran. C. R. Acad. Sci. Paris *276*:697-700. OFD:18

754   Golshani, Farrokh and Philippe Janvier (1974) Some aspects of the fish fauna in the Late Devonian seas of Iran. Rep. Geol. Surv. Iran #31:49-54. OFD:18

755   Gomi, T., A. Kimura, H. Tsuchiya, T. Hashimoto, and H. Fujita (1984) Differentiation of pulmonary alveolar epithelial cells in some lower vertebrates. Zool. Sci. (Tokyo) *1*:1004. (Abstract) DO+:1 10

756   Good, Robert A., Joanne Finstad, Bernard Pollara, and Ann E. Gabrielsen (1966) Morphologic studies on the evolution of the lymphoid tissues among the lower vertebrates. In R. T. Smith, P. A. Miescher, and Robert A. Good (eds): Phylogeny and Immunity. Gainsville: Univ. Fla. Press, pp.149-170. LO:1 11 12

757   Goodrich, Edwin S. (1902) On the pelvic girdle and fin of *Eusthenopteron*. Quart. J. Microsc. Sci. N.S. *45*:311-324. O(CN):1 4 17

758   Goodrich, Edwin S. (1904) On the dermal fin-rays of fishes - living and extinct. Quart. J. Microsc. Sci. *47*:465-522. OPLN:1 4 6 17

759   Goodrich, Edwin S. (1907) On the scales of fish, living and extinct, and their importance in classification. Proc. Zool. Soc. London *1907*:751-774. OPLN:1 3

760   Goodrich, Edwin S. (1909) Part IX. Vertebrata craniata. In E. Ray Lankester (ed): A Treatise on Zoology. London: Adam and Charles Black, pp.230-518. (Dipnoi:230-258). OPLN:1 3 4 6 9 11

761   Goodrich, Edwin S. (1911) On the segmentation of the occipital region of the head in the batrachian Urodela. Proc. Zool. Soc. London *1911*:101-120. O(NLP):1 4 5 6 15

762   Goodrich, Edwin S. (1924) The origin of land vertebrates. Nature *114*:935-936. DO:4 11 17

763   Goodrich, Edwin S. (1925) On the cranial roofing-bones in the Dipnoi. J. Linnean Soc. London Zool. *36*:78-86. FDN:1 4 17

764   Goodrich, Edwin S. (1930) Studies on the Structure and Development of Vertebrates. London: MacMillan and Co. Reissued (1958) New York: Dover Publications.

765   Goodrich, Samuel G. (1870) Johnson's Natural History, *2*:418. New York: A. J. Johnson. OPLN:G(1 3 18 20)

766   Goossens, N., K. Dierickx, and F. Vandesande (1978) Immunocytochemical study of the neurohypophysial hormone producing system of the lungfish, *Protopterus aethiopicus*. Cell Tiss. Res. *190*:69-77. P:1 6 8

767   Göppert, Ernst (1895) Untersuchungen zur Morphologie der Fischrippen. Gegenbaurs Morphol. Jahrb. *23*:145-217. OD:1 4 5 17

768   Göppert, Ernst (1904) Der Kehlkopf von *Protopterus annectens* (Owen). Anatomische Untersuchung. Denkschr. Med.-Naturwiss. Ges. Jena (Festschr. siebzigsten Geburtstage von Ernst Haeckel) *11*:115-132. P(L):1 4 5 10

769   Göppert, Ernst (1937) Kehlkopf und Trachea. In Louis Bolk, Ernest Göppert, Erich Kallius, and Wilhelm Lubosch (eds): Handbuch der vergleichenden Anatomie der Wirbeltiere. Berlin and Wien: Urban und Schwarzenberg, *III*:797-866. (Dipnoi:798-799). OPL:4 5 10

770   Gorbman, Aubrey and Howard A. Bern (1962) A Textbook of Comparative Endocrinology. New York: John Wiley and Sons, Inc. OPLN:1 8

771   Gorbman, Aubrey and M. Hyder (1973) Failure of mammalian TRH to stimulate thyroid function in the lungfish. Gen. Comp. Endocrinol. *20*:588-589. P:2 8

772 Gorizdro-Kulczycka, Zinaida (1950) Dwudyszne ryby dewonskie Gor Swietokrzyskich. (Les Dipneustes devoniens du massif de St. Croix). Acta Geol. Polonica *1*:53-105. FD*:18

773 Gosline, William A. (1944) The problem of the derivation of the South American and African fresh-water fish faunas. An. Acad. Bras. Ciênc. Rio *16*:211-223. DO:17 18

774 Gosline, William A. (1975) A reexamination of the similarities between the freshwater fishes of Africa and South America. Mem. Mus. Natl. Hist. Natur. Paris *88A*:146-154. OD:18

775 Gould, Stephan Jay (1977) The telltale wishbone. Natur. Hist. *86*:26-36. OD:17

776 Grafflin, Allan L. (1937) The structure of the nephron in fishes. Anat. Rec. *68*:287-304. OL:1 13 17 18

777 Graham-Smith, W. (1936) The tail of fishes. Proc. Zool. Soc. London *1936*:595-608. OP:1 4 13 17

778 Graham-Smith, W. and T. Stanley Westoll (1937) On a new long-headed dipnoan fish from the Upper Devonian of Scaumenac Bay, P.Q., Canada. Trans. Roy. Soc. Edinburgh *59*:241-266. FD:1 3 4 17 21

779 Graham-Smith, W. (1978) On the lateral lines and dermal bones in the parietal region of some crossopterygian and dipnoan fishes. Philos. Trans. Roy. Soc. London *282B*:41-105. (Dipnoi:85-91). FDO:1 4 7 17

780 Gray, John Edward (1839) New anomalous reptile. Ann. Natur. Hist. *2*:309. L:1

781 Gray, John Edward (1856) Observations on a living African *Lepidosiren* in the Crystal Palace. Proc. Zool. Soc. London *24*:342-348. P:1 9 10 18 19 20 21 24

782 Gray, John Edward (1858) On *Lepidosiren*. A letter to J. E. Gray from General Perronet Thompson. Proc. Zool. Soc. London *1858*:535. P:18 19

783 Gray, John Edward (1860) On the mud-fish of the Nile (*Lepidosiren annectens*?). Ann. Mag. Natur. Hist. *5*:70-71. P:1 18

784 Greene, J. Reay (1861) On the mutual relations of the cold-blooded Vertebrata. Proc. Linnean Soc. London *5*:218-228. PO:1 17

785 Greenwood, P. Humphry (1951) Fish remains from Miocene deposits of Rusinga Island and Kavirondo Province, Kenya. Ann. Mag. Natur. Hist. *4*:1192-1201. FPO:4 18

786 Greenwood, P. Humphry (1955) The fishes of Uganda. I. Uganda J. *19*:137-155. OP:18

787 Greenwood, P. Humphry (1958) The Fishes of Uganda. Kampala: Uganda Society. (*Protopterus*:12-17, 121). OP:1 3 9 10 14 15 18 19 20 21 23

788 Greenwood, P. Humphry (1958) Reproduction in the East African lung-fish *Protopterus aethiopicus* Heckel. Proc. Zool. Soc. London *130*:547-567. P:9 10 14 15 18 19

789 Greenwood, P. Humphry (1959) Quaternary fish-fossils. Explor. Parc Natl. Albert, Mission de Heinzelin de Braucourt *4*:1-80. OFP:4 18

790 Greenwood, P. Humphry and O. Oliva (1959) Does a lungfish breathe through its nose? Discovery (New Haven) *20*:18-19. P:9 10 18 19

791 Greenwood, P. Humphry (1974) Review of Cenozoic freshwater fish faunas in Africa. Ann. Geol. Surv. Egypt *4*:211-232. OFP:18

792 Greer, Brenda (1974) Conditioning of fish. Thesis, supervised study, Mary Baldwin College, Staunton, Virginia. P:19 21

793 Gregory, E. H. (1905) Die Entwickelung der Kopfhöhlen und des Kopfmesoderms bei *Ceratodus forsteri*. Denkschr. Med.-Naturwiss. Ges. Jena *4*:641-660. N:1 4 12 15

794 Gregory, William King (1915) Present status of the problem of the origin of the tetrapoda, with special reference to the skull and paired limbs. Ann. New York Acad. Sci. *26*:317-383. OFD(LN):1 4 17

795 Gregory, William King (1933) Fish skulls: a study of the evolution of natural mechanisms. Trans. Amer. Philos. Soc. *23*:75-481. (Dipnoi:104-105). FD(NPL):1 4 17 21

796 Gregory, William King and Henry C. Raven (1941) On the probable mode of transformation of rhipidistian paddle into tetrapod limb. Trans. New York Acad. Sci. *3*:153-158. O(N):1 4 17

797 Greil, Alfred (1906) Über die Entstehung der Kiemendarmderivate von *Ceratodus forsteri*. Anat. Anz. *29*:115-131. N(LP):1 5 6 8 9 15

798 Greil, Alfred (1906) Über die Homologie der Anamnierkiemen. Anat. Anz. *28*:257-272. ON:1 9 15 17

799 Greil, Alfred (1907) Über die Bildung des Kopfmesoderms bei *Ceratodus forsteri*. Anat. Anz. *30*:59-72. N:1 4 5 6 11 12 15

800 Greil, Alfred (1908) Über die erste Anlage der Gefässe und des Blutes bei Holo- und Meroblastiern (speziell bei *Ceratodus forsteri*). Anat. Anz. *32*:7-64. N:1 4 5 11 15

801 Greil, Alfred (1908) Entwickelungsgeschichte des Kopfes und des Blutgefässsystemes von *Ceratodus forsteri*. I. Gesammtenentwickelung bis zum Beginn der Blutzirkulation. Denkschr. Med.-Naturwiss. Ges. Jena *4*:661-934. N:1 3 4 5 6 7 9 11 12 13 15

802 Greil, Alfred (1913) Entwickelungsgeschichte des Kopfes und des Blutgefässsystemes von *Ceratodus forsteri*. II. Die epigenetischen Erwerbungen während der Stadien 39-48. Denkschr. Med.-Naturwiss. Ges. Jena *4*:935-1492. N:1 3 4 5 6 7 8 9 11 12 13 15

803 Griffiths, Mervyn (1938) Studies on the pituitary body. II. Observations on the pituitary in Dipnoi and speculations concerning the evolution of the pituitary. Proc. Linnean Soc. N.S.W. *63*:89-94. PLN:1 8 11 17

804 Grigg, Gordon C. (1965) Aspects of respiration in the Queensland lungfish, *Neoceratodus forsteri* (Krefft). Newsl. Aust. Soc. Limnol. *4*:8-9. N:2 9 10 17 19

805 Grigg, Gordon C. (1965) Studies on the Queensland lungfish, *Neoceratodus forsteri* (Krefft). I. Anatomy, histology, and functioning of the lung. Aust. J. Zool. *13*:243-253. N:1 2 5 9 10 11 19

806 Grigg, Gordon C. (1965) Studies on the Queensland lungfish, *Neoceratodus forsteri* (Krefft). II. Thermal acclimation. Aust. J. Zool. *13*:407-411. N:2 9 19

807 Grigg, Gordon C. (1965) Studies on the Queensland lungfish, *Neoceratodus forsteri* (Krefft). III. Aerial respiration in relation to habits. Aust. J. Zool. *13*:413-421. N:9 10 19

808 Grigg, Gordon C. (1965) Spawning behavior in the Queensland lungfish, *Neoceratodus forsteri*. Aust. Natur. Hist. *15*:75. N:14 19

809 Grigg, Gordon C. (1965) The prehistoric lungfish. Wildlife Aust. *3*:30-31. NPLFD:1 3 4 10 14 15 18 19 21

810 Grigg, Gordon C. (1972) The Queensland lungfish—
a window to the past. Univ. Sydney News, March 29,
l972:4-5,7. N:1 10 11 19 21

811 Grigg, Gordon C. (1973) The lungfish—creature from
the past. Animal Kingdom 76:22-25. Also in Koolewong 4, 6/75:11-13. N(PL):G(1 3 4 9 10 19 21 24)

812 Grigorjev, N. I., N. V. Petropavlovskaia, L. D. Vaver,
E. N. Merabishvili, V. V. Orlov, R. I. Volkova, and V.
D. Borschukov (1974) Stable cytological and histologi-
cal signs in large-cell lower vertebrates. Arkh. Anat.
Gistol. Ambriol. 67:5-13. [In Russian]. OD:1

813 Grodziński, Zygmunt (1972) The yolk of Neoceratodus forsteri Krefft (Dipnoi-Pisces). Acta Biol. Cracov.
Ser. Zool. 15:193-199. N:1 14

814 Groll, Hans E. (1969) Der Sprung ans Land. Del-
phin 16:12-14. LPNFD:1 4 9 15 17 20

815 Groodt, Marie H. A. de, M. Sebruyns, and A. Lagasse (1958) Elektronenmikroskopische Morfologie van
de Bloed-lucht-barrière bij een Longvis. Natuurwet.
Tijdschr. 40:215-219. P:1 10 11

816 Groodt, Marie H. A. de, M. Sebruyns, and A. Lagasse (1958) L'ultrastructure des alveoles pulmonaires
du Protopterus dolloi et de l'axolotl. Meded. Belg. Na-
tuurkund. Veren. #83:5-7. PO:1 10 11

817 Groodt, Marie H. A. de, M. Sebruyns, and A. Lagasse (1959) Contribution à l'étude de l'ultrastructure
comparée des alvéoles pulmonaires. Bull. Soc. Sci. Vét.
Méd. Comp. Lyon 61:43-53. P:1 10 11

818 Groodt, Marie H. A. de, A. Lagasse, and M. Sebruyns (1960) Elektronenmikroskopische Morphologie
der Lungenalveolen des Protopterus und Amblystoma.
Verh. IV. Internat. Conf. Electr. Microsc.:417-421. PO:1
10 11

819 Groodt-Lasseel, Marie H. A. de (1981) The presence
and origin of Kupffer cells in the liver of a lung fish.
Anat. Rec. 199:65A. (Abstract) P:1 11 12

820 Gross, Walter (1956) Über Crossopterygier und
Dipnoer aus dem baltischen Oberdevon im Zusammenhang einer vergleichenden Untersuchung des Porenkanalsystems paläozoischer Agnathen und Fische. Kgl.
Sven. Vetenskapsakad. Handl. 5:1-140. FDO*:1 3 4 7

821 Gross, Walter (1964) Über die Randzähne des
Mundes, die Ethmoidalregion des Schädels und die
Unterkiefersymphyse von Dipterus oervigi n. sp. Palä-
ontol. Z. 38:7-25. FD:1 4 6

822 Gross, Walter (1965) Über den Vorderschädel von
Ganorhynchus splendens Gross (Dipnoi, Mitteldevon).
Paläontol. Z. 39:113-133. FD:1 4 7

823 Grynfeltt, Édouard (1911) Études anatomiques et
histologiques sur l'oeil du Protopterus annectens. Bull.
Mens. Acad. Sci. Lett. Montpelier 1911:210-232.
P:1 6 7

824 Guenther, Konrad (1931) A naturalist in Brazil:
The Record of a Year's Observations of her Flora, her
Fauna, and her People. Boston: Houghton Mifflin Co.
OL:G(10 14 19)

825 Gulliver, George (1862) On the red corpuscles of the
blood of Vertebrata, and on the zoological import of the
nucleus, with plans of their structure, form, and size
(on a uniform scale), in many of the different orders.
Proc. Zool. Soc. London 1862:91-103. OP:1 11

826 Gulliver, George (1873) Measurements of the red
blood-corpuscles of Batrachians. Proc. Zool. Soc. London 1873:162-165. PO:1 11

827 Gulliver, George (1875) Observations on the sizes
and shapes of the red corpuscles of the blood of Vertebrates, with drawings of them to a uniform scale, and
extended and revised tables of measurements. Proc.
Zool. Soc. London 1875:474-4 95. OP:1 11

828 Gunby, Phil (1978) Primitive creature holds a metabolic secret. J. Amer. Med. Assoc. 239:817. P:G(2 20)

829 Günther, Carl Albert Ludwig Gotthilf (1870) Catalogue of the Fishes in the British Museum. Vol. 8.
London: British Museum, pp.321-323. OPLN:1

830 Günther, Carl Albert Ludwig Gotthilf (1871) The
new ganoid fish (Ceratodus) recently discovered in
Queensland. Nature (London) 4:406-408, 428-429, 447.
N(L):1 4 12 14 17

831 Günther, Carl Albert Ludwig Gotthilf (1871) Description of Ceratodus, a genus of ganoid fishes, recently discovered in rivers of Queensland, Australia.
Trans. Roy. Soc. London 161:511-571. Summary in Proc.
Roy. Soc. London 19:377-379. N(PL):1 3 4 9 11 12 13 14

832 Günther, Carl Albert Ludwig Gotthilf (1871) Ceratodus und seine Stelle in System. Arch. Naturgeschichte 1871:325-344. English summaries in Ann.
Mag. Natur. Hist. 7:222-227 and Amer. J. Sci. 1:387-
388. N:4 12 14 17

833 Günther, Carl Albert Ludwig Gotthilf (1872) An
account of a ganoid fish from Queensland (Ceratodus).
Pop. Sci. Rev. 11:257-266. N:G(1 3 4 9 10 11 17 18 21)

834 Günther, Carl Albert Ludwig Gotthilf (1880) An
Introduction to the Study of Fishes. Edinburgh: Adam
and Charles Black. (Dipnoi:355-359). OPLN:G(1 10 18
20)

835 Günther, Carl Albert Ludwig Gotthilf (1880) The
Voyage of H.M.S. Challenger. Zoology. Vol. I, Part IV:
Report on the shore fishes procured during the Voyage
of H.M.S. Challenger in the years 1873-1876. Prepared
under the supervision of Sir C. Wyville Thompson.
(Neoceratodus:30-32). ON:3 18 23

836 Günther, Carl Albert Ludwig Gotthilf (1894) Re-
port on the collection of reptiles and fishes made by
Dr. J. W. Gregory during his expedition to Mount
Kenia. Proc. Zool. Soc. London 1894:84-91. OP:18

837 Günther, Carl Albert Ludwig Gotthilf (1894) On
the pelvic limbs of Lepidosiren. Proc. Zool. Soc. London
1894:316. L:1 18

838 Günther, Carl Albert Ludwig Gotthilf (1896) Capture of a specimen of Lepidosiren in the River Amazons. Nature (London) 54:270. L:18

839 Günther, Carl Albert Ludwig Gotthilf (1900) The
Presidents's Anniversary Address: Correspondence of
William Swainson, naturalist. Proc. Linnean Soc. Lon-
don 1900:14-61. OP

840 Gupta, Vishwa Jit and Robert H. Denison (1966)
Devonian fishes from Kashmir, India. Nature (London)
211:177-178. FDO:4 18

841 Gupta, Vishwa Jit and Philippe Janvier (1979) A
review of the Devonian vertebrate localities of the
Indian Himalayas (Kashmire, Ladakh and Kumaun),
with remarks on their stratigraphical and paleobiogeo-
graphical significance. Cont. Himalayan Geol. 1 :78-
83. OFD+:18

842 Guy, O., D. C. Bartelt, J. Amic, E. Colomb, and C.
Figarella (1976) Activation peptide of human trypsinogen 2. FEBS Lett. 62:150-153. OP:2 12 17

843 Guyénot, M. Émile (1953) L'anatomie comparée des Vertébrés et l'évolution. Bull. Soc. Zool. Fr. 78:291-304. OD:17

844 Guyton, Jack S. (1935) The structure of the nephron in the South American lungfish, Lepidosiren paradoxa. Anat. Rec. 63:213-229. L(P):1 13 22

845 Gwahaba, J. J. (1975) The distribution, population density and biomass of fish in an equatorial lake, Lake George, Uganda. Proc. Roy. Soc. London 190B:393-414. OP:18

846 Gyldenholm, A. O. and J. J. Scheel (1971) Chromosome numbers of fishes. I. J. Fish. Biol. 3:479-486. OL:1

847 Haagner, A. K. (1938) Some notes on the African lungfish. Unpublished Manuscript. P:18 19 20

848 Haas, Richard (1982) Transplantation reactions in the African lungfish, Protopterus amphibius. Transplantation 33:249-253. P:3 11 22

849 Haeckel, Ernst (1866) Generelle Morphologie der Organismen. Berlin: Georg Reimer, p.CXXIX. OPL:G(1 17)

850 Haeckel, Ernst (1893) Zur Phylogenie der australischen Fauna. Denkschr. Med.-Naturwiss. Ges. Jena 4:XVI-XXIV. ON(PL):3 4 11 17

851 Haeckel, Ernst (1895) Systematische Phylogenie der Wirbelthiere. Dritter Theil: Des Entwurfs einer systematischen Stammesgeschichte. Berlin: Georg Reimer, pp.257-265. OFDPLN:G(1 4 9 11 12 13 17)

852 Haines, R. Wheeler (1937) The posterior end of Meckel's cartilage and related ossifications in bony fishes. Quart. J. Microsc. Sci. 80:1-38. OP:4 15 17

853 Halkett, Andrew (1899) The dark continent fish. Letter to The Fishing Gazette Feb. 4, 1899, p. 71, in response to article, Digging for fish, in The Fishing Gazette, Jan. 7, 1899:7. P(LN):G(10 20)

854 Halkett, Andrew (1901) An African Dipnoid fish (Protopterus annectens). Ottawa Natur. 15:184-187. P(LN):G(1 20)

855 Halstead, Lucien Beverley (1978) The cladistic revolution - can it make the grade? Nature (London) 276:759-760. OD:17

856 Halstead, Lucien Beverley, Errol Ivor White, and G. T. MacIntyre (1979) The salmon, the lungfish and the cow: a reply. Nature (London) 277:176. OD:17

857 Hancock, Albany and Thomas Atthey (1871) A few remarks on Dipterus and Ctenodus and their relationship to Ceratodus forsteri, Krefft. The Natural History Transactions of Northumberland and Durham 4:397-407. Same paper published in Ann. Mag. Natur. Hist. 7:190-198. Amer. J. Sci. 1:388. (Abstract) FD(N):1 4 17

858 Hanke, Wilfred (1970) Hormone. Fortschr. Zool. 20:318-380. (Protopterus:329-330). OP:2 8 13 20

859 Hanke, Wilfred and Peter A. Janssens (1983) The role of hormones in regulation of carbohydrate metabolism in the Australian lungfish Neoceratodus forsteri. Gen. Comp. Endocrinol. 51:364-369. N(P):2 8 12

860 Hansen, Georg Nørgaad, Bente Langvad Hansen, and Lotte Hummer (1980) The cell types in the adenohypophysis of the South American lungfish, Lepidosiren paradoxa, with special reference to immunocytochemical identification of the corticotropin-containing cells. Cell Tissue Res. 209:147-160. L(P): 1 8

861 Hansen, Georg Nørgaard and Bente Langvad Hansen (1981) Comparative immunocytochemical localization of prolactin and somatotropin in the pituitaries of Lepidosiren paradoxa, Rana temporaria and Ambystoma mexicanum. Cell Tissue Res. 217:127-141. LO:1 8

862 Hansen, Georg Nørgaard and Bente Langvad Hansen (1985) Immunocytochemical demonstration of mammalian lutropin-like material in the pituitary of the lungfish, Lepidosiren paradoxa. Cell Tissue Res. 239:355-358. L:1 8

863 Harald (1914) Vom australischen Molchfisch Ceratodus (Neoceratodus) nach Berichten von R. Semon. Wochenschr. Aquar.-Terr. Kunde 11:635-636. N:18 21 24

864 Harald (1914) Eier vom australischen Molchfisch (nach R. Semon). Wochenschr. Aquar.-Terr. Kunde 11:800-801. N:1 4 15

865 Harshbarger, John C. (1977) Activities Report, Registry of Tumors in Lower Animals: 1976 Supplement, Smithsonian Institution, Washington, D.C.:1-42. (Protopterus:17-18). OP:12 22

866 Harshbarger, John C. (1982) Activities Report, Registry of Tumors in Lower Animals: 1981 Supplement, Smithsonian Institution, Washington, D.C.:1-52. (Protopterus:22). OP:14 22

867 Haslewood, Geoffrey A. D. (1961) Isolation of 5 alpha-bufol from the Australian lungfish, Neoceratodus forsteri. 7th Int. Congr. Biochem., Tokyo:991. (Abstract) N:2 12

868 Haslewood, Geoffrey A. D. (1969) New information about bile alcohols. In Leon Schiff, James B. Carey, Jr., and John Dietschy (eds): Bile Salt Metabolism. Springfield: Charles C. Thomas, pp.151-159. OPLN:2 12 17

869 Haslewood, Geoffrey A. D. (1971) Examples of vertebrate evolution as indicated by bile salt types and by general morphology. In Ernest Schoffeniels (ed): Biochemical Evolution and the Origin of Life. New York: North-Holland Pub. Co., pp.191-202. ONPL:2 12 17

870 Hasse, Carl (1892) Die Entwicklung der Wirbelsäule der Dipnoi. Z. Wiss. Zool. 55:533-542. P(LN):1 4 15

871 Haswell, William A. (1882) On the structure of the paired fins of Ceratodus, with remarks on the general theory of the vertebrate limb. Proc. Linnean Soc. N.S.W. 7:2-11. N:1 4 17

872 Haug, Émile (1904) Sur la faune des couches à Ceratodus crétacées du Djoua, près Timassânine (Sahara). C. R. Acad. Sci. Paris 138:1529-1531. C:4 18

873 Hawkins, Waterhouse (1856) Lepidosiren annectens, or mud-fish, of the Gambia. The Illustrated London News, suppl. Sept. 20, 1856:303. P:1 10 19 20 21

874 Hay, Alastair W. M. (1975) Comparative aspects of vitamin D transport. In R. V. Talmage, M. Owen, and J. A. Parson (eds): Calcium-regulating Hormones. Proc. Fifth Parathyroid Conf., Oxford, England. New York: American Elsevier Pub. Co. (Excerpta Med. Int. Congr. Ser. Amsterdam, #346), pp.405-407. PO:2

875 Hay, Alastair W. M. and Graham Watson (1976) The plasma transport proteins of 25-hydroxycalciferol in fish, amphibians, reptiles and birds. Comp. Biochem. Physiol. 53B:167-172. OP:2

876 Hay, Alastair W. M. and Graham Watson (1977) Vitamin D₂ in vertebrate evolution. Comp. Biochem. Physiol. 56B:375-380. OP:2 17

877 Hay, Alastair W. M. and Graham Watson (1977) Binding properties of serum vitamin D transport pro-

teins in vertebrates for 24R, 25-dihydroxycholecal-ciferol and 24S, 25-dihydroxycholecalciferol in vitro. Comp. Biochem. Physiol. *58B*:43-48. OP:2 17

878 Hay, Oliver Perry (1899) On some changes in the names, generic and specific, of certain fossil fishes. Amer. Natur. *33*:783-792. FD

879 Hayashida, Ted (1970) Immunological studies with rat pituitary growth hormone (RGH). II. Comparative immunochemical investigation of GH from representatives of various vertebrate classes with monkey antiserum to RGH. Gen. Comp. Endocrinol. *15*:432-452. OP:2 8 11 17

880 Hayashida, Ted (1972) Comparative immunochemical studies of pituitary growth hormones. Proc. 2nd Internat. Symp. Milan, 5/5-7/71. (Excerpta Med. Int. Congr. Ser. #244) pp.25-37. OP:2 8 17

881 Hayashida, Ted (1977) Immunochemical and biological studies with growth hormone in a pituitary extract of the coelacanth, *Latimeria chalumnae* Smith. Gen. Comp. Endocrinol. *32*:221-229. O(P):2 4 8 17

882 Hecht, Max K., Peter Charles Goody, and Bessie M. Hecht (eds) (1977) Major Patterns in Vertebrate Evolution. New York: Plenum Press.

883 Heckel, Edouard (1888) Sur le *Protopterus annectens*, Owen. Le Naturaliste *10*:233-234. P:3 18 19 20 21 22 24

884 Heckel, Johann Jakob (1845) Bemerkung über *Lepidosiren paradoxa*. Briefliche Mittheilung. Müller's Arch. Anat. Physiol. *1845*:534-535. L(P):3 7 17

885 Heckel, Johann Jakob (1851) Über eine neue Fisch-Species aus dem Weissen Nil, *Protopterus aethiopicus*. Sber. K. Akad. Wiss. Wien 7:685-689. P(L):18 19 20 21

886 Hector, James (1874) On a specimen of *Ceratodus*. Trans. Proc. New Zealand Inst. 7:490-492. N:G(1 18 21)

887 Hegedus, Arthur M. (1970) Australian lungfish spawns. Anchor *4*:207-9. N:3 14 19

888 Heller, Hans and B. K. Follett (1963) Neurohypophyseal hormones of Amphibia and Choanichthyes. Gen. Comp. Endocrinol. *3*:706. (Abstract) OPN:2 8

889 Heller, Hans and Peter J. Bentley (1965) Phylogenetic distribution of the effects of neurohypophysial hormones on water and sodium metabolism. Gen. Comp. Endocrinol. *5*:96-108. OP:2 8 17

890 Henderson, I. W. and H. O. Garland (1980) The interrenal gland in fishes. Part 2. Physiology. In I. Chester Jones and I. W. Henderson (eds): General and Clinical Endocrinology of the Adrenal Cortex. London: Academic Press, pp.473-523. (Dipnoi:514-515). OLPN:2 8 17

891 Henle, Jakob (1839) Vergleichend-anatomische Beschreibung des Kehlkopfs mit besonderer Berücksichtigung des Kehlkopfs der Reptilien. Leipzig: Leopold Voss, pp.1-70. (*Lepidosiren*:5-6). OL:1 4 5 10 17

892 Henrichsen, I. G. C. (1972) A catalogue of fossil vertebrates in the Royal Scottish Museum, Edinburgh. Part Three: Actinistia and Dipnoi. Roy. Scott. Mus. Inf. Ser. Geol. *3*:1-26. ONFD:18

893 Herald, Earl S. (1961) Living Fishes of the World. New York: Doubleday and Co., Inc., pp.288-289. OPNL:G(1 3 13 14 15 18 19 20)

894 [see Johan Müller # 1434]

895 Hermodson, Mark A., Ross W. Tye, Gerald R. Reeck, Hans Neurath, and Kenneth A. Walsh (1971) Comparison of the amino terminal sequences of bovine, dogfish, and lungfish trypsinogens. FEBS Lett. *14*:222-224. PO:2 12 17

896 Herrick, C. Judson (1921) A sketch of the origin of the cerebral hemispheres. J. Comp. Neurol. *32*:429-454. OPLN:1 6 7 17

897 Hertwig, Oscar (1874) Über das Zahnsystem der Amphibien und seine Bedeutung für die Genese des Skelets der Mundhöhle. Arch. Mikrosk. Anat. *11*:1-208. O(LN):1 4 17

898 Hertwig, Oscar (1906) Die Lehre von den Keimblättern. In Oscar Hertwig (ed): Handbuch der Entwickelungslehre der Wirbeltiere. Jena: Gustav Fischer, *1*:699-1018. (Dipnoi:770-773). ON:6 15

899 Hertwig, Richard (1906) Eireife, Befruchtung und Furchungsprozess. In Oscar Hertwig (ed): Handbuch der Entwickelungslehre der Wirbeltiere. Jena: Gustav Fischer, *1*:477-698. (Dipnoi:640-644). LNO:1 14 15

900 Hesse, Richard (1910) Der Tierkörper als selbständiger Organismus. Vol. I of Richard Hesse and Franz Doflein (eds): Tierbau und Tierleben in ihrem Zusammenhang betrachtet. Leipzig: B. G. Teubner, *1*:193, 375-376. OPN:1 9 10 20

901 Hewell, Jamie L. (1974) Urea accumulation and other effects of estivation on the African lungfish, *Protopterus*. Thesis, Supervised Study, Mary Baldwin College, Staunton, Virginia. P:1 2 4 5 12 13 20

902 Higashi, K. and S. Sasa (1984) Histological study of the gallbladder of the lungfish *Protopterus aethiopicus*. Acta Anat. Nippon *59*:480. (Abstract) [in Japanese]. P+:1 12

903 Hilgendorf, Franz (1886) Über Fischzähne. Sber. Ges. Naturforsch. Fr. Berlin *6*:87-94. ON:4

904 Hill, Dorothy, G. Playford, and J. T. Woods (1970) Cainozoic fossils of Queensland. Queensland Paleontographical Soc. 1-36. Brisbane. OC:4 18

905 Hill, W. C. Osman (1926) A comparative study of the pancreas. Proc. Zool. Soc. London *1926*:581-631. (Dipnoi: 625-626). OPLN:1 8 12

906 Hillaby, John (1967) Fish with lungs. New Sci. *35*:87-88. Reprinted in Aust. Fish. Newsl. Dec., 1967:15. [Sanctuary for lungfish.] N(LP):G(1 3 10 15 18 21)

907 Hills, Edwin Sherbon (1929) The geology and palaeontography of the Cathedral Range and the Blue Hills, in north-western Gippsland. Proc. Roy. Soc. Victoria (N.S.) *41*:176-201. OFD:1 4 18

908 Hills, Edwin Sherbon (1931) The Upper Devonian fishes of Victoria, Australia, and their bearing on the stratigraphy of the state. Geol. Mag. *68*:206-231. OFD:3 4 18. See also Quart. J. Geol. Sci. London *88*:850-858.

909 Hills, Edwin Sherbon (1933) On a primitive Dipnoan from the Middle Devonian rocks of New South Wales. Ann. Mag. Natur. Hist. *11*:634-643. FD:4 18

910 Hills, Edwin Sherbon (1934) Tertiary fresh water fishes from Southern Queensland. Mem. Queensl. Mus. *10*:157-174. CO:4 18

911 Hills, Edwin Sherbon (1935) Records and descriptions of some Australian Devonian fishes. Proc. Roy. Soc. Victoria *48*:161-171. FDO:4 18

912 Hills, Edwin Sherbon (1941) The cranial roof of *Dipnorhynchus sussmilchi* (Eth. fil). Rec. Aust. Mus. Sydney *31*:45-55. FD(N):1 4 7

913 Hills, Edwin Sherbon (1943) Tertiary fresh-water fishes and crocodilian remains from Gladstone and Duaringa, Queensland. Mem. Queensl. Mus. *12*:96-100. CO:3 18

914 Hills, Edwin Sherbon (1943) The ancestry of the Choanichthyes. Aust. J. Sci. *6*:21-23. FD:1 4 7

915 Hills, Edwin Sherbon (1958) A brief review of Australian fossil vertebrates. In T. Stanley Westoll (ed): Studies on Fossil Vertebrates. London: Athlone Press, pp.86-104. CFD:18

916 Hinegardner, Ralph (1976) The cellular DNA content of sharks, rays and some other fishes. Comp. Biochem. Physiol. 55B:367-370. OPLN:1 17

917 Hines, H. J. G. (1947) T. L. Bancroft Memorial Lecture: Thomas Lane Bancroft, pharmacologist. Proc. Roy. Soc. Queensland 67:75-78. ON:15 16

918 Hippel, E. V. (1946) Stomach contents of crocodiles. Uganda J. 10:148-149. OP:22

919 Hirasaka, Kyosuke (1954) The sensory canal system of the Australian lung-fish, Ceratodus forsteri. J. Fac. Sci. Niigata Univ. Ser. II 2:11-29. N(PLC):1 7 15

920 Hirschfeld, Sue E. and Larry G. Marshall (1976) Revised faunal list of the La Venta fauna (Friasian-Miocene) of Colombia, South America. J. Paleontol. 50:433-436. OFL:18

921 Hirt, A. (1934) Sympathisches Nervensystem und Nebenniere. I. Die vergleichende Anatomie des sympathischen Nervensystems. In Louis Bolk, Ernest Göppert, Erich Kallius, and Wilhelm Lubosch (eds): Handbuch der vergleichenden Anatomie der Wirbeltiere. Berlin and Wien: Urban und Schwarzenberg, II.1: 685-776. (Dipnoi:703-704). OPL:6 10 11

922 Hochachka, Peter W. (1968) Action of temperature on branch points in glucose and acetate metabolism. Comp. Biochem. Physiol. 25:107-118. LO:2

923 Hochachka, Peter W. (1968) Short Communication: The nature of the thermal optimum for lungfish lactate dehydrogenase. Comp. Biochem. Physiol. 27:609-611. L:2 5

924 Hochachka, Peter W. (1968) Short communication: Lactate dehydrogenase function in Electrophorus swimbladder and in the lungfish lung. Comp. Biochem. Physiol. 27:613-615. LO:2 9 10 17

925 Hochachka, Peter W. and George N. Somero (1968) The adaptation of enzymes to temperature. Comp. Biochem. Physiol. 27:659-668. OL:2 5

926 Hochachka, Peter W. and George N. Somero (1971) Biochemical adaptation to the environment. In William S. Hoar and David J. Randall (eds): Fish Physiology. New York: Academic Press, 6:99-156. OPL:1 12 20

927 Hochachka, Peter W. and William C. Hulbert (1978) Glycogen 'seas', glycogen bodies, and glycogen granules in heart and skeletal muscle of two air-breathing, burrowing fishes. Can. J. Zool. 56:774-786. LO:1 2 5 10 20

928 Hochachka, Peter W. (1979) Cell metabolism, air breathing, and the origins of endothermy. In Stephen C. Wood and Claude Lenfant (eds): Lung Biology in Health and Disease. New York: Marcel Dekker. Vol. 13: Evolution of Respiratory Processes: A Comparative Approach: 253-288. LO:2 5 11

929 Hochachka, Peter W., Kenneth Bruce Storey, Christopher J. French, and David E. Schneider (1979) Hydrogen shuttles in air versus water breathing fishes. Comp. Biochem. Physiol. 63B:45-56. LO:2 5 11

930 Hochachka, Peter W. and Jeff F. Dunn (1983) Metabolic arrest: the most effective means of protecting tissues against hypoxia. In Hypoxia, Exercise, and Altitude: Proceedings of the Third Banff International Hypoxia Symposium, New York: Alan Liss, Inc., pp.297-309. OP:2 5 6 11

931 Hoeven, Jan van der (1838) Over Lepidosiren paradoxa, een nieuw geslacht van Reptilia. Tijdschr. Na-tuurl. Geschied. Physiol. Leiden 4:407-408. L:1 3 4 9 17

932 Hoeven, Jan van der (1839) Nader berigt over Lepidosiren. Tijdschr. Natuurl. Geschied. Physiol. Leiden 6:61-62. P(L):1 4 9 11

933 Hoffman, A., J. G. Disney, A. Pinegar and J. D. Cameron (1974) The preservation of some East African freshwater fish. Afr. J. Trop. Hydrobiol. Fisheries 3:1-13. PO:23

934 Hoffstetter, Robert (1971) Los Vertebrados Cenozoicos de Colombia: yacimientos, faunas, problemas planteados (con dos mapas de localidades). Geologia Colombiana 8:37-62. OFL:18

935 Hofweber, Herbert (1926) Über die Funktion des von Wiedersheim als "dorsaler Larynx" gedeuteten Gebildes bei Lepidosiren paradoxa. Zool. Jahrb. Abt. Anat. 48:95-118. L(PN):1 9 10 17 21

936 Hogg, John (1841) On the existence of branchiae in the young Caeciliae; and on a modification and extension of the branchial classification of the Amphibia. Ann. Mag. Nat. Hist. 7:355-363. Translation in Frohriep Notizen 1841:193-200 , 212-215. OPL:7 9 17

937 Hoier, R. (1950) À travers plaines et volcans au Park National Albert. Inst. Parcs Natl. Congo Belge (Brussels). (Protopterus:135-6). OP:3 18 20 21 24

938 Hollaender, Ludwig (1887) Die Anatomie der Zähne des Menschen und der Wirbelthiere sowie deren Histologie und Entwickelung, nach Charles S. Tomes' Manual of Dental Anatomy Human and Comparative. Berlin: August Hirschwald. (Dipnoi:169). OL(N):4

939 Holly, Maximilian (1930) Synopsis der Süsswasserfische Kameruns. Sber. K. Akad. Wiss. Wien 139:195-281. OP:18

940 Holly, Maximilian (1933) Das Tierreich. Pisces, 2: Dipnoi. Berlin: Walter de Gruyter Co. pp.1-20. OPLN:1 4 6 11 15 18 19 20

941 Holly, Maximilian (1936) Die Lungenfische (Dipnoi). Blätt. Aquar. Terrkd. 47:218-220. NLP:G(1 3 4 5 6 10 11 12 18 19)

942 Holman, J. Alan (1970) Possible habits of juvenile prototetrapods. Michigan Academician 3:101-103. D:17 18 19

943 Holmberg, Eduardo Ladislau (1887) Viaje á Misiones. Bol. Acad. Nac. Cien. Cordoba 10:1-372. (Lepidosiren:35). OL:18

944 Holmes, E. Bruce (1975) A reconsideration of the phylogeny of the tetrapod heart. J. Morphol. 147:209-228. OPD:1 11 17

945 Holmes, E. Bruce (1985) Are lungfishes the sister group of tetrapods? Biol. J. Linn. Soc. 25:379-397. NFD:1 17

946 Holmes, W. (1950) The adrenal homologues in the lungfish Protopterus. Proc. Roy. Soc. London 137B:549-562. P:1 8 11 13

947 Holmes, W. and D. E. Moorhouse (1956) The perirenal tissue of Protopterus. A contribution to the history of the adrenal. Quart. J. Microsc. Sci. 97:123-154. P:1 8 18

948 Holmgren, Nils (1922) Points of view concerning forebrain morphology in lower vertebrates. J. Comp. Neurol. 34:391-440. PLO(N):1 6 17

949 Holmgren, Nils and C. J. van der Horst (1925) Contribution to the morphology of the brain of Ceratodus. Acta Zool. (Stockholm) 6:59-165. N:1 6

950 Holmgren, Nils and C. J. van der Horst (1927) Over de Voorhersenen van Ceratodus. Tijdschr. Nederland.

Dierkund. Vereenig. *20*:II verslagen:V-VI. (Abstract)N(P):1 6 15 17

951 Holmgren, Nils (1928) Some observations about the growth of the tail in *Lepidosiren*. Acta Zool. (Stockholm) *9*:321-325. L:16

952 Holmgren, Nils (1933) On the origin of the tetrapod limb. Acta Zool. (Stockholm) *14*:185-295. ON:1 4 17

953 Holmgren, Nils and Erik Stensiö (1936) Kranium und Visceralskelett der Akranier, Cyclostomen und Fische. In Louis Bolk, Ernest Göppert, Erich Kallius, and Wilhelm Lubosch (eds): Handbuch der vergleichenden Anatomie der Wirbeltiere. Berlin and Wien: Urban und Schwarzenberg, *IV*:233-500. (Dipnoi: 363-387). NPLO:1 4 17

954 Holmgren, Nils (1939) Contribution to the question of the origin of the tetrapod limb. Acta Zool. (Stockholm) *20*:1-36. NO:4 15 17

955 Holmgren, Nils (1941) General morphology of the lateral sensory line system of the head in fish. Kgl. Sven. Vetenskapsakad. Handl. *20*:1-46. ONP:1 6 7 17

956 Holmgren, Nils and Torsten Pehrson (1949) Some remarks on the ontogenetical development of the sensory lines on the cheek in fishes and amphibians. Acta Zool. (Stockholm) *30*:249-314. (Dipnoi:259-265). ONPF:1 7 15 17

957 Holmgren, Nils (1949) Contributions to the question of the origin of tetrapods. Acta Zool. (Stockholm) *30*:459-484. NPO:1 4 15 17

958 Holmgren, Nils (1949) On the tetrapod limb problem - again. Acta Zool. (Stockholm) *30*:485-508. ONP:1 4 15 17

959 Holmgren, Uno (1959) On the pineal area and adjacent structures of the brain of the dipnoan fish, *Protopterus annectens* (Owen). Breviora *109*:1-11. P:1 6 8

960 Honma, Yoshiharu (1969) Some evolutionary aspects of the morphology and role of the adenohypophysis in fishes. Gunma Symp. Endocrinol. *6*:19-37. OP:1 8 17

961 Hopley, Catherine C. (1891) Observations on a remarkable development in the mudfish. Amer. Natur. *25*:487-489. P:16

962 Hosch, Friedrich (1904) Das Sehorgan von *Protopterus annectens*. Arch. Mikrosk. Anat. *64*:99-110. P:1 6 7 20

963 Howchin, Walter (1925) The Building of Australia and the Succession of Life. Part I. Adelaide: R. E. E. Rogers, pp. 317-318 OC:G(3 4 18)

964 Howell, A. Brazier (1933) Morphogenesis of the shoulder architecture. Part II. Pices. Quart. Rev. Biol. *8*:434-456. OD:4 15 17

965 Howell, Barbara J. (1970) Acid-base balance in transition from water breathing to air breathing. Fed. Proc. *29*:1130-1134. NLPO:2 3 9 10 11 17

966 Howes, G. B. (1887) On the skeleton and affinities of the paired fins of *Ceratodus*, with observations upon those of the Elasmobranchii. Proc. Zool. Soc. London *1887*:3-26. N:1 4 17

967 Howes, George Bond (1887) On a hitherto unrecognized feature in the larynx of the anurous Amphibia. Proc. Zool. Soc. London *1887*:491-501. O(PL):1 10

968 Howes, George Bond (1888) Dr. Giglioli and *Lepidosiren*. Nature (London) *38*:126. L

969 Howes, George Bond (1891) On some hermaphrodite genitalia of the codfish, (*Gadus morrhua*), with

remarks upon the morphology and phylogeny of the vertebrate reproductive system. J. Linnean Soc. London *23*:539-558. O(P):1 14

970 Howes, George Bond (1894) *Lepidosiren paradoxa*. Nature (London) *49*:576. L:11

971 Hubbard, G. B. and K. C. Fletcher (1985) A seminoma and a leiomyosarcoma in an albino African lungfish (*Protopterus dolloi*). J. Wildl. Dis. *21*:72-74. P:12 13 14 22

972 Hubbs, Carl L. (1919) The Amphibioidei, a group of fishes proposed to include the Crossopterygii and the Dipneusti. Science N.S. *49*:569-570. DO

973 Huet, H. (1943) La pêche en eau douce au Congo belge. I. Considérations générales d'hydrobiologie piscicole équatoriale. Bull. Agric. Congo Belge *34*:111-118. O:18

974 Huggins, A. K., G. Skutsch, and E. Baldwin (1969) Ornithine-urea cycle enzymes in teleostean fish. Comp. Biochem. Physiol. *28*:587-602. O(PN):2 13 17

975 Hughes, George M. (1967) Evolution between air and water. In Anthony V. S. De Reuck and Ruth Porter (eds): Development of the Lung. London: Ciba Foundation Symposium, J. and A. Churchill, Ltd., pp.64-80. OP:1 2 9 10 11 17

976 Hughes, George M. (1970) Ultrastructure of the airbreathing organs of some lower vertebrates. 7th Congr. Int. Microsc. Electron. Grenoble *3*:599.PO:1 9 10

977 Hughes, George M. (1973) Ultrastructure of the lung of *Neoceratodus* and *Lepidosiren* in relation to the lung of other vertebrates. Folia Morphol. (Prague) *21*:155-161. NL(PO):1 5 9 10 11 17

978 Hughes, George M. and Miriam Morgan (1973) The structure of fish gills in relation to their respiratory function. Biol. Rev. (Cambridge) *48*:419-475. ONLP:1 9 11

979 Hughes, George M., J. W. Ryan and Una Ryan (1974) Freeze-fractured lamellate bodies of *Protopterus* lung: a comparative study. J. Physiol. (London) *236*:15P-16P. P:1 10

980 Hughes, George M. and E. R. Weibel (1976) Morphometry of fish lungs. In George M. Hughes (ed): Respiration of Amphibious Vertebrates. New York: Academic Press, pp.213-232. OL:1 10

981 Hughes, George M. (1976) On the respiration of *Latimeria chalumnae*. J. Linnean Soc. London *59*:195-208. O(N):1 9

982 Hughes, George M. (ed) (1976) Respiration of Amphibious Vertebrates. New York: Academic Press.

983 Hughes, George M. and E. R. Weibel (1978) Visualization of layers lining the lung of the South American lungfish (*Lepidosiren paradoxa*) and a comparison with the frog and rat. Tissue Cell *10*:343-353. LO:1 10

984 Hughes, George M. (1978) A morphological and ultrastructural comparison of some vertebrate lungs. In E. Klika, (ed): XIX Congressus Morphologicus Symposia, Prague, pp.393-405. LPO:1 2 10

985 Hughes, George M. and G. A. Vergara (1978) Static pressure-volume curves for the lung of the frog (*Rana pipiens*). J. Exp. Biol. *76*:149-165. O(P):2 10

986 Hughes, George M. (1980) Ultrastructure and morphometry of the gills of *Latimeria chalumnae*, and a comparison with the gills of associated fishes. Proc. Roy. Soc. London *208B*:309-328. O(N):1 10

987 Hughes, George M. (1979) The Vertebrate Lung. J. J. Head, (ed) Carolina Biology Readers, #59:1-16. USA:

Oxford Univ. Press. OL:1 10

988 Hulot, A. (1950) Le régime alimentaire des poissons du Centre Africain.Intérêt éventuel de ces poissons en vue d'une zootechnie économique. Bull. Agric. Congo Belge 41:145-176. OP:18 21 23

989 Humphrey, G. M. (1872) The muscles of Lepidosiren annectens, with the cranial nerves. J. Anat. Physiol. 6:253-269. P:1 4 5 6

990 Humphrey, G. M. (1872) The muscles of Ceratodus. J. Anat. Physiol. 6:279-287. N:1 5

991 Hussakof, Louis (1908) Catalogue of types and figured specimens of fossil Vertebrates in the American Museum of Natural History. Bull. Amer. Mus. Natur. Hist. 25:1-103. (Dipneusti:50-58). CFDO:4 18

992 Hussakof, Louis (1916) The lungfish remains of the coal measures of Ohio, with special reference to the supposed amphibian Eurythorax of Cope. Bull. Amer. Mus. Natur. Hist. 35:127-133. FD:3 4 18

993 Huxley, Thomas Henry (1876) Contributions to morphology. Ichthyopsida. No. 1: On Ceratodus forsteri, with observations on the classification of fishes. Proc. Zool. Soc. London 1876:24-59. Reviewed in Zool. Rec. 13, Pices:7. N:1 4 6 7 9 17 21

994 Huxley, Thomas Henry (1876) Lecture on the evidence as to the origin of existing vertebrate animals. Nature (London) 13:410-412. NPO:1 4 9 11 17

995 Huxley, Thomas Henry (1876) On the position of the anterior nasal apertures in Lepidosiren. Proc. Zool. Soc. London 1876:180-181. P:1 9

996 Huxley, Thomas Henry (1883) Contributions to morphology. Ichthyopsida. No. 2: On the oviducts of Osmerus; with remarks on the relations of the teleostean with the ganoid fishes. Proc. Zool. Soc. London 1883:132-139. DO:1 14

997 Hyrtl, Joseph (1845) Monograph on Lepidosiren paradoxa. Abh. K. Bohm. Ges. Wiss. 3:605-668. Prague: Friedrich Ehrlich. L:1 3 4 5 6 7 9 10 11 12 13 14

998 Idler, David R., G. B. Sangalang, and B. Truscott (1972) Corticosteroids in the South American lungfish. Gen. Comp. Endocrinol. Suppl. 3:238-244. L:2 8 17

999 Idler, David R. and B. Truscott (1972) Corticosteroids in fish. In David. R. Idler (ed): Steroids in Nonmammalian Vertebrates. New York: Academic Press, pp.126-252. (Dipnoi:160-163). OPL:2 8 17 20

1000 Idler, David R. (1973) Comments on 'Structure and Function of the Adrenal Gland of Fishes' by David Gordon Butler. Amer. Zool. 13:881-884. OL:8

1001 Ihering, Hermann von (1902) Natterer e Langsdorff: Exploradores antigos do Estado de São Paulo. Riv. Mus. Paulista (São Paulo) 5:13-34. O(L)

1002 Illidge, Thomas (1893) On Ceratodus forsteri. Proc. Roy. Soc. Queensland 10:40-44. N:1 3 10 15 19 21

1003 Illidge, Thomas (1902) On Ceratodus. Brisbane Courrier, Aug. 6, 1902:10. N:19 22

1004 Imaki, Humi and Walter Chavin (1972) Ultrastructure of lungfish integumental melanophores. Amer. Zool. 12:730 (Abstract). PLN:1 3

1005 Imaki, Humi and Walter Chavin (1975) Ultrastructure of the integumental melanophores of the Australian lungfish, Neoceratodus forsteri. Cell Tissue Res. 158:363-373. N:1 3

1006 Imaki, Humi and Walter Chavin (1975) Ultrastructure of the integumental melanophores of the South American lungfish (Lepidosiren paradoxa) and the African lungfish (Protopterus sp.). Cell Tissue Res. 158:375-389. LP:1 3

1007 Imaki, Humi and Walter Chavin (1984) Ultrastructure of mucous cells in the sarcopterygian integument. SEM/1984/I:409-422. Diss. Abstr. Int. 44:1027-B. [1983]. (Abstract)NPLO:1 3 18

1008 Imms, A. D. (1904) Notes on the gill-rakers of the spoonbill sturgeon, Polydon spathula. Proc. Zool. Soc. London 1904:22-35. O(NPL):1 4 9 21

1009 Inger, Robert F. (1957) Ecological aspects of the origins of the tetrapods. Evolution 11:372-376.OD:17 18 19

1010 Ionescu-Varo, Mircea and Mircea Tufescu (1983) Quantitative remarks on immune evolution in the animal series. Rev. Roum. Biol. Ser. Biol. Anim. 27:29-39. OD:11 17

1011 Irvine, Frederick Robert (1947) The Fishes and Fisheries of the Gold Coast. London: The Crown Agents for the Colonies. (Protopterus: section 95). PO:1 3 10 18 19 20 24

1012 Isaacks, Russell E., Hyun Dju Kim, and Donald R. Harkness (1978) Relationship between phosphorylated metabolic intermediates and whole blood oxygen affinity in some air-breathing and water-breathing teleosts. Can. J. Zool. 56:887-890 or Amer. Zool. 17:889. (Abstract) LO:2 10 11

1013 Isaacks, Russell E., Hyun Dju Kim, and Donald R. Harkness (1978) Inositol diphosphate in erythrocytes of the lungfish, Lepidosiren paradoxa, and 2,3-diphosphoglycerate in erythrocytes of the armored catfish, Pterygoplichtys sp. Can. J. Zool. 56:1014-1016. LO:2 11

1014 Isaacks, Russell E. and Donald R. Harkness (1980) Erythrocyte organic phosphates and hemoglobin function in birds, reptiles, and fishes. Amer. Zool. 20:115-129. OL:2 11

1015 Isaacks, Russell E. and Hyun Dju Kim (1984) Erythrocyte phosphate composition and osmotic fragility in the Australian lungfish, Neoceratodus fosteri, and Osteoglossid, Scleropages schneichardti. Comp. Biochem. Physiol. 79A:667-671. Amer. Zool. 23:977. [1983]. (Abstract) NO(PL):2 11

1016 Ishikawa, C. and K. Matsuüra (1897) Preliminary Catalogue of Fishes, including Dipnoi, Cyclostomi, and Cephalochorda, in the collection of the Natural History Department, Imperial Museum. Tokyo: Imperial Museum. (Ceratodus:63). OC

1017 Ishiyama, M. and T. Ogawa (1983) Existence of true enamel on tooth plates of the lungfish Lepidosiren paradoxa. Kaibogaku Zasshi 58:157-161. [in Japanese]. L+:4

1018 Jack, Robert Logan and Robert Etheridge, Jr.(1892) The Geology and Palaeontology of Queensland and New Guinea. London: Dulau and Co. (Ceratodus:646-647). OCN:4 18

1019 Jackson, Frederick John (1916) African lung fish. East Afr. Natur. Hist. Soc. 5:3-4. P:14 18 19

1020 Jackson, P. B. N. (1958) A lungfish (Protopterus) from the Middle Zambezi. Nature (London) 182:123-124. P:4 18

1021 Jackson, P. B. N. (1959) New records and little-known species of fish from Rhodesia and Nyasaland. Occas. Pap. Natl. Mus. S. Rhodesia 23B:295-305. PO:18

1022 Jackson, P. B. N. (1971) The African Great Lakes Fisheries: past, present and future. Afr. J. Trop. Hydrobiol. Fisheries 1:35-49. OP:23

1023 Jacobs, Jeff (1976) The lungfishes, with some notes on the care of one species in captivity. Aquarist *41*:326-328. (Nov., 1976). PLN:1 3 4 9 10 14 15 18 20 21

1024 Jacobshagen, Eduard (1911) Untersuchungen über das Darmsystem der Fische und Dipnoer. Z. Naturwiss. Jena *47*:529-568. OLPN:1 12

1025 Jacobshagen, Eduard (1915) Zur Morphologie des Spiraldarms. (Two articles). Anat. Anz. *48*:220-235, 241-254. (*Protopterus*:228-233). OP(NL):1 5 11 12

1026 Jacobshagen, Eduard (1929) Zur Kenntnis und Charakterisierung des Rumpfdarmbaues der Lungenfische. Gegenbaurs Morphol. Jahrb. *63*:292-313. PNL:1 9 10 11 12 13

1027 Jacobshagen, Eduard (1934) Das Problem des Spiraldarms. II. Jahrb. Morphol. Mikrosk. Anat. (I), Gegenbaurs Morphol. Jahrb. *73*:392-445. DO*:1 12 17

1028 Jacobshagen, Eduard (1937) IV. Mittel- und Enddarm. Rumpfdarm. A. Einleitung. In Louis Bolk, Ernest Göppert, Erich Kallius, and Wilhelm Lubosch (eds): Handbuch der vergleichenden Anatomie der Wirbeltiere. Berlin and Wien: Urban und Schwarzenberg, *III*:563-724. OPLN:1 12

1029 Jacobshagen, Eduard (1955) Wie kam es zum Wurzelbau und zur Befestigung der Menschen- und der Säugetierzähne? Anat. Anz. *102*:249-270. (*Lepidosiren*:255-256). OLF:1 4 17

1030 Jaekel, Otto (1890) Über *Phaneropleuron* und *Hemictenodus*, n.g. und Dipnoer. Sber. Ges. Naturforsch. Fr. Berlin *1890*:1-8. FDC(NP):4

1031 Jaekel, Otto (1903) Über die Epiphyse und Hypophyse. Sber. Ges. Naturforsch. Fr. Berlin *1903*:27-58. OP:6

1032 Jaekel, Otto (1927) Der Kopf der Wirbeltiere. Z. Ges. Anat. *27*:815-934. OFD:1 4 7

1033 Jain, Sohan L. (1968) Vomerine teeth of *Ceratodus* from the Maleri Formation (Upper Triassic, Deccan, India). J. Paleontol. *42*:96-99. C:1 4 18

1034 Jain, Sohan L. (1983) Spirally coiled 'coprolites' from the Upper Triassic Maleri Formation, India. Paleontol. *26*:813-829. NCO(P):1 12 18

1035 James, W. Warwick (1957) A further study of dentine. Trans. Zool. Soc. London *29*:1-66. (*Protopterus* and *Lepidosiren*:17). OPL:4

1036 Janssens, Peter A. (1964) The metabolism of the aestivating African lungfish. Comp. Biochem. Physiol. *11*:105-117. P:2 19 20

1037 Janssens, Peter A. (1965) Short Communication: Phosphorylase and glucose-6-phosphatase in the African lungfish. Comp. Biochem. Physiol. *16*:317-319. P:2 20

1038 Janssens, Peter A., G. P. Vinson, I. Chester Jones, and W. Mosley (1965) Amphibian characteristics of the adrenal cortex of the African lungfish (*Protopterus sp.*). J. Endocrinol. *32*:373-382. P:1 2 8 11 13

1039 Janssens, Peter A. and Philip P. Cohen (1966) Ornithine-urea cycle enzymes in the African lungfish, *Protopterus aethiopicus*. Science (Washington) *152*:358-359. P:2 13

1040 Janssens, Peter A. and Philip P. Cohen (1968) Nitrogen metabolism in the African lungfish. Comp. Biochem. Physiol. *24*:879-886. P:2 13 20

1041 Janssens, Peter A. and Philip P. Cohen (1968) Biosynthesis of urea in the estivating African lungfish and in *Xenopus laevis* under conditions of water-shortage. Comp. Biochem. Physiol. *24*:887-898. PO:2 13 20

1042 Janvier, Philippe (1974) Preliminary report on Late Devonian fishes from Central and Eastern Iran. Rep. Iran Geol. Surv. *31*:5-47. OFD:4 18

1043 Janvier, Philippe and Michel Martin (1978) Les Vertébrés Dévoniens de l'Iran Central. I. Dipneustes. Géobios *11*:819-833. FD:1 4 7 8

1044 Janvier, Philippe, F. Lethiers, O. Monod and Ö. Balkas (1984) Discovery of a vertebrate fauna at the Devonian-Carboniferous boundary in S. E. Turkey (Hakkari Province). J. Pet. Geol. 7:147-168. OFD:4 18

1045 Jardine, William (1841) Remarks on the structure and habits of *Lepidosiren annectens*. Ann. Mag. Natur. Hist. 7:21-26. P(L):1 18 19 20

1046 Jarvik, Erik (1942) On the structure of the snout of crossopterygians and lower gnathostomes in general. Zool. Bidr. Uppsala *21*:235-675. (Dipnoi:270-284, 391-392, 620-621). OPLNFD:1 4 6 11 15 17

1047 Jarvik, Erik (1955) The oldest tetrapods and their forerunners. Sci. Monthly, March, *80*:141-154. DO:1 4 17

1048 Jarvik, Erik (1959) Dermal fin-rays and Holmgren's principle of delamination. Kgl. Sven. Vetenskapsakad. Handl. 6:3-51. ONPFD:1 3 4 17

1049 Jarvik, Erik (1964) Specializations in early vertebrates. Ann. Soc. Roy. Zool. Belg. *94*:11-95. (Dipnoi:41-47). PNFDO:4 17

1050 Jarvik, Erik (1967) On the structure of the lower jaw in dipnoans: with a description of an early Devonian dipnoan from Canada, *Melanognathus canadensis* gen. et sp. nov. J. Linnean Soc. London Zool. *47*:155-183. NFD:1 4 17

1051 Jarvik, Erik (1968) The systematic position of the Dipnoi. In Tor Ørvig (ed): Nobel Symposium 4: Current Problems of Lower Vertebrate Phylogeny. Stockholm: Almquist and Wiksell, pp.223-246. FDPLN:1 3 4 7 10 17

1052 Jarvik, Erik (1968) Aspects of vertebrate phylogeny. In Tor Ørvig (ed): Nobel Symposium 4: Current Problems of Lower Vertebrate Phylogeny. Stockholm: Almquist and Wicksell, pp.497-527 OFDN:17

1053 Jarvik, Erik (1980) Basic Structure and Evolution of Vertebrates. Vol. I (1980), Vol. 2 (1981). New York: Academic Press. OD:17

1054 Jeener, R. (1930) Evolution des centres diencéphaliques périventriculaires des Téléostomes. Proc. Kgl. Akad. Wetenskhap. Amsterdam, Sect. Sci. *33*:755-770. PNO:1 6 17

1055 Jenkin, Penelope M. (1928) Note on the sympathetic nervous system of *Lepidosiren paradoxa*. Proc. Roy. Soc. Edinburgh *48*:55-69. L:1 6

1056 Jensen, J. A. (1984) Continuing study of new Jurassic/Cretaceous vertebrate faunas from Colordao and Utah. Res. Reports, Natl. Geograph. Soc. *16*:373-380. OFD+:18

1057 Jepps, Margaret W. (1927) Note on a Haemogregarine in *Lepidosiren paradoxa*. Parasitology *19*:285-287. L:11 22

1058 Jepps, Margaret W. (1929) Further note on *Haemogregarina lepidosirenis*. Parasitology *21*:282-287. L:1 11 22

1059 Jepps, Margaret W. (1929) A holostomid larva from the pericardiac cavity of *Lepidosiren paradoxa*. Parasitology *21*:322-323. L:1 11 22

1060 Jes, Harald (1972) Jahresbericht des Aquariums 1971. Z. Kölner Zoo *14*:137-145. ONP:3

1061 Jespersen, Åse (1969) On the male urogenital organs of *Neoceratodus forsteri*. Biol. Skr. Dan. Vidensk. Selsk. *16*:1-11. N(LP):1 13 14

1062 Jespersen, Åse (1971) Fine structure of the spermatozoon of the Australian lungfish *Neoceratodus forsteri* (Krefft). J. Ultrastruct. Res. 37:178-185. N(P):1 14

1063 Jesse, Mary Jane, Clarence Shub, and Alfred P. Fishman (1967) Lung and gill ventilation of the African lung fish. Respir. Physiol. *3*:267-287. P:1 2 9 10 11

1064 Jobert, M. (1878) Mémoire á la respiration aérienne de quelques Poissons du Brésil. C. R. Acad. Sci. Paris 86:935-938. O(L):10

1065 Johansen, Kjell and Claude Lenfant (1967) Respiratory function in the South American lungfish, *Lepidosiren paradoxa* (Fitz). J. Exp. Biol. *46*:205-218. L:1 2 9 10 11 19

1066 Johansen, Kjell, Claude Lenfant, and Gordon C. Grigg (1967) Respiratory control in the lungfish *Neoceratodus forsteri* (Krefft). Comp. Biochem. Physiol. *20*:835-854. Fed. Proc. *25*:389. [1966]. (Abstract) N:2 9 10 11 17 19

1067 Johansen, Kjell and Ola B. Reite (1967) Effects of acetylcholine and biogenic amines on pulmonary smooth muscle in the African lungfish, *Protopterus aethiopicus*. Acta Physiol. Scand. 71:248-252. P:2 5 9

1068 Johansen, Kjell and Ola B. Reite (1968) Influence of acetylcholine and biogenic amines on branchial, pulmonary and systemic vascular resistance in the African lungfish, *Protopterus aethiopicus*. Acta Physiol. Scand. 74:465-471. P: 2 11

1069 Johansen, Kjell and David Hansen (1968) Functional anatomy of the hearts of lungfishes and amphibians. Amer. Zool. 8:191-210. PLNO:1 9 10 11

1070 Johansen, Kjell and Claude Lenfant (1968) Respiration in the African lungfish *Protopterus aethiopicus*. II. Control of breathing. J. Exp. Biol. 49:453-468. P:2 9 10 11

1071 Johansen, Kjell (1968) Air-breathing fishes. Sci. Amer. *219*:102-111. PNO:1 9 10 11 17 18 19

1072 Johansen, Kjell, Claude Lenfant, and David Hanson (1968) Cardiovascular dynamics in the lungfishes. Z. Vergl. Physiol. *59*:157-186. NLP:1 2 9 10 11

1073 Johansen, Kjell and Ragnar Hol (1968) A radiological study of the central circulation in the lungfish, *Protopterus aethiopicus*. J. Morphol. *126*:333-348. P:1 2 11

1074 Johansen, Kjell (1970) Cardiorespiratory adaptations in the transition from water breathing to air breathing. Introduction. Fed. Proc. 29:1118-1119. O:9 11

1075 Johansen, Kjell, Claude Lenfant, and David Hanson (1970) Phylogenetic development of pulmonary circulation. Fed. Proc. 29:1135-1140. NPO:1 2 9 10 11

1076 Johansen, Kjell (1970) Air breathing in fishes. In William S. Hoar and David J. Randall (eds): Fish Physiology. New York: Academic Press, 4:361-411. OPLN:1 2 9 10 11 18 19

1077 Johansen, Kjell (1971) Comparative physiology: gas exchange and circulation in fishes. Annu. Rev. Physiol. 33:569-612. OPLN:1 6 7 9 10 11

1078 Johansen, Kjell (1973) Adaptations to environment of cardiovascular functions. Acta Physiol. Scand. Suppl. *396*:35. (Abstract) DO:3 6 9 10 11 18

1079 Johansen, Kjell, Jens Peter Lumholt, and Geoffrey M. O. Maloiy (1976) Importance of air and water breathing in relation to size of the African lungfish, *Protopterus amphibius* Peters. J. Exp. Biol. 65:395-399. P:2 9 10 19

1080 Johansen, Kjell, Gunnar Lykkeboe, Roy E. Weber, and Geoffrey M. O. Maloiy (1976) Respiratory properties of blood in awake and estivating lungfish, *Protopterus amphibius*. Respir. Physiol. 27:335-345. P:2 11 20

1081 Johansen, Kjell, Charlotte P. Magnum and Gunnar Lykkeboe (1978) Respiratory properties of the blood of Amazon fishes. Can. J. Zool. 56:898-906. LO:2 9 10 11

1082 Johansen, Kjell and Warren Burggren (1980) Cardiovascular function in the lower vertebrates. In G. H. Burne (ed): Hearts and Heart-like Organs, Vol. 1. Comparative Anatomy and Development. New York: Academic Press, pp.1-118. (Dipnoi:75-82). PNO(L):1 2 9 10 11

1083 Johansen, Kjell (1984) A phylogenetic overview of cardiovascular shunts. In Kjell Johansen and Warren W. Burggren (eds): Cardiovascular Shunts: Phylogenetic, Ontogenetic and Clinical Aspects. 5. Alfred Benzon Symposium #21. (Abstract) OD:10 11

1084 Johnels, Alf G. (1953) Notes on fishes from the Gambia River. Ark. Zool. 6:327-411. OP:14 15 18 19

1085 Johnels, Alf G. and Gustav S. O. Svensson (1954) On the biology of *Protopterus annectens*. Ark. Zool. 7:131-164. P(LN):9 10 14 16 18 19 20 21

1086 Johnston, T. Harvey and Thomas Lane Bancroft (1915) Notes on an exhibit of specimens of *Ceratodus*. Proc. Roy. Soc. Queensland 27:58-59. N:1 15

1087 Johnston, T. Harvey (1916) A census of the endoparasites recorded as occurring in Queensland, arranged under their hosts. Proc. Roy. Soc. Queensland 28:31-79. (*Neoceratodus*:62). ON:22

1088 Jollie, Malcolm T. (1977) Segmentation of the vertebrate head. Amer. Zool. *17*:323-333. OD:4 17

1089 Jones, Thomas Rymer (1861) General Outline of the Organization of the Animal Kingdom and Manual of Comparative Anatomy. London: John van Voorst. (Dipnoi:670-671). OPL:G(1 7 18)

1090 Jones, Tudor (1932) The primitive conducting mechanisms of the vertebrate heart. An introduction to the study of their appearance and development in *Lepidosiren paradoxa*. Trans. Roy. Soc. Edinburgh 57:225-240. J. Anat. 67:197-198. (Abstract) L:1 6 11 15

1091 Jones, Tudor (1938) Neurogenesis and the development of "synapses", with particular reference to the conditions in *Lepidosiren paradoxa*. J. Mental Sci. 84:451-494. L:1 6 15

1092 Jordan, David Starr (1963) The Genera of Fishes and a Classification of Fishes. Stanford: Stanford Univ. Press. OCNLP

1093 Jordan, Harvey Ernest and C. C. Speidel (1931) Blood formation in the African lungfish, under normal conditions and under conditions of prolonged estivation and recovery. J. Morphol. Physiol. 51:319-371. P:1 11 20

1094 Jorgensen, J. M. (1984) On the morphology of the electroreceptors of the two lungfish *Neoceratodus forsteri* and *Protopterus annectens*. Vidensk. Medd. Dan. Naturhist. Foren. *145*:77-86. NP*:1 3 7

1095 Jubb, Rex A. (1961) An Illustrated Guide to the Freshwater Fishes of the Zambezi River, Lake Kariba, Pungwe, Sabi, Lundi, and Limpopo Rivers. Bulawayo: Stuart Manning. (*Protopterus*:73). OP:G(1 3 18 23)

1096 Jubb, Rex A. and Brian G. Gardiner (1975) A preliminary catalogue of identifiable fossil fish material from Southern Africa. Ann. S. Afr. Mus. 67:381-440. (*Ceratodus*:410-411). OC:18

1097 Junghans, W. (1915) *Lepidosiren paradoxus*. Blätt. Aquar.-Terrkd. 26:113-115. L:19 20 21

1098 Jurgens, J. D. (1977) Respirasieprobleme van die eerste landwerweldiere. Tydskr. Natuurwet. 17:2-8. PLNO:9 10 18

1099 Kälin, J. A. (1938) III. Extremitätenskelett. A. Die paarigen Extremitäten der Fische (Pterygia). In Louis Bolk, Ernest Göppert, Erich Kallius, and Wilhelm Lubosch (eds): Handbuch der vergleichenden Anatomie der Wirbeltiere. Berlin and Wien: Urban und Schwarzenberg, V:1-70. (Dipnoi:19-25). NPLO:1 4

1100 Kappers, C. U. Ariëns, G. Carl Huber and Elizabeth Caroline Crosby (1960) The Comparative Anatomy of the Nervous System of Vertebrates, Including Man.Vol. 1. New York: Hafner Pub. Co.OD:1 6

1101 Kathariner, Ludwig (1899) Findet sich eine "Trägerfunction" der paarigen Flossen nur bei den Dipnoern? Zool. Anz. 22:345-346. N:19

1102 Keast, J. Allen (1977) Zoogeography and phylogeny: the theoretical background and methodology to the analysis of mammal and bird fauna. In Max K. Hecht, Peter Charles Goody, and Bessie M. Hecht (eds): Major Patterns in Vertebrate Evolution. pp.249-312. (*Ceratodus, Neoceratodus*:260-261). OD:18

1103 Keller, Conrad (1880) Über *Ceratodus*. Vierteljahresschr. Naturforsch. Ges. Zurich 25:415-416. N(FD):1 3 4 9 10 17

1104 Kellicott, William Erskine (1904) The development of the vascular system of *Ceratodus*. Biol. Bull. (Woods Hole) 6:320-321. N:11 15

1105 Kellicott, William Erskine (1905) The development of the vascular system of *Ceratodus*. Anat. Anz. 26:200-208. N:1 11 15 17

1106 Kellicott, William Erskine (1905) The development of the vascular and respiratory systems of *Ceratodus*. Mem. New York Acad. Sci. 2:131-250. N:1 9 10 11 15 17

1107 Kemp, Anne (1977) The development of *Ceratodus forsteri* Krefft, with particular reference to tooth formation. Thesis, University of Queensland, Australia. N(PL):4 14 15 19

1108 Kemp, Anne (1977) The pattern of tooth plate formation in the Australian lungfish, *Neoceratodus forsteri* Krefft. Zool. J. Linn. Soc. 60:223-258. N(FD):1 4 15

1109 Kemp, Anne (1979) The histology of tooth formation in the Australian lungfish, *Neoceratodus forsteri* Krefft. Zool. J. Linn. Soc. 66:251-287. N(LPFD):1 4 15 16

1110 Kemp, Anne (1981) The use of the Australian lungfish, (*Neoceratodus forsteri*) for the control of submerged aquatic weeds. Proc. 6th Austral. Weeds Conf., Vol. 1: Biological Control of Weeds. 5 pp.N:21 24

1111 Kemp, Anne (1981) Rearing of embryos and larvae of the Australian lungfish, *Neoceratodus forsteri*, under laboratory conditions. Copeia 1981:776-784. N:15 21 22

1112 Kemp, Anne and Ralph E. Molnar (1981) *Neoceratodus forsteri* from the Lower Cretaceous of New South Wales, Australia. J. Paleontol. 55:211-217. FN:4 18

1113 Kemp, Anne (1981) *Neoceratodus djelleh*, a new ceratodont lungfish from Duaringa, Queensland. Alcheringa 6:151-155. FN:4 18

1114 Kemp, Anne (1982) Australian Mesozoic and Cenozoic lungfish. In P. V. Rich and E. M. Thompson (eds): The Fossil Vertebrate Record of Australasia. Clayton, Victoria: Monash Univ. Offset Printing Unit, pp.133-143. C:4 18

1115 Kemp, Anne (1982) The embryological development of the Queensland lungfish, *Neoceratodus forsteri*, (Krefft). Mem. Queensld. Mus. 20:553-597. N(PL):3 4 5 6 7 10 13 15

1116 Kemp, Anne (1982) *Ceratodus nargun*, a new Early Cretaceous ceratodont lungfish from Cape Lewis, Victoria. Proc. Roy. Soc. Vict. 95:23-24. C:18

1117 Kemp, Anne (1983) Skull development and roofing patterns in Australian ceratodont lungfish. Amer. Zool. 23:1009. (Abstract) NFD:4

1118 Kemp, Anne (1984) Spawning of the Australian lungfish, *Neoceratodus forsteri* (Krefft) in the Brisbane River and in Enoggera Reservoir, Queensland. Mem. Queensl. Mus. 21:391-399. N:14 18 19

1119 Kemp, Anne (1984) A comparison of the developing dentition of *Neoceratodus forsteri* and *Callorhynchus milii*. Proc. Linn. Soc. N.S.W. 107:245-262. NO:4 15

1120 Kenemans, Peter (1973) The pattern of ventricular grooves in the brain stem of some fish. Acta Morphol. Neerl.-Scand. 11:371-372. (Abstract) PO:1 6

1121 Kenny, Alexander D., Samarendra N. Baksi, Sara M. Galli-Gallardo, and Peter K. T. Pang (1977) Vitamin D metabolism in amphibia and fish. Fed. Proc. 36:1097. (Abstract) DO:2 13

1122 Kerr, John Graham (1898) The *Lepidosiren* of South America. Natur. Sci. 12:3. (Abstract) L:G(3 10 15 18 19 20 21)

1123 Kerr, John Graham (1898) *Lepidosiren* development. Amer. Natur. 32:206-207. (Abstract) L:15

1124 Kerr, John Graham (1898) On the dry-season habits of *Lepidosiren*. Proc. Zool. Soc. London 1898:41-44. L:18 19 20

1125 Kerr, John Graham (1898) Exhibition of *Lepidosiren* and other Paraguayan fishes. Proc. Zool. Soc. London 1898:492. LO:3 15 18

1126 Kerr, John Graham (1900) The external features in the development of *Lepidosiren paradoxa*. Trans. Roy. Soc. London 192:299-330. Summary in J. Roy. Microsc. Soc. London 1900:301-302, in Proc. Roy. Soc. London 65:160-161 [1891], and in Zool. Anz. 22:292-294. [1899] L:1 3 6 9 11 14 15 18 19 20 21

1127 Kerr, John Graham (1900) Note on hypotheses as to the origin of the paired limbs of vertebrates. Proc. Camb. Philos. Soc. 10:227-235. LO(PN):1 4 15 17

1128 Kerr, John Graham (1901) The development of *Lepidosiren paradoxa*. Part II. With a note upon the corresponding stages in the development of *Protopterus annectens*. Quart. J. Microsc. Sci. 45:1-40. L(P):1 15

1129 Kerr, John Graham (1901) The origin of the paired limbs in vertebrates. Rep. Brit. Assoc. Advan. Sci. 1901:693-695. LO(P):1 4 17

1130 Kerr, John Graham (1901) On the male genitourinary organs of the *Lepidosiren* and *Protopterus*. Proc. Zool. Soc. London 1901:484-498. LP:1 13 14 17

1131 Kerr, John Graham (1902) The development of *Lepidosiren paradoxa*. Part III. Development of the skin and its derivatives. Quart. J. Microsc. Sci. *46*:417-459. L:1 3 6 7 15

1132 Kerr, John Graham (1902) The genito-urinary organs of dipnoan fishes. Proc. Cambridge Philos. Soc. *11*:329-333. LP(N):1 12 13 14 15 17

1133 Kerr, John Graham (1902) The early development of muscles and motor nerves in *Lepidosiren*. Rep. Brit. Assoc. Advan. Sci. *1902*:655-657. L:1 5 6 15

1134 Kerr, John Graham (1904) On some points in the early development of motor nerve trunks and myotomes in *Lepidosiren paradoxa* (Fitz.). Trans. Roy. Soc. Edinburgh *41*:119-128. L:1 5 6 15

1135 Kerr, John Graham (1905) The embryology of certain of the lower fishes, and its bearing upon vertebrate morphology. Proc. Roy. Phys. Soc. Edinburgh *16*:191-215. LO:1 3 6 9 10 12 15 17

1136 Kerr, John Graham (1908) Note on swim-bladder and lungs. Proc. Roy. Phys. Soc. Edinburgh *17*:170-174. NLO:1 9 10 17

1137 Kerr, John Graham (1908) Note on the cause of disappearance of the fifth aortic arch in air-breathing vertebrates. Proc. Roy. Phys. Soc. Edinburgh *17*:167-168. L:1 11 15 17

1138 Kerr, John Graham (1909) Normal plates of the development of *Lepidosiren paradoxa* and *Protopterus annectens*. In F. Keibel (ed): Normentafeln zur Entwicklungsgeschichte der Wirbeltiere. Jena: Gustav Fischer, pp.1-27. LP:3 4 5 8 9 12 13 14 15

1139 Kerr, John Graham (1910) On certain features in the development of the alimentary canal in *Lepidosiren* and *Protopterus*. Quart. J. Microsc. Sci. *54*:483-518. LP:1 8 9 12 15

1140 Kerr, John Graham (1919) Textbook of Embryology. Vol. II. Vertebrata. London: MacMillan and Co., Ltd.OLPN:1 3 4 5 6 7 8 9 11 13 14 15

1141 Kerr, John Graham (1924) The teeth of Dipnoi and their relation to the general problems of tooth structure. Dent. Rec. *44*:295-298. LPN:1 4 15 17

1142 Kerr, John Graham (1925) Limbs and pigment cells. Nature (London) *115*:154. (Letter to Editor). PL:1 3

1143 Kerr, John Graham (1925) On embryology, evolution and religion. Nature (London) *116*: Suppl., July 11:80. O

1144 Kerr, John Graham (1932) Archaic fishes - *Lepidosiren*, *Protopterus*, *Polypterus* - and their bearing upon problems of vertebrate morphology. Z. Naturwiss. Jena *67*:419-433. LPO(N):5 7 9 12 15 17

1145 Kerr, John Graham (1950) A Naturalist in the Gran Chacao. Cambridge: Cambridge Univ. Press. (*Lepidosiren* Expedition:169-229). LO:10 15 18 19 20 21 23

1146 Kerr, Thomas (1933) On the pituitary in *Lepidosiren* and its development. Proc. Roy. Soc. Edinburgh *53*:147-150. L:1 8 15

1147 Kerr, Thomas (1942) A comparative study of some teleost pituitaries. Proc. Zool. Soc. London *112*:37-56. O(LPN):1 8 17

1148 Kerr, Thomas (1955) The scales of modern lungfish. Proc. Zool. Soc. London *125*:335-345. NPL:1 3

1149 Kerr, Thomas and van Oordt, P. G. W. J. (1966) The pituitary of the African lungfish *Protopterus sp.* Gen. Comp. Endocrinol. 7:549-558. P:1 8

1150 Kesteven, H. Leighton (1931) The evolution of the Anamniota. Rec. Aust. Mus. Sydney *18*:167-200. NPLO:1 4 6 10 11 15 17

1151 Kesteven, H. Leighton (1931) Contributions to the cranial osteology of the fishes. No. VII. The skull of *Neoceratodus forsteri*: a study in phylogeny. Rec. Aust. Mus. Sydney *18*:236-265. N:1 4 6 11 17

1152 Kesteven, H. Leighton (1942) The evolution of the skull and the cephalic muscles: a comparative study of their development and adult morphology. Part II. The Amphibia. Mem. Aust. Mus. Sydney *8*:1-316. 1942-45. (Dipnoan muscles:133-144, Dipnoan skull:200-204). ON:1 4 5 6 15 17

1153 Kesteven, H. Leighton (1945) The cranial nerves of *Neoceratodus*. Proc. Linnean Soc. N.S.W. *70*:25-33. N:1 6

1154 Kesteven, H. Leighton (1950) The origin of the tetrapods. Proc. Roy. Soc. Victoria *59*:93-138. OFD:1 4 17

1155 Khabakov, Aleksandr V. (1931) Ob ostatkakh dvoiakodyshashchikh (sem. Ceratodontidae) iz nizhnego Triasa gory Bogdo. (Ceratodontidae from the Lower Triassic of the Mt. Bogdo, Kalmyk steppes, USSR). Tr. Paleontol. Inst. Akad. Nauk SSSR *1*:45-56. C*:18

1156 Khalil, L. F. (1971) Check list of the helminth parasites of African freshwater fishes. Commonw. Inst. Helminthol. Technical Communication #42:1-79. Slough: Commonwealth Agricultural Bureaux. (*Protopterus*:8). OP:22

1157 Kharchenko, E. P. and N. N. Nalivaeva (1980) Some evolutionary aspects of the structural organization of chromosomes: a review. J. Evol. Biochem. Physiol. (Engl. transl. Zh. Evol. Biokhim. Fiziol.) *16*:358-366. [1981] LO:1 17

1158 Kim, Hyun Dju and Russell E. Isaacks (1978) The osmotic fragility and critical hemolytic volume of red blood cells of Amazon fishes. Can. J. Zool. *56*:860-862. LO:2 11

1159 Kim, Hyun Dju and Russell E. Isaacks (1978) The membrane permeability of nonelectrolytes and carbohydrate metabolism of Amazon fish red cells. Can. J. Zool. *56*:863-869. LO:2 11 20

1160 Kimura, A., T. Gomi, H. Tsuchiya, T. Hashimoto, and H. Fujita (1984) Electron microscopic observation on the blood-air barrier of the lung in the lower vertebrates. Zool. Sci. (Tokyo) *1*:985. (Abstract) DO+:1 10 11 17

1161 Kindahl, Märtha (1938) Zur Entwicklung der Exkretionsorgane von Dipnoërn und Amphibien. Acta Zool. (Stockholm) *19*:1-190. (Dipnoi:6-31, 92-120). NPLO:1 13 15 17

1162 Kingsbury, Benjamin Freeman (1895) The lateral line system of sense organs in some American Amphibia, and comparison with the dipnoans. Trans. Amer. Microsc. Soc. *17*:115-154. (Dipnoi:132-137). OPLN:1 6 7 17

1163 Kisselewa, S. (Z.N.) (1928) Zur Kenntnis des Skeletts von *Lepidosiren paradoxa*. Bull. Soc. Imp. Natur. Moscow *37*:65-87. L(PN):1 4 17

1164 Kisselewa, Z. N.(1929) Sravnitel'no-anatomicheskoe izuchenie skeleta Dipnoi. (Comparative anatomical study of the dipnoan skeleton). Tr. Nauchno-Issled. Inst. Zool. Mosk. *3*:1-35. (German summary in same issue: 36-44). PLN:1 4

1165 Kitzan, Sonja and Phillip R. Sweeny (1968) A light and electron microscope study of the structure of *Protopterus annectens* epidermis. I. Mucus production. Can. J. Zool. *46*:767-772. P:1 3

1166 Klaatsch, Hermann (1890) Zur Morphologie der Fischschuppen und zur Geschichte der Hartsubstanzgewebe. Gegenbaurs Morphol. Jahrb. *16*:97-202, 209-258. (Dipnoi:208-218, 222-223). PLNO:1 3

1167 Klaatsch, Hermann (1893) Über die Wirbelsäule der Dipnoer. Anat. Anz. *8*:130-133. PN:1 4

1168 Klein, von (1864) Beiträge zur Anatomie der *Lepidosiren annectens*. Württemb. Naturwiss. Jahresh. *20*:134-144. P:1 4 9 11 12 13

1169 Kleine, R. (1967) Besonderheiten des Exkretionsstoffwechsels der Lungenfische. Naturwiss. Rundsch. *20*:254. P:2 13 20

1170 Klika, E. and A. Lelek (1967) A contribution to the study of the lungs of *Protopterus annectens* and *Polypterus senegalensis*. Folia Morphol. (Prague) *15*:168-175. PO:1 9 10

1171 Klitgaard, Torben U. (1978) Morphology and histology of the heart of the Australian lungfish, *Neoceratodus forsteri* (Krefft). Acta Zool. (Stockholm) *59*:187-198. N(LP):1 11

1172 Knight, Wilbur C. (1898) Some new Jurassic vertebrates from Wyoming. Amer. J. Sci. *5*:186. CO:4 18

1173 Kobayashi, Ryoko, Yutaka Kobayashi, and C. H. W. Hirs (1978) Identification of a binary complex of procarboxypeptidase A and a precursor of protease E in porcine pancreatic secretion. J. Biol. Chem. *253*:5526-5530. O(P):2 12

1174 Koken, Ernst Friedrich Rudolf Carl (1891) 3. Neue Untersuchungen an tertiären Fisch-Otolithen. II. Z. Dtsch. Geol. Ges. *43*:77-171. ON:1 7

1175 Kölliker, Albert von (1860) Histologisches über *Rhinocryptis* (*Lepidosiren annectens*) Pet. Würzburg. Naturwiss. Z. Phys.-Med. Ges. *1*:11-19. P:1 3

1176 Kölliker, Albert von (1887) Über die Entstehung des Pigmentes in den Oberhautgebilden. Z. Wiss. Zool. *45*:713-717. O(P):1 3

1177 König, Clemens (1911) Die geographische Verbreitung des australischen Lungenfisches. Natur. Wochenschr. *10*:104-107. N:18

1178 Kramer, Donald L., C. C. Lindsey, G. E. E. Moodie, and E. D. Stevens (1978) The fishes and the aquatic environment of the Central Amazon Basin, with particular reference to respiratory patterns. Can. J. Zool. *56*:717-729. OL:10 18

1179 Krauss, Ferdinane (1864) Über einen lebendigen Lungenfisch (*Lepidosiren annectens* Owen). Württemb. Naturwiss. Jahresh. *20*:126-133. P:3 19 20 21

1180 Krawetz, L. (1910) Entwickelung des Knorpelschädels von *Ceratodus*. Bull. Soc. Imp. Natur. Moscow *24*:332-365. N:1 4 6 15

1181 Krefft, Gerard (1870) Description of a gigantic amphibian allied to the genus *Lepidosiren*, from the Wide-Bay District, Queensland. Proc. Zool. Soc. London *1870*:221-224. Summary in Nature (New York) *2*:38. Translation [1871] in Arch. Naturgeschichte *37*:320-324. N:1 3 4 18 24

1182 Krefft, Gerard and Carl Albert Ludwig Gotthilf Gunther (1872) Le genre *Ceratodus* retrouvé vivant en Australie. J. de Zool. *1*:176-178. N:1 3 4 12

1183 Krefft, Gerard (1874) Fossil tooth of *Ceratodus palmeri*. Nature (London) *9*:293. C:4 18 24

1184 Krietsch, Peter (1968) Eine ichthyologische Kostbarkeit: *Protopterus amphibius* (Peters, 1844). Monatsschr. Ornithol. Vivarienkd. Ausg. B. Aquarien Terrarien *15*:56-60. P:G(3 7 9 16 18 19 21)

1185 Krumbein, Wolfgang E. and Norbert Wilczewski (1973) Eine Dipnoer-Zahnplatte aus dem Bundsandstein Helgolands. Neues Jahrb. Geol. Paläontol. Monatsh. *5*:279-283. C:1 4 18

1186 Krupina, N. I. (1979) Novyy vid dipnoy iz famena Zakavkaz'ya. (A new dipnoan species from the Famennian of Transcausasia). Paleontol. Zh. *2*:145-147. Translation in Paleontol. J. (Moscow) *13*:261-263. FD:4 18

1187 Krupina, N. I. (1980) A new Dipnoi genus from the Famennian deposits of the Central Devonian field Orel Oblast USSR. Paleontol. Zh.:140-143. FD+:18

1188 Kryzanovsky, S. G. (1934) Die Pseudobranchie: Morphologie und biologische Bedeutung. Zool. Jahrb. *58*:171-238. (*Neoceratodus*:191-193). ON:1 7 11

1189 Kryzanovsky, S. G. (1934) Die Atmungsorgane der Fischlarven (Teleostomi). Zool. Jahrb. Abt. Anat. Ont. *58*:21-60. ON(LP):1 9 11 15

1190 Kudhongania, W. A. and Almo J. Cordone (1972) Bathymetric distribution pattern and biomass estimate of the major demersal fishes in Lake Victoria, as derived from exploratory bottom trawling, and in relation to fishery development aspects. Manuscript seen at EAFFRO, August 1972. PO:18 23

1191 Kudhongania, W. A. (1973) Past trends and rece. research on the fisheries of Lake Victoria in relation to possible future developments. Afr. J. Trop. Hydrobiol. Fisheries, Sp. Issue *II*:93-106. OP:23

1192 Kuhlenbeck, Hartwig (1929) Über die Grundbestandteile des Zwischenhirnbauplans der Anamnier. Gegenbaurs Morphol. Jahrb. *63*:50-95. (*Protopterus*:78-81). PO:1 6

1193 Kuhlenbeck, Hartwig (1975) The Central Nervous System of Vertebrates. Vol. 4, Spinal Cord and Deuterencephalon: 130-132 (Spinal Cord), 436-444 (Medulla Oblongata and Pons), 706-712 (Cerebellum), 867-874 (Mesencephalon). Basel: S. Karger. PNO:1 6

1194 Kuhlenbeck, Hartwig (1977) The Central Nervous System of Vertebrates. Vol. 5, Derivatives of the Prosencephalon: Diencephalon and Telencephalon:206-217 (Diencephalon), 591-602 (Telencephalon). Basel: S.

1195 Kuhn, Oskar (1939) Beiträge zur Keuperfauna von Halberstadt. Palaeontol. Z. *21*:258-286. OC:4 18

1196 Kutscher, Fritz (1973) Beiträge zur Sedimentation und Fossilführung des Hünsrückschiefers. 37: Zusammenstellung der Agnathen und Fische des Hünsruckschiefer-Meeres. Notizbl. Hess. Landesamt. Bodenforsch. *101*:46-79. OFD:4 18

1197 Kutscher, Fritz (1978) Walter Robert Gross und die Fische des Hunsrückschiefers (Forscher, Liebhaber und Sammler der Hunsrükschiefer-Fossilien. 8). Mitt. Pollichia *66*:5-10. OFD:18

1198 Kyle, Harry Macdonald (1900) On the presence of nasal secretory sacs and a naso-pharyngeal communication in Teleostei, with especial reference to *Cynoglossus semilaevis*, Gthr. J. Linnean Soc. London *27*:541-556. O(N):1 7 15

1199 Lachiver, F., F. Boulu and A. Brisson-Martin (1974) Composition en acides aminés iodés de la thyroglobuline chez quelques Vertébrés inférieurs. Gen. Comp. Endocrinol. 22:373. (Abstract) PO:2 8

1200 Lachmann, Hermann (1891) Der Schlammfisch (Protopterus annectens Owen). Zool. Gart. 32:129-134. P:G(1 3 9 10 18 19 20 21)

1201 Laerm, Joshua (1979) The origin and homology of the chondrostean vertebral centrum. Can. J. Zool. 57:475-485. O(N):1 4

1202 Lagios, Michael D. (1975) The pituitary gland of the coelacanth Latimeria chalumnae Smith. Gen. Comp. Endocrinol. 25:126-146. O(L):1 8 17

1203 Lagios, Michael D. and John E. McCosker (1977) A cloacal excretory gland in the lungfish Protopterus. Copeia 1977:176-178. P:1 13

1204 Lagios, Michael D. (1980) Latimeria and the Chondrichthyes as sister taxa: a rebuttal to recent attempts at refutation. Copeia 1982:942-948. O(D):17

1205 Laguesse, Édouard (1890) Note sur la rate et le pancréas du Protoptère et de la Lamproie. Mem. Soc. Biol. 42:425-426. PO:1 12

1206 Laguesse, Édouard (1890) Sur la présence de vaisseaux dans l'épithélium intestinal (chez le Protoptère). Mem. Soc. Biol. 42:292-293. P:1 11 12

1207 Lahiri, Sukhamay, Clarence Shub, and Alfred P. Fishman (1968) Respiratory properties of blood of the African lungfish (Protopterus). Proc. 24th Int. Union Physiol. Sci. (Wash., D.C.) 7:251. (Abstract) P:2 9 11

1208 Lahiri, Sukhamay, Jan Peter Szidon, and Alfred P. Fishman (1970) Potential respiratory and circulatory adjustments to hypoxia in the African lungfish. Fed. Proc. 29:1141-1148. P:1 2 6 9 10 11 17 19 20

1209 Lake, John S. (1971) Freshwater Fishes and Rivers of Australia. Melbourne: Thomas Nelson (Australia) Ltd. ON:G(18 19 21)

1210 Lake, John S. (1978) Australian Freshwater Fishes. Melbourne: Thomas Nelson (Australia) Ltd. ON:G(18 19 21)

1211 Lane, E. B. and M. Whitear (1982) Sensory structures at the surface of fish skin. I. Putative chemoreceptors. Zool. J. Linn. Soc. 75:141-152. PO:1 3 7

1212 Lane, Frank W. (1945) Fish that lives four years without a meal. Country Life, Aug. 10:241. P:G(19 20)

1213 Langston, Wann, Jr. (1963) Fossil vertebrates and the Late Paleozoic Red Beds of Prince Edward Island. Bull. Natl. Mus. Canada #187 (Geol. Ser. #56):1-36. OFD:18 20

1214 Lankester, Edwin Ray (1879) On the hearts of Ceratodus, Protopterus, and Chimaera, with an account of undescribed pocket valves in the conus arteriosus of Ceratodus and of Protopterus. Trans. Zool. Soc. London 10:493-505. Proc. Zool. Soc. London 1878:634. (Abstract) NPO:1 11

1215 Lankester, Edwin Ray (1894) The limbs of Lepidosiren paradoxa. Nature (London) 49:555. L(P):1

1216 Lankester, Edwin Ray (1894) Lepidosiren paradoxa. Nature (London) 49:601. L:1

1217 Lankester, Edwin Ray (1896) On the Lepidosiren of Paraguay, and on the external characters of Lepidosiren and Protopterus. Trans. Zool. Soc. London 14:11-24. LP(N):1 16 18 21 22

1218 Lankester, Edwin Ray (1897) On Lepidosiren articulata and L. paradoxa. Amer. Natur. 31:72. L:1

1219 Lannan, John (1967) Strange breathers used in eye, biology research: lungfish help solve mysteries. Boston Sunday Herald Traveler, Aug. 6. P:1 6 7 13

1220 Lapparent, Albert F. de (1949) Sur la stratigraphie et la paléontologie du Djoua (Sahara central). C. R. Acad. Sci. Paris 228:1040-1042. OC:18

1221 Larsell, Olof (1967) Dipnoi. In Jan Jansen (ed): The Comparative Anatomy and Histology of the Cerebellum, from Myxinoids through Birds. Minneapolis: Univ. Minn. Press, pp.62-65. N:1 6

1222 Lauder, George Varick, Jr. (1980) On the evolution of the jaw adductor musculature in primitive gnathostome fishes. Breviora #460:1-10. OD:5 17

1223 Laurent, Pierre and Suzanne Dunel (1978) Relations anatomiques des ionocytes (cellules à chlorure) avec le compartiment veineux branchial: définition de deux types d'épithélium de la branchie des Poissons. C. R. Acad. Sci. Paris 286:1447-1450. OPL:1 9 11

1224 Laurent, Pierre, Richard G. DeLaney and Alfred P. Fishman (1978) The vasculature of the gills in the aquatic and aestivating lungfish (Protopterus aethiopicus). J. Morphol. 156:173-208. P(LN):1 9 10 11 20

1225 Laurent, Pierre, Richard G. DeLaney and Alfred P. Fishman (1978) Adaptation du système vasculaire à la respiration bimodale chez un poisson pulmoné: Protopterus aethiopicus. J. Physiol. (Paris) 74:35A. (Abstract). Also Physiologist 22:75. [1979]. (Abstract). See also Adv. Physiol. Sci. 20:305-306. [1980] P(L):1 2 6 8 9 10 11

1226 Laurent, Pierre and Suzanne Dunel (1980) Morphology of gill epithelia in fish. Amer. J. Physiol. 7:R147-R159. OPL:1 9 11

1227 Laurent, Pierre (1984) Organization and control of the respiratory vasculature in lower vertebrates: are there anatomical gill shunts? In Kjell Johansen and Warren W. Burggren (eds): Cardiovascular Shunts: Phylogenetic, Ontogenetic and Clinical Aspects.7. Alfred Benzon Symposium #21. (Abstract) PLO:8 10 11

1228 Lavocat, René (1948) Découverte de Crétacé à Vertébrés dans le soubassement de la Hammada du Guir (Sud marocain). C. R. Acad. Sci. Paris 226:1291-1292. CO:18

1229 Lavocat, René (1955) Découverte de Dipneustes du genre Protopterus dans le Tertiaire ancien de Tamaguilelt (Soudan français). C. R. Acad. Sci. Paris 240:1915-1917. FP:18

1230 Lawrence, Sarah P. (1976) Pigment analysis of the blue-green bones and green mature eggs of the lungfish, Protopterus annectens. Thesis, Supervised Study, Mary Baldwin College, Staunton, Virginia. P:2 4 14

1231 Lebied, B. (1946) Terminal abnormalities in the pectoral and pelvic fins of Protopterus. Acta Trop. 3:272-273. P:16 17

1232 Léger, Louis (1897) Mutilation pathologique et régéneration chez le Protoptère. C. R. Soc. Biol. Paris 4:543-545. P:16

1233 Lehman, Jean-Pierre (1955) Les Dipneustes du Dévonien Supérieur du Groenland. C. R. Acad. Sci. Paris 240:995-997. FD:4 18

1234 Lehman, Jean-Pierre (1956) L'évolution des Dipneustes et l'origine des Urodèles. Colloq. Internat. Cent. Natl. Rech. Sci. Paris 60:69-76. DO:4 17

1235 Lehman, Jean-Pierre, C. Chateau, M. Laurain, and M. Nauche (1959) Paléontologie de Madagascar. XXVIII. Les Poissons de la Sakamena Moyenne. Ann. Paléontol. 45:177-219. C(N):1 3 4 7 18 20

1236 Lehman, Jean-Pierre (1959) Les Dipneustes du Dévonien Supérieur du Groenland. Medd. Grønland 160:3-58. FD:4 18

1237 Lehman, Jean-Pierre (1966) Actinopterygiens, Crossopterygiens, Dipneustes. In Jean Piveteau (ed): Traité de Paléontologie. Paris: Masson and Cie, 4:1-420. (Dipnoi:244-300). CFDO(NPL):3 4

1238 Lehman, Jean-Pierre (1971) Nouveaux Vertébrés fossiles du Trias de la série de Zarzaïtine. Ann. Paléontol. 57:71-93. (Ceratodus:84). OC:4 18

1239 Lehman, Jean-Pierre (1975) À propos de Ceratodus sturii Teller, 1891. Bull. Mus. Natl. Hist. Natur. Paris Terre 50:241-246. C:1 4

1240 Lehmann, W. M. and T. Stanley Westoll (1952) A primitive dipnoan fish from the Lower Devonian of Germany. Proc. Roy. Soc. London 140B:403-421. FD:1 17 18

1241 Lehmann, W. M. (1956) Dipnorhynchus lehmanni Westoll, ein primitiver Lungenfisch aus dem rheinischen Unterdevon. Paläontol. Z. 30:21-25. FD:4

1242 Leiner, Michael and Dora Schmidt (1957) The histology of the islet-system in the pancreas of the lungfish Protopterus annectens Ow. Photogr. Forsch. 7:129-138. P:1 8

1243 Leloup, Jacques (1958) Contribution à l'étude du fonctionnement thyroïdien d'un Dipneuste: Protopterus annectens Owen. C. R. Acad. Sci. Paris 246:474-477. P:2 8

1244 Leloup, Jacques (1958) Influence de "l'estivation" sur le fonctionnement thyroïdien du Protoptère (Protopterus annectens Owen). C. R. Acad. Sci. Paris 246:830-833. P:2 8 20

1245 Leloup, Jacques (1958) Sur la répartition des hormones thyroïdiennes (thyroxine et 3:5:3' triiodothyronine) entre les hématies et le plasma du sang de quelques Poissons (Dipneustes et Téléostéens). J. Physiol. (Paris) 50:368-370. PO:2 8 11

1246 Leloup, Jacques (1961) Variations spécifiques de la liaison de la thyroxine avec les protéines du plasma chez les Poissons. J. Physiol. (Paris) 53:403-405. PO:2 8 11

1247 Leloup, Jacques (1963) Fonctionnement thyroïdien du Protoptère en relation avec le changement de milieu. J. Physiol. (Paris) 55:285-286. P:2 8 20

1248 Leloup, Jacques (1964) Biochimie comparée des hormones thyroïdiennes. In C. Chagas and L. C. Lobo (eds): Colloquio sobre a Tiroide. Paru, pp.47-80. OP:2 8

1249 Lenfant, Claude, Kjell Johansen, and Gordon C. Grigg (1966) Respiratory properties of blood and pattern of gas exchange in the lungfish Neoceratodus forsterii (Krefft). Respir. Physiol. 2:1-21. Fed. Proc. 25:325. (Abstract) N(PL):2 9 10 11 18

1250 Lenfant, Claude and Kjell Johansen (1967) Gas exchange and response to environment in the lungfish Protopterus aethiopicus (Heck). Fed. Proc. 26:441. (Abstract) P:2 9 10 11 20

1251 Lenfant, Claude and Kjell Johansen (1968) Respiration in the African lungfish Protopterus aethiopicus. I. Respiratory properties of blood and normal patterns of breathing and gas exchange. J. Exp. Biol. 49:437-452. P:2 9 10 11

1252 Lenfant, Claude, Kjell Johansen, and David Hanson (1970) Bimodal gas exchange and ventilation-perfusion relationship in lower vertebrates. Fed. Proc. 29:1124-1129. PLNO:2 10 11 17

1253 Leuckart, Friedrich Sigismund (1840) Über das Gen. Lepidosiren. Frohriep's Notizen 13:17-19. LP:1

1254 Leure-duPree, A. E. (1973) Electron microscopic observations of the retina of the African lungfish Protopterus aethiopicus. Anat. Rec. 175:370-371. P:1 7

1255 Ley, Willy (1941) The Lungfish and the Unicorn. New York: Modern Age Books. ON:1 17

1256 Liem, Karel F. (1981) Larvae of air-breathing fishes as countercurrent flow devices in hypoxic environments. Science (Washington) 211:1177-1179. ON:9 11 19

1257 Linck, Otto (1936) Ein Lebensraum von Ceratodus im Stubensandstein des Strombergs mit Ceratodus rectangulus n. sp. und anderen Arten. Jahresh. Vaterl. Naturk. Württemberg 92:45-68. C:1 3 16 18

1258 Linck, Otto (1938) Nachtrag zu: Ein Lebensraum von Ceratodus im Stubensandstein des Strombergs usw. Jahresh. Vaterl. Naturk. Württemberg 94:4-14. C:1 4 18

1259 Linck, Otto (1962) Neuer Beitrag zur Kenntnis der Ceratodontiden der germanischen Trias. Jahresh. Vaterl. Naturk. Württemberg 117:195-209. C:1 4 18

1260 Linck, Otto (1963) Schädelknochen von Ceratodus Agassiz aus dem Stubensandstein (Trias, Mittl. Keuper 4) Württembergs und ihre Bedeutung. Paläontol. Z. 37:268-276. Abstract, same issue, p.16. C(N):1 4 18

1261 Lindsey, Casimer Charles (1978) Form, function, and locomotory habits in fish. In William S. Hoar and David J. Randall (eds): Fish Physiology. New York: Academic Press, 7:1-100. (Dipnoi:43). OPN:19

1262 Lison, L. (1941) Sur la structure des dents des Poissons Dipneustes. La Pétrodentine. C. R. Soc. Biol. Paris 135:431-433. P:1 4

1263 Lison, L. (1941) Recherches sur la structure et l'histogenèse des dents des Poissons Dipneustes. Arch. Biol. 52:279-320. P:1 4 15

1264 Lison, L. (1954) Les Dents. In Pierre-P. Grassé (ed): Traité de Zoologie. Paris: Masson et Cie, 12:791-853. OPN:1 4 15

1265 Litman, Gary W., Dominique Frommel, Andreas Rosenberg, and Robert A. Good (1971) Circular dichroic analysis of immunoglobulins in phylogenic perspective. Biochim. Biophys. Acta 236:647-654. PO:2 11 17

1266 Litman, Gary W., Andreas Rosenberg, Dominique Frommel, Bernard Pollara, Joanne Finstad, and Robert A. Good (1971) Biophysical studies of the immunoglobulins. The circular dichroic spectra of the immunoglobulins: a phylogenetic comparison. Int. Arch. Allergy Appl. Immunol. 40:551-575. PO:2 11 17

1267 Litman, Gary W., An-Chuan Wang, Hugh H. Fudenberg, and Robert A. Good (1971) N-terminal amino-acid sequence of African lungfish immunoglobulin light chains. Proc. Nat. Acad. Sci. USA 68:2321-2324. P:2 11

1268 Litman, Gary W. (1975) Relationship between structure and function of lower vertebrate immunoglobulins. In W. H. Hildemann and A. A. Benedict (eds): Immunologic Phylogeny. New York: Plenum Press, pp.217-228. ONP:2 11 17

1269 Little, G. J. and P. P. Giorgi (1984) Ultrastructure of the optic nerve of the Queensland lungfish Neoceratodus forsteri. J. Anat. 139:188. (Abstract) N:1 7

1270 Littrell, Lincoln (1971) African lungfishes. Trop. Fish Hobbyist 19:40-57. P:G(1 3 14 18 19 20 23)

1271 Liu, Hsien-t'ing and Hsiang-k'uei Yeh (1957) Two

new species of *Ceratodus* from Szechuan, China. Vertebr. Palasiat. *1*:305-309. [in Chinese]. C:18

1272 Liu, Hsien-t'ing and Hsiang-k'uei Yeh (1960) New *Ceratodus* from Shenmu, N. Shensi. Vertebr. Palasiat. *4*:14-16. C:1 4 18

1273 Livingston, John A. (1980) On the relevance of lungfish, lilacs, wolves, and spirit levels in resource-constrained economies: can North American societies adapt to the resource constraints confronting them? J. Soil Water Conserv. *35*:165-170. OP

1274 Locket, Nigel A. (1970) Mitosis in mature lungfish retina. Zool. J. Linn. Soc. *49*:1-4. P:1 6 7

1275 Locket, Nigel A. (1970) Landolt's Club in the retina of the African lungfish, *Protopterus aethiopicus*, Heckel. Vision Res. *10*:299-306. P:1 6 7

1276 Lombardini, J. B., Peter K. T. Pang, and Robert W. Griffith (1979) Amino acids and taurine in intracellular osmoregulation in marine animals. Occas. Pap. Calif. Acad. Sci. #134:160-169. LO:2 18

1277 Lomholt, Jens Peter, Kjell Johansen, and Geoffrey M. O. Maloiy (1975) Is the aestivating lungfish the first vertebrate with suctional breathing? Nature (London) *257*:787-788. P:2 10 20

1277a Long, John A. (1982) The history of fishes on the Australian Continent. In P.V. Rich and E.M. Thompson (eds): The Fossil Vertebrate Record of Australia. Clayton: Monash University Offset Printing Unit, pp.54-85.

1278 Longman, Heber A. (1918) Exhibit of specimen of *Neoceratodus forsteri*. Proc. Roy. Soc. Queensland *30*:xi-xii. N:18

1279 Longman, Heber A. (1928) Discovery of juvenile lung-fishes, with notes on *Epiceratodus*. Mem. Queensl. Mus. *9*:160-173. N:1 3 9 10 15 18 19 21

1280 Løvtrup, Søren (1977) Phylogenetics: some comments on cladistic theory and method. In Max K. Hecht, Peter Charles Goody, and Bessie M. Hecht (eds): Major Patterns in Vertebrate Evolution. New York: Plenum Press, pp.805-822. OD:17

1281 Lubosch, Wilhelm (1926) Über das perennierende Kalkskelett der Wirbeltiere. Verh. Physik.-Med. Ges. Würzburg *51*:72-88. OD*:4 15

1282 Lüling, Karl Heinz (1959) Einige Notizen über die afrikanischen Lungenfische. Aquarien Terrarien Z. *12*:12-14. P:16 18 19 21

1283 Lüling, Karl Heinz (1959) Einige Notizen über die afrikanischen Lungenfische. Aquarien Terrarien Z. *12*:44-46. P:1 3

1284 Lüling, Karl Heinz (1961) Untersuchungen an Lungenfischen, insbesondere an afrikanischen Protopteriden. Bonn. Zool. Beitr. *12*:87-112. P:1 10 14 18 19 20

1285 Lüling, Karl Heinz (1966) Fische mit Lungen. Neptune *6*:80-83. P(NL):3 4 7 9 10 11 15 16 18 19 20 21 24

1286 Lüling, Karl Heinz (1971) Lungenfische. Aqua Terra *8*:32-36. NP(L):G(1 3 7 10 18 20)

1287 Lüling, Karl Heinz (1971) Lungenfische. Aqua Terra *8*:37-38. NPL:G(1 2 10 14 15 19 20 21)

1288 Lüling, Karl Heinz (1973) Südamerikanische Fische und ihr Lebensraum. Elberfeld: Engelbert Pfriem Verlag, pp.1-84. (*Lepidosiren*:68). OL:20

1289 Lüling, Karl Heinz (1975) Lungenfische sind interessante Pfleglinge. Aquarium Aqua. Terra. *9*:378-380. P:G(1 3 9 10 15 19)

1290 Lumholtz, Carl (1889) Among Cannibals. An Account of Four Years Travels in Australia and of Camp Life with the Aborigines of Queensland. London: John Murray. (*Neoceratodus*:385). ON:9 10 18 19 21

1291 Lund, Richard (1970) Fossil fishes from Southwestern Pennsylvania, Part I: Fishes from the Duquesne Limestones (Conemaugh, Pennsylvania). Ann. Carnegie Mus. *41*:231-261. OFD:1 4 18 21

1292 Lund, Richard (1973) Fossil fishes from Southwestern Pennsylvania, Part II: *Monongahela dunkardensis*, new species, (Dipnoi, Lepidosirenidae) from the Dunkard Group. Ann. Carnegie Mus. *44*:71-101. FD:1 4 18

1293 Lund, Richard (1975) Vertebrate-fossil zonation and correlation of the Dunkard Basin. In Israel Charles White Symposium: The Age of the Dunkard, pp.171-182. West Virginia Geological Survey. OFD:18

1294 Lund, Richard (1976) General geology and vertebrate biostratigraphy of the Dunkard Basin. In H. Falke (ed): The Continental Permian in Central, West, and South Europe. Dordrecht-Holland: D. Reidel Pub. Co., pp.225-339. OFD:18

1295 Luther, Alex. (1913) Über die vom N. Trigeminus versorgte Muskulatur der Ganoiden und Dipneusten. Acta Soc. Sci. Fenn. *41*:1-72. NPLO:1 4 5 6 21

1296 Luther, Alex (1938) Die Visceralmuskulatur der Acranier, Cyclostomen und Fische. A. Acranier, Cyclostomen, Selachier, Holocephalen, Ganoiden und Dipnoer. In Louis Bolk, Ernest Göppert, Erich Kallius, and Wilhelm Lubosch (eds): Handbuch der vergleichenden Anatomie der Wirbeltiere. Berlin and Wien: Urban und Schwarzenberg, *V*:468-542. (Dipnoi:515-517). ONPL:1 4 5

1297 Lütken, Christian Frederick (1871) Sur les limites et la classification des ganoides. Arch. Sci. Physiques et Natur. *40*:283-296. Summary in Ann. Mag. Natur. Hist. *7*:329-339. O(D):1

1298 Lütken, Christian Frederick (1873) Über die Begrenzung und Eintheilung der Ganoiden. Paleontographica *22*:1-54. O(D):1

1299 Lydekker, Richard (1895) The New Natural History. Vol. *5*:325-330. New York: Merrill and Baker. NLP:G(1 4 10 14 18)

1300 MacDonagh, Emiliano J. (1945) Hallazgo de una *Lepidosiren paradoxa* en el delta del Paraná. Notas Mus. La Plata *10*:11-16. L:1 3 7 18 21

1301 Maclaren, R. I. R. (1954) Nigerian fishes and their palatability. Nigerian Field *19*:4-15. PO:24

1302 Macleay, William Sharpe (1881) Descriptive catalogue of Australian fishes. Proc. Linnean Soc. N.S.W. *6*:202-387, and Sydney: F. W. White. (*Ceratodus*:347-348). ON:G(1 3 18)

1303 Macleay, William Sharpe (1883) Notes on a collection of fishes from the Burdekin and Mary Rivers, Queensland. Proc. Linnean Soc. N.S.W. *8*:199-213. ON:18 21

1304 Macleay, William Sharpe (1883) On some newly observed habits of *Ceratodus forsteri*. Zoologist *1883*:506-507. N:14 19 21

1305 Magalhães, Agenor Couto de (1931) Monographia Braziliera de Peixes Fluviaes. São Paulo: Romiti, Lanzara and Zanin, pp.1-260. (*Lepidosiren*:213-231). LO:1 18 19

1306 Maina, John N. and Geoffrey M. O. Maloiy (1985) The morphometry of the lung of the African lungfish

(*Protopterus aethiopicus*): its structural-functional correlations. Proc. Roy. Soc. London *224B*:399-420. P(LN):1 10 17

1307 Maitland, Robert T. (1863) De Moddervisch (*Lepidosiren annectens*). Nederland. Tijdschr. Dierk. Amsterdam *1*:LXVII-LXIX. PO:G(3 20)

1308 Mangum, Charlotte P., M. S. Haswell, and Kjell Johansen (1977) Low salt and high pH in the blood of Amazon fishes. J. Exp. Zool. *200*:163-168. LO:2 11

1309 Mangum, Charlottte P., M. S. Haswell, Kjell Johansen, and D. W. Towle (1978) Inorganic ions and pH in the body fluids of Amazon animals. Can. J. Zool. *56*:907-916. LO:2 11 13

1310 Manski, Wladyslaw, S. P. Halbert, and P. Javier (1967) On the use of antigenic relationships among species for the study of molecular evolution. Int. Arch. Allergy Appl. Immunol. *31*:475-489. OP:2 17

1311 Marchalonis, John J. (1969) Isolation and characterization of immunoglobulin-like proteins of the Australian lungfish (*Neoceratodus forsteri*). Aust. J. Exp. Biol. Med. Sci. *47*:405-419. N:2 11

1312 Marchalonis, John J. and J. L. Atwell (1973) Phylogenetic emergence of distinct immunoglobulin classes. Inst. Nat. Sante Rech. Med. Colloque L'étude phylogenetique et ontogenique de la réponse immunaire et la théorie immunologique, Paris, France: 153-162. Pub. by Inst. Nat. de la Santé et de la Rech. Med., Paris. ON:2 11 17

1313 Marchelidon, J., A. Brisson-Martin, and F. Lachiver (1972) Composition en acides aminés de la thyroglobuline de divers Poissons. Gen. Comp. Endocrinol. *18*:601-602. (Abstract) PO:2 8

1314 Marcus, H. (1930) Über die Bildung von Geruchsorgan, Tentakel und Choanen bei *Hypogeophis*, nebst Vergleich mit Dipnoern und *Polypterus*. Z. Ges. Anat. Abt. I, Z. Anat. Gesch. Entwickl. *91*:657-691. O(N)*:1 7 15

1315 Marcus, H. (1937) B. Lungen. In Louis Bolk, Ernest Göppert, Erich Kallius, and Wilhelm Lubosch (eds): Handbuch der vergleichenden Anatomie der Wirbeltiere. Berlin and Wien: Urban and Schwarzenberg, *III*:909-988. OLNP:1 5 9 11

1316 Margo, Theodor (1895) Studien über *Ceratodus*. Math. Naturwiss. Ber. Ungarn Budapest *12*:195-207. N:1 3 4 7 11 12 19 21

1317 Marlier, G. (1938) Considerations sur les organs accessoires servant à la respirations aerienne chez les Teleosteens. Ann. Soc. Roy. Zool. Belg. *69*:163-185. OP+:1 9

1318 Marlier, G. (1953) Étude biogeographique du Bassin de la Ruzizi, basée sur la distribution des Poissons. Ann. Soc. Roy. Zool. Belg. *84*:175-224. OP:18 19 21

1319 Marlier, G. (1957) L'enkystement du *Protopterus aethiopicus* Heckel. Ann. Soc. Roy. Zool. Belg. *87*:211-216. P:19 20

1320 Marno, Ernst (1873) Der äthiopische Schuppenmolch, *Protopterus aethiopicus*. Zool. Gart. *14*:441-444. P:3 16 17 18 20 24

1321 Marno, Ernst (1873) Nachrichten über *Protopterus annectens*. Lotos *23*:119-123. P:18 19 20 24

1322 Marsh, Othniel Charles (1878) New species of *Ceratodus*, from the Jurassic. Amer. J. Sci. *15*:76. Also in Ann. Mag. Natur. Hist. *1*:184. C:4 18

1323 Marten, Gerald G. (1979) Predator removal: effect on fisheries yields in Lake Victoria (East Africa). Science (Washington) *203*:646-648. OP:23

1324 Marten, Gerald G. (1979) Impact of fishing on the inshore fishery of Lake Victoria (East Africa). J. Fish. Res. Board Can. *36*:891-900. OP:23

1325 Martin, Michel (1979) *Arganodus atlantis* et *Ceratodus arganensis*, deux nouveaux Dipneustes du Trias supérieur continental marocain. C. R. Acad. Sci. Paris *289D*:89-92. C:18

1326 Martin, Michel (1980) Revision of *Ceratodus concinnus* Plieninger. Stuttg. Beitr. Naturkd. ser. B (Geol. Paläontol.) *56*:1-15. C:1 4 18

1327 Martin, Michel (1980) La phylogenie des Ceratodontides: quelques hypotheses de travail. 105e Congr. Soc. sav. Caen, Section des Sciences, 3:47-59. Paris. C:1 4

1328 Martin, Michel (1981) Les Ceratodontiformes (Dipnoi) de Gadoufaoua (Aptien supérieur, Niger). Bull. Mus. Natl. Hist. Natur. Paris (4) *3*:267-283. C:4 18

1329 Martin, Michel (1981) Über drei Zahnplatten von *Ceratodus* aus der ägyptischen Kreide. Mitt. Bayer. Staatsslg. Paläont. Hist. Geol. *21*:73-80. C:1 4

1330 Martin, Michel (1981) Les Dipneustes et Actinistiens du Trias supérieur continental marocain. Stuttg. Beitr. Naturkd. ser B (Geol. Paläontol.) *69*:1-29. CO(N):1 4 7 18

1331 Martin, Michel (1981) Les Dipneustes mésozoïques malgaches, leurs affinités et leur intérêt paléobiogéographique. Bull. Soc. Geol. Fr. *23*:579-585. C:18

1332 Martin, Michel, Denise Sigogneau-Russell, Paul Coupatez, and Georges Wouters (1981) Les Cératodontidés (Dipnoi) du Rhétien de Saint-Nicolas-de-Port (Meurthe-et-Moselle). Géobios *14*:773-791. C:4 18

1333 Martin, Michel (1982) Nouvelles données sur la phylogénie et la systématique des Dipneustes postpaléozoiques. C. R. Acad. Sci. Paris *294* sér. II:611-614. Also same volume number, sér. III:413-416. C:4

1334 Martin, Michel and Rucha Ingavat (1982) First record of an Upper Triassic Ceratodontid (Dipnoi, Ceratodontiformes) in Thailand and its paleogeographical significance. Géobios *15*:111-114. C:1 4 18

1335 Martin, Michel (1982) Revision von *Tellerodus sturii* (Teller 1891). Verh. Geol. B.A. *1982*:21-31. C:1 4

1336 Martin, Michel (1982) Les Dipneustes: des cousins des quadrupèdes? Pour la Science *59* (Sept.):12-23. LPNFD:1 4 9 10 14 17 18 19 20

1337 Martin, Michel (1982) La coupure du Jurassique dans l'histoire des Ceratodontiformes. 9e Reunion Ann. Sci. Terre Paris:416. (Abstract) C:4 17 18

1338 Martin, Michel (1982) Nouvelles données sur la phylogénie et la systématique des Dipneustes postpaléozoiques, conséquences stratigraphiques et paléogéographiques. Géobios Mém. Spéc. *6*:53-64. Lyon. FDCNPL:4 17 18

1339 Martin, Michel (1983) Les Dipneustes actuels, des fossiles vivants? Bull. Soc. Zool. Fr. *108*:670-671. (Abstract) DFD:17 18

1340 Martin, Michel (1983) Les Dipneustes une sousclasse à la recherche d'une evolution. In Eric Buffetaut, J.M. Mazin and E. Salmon (eds): Actes du Symposium Paléontologique G. Cuvier, Montbeliard, pp.363-374. FDC:17

1341 Martin, Michel (1984) Révision des Arganodontidés et des Néocératodontidés (Dipnoi, Ceratodontiformes) du Crétacé africain. Neues Jahrb. Geol. Paläontol. Abh. *169*:225-260. FNO:4 17 18

1342 Martin, Michel (1984) Deux Lepidosirenidae (Dipnoi) crétacés du Sahara, *Protopterus humei* (Priem) et

Protopterus protopteroides (Tabaste). Paläont. Z. *58*:265-277. FP:4 18

1343 Martínez Achenbach, Guillermo (1971) Aspectos salientes en el comportamiento de dos ejemplares cautivos de *Lepidosiren paradoxa* Fitzinger, 1837 (Osteichthyes, Dipnoi, Lepidosirenidae). Acta Zool. Lilloana *28*:75-90. Comun. Mus. Prov. Cienc. Nat. Florentino Ameghino 4, Zool. Santa Fe, Argentina. L:1 4 7 10 19 21

1344 Martins Mimura, Olga (1975) Contribuição para o conhecimento do pâncreas de Dipnóicos. An. Acad. Brasil Ciênc. *47*:567-568. (Abstract) L:1 12

1345 Martins Mimura, Olga and I. Mimura (1977) Timo de *Lepidosiren paradoxa* (Fitz. 1836) Peixe Dipnóico. Bol. Fisiol. Anim. Univ. São Paulo *1*:29-38. L+:1 8

1346 Martins Mimura, Olga (1978) Ocurrencia do sistema neurossecretor caudal em *Lepidosiren paradoxa* (Peixe Dipnóico) em fasse estival. Bol. Fisiol. Anim. Univ. São Paulo *2*:43-48. L:2 6 8 20

1347 Mârza, Vasile D. (1978) Relationship between specialized cells, capillaries and intermediary cytofibrillary elements. XIth Note: Biological evolution of the emunctory subsystem and stereotype in vertebrates. Rev. Roum. Morphol. Embryol. *24*:283-304. OD+:1 11 13 17

1348 Mârza, Vasile D. (1982) The vascular biological stereotype and the achievement problem of the neurohumoral integration during phylogenesis. Anat. Anz. *152*:275-291. OD:11 17

1349 Masahito, Prince, T. Ishikawa, and S. Takayama (1984) Spontaneous spermatocytic seminoma in African lungfish, *Protopterus aethiopicus* Heckel. J. Fish Dis. *7*:169-172. P:14 22

1350 Masseyeff, R., René Godet, and J. Gombert (1963) Les protéines sériques de *Protopterus annectens*. Étude électrophorétique et immuno-électrophorétique. C. R. Soc. Biol. Paris *157*:167-172. P:2 11 20

1351 Masson, A. Guy and Brian R. Rust (1984) Freshwater shark teeth as paleoenvironmental indicators in the Upper Pennsylvanian Morien Group of the Sydney Basin, Nova Scotia. Can. J. Earth Sci. *21*:1151-1155. FDO:4 18

1352 Matthes, Ernst (1934) 2. Geruchsorgan. In Louis Bolk, Ernest Göppert, Erich Kallius, and Wilhelm Lubosch (eds): Handbuch der vergleichenden Anatomie der Wirbeltiere. Berlin and Wien: Urban und Schwarzenberg, *II*:879-948. (Dipnoi:892). NP:1 7

1353 Matthes, H. (1964) Les Poissons du Lac Tumba et de la region d'Ikela. Ann. Mus. Roy. Afr. Cent. Sér. Quarto Zool. #126:1-204. (*Protopterus*:5,9,18-19). OP:1 3 18 24

1354 Matty, A. J. (1968) Thyroid cycles in fish. Symp. Zool. Soc. London #2:1-15. OP:8

1355 Maurer, Friedrich (1912) Die ventrale Rumpfmuskulatur der Fische. Jenaische Z. Naturwiss. *49*:1-118. (Dipnoer:88-101). PNO(L):1 5

1356 Mauro, N. A. and Russell E. Isaacks (1985) Variation in the oxidation of glutamate and glucose by vertebrate and invertebrate erythrocytes. Amer. Zool. *25*:48A. (Abstract) DO:2 11

1357 Mayer, Gaston (1951) Palaeontologische Notizen aus dem Kraichgauer Hauptmuschelkalk. Beitr. Naturkd. Forsch. Südwestdtsch. *10*:105-109. C:1 4 18

1358 McAllister, Don E. (1968) The evolution of branchiostegals and associated opercular, gular, and hyoid bones, and the classification of teleostome fishes, living and fossil. Bull. Can. Natl. Mus. *221*:1-239. (Dipnoi:13-17). OFDN(LP):1 4 17

1359 McCulloch, Allan R. and Gilbert P. Whitley (1926) A list of the fishes recorded from Queensland waters. Mem. Queensl. Mus. *8*:125-182. ON:18

1360 McCulloch, Allan R. (1929) A check-list of the fishes recorded from Australia. Mem. Aust. Mus. Sydney *5*:1-534. (*Neoceratodus*:32-33). ON:18

1361 McDonnell, Robert (1859) Notiz über *Lepidosiren annectens*. Z. Wiss. Zool. *10*:409-411. P:1 6 10 11 12 19 20 21

1362 McDonnell, Robert (1860) Observations on the habits and anatomy of the *Lepidosiren annectens*. Natur. Hist. Rev. *7*:93-112. P:1 3 9 10 11 18 19 20 21

1363 McDonnell, Robert (1864) On the system of the "lateral line" in fishes. Trans. Roy. Irish Acad. *24*:161-187. OP:1 7

1364 McDowall, R. M. (1980) Freshwater fishes and plate tectonics in the southwest Pacific. Palaeogeogr. Palaeoclimatol. Palaeoecol. *31*:337-351. ON:18

1365 McMahon, Brian R. (1969) A functional analysis of the aquatic and aerial respiratory movements of an African lungfish, *Protopterus aethiopicus*, with reference to the evolution of the lung-ventilation mechanism in vertebrates. J. Exp. Biol. *51*:407-430. P:1 4 5 9 10 17

1366 McMahon, Brian R. (1970) The relative efficiency of gaseous exchange across the lungs and gills of an African lungfish *Protopterus aethiopicus*. J. Exp. Biol. *52*:1-15. P:2 9 10 19

1367 Meaders, Hollon (1975) Observations on the growth and structure of the tooth plates in the African lungfish, *Protopterus*. Thesis, Supervised Study, Mary Baldwin College, Staunton, Virginia. P:1 4 16 21

1368 Mednikov, B. M. and A. S. Antonov (1974) O statuse dvoiakodyshashchikh ryb (Dipnoi) i ikh polozhenie v sisteme. (Status of lungfishes (Dipnoi) and their taxonomic position). Dokl. Akad. Nauk SSSR. Ser. Biol. *218*:1485-1487. Translation in Dokl. Biol. Sci. *218*:474-476. DP:1 17

1369 Mednikov, B. M., Y. S. Reshetnikov and K. A. Savvaitova (1976) Molecular hybridization: an approach to disputable issues in fish taxonomy. II Congr. Europ. Ichthyol. Paris 8 Sept. 1976 In J. C. Hurean and K. E. Banisters (eds): Acts of the 2nd European Ichthyological Congress organized with the National Museum of Natural History, Paris, UNESCO. OD+:1 17

1370 Mednikov, B. M., E. A. Shubina and C. Y. Filippovich (1976) Divyergyentsya gyenomov amfibiy i ikh sistyematicheshiy status. (Divergent amphibian genomes and their systematic status). Biol. Nauki Kazakhskii Gosudarstvennyi Universit. *19*:21-26. OP:1 17

1371 Meek, Alexander (1916) The Migrations of Fish. London: Edward Arnold, pp.1-427. (Dipnoi:55-58). OPLN:10 18 20

1372 Meerwarth, Hermann (1897) Briefliche Mitteilungen über *Lepidosiren paradoxa*. Zool. Gart. *38*:282. L:10 19 21

1373 Meinke, Deborah Kay and Keith Stewart Thomson (1983) The distribution and significance of enamel and enameloid in the dermal skeleton of osteolepiform rhipidistian fishes. Paleobiology *9*:138-149. O(FDNL): 1 4

1374 Melville, A. G. (1847) On the *Lepidosiren*. Rep. Brit. Assoc. *17*:78. P:1

1375 Melville, A. G. (1860) On the *Lepidosiren*. Roy. Dublin Soc. *2*:405-406 and Natur. Hist. Rev. *7*:110-112. P:1 3 4 10 11 12

1376 Merciai, Giuseppe (1906) *Lepidosiren paradoxa* Fitzg. Riv. Ital. Sci. Natur. Siena *26*:59-61. L:1 4 9 11 12 15

1377 Merle, René (1913) Un poisson aérien: le Protoptère. La Nature *41*:225-226. P:G(3 18 20)

1378 Mészáros, Béla and Ilona Kató (1976) A halek evoluciója a kariológia tükrében. (On the evolution of fishes as seen from a karyological point of view). Acta Biol. Debrecina *13*:255-274. ONL:1 17

1379 Meunier, François-Jean and Yves François (1980) L'organisation spatiale des fibres collagènes et la minéralisation des écailles des Dipneustes actuels. Bull. Soc. Zool. Fr. *105*:215-226. NPL:1 3

1380 Meunier, François-Jean (1980) Have the incompletely or nonmineralized basal plate any relationships with the typical organisation of collagenous fibers in the osteichthyan scales? Calcif. Tissue Int. *31* (Suppl.):97. (Abstract) ON:1 3

1381 Meunier, François-Jean and Jacqueline Géraudie (1980) Les structures en contre-plaqué du derme et des écailles des Vertébrés inférieurs. Année Biol. *19*:1-18. ONP:1 3

1382 Meunier, François-Jean and Jacqueline Géraudie (1983) Le squelette dermique des nageoires des Dipneustes: les camptotriches. Bull. Soc. Zool. Fr. *108*:671-672. (Abstract) PLNFD:4 17

1383 Meunier, François-Jean (1984) Spatial organization and mineralization of the basal plate of elasmoid scales in Osteichthyans. Amer. Zool. *24*:953-964. OPNL:1 3

1384 Meyer, Adolf Bernhard (1866) Der fischartige Schuppenmolch (*Protopterus annectens* Ow) und sein Cocon. Zool. Gart. *7-8*:392-394. P:20

1385 Meyer, Adolf Bernhard (1875) *Ceratodus forsteri* and *C. miolepis*. Ann. Mag. Nat. Hist. *15*:368. N:1 3

1386 Meyer, Hermann von and Theodor Plieninger (1844) Beiträge zur Paläontologie Württemberg's. Stuttgart: Schweizerbart. (*Ceratodus*:85-89). CO:1 4 18

1387 Meyer, Hermann von (1848) Fossile Saurier des Muschelkalkes, II. Neues Jahrb. Min. Geogn. Geol. Petrefaktn-Kd. Stuttg. *1848*:465-473. CO:4 18

1388 Mezhnin, F. I. (1980) The evolution of the suprarenal body in the phylogeny of Cyclostomata and Pisces. J. Ichthyol. *20*:80-93. OP:1 8 17

1389 Miall, Louis Compton (1878) On the genus *Ceratodus*, with special reference to the fossil teeth found at Malédi, Central India. Mem. Geol. Surv. India, Paleontol. Indica *1*:9-17. C(FDLPN):1 4 18

1390 Miall, Louis Compton (1878) Monograph of the Sirenoid and Crossopterygian ganoids. Palaeontograph. Soc. *32*:1-34. PLNO:1 4 9 11 12 18

1391 Miles, Albert Edward William and D. F. G. Poole (1967) The history and general organization of dentitions. In Albert Edward William Miles (ed): Structural and Chemical Organization of Teeth. New York: Academic Press, *1*:3-44. OP:4

1392 Miles, Roger S. (1975) The relationships of the Dipnoi. Colloq. Internat. Cent. Natl. Rech. Sci., Problèmes Actuels de Paléontologie (Évolution des Vertébrés) #218:133-148. D:1 4 17

1393 Miles, Roger S. (1977) Dipnoan (lungfish) skulls and the relationships of the group: a study based on new species from the Devonian of Australia. Zool. J. Linn. Soc. *61*:1-328. Reviewed by Gavin Young in Alcheringa *3*:90. [1979] FDNPL*:1 4 5 6 7 11 17 18

1394 Miller, Agnes E. (1923) The cleavage of the egg of *Lepidosiren paradoxa*. Quart. J. Microsc. Sci. *67*:497-505. L:1 15

1395 Miller, Agnes E. (1930) Notes on the tail skeleton of *Lepidosiren paradoxa*, with remarks on the affinities of *Palaeospondylus*. Proc. Zool. Soc. London *1930*:782-789. L:1 4 15 17

1396 Miller, Agnes E. (1952) Note on the evolutionary history of the paired fins of elasmobranchs. Proc. Roy. Soc. Edinburgh *65B*:27-35. O(N):1 4

1397 Miller, Agnes E. (1962) Studies in dipnoan structure. Thesis, University of Glasgow. LN:1 4 15 17

1398 Miller, Robert Rush (1954) The scientific name of the Australian lungfish. Turtox News *32*:69. N

1399 Milne-Edwards, Henri (1857) Leçons sur la Physiologie et l'Anatomie Comparée de l'Human et des Animaux. *II*:365-367. Paris: V. Masson. OL:G(1 3 10)

1400 Milne-Edwards, Alphonse (1840) Remarque sur les affinités naturelles du *Lepidosiren*. Ann. Sci. Natur. *14*:159-162. Translation in Ann. Mag. Natur. Hist. *6*:466-468. [1841] PL:1 9 11 12 17

1401 Minick, Merlyn C. and Walter Chavin (1972) Effects of vertebrate insulins upon serum FFA and phospholipid levels in the goldfish, *Carassius auratus*. Comp. Biochem. Physiol. *41A*:791-804. O(P):2 8 11

1402 Minikh, M. G. (1978) Tafonomii dvoyakodyshashchikh ryb v triase vostoka yevropeyskoy chasti SSSR. (Taphonomy of Dipnoi fish remains from the Triassic of the eastern European USSR). In Voprosy tafonomi i paleobiologii, B. S. Sokolov, chairperson. Tr. Dokl. Sess. Vses. Paleontol. O-vo *20*:94-100. 1974: 29. OC+:18

1403 Mirsky, A. E. and Hans Ris (1951) The desoxyribonucleic acid content of animal cells and its evolutionary significance. J. Gen. Physiol. *34*:451-462. PO(LN):1 17

1404 Mohsen, Tahsin and René Godet (1960) Action of thyroxine on the rate of oxygen consumption of the lung-fish (*Protopterus*). Nature (London) *185*:108. P:2 8 10

1405 Mohsen, Tahsin (1965) Additional notes on *Polypterus* and *Protopterus*. Turtox News *43*:31. PO:G(1 3 9)

1406 Mohsen, Tahsin (1970) Sur l'importance des réserves lipidiques dans l'apparition d'oedèmes chez les Protoptères thyroïdectomisés. C. R. Acad. Sci. Paris *271*:2120-2122. P:2 8 12 20

1407 Mohsen, Tahsin and Georgette Jadoun (1972) Sur les centres automatogènes du coeur de *Protopterus annectens* (Poisson Dipneuste). C. R. Acad. Sci. Paris *274*:2116-2119. P:1 2 6 11 17

1408 Mohsen, Tahsin (1973) Sur la numération érythrocytaire, le taux d'hémoglobine et l'hématocrite de *Protopterus annectens* (Poisson Dipneuste) en phase aquatique. Bull. Inst. Fondam. Afr. Noire, sér. A Sci. Natur. *35*:450-461. P:2 11

1409 Mohsen, Tahsin and René Godet (1973) Sur la circulation céphalique et hypophysaire chez le Dipneuste *Protopterus annectens*. Bull. Inst. Fondam. Afr. Noire, sér. A Sci. Natur. *35*:705-715. P:1 8 11

1410 Mohsen, Tahsin, Hani Lattouf and Georgette Jadoun (1974) Action des hormones thyroidiennes sur le coeur isolé de Protoptères (*Protopterus annectens*) normaux et thyroidectomisés. Ann. Fac. Sci. Univ. Dakar *27*:49-57. P:2 8 11 20

1411 Mohsen, Tahsin (1974) Sur les facteurs qui interviennent dans la régulation de l'activité cardiaque chez *Protopterus annectens* (Poisson Dipneuste). Ann. Fac. Sci. Univ. Dakar *27*:45-48. P:2 6 8 11 20

1412 Mohsen, Tahsin (1974) L'importance du fonctionnement thyroïdien dans la régulation de l'érythropoïèse chez *Protopterus annectens* (Poisson Dipneuste). Bull. Inst. Fondam. Afr. Noire sér. A Sci. Natur. *36*:403-406. P:2 8 11

1413 Mohsen, Tahsin, Georgette Jadoun and Hani Lattouf (1974) Effet chronotrope positif de l'acétylcholine sur le coeur isolé de *Protopterus annectens* (Poisson Dipneuste). Bull. Inst. Fondam. Afr. Noire sér. A Sci. Natur. *36*:722-726. P:2 8 11 20

1414 Mohsen, Tahsin, Hani Lattouf and Georgette Jadoun (1974) Variations des effets de l'adrénaline sur le coeur isolé de *Protopterus annectens* (Poisson Dipneuste) selon la dose et selon la phase du cycle biologique de l'animal. C. R. Soc. Biol. Paris *168*:915-919. P:2 8 11 20

1415 Mohsen, Tahsin, P. Anthonioz and Georgette Jadoun (1976) Sur la présence dans le coeur de *Protopterus annectens* (Poisson Dipneuste) de cellules nodales et conductrices histologiquement distinctes des cellules myocardiques ordinaires. C. R. Soc. Biol. Paris *170*:712-715. P:1 5 6 11

1416 Mok, Hin-Kiu (1981) The posterior cardinal veins and kidneys of fishes, with notes on their phylogenetic significance. Jpn. J. Ichthyol. *27*:281-290. LPO:1 11 13 17

1417 Mollier, Siegfried (1894) Die paarigen Extremitäten der Wirbeltiere. I. Das Ichthyopterygium. Anatom. Hefte, Wiesbaden *3*:3-160. (Dipnoi:86-128). ON:1 4 5 6 17

1418 Monod, Olivier, Metin Meshur, Michel Martin, and Maurice Lys (1983) Découverte de Dipneustes triasiques (Ceratodontiformes, Dipnoi) dans la Formation de Cenger ("Arkoses rouges") du Taurus lycien (Turquie occidentale). Géobios #16:161-168. C:4 18

1419 Mookerjee, H. K., D. N. Ganguly, and S. K. Brahma (1954) On the development of the centrum and arches in the Dipnoi, *Protopterus annectens*. Anat. Anz. *100*:217-230. P:1 4 15

1420 Moore, Carolyn M. (1976) A study of the structure of the axial endoskeleton of the limbs of estivated and nonestivated African lungfish, *Protopterus aethiopicus*. Thesis, Supervised Study, Mary Baldwin College, Staunton, Virginia. P:1 4 16 20

1421 Moorhouse, D. E. (1956) Experimental alteration of the peri-renal tissue of *Protopterus*. Quart. J. Microsc. Sci. *97*:519-534. P:1 2 8

1422 Moraes, Sérgio de (1970) A piscicultura e o controle biológico nos arrozais. Lavoura Arrozeira *294*:17-18. OP:21 23

1423 Morescalchi, Alessandro (1970) Karyology and vertebrate phylogeny. Boll. Zool. *37*:1-28. OD:1

1424 Morescalchi, Alessandro (1971) Comparative karyology of the Amphibia. Boll. Zool. *38*:317-320. O(D):1

1425 Morescalchi, Alessandro (1973) Amphibia. In A. B. Chiarelli and Ernesto Capanna (eds): Cytotaxonomy and Vertebrate Evolution. London: Academic Press, pp.233-348. OD:1

1426 Morescalchi, Alessandro (1977) Phylogenetic aspects of karyological evidence. In Max K. Hecht, Peter Charles Goody, and Bessie M. Hecht (eds): Major Patterns in Vertebrate Evolution. New York: Plenum Press, pp.149-167. OD:1

1427 Morris, Charles (1885) On the air-bladder of fishes. Proc. Acad. Natur. Sci. Phil. *1885*:124-135. NLPO:1 10 17

1428 Morris, John (1854) A Catalogue of British Fossils. London: John Morris. (*Ceratodus*:320). OC

1429 Moy-Thomas, James A. (1934) On the teeth of the larval *Belone vulgaris*, and the attachment of teeth in fishes. Quart. J. Microsc. Sci. *76*:481-498. (Dipnoi:492-493). ONL:1 4 15

1430 Moy-Thomas, James A. and Roger S. Miles (1971) Paleozoic Fishes, 2nd edition. Philadelphia: W.B. Saunders Co. (Dipnoi:141-160). FDO(NPL):3 4

1431 Mugaas, J. N., M. C. Khosla, and H. Nishimura (1979) Biochemistry of renin and angiotensin in primitive vertebrates. Fed. Proc. *38*:882. (Abstract) PLO:2 8 11 13

1432 de Muizon, Christian, Mireille Gayet, Alain Lavenu, Larry G. Marshall, Bernard Sigé, and Carlos Villaroel (1983) Late Cretaceous vertebrates, including mammals, from Tiupampa, South central Bolivia. Géobios #16:747-753. OFL:4 18

1433 Müller, Arno Hermann (1966) Lehrbuch der Paläozoologie. Vol. 3, part 1: Fische im weiteren Sinne und Amphibien. Jena: Gustav Fischer. (Dipnoi:380-397). FDC(NPL):1 3 10 12 18 20 21

1434 Müller, Johannes (1840) Berichte über die Fortschritte der vergleichenden Anatomie im Jahre 1839. Arch. Anat. Physiol., *1840*:CLIX-CXCVIII. LPO:G(1 4 6 9 10 12 22)

1435 Müller, Johannes (1844) *Lepidosiren annectens* oder *Rhinocryptis amphibius*. Ber. K.-Preuss. Akad. Wiss. Berlin *1844*:411-414. P(L):1 4 18

1436 Müller, Johannes (1844) Über den Bau und die Grenzen der Ganoiden. Ber. Akad. Wiss. Berlin *1844*:67-85. O(L):1

1437 Müller, Johannes (1845) Mémoire sur les Ganoïdes et sur la classification naturelle des Poissons. Ann. Sci. Natur. *4*:5-53. O(L):1

1438 Müller, Johannes (1845) Über den Bau und die Grenzen der Ganoiden, und über das natürliche System der Fische. Archiv Naturgeschichte *1845*:91-142. D

1439 Muller, R. G. and R. S. Benda (1981) Comparison of bottom trawl stock densities in the inner Kavirondo Gulf of Lake Victoria. J. Fish. Biol. *19*:399-401. PO:23

1440 Munk, Ole (1964) The eye of *Calamoichthys calabaricus* Smith, 1865 (Polypteridae, Pisces) compared with the eye of other fishes. Vidensk. Medd. Dansk Naturhist. Foren. Kjobenhavn *127*:113-126. (*Protopterus*:118-120). OP(LN):1 6 7

1441 Munk, Ole (1969) On the visual cells of some primitive fishes with particular regard to the classification of rods and cones. Vidensk. Medd. Dansk Naturhist. Foren. Kjobenhavn *132*:25-30. NPLO:1 7 17

1442 Munro, Ian S. R. (1956) Handbook of Australian

fishes. Aust. Fish. Newsl. *15*:15-18. ON:G(1 3 4 15 18 21)

1443　Murray, J. A. (1906) Zahl und Grössenverhält-nisse der Chromosomen bei *Lepidosiren paradoxa* Fitz. Anat. Anz. *29*:203-208. L:1

1444　Musisi, L. M. (1977) Studies on the feeding biology and digestive system of the East African Lungfish, *Protopterus aethiopicus* (Heckel). MSc. Thesis, Maker-ere University, Kampala, Uganda. (Abstract) P*:1 2 12 16 21 22 23

1445　Nair, M. G. K. (1969) The cardiac conducting sys-tem of the lungfish, *Protopterus aethiopicus*. Proc. In-dian Sci. Congr. Assoc. *56*:500. (Abstract) P:1 5 6 11

1446　Nair, M. G. K. (1976) Some observations on the anatomy of the heart of the African lung fish, *Protop-terus aethiopicus* Heckel. Proc. Indian Acad. Sci. *84B*:6-11. P(NL):1 5 6 11

1447　Natterer, Johann (1837) *Lepidosiren paradoxa*, eine neue Gattung aus der Familie der fischähnlichen Reptilien. Ann. Wien Mus. *II*:165-170. Summary in Isis *1838*:346-347. L:1 3 4 7 18 21 24

1448　Negus, Victor Ewings (1932) Studies of the larynx of Dipnoi or lung fish; and evidence derived therefrom concerning laryngeal paralysis in man. Acta Oto-Lar-yngol. *17*:261-274. PL:1 5 9 10 17

1449　Nelson, Gareth J. (1969) Gill arches and the phy-logeny of fishes, with notes on the classification of vertebrates. Bull. Amer. Mus. Natur. Hist. *141*:475-552. DNO:1 4 17

1450　Neumayer, Ludwig (1903) Die Entwickelung des Darmkanales von *Ceratodus forsteri*. Anat. Anz. *23*, Ergh.:139-142. Or: Verh. Anat. Ges. *17*:139-142.N:12 15

1451　Neumayer, Ludwig (1904) Recherches sur le dével-oppement du foie, du pancréas et de la rate chez *Cera-todus*. C. R. Assoc. Anat. (Toulouse) Nancy, *6*:73-77. N:11 12 15

1452　Neumayer, Ludwig (1904) Die Entwickelung des Darmkanales, Lunge, Leber, Milz und Pankreas bei *Ceratodus forsteri*. Denkschr. Med.- Naturwiss. Ges. Jena *4*:377-422. N:10 11 12 15

1453　Neurath, Hans and K. A. Walsh (1970) Evolution-ary interrelationships of proteolytic enzymes as a tool for probing internal structure. Symp. Int. Congr. Biochem. *8*:68-70. (Abstract) OP:2 17

1454　Newberry, John Strong (1875) Descriptions of fos-sil fishes. Rep. Geol. Surv. Ohio, Paleontol. *2*:3-64. (*Protopterus*:24-27). FD(P):G(19 20 21)

1455　Newman, Edward (1856) Note on *Lepidosiren an-nectens* Owen. Proc. Linnean Soc. London *1*:73-74. P:1 3 4 7 17

1456　Newman, Edward (1859) Is the mud-fish a fish or an amphibian? Zoologist *17*:6450-6461. PL:1 10 19 22

1457　Newman, Edward (1872) The Barramunda, a new ganoid fish from Queensland. Zoologist *7*:3188-3189. N:18

1458　Nichols, John Treadwell and Ludlow Griscom (1917) Fresh-water fishes of the Congo Basin obtained by the American Museum Congo Expedition, 1909-1915. Bull. Amer. Mus. Natur. Hist. *37*:653-756. (*Pro-topterus*:665). OP:1 18 19 20

1459　Nicklanovich, Michael D. (1973) An augury of lungfish guts. In From Cell to Philosopher. Englewood Cliffs: Prentice-Hall, Inc., pp.541-544. O

1460　Nicoll, Charles S. and Howard A. Bern (1965) Pi-geon crop-stimulating activity (prolactin) in the ade-nohypophysis of lungfish and tetrapods. Endocrinology *76*:156-160. PO:2 8 17

1461　Nicoll, Charles S., Howard A. Bern, and Donna Brown (1966) Occurrence of mammotrophic activity (prolactin) in the vertebrate adenohypophysis. J. En-docrinol. *34*:343-354. OP:2 8 17

1462　Nicoll, Charles S. and Howard A. Bern (1968) Fur-ther analysis of the occurrence of pigeon crop sac-stim-ulating activity (prolactin) in the vertebrate adenohypophysis. Gen. Comp. Endocrinol. *11*:5-20. OP:2 8 17

1463　Nieuwenhuys, Rudolf and Marion Hickey (1965) A survey of the forebrain of the Australian lungfish *Neoceratodus forsteri*. J. Hirnforsch. 7:433-452. N:1 6

1464　Nieuwenhuys, Rudolf (1967) Comparative anat-omy of the cerebellum. In C. A. Fox and R. S. Snider (eds): Progress In Brain Research. New York: Ameri-can Elsevier Publishing Co., Inc., *25*:1-93. OPN:1 6

1465　Nieuwenhuys, Rudolf (1969) A survey of the struc-ture of the forebrain in higher bony fishes (Oste-ichthyes). Ann. New York Acad. Sci. *167*:31-64. (*Neocer-atodus* and *Protopterus*:46-54). ONP(L):1 6

1466　Nieuwenhuys, Rudolf (1974) Topological analysis of the brain stem: a general introduction. J. Comp. Neurol. *156*:255-276. LO:1 6

1467　Nieuwenhuys, Rudolf (1975) The fundamental morphological pattern of the brain stem. Exp. Brain Res. *23*(Suppl.):149. (Abstract) LO:1 6

1468　Nieuwenhuys, Rudolf (1979) Topological analysis of the brain stem of the lungfish *Lepidosiren paradoxa*. J. Comp. Neurol. *187*:589-611. L:1 6

1469　Nigrelli, Ross F. and Sophie Jakowska (1953) Spontaneous neoplasms in fishes. VII. A spermatocy-toma and renal melanoma in an African lungfish, *Pro-topterus annectens* (Owen). Zoologica (New York) *38*:109-112. Cancer Res. *12*:286. (Abstract) P:1 13 14 22

1470　Nikolsky, Georgii Vasil'evich (1963) The Ecology of Fishes. Translated by L. Birkett. New York: Aca-demic Press, Inc. OP:21

1471　Nishimura, Hiroko, Mizuho Ogawa, and Wilbur Sawyer (1973) Renin-angiotensin system in primitive bony fishes and a holocephalian. Amer. J. Physiol. *224*:950-956. Fed. Proc. *31*:381. [1972]. (Abstract) PLO:2 11 13 17

1472　Nishimura, Hiroko and Mizuho Ogawa (1973) The renin-angiotensin system in fishes. Amer. Zool. *13*:823-838. PLO:2 11 13 17

1473　Nishimura, Hiroko (1978) Physiological evolution of the renin-angiotensin system. Jap. Heart J. *5*:806-822. PNO:2 11 13 17

1474　Noakes, David L. G. (1980) Comparative aspects of behavioral ontogeny: a philosophy from fishes. In Klaus Immelmann, George W. Barlow, Lewis Petri-novitch and Mary Main (eds): Behavioral Develop-ment: The Bielefeld Interdisciplinary Project. London: Cambridge Univ. Press, pp.490-508. Translated as Ver-haltensentwicklung bei Mensch und Tier: das Biele-feld Projekt. Berlin: Verlag Paul Parey. [1982] OD:15 19

1475　Norman, John Roxborough (1945) A Draft Synop-sis of the Orders, Families and Genera of Recent Fishes and Fish-like Vertebrates. London: British Museum of Natural History. (Dipnoi:605-606). PLNFD

1476 Norman, John Roxborough and P. Humphrey Greenwood (1963) A History of Fishes. New York: Hill and Wang, Inc. ONPLFD:G(1 4 18)

1477 Northcutt, Richard Glenn and Timothy J. Neary (1975) Observations on the optic tectum of the coelacanth, *Latimeria chalumnae*. Amer. Zool. *15*:806. (Abstract) O(N):1 6

1478 Northcutt, Richard Glenn (1977) Retinofugal projections in the lepidosirenid lungfishes. J. Comp. Neurol. *174*:553-574. PL:1 6 7 17

1479 Northcutt, Richard Glenn, Timothy J. Neary, and David G. Senn (1978) Observations on the brain of the coelacanth *Latimeria chalumnae*: external anatomy and quantitative analysis. J. Morphol. *155*:181-192. O(L):1 67

1480 Northcutt, Richard Glenn (1980) Retinal projections in the Australian lungfish. Brain Res. *185*:85-90. N(PL):1 6 7

1481 Novitskaya, L. I. (1971) O diagnosticheskoy otsenke ornamenta beschelyustnykh i ryb. (Diagnostic evaluation of the ornamentation of Agnatha and Pisces). Paleontol. Zh. #4:82-96. Translation in Paleontol. J. 5:494-506. O(FD): 1 3 4

1482 Novitskaya, L. I. and N. I. Krupina (1985) Ethmoids of Paleozoic Dipnoi. Paleontol. Zh. *1985*:92. [in Russian]. FD+:4

1483 Ochev, V. G. and B. N. Smagin (1974) O mestonakhozhdeniyakh Triasovykh pozvonochnykh u Ozera Inder. (Occurrence of Triassic vertebrates near Lake Inder). Mosk. O-vo. Ispyt. Prir. Byull. Otd. Geol. *49*:74-81. OFD+:18

1484 O'Connor, D. (1896) On the redistribution of *Ceratodus*. Proc. Roy. Soc. Queensland *11*:ii and xvi. N:18

1485 O'Connor, D. (1897) Report on preservation of *Ceratodus*. Proc. Roy. Soc. Queensland *12*:101-102. N:18

1486 O'Connor, D. (1898) Letter read on biology of *Ceratodus forsteri*. Proc. Zool. Soc. London *1898*:492-493. N:18 21

1487 O'Connor, D. (1898) Report of live *Ceratodus forsteri*. Proc. Zool. Soc. London *1898*:586. N

1488 O'Connor, D. (1899) On a shipment of *Ceratodus* to England. Proc. Roy. Soc. Queensland *14*:iv. N

1489 O'Connor, D. (1902) On *Ceratodus*. Brisbane Courrier, July 26, *1902*:11. N:16 18

1490 O'Connor, D. (1910) Notes on the *Ceratodus*. Rep. Aust. Assoc. Advan. Sci. *12*:383-384. N:4 18 19 20

1491 Oduleye, S. O. (1977) Unidirectional water and sodium fluxes and respiratory metabolism in the African lung-fish, *Protopterus annectens*. J. Comp. Physiol. *119B*:127-139. P:2 9 10

1492 Oertle, G. F. (1928) Das Vorkommen von Fischen in der Trias Württembergs. Neues Jahrb. Min. Geol. Paläontol. Stuttgart B *60*:325-472. (*Ceratodus*:347-357). CO:4 18

1493 Ogilby, J. Douglas (1912) On some Queensland fishes. Mem. Queensl. Mus. *1*:26-65. (*Neoceratodus*:65). ON:1 3 18

1494 Ogilby, J. Douglas (1915) An essay. In The Commercial Fishes and Fisheries of Queensland. Brisbane: Government Printer pp.1-61.NO:G(18)

1495 Ogilby, J. Douglas (1918) Ichthylogical notes (No. 4). Mem. Queensl. Mus. *6*:97-105. (*Neoceratodus*:103-104). NO:18

1496 Oguro, C. and Peter K. T. Pang (1974) Endocrine control of calcium regulation in lower vertebrates. Amer. Zool. *14*:1295. (Abstract) LO:2 8 12

1497 Ohno, Susumu and N. B. Atkin (1966) Comparative DNA values and chromosome complements of eight species of fishes. Chromosoma (Berlin) *18*:455-466. LO:1

1498 Ohno, Susumu (1970) Evolution by Gene Duplication. New York: Springer-Verlag, Inc. OL:1 17

1499 Okedi, John (1970) Maturity, sex ratio and fecundity of the lung fish (*Protopterus aethiopicus* Heckel) from Lake Victoria. Rep. E. Afr. Freshw. Fish. Res. Org. *1970*:17–20. P:1 14 16

1500 Oken, Laurent (1838) Über *Lepidosiren paradoxa*. Isis *1838*:346-347. L:1

1501 Oken, Laurent (1841) Über *Lepidosiren paradoxa*. Isis *1841*:462-469. L:1 4 9 17

1502 Oken, Laurent (1843) R. Owen: Beschreibung der *Lepidosiren annectens*. Isis *1843*:440-444. P(L):1 3 4 6 11 14

1503 Okuno, R. (1961) '*Epiceratodus*', the Australian lungfish. Nature Study 7:64-67. [in Japanese]. N(PLO):G(1 10 17) See also K. Inoue, Umi to Shizoku, II:5.

1504 Okuno, R. (1962) A story of the lungfishes. Umi to Shizoku, The Sea and its Inhabitants, *III*:2-4, 7. [in Japanese]. LPN:G(1 10 17 20)

1505 Oldham, Thomas (1859) On some fossil fish-teeth of the genus *Ceratodus*, from Maledi, South of Nagpur. Mem. Geol. Surv. India *1*:295-309. C:1 4 12 18

1506 Olivereau, Madeleine (1959) Anatomie et histologie de la glande thyroïde chez *Protopterus aethiopicus* Heckel et *Protopterus annectens* Owen. Acta Anat. *36*:77-92. P:1 8 17

1507 Olson, Everett Claire (1946) Fresh- and brackish-water vertebrate-bearing deposits of the Pennsylvanian of Illinois. J. Geol. *54*:281-305. OFD:4 18

1508 Olson, Everett Claire (1951) Fauna of upper Vale and Choza: 1-5. Fieldiana Geol. *10*:89-128. (Dipnoi:104-124). OFD(PL):1 4 18

1508A Olson, Everett Claire (1952) The evolution of a Permian vertebrate chronofauna. Evolution 6:181-196.

1509 Olson, Everett Claire (1958) Fauna of the Vale and Choza: 14: Summary, review, and integration of the geology and the faunas. Fieldiana Geol. *10*:397-448. OFD:18

1510 Olson, Everett Claire and Peter Paul Vaughn (1970) The changes of terrestrial vertebrates and climates during the Permian of North America. Forma Functio 3:113-138. FDC:18 20

1510A Olson, Everett Claire (1971) Vertebrate Paleozoology. New York: Wiley Interscience. (Dipnoi:243-249; 581-585).

1511 Olson, Everett Claire and Eleanor Daly (1972) Notes on *Gnathorhiza* (Osteichthyes, Dipnoi). J. Paleontol. *46*:371-376. FD:1 4 18

1512 Olson, Everett Claire and Kathryn Bolles (1975) Permo-Carboniferous fresh water burrows. Fieldiana Geol. *33*:271-290. OFD(P):20

1513 Ono, R. Dana (1982) Dual motor innervation in the axial musculature of fishes. J. Fish Biol., 22:395-408. OD:5 6 17

1514 Oordt, P. G. W. J. van and T. Kerr (1967) Comparative morphology of the pituitary in the lungfish, *Protopterus aethiopicus*. J. Endocrinol. 37:viii-ix. P:1 8

1515 Orbigny, Charles d' (1846) Dictionnaire Universel d'Histoire Naturelle. Paris: Renard, Martinet and Co. (*Lepidosiren*:301-303). OL(P):G(1 3 4 7 9)

1516 Orsini, J. C. and Mireille Dupé (1971) Le potentiel évoqué à la surface du bulbe olfactif d'un Dipneuste et ses variations avec le mode de vie. C. R. Soc. Biol. Paris 165:1942-1945. P:6 7 8 20

1517 Orton, Grace L. (1954) Original adaptive significance of the tetrapod limb. Science (Washington) 120:1042-1043. OPF:4 17 19 20

1518 Ørvig, Tor (1957) Remarks on the vertebrate fauna of the Lower Upper Devonian of Escuminac Bay, P. Q., Canada, with special reference to the porolepiform Crossopterygians. Ark. Zool. 10:367-426. OFD:1 3 17

1519 Ørvig, Tor (1961) New finds of Acanthodians, Arthrodires, Crossopterygians, Ganoids and Dipnoans in the Upper Middle Devonian Calcareous Flags (Oberer Plattenkalk) of the Bergish Gladbach-Paffrath Trough. Paläontol. Z. 35:10-27. FDO:1 4 7

1520 Ørvig, Tor (1967) Phylogeny of tooth tissues: evolution of some calcified tissues in early vertebrates. In Albert Edward William Miles (ed): Structural and Chemical Organization of Teeth. New York: Academic Press, 1:45-110. O(PN):1 4 17

1521 Ørvig, Tor, ed. (1968) Current Problems of Lower Vertebrate Phylogeny. Nobel Symposium 4. Stockholm: Almqvist and Wiksell.

1522 Ørvig, Tor (1969) Cosmine and cosmine growth. Lethaia 2:241-260. FDO:1 3 16

1523 Ørvig, Tor (1971) Comments on the lateral line system of some brachythoracid and ptyctodontid arthrodires. Zool. Scripta 1:5-35.O(P):1 7 15

1524 Ørvig, Tor (1976) Palaeohistological notes. 4. The interpretation of osteodentine, with remarks on the dentition in the Devonian dipnoan *Griphognathus*. Zool. Scripta 5:79-96. PNFDO:1 4 15

1525 Osborn, Henry Fairfield (1889) A contribution to the internal structure of the amphibian brain. J. Morphol. 2:51-96. O(PN):1 6

1526 Ostrom, John H. (1970) Stratigraphy and paleontology of the Cloverly Formation (Lower Cretaceous) of the Bighorn Basin area, Wyoming and Montana. Peabody Mus. Natur. Hist. Yale Univ. Bull. #35:1-234. (*Ceratodus*:53-55). OC:4 18

1527 Owen, Richard (1839) A new species of the genus *Lepidosiren*. Proc. Linnean Soc. London 1:27-32. Summary In Isis 1839:604-607. Summarized in French in Ann. Sci. Natur. (Zool.) 11:371-378. P:1 4 5 6 11 12 13 14

1528 Owen, Richard (1840) Odontography. London: Hippolyte Bailliere 1840-1845. (*Protopterus*:166-170). OP:1 4

1529 Owen, Richard (1841) Description of the *Lepidosiren annectens*. Trans. Linnean Soc. London 18:327-361. Summary in Isis 1843:440-444. P:1 3 4 5 67 9 10 11 12 13 14

1530 Owen, Richard (1841) On the microscopic structure of the teeth of *Lepidosiren annectens*. Ann. Mag. Natur. Hist. 7:211-212. P:1 4

1531 Owen, Richard (1853) Descriptive Catalogue of the Osteological Series contained in the Museum of the Royal College of Surgeons of England 1:85-89. London: Taylor and Francis. OP:1 4 7

1532 Owen, Richard (1858) Professor Owen's Lectures on Palaeontology. Ann. Mag. Natur. Hist. 1:317-320. OL:4 17

1533 Owen, Richard (1859) Descriptive Catalogue of the Specimens of Natural History in Spirit contained in the Museum of the Royal College of Surgeons of England. Vertebrata. London: Taylor and Francis. (Dipnoi:57-58). OP:1 18 20

1534 Owen, Richard (1866) On the Anatomy of Vertebrates. London: Longman, Green and Co. Review in J. Anat. Physiol. 1:120-141. OD:1

1535 Owen, Richard (1882) On the homology of the co-nario-hypophysial tract, or the so-called pineal and pituitary glands. J. Linnean Soc. London 16:131-149. OP:1 8

1536 Özeti, Neclâ (1971) Amphibia'nin kökeni ve omurgalilarin sudan karaya geçisi. (Origin of Amphibia and their transition from water to land). Turk. Biol. Derg. 21:91-105. [in Turkish]. PLFDO:1 4 17

1537 Ozon, R. (1966) Isolement et identification de stéroïdes chez les Vertébrés inférieurs et les Oiseaux. Ann. Biol. anim. Biochim. Biophys. 6:537-551. PO:2 8 14

1538 Pack, Allen I., Raymond J. Galante and Alfred P. Fishman (1984) Breuer-Hering reflexes in the African lungfish (*Protopterus annectens*). Fed. Proc. 43:433. (Abstract) P:6 10 19

1539 Packard, Gary C. (1974) The evolution of air-breathing in Paleozoic gnathostome fishes. Evolution 28:320-325. FDNO:10 13 17 18

1540 Packard, Gary C. (1976) Devonian amphibians: did they excrete carbon dioxide via skin, gills, or lungs? Evolution 30:270-280. O(NLP):2 9 10 11

1541 Padoa, E. (1929) Ghiandole pluricellulari ed organi di senso cutanei in *Protopterus annectens* Ow. Monit. Zool. Ital. 40:270-277. P:1 3 6 7

1542 Palissa, Alfred (1971) Zur vergleichenden Ökophysiologie der Atmung. Biol. Rundsch. 9:345-366. OP:2 9 10 11

1543 Palmen, Johan Axel (1898) Lungfisken, *Protopterus annectens*. Medd. Soc. Fauna Flora Fenn. 24:66. P

1544 Panchen, Alec L. (1967) The nostrils of choanate fishes and early tetrapods. Biol. Rev. (Cambridge) 42:374-420. PLNOFD:1 4 7 9 17

1545 Panchen, Alec L. (1980) The Terrestrial Environment and the Origin of Land Vertebrates. The Systematics Assoc. Spec. Vol. #15. New York: Academic Press.

1546 Pander, Christian Heinrich (1858) Über die Ctenodipterinen des Devonischen Systems. (Monographie) St. Petersburg. Kais. Akad. Wiss. 8:1-53. FD:3 4

1547 Pang, Peter K. T. (1971) Calcitonin and ultimobranchial glands in fishes. J. Exp. Zool. 178:89-100. NO:2 8 11

1548 Pang, Peter K. T., Nancy B. Clark, and Keith Stewart Thomson (1971) Hypocalcemic activities in the ultimobranchial bodies of lungfishes, *Neoceratodus forsteri* and *Lepidosiren paradoxa* and teleosts, *Fundulus heteroclitus* and *Gadus morhua*. Gen. Comp. Endocrinol. 17:582-585. NLO:2 8

1549 Pang, Peter K. T., Wilbur H. Sawyer, and C. Casals (1974) Circulating levels of arginine vasotocin (AVT) in lower vertebrates. Amer. Zool. 14:1244. (Abstract) LO:2 8 13

1550 Pang, Peter K. T. and Wilbur H. Sawyer (1975) Parathyroid hormone preparations, salmon calcitonin, and urine flow in the South American lungfish, *Lepidosiren paradoxa*. J. Exp. Zool. *193*:407-412.L:2 8 11 13

1551 Pang, Peter K. T. (1977) Osmoregulatory functions of neurohypophysial hormones in fishes and amphibians. Amer. Zool. *17*:739-749. OPLN:2 8 11 13

1552 Pang, Peter K. T., May Yang, Chitaru Oguro, John G. Phillips, and John A. Yee (1980) Hypotensive actions of parathyroid hormone preparations in vertebrates. Gen. Comp. Endocrinol. *41*:135-138. LO:2 8 11

1553 Pang, Peter K. T., M. C. M. Yang, A. D. Kenny, and T. E. Turner, Jr. (1982) Structure and vascular activity relationship of parathyroid hormone and some hypotensive peptides. Clin. Exp. Hypertens. *4*:189-199. O(L):2 8 13

1554 Pang, Peter K. T. (1983) Evolution of control of epithelial transport in vertebrates. J. Exp. Biol. *106*:283-299. O(D):2 8 11 15 17

1555 Pang, Peter K. T., Philip B. Furspan, and Wilbur H. Sawyer (1983) Evolution of neurohypophyseal hormone actions in vertebrates. Amer. Zool. *23*:655-662. ODL:2 8 11 13 17

1556 Parker, William Kitchen (1879) On the structure and development of the skull in the urodelous Amphibia. J. Linnean Soc. London *14*:717-719. O(NL):1 4 7 15

1557 Parker, William Newton (1888) Preliminary note on the anatomy and physiology of *Protopterus annectens*. Nature (London) *39*:19-21. Amer. Natur. *23*:57-58. [1889]. (Abstract) P:1 4 5 8 9 10 11 12 13 14 16 20

1558 Parker, William Newton (1888) On the African Mudfish (*Protopterus annectens*). Trans. Cardiff Natur. Soc. *20*:69-77. P(LN):1 3 10 11 16 19 20 21

1559 Parker, William Newton (1889) Zur Anatomie und Physiologie von *Protopterus annectens*. Ber. Naturforsch. Ges. Freiburg Breisgau *4*:83-108. P:1 3 5 6 7 10 11 12 13 14

1560 Parker, William Newton (1889) On the occasional persistence of the left posterior cardinal vein in the frog, with remarks on the homologies of the veins in the Dipnoi. Proc. Zool. Soc. London *1889*:145-151. OP:1 11 17

1561 Parker, William Newton (1891) On the anatomy and physiology of *Protopterus annectens*. Proc. Roy. Soc. London *39*:549-554. P:1 3 4 5 6 8 11 12 13 14 18 19 20

1562 Parker, William Newton (1892) On the anatomy and physiology of *Protopterus annectens*. Trans. Roy. Irish Acad. *30*:109-216. P:1 3 4 5 6 7 8 10 11 12 13 14 18 19 20

1563 Parkinson, James (1811) *Trionyx* Parkinson. In Organic Remains of a Former World: an Examination of the Mineralized Remains of the Vegetables and Animals of the Antediluvian World, Generally Termed Extraneous Fossils. *3*:269. London: Sherwood, Neely and Jones, Paternoster-Row. O(C):4

1564 Parrish, J. Michael and Robert A. Long (1983) Vertebrate paleoecology of the Late Triassic Chinle Formation, Petrified Forest and vicinity, Arizona. Geol. Soc. Amer. *15*:285. (Abstract) OC:18

1565 Parsons, C. W. (1935) Breeding in captivity of the South American lung-fish. Nature (London) *136*:954. L:14

1566 Pascual, Rosendo and Pedro Bondesío (1976) Notas sobre Vertebrados de la Frontera Cretácica-Terciaria. III: Ceratodontidae (Peces Osteichthyes, Dipnoi) de la Formación Coli-Toro y de otras unidades del Cretacio Tardío de Patagonia y sur de Mendoza. Sus implicancias paleobiogeográficas. VI Congr. Geol. Argent. *1*:565-577. C:4 18

1567 Pasteels, J., Paul Brien, and Jean Bouillon (1961) Gastrulation chez *Protopterus dolloi* Boulenger. C. R. Assoc. Anatomists, 47ième Réunion (Naples), Bull. Assoc. Anat. *110*:610-613. P:1 15

1568 Pasteels, J. (1962) Gastrulation du *Protopterus dolloi* Blgr. Ann. Mus. Roy. Afr. Cent. sér. Quarto Zool. *108*:173-184. P:1 15

1569 Patterson, Colin (1975) The distribution of Mesozoic freshwater fishes. Mem. Mus. Natl. Hist. Natur. Paris Zool. *88A*:156-174. OC(PLN):18

1570 Patterson, Colin (1980) Origin of tetrapods: historical introduction to the problem. In Alec L. Panchen (ed): The Terrestrial Environment and the Origin of Land Vertebrates. London: Academic Press, pp.159-175. LPNO:1 17

1571 Pattle, R. E. (1973) Inter-species differences in surface properties of the lung. Proc. Roy. Soc. Med. *66*:385-386. PLO:1 2 10 17

1572 Pattle, R. E. (1976) The lung surfactant in the evolutionary tree. In George M. Hughes (ed): Respiration of Amphibious Vertebrates. New York: Academic Press, pp.233-256. OPLN:1 2 10

1573 Paulson, O. (1865) Die Epidermis von *Protopterus annectens*. Bull. Acad. St. Petersbourg *8*:141-145. P:1 3 6 20

1574 Payne, A. I. (1974) Some characteristics of the fish fauna of a dam in the Lake Victoria region of Tanzania including the effects of multispecific stocking with *Tilapia* species. Afr. J. Trop. Hydrobiol. Fisheries *3*:111-222. O(P):21

1575 Pedersen, Roger Arnold (1969) Ribosomal gene multiplicity and DNA content in vertebrates. Amer. Zool. *9*:607. (Abstract) NO:1 2

1576 Pedersen, Roger Arnold (1971) Specific gene multiplicity in evolution and development. Diss. Abstr. Int. B Sci. Eng. *31*:5814. (Abstract) NO:1 2

1577 Pedersen, Roger Arnold (1971) DNA content, ribosomal gene multiplicity, and cell size in fish. J. Exp. Zool. *177*:65-78. PLNO:1 2 17

1578 Pedler, C. (1969) Rods and cones - a new approach. Int. Rev. Gen. Exp. Zool. *4*:219-274. (*Protopterus*:237). OP:1 7

1579 Pegueta, V. P. (1968) Razvitie zameshchaiushchikh kostei u sovremennykh anamnia v ontogeneze. (Development of "substituting bones" in contemporary anamniotes). Akad. Med. Nauk SSSR Inst. Gerontol. Kiev *1968*:72-73. DO:4

1580 Pegueta, V. P. (1968) Dokazana li poteria enkhondral'noi ossifikatsii v filogeneze nizshikh posvonochnykh? (Is the loss of endochondral ossification indicated in the phylogeny of lower vertebrates?). Akad. Nauk Ukr. SSR Biol. Zool. Cytol. *1968*:99-101. OD:4 17

1581 Péguéta, V. P. (1969) La microstructure des os cartilagineux chez Dipneustes actuels. Résumé des Communications et Démonstrations Présentées au Cours de la 54e Réunion de l'Association des Anatomistes, Sofia, Avril, 1969. (Abstract) LPN:1 4 16

1582 Pegueta, V. P. (1974) Do pytannya pro polozhennya v systemi ryb dvoyakodykhayuchykh ta khryashchovykh ganoyidiv. (The problem of the position of Dipnoi and Chondrostei in the system of fishes). Dopov. Akad. Nauk Ukr. Rsr. ser. B Geol. Geofix. Khim. Biol. *36*:940-942. D:1 17

1583 Pehrson, Torsten (1949) The ontogeny of the lateral line system in the head of dipnoans. Acta Zool. (Stockholm) *30*:153-182. PN:1 7 15

1584 Pellegrin, Jacques (1904) Poissons du Chari et du

Lac Tchad, récoltés par la Mission Chevalier-Decorse. Bull. Mus. Natl. Hist. Natur. Paris *10*:309-316. OP:18

1585 Pellegrin, Jacques (1904) Mission scientifique de Ch. Alluaud en Afrique Orientale (Juin 1903-Mai 1904). Poissons. II. Systématique. Mem. Soc. Zool. Fr. *17*:174-185. OP:18

1586 Pellegrin, Jacques (1907) Les Poissons du Lac Tchad. Rev. Sci. Paris 7:614-618. OP:18 20 24

1587 Pellegrin, Jacques (1919) Poissons du Gribingui recueillis par M. Baudon. Description de sept espèces nouvelles. Bull. Soc. Zool. Fr. *44*:201-214. OP:18

1588 Pellegrin, Jacques (1923) Les Poissons des Eaux Douces de l'Afrique Occidentale. Paris: Émile Larose, Libraire-éditeur. (*Protopterus*:40-41). OP:1 18

1589 Pellegrin, Jacques (1928) Poissons du Chiloango et du Congo recueillis par l'expédition du Dr. H. Schouteden (1920-22). Ann. Mus. Congo Belge, sér. 1 Zool. *3*:1-50. (*Protopterus*:5). OP:18

1590 Percival, A. Blayney (1919) Death of the lung fish. J. East Afr. Uganda Natur. Hist. Soc. *15*:495-496. P:18 19 20 21

1591 Percy, H. E., Richard C. Percy, and M. W. Ridley (1953) An expedition to the Tana River, Kenya Colony. Oryx *2*:110-119. OP:18

1592 Percy, Richard C., H. E. Percy, and M. W. Ridley (1953) The water-holes at Ijara, Northern Province, Kenya. J. East Afr. Natur. Hist. Soc. *22*:2-14. PO:1 16 18 21

1593 Percy, Richard C. (1962) The post-notochordal tail in Dipnoi and Urodela. Trans. Zool. Soc. London *29*:357-390. PO:1 4 5 6 15

1594 Pérez-Gonzales, Maria Dolores and C. N. Grinkraut (1963) Estudo comparativo do comportamento e do metabolismo respiratório de peixes de respiração aérea. Ciênc. Cult. (São Paulo) *15*:279-280. (Abstract) LO:2 10 18 19 20

1595 Pérez-Gonzales, Maria Dolores and C. N. Grinkraut (1971) Comportamento e metabolismo respiratório da *Lepidosiren paradoxa* durante a vida aquática o em estivação. Bol. Zool. Biol. Marinha N.S. (São Paulo) #28:137-164. Ciênc. Cult. (São Paulo) *20*:393-394. [1968]. (Abstract) L:2 9 10 18 19 20 21

1596 Perkins, Philip Lawrence (1971) The dipnoan fish *Dipterus* from the Middle Devonian (Givetian) of Alaska. J. Paleontol. *45*:554-555. FD:18

1597 Perkins, Philip Lawrence (1973) Mandibular mechanics and feeding groups in the Dipnoi. Diss. Abstr. Int. *34B*:335-336. (Abstract) NPLFD:4 19 21

1598 Pernkopf, Eduard and Joseph Lehner (1937) III. Vorderdarm. A. Vergleichende Beschreibung des Vorderdarmes bei den einzelnen Klassen der Kranioten. In Louis Bolk, Ernest Göppert, Erich Kallius, and Wilhelm Lubosch (eds): Handbuch der vergleichenden Anatomie der Wirbeltiere. Berlin and Wien: Urban and Schwarzenberg, *III*:349-476. (Dipnoi: 368-371). OPNL:1 12

1599 Perret, Auguste (1900) Les Dipneustes. Rev. Scien. *13*:786-788. PLN(FD):1 3 6 9 12 18 20 21

1600 Peters, Wilhelm Carl Hartwig (1845) Über einen dem *Lepidosiren annectens* verwandten Fisch von Quellimane. Arch. Anat. Physiol. *1845*:1-14. Summary in Ann. Mag. Natur. Hist. *16*:348-350. P(L):1 3 4 9 11 12 18 19 20

1601 Peters, Wilhelm Carl Hartwig (1866) Über die systematische Stellung der Lepidosirenen. Ber. K.-Preuss. Akad. Wiss. Berlin 1866:12-13. Summary in Ann. Mag. Natur. Hist. *17*:473. PL:1 4 9 17

1602 Peters, Wilhelm Carl Hartwig (1868) Reise nach Mossambique. Berlin: Georg Reimer, pp.1-116 (Dipnoi:1-6). OP:1 3 4 13 14 18 20 24

1603 Peters, Wilhelm Carl Hartwig (1870) Über *Ceratodus forsteri* Krefft. Sber. Ges. Naturforsch. Fr. Berlin *1870*:29. N:1 3

1604 Petit, G. (1936) Remarques sur la répartition géographique des Dipneustes. C. R. Som. Séances Soc. Biogeog. *13*:42-46. PLN:1 17 18

1605 Pettit, Auguste (1896) Remarques anatomiques et physiologiques sur les capsules surrénales des Téléostéens et des Dipnoïques. Bull. Mus. Hist. Natur. *1896*:19-22. PO:1 8

1606 Pettit, Michael J. and Thomas L. Beitinger (1980) Thermal responses of the South American lungfish, *Lepidosiren paradoxa*. Copeia *1980*:130-136. L:2 18

1607 Peyer, Bernhard (1917) Über rezente und triassische Gebisse von Ceratodontidae. II. Das Gebiss von *Ceratodus parvus* Ag. nebst Beiträgen zur Kenntnis triassischer Ceratodontiden. Z. Dtsch. Geol. Ges. *69*:18-79. C:1 4 16 18

1608 Peyer, Bernhard (1925) Ergebnisse der Forschungsreisen Prof. E. Stromers in den Wüsten Ägyptens. II. Wirbeltier-Reste der Baharîje-Stufe (unterstes Cenoman).6. Die *Ceratodus*-Funde. Abh. Bayer. Akad. Wiss. München *30*:1-22. C:1 4 18

1609 Peyer, Bernhard (1931) Hartgebilde des Integumentes. IN Louis Bolk, Ernest Göppert, Erich Kallius, and Wilhelm Lubosch (eds): Handbuch der vergleichenden Anatomie der Wirbeltiere. Berlin and Wien: Urban und Schwarzenberg, *I*:703-752. ON:3

1610 Peyer, Bernhard (1937) Zähne und Gebiss. In Louis Bolk, Ernest Göppert, Erich Kallius, and Wilhelm Lubosch (eds): Handbuch der vergleichenden Anatomie der Wirbeltiere. Berlin and Wien: Urban und Schwarzenberg, *III*:49-114. (Dipnoi:73-75). ONC:1 4

1611 Peyer, Bernhard (1943) Über Wirbeltierfunde aus dem Rhät von Hallau (Kt. Schaffhausen). Eclogae Geol. Helv. *36*:260-263. CO:4 18

1612 Peyer, Bernhard (1959) Über die Vomerzähne von *Ceratodus parvus* und über die verschiedenen Altersstadien seiner Zahnplatten. Vierteljahresschr. Naturforsch. Ges. Zurich *104*:148-156. C:1 4 15 17

1613 Peyer, Bernhard (1968) Comparative Odontology. Translated by Rainer Zangerl. Chicago: Univ. Chicago Press, pp.1-347. (Dipnoi:110-118). OCFD:1 4 15 18

1614 Pfeffer, Georg Johann (1897) Zur Faunistik Deutsch-Ost-Afrikas. 2. Fische. Arch. Naturgeschichte *63*:60-62. OP:18

1615 Pfeiffer, Wolfgang (1968) Gasstoffwechsel der Fische, Amphibien und Reptilien. Fortschr. Zool. *19*:105-140. OPLN:10 19

1616 Pfeiffer, Wolfgang (1968) Retina und Retinomotorik der Dipnoi und Brachiopterygii. Z. Zellforsch. Mikrosk. Anat. *89*:62-72. PO:1 6 7

1617 Pfeiffer, Wolfgang (1968) Die Fahrenholzschen Organe der Dipnoi und Brachiopterygii. Z. Zellforsch. Mikrosk. Anat. *90*:127-147. PLNO:1 3 7 19

1618 Pfeiffer, Wolfgang (1969) Das Geruchsorgan der rezenten Actinistia und Dipnoi (Pisces). Z. Morphol. Tiere *64*:309-337. PLNO:1 6 7

1619 Pfeiffer, Wolfgang (1971) Bau, Leistung und biologische Bedeutung des Geruchsorgans der Knochenfische. Naturwiss. Rundsch. 24:417-423. PNO:1 7

1620 Phelps, Charles, Martha Farmer, Hans J. Fyhn, Unni E. H. Fyhn, Robert L. Garlick, Robert Noble and Dennis A. Powers (1979) Equilibria and kinetics of oxygen and carbon monoxide binding to the hemoglobin of the South American lungfish, Lepidosiren paradoxa. Comp. Biochem. Physiol. 62A:139-143. L(P):2 10 11

1621 Phillips, J. G. and I. Chester Jones (1957) The identity of adrenocortical secretions in lower vertebrates. J. Endocrinol. 16:iii. PO:2 8

1622 Phleger, C. F. and B. S. Saunders (1978) Swimbladder surfactants of Amazon air-breathing fishes. Can. J. Zool. 56:946-952. LO:2 10

1623 Pickering, B. T. and Susan McWatters (1966) Neurohypophysial hormones of the South American lungfish Lepidosiren paradoxa. J. Endocrinol. 36:217-218. L:2 8

1624 Pidoplichko, I. G. and Y. N. Kurazhskovski (1956) Palyeogyeografichne znachyennya podviynodikhayuchikh khryebyetnykh. (Paleographic importance of Dipnoi). Trav. Mus. Zool. Acad. Sci. Ukr. 27:144-153. FDO:18

1625 Pienaar, U. de V. (1981) Another important ichthyological find in the Kruger National Park (Protopterus annectens brieni). Koedoe 24:189-192. P:18

1626 Pinkus, Felix (1894) Über einen noch nicht beschriebenen Hirnnerven des Protopterus annectens. Anat. Anz. 9:562-566. P:1 6

1627 Pinkus, Felix (1895) Die Hirnnerven des Protopterus annectens. Morphol. Arb. 4:275-346. P:1 6

1628 Pinsof, J. D. (1983) A Jurassic lungfish (Dipnoi, Ceratodontidae) from western South Dakota. Proc. South Dakota Acad. Sci. 62:75-77. C+:18

1629 Pinto, Cesar (1928) Myxosporideos e outros protozoários intestinais de Peixes observados na América do Sul. Arch. Inst. Biol. São Paulo 1:101-136. LO:14 22

1630 Pitman, Charles Robert Senhous (1934) A report on a faunal survey of Northern Rhodesia. Livingstone, Northern Rhodesia: Government Printer. OP:18

1631 Pitman, Charles Robert Senhous (1956) Aestivating Protopterus. Uganda J. 20:99. P:20

1632 Pitman, Charles Robert Senhous (1957) Further notes on aquatic predators of birds. Bull. Brit. Ornithol. Club 77:89-97. P:19 21

1633 Piveteau, Jean (1966) Traité de Paléontologie. Vol. 3, Actinoptérygiens, Crossoptérygiens, Dipneustes. Vol. 4, L'Origine des Vertébrés, leur Expansion dans les Eaux Douces et le Milieu Marin. Paris: Masson et Cie.

1634 Plane, M. and C. G. Gatehouse (1968) A new vertebrate fauna from the Tertiary of Northern Australia. Aust. J. Sci. 30:272-273. CO:4 18

1635 Plessis, Jacqueline (1958) Note préliminaire sur le sang de Protopterus annectens (Owen, 1839). Bull. Mus. Natl. Hist. Natur. Paris, 30:345-351. P:1 11 22

1636 Poll, Max (1933) Contribution à la faune ichtyologique du Katanga. Ann. Mus. Congo Belge sér. Quarto Zool. 3:105-151. (Protopterus:108). OP:1 18

1637 Poll, Max (1938) Les Protoptères. Bull. Cercle Zool. Congolais 15:16-28. PLN:1 14 15 16 18 19 20

1638 Poll, Max (1938) Caractères et distribution géographique des Protoptères du Congo belge. Ann. Soc. Roy. Zool. Belg. 69:157-168. P:1 3 18

1639 Poll, Max (1938) Poissons du Katanga (bassin du Congo) récoltés par le professeur Paul Brien. Rev. Zool. Bot. Afr. 30:389-423. (Protopterus:390-398). PO:1 18 19 20

1640 Poll, Max (1939) Les poissons du Stanley-Pool. Ann. Mus. Congo Belge sér. 1 Zool. 4:5-151. (Protopterus:11). OP:1 3 14 16 18 20 21 24

1641 Poll, Max (1939) Exploration du Parc National Albert, Mission H. Damas. Inst. Parcs Natl. Congo belge (Brussels), Poissons 6:1-71. (Protopterus:15-18). OP:18

1642 Poll, Max (1939) Exploration du Parc National Albert, Mission G. F. de Witte. Inst. Parcs Natl. Congo belge (Brussels), Poissons 24:1-81. (Protopterus:19, 57). OP:1 3 14 16 18 20 21 24

1643 Poll, Max (1943) La pêche en eau douce au Congo belge. II. Aperçu général sur les poissons d'eau douce du Bassin du Congo. Bull. Agric. Congo Belge 34:119-132. OP:1 18

1644 Poll, Max (1946) Revision de la faune ichthyologique du Lac Tanganika. Ann. Mus. Congo Belge sér. 1 Zool. 4:141-364. (Protopterus:162-163). OP:18

1645 Poll, Max (1948) Poissons recueillis au Katanga par H. J. Bredo. Bull. Mus. Roy. Hist. Natur. Belge 24:1-24. OP:1 18

1646 Poll, Max and H. Renson (1948) Les poissons, leur milieu et leur pêche au Bief Supérieur du Lualaba. Bull. Agric. Congo Belge 34:427-466. OP:14 18

1647 Poll, Max (1952) Les Vertébrés. Exploration hydrobiologique du Lac Tanganika (1946-47). Inst. Roy. Sci. Natur. Belg. 1:103-165. PO:18

1648 Poll, Max (1952) Ségrégation géographique et formation des espèces. Ann. Soc. Roy. Zool. Belg. 83:211-224. OD:17 18

1649 Poll, Max (1953) Les poissons d'aquarium du Congo belge. Bull. Soc. Roy. Zool. Antwerp #2:1-48. (Protopterus:2-6). PO:1 3 18

1650 Poll, Max (1953) Poissons non Cichlidae. Exploration hydrobiologique du Lac Tanganika (1946-47). Inst. Roy. Sci. Natur. Belg. 3:1-251. (Protopterus:13, 22-23). OP:1 3 18 21

1651 Poll, Max (1954) Zoogéographie des Protoptères et des Polyptères. Bull. Soc. Zool. Fr. 79:282-289. PO:1 17 18

1652 Poll, Max (1957) Les genres des poissons d'eau douce de l'Afrique. Ann. Mus. Congo Belge sér. Quarto Zool. 54:5-191. (Protopterus:19-20). OP:1 18

1653 Poll, Max (1959) Recherches sur la faune ichthyologique de la région du Stanley Pool. Ann. Mus. Congo Belge sér. Quarto Zool. 71:77-174. (Protopterus:118-119, 154-159). PO:10 14 18 20

1654 Poll, Max (1959) Aspects nouveaux de la faune ichthyologique du Congo belge. Bull. Soc. Zool. Fr. 84:259-271. PO:14 18 20

1655 Poll, Max (1960) Les poissons à respiration aérienne. Congo-Tervuren 6:113-118. PO(LN):1 9 10 17 18 20

1656 Poll, Max (1961) Revision systématique et raciation géographique des Protopteridae de l'Afrique Centrale. Ann. Mus. Roy. Afr. Cent. sér. Quarto Zool. 103:1-50. P:1 14 15 18 20

1657 Poll, Max (1965) Une pluie de poissons en Afrique. Congo-Tervuren 11:11-14. P:18

1658   Poll, Max (1967) Contribution à la faune ichthyologique de l'Angola. Subsídios para o Estudo da Biologia na Lunda, Museu do Dondo. Companhia Diamantes de Angola, Serviços Culturais 75:15-376. (Protopterus:18-30). OP:18

1659   Poll, Max (1967) Notice sur George-A. Boulenger. Annu. Acad. Roy. Belg. 1967:3-40. Bruxelles: Palais des Academies. O

1660   Poll, Monique (1962) Étude sur la structure adulte et la formation des sacs pulmonaires des Protoptères. Ann. Mus. Roy. Afr. Cent. sér. Quarto Zool. 108:129-172. P(NL):1 6 10 11 15

1661   Pollard, Jack (1980) G. P. Whitley's Handbook of Australian Fishes. Sydney: Jack Pollard Pty., Ltd. (Neoceratodus:334-335). NO:G(1 3 10 18)

1662   Poole, D. F. G. (1967) Phylogeny of tooth tissues: enameloid and enamel in recent vertebrates, with a note on the history of cementum. In Albert Edward William Miles (ed): Structural and Chemical Organization of Teeth. New York: Academic Press, 1:111-149. OP:4 17

1663   Poole, D. F. G. (1968) An introduction to the phylogeny of calcified tissues. International Symposium on Dental Morphology 2:65-79. OP+:4 17

1664   Popov, L. S. and B. M. Mednikov (1977) Comparative characteristics of DNA pyrimidine sequences of shark, Protopterus and perch. Mol. Biol. (Moscow) 11:286-293. [in Russian]. Translation in Mol. Biol. (Moscow) 11:216-222. PO*:2

1665   Popov, L. S. (1978) Use of benzoylated DEAE-cellulose for the fractionation of high-polymer DNA. Translated from Biokhimiya 43:511-515. PO:2 17

1666   Powers, Dennis A., Hans J. Fyhn, Unni E. H. Fyhn, Joseph P. Martin, Robert L. Garlick, and Stephen C. Wood (1979) A comparative study of the oxygen equilibria of blood from 40 genera of Amazonian fishes. Comp. Biochem. Physiol. 62A:67-85. OL:2 10 11 18

1667   Powers, Dennis A., Joseph P. Martin, Robert L. Garlick, Hans J. Fyhn, and Unni E. H. Fyhn (1979) The effect of temperature on the oxygen equilibria of fish hemoglobins in relation to environmental thermal variability. Comp. Biochem. Physiol. 62A:87-94. LO:2 10 11 18

1668   Price, Llewellyn Ivor (1960) Dentes de Theropoda num testemunho de Sonda no Estado do Amazonas. An. Acad. Bras. Ciênc. 32:79-84. OFD:18

1669   Priem, Fernand (1924) Paléontologie de Madagascar. XII. Les Poissons fossiles. Ann. Paléontol. 13:107-132. CO:1 4 18

1670   Prince, Jack H. (1956) Comparative Anatomy of the Eye. Springfield: Charles C. Thomas. OPLN:1 6 7

1671   Prince, Jack H. (1972) From tiger snake to multiple sclerosis. Koolewong 1:7-9. OLN:1 6

1672   Probatov, A. N. (1966) Ob Afrikanskikh dvoyakodyshashchikh rybakh, kak ob 'ektakh oranzhereinogo' rybovodstva. (African lungfishes as objects of pond culture). Ref. Zh. Biol. 1967:102-104. P*:23

1673   Probatov, A. N. (1969) On the possible use of Dipnoi in fish culture. Trudy Vses. Nauchno-Issled Inst. Prud. Ryb. Khoz. 16:282-287. P+:23

1674   Puigserver, A. and P. Desnuelle (1975) Dissociation of bovine 6S procarboxypeptidase A by reversible condensation with 2,3-dimethyl maleic anhydride: application to the partial characterization of subunit III. Proc. Nat. Acad. Sci. USA 72:2442-2445. O(L):2

1675   Purkerson, M. L., J. U. M. Jarvis, S. A. Luse, and E. W. Dempsey (1974) X-ray analysis coupled with scanning and transmission electron microscopic observations of spermatozoa of the African lungfish, Protopterus aethiopicus. J. Zool. (London) 172:1-12. P:1 14

1676   Purkerson, M. L., J. U. M. Jarvis, S. A. Luse, and E. W. Dempsey (1975) Electron microscopy of the intestine of the African lungfish, Protopterus aethiopicus. Anat. Rec. 182:71-90. P:1 12

1677   Purser, George Leslie (1916) The early development of the spleen of Lepidosiren and Protopterus. Quart. J. Microsc. Sci. 62:231-241. LP:1 11 12 15

1678   Putnam, Frederic Ward (1871) The new Australian fish. Bull. Essex Inst. 1:40-41. N

1679   Putnam, Jerry L. and Lawrence S. Dillon (1967) Heart structure and the ancestry of amphibians. Amer. Zool. 7:210. (Abstract) OP:1 11 17

1680   Putnam, Jerry L. (1976) Heart anatomy and the relationship of extant amphibians. Amer. Zool. 16:216. (Abstract) O(P):1 11 17

1681   Quenstedt, Friedrich August (1852) Handbuch der Petrefaktenkunde. Tübingen: H. Laupp'schen. (Ceratodus:186-188). CO:1 4 18

1682   Quenstedt, Friedrich August (1858) Der Jura. Tübingen: H. Laupp'schen. (Ceratodus:34). OC:18

1683   Quinlan, Alician V. (1980) The thermal sensitivity of generic Michaelis-Menton processes without catalyst denaturation or inhibition. J. Thermal Biol. 6:103-114. OL:2 5

1684   Rabiner, S. Frederick, Ira D. Goldfine, Arlene Hart, Louis Summaria, and Kenneth C. Robbins (1969) Radioimmunoassay of human plasminogen and plasmin. J. Lab. Clin. Med. 74:265-273. O(D):2 11

1685   Rabl, Carl (1901) Gedanken und Studien über den Ursprung der Extremitäten. Z. Wiss. Zool. 70:474-558. OPN:1 4 17

1686   Rabl, Hans (1931) Integument der Anamnier. In Louis Bolk, Ernest Göppert, Erich Kallius, and Wilhelm Lubosch (eds): Handbuch der vergleichenden Anatomie der Wirbeltiere. Berlin und Wien: Urban und Schwarzenberg, I:271-374. OLP:1 3

1687   Rafn, Svend and Karl Georg Wingstrand (1981) Structure of intestine, pancreas, and spleen of the Australian lungfish, Neoceratodus forsteri (Krefft). Zool. Scripta 10:223-240. N(PL):1 8 11 12

1688   Rahn, Hermann and Barbara J. Howell (1976) Bimodal gas exchange. In George M. Hughes (ed): Respiration of Amphibious Vertebrates. New York: Academic Press, pp.271-286. LPO:2 9 10

1689   Rai, Bhuwan Prakash (1972) Gonadotrops in agnatha, fishes and amphibia. Acta Anat. 81:42-52. OP:1 8

1690   Ramsay, Edward Pierson (1871) Letter read on Ceratodus forsteri. Proc. Zool. Soc. London 1871:7-8. N:12 18 19 20 21

1691   Ramsay, Edward Pierson (1873) Exhibition of Ceratodus forsteri. Proc. Zool. Soc. London 1873:686. N

1692   Ramsay, Edward Pierson (1876) Notes on living Ceratodus. Proc. Zool. Soc. London 1876:698-699. N:3 7 19 21

1693   Rankin, J. C. and M. M. Babiker (1974) Renal actions of neurohypophysial hormones in fish. 2. Tubular effects. Gen. Comp. Endocrinol. 22:380. (Abstract) PO:2 8 13

1694 Rauther, Max (1937) Pharynx und Epitheliale Organe der Pharynx und Kiemen der Anamnier-Kiemendarmderivate der Cyclostomen und Fische. In Louis Bolk, Ernest Göppert, Erich Kallius, and Wilhelm Lubosch (eds): Handbuch der vergleichenden Anatomie der Wirbeltiere. Berlin und Wien: Urban and Schwarzenberg, *III*:211-278. OD:1 9

1695 Rauther, Max (1940) Echte Fische. Teil 1: Anatomie, Physiologie und Entwicklungsgeschichte. In Heinrich Georg Bronns (ed): Klassen und Ordnungen des Tierreichs, 6. Band: Wirbeltiere. 1. Abteilung: Pices. 2. Buch: Echte Fische. Teil 1:1-1050. Leipzig: Akademischer Verlag. (Dipnoi:229-230, 292-295, 362-364, 721-727, 736-740, 764-767, 920-921, 968-970). ONPLFD:1 3 4 9 10 12 15 21

1696 Reeck, Gerald Russell, William P. Winter, and Hans Neurath (1970) Pancreatic enzymes of the African lungfish *Protopterus aethiopicus*. Biochemistry *9*:1398-1403. P:2 12

1697 Reeck, Gerald Russell (1971) Phylogenetic variations among proteolytic enzymes: studies on pancreatic enzymes of the African lungfish and bovine carboxypeptidase B. Diss. Abstr. Int. B Sci. Eng. *32*:1360-1361. (Abstract) P:2 12

1698 Reeck, Gerald Russell and Hans Neurath (1972) Pancreatic trypsinogen from the African lungfish. Biochemistry *11*:503-510. P:2 12 17

1699 Reeck, Gerald Russell and Hans Neurath (1972) Isolation and characterization of pancreatic procarboxypeptidase B and carboxypeptidase B of the African lungfish. Biochemistry *11*:3947-3955. P:2 12

1700 Reed, John Wallace (1985) Devonian dipnoans from Red Hill, Nevada. J. Paleontol. *59*:1181-1193. FD:1 4 18

1701 Reed, William, John Burchard, A. J. Hopson, Jonathan Jenness, and Ibrahim Yaro (1967) Fish and Fisheries of Northern Nigeria. Zaria, Northern Nigeria: Ministry of Agricul., pp. 1-229. (*Protopterus*:8-9). OP:1 14 20 24

1702 Reichenbach-Klinke, H. (1966) Eine neue Art der Polystomatidengattung *Eupolystoma* Kaw, 1950 (Monogena, Polystomatidae) von den Kiemen des australischen Lungenfisches *Neoceratodus forsteri* Krefft. Zool. Anz. *176*:142-146. N:3 9 22

1703 Reichlin, Morris and Bonnie J. Davis (1979) A precipitin reaction between human serum and fish hemoglobins. Comp. Biochem. Physiol. *62A*:105-107. LO:2 11

1704 Reifenrath, R., A. Vatter, and C. Lin (1981) Surface properties of pulmonary surfactant-evolutionary and physiological aspects. In P. von Wichert (ed): Progress in Respiration Research. Importance of Surfactant Defects. *15*:49-56. OD:2 10 17

1705 Reinhard, F. G. (1980) Suppression of DNA synthesis by peptide(s) from the brain of estivating lungfish, *Protopterus annectens* Owen. Cryobiology *18*:103. (Abstract) P:2 6 20

1706 Reite, Ola Bodvar (1969) The evolution of vascular smooth muscle responses to histamine and 5-hydroxytryptamine. I. Occurrence of stimulatory actions in fish. Acta Physiol. Scand. *75*:221-239. OP:2 5 11 17

1707 Remane, Adolf (1936) Wirbelsäule und ihre Abkömmlinge. In Louis Bolk, Ernest Göppert, Erich Kallius, and Wilhelm Lubosch (eds): Handbuch der vergleichenden Anatomie der Wirbeltiere. Berlin and Wien: Urban und Schwarzenberg, *IV*:1-206. (Dipnoi:74-76). OPN:1 4

1708 Reno, Harley W., Frederick R. Gehlbach, and Robert A. Turner (1972) Skin and aestivational cocoon of the aquatic amphibian, *Siren intermedia* Le Conte. Copeia *1972*:625-631. Texas Rep. Biol. Med. *29*:427. (Abstract) O(P):1 3 20

1709 Retzius, Gustaf (1881) Einige Beiträge zur Histologie und Histochemie der Chorda dorsalis. Arch. Anat. Entwickelungsgesch. *1881*:89-110. OPN:1 4

1710 Ribeiro, Alipio de Miranda (1909) Fauna Braziliense: Peixes. Rio de Janiero: Imprensa Nacional, *III*:1-505. (*Lepidosiren*:5-19). LO:1 3 7 9 10 14 18 19 20 21 24

1711 Ribeiro, Alipio de Miranda (1909) Fauna Braziliense: Peixes III. Eleutherobranchios Spirophoros. Arch. Mus. Nac. Rio de Janeiro *15*:171-185. L:10 11 14 18 19 20 21 24

1712 Ribeiro, Paulo de Miranda (1961) Catálogo dos Peixes do Museu Nacional, Vol. VI. Rio de Janeiro: Publ. Avulsas Mus. Nac. *38*:1-10. ONLP:18

1713 Richardson, Linsdall (1906) On the occurrence of *Ceratodus* in the Rhaetic at Garden Cliff Westbury-on-Severn, Gloucestershire, with some remarks upon its distribution in British Formations. Proc. Cotteswold Natur. Field Club *15*:267-271. C:4 18

1714 Ridewood, Walter George (1894) On the hyoid arch of *Ceratodus*. Proc. Zool. Soc. London *1894*:632-640. N(P):1 4

1715 Ridewood, Walter George (1896) The teeth of fishes. Natur. Sci. (London) *8*:380-391. ONP:1 4

1716 Riggs, Austen (1970) Properties of fish hemoglobins. In William S. Hoar and David J. Randall (eds): Fish Physiology. New York: Academic Press, *4*:209-252. (Dipnoi:245-246). OPLN:2 11

1717 Riggs, Austen (1979) Studies of the hemoglobins of Amazonian fishes: an overview. Comp. Biochem. Physiol. *62A*:257-271. LO:2 11

1718 Ritchie, Alexander (1971) Fossil fish discoveries in Antarctica. Aust. Natur. Hist. *17*:65-71. OFD:18

1719 Ritchie, Alexander (1981) First complete specimen of the dipnoan *Gosfordia truncata* Woodward from the Triassic of New South Wales. Rec. Aust. Mus. *33*:606-615. FD:1 3 4 17

1720 Robert, Maurice (1946) Le Congo Physique. Liège: H. Vaillant-Carmanne, pp.1-449. (*Protopterus*:402-403). OP:18 20 23

1721 Roberts, Tyson (1967) A provisional check-list of the fresh-water fishes of the Volta Basin, with notes on species of possible economic importance. J. West Afr. Sci. Assoc. *12*:10-18. OP:18 23 24

1722 Robertson, Jane I. (1913) The development of the heart and vascular system of *Lepidosiren paradoxa*. Quart. J. Microsc. Sci. *59*:53-132. L:1 11 15 17

1723 Rochon-Duvigneaud, A. (1941) L'oeil de *Lepidosiren paradoxa*. C. R. Acad. Sci. Paris *212*:307-309. L(P):1 7

1724 Rode, Karl (1938) Der erste Lungenfisch aus dem deutschen Oberkarbon. Z. Dtsch. Geol. Ges. *90*:615-620. FD:4 18

1725 Rodewald, Karin, Anton Stangl, and Gerhard Braunitzer (1984) Primary structure, biochemical and physiological aspects of hemoglobin from South American lungfish (*Lepidosiren paradoxus*, Dipnoi). Z. Physiol. Chem. *365*:639-649. L:2 11 17

1726 Rohon, Joseph Victor (1898) Bau der obersilurischen Dipnoer-Zähne. Sber. Böhm. Ges. *1898*:1-18. FD:1 4 18

1727 Rohon, Joseph Victor (1899) Teeth of fossil Dipnoi. J. Roy. Microsc. Soc. London *1899*:474. (Abstract) FD:1 4

1728 Román, Benigno (1968) Consideraciones sobre la filogenía de los Peces. Misc. Zool. Mus. Zool. *2*:155-171. OD:1 17

1729 Romer, Alfred Sherwood and Homer J. Smith (1934) American Carboniferous dipnoans. J. Geol. *42*:700-719. FD(PL):1 4 18

1730 Romer, Alfred Sherwood (1936) The dipnoan cranial roof. Amer. J. Sci. *32*:241-256. FDN:1 4 17

1731 Romer, Alfred Sherwood (1942) Cartilage an embryonic adaptation. Amer. Natur. *76*:394-404. OD:4 15 17

1732 Romer, Alfred Sherwood (1945) The Late Carboniferous vertebrate fauna of Kounova (Bohemia) compared with that of the Texas Redbeds. Amer. J. Sci. *243*:417-442. OFD:18

1733 Romer, Alfred Sherwood and Everett C. Olson (1954) Aestivation in a Permian lungfish. Breviora #30:1-8. FD(LP):1 17 18 20

1734 Romer, Alfred Sherwood (1955) Herpetichthyes, Amphibioidei, Choanichthyes or Sarcopterygii. Nature (London) *176*:126. D:1 17

1735 Romer, Alfred Sherwood (1958) The Texas Permian Redbeds and their vertebrate fauna. In T. Stanley Westoll (ed): Studies on Fossil Vertebrates. London: Athlone Press, pp.157-179. OFD:18

1736 Romer, Alfred Sherwood (1962) Vertebrate evolution. Copeia *1962*:223-227. OFD:1 17

1737 Romer, Alfred Sherwood (1965) Possible polyphylety of the vertebrate classes. Zool. Jahrb. Abst. Syst. *92*:143-156. OD:17

1737a Romer, Alfred Sherwood (1966) Vertebrate Paleontology, 3rd edition. Chicago: Univ. Chicago Press. (Dipnoi:75-77).

1738 Röse, Carl (1892) Über Zahnbau und Zahnwechsel der Dipnoer. Anat. Anz. 7:821-839. PN:1 3 4 12 15

1739 Rosen, Donn E., Peter L. Forey, Brian G. Gardiner, and Colin Patterson (1981) Lungfishes, tetrapods, paleontology, and plesiomorphy. Bull. Amer. Mus. Natur. Hist. *167*:159-276. FDNLPO:1 4 7 17

1740 Rosenberg, H., A. H. Ennor, D. D. Hagerman and Sadako Sugai (1962) L-threonine ethanolamine phosphate: a compound newly isolated from fish. Biochem. J. *84*:536-541. NO:2

1741 Ross, Lawrence S. (1966) Lunar lungfish. N. Engl. J. Med. *274*:1388. O

1742 Roth, Anton (1973) Electroreceptors in Brachiopterygii and Dipnoi. Naturwissenschaften *60*:106. LO:2 7 19

1743 Roth, Anton and Herta Tscharntke (1976) Ultrastructure of the ampullary electroreceptors in lungfish and Brachiopterygii. Cell Tissue Res. *173*:95-108. PO:1 6 7 19

1744 Roughley, Theodore Cleveland (1951) Fish and Fisheries of Australia. Sydney: Angus and Robertson. (*Epiceratodus forsteri*:158-160). ON:1 7 9 10 14 15 18 21

1745 Roughley, Theodore Cleveland (1916) Fishes of Australia and their Technology. Tech. Mus., Sydney, Tech. Ed. series #21. Sydney: William Applegate Gullick, Government Printer. (*Neoceratodus*:191-195). NO (C):1 3 4 15 18 19 21

1746 Roux, C. (1967) Une collection de poissons d'eau douce recueillis dans la région de La Maboké (République Centrafricaine). Cahiers de La Maboké. Cybium (Bulletin de l'Association des Amis du Laboratoire des Pêches Coloniales, Paris), N.S. *5*:105-119. PO:1 9 18 19 20 21 24

1747 Rudebeck, Birger (1944) Does an accessory olfactory bulb exist in Dipnoi? Acta Zool. (Stockholm) *25*:89-96. P(LN):1 6 7 15 17

1748 Rudebeck, Birger (1945) Contributions to forebrain morphology in Dipnoi. Acta Zool. (Stockholm) *26*:9-156. PLN:1 6 17

1749 Rudel, A. (1935) Notes on rearing young *Ceratodus*. Mem. Queensl. Mus. *10*:231-232. N:16 18 21

1750 Russell, Denise, Donald Russell, Philippe Taquet, and Herbert Thomas (1976) Nouvelles récoltes de Vertébrés dans les terrains continentaux du Crétacé supérieur de la région de Majunga (Madagascar). Bull. Soc. Geol. Fr. Suppl. *18*:204-208. CO:18

1751 Rykov, S. P. and M. G. Minikh (1969) O novykh nakhodkakh Dipnoi v razreze gory "Bolshoe Bogdo". (On recent finds of Dipnoi in quarry of Mt. Bogdo). Dokl. Akad. Nauk SSSR *188*:414-416. Translation in Acad. Sci. USSR, Dokl., Earth Sci. Sect. *188*:55-56. [1970] C:4 18

1752 Sabatier, Armand (1904) Sur les mains scapulaires et pelviennes des Poissons holocéphales et chez les Dipneustes. C. R. Acad. Sci. Paris *138*:249-252. PLO:1 4

1753 Sage, Martin and Howard A. Bern (1972) Assay of prolactin in vertebrate pituitaries by its dispersion of xanthophore pigment in the teleost *Gillichthys mirabilis*. J. Exp. Zool. *180*:169-174. OP:2 8 17

1754 Saint-Hilaire, Albert Geoffroy (1863) À propos de *Lepidosiren annectens*. C. R. Acad. Sci. Paris *57*:541. [See also M. Serres #1903] P:19 20

1755 Saint-Hilaire, Auguste de (1846) Sur le Minhocâo des Goyanais. C. R. Acad. Sci. Paris *23*:1145-1147. Translation [1847] in Ann. Mag. Natur. Hist. *19*:140-141, and Amer. J. Sci. and Arts *4*:130-131. L:1 18

1756 Saint-Hilaire, Auguste de (1847) Voyage aux Sources du Rio de S. Francisco et dans la Province de Goyaz. Paris: Arthus Bertrand. OL:18

1757 Saito, Hiroaki (1984) The development of the spleen in the Australian lungfish, *Neoceratodus forsteri* Krefft, with special reference to its relationship to the "Gastro"-enteric vasculature. Amer. J. Anat. *169*:337-360. Acta Anat. Nippon *59*:480. (Abstract) N:1 11 12 15

1758 Saito, Hiroaki (1985) The development of the intra-intestinal artery in the Australian lungfish, *Neoceratodus forsteri*. Anat. Anz. *159*:291-303. N:1 11 12 15

1759 Salensky, Wladimir Wladimirowitsch (1898) Istoriia rozuitiva ikhtiopetepugiia Ganoid i Dipnoi. (History of the development of the ichthyopterygium in Ganoids and Dipnoi). Annu. Mus. Zool. Acad. Imp. Sci. St. Petersburg *3*:215-275. ON:1 4 5 15 17

1760 Salensky, Wladimir Wladimirowitsch (1898) Zur Entwicklungsgeschichte des Ichthyopterygiums. Proc. Int. Congr. Zool. *1898*:177-183. ON:1 4 5 15 17

1762 Sanders, Alfred (1888) Contributions to the anatomy of the central nervous system in vertebrated animals. Part I: Ichthyopsida. Section I: Pices. Subsection III: Dipnoi. Proc. Roy. Soc. London *43*:420-423. N(P):1 6

1763 Sanders, Alfred (1889) Contributions to the anatomy of the central nervous system in *Ceratodus forsteri*. Ann. Mag. Natur. Hist. *3*:157-188. N(P):1 6

1764 Sandon, H. (1950) An illustrated guide to the freshwater fishes of the Sudan. Sudan Notes and Records, London. OP:G(1 18 20)

1765 Sarasin, Fritz (1905) La sortie du *Protopterus annectens* de sa motte de terre. Arch. Sci. Phys. Natur. (Genève) *20*:594-595. P:18 20

1766 Satchell, G.H. (1971) Circulation in Fishes. London: Cambridge Univ. Press. OPLN:1 2 9 10

1767 Satchell, G.H. (1976) The circulatory system of air-breathing fish. In George M. Hughes (ed): Respiration of Amphibious Vertebrates. New York: Academic Press, pp.105-124. PLNO:1 2 9 10 11

1768 Säve-Söderbergh, Gunnar (1937) On *Rhynchodipterus elginensis* n.g., n.s., representing a new group of Dipnoan-like Choanata from the Upper Devonian of East Greenland and Scotland. Ark. Zool. *29*:1-8. FD:4 18

1769 Säve-Söderbergh, Gunnar (1951) Nagot om fossila lungfiskar. Uppsala Univ. Arsskr. *1951*:1-20. FD(NPL):1 4 17

1770 Säve-Söderbergh, Gunnar (1952) On the skull of *Chirodipterus wildungensis* Gross, an Upper Devonian dipnoan from Wildungen. Kgl. Sven. Vetenskapsakad. Handl. *3*:5-29. FD:1 4 17

1771 Sawaya, Paulo (1946) Sôbre a biologia de alguns peixes de respiração aérea (*Lepidosiren paradoxa* Fitz. e *Arapaima gigas* Cuv.). Bol. Fac. Filos. Ciênc. Letras Univ. São Paulo sér. Zool. *11*:255-285. LO(P):2 3 9 10 18 19 20 21

1772 Sawaya, Paulo (1947) Metabolismo respiratório de peixes de respiração aérea (*Lepidosiren paradoxa* Fitz.). Bol. Fac. Filos. Ciênc. Letras Univ. São Paulo ser. Zool. *12*:43-49. L:2 9 10 19

1773 Sawaya, Paulo and Naomi Shinomiya (1970) The blood sugar level in *Lepidosiren paradoxa*. In Proceedings of the 22nd Annual Meeting of Sociedade Brasileira para o Progresso da Ciência: 36l. (Abstract) L+:2 11

1774 Sawaya, Paulo and Naomi Shinomiya (1972) Biologia da Tambaki-M'Boya, *Lepidosiren paradoxa* (Fitz. 1836) Peixe, Dipnoico: metabolismo da glicose. Bol. Zool. Biol. Marinha Nova Ser. (São Paulo) *29*:1-44. L(PN):2 10 11 12 18 19 20 21 24 See also pp.65-118 in same issue.

1775 Sawaya, Paulo (1975) Reação da *Lepidosiren paradoxa* em estivação ao enantato e ao propionato de testosterona. An. Acad. Brasil. Ciênc. *47*:567-568. (Abstract) L:2 8 20

1776 Sawaya, Paulo and Olga Martins Mimura (1977) O pancreas de *Lepidosiren paradoxa* (Fitz. 1836) nas fases aquatica e estival. Bol. Fisiol. Anim. São Paulo *1*:79-90. L+:1 8 12 20

1777 Sawaya, Paulo and Olga Martins Mimura (1979) Desenvolvimento de novos orgãos induzidos pela testosterona em Peixes Dipnóicos (*Lepidosiren paradoxa*) (Fitz. 1836). (New organ development induced by parenteral administration of testosterone in dipnoan fishes). Ciênc. Cult. (São Paulo) *27*:542-545. L:8 11 16 20

1778 Sawaya, Paulo, I. Mimura, and Olga Martins Mimura (1981) Gills and lungs of *Lepidosiren paradoxa*, Pices, Dipnoi, histophysiology. Bol. Fisiol. Anim. (São Paulo) *5*:107-120. L+:1 9 10

1779 Sawyer, Wilbur H. and H. B. van Dyke (1963) Principles resembling oxytocin in neurohypophyses of fishes. Fed. Proc. *22*:386. (Abstract) PO:2 8

1780 Sawyer, Wilbur H. (1964) Vertebrate neurohypophysial principles. Endocrinology *75*:981-990. OP:8 17

1781 Sawyer, Wilbur H. (1966) Diuretic and natriuretic responses of lungfish (*Protopterus aethiopicus*) to arginine vasotocin. Amer. J. Physiol. *210*:191-197. P:2 8 13

1782 Sawyer, Wilbur H. (1966) Neurohypophysial principles of vertebrates. In Geoffrey Winfield Harris and Bernard Thomas Donovan (eds): The Pituitary Gland, *3*:307-329. London: Butterworths. PO:2 8 17

1783 Sawyer, Wilbur H. (1967) Evolution of antidiuretic hormones and their functions. Amer. J. Med. *42*:678-686. OP:2 8 11 13 17

1784 Sawyer, Wilbur H. (1969) The active neurohypophysial principles of two primitive bony fishes, the bichir (*Polypterus senegalis*) and the African lungfish (*Protopterus aethiopicus*). J. Endocrinol. *44*:421-435. PO:2 8 17

1785 Sawyer, Wilbur H. (1970) Vasopressor, diuretic, and natriuretic responses by lungfish to arginine vasotocin. Amer. J. Physiol. *218*:1789-1794. Proc. Int. Congr. Physiol. Sci. 7:388. [1968] (Abstract) P:2 8 11 13 17

1786 Sawyer, Wilbur H. and Peter K. T. Pang (1972) Neurohypophysial hormones and water and sodium balances in the South American lungfish (*Lepidosiren paradoxa*). Int. Congr. Endocrinol. Ser. #256:137. (Abstract) L(P):2 8 11 13

1787 Sawyer, Wilbur H. (1972) Lungfishes and amphibians: endocrine adaptation and the transition from aquatic to terrestrial life. Fed. Proc. *31*:1609-1614. PLO:2 8 13 17 18

1788 Sawyer, Wilbur H. (1972) Hydromineral regulation in animals. Part II. Neurohypophysial hormones and water and sodium excretion in the African lungfish. Gen. Comp. Endocrinol. Suppl. 3:345-349. P:2 8 11 13

1789 Sawyer, Wilbur H. (1973) Discussion: endocrines and osmoregulation among fishes. Amer. Zool. *13*:819-821. OD:2 18

1790 Sawyer, Wilbur H. and Peter K. T. Pang (1975) Endocrine adaptation to osmotic requirements of the environment: endocrine factors in osmoregulation by lungfishes and amphibians. Gen. Comp. Endocrinol. *25*:224-229. O(D):2 8 9 13 18

1791 Sawyer, Wilbur H., John R. Blair-West, Pamela A. Simpson, and Marion K. Sawyer (1976) Renal responses of Australian lungfish to vasotocin, angiotensin II, and NaCl infusion. Amer. J. Physiol. *231*:593-602. N(P):1 2 8 11 13

1792 Sawyer, Wilbur H. (1977) Evolution of neurohypophyseal hormones and their receptors. Fed. Proc. *36*:1842-1847. ODN:2 8 17

1793 Sawyer, Wilbur H. (1977) Evolution of active neurohypophysial principles among vertebrates. Amer. Zool. *17*:727-737. ODN:2 8 17

1794 Sawyer, Wilbur H., Peter K. T. Pang, and Sarah M. Galli-Gallardo (1978) Environment and osmoregulation among lungfishes and amphibians. In Ivan Assenmacher and Donald Sanke Farner (eds): Environmental Endocrinology. Berlin: Springer Verlag, pp.210-216. PLNO:2 8 11 13 17

1795 Sawyer, Wilbur H. and Peter K. T. Pang (1980) Neurohypophysial peptides and epithelial sodium transport in fishes. In Brahim Lahlou (ed): Epithelial Transport in the Lower Vertebrates. New York: Cambridge Univ. Press, pp.331-336. OLP:2 8 11 13

1796 Sawyer, Wilbur H. and Peter K. T. Pang (1980) Evolution of responses to arginine-vasotocin among the vertebrates. In Sho Yoshida, Leonard Share, and Kinji Yagi (eds): Antidiuretic Hormone. Baltimore: Univ. Park Press, pp.69-77. ONL:2 8 11 13

1797 Sawyer, Wilbur H., M. Uchiyama and Peter K. T. Pang (1982) Control of renal functions in lungfishes. Fed. Proc. 41:2361-2364. PNL:1 2 8 11 13

1798 Schaeffer, Bobb (1952) Rates of evolution in the Coelacanth and dipnoan fishes. Evolution 6:101-111. FDO:1 3 4 17

1799 Schaeffer, Bobb (1967) Osteichthyan vertebrae. J. Linnean Soc. London 47:185-195. OFDP:1 4 15

1800 Schaeffer, Bobb (1968) The origin and basic radiation of the Osteichthyes. In Tor Ørvig (ed): Nobel Symposium 4: Current Problems of Lower Vertebrate Phylogeny. Stockholm: Almqvist and Wiksell, pp.207-222. FDO(N):1 4 17

1801 Schaeffer, Bobb (1969) Adaptive radiation of the fishes and the fish-amphibian transition. Ann. New York Acad. Sci. 167:5-17. ONPLFD:1 6 17

1802 Schaeffer, Bobb (1971) Late Permian and Early Triassic fish assemblages. Bull. Can. Pet. Geol. 19:352-353. (Abstract) CO:17

1803 Schaeffer, Bobb (1972) Mesozoic fishes and climate. In S. J. Olson (ed): Proc. of the North American Paleontol. Conv., Part D: Paleoclimatology. Lawrence: Allen Press, Inc., pp.376-388. CO:18

1804 Scharrer, Berta and Sarah Wurzelmann (1967) Ultrastructural study of nucleolar activity in oocytes of the lungfish, Protopterus aethiopicus. Anat. Rec. 157:316. (Abstract) P:1 14

1805 Scharrer, Berta and Sarah Wurzelmann (1969) Ultrastructural study on nuclear-cytoplasmic relationships in oocytes of the African lungfish, Protopterus aethiopicus. I. Nucleolo-cytoplasmic pathways. Z. Zellforsch. Mikrosk. Anat. 96:325-343. P:1 14

1806 Scharrer, Berta and Sarah Wurzelmann (1969) Ultrastructural study on nuclear-cytoplasmic relationships in oocytes of the African lungfish, Protopterus aethiopicus. II. The microtubular apparatus of the nuclear envelope. Z. Zellforsch. Mikrosk. Anat. 101:1-12. P:1 14

1807 Scheuermann, Dieter W. (1976) Electron microscopic study on phosphatidic acid phosphatase activity of the Protopterus lung. XXI Congr. Morphol. Prague, Argumenta Communicationum: 161. (Abstract) P:1 2 9 10

1808 Scheuermann, Dieter W. (1977) Ultrastructural study on the innervation of the heart of Protopterus. Acta Anat. 99:312-313. (Abstract) P:1 6 11

1809 Scheuermann, Dieter W. (1978) Elektronenmikroskopische Untersuchungen über das Vorkommen und die Lokalisation der phosphatidsauren Phosphatase an der Lunge des Protopterus. In E. Klika (ed): XXI. Colloquium Scientificum Facultatis Medicae Universitatis Carolinae, and XIX. Congressus Morphologicus Symposia. pp.363-369. P:1 2 10

1810 Scheuermann, Dieter W. (1978) Onderzoek naar de innervatie van de sinus venosus en van de aurikels bij Protopterus annectens. Ned. Tijdschr. Geneeskd. 122:461. (Abstract) P:1 2 5 6 11

1811 Scheuermann, Dieter W. (1978) Über den Feinbau des Myokards von Protopterus annectens. Verh. Anat. Ges. 72:297-307. P:1 5 6 11

1812 Scheuermann, Dieter W. (1979) Untersuchungen hinsichtlich der Innervation des Sinus venosus und des Aurikels von Protopterus annectens. Acta Morphol. Neerl.-Scand. 17:231-232. P:1 2 5 6 11

1813 Scheuermann, Dieter W. (1980) A study of chromaffin cells in the heart of Protopterus. Folia Morphol. (Prague) 28:93-98. V. Congr. Anat. Europen. Prague, Argumenta Communicationum:362. [1979]. (Abstract) P:1 2 8 11

1814 Scheuermann, Dieter W., Christiane Stilman, and Marie H. A. de Groodt-Lasseel (1980) Fine structure and innervation of the chromaffin tissue of Dipnoi. In P. C. Brederoo (ed): Electron Microscopy 1980. Vol. 3: Analysis. The VIIth European Congress on Electron Microscopy Foundation, Leiden, pp.114-115. P:1 6 8 11

1815 Scheuermann, Dieter W. and Marie H. A. de Groodt-Lasseel (1980) Localization of catalase and peroxidase activity in the liver of Protopterus annectens. Eur. J. Cell Biol. 22:167. (Abstract) P:2 11 12

1816 Scheuermann, Dieter W. and Marie H. A. de Groodt-Lasseel (1981) On the endogenous peroxidase (E. P.) in the liver of Protopterus. Kurzfass. 76 Versamml. Anat. Ges. Varna-Goldstrand:82. (Abstract) P:1 2 11 12

1817 Scheuermann, Dieter W., Christiane Stilman, C. Reingold, and Marie H. A. de Groodt-Lasseel (1981) Microspectrofluorometric study of FIF-cells in the auricle of the heart of Protopterus. Kurzfass. 76 Versamml. Anat. Ges. Varna-Goldstrand:93. (Abstract) P:2 6 8 11

1818 Scheuermann, Dieter W. (1981) The presence of peroxidase positive cells in the liver of a lung fish. Anat. Anz. 149:101. (Abstract) P:2 12

1819 Scheuermann, Dieter W. (1981) Development of macrophages with different patterns of peroxidase activity in the liver of Dipnoi. Acta Anat. 111:134. (Abstract) P:2 12

1820 Scheuermann, Dieter W., Christiane Stilman, C. Reinhold, and Marie H. A. de Groodt-Lasseel (1981) Microspectrofluorometric study of monoamines in the auricle of the heart of Protoperus aethiopicus. Cell Tiss. Res. 217:443-449. P:1 2 8 11

1821 Scheuermann, Dieter W. (1981) Mononuclear phagocytes developing in the liver of a lung fish. 20. Tagung für Elektronenmikrosk:48. (Abstract) P:1 11 12

1822 Scheuermann, Dieter W. and Marie H. A. de Groodt-Lassel (1981) Cytochemical localization of endogenous peroxidase in the liver of a lungfish. IX. Mtg. of Anatomists, Histologists, and Embryologists of the U.S.S.R., Minsk:440. (Abstract) [in Russian]. P:2 11 12

1823 Scheuermann, Dieter W., M. Haverhals-Gunzburg, A. de Mazière, P. Aertgeerts, and Marie H. A. de Groodt-Lasseel (1982) Ventricular myocard cell junctions in Protopterus. 77. Versamml. Anat. Ges.:125. (Abstract) P:1 5 11

1824 Scheuermann, Dieter W. and F. van Meir (1982) Intramembraneuze partikels in de celmembraan van de hartspier van een longvis. 125e Anatomendag:10.

(Abstract) P:1 5 11

1825 Scheuermann, Dieter W. and Christiane Stilman (1982) Dopamine-containing cells in the heart of *Lepidosiren paradoxa*. First Eur. Congr. Cell Biol., Paris:143. (Abstract) L:1 8 11

1826 Scheuermann, Dieter W. and Marie H. A. de Groodt-Lasseel (1982) Tissue macrophages developing in the liver of *Protopterus*. Verh. Anat. Ges. 76:319-320. P:1 11 12

1827 Scheuermann, Dieter W., M. Haverhals-Gunzburg, A. de Mazière, P. Aertgeerts and Marie H. A. de Groodt-Lasseel (1983) Cell membrane specializations in *Protopterus* cardiac muscle. Verh. Anat. Ges. 77:597-599. P:1 5 11

1828 Scheuermann, Dieter W., F. van Meir, and Marie H. A. de Groodt-Lasseel (1983) Analysis of particle patterns in cardiac muscle cells of a dipnoan fish. Acta Morphol. Neerl.-Scand. 21:308. (Abstract) P:1 5 11

1829 Scheuermann, Dieter W. and A. de Mazière (1984) Gap junctions in the heart of the adult *Protopterus aethiopicus*. Acta Morphol. Neerl.-Scand. 22:123-131. Anat. Rec. 202:168A. (Abstract) P:1 5 11

1830 Scheuring, Ludwig (1929) Die Wanderungen der Fische. Ergeb. Biol. 5:405-691. (Dipnoi:442-443). ONLP:20

1831 Schiefferdecker, Paul (1886) Studien zur vergleichenden Histologie der Retina. Arch. Mikrosk. Anat. Ent.-Mech. 28:305-396. (Dipnoi:337-340). ONP:1 7

1832 Schlumberger, M. (1862) Dent de *Ceratodus runcinatus*, Plien. Bull. Soc. Geol. Fr. sér. II, 19:707-708. C:1 4

1833 Schmalhausen, Ivan Ivanovich (1916) Zur Morphologie der unpaaren Flossen. II. Bau und Phylogenese der unpaaren Flossen und insbesonders der Schwanzflosse der Fische. Z. Wiss. Zool. 104:1-80. (Dipnoi:46-51). ONLP:1 4 5 21

1834 Schmalhausen, Ivan Ivanovich (1916) On the median fin of the Dipnoi. Rev. Zool. Russe 1:65-74. PD:1 4 5 6 15

1835 Schmalhausen, Ivan Ivanovich (1916) K voprosu o morfologicheskom znachenii neparnago plavnika Dipnoi. (The morphological significance of the median fins of the Dipnoi). Rev. Zool. Russe 1:75-79. PD:1 4 5 6 15

1836 Schmalhausen, Ivan Ivanovich (1923) Der Suspensorialapparat der Fische und das Problem der Gehörknöchelchen. Anat. Anz. 56:534-543. NO:1 4 7 11 15

1837 Schmalhausen, Ivan Ivanovich (1923) Über die Autostylie der Dipnoer und der Tetrapoda. Anat. Anz. 56:543-550. NPO:1 4 6 11 15 17

1838 Schmalhausen, Ivan Ivanovich (1968) The Origin of Terrestrial Vertebrates. English Edition translated by Leon Kelso; Keith S. Thomson (ed). New York: Academic Press, pp.1-314. (Dipnoi:29-33). FDPN:1 4 6 11 17 21

1839 Schmeltz, J. D. E. (1876) Notizen über *Ceratodus forsteri*. J. Mus. Godeffroy 8:138. N:3 18 23

1840 Schmidt, Martin (1958) Die Lebewelt unserer Trias. Oehringen: Ferdinand Rau. CO:18

1841 Schmidt, Wilhelm J. (1966) Eisenoxyd-Färbung der Zahnplatten des *Protopterus annectens*. Zool. Anz. 177:111-116. P:1 2 4

1842 Schmidt, Wilhelm J. and A. Keil (1971) Polarizing Microscopy of Dental Tissues. Oxford: Pergamon Press.

(Dipnoi:240-244). OPN:1 4

1843 Schneider, Anton (1879) Beiträge zur vergleichenden Anatomie und Entwicklungsgeschichte der Wirbelthiere. Berlin: G. Reimer, pp.1-164. (Dipnoi:124). OD:1 4 5

1844 Schneider, Anton (1886) Über die Flossen der Dipnoi und die Systematik von *Lepidosiren* und *Protopterus*. Zool. Anz. 9:521-524. NPL:1 4

1845 Schneider, Anton (1887) Über die Dipnoi und besonders die Flossen derselben. Zool. Beitr. 2:97-105. PLN:1 4 15

1846 Schnitzlein, Harold N. (1966) The olfactory tubercle of the African lungfish, *Protopterus*. Ala. J. Med. Sci. 3:39-45. P:1 6 7

1847 Schnitzlein, Harold N. (1966) The primordial amygdaloid complex of the African lungfish, *Protopterus*. In Rolf Hassler and Heinz Stephan (eds): Evolution of the Forebrain: Phylogenesis and Ontogenesis of the Forebrain. Stuttgart: Georg Thieme, pp.40-49. P:1 6 7 17

1848 Schnitzlein, Harold N. (1967) Amygdala of fishes. In Harold N. Schnitzlein, H. H. Hoffman, E. G. Hamel, Jr. and N. C. Ferrer (eds): Parallelisms in fiber relations and variations in nuclear patterns in the phylogeny of the amygdala. Arch. Méx. Anat. #26:25-63. PO:1 6 7 17

1849 Schnitzlein, Harold N. (1967) The basic phylogenetic pattern of the striatal complex. Part I - Lungfish. Anat. Rec. 157:317-318. (Abstract) D:1 6

1850 Schnitzlein, Harold N. and Elizabeth C. Crosby (1967) The telencephalon of the lungfish, *Protopterus*. J. Hirnforsch. 9:105-149. P(L):1 6

1851 Schnitzlein, Harold N. and Gerald G. Whitt (1968) A comparison of the medial hemisphere wall in two dipnoan fishes. Anat. Rec. 160:423. (Abstract) PN:1 6

1852 Schnitzlein, Harold N. (1968) Introductory remarks on the telencephalon of fish. IN D. Ingle (ed): The Central Nervous System and Fish Behavior. Chicago: Univ. Chicago Press, pp.97-100. PO:6

1853 Schnitzlein, Harold N. and Elizabeth C. Crosby (1968) The epithalamus and thalamus of the lungfish, *Protopterus*. J. Hirnforsch. 10:351-371. P:1 6 7 17

1854 Schnitzlein, Harold N. (1982) Telencephalon of fishes. In Elizabeth C. Crosby and Harold N. Schnitzlein (eds): Comparative Correlative Neuroanatomy of the Vertebrate Telencephalon. New York: Macmillan Pub. Co., Inc., pp.3-160. (Dipnoi:142-156). OPNL:1 6

1855 Scholler, Hubert (1954) Johann Natterer zum Gedächtnis. Ann. Naturhist. Mus. Wien 60:36-42. O

1856 Schultze, Hans-Peter (1969) *Griphognathus* Gross, ein langschnauziger Dipnoer aus dem Oberdevon von Bergisch-Gladbach (Rheinisches Schiefergebirge) und von Lettland. Geol. Paläontol. 3:21-79. FD:1 4 18

1857 Schultze, Hans-Peter (1970) Die Histologie der Wirbelkörper der Dipnoer. Neues Jahrb. Geol. Paläontol. Abh. 135:311-336. FDP:1 4

1858 Schultze, Hans-Peter (1975) Die Lungenfisch-Gattung *Conchopoma* (Pices, Dipnoi). Senckenb. Lethaea 56:191-231. FD:1 4

1859 Schultze, Hans-Peter (1975) Das Axialskelett der Dipnoer aus dem Oberdevon von Bergisch-Gladbach (Westdeutschland). Colloq. Internat. Cent. Nat. Res. Sci. Problemes Actuels de Paleontologie (Evolution des Vertébrés) #218:149-157. FD:1 4

1860 Schultze, Hans-Peter (1976) Paleozoic Vertebrates. In Bernhard Grzimek (ed): Grzimek's Encyclopedia of Evolution. New York: Van Nostrand Reinhold Co., pp.217-238. OFD:G(3 4 7 10 18 20)

1861 Schultze, Hans-Peter (1977) The origin of the tetrapod limb within the Rhipidistian fishes. In Max K. Hecht, Peter Charles Goody, and Bessie M. Hecht (eds): Major Patterns in Vertebrate Evolution. New York: Plenum Press, pp.541-544. OD:1 4 17

1862 Schultze, Hans-Peter (1977) Ausgangsform und Entwicklung der rhombischen Schuppen der Osteichthyes (Pisces). Paläont. Z. *51*:152-168. OD:1 3

1863 Schultze, Hans-Peter (1977) *Megapleuron zangerli*: a new dipnoan from the Pennsylvanian, Illinois. Fieldiana Geol. *33*:375-396. FD:1 4 15 17

1864 Schultze, Hans-Peter and Linda Trueb (1981) Book review: Basic Structure and Evolution of Vertebrates, by Erik Jarvik, Academic Press, New York, 1981. J. Vert. Paleontol. *1*:389-397. OD:17

1865 Schultze, Hans-Peter (1981) Hennig und der Ursprung der Tetrapoda. Paläont. Z. *55*:71-86. OD:1 4 17

1866 Schultze, Hans-Peter (1981) A dipnoan tooth plate from the Lower Cretaceous of Kansas, USA. Trans. Kans. Acad. Sci. *84*:187-195. C:4 18

1867 Schultze, Hans-Peter (1981) Das Schädeldach eines ceratodontiden Lungenfisches aus der Trias Süddeutschlands (Dipnoi, Pices). Stuttgarter Beitr. Naturk. ser B *70*:1-31. C:4 18

1868 Schultze, Hans-Peter (1982) A dipterid dipnoan from the Middle Devonian of Michigan, U.S.A. J. Vert. Paleontol. *2*:155-162. FD:1 3 4 18

1869 Schultze, Hans-Peter (1985) Marine to onshore vertebrates in the Lower Permian of Kansas and their paleoenvironmental implications. Univ. Kans. Paleontol. Contrib. Paper #113:1-18. OFD:18 20

1870 Schulz, W. A. (1903) Überblick über die Geschichte der Auffindung von *Lepidosiren paradoxa*. Verh. Zool.-Bot. Ges. Wien *53*:588-591. L(P):1 3 18 24

1871 Schulze, Franz Eilhard (1889) Über die Lebensweise von *Protopterus annectens*. Sber. Ges. Naturforsch. Fr. Berlin *1889*:127. P:20

1872 Sclater, Philip Lutley (1866) Comments concerning the scarcity of *Lepidosiren*. Proc. Zool. Soc. London *1866*:34-35. L:18 20

1873 Sclater, Philip Lutley (1870) Exhibit of preserved *Ceratodus*. Proc. Zool. Soc. London *1870*:747. N:18

1874 Sclater, Philip Lutley (1873) Exhibit of six preserved *Ceratodus*. Proc. Zool. Soc. London *1873*:686. N:18 21

1875 Sclater, Philip Lutley (1894) Comments concerning reproduction in *Protopterus*. Proc. Zool. Soc. London *1894*:353-354. P:15 16 19

1876 Sclater, Philip Lutley (1896) Exhibit of a model of *Ceratodus*. Proc. Zool. Soc. London *1896*:786. N

1877 Sclater, Philip Lutley (1898) Display and description of living *Neoceratodus*. Proc. Zool. Soc. London *1898*:492-493. N:18 21

1878 Sclater, Philip Lutley (1906) Rare living animals in London. VI. Forster's Lung-fish. Knowledge N.S. *3*:379-380. N:G(4 18 21)

1879 Seal, U. S. and R. P. Doe (1965) Vertebrate distribution of corticosteroid-binding globulin and some endocrine effects on concentration. Steroids *5*:827-841. OL:2 8 11

1880 Sebruyns, M. (1942) Intraëpitheliale bloedhaarvaten in het darmepitheel van *Protopterus dolloi*. Natuurwet. Tijdschr. *24*:193-201. P:9 11 12

1881 Seddon, George (1969) Conodont and fish remains from the Gneudna Formation, Carnarvon Basin, Western Australia. J. Proc. Roy. Soc. West. Aust. *52*:21-30. OFD:4 18

1882 Seeley, Harry Govier (1897) On *Ceratodus kannemeyeri* (Seeley). Geol. Mag. (Decade IV) *4*:543-544. C:1 4 18

1883 Segers, L. G. (1967) Presence de *Protopterus annectens* Owen au Nord Nigeria. Biol. Jaarboek. *35*:274-276. P:18 20

1884 Selezneva, A. A. (1982) Nature of the branchiostegal series of paleoniscid fishes (Lower Actinopterygii). J. Ichthyol. *22*:75-83. O(FD):4 17

1885 Selezneva, A. A. (1985) Intensification of respiration as a base of evolutionary development of Actinopterygii. Vopr. Ikhtiol. *25*:26-34. [in Russian]. OD*:4 9 17

1886 Semichon, Louis (1913) Observations sur l'ovaire de *Protopterus annectens* Owen (Poissons Dipnés). Bull. Mus. Natl. Hist. Natur. Paris *19*:7-9. P:1 14

1887 Semon, Richard (ed) (1893) Zoologische Forschungsreisen in Australien und dem Malayischen Archipel. Denkschr. Med.-Naturwiss. Ges. Jena Vol. 4, 1893-1913. Gustav Fischer. N:1 4 5 6 15

1888 Semon, Richard (1893) Verbreitung, Lebensverhältnisse und Fortpflanzung des *Ceratodus forsteri*. Denkschr. Med.-Naturwiss. Ges. Jena *4*:11-28. N:10 16 17 18 19 20 21 24

1889 Semon, Richard (1893) Die äussere Entwickelung des *Ceratodus forsteri*. Denkschr. Med.-Naturwiss. Ges. Jena *4*:29-50. N:1 3 5 6 7 9 11 13 15 19 21

1890 Semon, Richard (1894) Vermeintliche "äussere" Kiemen bei Ceratodusembryonen. Anat. Anz. *10*:332-333. N:1 9 15

1891 Semon, Richard (1898) Die Entwickelung der paarigen Flossen des *Ceratodus forsteri*. Denkschr. Med.-Naturwiss. Ges. Jena *4*:59-111. N:1 4 5 6 15

1892 Semon, Richard (1899) Über die Entwickelung der Zahngebilde der Dipnoer. Sber. Ges. Morphol. Physiol. München *15*:75-85. NPF:1 4 15 20

1893 Semon, Richard (1899) Weitere Beiträge zur Physiologie der Dipnoerflossen, auf Grund neuer, von Mr. Arthur Thompson, an gefangenen Exemplaren von *Ceratodus* angestellten Beobachtungen. Zool. Anz. *22*:294-300. NP:1 17 19

1894 Semon, Richard (1899) In the Australian Bush and on the Coast of the Coral Sea, being the Experiences and Observations of a Naturalist in Australia, New Guinea and the Moluccas. London: Macmillan and Co. (*Neoceratodus*: 1-205). ON:10 15 18 19 21

1895 Semon, Richard (1901) Zur Entwicklungsgeschichte des Urogenitalsystems der Dipnoer. Zool. Anz. *24*:131-135. N:1 13 14 15 17

1896 Semon, Richard (1901) Die Furchung und Entwickelung der Keimblatter bei *Ceratodus forsteri*. Denkschr. Med.-Naturwiss. Ges. Jena *4*:301-332. N(L):1 3 4 5 6 7 9 11 15 17

1897 Semon, Richard (1901) Die Zahnentwickelung des *Ceratodus forsteri*. Denkschr. Med.-Naturwiss. Ges. Jena *4*:113-135. N(PFD):1 4 15 16

1898 Semon, Richard (1901) Die "ektodermale Mediannaht" des *Ceratodus*. Arch. Entwicklungsmech. Organismus (Wilhelm Roux) *11*:310-320. N:12 15

1899 Semon, Richard (1901) Über das Verwandtschaftsverhältniss der Dipnoer und Amphibien. Zool. Anz. *24*:180-188. NPLO:1 3 4 5 6 9 10 11 13 15 17

1900 Semon, Richard (1901) Normentafel zur Entwicklungsgeschichte des *Ceratodus forsteri*. In F. Keibel (ed): Normentafeln zur Entwicklungsgeschichte der Wirbelthiere, *3*:1-38. N:3 6 7 8 9 10 11 12 13 14 15 16

1901 Semon, Richard (1908) Beobachtungen über den australischen Lungenfisch im Freileben und in der Gefangenschaft. Blätt. Aquar.-Terrkunde *1908*:1-6. N:10 18 19 21 24

1902 Senn, David G. (1976) Brain structure in *Calamoichthyes calabaricus* Smith 1865 (Polypteridae, Brachiopterygii). Acta Zool. (Stockholm) *57*:121-128. O(P):1 6

1903 Serres, Marcel de (1863) Recherches sur quelques points de l'organisation du *Lepidosiren annectens*; description du cerveau (première note). C. R. Acad. Sci Paris *57*:540-547. P:1 6 7 15

1904 Serres, Marcel de (1863) Recherches sur quelques points de l'organisation du *Lepidosiren annectens*; description du cerveau. C. R. Acad. Sci. Paris *57*:577-580. P:1 6 15

1905 Sewertzoff, A. N. (1902) Zur Entwickelungsgeschichte des *Ceratodus forsteri*. Anat. Anz. *21*:593-608. N(P):1 4 6 15

1906 Shah, S. C. and P. P. Satsangi (1967) A new *Ceratodus* species from the Maleri Beds, Andhra Pradesh. Rec. Geol. Surv. India *98*:175-178. C:18

1907 Shann, E. W. (1924) Further observations on the myology of the pectoral region in fishes. Proc. Zool. Soc. London *1924*:195-215. LO:1 4 5

1908 Sharma, Moti L. (1966) Studies on the changes in the pattern of nitrogenous excretion of *Orconectes rusticus* under osmotic stress. Comp. Biochem. Physiol. *19*:681-690. O(P):1 13 18

1909 Shelton, John W. (1971) Lungfish burrows in dolomite of the Wellington Formation. Okla. Geol. Notes *31*:50. FD:18 20

1910 Shepherd, C. E. (1914) On the location of the sacculus and its contained otoliths in fishes. Zoologist *18*:103-109. NLO:1 7

1911 Shinomiya, Naomi (1970) Sôbre a biologia da *Lepidosiren paradoxa*. Proc. 22nd Ann. Mtg. Soc. Brasil. Prog. Ciênc. *1970*:288. (Abstract) L+

1912 Shipley, Arthur Everet (1906) John Samuel Budgett. In Joseph James Fletcher (ed): The Macleay Memorial Volume, Linnean Soc. N.S.W. pp.1-55. OP:1 14 15 16 18 20

1913 Shipman, Pat (1975) Implications of drought for vertebrate fossil assemblages. Nature (London) *257*:667-668. OD:18

1914 Shufeldt, R. W. (1893) On *Protopterus annectens*. Science *22*:2-3. P:1 17 19 20 21

1915 Sigé, Bernard (1968) Dents de micromammifères et fragments de coquilles d'oeufs de dinosauriens dans la faune de Vertébrés du Crétacé supérieur de Laguna Umayo (Andes péruviennes). C. R. Acad. Sci. Paris *267*:1495-1498. OFL:4 18

1916 Silva Coelho, Lina Maria de Petrini da and Paulo Sawaya (1972) Fisioecologia de Tambaky M'Boya, *Lepidosiren paradoxa* (Fitzinger) da Amazônia (Peixe-Dipnóico): estrutura do tegumento. Bol. Zool. Biol. Marinha N.S. (São Paulo) *29*:65-118. L(P):1 3 9 11 16 20

1917 Singh, B. N. (1976) Balance between aquatic and aerial respiration. In George M. Hughes (ed): Respiration of Amphibious Vertebrates. New York: Academic Press, pp.125-164. OPL:2 9 10

1918 Singh, B. R. and K. P. Singh (1979) A histochemical study on the skin of *Lepidosiren paradoxa* (Fitz.). Arch. Biol. *90*:421-436. L(P):1 3

1919 Singh, K. P., R. N. Thakur and B. R. Singh (1981) Histochemical observations on the gills of *Lepidosiren paradoxa* (Fitz). Folia Morphol. *29*:263-269. L:1 9

1920 Siwe, Sture A. (1926) Pankreasstudien. Gegenbaurs Morphol. Jahrb. *57*:84-307. (*Neoceratodus*:128-129). ON:1 8 12 15

1921 Smith, Grafton Elliot (1908) The cerebral cortex in *Lepidosiren*, with comparative notes on the interpretation of certain features of the forebrain in other vertebrates. Anat. Anz. *33*:513-540. LO(P):1 6 17

1922 Smith, G. M. and C. W. Coates (1936) Cutaneous melanosis in lungfishes (Lepidosirenidae). Biol. Bull. (Woods Hole) *71*:282-285. L:1 3 22

1923 Smith, G. M. and C. W. Coates (1937) On the histology of the skin of the lungfish *Protopterus annectens* after experimentally induced aestivation. Quart. J. Microsc. Sci. *79*:487-491. P:1 3 10 20

1924 Smith, Homer W. (1930) Lung-fish. Sci. Monthly *31*:467-470. P:G(1 2 13 17 18 19 20)

1925 Smith, Homer W. (1930) Metabolism of the lungfish, *Protopterus aethiopicus*. J. Biol. Chem. *88*:97-130. P:2 9 13 20

1926 Smith, Homer W. (1931) Observations on the African lung-fish, *Protopterus aethiopicus*, and on evolution from water to land environments. Ecology *12*:164-181. P(NL):1 2 9 10 13 14 19 20

1927 Smith, Homer W. (1931) The regulation of the composition of the blood of teleost and elasmobranch fishes, and the evolution of the vertebrate kidney. Copeia *1931*:147-152. OD:13 17

1928 Smith, Homer W. (1932) Water regulation and its evolution in the fishes. Quart. Rev. Biol. 7:1-26. OP:1 13 17

1929 Smith, Homer W. (1932) Kamongo. New York: The Viking Press. P:18 20

1930 Smith, Homer W. (1935) The metabolism of the lung-fish. I. General considerations of the fasting metabolism in active fish. J. Cell. Comp. Physiol. 6:43-67. P:2 10 21

1931 Smith, Homer W. (1935) The metabolism of the lung-fish. II. Effect of feeding meat on metabolic rate. J. Cell. Comp. Physiol. 6:335-349. P:2 9 16 21

1932 Smith, Homer W. (1935) Lung-fish. Aquarium *1*:241-243. P:G(13 19 20)

1933 Smith, Homer W. (1939) The lungfish. Natur. Hist. *44*:224-225. P:16 20

1934 Smith, Homer W. (1953) From Fish to Philosopher. Boston: Little, Brown and Company. (Chap. VI. The Lungfish:71-84). P:2 10 13 14 18 19 20

1935 Smith, I. C. (1955) Giant nerve fibers in *Protopterus*. J. Physiol. (London) *129*:42P-43P. P:1 6

1936 Smith, Malcolm (1938) George Albert Boulenger, 1858-1937. Copeia *1938*:1-3. O

1937 Smith, Moya Meredeith and M. H. Hobdell (1973) Comparisons between the microstructure of scales of *Latimeria chalumnae* and extant dipnoan and teleostean scales. J. Dent. Res. *52*:957. (Abstract) ONP:1 3

1938 Smith, Moya Meredeith (1977) The microstructure of the dentition and dermal ornament of three dipnoans from the Devonian of Western Australia: a contribution towards dipnoan interrelations, and morphogenesis, growth and adaptation of the skeletal tissues. Philos. Trans. Roy. Soc. London *281B*:29-72. J. Dent. Res. *56*:D109. (Abstract) FD(N):1 3 4 17

1939 Smith, Moya Meredeith (1978) Enamel in the oral teeth of *Latimeria chalumnae* (Pisces: Actinistia): a scanning electron microscope study. J. Zool. (London) *185*:355-369. O(NPL):1 4 17

1940 Smith, Moya Meredeith (1979) Structure and histogenesis of tooth plates in *Sagenodus inaequalis* Owen considered in relation to the phylogeny of post-Devonian dipnoans. Proc. Roy. Soc. Lond. *204B*:15-39. FD(NPL):1 4 17

1941 Smith, Moya Meredeith (1979) SEM of the enamel layer in oral teeth of fossil and extant crossopterygian and dipnoan fishes. SEM/1979/II:483-490. LO:1 4 15 17

1942 Smith, Moya Meredeith (1984) Cathodoluminescence as an indicator of growth increments in the dentine in tooth plates of Triassic lungfish. Neues Jahrb. Geol. Paläontol. Monatsh. *84*:39-45. FD+:4 15 16

1943 Smith, Moya Meredeith (1984) Petrodentine in extant and fossil dipnoan dentitions: microstructure, histogenesis and growth. Proc. Linnean Soc. N.S.W. *107*:367-407. PLNCFD:1 4 16

1944 Smith, Moya Meredeith (1985) The pattern of histogenesis and growth of tooth plates in larval stages of extant lungfish. J. Anat. *140*:627-643. P(N):4 15

1945 Soffié, M., M. Lannoye, M. Weyers and M. Citta (1970) Recherches sur la respiration aérienne de deux sous-espèces de Protoptères (*Protopterus aethiopicus mesmaekersi* Poll et *Protopterus aethiopicus aethiopicus* Heckel). Bull. Acad. Roy. Belg. *56*:580-595. P:2 9 10 19

1946 Sokabe, Hirofumi and Mizuho Ogawa (1974) Comparative studies of the juxtaglomerular apparatus. Int. Rev. Cytol. *37*:271-327. OPL:1 13 17

1947 Solger, Friederich B. (1880) Neue Untersuchungen zur Anatomie der Seitenorgane der Fische. III. Die Seitenorgane der Knochenfische. Arch. Mikrosk. Anat. *18*:364-390. (Dipnoi:365-367). ONLP:1 3 6 7

1948 Souza Cunha, Fausto Luiz de (1979) Sur l'évidence des restes de *Ceratodus africanus* Haug proviennent de gisements Crétacé (Cénomanien) de la Baía de São Marcos, Ma, Brésil. An. Acad. Bras. Ciênc. *51*:361-362. (Abstract) C:4 18

1948a Souza Cunha, Fausto Luiz de and Candido Simoes Ferreira (1980) Um Dipnoi na Formacion Itapecuru (Cenomaniano), Maranhao, Brasil. Actas Congr. Argent. Paleontol. Bioestratigr. *2*:1-9.

1949 Spencer, W. Baldwin (1892) Note on the habits of *Ceratodus forsteri*. Proc. Roy. Soc. Victoria *4*:81-84.

Summarized in Nature *45*:425. N:10 18 19 21

1950 Spencer, W. Baldwin (1892) A trip to Queensland in search of *Ceratodus*. Victorian Natur. *9*:16-32. N:10 14 18 19

1951 Spencer, W. Baldwin (1893) Contributions to our knowledge of *Ceratodus*. Part I. The blood vessels. In Joseph James Fletcher (ed): Macleay Memorial Volume. Linnean Soc. N.S.W., pp.1-34. N:1 11

1952 Spencer, W. Baldwin (1898) Der Bau der Lungen von *Ceratodus* und *Protopterus*. Denkschr. Med.-Naturwiss. Ges. Jena *4*:51-58.NP:1 9 11 17

1953 Spencer, W. Baldwin (1928) *Ceratodus*. In The Australian Encyclopedia. Sydney: Angus and Robertson, *1*:248-250. N(PL):G(3 4 9 11 12 15 16 18 21 24)

1954 Sprenkel, H. Berkelbach van der (1934) II. Nebenniere und Paraganglien. In Louis Bolk, Ernest Göppert, Erich Kallius, and Wilhelm Lubosch (eds): Handbuch der vergleichenden Anatomie der Wirbeltiere. Berlin and Wein: Urban und Schwarzenberg, *2*:777-816. OD:1 6 13

1955 Stadtmüller, Franz (1927) Über das Kiemenfilter der Dipnoer. Gegenbaurs Morphol. Jahrb. *57*:489-529. NPL:1 4 9 17

1955a Stahl, Barbara J. (1974) Vertebrate History: Problems in Evolution. New York, McGraw Hill. (Dipnoi:127-142).

1956 Stallknecht, Helmut (1963) The Australian lungfish. Trop. Fish Hobbyist *11*:64-68. N(PL):G(3 9 10 14 18 20 21)

1957 Stanbury, Peter (1978) Australia's Animals: Who Discovered Them? The Macleay Museum, Univ. Sydney. ON:14 18 19

1958 Stannius, Hermann (1854) Handbuch der Anatomie der Wirbelthiere. Berlin: Veit Comp.

1959 Starkey, Phyllis M. and Alan J. Barrett (1982) Evolution of alpha$_2$ macroglobulin: the demonstration in a variety of vertebrate species of a protein resembling human alpha$_2$ macroglobulin. Biochem. J. *205*:91-95.PO:2 11 17

1960 Stead, David G. (1906) Fishes of Australia: A Popular and Systematic Guide to the Study of the Wealth Within our Waters. Sydney: William Brooks and Co., Ltd. (*Neoceratodus*:228-230). ON:G(3 4 10 18 20)

1961 Steindachner, Franz (1861) Vorläufige Mittheilung *Leucifer uracanthus* n. sp., *Ophianoplus sarsii* n. sp. und über die äusseren Kiemen—Anhänge der *Protopterus*—Arten. Verh. Zool.-Bot. Ges. Wien *11*:365-366.P(L):1 9 15

1962 Stensiö, Erik Anderson (1921) Triassic Fishes from Spitzbergen. Part I. Vienna: A. Holzhausen. (*Ceratodus*:42-43). CO:4 18

1963 Stensiö, Erik Anderson (1947) The sensory lines and dermal bones of the cheek in fishes and amphibians. Kgl. Sven. Vetenskapsakad. Handl. *24*:3-195. NPLO:1 3 4 7 15 17

1964 Stephan, P. (1906) Le fonctionnement des grandes cellules à granulations éosinophiles du tissu lymphoïde du Protoptère. C. R. Soc. Biol. Paris *1906*:501-503. P:1 11 12 13 20

1965 Stephenson, W. (1953) The natural history of Somerset Dam and its fishing potentialities. Reprinted from Ichthyological Notes #2 (and other Papers) issued by Department of Harbours and Marine, Queensland. (*Neoceratodus*:36). NO:18

1966 Sterba, Günther (1959) Süsswasserfische aus aller Welt. Leipzig: Urania-Verlag. (Dipneusti:616-622). Translated and revised by Denys W. Tucker. London: Vista Books. [1962] OLPN:G(3 4 10 14 15 18 19 20 21)

1967 Stirton, Ruben Arthur, Richard H. Tedford, and Alden H. Miller (1961) Cenozoic stratigraphy and vertebrate paleontology of the Tirari Desert, South Australia. Rec. S. Aust. Mus. Adelaide 14:19-61. OFN:4 18

1968 Stirton, Ruben Arthur, Richard H. Tedford, and Michael O. Woodburne (1968) Australian Tertiary deposits containing terrestrial mammals. Univ. Cal. Publ. Geol. Sci. 77:1-30.OFN:18

1969 Stivens, Dal (1974) The story of 'Forster's new horny tooth'. Wildlife (London) 16:410-411. N:G(1 3 4 10 19)

1970 Stivens, Dal (1975) Bahník Australskg (Neoceratodus forsteri) - "zivoucí fosilie" z devonského období. Ziva 23:68-70. NFD:G(1 3 4 10 11 17 18 19)

1971 Stoddart, W. W. (1875) Ceratodus forsteri. Proc. Bristol Natur. Soc. NS 1:145-149. N(LFD):G(1 3 4 10 11 14 18 19 21)

1972 Stormer, Leif (1977) Arthropod invasion of land during late Silurian and Devonian times. Science (Washington) 191:1362-1364. OD:18 20

1973 Striegnitz, H. J. (1942) Aufbau und Struktur der Zähne von Lepidosiren paradoxa. Z. Mikrosk.-Anat. Forsch. 51:119-144. L:1 4

1974 Striegnitz, H. J. (1947) Aufbau und Konstruktion weiterer Lungenfischzähne. Anat. Anz. 96:166-182. PLNFD:1 4 17

1975 Stromer, Ernst (1910) Über das Gebiss der Lepidosirenidae und die Verbreitung tertiarer und mesozoischer Lungenfische. Festschrift zum sechzigsten Geburtstag Richard Hertwigs 2:611-624. FLP:1 4 17 18

1976 Stromer, Ernst (1914) Mitteilungen über Wirbeltierreste aus dem Mittelpliocän des Natrontales (Ägypten). 4. Fische: a) Dipnoi: Protopterus. Z. Dtsch. Geol. Ges, 66:420-425. FLP:1 4 17 18

1977 Stromer, Ernst (1917) Über rezente und triassische Gebisse von Ceratodontidae. I. Das Gebiss von Epiceratodus forsteri Krefft sp. Z. Dtsch. Geol. Ges. 69:1-17. N(LP):1 4 21

1978 Stromer, Ernst and Wilhelm Weiler (1930) Ergebnisse der Forschungsreisen Prof. E. Stromers in den Wüsten Ägyptens. VI. Beschreibung von Wirbeltier-Resten aus dem nubischen Sandsteine Oberägyptens und aus ägyptischen Phosphaten nebst Bemerkungen über die Geologie der Umgegend von Mahamîd in Oberägypten. Abh. Bayerischen Akad. Wiss. München (NF) 7:12-42. (Ceratodus:25-26). CO:1 4 18

1979 Stromer, Ernst (1938) Der Wüstenfisch Ceratodus Ag. 1838 und seine meso- und känozoischen Verwandten. Neues Jahrb. Min. Geol. Paläontol. Stuttgart 80:248-263. CPLN(FD):4 10 18 21

1980 Stuhlmann, Franz (1889) Bemerkungen über die Süsswasserfauna von Quilimane. Sber. Akad. Berlin 1889:453-466. PO:3 10 14 18 19 20 21 22

1981 Stuhlmann, Franz (1889) Zweiter Bericht über eine mit Unterstützung der königlichen Akademie der Wissenschaften nach Ost-Africa unternommene Reise. II. Weitere Studien über die Süsswasserfauna von Sansibar. Sber. Akad. Berlin 1889:645-660. PO:1 3 4 10 18 20 21 22 23 24

1982 Stuhlmann, Franz (1891) Beiträge zur Fauna centralafrikanischer Seen. 1. Süd-Creek des Victoria-Niansa. Zool. Jahrb. Abt. Syst. 5:924-926. OP:1 9 15 18

1983 Stur, Dionys (1886) Vorlage des ersten fossilen Schädels von Ceratodus aus den obertriadischen Reingrabner Schiefern von Pölzberg nördlich bei Lunz. Verh. Geol. Reichsanst 1886:381-383. C:4 18

1984 Suga, S. and Y. Taki (1981) Fluoride concentration in the enameloid of primitive bony fishes. J. Dent. Res. 60:488. NLPO:2 4 17

1985 Sutton, J. Bland (1890) Evolution and Disease. London: Walter Scott. O(P):16

1986 Svensson, Gustav S. O. (1933) Fresh water fishes from the Gambia River. Kgl. Sven. Vetenskapsakad. Handl. 12:1-101. (Protopterus:27-28). OP:14 15 16 18 19 20

1987 Swan, Henry (1963) Kamango and anabolone. Arch. Surg. 87:715-716. P:2 12 20

1988 Swan, Henry and F. G. Hall (1966) Oxygen-hemoglobin dissociation in Protopterus aethiopicus. Amer. J. Physiol. 210:487-489. P:2 11 18 20

1989 Swan, Henry, Dalton Jenkins and Kerwin Knox (1968) Anti-metabolic extract from the brain of Protopterus aethiopicus. Nature (London) 217:671. P:2 6 20

1990 Swan, Henry, Dalton Jenkins and Kirvin Knox (1969) Metabolic torpor in Protopterus aethiopicus: an anti-metabolic agent from the brain. Amer. Natur. 103:247-258. P:2 6 20

1991 Swan, Henry (1974) Thermoregulation and Bioenergetics: Patterns for Vertebrate Survival. New York: American Elsevier Pub. Co. (Chapter 13, Aestivation, and the aestivating poikilotherm, Kamango:254-280). PLO(N):2 6 9 10 11 17 18 20 21

1992 Swan, Henry, F. G. Reinhard, D. L. Caprio and Christopher L. Schätte (1981) Hypometabolic brain peptide from vertebrates capable of torpor. Cryobiology 18:598-602. Cryobiology 18:102. (Abstract). See also Science (Washington) 195:84-85. [1977] PO:2 6 20

1993 Swan, Henry (1981) Neuroendocrine aspects of hibernation. IN Survival in the Cold: Hibernation and Other Adaptations, Internat. Symp. Prague, July, 1980:121-138. New York: Elsevier North Holland, Inc. O(P):2 6 20

1994 Szarski, Henryk (1962) The origin of the Amphibia. Quart. Rev. Biol. 37:189-241. OD:4 7 9 10 11 17

1995 Szarski, Henryk and R. Cybulska (1967) Liver cell size in Protopterus dolloi Blngr. (Dipnoi). Bull. Acad. Polon. Sci. Ser. Biol. 15:217-220. P:1 12

1996 Szarski, Henryk (1976) Cell size and nuclear DNA content in vertebrates. Int. Rev. Cytol. 44:93-111. OLPN:1 17

1997 Szarski, Henryk (1977) Sarcopterygii and the origin of tetrapods. In Max K. Hecht, Peter Charles Goody, and Bessie M. Hecht (eds): Major Patterns in Vertebrate Evolution. New York: Plenum Press, pp.517-540. OD:17

1998 Szarski, Henryk (1982) Nowe poglady na pokrewieństwa kregowców ladowych. (Actual views on tetrapod affinities). Przegl. Zool. 26:281-284. [in Polish]. FDNLPO:1 4 7 17

1999 Szarski, Henryk (1983) Cell size and the concept of wasteful and frugal evolutionary strategies. J. Theor. Biol. 105:201-209. DO:1 17 18

2000 Szidon, Jan Peter, Sukhamay Lahiri, Maurice Lev, and Alfred P. Fishman (1969) Heart and circulation of the African lungfish. Circ. Res. *25*:23-38. P:1 9 10 11

2001 Tabaste, Nicole (1963) Étude de restes de Poissons du Crétacé Saharien. Mém. Inst. Français Afr. Noire sér. A Sci. Natur. #68:437-485. (Les Dipneustes:440-458). CO:1 4 18

2002 Tagliani, Giulio (1905) Le fibre del Mauthner nel midollo spinale de'Vertebrati inferiori (anamni). Arch. Zool. Ital. *2*:385-435. (Dipnoi:406-408). OPN:1 6

2003 Tamai, Y., H. Kojima, K. Abe, and A. Suzuki (1984) Evolutionary change of glycolipids and myelin-proteins in the brain of the primitive bony fishes. Neurochem. Res. *9*:1120. (Abstract) DO:2 6 17

2004 Tanaka, Yasukazu and Yoriko Saito (1981) Lamellar inclusion bodies in lung-fish thrombocytes. J. Electron Microsc. *30*:63-66. LP:1 11 20

2005 Tanaka, Yasukazu and Yoriko Saito (1982) A comparative anatomical study of three different intestinal spleens and their significance in vertebrate hematopoiesis. Acta Haematol. Jpn. *45*:1017-1030. [in Japanese]. LPO*:1 11 12

2006 Tanaka, Yasukazu (1985) An anatomical study on the spleen of archaic fishes. 1. Coelacanthiformes and Dipneusti. Acta Haematol. Jpn. *48*:710-723. [in Japanese]. DO*:1 11 12

2007 Taquet, Philippe (1970) Sur le gisement de Dinosauriens et de Crocodiliens de Gadoufaoua (République de Niger). C. R. Acad. Sci. Paris *271*:38-40. OC:18

2008 Tate, Ralph (1886) Post-Miocene climate in South Australia. Trans. Roy. Soc. S. Aust. *9*:49-59, 203. OC:18

2009 Teixeira, Carlos (1949) La faune de poissons du Karroo de l'Angola et du Congo Belge. Bol. Mus. Lab. Minerol. Geol. Univ. Lisboa #17:27-31. CO:4 18

2010 Teixeira, Carlos (1954) Sur un Ceratodontidé du Karroo de l'Angola. Mem. Acad. Ciênt. Lisboa cl. Ciênc. *7*:55-60. C(N):4 18

2011 Teller, Friedrich Joseph (1891) Über den Schädel eines fossilen Dipnoers *Ceratodus sturii* nov. sp. aus den Schichten der Oberen Trias der Nordalpen. Abhandl. der Kaiser König. Geolog. Reichsanstalt *15*:1-38. C+:4 18

2012 Tennent, J. Emerson (1861) Natural History of Ceylon, with Narratives and Anecdotes. London: Longman and Co. (*Protopterus*:352). OP:G(20)

2013 Theisen, Birgit (1972) Ultrastructure of the olfactory epithelium in the Australian lungfish *Neoceratodus fosteri*. Acta Zool. (Stockholm) *53*:205-218. N:1 7

2014 Thenius, Erich (1974) Coelacanths and lungfishes. In Bernhard Grzimek (ed): Grzimek's Animal Life Encyclopedia. New York: Van Nostrand Reinhold Co., *5*:261-268. NPLFDO:G(1 3 4 9 11 12 18 20 21)

2015 Thomas, J. D. (1958) Two new digenetic trematodes, *Heterorchis protopteri*, n. sp. (Fellodistomidae) and *Acanthostomium bagri*, n. sp. (Acanthostomidae: Acanthostominae) from West Africa. Proc. Helminthol. Soc. Wash. *25*:8-14. P:12 22

2016 Thomas, Susan F. (1976) Histological observations of the regenerating limb in the African lungfish *Protopterus*. Thesis, Supervised Study, Mary Baldwin College, Staunton, Virginia. P:1 3 4 5 6 7 11 16

2017 Thomasset, Jean-Jaques (1928) Essai de classification des variétès de dentine chez les Poissons. C. R. Acad. Sci. Paris *187*:1075-1076. NO:4

2018 Thomasset, Jean-Jacques (1930) Recherches sur les tissus dentaires des Poissons fossiles. Arch. Anat. Histol. Embryol. *10-11*:5-153. (Dipneustes:137). CO(LP):4

2019 Thomson, James M. (1978) Vertebrates of the Brisbane River Valley. Proc. Roy Soc. Queensland *89*:121-128. NO:10 18

2020 Thomson, Keith Stewart (1965) On the relationships of certain Carboniferous Dipnoi; with descriptions of four new forms. Proc. Roy. Soc. Edinburgh *69B*:221-245. FD:1 4

2021 Thomson, Keith Stewart (1965) The nasal apparatus in Dipnoi, with special reference to *Protopterus*. Proc. Zool. Soc. London. *145*:207-238.PLN:1 4 6 7 10 11 15 17

2022 Thomson, Keith Stewart (1966) The snout anatomy of Rhipidistia and Dipnoi, with reference to tetrapod ancestry. Amer. Dissertation D. *11*:15. (Abstract) FD+:1 4

2023 Thomson, Keith Stewart (1967) Mechanisms of intracranial kinetics in fossil rhipidistian fishes (Crossopterygii) and their relatives. J. Linnean Soc. London Zool. *46*:223-253. O(FD):1 4 10

2024 Thomson, Keith Stewart (1967) A new genus and species of marine dipnoan fish, from the Upper Devonian of Canada. Postilla #106:1-6. FD:4 18 21

2025 Thomson, Keith Stewart (1968) Experiments on lungfish respiration. Discovery (New Haven) *4*:13-18. PL:9 10 17 18 19

2026 Thomson, Keith Stewart (1968) Lung ventilation in dipnoan fishes. Postilla #122:1-6. P:5 9 10

2027 Thomson, Keith Stewart (1969) Gill and lung function in the evolution of the lungfishes (Dipnoi): an hypothesis. Forma Functio *1*:250-262. PLNFD:1 2 9 10 17

2028 Thomson, Keith Stewart (1969) The biology of the lobe-finned fishes. Biol. Rev. (Cambridge) *44*:91-154. PLN:1 2 4 9 10 11 13 14 17 18 20 21

2029 Thomson, Keith Stewart (1969) The environment and distribution of Paleozoic sarcopterygian fishes. Amer. J. Sci. *267*:457-464. FDO:17 18

2030 Thomson, Keith Stewart and Ken S.W. Campbell (1971) The structure and relationships of the primitive Devonian lungfish - *Dipnorhynchus sussmilchi* (Etheridge). Bull. Peabody Mus. Natur. Hist. Yale Univ. #38:1-109. FD:1 3 4 6 7 17 18 21

2031 Thomson, Keith Stewart (1971) The adaptation and evolution of early fishes. Quart. Rev. Biol. *46*:139-166. OD:10 13 17 18

2032 Thomson, Keith Stewart (1972) An attempt to reconstruct evolutionary changes in the cellular DNA content of lungfish. J. Exp. Zool. *180*:363-372.FDPLN:1 4 17

2033 Thomson, Keith Stewart (1975) On the biology of cosmine. Bull. Peabody Mus. Natur. Hist. Yale Univ. #40:1-59. O(FD):1 3 4 7

2034 Thomson, Keith Stewart and Karin Muraszko (1978) Estimation of cell size and DNA content in fossil fishes and amphibians. J. Exp. Zool. *205*:315-320. OD:1 17

2035 Thomson, Keith Stewart (1980) The ecology of Devonian lobe-finned fishes. In Alec L. Panchen (ed): The Terrestrial Environment and the Origin of Land Vertebrates. New York: Academic Press, pp.187-122. FDO:17 18

2036 Thomson, Keith Stewart (1981) A radical look at fish-tetrapod relationships. Paleobiology 7:152-156. OD:17

2037 Thors, Frans (1973) The brain stem of the Dipnoan Lepidosiren paradoxa. Acta Morphol. Neerl.-Scand. 11:373-374. (Abstract) L:1 6

2038 Thors, Frans and Rudolf Nieuwenhuys (1979) Topological analysis of the brain stem of the lungfish Lepidosiren paradoxa. J. Comp. Neurol. 187:589-612.L(NP):1 6

2039 Thurmond, John T. (1974) Lower vertebrate faunas of the Trinity Division in North-central Texas. Geoscience and Man 8:103-109. CO:4 18

2040 Tiegs, O. W. (1931) A study of the neurofibril structure of the nerve cell. J. Comp. Neurol. 52:189-222. LO:1 6

2041 Tiwari, Vijay and R. K. Gaur (1978) Functional significance of fibro-cartilage plug in the heart of Protopterus aethiopicus. Anat. Rec. 190:561. (Abstract) P:1 2 5 6 11

2042 Tomes, Charles S. (1923) A Manual of Dental Anatomy Human and Comparative. Eighth Edition. New York: The Macmillan Company. [See also Ludwig Hollaender #938] OL(N):1 4

2043 Tortonese, Enrico and Gianna Arbocco (1955) I Prototteri della Somalia Italiana. Doriana 2:1-8. P:1 3 18

2044 Tortonese, Enrico (1955) Una nuova specie vivente di Dipnoo. Natura (Milano) 46:187-188. P:1 18

2045 Toyozumi, Y. (1984) Comparative anatomy and evolution of the phonatory organ in vertebrates. Otol. Fukuoka 31:47-68. [in Japanese]. DO*:1 10 17

2046 Traquair, Ramsay Heatley (1871) On the restoration of the tail in Protopterus annectens. Rep. Brit. Assoc. Advan. Sci. 1871:143. P:1 4 5 6 16

2047 Traquair, Ramsay Heatley (1873) On a new genus of fossil fish of the order Dipnoi. Geol. Mag. (Decade I) 10:552-555. FD:1 4

2048 Traquair, Ramsay Heatley (1878) On the genera Dipterus, Palaedaphus, Holodus and Cheirodus. Ann. Mag. Natur. Hist. 2:1-17. FDN(LP):1 4 17

2049 Traquair, Ramsay Heatley (1888) Notes on the nomenclature of the fishes of the Old Red Sandstone of Great Britain. Geol. Mag. (Decade III) 5:507-517. FDO:3 4 18

2050 Traquair, Ramsay Heatley (1890) List of the fossil Dipnoi and Ganoidei of Fife and the Lothians. Proc. Roy. Soc. Edinburgh 17:385-400. FDO

2051 Traquair, Ramsay Heatley (1900) Presidential Address: On evolution and the Dipnoi. Rep. Brit. Assoc. Advan. Sci. 1900:768-783. OFD(NPL):1 17

2052 Tretjakoff, Dmitri Konstantinovich (1936) Tkanevoi sostav cheshui ryb. (Histology of fish scales). Arkh. Anat. Gistol. Embriol. 15:89-104. German translation:174-178. N:1 3 17

2053 Trewavas, Ethelwynn (1954) The presence in Africa east of the Rift Valleys of two species of Protopterus, P. annectens and P. amphibius. Ann. Mus. Congo Belge sér. Quarto Zool. 1:83-100. P:1 4 18

2054 Trewavas, Ethelwynn, Errol Ivor White, N. S. Marshall, and Denys W. Tucker (1955) Answer to Romer's Herpetichthyes, Amphibioidei, Choanichthyes or Sarcopterygii. Nature (London) 176:126-127. D:17

2055 Tribolet, Frédéric-Maurice de (1898) Les fossiles vivants. Bull. Soc. Neuchatel. Sci. Natur. 27:47-53. NCO:G(17)

2056 Tripathi, C. (1975) Observations on the Maleri-Kota beds of the Adilabad District, Andhra Pradesh. Rec. India Geol. Surv. 106:1-12. CO:4 18

2057 Troschel, Franz Hermann (1871) Über eine Queensland neu entdeckte Fischgattung. Verh. Naturh. Ver. Preuss Reinl. Westphal. 28:90. N(C):18

2058 Tucker, Richard (1972) Some functional and morphological adaptations in the gills of Dipnoi. Z. Morphol. Tiere 73:279-296. N:1 9 18

2059 Ueck, M. (1969) Ultrastrukturbesonderheiten der pinealen Sinneszellen von Protopterus dolloi. Z. Zellforsch. Mikrosk. Anat. 100:560-580. P:1 6 7

2060 Ueda, Shintaro, Nobuyashi Ishii, Shoichi Masumoto, and Kazuhiro Hayashi (1980) Comparative morphological studies of the lungs: ultrastructure of the lungs of lung-fish. J. Clin. Electron Microsc. 13:461-462. (Abstract) O(L):1 10

2061 Umlauff, Heinrich (1895) Der Molchfisch (Protopterus annectens). Blätt. Aquarien Terrarien-Freunde 6:85-88. P:19 20

2062 Urist, Marshall R., S. Uyeno, E. King, M. Okada, and S. Applegate (1972) Calcium and phosphorus in the skeleton and blood of the lungfish Lepidosiren paradoxa, with comment on humoral factors in calcium homeostasis in the Osteichthyes. Comp. Biochem. Physiol. 42A:393-408. L:2 4 8 11 17

2063 Urist, Marshall R. (1973) Testosterone-induced development of limb gills of the lungfish, Lepidosiren paradoxa. Comp. Biochem. Physiol. 44A:131-135.L:8 9 16

2064 Vaillant, Léon (1892) Sur le genre Megapleuron. C. R. Acad. Sci. Paris 114:1083-1084. FD(N):3

2065 Vaillant, Léon (1896) Sur le mode de formation des coprolithes hélicoïdes, d'après les faits observés à la ménagerie des reptiles sur les Protoptères. C. R. Acad. Sci. Paris 122:742-743. P:9 12 17

2066 Vaillant, Léon (1899) Protopterus retropinnis et Ectodus foae, espèces nouvelles de l'Afrique Équatoriale. Bull. Mus. Natl. Hist. Natur. Paris 5:219-222. O

2067 Van Couvering, Judith Anne Harris (1977) Early records of freshwater fishes in Africa. Copeia 1977:163-166. FPO:18

2068 Vanderplank, F. L. (1969) The African lungfish. Aquarist Pondkeeper 34:271. P:G(10 15 18 19 20 21)

2069 Vanhöffen-Königsberg, Ernst (1890) Über die Ceratodusflosse. Verh. Ges. Dtsch. Naturforsch. Artze 63:134-135. N(PL):4 17

2070 Vassiliades, G. and J. Richard (1971) Heterorchis senagalensis n.sp. (Trematoda; Fellodistomatidae), parasite de Protopterus annectens Owen, 1839 (Poisson; Lepidosirenidae). Bull. Mus. Natl. Hist. Natur. Paris sér. 2, 42:1288-1292. P:12 22

2071 Vaughn, Peter Paul (1964) Evidence of aestivating lungfish from the Sangre de Cristo Formation, Lower Permian of Northern New Mexico. Los Angeles County Mus., Contrib. Sci. #80:1-8. FD:18 20

2072 Vaughn, Peter Paul (1969) Early Permian Vertebrates from Southern New Mexico and their paleozoogeographic significance. Los Angeles County Mus., Contrib. Sci. #166:1-22. OFD:18

2073 Vervoort, A. (1980) Tetraploidy in *Protopterus* (Dipnoi). Experientia (Basel) *36*:294-295. P:1

2074 Vianna, Antonio (1949) Um peixe do lusitaniano do cabo Mondego. Port. Ser. Geol., Com. *30*:13-21. (*Protopterus microstomus*). OFP*:18

2075 Vincent, Swale (1897) On the morphology and physiology of the suprarenal capsules in fishes. Anat. Anz. *13*:39-48. OPL:1 8

2076 Vinciguerra, Decio (1897) Pesci raccolti dal cap. V. Bottego durante la sua Seconda Spedizione nelle regioni dei Somali e dei Galla. Ann. Mus. Civ. Storia Natur. Genova *37*:343-364. OP:1 18

2077 Vis, Charles W. de (1884) *Ceratodus forsteri* post-Pliocene. Proc. Roy. Soc. Queensland *1*:40-43. CFN:1 18

2078 Vogel, Zdenek (1972) Bahník australský poprvé v Praze. Ziva *20*:106-107. Reprinted in Aquarien Terrarien *20*:76-78. [1973; In German] N(PL):G(1 3 10 15 16 18 19 21)

2079 Vollrath, Paul (1923) *Ceratodus elegans* n. sp. aus dem Stubensandstein. Jahresber. Oberrhein. Geol. Ver. Stuttgart N.S. *12*:158-162. C:1 4 18

2080 Volz, Wilhelm (1896) Neue Funde aus dem Muschelkalk Oberschlesiens. Z. Dtsch. Geol. Ges. *48*:976-982. CO:1 4 18

2081 Vorob'yeva, Emilia I. (1971) Etmoidnay oblast-'Panderichthys i nekotorye problemy morfologii kisteperykh. (The ethmoid region of *Panderichthys* and some problems in lungfish morphology). Tr. Paleontol. Inst. Akad. Nauk SSSR *130*:142-159. O(D):4 17

2082 Vorob'yeva, Emilia I. and D. V. Obruchev (1964) Subclass Sarcopterygii. In D. V. Obruchev (ed): Fundamentals of Paleontology. Vol. IX, Agnatha, Pisces, sections 268-317. CNPL:G(1 4 14 20 21)

2083 Vorob'yeva, Emilia I. (1967) Triasovvy tseratod iz yuzhnoy fergany i nekotoryye zamechaniya o sisteme i filogenii tseratodontid. (A Triassic Ceratod from South Fergana and remarks on the systematics and phylogeny of Ceratodontids). Paleontol. Zh. *1967*:102-111. Translation in Paleontol. J. *1967*:80-87. C:3 4 16 18

2084 Vorob'yeva, Emilia I. and M. G. Minikh (1968) Opyt primeneniya biometrii k izucheniyu zubnykh plastinok tseratodontid. (Experimental application of biometry to the study of Ceratodontid dental plates). Paleontol. Zh. *1968*:76-87. Translation in Paleontol. J. *1968*:217-227. C:1 4 18

2085 Vorob'yeva, Emilia I. and L. A. Liarskaia (1968) Ostatki kistyepyerykh i dvoiakodysha shchikh iz amatskikh sloev Latvii i ikh zakhoronenie. (Remains of Dipnoi from Amatski, Latvia, and their preservation). Akad. Nauk SSSR Otdel. Obshch. Biol. *1968*:71-86. FD:18

2086 Vorob'yeva, Emilia I. (1972) Novyi rod dvoiakodyschchikh iz emiaksinskoi suity jakutii. (New genus of Dipnoi from the Paleozoic Emjakinski Suite in Jakutija). Paleontol. J. *1972*:94-100. Translation in Paleontol. J. *1972*:229-234. FD(C):4 7 16 18 21

2087 Vorob'yeva, Emilia I. (1974) O filogeneticheskikh sviasiakh iskopaiemykh kisteperykh ryb (Crossopterygii) gruppy rhipidistia. (Phylogenetic relationships of the crossopterygian Rhipidistian group). Ichthyologia 6:111-117. OD:17

2088 Vorob'yeva, Emilia I. (1975) K voprosu o sootnoshyenii i kosto v filogyenyezye dryevnyeyshikh nizshikh pozvonochnykh. (Relationship between cartilage and

2089 Wächtler, K. (1980) The regional production of acetylcholine in the brains of lower and higher vertebrates. Comp. Biochem. Physiol. *65C*:1-16. LO:2 6 17

2090 Wade, Robert Thompson (1930) The fossil fishes of the Australian Mesozoic rocks. J. Proc. Roy. Soc. N.S.W. *64*:115-147. FDCO:17 18

2091 Wade, Robert Thompson (1935) The Triassic Fishes of Brookvale, New South Wales. London: British Museum of Natural History. (*Ceratodus*:1-3). OC:1 3 4

2092 Wager, Vincent A. (1958) The lung fish. Afr. Wildlife *12*:151-154. P:G(10 15 16 18 19 20 21)

2093 Wagner, Günter P. (1980) Empirical information about the mechanism of typogenic evolution. Naturwiss. *67*:258-259. D:17

2094 Waldeyer-Hartz, Wilhelm von (1906) Die Geschlechtszellen. In Oscar Hertwig (ed): Handbuch der Entwicklungslehre der Wirbeltiere. Jena: Gustav Fischer, *1*:86-476. (Dipnoi:124-127). OPN:1 13 14

2095 Waldman, Michael (1971) Fish from the freshwater Lower Cretaceous of Victoria, Australia, with comments on the paleo-environment. Spec. Pap. Paleontol. #9:1-124. London: Palaeontol. Assoc. (*Ceratodus*:7-10). OC:3 4 18

2096 Waldman, Michael (1973) The fossil lake-fauna of Koonwarra, Victoria. Aust. Natur. Hist. *17*:317-321. CO:18

2097 Walker, F. G. (1922) *Ceratodus* in the Upper Coomera River. Brisbane Courrier, Jan. 14. N:18

2098 Walker, S. F. (1929) On *Ceratodus* in the Coomera River. Brisbane Courrier, Feb. 14. N:18

2099 Walliker, D. (1969) Myxosporidea of some Brazilian freshwater fishes. J. Parasitol. *55*:942-948. LO:22

2100 Walls, Gordon Lynn (1942) The vertebrate eye and its adaptive radiation. Cranbrook Inst. Sci. Bull. No. 19. PLNO:1 6 7 20

2101 Walter, Georg (1889) Über die Schalenhäute von *Protopterus annectens*. Z. Physiol. Chem. *13*:464-476. P:1 2 3 20

2102 Walter, J. A. (1873) *Lepidosiren* und ihre Stelle im System. Lotos *23*:36-43. LPN:1 9 17

2103 Wang, Junqing (Chun-ching) (1981) A tooth plate of Dipnoan from Qujing, Yunnan. Vertebr. Palasiat. *19*:197-199. [In Chinese, with English summary, p. 199]. FD:4 18

2104 Ward, James W. (1969) Comparative hematological studies on *Neoceratodus forsteri*, *Lepidosiren paradoxa*, *Lepiosteus osseus*, *Synodus foetens*, *Micropogon undulatus*, and *Opsanus beta*. Anat. Rec. *163*:281. (Abstract) NLO:1 11

2105 Ward, James W. (1969) Hematological studies on the Australian lungfish, *Neoceratodus forsteri*. Copeia *1969*:633-635. Assoc. Southeast Biol. Bull. *15*:28. [1968]. (Abstract) N(L):1 11

2106 Warthin, Aldred S., Jr. (1928) Fossil fishes from the Triassic of Texas. Contrib. Mus. Paleontol. Univ. Mich. *3*:15-18. CO:1 4 18

2107 Wasawo, David P. S. (1959) A dry season burrow of *Protopterus aethiopicus* Heckel. Rev. Zool. Bot. Afr. *60*:65-71. P:18 19 20

2108 Wasawo, David P. S. (1964) Some problems of Uganda swamps. Proc. Pap. International Union for

Conservation of Nature and Natural Resources (IUCN) Pub. N.S. *4*:196-204. P*:18

2109 Watson, David Meredith Sears and Henry Day (1916) II. Notes on some Palaeozoic fishes. Manchester Mem. *60*:1-53. FDO(N):1 4 17

2110 Watson, David Meredith Sears and E. Leonard Gill (1923) The structure of certain Paleozoic Dipnoi. J. Linnean Soc. London. Zool. *35*:163-216. FD(N):1 4

2111 Weber, Roy E., Kjell Johansen, Gunnar Lykkeboe and Geoffrey M. O. Maloiy (1977) Oxygen-binding properties of hemoglobins from estivating and active African lungfish. J. Exp. Zool. *199*:85-96. P:2 11 20

2112 Weiler, Wilhelm (1926) Mitteilungen über die Wirbeltierreste aus dem Mittel-pliozän des Natrontales (Ägypten). Sber. Math.- Naturwiss. Abt. Bayerische Akad. Wiss. München *1926*:317-340. FP*:4 18

2113 Weiler, Wilhelm (1959) Über Ossiculithen und Otolithen bei Fischen. Paläontol. Z. *33*:148-151. ONP:1 7

2114 Weir, J. S. (1962) The lung-fish *Protopterus* in Central Africa, south of the Zambezi. Occas. Pap. Natl. Mus. S. Rhodesia *3*:770-779. P:1 18

2115 Weitzel, Karl (1926) *Conchopoma gadiforme* Kner, ein Lungenfisch aus dem Rotliegenden. Abh. Senckenb. Naturf. Ges. Frankfurt *40*:159-178.FD(N):3 4 7 17 18

2116 Welcomme, R. L. (1971) A description of certain indigenous fishing methods from southern Dahomey. Afr. J. Trop. Hydrobiol. Fish. *2*:129-140. OP:23

2117 Welcomme, R. L. (1973) A brief review of the floodplain fisheries of Africa. Afr. J. Trop. Hydrobiol. Fish. Special Issue *1*:67-76. OP:18

2118 Welsby, Thomas (1905) Schnappering and Fishing in the Brisbane River and Moreton Bay Waters, a Wandering Discourse on Fishing Generally. Brisbane: Outridge Printing Co. (*Ceratodus*:175-90). NO:G(1 3 15 18 19 21 22)

2119 Welsby, Thomas (1923) The *Ceratodus* fish. Brisbane Courier, Feb. 15. N:18

2120 Weltner, W. (1896) Der Afrikanische Molch- oder Schlammfisch, *Protopterus annectens*, Owen. Blätt. Aquarien Terrarien Freunde 7:220-226. P(N):G(1 3 9 10 19 20)

2121 Werner, Franz (1906) Ergebnisse der mit Subvention aus der Erbschaft Treitl unternommenen zoologischen Forschungsreise Dr. F. Werner's nach dem ägyptischen Sudan und Nord-Uganda. Sber. Akad. Wiss. Math.-Naturwiss. Kl. Wien *115*:1097-1158. (*Protopterus*:1121-1123).OP:1 3 18 24

2121a Westoll, T. Stanley (1937) The Old Red Sandstone fishes of the north of Scotland particularly of Orkney and Shetland. Proc. Geol. Soc. Lond. *48*:13-45.

2122 Westoll, T. Stanley (1943) The origin of tetrapods. Biol. Rev. Cambridge Phil. Soc. *18*:78-98. OD:1 17

2123 Westoll, T. Stanley (1943) The origin of the primitive tetrapod limb. Proc. Roy. Soc. London *131*:373-393. OD:1 4 17

2124 Westoll, T. Stanley (1948) Evolutionary trends in the Dipnoi. C. R. Cong. Int. Zool. *13*:513-516. FD:1 3 4 17

2125 Westoll, T. Stanley (1949) On the evolution of the Dipnoi. In Glenn Lowell Jepsen, George Gaylord Simpson and Ernst Mayr (eds): Genetics, Paleontology and Evolution. Princeton: Princeton Univ. Press, pp.121-

184. Reissued by Atheneum, New York. [1963] FDNLP:1 3 4 7 17

2126 Westoll, T. Stanley (1979) Devonian fish biostratigraphy. In Michael Robert House, Colin Thomas Scrutton, and Michael G. Bassett (eds): The Devonian System. London: Spec. Pap. Palaeontol. #23:341-353. (Dipnoi:347-349). FDO:3 4 17

2127 White, Errol Ivor (1925) Two new fossil species of *Epiceratodus* from South Australia. Ann. Mag. Natur. Hist. *16*:139-146. FN(C):1 4 18

2128 White, Errol Ivor (1926) On the occurrence of the genus *Epiceratodus* in the Upper Cretaceous of New South Wales. Ann. Mag. Natur. Hist. *17*:677-682. FN(C):4 17

2129 White, Errol Ivor (1962) A dipnoan from the Assise de Mazy of Hingeon. Bull. Inst. Roy. Sci. Natur. Belgique *38*:1-7. FD:1 4 18

2130 White, Errol Ivor (1965) The head of *Dipterus valenciennesi*. Bull. Brit. Mus. (Natur. Hist.) Geol. *11*:3-45. FD(N):1 4 21

2131 White, Errol Ivor (1966) Presidential Address: A little on lungfishes. Proc. Linnean Soc. London *177*:1-10. FD:1 4 17

2132 White, Peter T. and Iain R. F. Brown (1981) The osmotic fragility of the erythrocytes of the African lungfish *Protopterus aethiopicus* Heckel. Comp. Biochem. Physiol. *70A*:335-340. P:2 11 20

2133 Whiting, H. P. and Quentin Bone (1980) Ciliary cells in the epidermis of the larval Australian Dipnoan, *Neoceratodus*. Zool. J. Linn. Soc. *68*:125-137. N(PL):1 3 9 15 19 22

2134 Whitley, Gilbert Percy (1927) The Queensland lungfish. Aust. Mus. Mag. *3*:50-52. N:G(1 10 15 19 21)

2135 Whitley, Gilbert Percy (1929) The discovery of the Queensland lungfish. Aust. Mus. Mag. *3*:363-364. N:1

2136 Whitley, Gilbert Percy (1930) The teeth of fishes. Aust. Mus. Mag. *4*:92-99. N:G(4)

2137 Whitley, Gilbert Percy (1933) *Ompax spatuloides* Castelnau, a mythical Australian fish. Amer. Natur. *67*:563-567. O(N)

2138 Whitley, Gilbert Percy (1940) Mystery animals of Australia. Mag. Aust. Mus. 7:132-139. O(N)

2139 Whitley, Gilbert Percy (1940) The fishes of Australia. Part I: The sharks, rays, devil-fish and other primitive fishes of Australia and New Zealand. Roy. Zool. Soc. N.S.W., Sydney. 1-280. (*Neoceratodus*:239-245). ON:1 15 18 19

2140 Whitley, Gilbert Percy (1960) Freshwater Fishes of Australia. Brisbane: Jacaranda Press. (*Neoceratodus*:17-18). ON:G(1 18)

2141 Whitt, Gerald G. (1969) The telencephalon of the Australian lungfish, *Epiceratodus*. Ala. J. Med. Sci. 6:165-191. N(PL):1 6 7

2142 Whitt, Gregory (1981) Evolution of isozyme loci and their differential regulation. In G. G. E. Scudder and J. L. Reveal (eds): Evolution Today, Proceedings of the Second International Congress of Systematic and Evolutionary Biology, pp.271-289. OL:2 17

2143 Wickbom, Torsten (1945) Cytological studies on Dipnoi, Urodela, Anura, and *Emys*. Hereditas *31*:241-345. NPO(L):1

2144 Wiedersheim, Robert (1880) Das Skelet und Nervensystem von *Lepidosiren annectens* (*Protopterus ang.*). Z. Naturwiss. Jena *14*:155-192. P(N):1 4 6

2145 Wiedersheim, Robert (1880) Zur Histologie der Dipnoër-Schuppen. Arch. Mikrosk. Anat. *18*:122-129. P(LN):1 3

2146 Wiedersheim, Robert (1886) Comparative Anatomy of Vertebrates. London: Macmillan and Co., Ltd.

2147 Wiedersheim, Robert (1887) Zur Biologie von *Protopterus*. Anat. Anz. 2:707-713. P:1 3 9 19 20 21

2148 Wiedersheim, Robert (1887) On the torpid state of *Protopterus*. Rep. Brit. Assoc. Advan. Sci. *57*:738-740. P:1 3 9 19 20

2149 Wiedersheim, Robert (1892) Die Phylogenie der Beutelknochen. Z. Wiss. Zool. *53*:41-66. OP(N):1 4 6 17

2150 Wiedersheim, Robert (1903) Über den Kehlkopf der Ganoiden und Dipnoër. Anat. Anz. *22*:522-535. PO:1 4 5 9

2151 Wiedersheim, Robert (1904) Über das Vorkommen eines Kehlkopfes bei Ganoiden und Dipnoern sowie über die Phylogenie der Lunge. Zool. Jahrb. Suppl. 7:1-66. PLNO:1 4 5 9 10 15

2152 Wiedersheim, Robert (1904) Nachträgliche Bemerkungen zu meinem Aufsatz über den Kehlkopf der Ganoiden und Dipnoer. Anat. Anz. *24*:651-652. P:1 4

2153 Wiegman, Arend Friedrich August (1839) *Lepidosiren* ist kein Reptil. Arch. Naturgeschichte *1839*:398-403. P(L):1

2154 Wijhe, Jan Willem van (1882) Über das Visceralskelett und die Nerven des Kopfes der Ganoiden und von *Ceratodus*. Niederländ. Arch. Zool. 5:207-320.ON:1 3 4 6 7

2155 Wild, Rupert (1978) Massengrab für Saurier. Kosmos *74*:790-797.OC(N):4 18

2156 Wilder, Burt G. (1876) On the brains of fishes. Proc. Acad. Natur. Sci. Phil. *1876*:51-53. OLPN:1 6

2157 Wilder, Burt G. (1887) The dipnoan brain. Amer. Natur. *21*:544-548.N(P):1 6

2158 Wiley, Edward O. (1979) Ventral gill arch muscles and the interrelationships of gnathostomes, with a new classification of the Vertebrata. Zool. J. Linn. Soc. *67*:149-180. NPLO:1 4 5 6 17

2159 Williams, K. A. W. (1971) The fishes found in the fresh waters of the Brisbane River and the associated systems of the Bremer and Stanley River. Queensl. Natur. *20*:51-53. ON:G(18)

2160 Williams, Michael E. (1972) The origin of "spiral coprolites". Univ. Kans. Paleontol. Contrib. Pap. 59:1-19. OFD(P):12

2161 Willnow, I. and R. Willnow (1979) Biomicroscopical investigations of the vascular system of the lungs of lungfishes. Microvasc. Res. *17*:89. (Abstract) PNL:1 10 11

2162 Wilson, Donald M. (1959) Function of giant Mauthner's neurons in the lungfish. Science (Washington) *129*:841-842. P:2 6 19

2163 Wilson, Gregg (1901) The first foundation of the lung of *Ceratodus* (preliminary notice). Proc. Roy. Phys. Soc. Edinburgh *14*:319-321. Also in J. Roy. Microsc. Soc. London *1901*:510-511. N(LP):9 15 17

2164 Wilson, Gregg (1901) Embryonic excretory organs of *Ceratodus*. (preliminary notice). Proc. Roy. Phys. Soc. Edinburgh *14*:321-323. N:13 15

2165 Wingstrand, Karl Georg (1956) The structure of the pituitary in the African lungfish, *Protopterus annectens* (Owen). Vidensk. Medd. Dansk Naturhist.

Foren. Kjobenhavn *118*:193-210. P(NL):1 8 17

2166 Wingstrand, Karl Georg (1959) Attempts at a comparison between the neurohypophysial region in fishes and tetrapods, with particular regard to amphibians. In Aubrey Gorbman (ed): Comparative Endocrinology, (Proceedings of a Symposium at Cold Spring Harbor). New York: John Wiley and Sons, Inc., pp.393-403. PO:1 8

2167 Wingstrand, Karl Georg (1966) Comparative anatomy and evolution of the hypophysis. In Geoffrey Wingfield Harris and Bernard Thomas Donovan (eds): The Pituitary Gland. Berkeley: Univ. of Calif. Press, *1*:58-126.OPL:1 8 17

2168 Winslow, Guy Monroe (1895) The chondrocranium in the Ichthyopsida. Bull. Essex Inst. Salem, Mass. *27*:87-141. Also published in Tufts College Studies No. *5*:147-200. [1898] OP:1 4 6 11 15 17

2169 Witte, F. and E. L. M. Witte-Maas (1981) Haplochromine cleaner fishes: a taxonomic and eco-morphological description of two new species. Revision of the haplochromine species (Teleostei, Cichlidae) from Lake Victoria. Part I. Neth. J. Zool. *31*:203-231. PO:22

2170 Wood, John George (1885) Animate Creation: Popular Edition of 'Our Living World', a Natural History. New York: Selmar Hess, *III*:180-184. P(L):G(1 3 4 9 10 16 19 20 21)

2171 Wood, Stephan C. and Claude J. M. Lenfant (1976) Physiology of fish lungs. In George M. Hughes (ed): Respiration of Amphibious Vertebrates. New York: Academic Press, pp.257-270. PNO(L):2 9 10

2172 Woodrow, Donald L. and Frank W. Fletcher (1968) Devonian dipnoan aestivation cylinders. Spec. Pap. Geol. Soc. Amer. #121:383-384. (Abstract) FD:20

2173 Woodrow, Donald L., Frank W. Fletcher, and William F. Ahrnsbrak (1973) Paleogeography and paleoclimate at the deposition sites of the Devonian Catskill and Old Red Facies. Bull. Geol. Soc. Amer. *84*:3051-3064. OFD:18 20

2174 Woodward, Arthur Smith (1889) Note on a tooth of *Ceratodus* from the Stormberg Beds of the Orange Free State, South Africa. Ann. Mag. Natur. Hist. 4:243. C:4 18

2175 Woodward, Arthur Smith (1890) The fossil fishes of the Hawkesbury series at Gosford. Mem. Geol. Surv. N.S.W., Paleontology #4:1-55. (Dipnoi:4-6).OFD:4 18

2176 Woodward, Arthur Smith (1890) A synopsis of the fossil fishes of the English Lower Oolites. Proc. Geol. Assoc. *11*:285-306. CO:4 18

2177 Woodward, Arthur Smith (1891) Catalogue of the Fossil Fishes in the British Museum (Natural History). Part II. Containing the Elasmobranchii (Acanthodii), Holocephali, Ichthodorulites, Ostracodermi, Dipnoi, and Teleostomi. London: British Mus. Natur. Hist., pp.1-553. (Dipnoi:234-275). OFDC:4 18

2178 Woodward, Arthur Smith (1893) Note on a case of subdivision of the median fin in a dipnoan fish. Ann. Mag. Natur. Hist. *11*:241-242.FD:1 4

2179 Woodward, Arthur Smith (1893) Palaeichthyological notes. I. On some ichthyolites from the Keuper of Warwickshire. Ann. Mag. Natur. Hist. *12*:281-287. CO:18

2180 Woodward, Arthur Smith (1906) On a tooth of *Ceratodus* and a dinosaurian claw from the Lower Jurassic of Victoria, Australia. Ann. Mag. Natur. Hist. *18*:1-3. CO:1 4 18

2181 Woodward, Arthur Smith (1906) Presidential Address: The study of fossil fishes. Proc. Geol. Assoc. *19*:266-282. OCFD:1 4 17

2182 Woodward, Arthur Smith (1908) The fossil fishes of the Hawkesbury series at St. Peters. Mem. Geol. Surv. N.S.W., Paleontology *10*:1-29. (Dipnoi:6-8). OFD:3 4 18

2183 Woodward, Henry (1904) The President's Address: The evolution of vertebrate animals in time. J. Roy. Microsc. Soc. London *1904*:137-164.OD:G(9 17 18)

2184 Worthington, Edgar Barton (1932) A Report on the Fisheries of Uganda. London: The Crown Agents for the Colonies. PO:1 12 18 19 21 23

2185 Worthington, Edgar Barton and C. K. Ricardo (1936) The fish of Lake Tanganyika (other than Cichlidae). Proc. Zool. Soc. London *1936*:1061-1112. (*Protopterus*:1066, 1078). OP:18 21

2186 Worthington, Edgar Barton (1937) On the evolution of fish in the great lakes of Africa. Int. Rev. Gesamten Hydrobiol. Hydrograph. *35*:304-317. OP:18

2187 Worthington, S. and Edgar Barton Worthington (1933) Inland Waters of Africa. London: Macmillan and Co., Ltd. OP:G(18 24)

2188 Wourms, John P. and Anne Kemp (1982) Scanning electron microscopy of gastrulation and development of the lungfish *Neoceratodus*. Amer. Zool. *22*:876. (Abstract) N:1 15

2189 Wright, D. E. (1974) Morphology of the gill epithelium of the lungfish, *Lepidosiren paradoxa*. Cell Tissue Res. *153*:365-381. L:1 9 11

2190 Wunder, Wilhelm (1931) Brutpflege und Nestbau bei Fischen. Ergeb. Biol. *7*:118-192. OLP:14 19

2191 Young, Chung-Chien (1941) On two new fossil fishes from Southwestern China. Bull. Geol. Soc. China *21*:91-96. CO:4 18

2192 Young, Chung-Chien (1942) Fossil vertebrates from Kuangyuan, N. Szechuan, China. Bull. Geol. Soc. China *22*:293-309. CO:4 18

2193 Young, Chung-Chien (1945) A review of the fossil fishes of China, their stratigraphical and geographical distribution. Amer. J. Sci. *243*:127-137. OC:18

2194 Yvroud, Marcelle (1971) Le canal nasolacrymal et son intérêt évolutif. Année Biol. *10*:465-509. OD:4 7 17

2195 Zaddach, G. (1893) Über Fische mit Athmungsorgane, Kiemen und Lungen. Schr. Physik.-ökonomisch. Ges. Konigsberg *14*:17-19. LP(FDC):1 4 10 17 20

2196 Zalenski, V. (1898) see Salensky, W.

2197 Zambrano, David and Fermin C. Iturriza (1972) Histology and ultrastructure of the neurohypophysis of the South American lungfish, *Lepidosiren paradoxa*. Z. Zellforsch. Mikrosk. Anat. *131*:47-62. L:1 6 8 11

2198 Zambrano, David (1972) Innervation of the teleost pituitary. Gen. Comp. Endocrinol. Suppl. *3*:22-31. OL:6 8

2199 Zambrano, David (1973) Evolution of the hypothalamic control of the pars distalis. Acta Physiol. Latinoamer. *23*:442-444. L:1 6 8 11 17

2200 Zambrano, David and Fermin C. Iturriza (1973) Hypothalamic-hypophysial relationships in the South American lungfish *Lepidosiren paradoxa*. Gen. Comp. Endocrinol. *20*:256-273. L(P):1 6 8 11 17

2201 Zambrano, David (1973) Innervation of the teleost and dipnoan pituitaries. Excerpta Med. Int. Congr. Ser. *273*:215-219. OL:6 8

2202 Zidek, Jiri (1972) Oklahoma paleoichthyology. Part I: A review and commentary. Okl. Geol. Not. *32*:171-187. FDO:18

2203 Zidek, Jiri (1975) Some fishes of the Wild Cow Formation (Pennsylvanian), Manzanita Mountains, New Mexico. Circ. New Mex. Bur. Mines, Mineral Resources #135:1-22. (*Proceratodus*:17-18). OC:4 18

2204 Ziegels, Jocelyne (1976) The vertebrate subcommissural organ: a structural and functional review. Arch. Biol. *87*:429-476. (*Neoceratodus*:438). ON:1 6

2205 Zittel, Karl Alfred von (1887) Über *Ceratodus*. Sber. Math.-Physik. Kl. Akad. Wiss. München *16*:253-265. C:1 4 18

2206 Zittel, Karl Alfred von (1887) Handbuch der Palaeontologie. Palaeozoologie, *3*:122-133. München: R. Oldenbourg. [see also Edward D. Cope #431A] FDNLP:G(4 10 18)

2208 Zottoli, Steven J. (1978) Comparative morphology of the Mauthner cell in fish and amphibians. In Donald S. Faber and Henri Korn (eds): Neurobiology of the Mauthner Cell. New York: Raven Press, pp.13-45. ONLP:1 6

2209 Zwilling, Robert, Hans Neurath, Lowell H. Ericsson and David L. Enfield (1975) The amino-terminal sequence of an invertebrate trypsin (crayfish *Astacus leptodactylus*): homology with other serine proteases. FEBS Lett. *60*:247-249. O(P):2 17

ACKNOWLEDGMENTS

I am grateful to Willy Bemis, editor of this volume who gave innumerable hours, wise counsel, and encouragement in the final preparation of the listing. His efforts and his high standards greatly enhanced the clarity and the accuracy of this bibliography.

Index

References to figures and tables are shown in italics.